THE YOGA DARSANA

OF

PATAÑJALI

with

The Sāṅkhya Pravacana Commentary of Vyāsa and
The Gloss of Vācaspati Miśra

THE YOGA DARSANA
OF
PATAÑJALI

with
The Sāṅkhya Pravacana Commentary of Vyāsa and The Gloss of Vācaspati Miśra

Translated by

Rāma Prasāda

With an introduction by

Rai Bahadur Śrīśa Chandra Vasu

LOGOS PRESS, NEW DELHI-110002

Cataloging in Publication Data—DK
Courtesy : D.K. Agencies (P) Ltd. <docinfo@dkagencies.com>

Patañjali.

[Yogasūtra. English & Sanskrit]

The Yoga darśana of Patañjali : with the Sāṅkya pravacana commentary of Vyāsa and the gloss of Vācaspati Miśra / translated by Rāma Prasāda; with an introduction by Śrīśa Chandra Vasu. p. cm.

In Sanskrit; translation and introd. in English. Reprint. Originally published : Allahabad : Panini Office, 1912.

Aphoristic work on the meditational fundamentals of the yoga school of Indic philosophy.

Includes index.

ISBN 81-7268-124-0

1. Yoga—Early works to 1800. I. Vyāsa. II. Vācaspatimiśra, 15th cent. III. Rāma Prasād. IV. Title.

DDC 181.45 22

ISBN : 81-7268-124-0

Originally published in 1912
Published in this form 2005
Reprinted 2015

Printed & Published by

LOGOS PRESS

Building No. 4788-90, Street No. 23, Ansari Road,
Darya Ganj, New Delhi-110 002 (India)
Phone : 23272187

INTRODUCTION

The aphorisms of Patañjali on the Yoga Sūtras are contained in four chapters and are nearly two hundred in number. The author of the aphorisms is said to be the same Patañjali who wrote the famous commentary on Pāṇini's aphorisms, under the name of the Mahābhāṣya or the Great Commentary. Another work is also attributed to him—the great work on Medicine. If so, he was not only a great Grammarian and a great Philosopher, but also Great Physician. He prescribed for the body, mind and spirit all the three. The age of Patañjali is now generally fixed at three centuries before Christ.[1]

The word Yoga comes from a Sanskrit root which means "to go to trance, to meditate." Others however derive it from a root which means to join; and Yoke in English is said to be the same word as Yoga. Both roots are feasible—in the case of the root to join, Yoga would mean the science that teaches the method of joining the human soul with God.

The philosophy of Patañjali is essentially Dualistic. The Jīvas or Puruṣas or human egos are separate individual entities and exist from eternity; so is also Prakṛti, and so also Īśvara or God. It thus believes in three Eternal co-existent principles, the God, the Man and the Matter.

But man is found to be involved in matter, to have fallen from its pristine state of purity. The aim of Yoga is to free (viyoga) man from the meshes of matter. But the highest form of matter is mind—the Citta (a term which would include that which is technically known as manas, as Ahaṁkāra and as Buddhi). The students of Sāṅkhya need not be told that the first product of Prakṛti or the root-matter is Mahat or the Great Principle—the Buddhi, then comes the Ahaṁkāra or I-principle—the matter through which can function the I-ness : and then the Manas or the matter which is the vehicle of thought. These three vehicles—the thought-vehicle (Manas), the I-vehicle (Ahaṁkāra), the Pure-Reason-vehicle (Buddhi)—constitute Citta or the subtlest form of Matter. To free man from the fetters of this Citta is thus the problem of Yoga.

The man when freed from all vehicles, remains in his own form called Svarūpa. It is not made of Prākṛtic matter. It is the body which belongs to man—is part of man from eternity—the body in which he dwells in Mukti in super-celestial worlds. It is the body in which the Triune God is directly active—Īśvara, Prāṇa and Śrī—or the Father, the Son and the Holy Ghost. This svarūpa—deha, is the body of Prāṇa—the body of Christ of the Gnostics. This is the incorruptible undecaying body, the spiritual body.

But when man is not in his Own-Form (Svarūpa), he functions naturally in the lower vehicles, and his form is there the form of his vehicles—whether it be of Buddhic, Ahaṁkāric

1. See Dr. Rajendra Lala Mitra's preface to his Edition of the Yoga Aphorisms of Patañjali and also his paper on Goṇikāputra and Gonardīya as names of Patañjali, pp. 261 *et seq.*, of the Journal of the Asiatic Society of Bengal for 1883.

or Mānasic matter. In fact the man of Psychology is this triad—Ahaṁkāra, Buddhi and Manas.

The human consciousness in whatever lower body it may function is always a dual consciousness—it must be alternately pleasurable or painful. Pleasure and pain are the marks of consciousness functioning in Citta. The Svarūpa consciousness is only above all pains.

Next to this primary division of all consciousness, as regards their nature; the consciousness as regards its quality is five-fold :—(1) it may be a true consciousness of some objective reality—something which is outside the man and his vehicles; or (2) it may be an incorrect consciousness of outward reality; or (3) it may be a hallucination; or (4) it may be non-perception of anything external but of rest; or (5) it may be the reviving of old perceptions. In other words, the consciousness looked at from the subejctive or emotional point of view is either pleasurable or painful; looked at from the objective or cognitional point of view it is—(i) true perceptions, (ii) false perceptions, (iii) hallucinations, (iv) sleep, and (v) memory.

Thus both the emotional and the intellectual aspects of the Citta—or the Triune Man are to be checked. But how is it to be checked. The answer is by constant practice and want of attachment or Dispassion. There must be constant exertion to keep the mind on one point. This is called Abhyāsa. The intellectual functioning of the Chitta is to be checked by Abhyāsa—putting the mind to think of one object, and as soon as it strays away from it to bring it back again to the same point. This practice or Abhyāsa, steadily persevered in, would make the mind one-pointed, with the help of Viveka or discrimination.

As regards the emotional sides of the mind, it must be checked by Vairāgya or dispassion. Pleasure or Pain, attraction or repulsion, love and hatred can be controlled only by this world-weariness—realisation that there is nothing in this world or the next worth striving after, worth desiring or worth hating. The highest form of Vairāgya will be attained when one will realise his separateness from all Prākṛtic vehicles—when he can say "I am not Body, or Desire, or mind, or Reason or I-ness."

The state of Samādhi or trance induced by Practice and Dispassion is two-fold—Samprajñāta and Asamprajñāta. In the first, the man has shut off from his consciousness all external impressions, but his internal self-initiated activities have not ceased. In the other, even these are stopped.

There are some entities whose consciousness is in a state of Samādhi naturally, who have not to acquire it by any exertion. These are the classes of beings called Videhas and Prakṛtilayas. Their consciousness is cosmic. The Videhas are Devas. They are Mukta from the beginning : but in some future Kalpa they may come into the world-cycle. The Prakṛtilayas are Adhikāri Puruṣas, the great office-holders in the cosmic hierarchy. They are the perfect ones of the past Kalpa.

In the case, however, of ordinary entities—for the Videhas and the Prakṛtilayas do not stand in need of Yoga—the method of suppressing Citta-functions consists in having faith, energy, retentive memory, meditation and wisdom. One must cultivate these qualities in order to become a successful Yogī.

The success is quicker according to the amount of energy put in by the person in his practice. But the best and the safest method of Yoga is the love of God. Loving God with all one's heart and soul, would quickly bring about the cessation of all mental functions. God is a spirit untouched by sorrow, action and its fruition. He is Omniscient, He is the Teacher of all, and from eternity. His mystic name is Om. One must recite this Om constantly meditating on its letters and their imports; and thus all obstacles to concentration will be removed, and the Inner Self will manifest itself. The obstacles to concentration are disease, languor, doubt, heedlessness, laziness, sensuality, delusion, etc., mentioned in I. 30. But when the mind is concentrated, there is no pain or despondency, no fidgetiness, no difficulty of breathing. To attain concentration and remove these obstacles, the aspirant must practise to fix his attention on One Point, One Truth. Of course the highest Truth is God and so the constant attitude of the mind should be God-pointed.

The aspirant must strictly regulate his conduct as regards others. He must show happiness and feel happiness when dealing with those who are happy. Let him have no feeling of jealousy towards them. He must show compassion towards those who are suffering. He must not be callous to the miseries of others. He must be complacent towards the virtuous, and hate not the sinner. These are the moral attributes that he must try to cultivate.

There are, however, some particular methods which quickly bring about concentration; one of them is the regulation of the breath. The monotony of slowly breathing in and breathing out brings about hypnosis. Fixing the attention on various parts of the body, such as the tip of the nose, palate, etc., are also helpful. The astral senses are developed by this means, and when the practitioner gets first-hand knowledge of astral sights, sounds, etc., his doubts are removed, and he feels more earnestness in pursuing the path.

If the astral development is not wanted, the practitioner may concentrate his attention on the light in the heart : and upon the thought "I am." This also steadies the mind.

Or he may fix his attention on some great and holy saint or sage—such as Zoroaster, the Buddha, the Christ, etc.

Or he may fix his attention on the objects of his dreams. Sometimes in dream he may be shown a great Deva or a great Teacher. Let him not reject it as fancy. By fixing his attention on it he may acquire steadiness of mind.

Or he may fix his attention on the ideas that pass through his mind just before he goes to sleep, the pictures that arise when one is half-awake and half-asleep—the hypnopompic (as Myers calls them). Or he may fix his attention on the pictures that one sees just before awakening—the hypnogogic. If he can fix his attention on these, he may easily pass into hypnosis.

By such concentration all mental impurities are removed, and the mind becomes like a pure crystal that reflects truly and correctly all objects that are presented to it. They are no longer distorted pictures or dim and dull reflections of outer verities. The mental vehicle is purified, and the knowledge that now arises is far more true than any knowledge that he had before. The mind, however, enters as an element in every such knowledge, and the past ideas and memories tinge such knowledge. This state is called Savitarka or mixed up trance. But when the mind reflects only the object, without adding to it anything from its own associations and storehouse, it is pure idea and is Nirvitarka Samādhi. In this state the light of the Self shines out on purified mind. It is not only a pure crystal that faithfully reflects the outer objects, but it is illumined, as if it were, by a light which was dormant within its own inmost centre. Such a mind is called the Truth-bearing mind. It has truth within it and truth without—a mass of truth—a tree carrying the fruit of truth—a female full with truth. Up to this time the objects of the mind were mere ideas and inferences, mere thoughts. Now the contents of the mind are things, the very things as it were, and not merely thoughts of things. The mind modifies itself, as it were, into the very thing itself; and thus the thing is known more truly and essentially than it was known ever before. In this state of mind, the time and space cannot impede the perception of the object. The object may be inside a box, behind a wall or hundreds of miles off, the mind faithfully reproduces it. The object may be the subtlest and the minutest, not visible even under the strongest microscope, the mind reproduces it. For it no longer depends upon the senses for its knowledge, but has become the all-sense itself. In this way the mind becomes the highest sensory :—by constant practice the mind gets into the habit of reflecting the trance objects. But even this habit is ultimately to be conquered if one wishes to rise to the higher levels of what is called the seedless trance.

The First Chapter thus, in fifty-one aphorisms, gives what may be called the theory or the science of Yoga. An ardent and intelligent person can learn enough from this chapter alone to become a practical Yogī. But for men of ordinary intellect, more detailed teaching is necessary. The Second Chapter enters into such teaching. It may be called the art of Yoga—the technique of it.

The art of Yoga consists in bringing under control and purifying the three lower vehicles of man, namely, the body, the mind and the spiritual Self—the astro-physical, mental and the causal bodies. The astro-physical body is to be purified and brought under control by what are called ascetic practices—early rising, bathing, fasting, bearing hardships, etc., in short, all that go under the name of Tapas—or austerities. The mental body must be purified and strengthened by study, by acquiring knowledge. An ignorant person cannot be a Yogī. The causal or spiritual body is to be developed by entire devotion to God. Thus an atheist cannot be a true Yogī.

These three helps—austerities, study and resignation to the will of God—facilitate trance and remove "afflictions." The "affliction" is the technical name of certain intellectual and emotional weaknesses to which all human beings are liable. They are five in number :—1. The first is the Nescience or Wrong Notion of things objective—mistaking the non-eternal for the eternal, the impure for the pure, the painful for the pleasurable, the non-Self for the Self. 2. The second is the wrong notion about things subjective—identifying one's Self with the vehicles in which the Self functions, taking the bodies for the soul. These two are intellectual defects. 3. The third is the emotional weakness. It is the desire natural of man, running after pleasant things. 4. The fourth also is emotional—hatred of things that give pain. Thus these two—love and hatred—are emotional defects. The fifth defect is neither intellectual nor emotional—it is instinctive—the instinct self-preservation—the instinctive fear of death—the love of life. These are the five "afflictions" of Yoga—Avidyā, Asmitā, Rāga, Dveṣa and Abhiniveśa—Nescience, Egoism, love and hatred and instinctive dread of death. These "afflictions" are destroyed by meditation and the methods already mentioned.

These "afflictions" are the root of the body of transmigration, the root of re-incarnation, of birth, life and suffering. The pleasure and pain which a man suffers are the result of his past acts, the virtuous acts are the seed of pleasure, the vicious of pain. The word "affliction" is thus a purely technical term, for it includes the high heavenly pleasure also which is the result of virtuous actions. But in the philosophy of Yoga—as well as that of Sāṅkhya—all such pleasures are also considered as pains : because philosophically the world is painful, all its experiences, even those which people call pleasurable, are painful to the philosopher. This is stated in the memorable aphorism, II, 15, p. 100.

All world-experience being thus painful, the philosopher seeks to find the root-cause of this experience and this is the conjunction of the knower and the knowable—the Self and the not-Self. Because man is tied with mind, and cannot extricate himself from the embraces of mind-matter that he suffers. When he masters the mind, and is not her slave, then there is no pain—there is no necessary experiencing of joy and sorrow. The non-ego to which the man is tied has the three well-known attributes or Guṇas—the Sattva, Rajas and Tamas—the Light, the Activity and the Inertia—is the source of all elements, and producer of all sensations and senses.

The Yoga system of cosmogony is the same as that of the Sāṅkhya, so far as the evolution of the world-elements out of the Primordial matter called Prakṛti is concerned. It is summarised in II. 19.

What is the nature of the Self ? This question naturally arises after one has learned the nature of the non-Self. The man is pure consciousness : and the non-Self exists for him. If man is pure consciousness, how does he perceive the non-Self? He knows the non-ego by a sort of reflex action. The mind catches the reflection of the non-Self; and the man becomes conscious of that reflection. The man is thus the seer of the pictures in the mind. The non-ego or the knowable thus exists for the sake of the Man. In the state of Mukti, there exists no knowable for that Man. Though to the Perfect Man there is no knowable, it does not mean that the knowable ceases to exist. It exists with regard to the other souls that have not reached perfection.

A question is often asked : If the ultimate goal is the separation of man from the non-Self, the knowable, why was this conjunction between the two brought about ? Why was man tied down to non-Self, to matter-mind ? The answer to this is : In order that Man may perfect his nature by acquiring all experiences and passing through them. Unless the Man learns all that the Matter-Mind has to teach, the conjunction is not broken. The effective cause of this conjunction lies in the Avidyā—the Wrong Notion. When, therefore, the Avidyā or Nescience is removed, the conjunction is removed and the Man shakes off the eternal burden. How is the Avidyā to be removed ? The Avidyā being Wrong Notion, can be removed only by Right Notion call Viveka-Khyāti or Discriminative knowledge. This discriminative knowledge has seven stages—four dealing with the phenomenal knowledge and three with the mental or subjective notions, as described in II. 27. It is on reaching this that the title of Adept or Kuśala is given to the Yogī.

The acquisition of this Adeptship is through the practice of eight-fold Yoga. The famous phrase Aṣṭāṅga Yoga refers to this. The eight accessories of Yoga are enumerated in II. 29. Five of these are external, as if, compared with the last three. The eight Aṅgas are so important that it can well bear repetition here.

First, Practise Restraint, *i.e.,* be moral. This restraint or Yama consists of five sub-divisions :—(a) do not kill or injure any being. Be kind to all. Ahiṁsā; (b) Speak and act truth; (c) Steal not, nor acquire illicit gains; (d) Practise continence and celibacy; (e) Be not avaricious. These are universal rules.

Second Niyama or Observance. This is also five-fold :—(a) Be clean in body and mind, (b) Be contented, (c) Practise asceticism and austerity, (d) Study sacred books, (e) Be devoted to God.

While practising Yama and Niyama, if obstacles arise, always try to think of the opposite quality. If he feels a strong desire to tell a falsehood, let him not fight the desire, by a frontal attack, by checking it. Let him substitute the opposite desire—the beauty of truthfulness. If he hates another, let him think of the good qualities of that man. If he is in danger of breaking the vow of celibacy, let him think of the glorious future of the Brahmacārī. Pratipakṣa Bhāvana—thinking of the contrary—is the key of success. It is the great strategy in this moral battle, and is embodied in II.33. The moral qualities mentioned in Yama, must be absolutely observed—no sophistical diminution of their absolute nature is allowed to the Yogī. To him the moral laws are absolute. Thus the first rule of Ahiṁsā says "kill not." This is an absolute rule. There cannot be any exceptions or reservations. The enemies of the country, the renegades of religion, the blasphemers of sages and saints, the murderer, the criminal—kill none. To Yogī the vow of non-killing is absolute. He must not kill even in self-defence of himself or of his near and dear ones. Hence the rule says : "They (Yama) are the great vow universal, and not limited by caste, country, age and condition." (II.31). So also with truth. One must not lie for the sake of one's country or State or Brāhmaṇa or cow, etc. Not only this : there are certain omissions which become as bad as actual commissions of these sins. He incurs sin if he causes another to do it or permits its being done.

The third Aṅga of Yoga is Āsana or posture. No particular posture is obligatory, but the posture must be such as is steady and easy; not painful or irksome. The various postures given in books of Haṭha Yoga such as Gheraṇḍa Saṁhitā or Śiva Saṁhitā are useful as physical exercises, for the otherwise sedentary Yogī.

The fourth Aṅga of Yoga is the much abused Prāṇāyāma or the Regulation of breath. The Yoga has come to mean, in the thoughts of many, posturing and nose-closing. But the right regulation of breath as a mental and physical effect was pointed out long ago. The Western science has come to recognise its advantages and Books of Breathing are not as rare now as they were when we first wrote about it in 1882.

The fifth Aṅga of Yoga is Pratyāhāra or Abstraction. It is a state of catalepsy when the senses do not come into contact with their objects. It is the state of the inhibition of the senses. A pistol may be fired near the ear of the Yogī and he will not hear it. Ammonia may be held under his nostrils and he will not smell it, and so on.

All the above five are Bahiraṅga or the external. The internal Yoga which has to deal with the mind and mind alone consists of the last three Aṅgas—Dhāraṇā, Dhyāna and Samādhi.

The Third Chapter gives a description of this Antaraṅga Yoga. The Dhāraṇā, Dhyāna and Samādhi are collectively called Saṁyama.

When the stage of catalepsy is reached, the Yogī fixes his mind on any particular portion of his body. This *holding* the mind in a particular part is Dhāraṇā or concentration.

The continuation of the mental effort to keep the mind there is Dhyāna or meditation.

This meditation (Dhyāna) turns into Samādhi or contemplation when the Self is lost as if it were, the object of meditation alone remains in the mind and shines out alone.

This Saṁyama—concentration, meditation and contemplative trance—is the great instrument of acquiring all knowledge of supersensuous verities. It is the strong searchlight of the mind which turned on any object, reveals its inmost core. It is the great light of wisdom—Prajñāloka.

This Saṁyama must be applied to plane after plane of nature, physical, astral, mental, etc. One cannot jump to a higher plane, leaving off an intermediate plane—the progress is gradual.

The Yogī who has mastered Saṁyama as regards a higher plane should not discrete this faculty by employing it in lower planes. He who by Saṁyama, has learnt communion with God, should not waste his faculty in thought-reading, clairvoyance, bringing messages from the dead to the living or *vice versa.* He should not squander his energy in hunting up the past records in the astral light, nor the shadows of the future in the Brāhmic Idea.

What is the state of mind in Samādhi and Nirodha? Is it a state of perfect quiescence of the mental body? As regards the mental body it is a state of perfect stillness so far as the vehicle is concerned, but it is a state of great *molecular* motion *in* the mental body itself. *The molecules* of the mental body are thrown in a very high state of vibration, though the body in all appearance is in perfect calm. This vibration of the molecules of the mental body, becomes by practice, rhythmic and this rhythmic flow is the mental peace of Samādhi. The swing of the vibration lies between one-pointedness and all-pointedness—between the contraction to a point and expansion to embrace a whole universe. That which appears to be the stillness of Samādhi is perhaps the highest activity possible. Even what is called one-pointedness is itself a state of utmost activity. When the mind is one-pointed it does not mean that on idea is indelibly impressed on the mind like an engraving on a stone, but that the mind is working so quickly that the image of one is formed in *no* time as it were, destroyed in *no* time as it were, and formed again. This quick succession of the same form is one-pointedness. In ordinary states one idea is followed by another idea. In one-pointedness the same idea vanishes and re-appears again and again. Thus what is called fixing the mind to a thought is really making the mind reproduce one thought over and over again, in the utmost quickness of succession, without the intrusion of any foreign thought.

The Third Chapter then gives a list of psychic powers and how to acquire them by applying Saṁyama. The power of knowing the past, present and future is by making Saṁyama on three-fold modifications which all objects are constantly undergoing (III. 13)

Methods are laid down as how to acquire the memory of past births, how to read the thoughts of others, how to disappear from sight, how to get strength, how to see through closed doors, how to know the solar system and astronomy, etc., etc. These methods have a meaning only for him who knows the practice of Saṁyama. Without that no amount of thinking on the solar plexus will give one a knowledge of internal anatomy, etc.

The Fourth Chapter deals with Kaivalya or final emancipation—the realisation by Man that he is separated from Mind-Matter.

The psychic powers or Siddhis are either innate, or produced through the means of medicinal drugs, or suggestion of Mantra, or asceticism or contemplation. Some are born psychics, as Kapila Swedenborg, etc. Temporary psychic powers may be acquired through anaesthetics, such as chloroform hashish, etc. Psychic faculties may be developed by the recitation of certain Mantras, or the suggestion of sound. Some persons have acquired psychic powers through austerities. The fifth or contemplation is the method of this Yoga system.

The born psychics are those who had practised Yoga in their past lives. They are like eggs in which bird has already fully formed—break the shell and the bird comes out. But ordinary men are eggs that require hatching for lives to develop the bird. The born psychics are like a field by the side of a reservoir of water on a higher level. It only requires the opening of the sluice to flood the field with water. It only requires some exciting cause to make a born psychic a developed Yogī. Ordinary men are, however, like fields, which are away from any source of water, and which require to be irrigated by bringing water from a distance, with great exertion, in this life. A Yogī, having attained the power of Samādhi, sets about destroying his past Karmas. All Karmas may be divided into three classes :—1. The acts done in the past whose consequences the man *must* suffer in the present life : the Karmas to expiate which he has taken the present birth or incarnation. They are the *ripe* Karmas (Prārabdha). 2. The Karmas done in the past, but which are not ripe, and will have to be expiated in some future life. They are the *stored* Karmas or *unripe* (Sañcita). 3. The Karmas which a man creates in his present life, and which have to be expiated in a future or the present life. This last kind of act—the fresh Karmas, can be stopped. By devotion to the Lord and doing everything in a spirit of service, no *fresh* Karmas are generated. The incurring of debt is stopped. The man, however, has to pay off past debts—the ripe and unripe Karmas. The ripe Karmas will produce their effects in the present life. The Yogī does not trouble himself about this. But the *unripe* or *stored* Karmas require a future birth. It is here that the Yoga is of the greatest practical importance. The Yogī is not bound to wait for future lives in order to get an opportunity to pay off the debt of Sañcita Karmas. He simultaneously *creates* the bodies that those Sañcita Karmas require—through those bodies expiates all his Karmas simultaneously. Every one of such body has a Citta or mentality of his own. This is the Nirmāṇa-citta or the Artificial mind—like the Pseudo-Personalities of hypnotic trance. These artificial minds arise simultaneously like so many sparks from the Ahaṁkāric matter of the Yogī's Self, and they ensoul the artificial bodies created for them. These artificial bodies with artificial minds in them walk through the earth in hundreds—they are distinguished from ordinary men by the fact that they are perfectly methodical in all their acts, and automatic in their lives. All these artificials are controlled by the consciousness of the Yogī. One consciousness controlling hundred automatons. Every one of these automatons has a particular destiny, a particular portion of the Sañcita Karma to exhaust. As soon as that destiny is fulfilled, the Yogī withdraws his ray from it, and the "man" dies a sudden death—a heart failure generally.

Now what is the difference between the ordinary mind and the Yoga-created mind—the natural Citta and the artificial Citta. The natural mind by experience gains a habit, the impressions are stored in it and they, as Vāsanās, become the seeds of desires and activities. The artificial mind is incapable of storing up impressions in it. It has no Vāsanās and consequently it disintegrates as soon as the body falls down.

The actions performed by the Yogī, through his ordinary or the extraordinary bodies—through the body with which he was born, or through the bodies which he gives birth to by Yoga power—are no actions in the ethical sense of the word. They are not Karmas—neither good nor bad. They are the paying up of the past debts, and not incurring of fresh liabilities. With ordinary men the actions are good or bad, or a mixture of both—white or black or grey, all such actions produce their effect—particular kind of birth, particular length of life period, particular kinds of life experiences—or produce their effect as tendencies to certain kind of actions. Both kinds of effects constitute the *fate* or the *destiny* of man.

Tendency is memory. The essence of memory is converted into tendency. The tendencies with which a man is born are the extracts of all the memories of a particular kind. The *events* of the past life are not remembered, but from the tendencies of the present life one can easily infer what those events must have been to give rise to these tendencies. The surgical portion may be forgotten because performed under chloroform, or in infancy, but from the nature of the cicatrix one can infer what must have been the nature of the operation. Therefore, the Smṛti (memory) and Saṁskāra (tendency or habit) are really one (Ekarūpatva)—IV.9. Acts produce habits, habits lead to acts—the circle of Vāsanā is eternal, and beginningless. Is it possible to break this chain of habits and acts, acts and habits ? Jñāna is the only means. Through Jñāna alone is possible to destroy this inexorable chain of causation.

Now what is this Jñāna or wisdom? It is the realisation of the distinction between the Puruṣa or Spirit, and Prakṛti or mind-matter energy. Puruṣa is pure consciousness or rather Citśakti—power of consciousness. By his proximity to Prakṛti (mind-energy-matter) it induces in the latter his quality. This induction takes place in the purest part of Prakṛti in the Buddhic-essence (the mental portion of Prakṛti) : Just as soft iron becomes magnetised by its promixity to iron. Thus Cit-śakti or consciousness is two-fold,—the pure consciousness of the spirit or spiritual consciousness and the consciousness of the Buddhisattva or mental consciousness. The pure Buddhisattva (devoid of Rajas and Tamas) reflects the spirit and appears likes spirit and is mistaken for it. The Jñāna consists in the discrimination of this difference realising that the Citta is the instrument and not the Self. In the state of Samādhi, when this highest knowledge is realised, then arises the positive activity of the Spirit. Up to this time the effort was in a sense negative only—separating the Spirit from mind-energy-matter. When this separation is realised, then the Spirit manifests its own attributes fully.

This manifestation of the attributes (dharma) of the Spirit on its own plane above the planes of Prakṛti (mind-energy-matter) is the highest form of Samādhi. It is positive Samādhi and is called Dharma-Megha Samādhi. Dharma means highest activity, above the shaper of causation, where the actions are neither white, black nor grey, an activity that leads to the highest end of Man—an activity which is the highest end of Man. It is called Megha or cloud, because this state of Samādhi rains such Dharma—is full of Dharma and Dharma alone. It is the cloud which showers all blessings on the lower planes—while the Man himself basks in the Light of the Eternal Sun. Every Mukta Yogī is a Dharma-Megha—the Cloud of Holiness—the showerer of good and nothing but good on all creation. A man who has become a Dharma-Megha—a Cloud of Holiness, is above all afflictions and Karmas, his mind is free from all taints, and there is nothing that is beyond the scope of his knowledge. Being the Cloud of Dharma all attributes are known to him. Then the man is in his Svarūpa—this is Kaivalya, this is Self-realisation—the state of true Freedom, though full of highest activity. Such a Man, the Dharma-Megha, the Cloud of Holiness, is a blessing to the thirsting humanity—nay a blessing to the whole creation.

Dated, 24th February 1910. **S.C.V.**

CONTENTS

1

Trance (Samādhi)

Sūtra 1

अथ योगानुशासनम् ।। १ ।।

अथ Atha, now. योग Yoga, of Yoga, or concentration, contemplation (Samādhi). अनुशासनम् Anuśāsanaṁ, a revised text, or explanation.

1. Now a revised text of Yoga.

ॐ नमो भगवते वासुदेवाय ।

यस्त्यक्त्वा रूपमाद्यं प्रभवति जगतोऽनेकधानुग्रहाय
प्रक्षीणक्लेशराशिर्विषमविषधरोऽनेकवक्त्रः सुभोगी ।
सर्वज्ञानप्रसूतिर्भुजगपरिकरः प्रीतये यस्य नित्यम्
देवोऽहीशः स वोऽव्यात्सितविमलतनुर्योगदो योगयुक्तः ।। १ ।।

अथ योगानुशासनम् । अथेत्ययमधिकारार्थः । योगानुशासनं शास्त्रमधिकृतं वेदितव्यम् । योगः समाधिः । स च सार्वभौमश्चित्तस्य धर्मः । क्षिप्तं मूढं विक्षिप्तमेकाग्रं निरुद्धमिति चित्तभूमयः । तत्र विक्षिप्ते चेतसि विक्षेपोपसर्जनीभूतः समाधिर्न योगपक्षे वर्तते । यस्त्वेकाग्रे चेतसि सद्भूतमर्थं प्रद्योतयति क्षिणोति च क्लेशान्कर्मबन्धनानि श्लथयति निरोधमभिमुखं करोति स संप्रज्ञातो योग इत्याख्यायते । स च वितर्कानुगतो विचारानुगत आनन्दानुगतोऽस्मितानुगत इत्युपरिष्टान्निवेदयिष्यामः । सर्ववृत्तिनिरोधे त्वसंप्रज्ञातः समाधिः ।। १ ।।

Vyāsa's Commentary

"Now"—This word here denotes undertaking. A text giving a revised critical teaching of Yoga is to be understood as having been undertaken.

Yoga is contemplation (Samādhi, trance), and it is a characteristic of the mind pervading all its planes. The planes of the mind are :—

Wandering (Kṣipta); Forgetful (Mūḍha); Occasionally steady or distracted (Vikṣipta); One-pointed (Ekāgra); and Restrained (Niruddha).

Of these the contemplation in the occasionally steady mind does not fall under the heading of Yoga, because of unsteadiness appearing in close sequence. That however, which in the one-pointed mind, fully shows forth an object existing as such in its most perfect form, removes the affections, loosens the bonds of karma and thus inclines it towards restraint, is said to be the Cognitive Trance (Samprañāta Samādhi). And we shall explain further that this is accompanied by philosophical curiosity (vitarka), meditation (vicāra), bliss (ānanda), and egoism (asmitā).

When however all the modifications come under restraint, the trance is ultra-cognitive (Asamprajñāta Samādhi).

Vācaspati's Gloss

Bhagavān Patañjali here composed the aphorism, "Now a revised text of Yoga," with the object of stating briefly the subject of the treatise he desired to write, so that it may attract the intelligent student and also that the reader may be able to understand with ease.

The word 'Now' (atha) the first of the sentence is explained :—" 'Now' :—This word here denotes undertaking."

The word 'now' does not here denote sequence, as it does in, "Now there is light."

The word 'anuśāsana' means here a text-book, the derivative meaning being that by which something is taught; and this cannot be begun in sequence of the performance of mental and physical restraint. On the contrary however the desire to know and the knowledge of realities appear in sequence of the desire to explain the knowledge of realities. As says the Veda :— "Therefore let him see the self, in the self" after having controlled the mind and the senses and become desireless, enduring and contemplative, (Br. U. IV. 4. 23).

Although it is possible that the questioning of a student the performance of purificatory actions (tapas), and employment of alchemy may serve as antecedents, they are not to be taken as such here, because the recognition and taking up of the study by a student are of no use in making a treatise on Yoga authoritative. Even if there should be no student for the time being, the work should be undertaken if authoritative. If however not authoritative, it should be given up, even though there be a student asking for it. The existence of an immediate sequence between the knowledge of truth and the desire to explain it is hereby refuted.

If, however, the meaning is to be taken to be undertaking, then by speaking of the Yoga to be discussed by undertaking the work, the whole meaning and object of the work is set forth; and the student is easily informed and set to work in the belief that trance is the means of the highest good, as set forth in the Vedas, the Smṛtis, the Itihāsas, and the Purāṇas.

The question arises, Is the word 'Now' to be taken to mean undertaking in all works? Because in that case it would mean the same in the Vedānta Sūtra.

Athāto Brahmajijñāsā.

"Now then a desire to know Brahma."—I. 1. 1.

To meet this objection the commentator specifies :-'This word *here,* etc.'

Another doubt arises. How is Patañjali, the author of the Yoga Teaching, when we have it in the Smṛti of the Yogī Yājñavalkya, that Hiraṇyagarbha and no other ancient was the original teacher of Yoga. For this reason the author of the aphorisms has used the word 'Anuśāsana' (revised text) which means teaching after it has already been taught, not only teaching.

Because the word 'Now' means here an undertaking, the Commentator says that the meaning is that, 'a text giving a revised critical teaching of Yoga is to be understood as having been undertaken.'

But why should it be said that a work teaching Yoga is undertaken here ? It is Yoga itself that is intended to be discussed here.

For this reason is it said :— 'Is to be understood, etc.' It is true that yoga is spoken of as the subject of discussion here. It can, however, be discussed only by means of a work treating of the subject. The action of the teacher works through the instrument and does not directly operate upon the object. With the object of specifically mentioning the action of the teacher, his work treating of the subject of Yoga is to be understood as having been undertaken. Yoga, however, is to be undertaken as the subject of the work.

It should also be known that the hearing of the sound of the word 'atha' (now) when used to denote undertaking, is considered auspicious, like the sight of jar full of water, which some one may be carrying.

The Commentator now removes the doubt as to the meaning of the word 'Yoga' which arises from its ordinary connotation. Thus says he, "Yoga is contemplation." The word 'Yoga' is derived from the root Yuj, to contemplate, and not from the root Yujir, to join, in which latter case it would mean conjunction.

Another question arises again. Trance (Samādhi) is to described later on as being only a branch of Yoga. How can it then be that a part only may be the whole ?

The Commentator adds for this reason :—'and it pervades all its planes.' It is the word 'and' (ca) which distinguishes the whole from the part.

The planes are the states to be mentioned later on, the Madhumatī, the Madhupratīkā, and the Viśokā. They are the states of the mind in which the potencies, only are left in residue in the mind. Yoga, defined as the restraint of mental modifications, is present in all these planes, *i.e.* in all these states of the mind. Not so the trance which is only a branch of it.

Yoga is given here only its root meaning of contemplation, because the statement is made here only as an incentive to study, without intending to emphasize the distinction between the whole and the part. The real meaning of the word 'Yoga' is only the restraint of mental modifications.

For the refutation of those who say that the restraint of mental modifications is dependent upon the self, by reason of the modifications themselves being cognitions and therefore dependent upon the self, it is said :—'and it is a characteristic of the mind.'

By the word 'mind' (citta) the internal organ, the will-to-know is hinted at. The power of consciousness, which is constant in its eternity and thus unchangeable, cannot have the faculty of knowledge for its characteristic. The will-to-be, which is the same as the will-to-know, however may. This is the meaning.

Grant that, but if the Yoga pervades all the mental planes, then, the wandering, the forgetful and the distracted planes of the mind too should be understood by the word 'Yoga' showing as they do the restraint of certain mental modification relatively to the others. To remove this doubt, the planes to be taken and rejected as falling within 'Yoga' are mentioned, beginning with the word, 'wandering, etc.'

The wandering plane or condition of the mind is that in which it is always thrown by disturbing Energy (Rajas) towards these and those objects, and is thus extremely unsteady.

In the *forgetful* condition, the mind is possessed of the modification of deep sleep on account of the excess of inertia (the quality of Tamas.)

The *occasionally steady or distracted* is differentiated from the *wandering*. The difference consists in the occasional steadiness of that which is for the most part unsteady. This excess of its unsteadiness is either required, or brought about by the obstacles of disease, disinclination, etc., to be mentioned later.

The *one-pointed* is that which moves along one line only.

The restrained mind is that in which all the mental modifications have been restrained, and exist only as potencies.

Of these, the *wondering* and the *forgetful* modifications are not denied here *expressly* the status of Yoga, being far removed as they are from that state, in as much as notwithstanding the existence of relative restraint in them, they do not even form links in the chain of causes which lead to the highest good, and because they are in conflict with the nature thereof. To the *occasionally steady,* however, the status of Yoga is expressly denied, because in this case it is possible to mistake it as such on account of its occasional manifestation of steadiness over existing objects of knowledge. In the occasionally steady mind the contemplation does not fall under the heading of Yoga consisting as it does only occasional steadiness of the mind over an existing object. Why ? Because it is followed in close sequence by its contrary state of unsteadiness and inapplication. Having fallen as it does in the midst of the manifestations of a contrary class, its very nature becomes difficult to distinguish from the very first as cause or effect. A seed which has remained in fire even for three or four seconds, will most certainly not sprout into leaves, even though sown.

Which contemplative mental state is then Yoga, if not the one which follows or is followed closely by unsteadiness ?

'That however which in the one-pointed mind, etc.'

The word 'existing as such' keep out an object whose existence is only fastened upon the reality. The words, 'in its most perfect form' are used to signify the best, *i.e.*, that which manifests its essence to its utmost capacity. This is mentioned because the phenomenon of deep sleep also has a mind directed towards the one point which is its then object; that is to say, the quality of inertia (tamas) which though characterized by the absence of all other mental phenomena, does still exist as such; and the excess of inertia is bad because it is the cause of the afflictions.

The word, 'fully' is used to qualify the words, 'shows forth,' because the showing forth, *i.e.*, the knowledge of the realities may be accomplished by verbal and inferential cognitions also. Knowledge so obtained however, is not competent to remove nescience (avidyā) which is directly present in the mind; whereas inferential and verbal knowledge are after all indirect, the object being absent. The word 'fully' (pra) signifies intensity, and therefore indicates direct perceptual knowledge. The present sight of two moons and the doubt as to any particular direction of space go on existing, even though inference and authority point the other way.

Egoism and the other afflictions have their root in nescience. The appearance of knowledge means the removal of nescience. Egoism and other afflictions are also removed on the appearance of knowledge, because they are contrary thereto, and because the cause of their existence is destroyed. For this reason the words, 'removes the afflictions' have been added to the description.

For the same reason does it loosen the bonds in the shape of actions (karma). It is non-antecedent action that is desired to be understood here, by using the word denoting the cause to mean the effect.

'Loosens' means renders unfit for the production of effects. It will be said further.

"It ripens into life-time, life-state and life-experience, if the root exists."—II. 13.

"And inclines it towards restraint" means that it was not so inclined before.

This cognitive trance is four-fold . Hence is it said,

'This is accompanied, etc.'

The ultra-cognitive trance is described by the words,

'When however all the modifications, etc.'

In the *cognitive* trance are restrained those mental modifications of real cognition, etc., which are of the nature of disturbing energy and inertia (rajas and tamas) : and this is done by resort to the class of mental modifications which are of the nature of the essence (sattva). In the *ultra-cognitive,* however, all modifications are restrained. This is the meaning.

The mental planes of Madhumatī, etc., which find their end in these two states, are all the planes. That which pervades all these planes is called Sārvabhauma, all-pervading.

Sūtra 2

योगश्चित्तवृत्तिनिरोधः ।। २ ।।

योगः Yogaḥ. yoga. चित्त Citta, of the mind, mental. वृत्ति Vṛtti, of the modifications, changes, various forms. निरोध Nirodhaḥ, restraint.

2. Yoga is the restraint of mental modifications.

तस्य लक्षणाभिधित्सयेदं सूत्रं प्रववृते। योगश्चित्तवृत्तिनिरोधः। सर्वशब्दाग्रहणात्संप्रज्ञातोऽपि योग इत्याख्यायते। चित्तं हि प्रख्याप्रवृत्तिस्थितिशीलत्वात् त्रिगुणम्। प्रख्यारूपं हि चित्तसत्त्वं रजस्तमोभ्यां संसृष्टमैश्वर्यविषयप्रियं भवति। तदेव तमसाऽनुविद्धमधर्माज्ञानावैराग्यानैश्वर्योपगं भवति। तदेव प्रक्षीणमोहावरणं सर्वतः प्रद्योतमानमनुविद्धं रजोमात्रया धर्मज्ञानवैराग्यैश्वर्योपगं भवति। तदेव रजोलेशमलापेतं स्वरूपप्रतिष्ठं सत्त्वपुरुषान्यताख्यातिमात्रं धर्ममेघ ध्यानोपगं भवति। तत्परं प्रसंख्यानमित्याचक्षते ध्यायिनः। चितिशक्तिरपरिणामिन्यप्रतिसंक्रमा दर्शितविषया शुद्धा चानन्ता च सत्त्वगुणात्मिका चेयमतो विपरीता विवेकख्यातिरिति। अतस्तस्यां विरक्तं चित्तं तामपि ख्यातिं निरुणद्धि। तदवस्थं संस्कारोपगं भवति स निर्बीजः समाधिः। न तत्र किंचित्संप्रज्ञायत इत्यसंप्रज्ञातः। द्विविधः स योगश्चित्तवृत्तिनिरोध इति।। २।।

Vyāsa

The following aphorism was composed with the object of formulating its definition :—

'Yoga is the restraint of mental modifications.'

Because the word, 'all' is not put in before (mental modifications) the Cognitive also is termed Yoga.

The mind is possessed of the 'three qualities,' showing as it does the nature of illumination, activity and inertia. Mental Essence manifesting as illumination loves power and objects of sense, when mixed up with disturbing energy (rajas) and inertia (tamas). The same pierced through by inertia (tamas) approaches vice, ignorance, and absence of desirelessness and supineness. The same shining all round with the veil of forgetfulness removed, but affected by a touch of disturbing energy, approaches virtue, knowledge, desirelessness, and masterfulness. The same becomes itself when the least impurity of disturbing energy (rajas) is removed. It then shows forth only the distinction of nature between the Essence of objective being and the conscious principle (puruṣa), and approaches the state of trance called the Cloud of Virtue (dharma-megha). This the thinkers call the Highest intellection. (Param prasaṅkhyānam).

The power of consciousness changes not. It goes not from object to object. The objects are shown to it. It is pure and infinite. This phenomenon (of the knowledge of the distinct nature of the two) is, however, of the nature of the Objective Essence, and is the opposite thereof. On this account the mind freed from attachment to that too, restrains even this form of manifestation. In that state it is possessed of residual potencies alone. That is the seedless trance. It is called the ultra-cognitive because nothing is cognized in that state.

This is the two-fold Yoga, the restraint of mental modifications.

Vācaspati's Gloss

The second aphorism is introduced by the words,

'This aphorism was composed, etc.'

The word 'its' refers to the two descriptions of Yoga, mentioned in the previous aphorism. "Yoga is the restraint of mental modifications."

That particular state of the mind in which the manifestations of real cognition, etc., have been restrained, is the state of Yoga.

The question arises, is not this definition bad, in as much as it does not cover the Cognitive Trance, in which that class of mental modifications which are of the very nature of its essence (sattva) are not restrained ?

For this reason the Commentator says :—"Because the word 'all' is not put in, etc." If the restraint of *all* the mental modifications were mentioned, the definition would not cover the Cognitive Trance. The restraint of mental modifications, however, which checks the operation of the vehicles of affliction, action and fruition, comprehends that too. In the Cognitive Trance also, the mental modifications caused by disturbing Energy (rajas) and inertia (tamas) are restrained. In fact, the Cognitive trance is the restraint of these modifications.

Why then does the one mind come into relationship with the wandering and other (more than one) planes ? Further, what is the object of restraining the modifications of the mind so conditioned? To meet this apprehended questioning, the Commentator first takes up the cause of the mind thus coming into relationship with different conditions (planes).

'The mind is possessed of the three qualities :—

The Essence (sattva) is there, because it has the nature of illumination. Disturbing Energy is there, because of its possessing the nature of activity. The quality of darkness (tamas) is there, because of its possessing the nature of inertia.

The mention of the nature of illumination is suggestive. All the other qualities, therefore, of the Essence of things (sattva), such as brightness, lightness, joy and others are indicated.

By activity other qualities of disturbing Energy, such as remorse and sorrow, etc., are indicated.

Inertia is the characteristic modification of the quality of Tamas, the opposite of the quality of activity. By the mention of inactivity are indicated heaviness, interception, helplessness, etc.

The meaning is that the mind although *one*, passes into more conditions than one, because it is made up of the three qualities (guṇas) and its modifications are various, because the 'qualities' being unequal, fall into a variety of combinations.

Now the Commentator illustrates so far as may be, these very planes of the mind, the wandering and others, possessing as they do differences of sub-states :—"Mental Essence, etc."

Mental Essence means the Objective Essence (sattva) which has evolved as mind. By saying that the mental essence has the nature of illumination, it is shown that the mind has the quality of Essence (sattva) for its chief factor.

When in the mind, the disturbing Energy and Inertia (rajas and tamas) are a little less predominant than its own Essene, but equal to each other, then to it are dear power and the objects of sense, such as sound, etc. The mind, on account of the Essence being its ruling factor, desires to dwell upon reality. But because the reality is veiled by Inertia (tamas) it mistakes the attainments of Attenuation (Aṇimā), etc., for the reality; and desires to dwell and dwells upon them for a moment. Being pushed away, however by Energy (rajas), even from this resting place, it finds not the rest sought after even there, but gets only a liking for them. As to sound, etc., why its love of them is well established as a matter of course, ever inclining as it does towards them by its own nature. It is the occasionally steady mind that is thus described.

While explaining the wandering mind, the author indicates the Forgetful mind also by words beginning with, 'The same pierced through thereafter by Inertia, etc.'

When Inertia flows into the mind and conquers Energy, then the Energy, having become incapable of driving the veil of the darkness of Inertia away from the Essence of the mind, it is rendered lazy by the Inertia, and approaches vice, etc. Ignorance is Untrue knowledge. Further, the knowledge in deep sleep is described as depending upon the notion of the absence of all other modifications. Therefore the state of forgetfulness (the Mūḍhā Bhūmi) is also indicated. The absence of masterfulness or supineness is the non-fulfilment of one's wishes everywhere. The meaning is that the mind becomes pervaded by vice, etc.

By the words, 'The same when the veil of forgetfulness, etc.,' the author means that, when the same mental Essence shines out in its own nature, then the mind approaches virtue, knowledge, desirelessness and masterfulness. Forgetfulness is inertia (tamas) and the same is the veil. When the veil is removed, it becomes as above described. It is for this reason that it illuminates all the specialized, the unspecialized, the undifferentiated phenomenal and noumenal states and the Puruṣa.

In as much as notwithstanding this, it may not be capable of manifesting virtue and masterfulness on account of the absence of activity, the Commentator says :—'When it is affected by a touch of rajas, etc.' The meaning is that because Energy is the cause of activity, virtue, etc., exist in that state.

This gives a comprehensive description of the mental Essence of the two classes of Yogīs who have reached the stage of Cognitive Trance, the Madhubhūmikās and the Prajñājyotiṣas of the middle path. Now the author describes the state of mind of the fourth class of Yogīs, the Dhyānās or thinkers who have passed the domain of things to be known :—

'The same mind becomes itself, when the least impurity of disturbing Energy is removed.' It is for this very reason that it becomes fixed in its own nature. Purified of the dross of disturbing Energy and Inertia (rajas and tamas) by the device of heating it with the re-agents of practice and desirelessness, the gold of the Essence of the will-to-know becomes established in its own nature, and becomes the master of the senses and their objects, It has thus fulfilled much of its work, but goes on working; as its great work with the achievement of the knowledge of the distinction between the Objective Essence and consciousness. The author says :—

"The same becomes itself when the least impurity of disturbing Energy is removed. It then shows forth only the distinction of nature between the Essence of Objective Nature and the conscious principle, and approaches the state of contemplation called the Cloud of Virtue." The Cloud of Virtue will be described later. He describes here a term better known among the Yogīs :—"This the thinkers, etc." The thinkers call the mind showing forth the distinction of the natures of the Objective Essence and the Conscious Principle, and having the Cloud of Virtue as the other end, by the name of the Highest Intellection. The mind is here spoken of as an abstraction, because the characteristic and the characterized are intended to be spoken of as one.

The Commentator now shows that the power of consciousness is the good and the faculty of discriminative knowledge is not the good. This is with the object of introducing the Inhibitive Trance (Nirodha Samādhi), which restraints the mental modifications of discriminative knowledge, and brings about the perfect freedom of the conscious principle :—

"The power of consciousness changes not, etc."

Impurity consists in identifying the self with pleasure and pain and forgetfulness. Pleasure and pain both cause pain to him who discriminates. Hence they too are to be given up like pain. Even the very beautiful gives pain having an end. Therefore that also has to be given up by him who discriminates. This impurity and end do not exist in the power of consciousness or the Puruṣa. Hence is it said to be pure and infinite.

But how is this power of consciousness pure when it takes the forms of pleasureable, painful and forgetful objects, sounds, etc., while cognizing them ? And how again is it infinite, when it takes up that form and also gives it up ? To meet this the author says :—

'The objects are shown to it.'

It is so described because the objective sounds, etc., are shown to it. It might be impure and finite if it took the forms of the objects in the same way as does the will-to-be. It is in fact the will-to-be that takes the forms of the objects, and presents them to the consciousness, which follows its forms. Thence is it said that the Puruṣa cognizes.

The doubt again arises, how can an object be known if the power of consciousness do not take possession of the will-to-be appearing as an object? If it does take possession, how can it be said that it has not taken the form of the object? For this reason says the author :—

"It goes not from object to object."

Going from object to object means motion, and the teaching is that consciousness does not move. But then how does it take possession of that form ? For this reason he says :—

"The power of consciousness changes not."

The three-fold change, indicated by characteristic, differentia and condition, does not exist in consciousness, that it may put on the form of action and thereby change in conjunction with the will-to-be. It will be described further on how it congizes, even though it moves not.

Thus it is established that the power of consciousness is the good. It has been said that the manifestation of discriminative knowledge is not the good, being as it is of the nature of the will-to-be. For this reason it is the opposite of the power of consciousness.

When even the manifestation of discrimination also is to be given up, what is to be said of the other modifications which are full of shortcomings? This is the meaning. Hence for this reason, the discussion of the Inhibitive Trance is properly introduced. Therefore the author says :—

"On this account the mind tends to turn from it, etc." The meaning is that it checks the indulgence of discriminative knowledge too, by the Higher desirelessness, which is the illumination of knowledge itself.

Now he describes what the aspect of the mind is when all its modifications have been restrained :—

"In that state, etc." That state means the state of Restraint (Nirodha). The nature of restraint or inhibition is described :—"It is the seedless."

The vehicle of actions with that of afflictions is the seed of life-state, life-period and life-experience. The seedless is that which has gone beyond that.

Now the author gives another name of the same which is better known to the Yogis and which is descriptive of the mental state, the ultra-cognitive.

"Nothing is cognized in that, etc."

Sūtra 3

तदा द्रष्टुः स्वरूपेऽवस्थानम्।। ३।।

तदा Tadā, then, at that time, at the time of concentration. द्रष्टुः Draṣṭuḥ, of the seer, of the soul. स्वरूपे Sva-rūpe, in his own nature, or state. अवस्थानम् Avasthānam, resting, standing, remaining, lying.

3. Then the seer stands *in his own nature.*

तदवस्थे चेतसि विषयाभावाद् बुद्धिबोधात्मा पुरुषः किंस्वभाव इति। तदा द्रष्टुः स्वरूपेऽवस्थानम्। स्वरूपप्रतिष्ठा तदानीं चितिशक्तिर्यथा कैवल्ये। व्युत्थानचित्ते तु सति तथापि भवन्ती न तथा।। ३।।

Vyāsa

There being no object of cognition in that state of the mind, what is the state of the conscious principle (puruṣa) who has identified himself with the cognitions of the Will-to-be? "Then the seer stands in his own nature." At that time the power of consciousness

is established in its own nature, as in the state of perfect freedom. In the outgoing mind it appears to be not so centred in its own nature, though in reality it is the same.

Vācaspati's Gloss

Now says he, in order to introduce the next aphorism :—

"There being no object of cognition in that state of the mind, etc." The word 'what' is inquisitive. The meaning is this. The conscious principle is always perceived as the very self of the cognitions of the Will-to-know taking on the forms of various objects. He is never perceived as separate from the cognitions of the Will-to-know. For this reason the knowledge of the will-to-be is of the very nature of the conscious principle, as light of the sun. And it does not exist when the mind is in a state of residual potency (saṁskāra). And no existence can last as such when it has given up its nature.

Let it be so. But then why does not the Puruṣa know the Will-to-be in its state or residual potency? To meet this he says :—"There being no object of cognition, etc."

It is not the Will-to-know alone, but the Will-to-know which has the objects of the Puruṣa to achieve that is the sphere of consciousness. The objects of the Puruṣa are discriminative knowledge and the experience of the objective world. These two no longer exist in the sate of inhibition (nirodha). Therefore the non-existence of objects in that state is established. The author gives the answer by the aphorism—"Then the seer stands in his own nature."

By the word 'svarūpa' (his own nature), the author excludes the appearances of the calm, the ruffled and the forgetful (the Śānta, the Ghora and the Mūḍha) which have been fastened upon it. The nature of the Puruṣa is consciousness alone, unaffected the contacts (of objects placed alongside), not the cognitive action of the Will-to-know appearing as calm, etc. This is of the nature of contacts. It is like the redness which appears in a crystal pure white by nature, when a Japā flower is placed in contact therewith. And it is not necessary that when the things placed in contact are removed, the thing with which they have beén placed in contact, should also disappear. That would mean encroachment of the one into the sphere of the other. The locative case is used, because the thing and the nature of the thing are conceived as being separate, although in reality the same, and not distinct.

The same meaning is rendered clear by the Commentator :—

"At that time the power of consciousness, etc." At that time, in the state of restraint and not in the state of outgoing.

Let that be so. But then the power of consciousness, not standing in its own nature when the Will-to-be is in the state of outgoing activity, and becoming established in that state when in the state of inhibition, becomes changeful. If it be said that it remains established in its own nature even in the state of outgoing activity, then there would be no difference between the states of outgoing activity and inhibition. For this reason says the author :—

'In the outwardly inclined mind, etc.'

The power of consciousness, constant because standing alone, is never disturbed in its own nature; and for this reason is the same inactivity as in the state of restraint. The mother-of-pearl does not for certain, put on and give up its true nature, while becoming the object of true or false knowledge. The knower, however, fancies it to be something different from what it really is.

In relation to the Inhibitive Trance, the Cognitive Trance also is a state of outgoing activity.

Sūtra 4

वृत्तिसारूप्यमितरत्र ।। ४ ।।

वृत्ति Vṛtti, with modifications. सारूप्यम् Sārūpyam, identification. इतरत्र itaratra, at other times, elsewhere.

4. Identification with modifications elsewhere.

कथं तर्हि ? दर्शितविषयत्वात् वृत्तिसारूप्यमितरत्र । व्युत्थाने याश्चित्तवृत्तयस्तदविशिष्टवृत्तिः पुरुषः । तथा च सूत्रम् । एकमेव दर्शनं ख्यातिरेव दर्शनमिति । चित्तमयस्कान्तमणिकल्पं संनिधिमात्रोपकारि दृश्यत्वेन स्वं भवति पुरुषस्य स्वामिनः । तस्माच्चित्तवृत्तिबोधे पुरुषस्यानादिः सम्बन्धो हेतुः ।। ४ ।।

Vyāsa

How then ? On account of objects being presented to it, identification with modifications takes place elsewhere. The conscious principle (puruṣa) is not unaffected by whatever may be the modifications of the mind in the state of outgoing activity. And so in the aphorism :—

"Knowledge is but one; discrimination alone is knowledge."

The mind is like a magnet energized by nearness alone. Being seen it becomes the possession of its lord, the puruṣa. Therefore the reason for knowing the modifications of the mind is the eternal relation of the puruṣa.

Vācaspati's Gloss

For the purpose of introducing another aphorism, the author puts the question, 'How then?' The meaning is this. In what manner does it shine then, if it is not perceived to be what it really is. Adding the word which explains the cause, he reads the aphorism :—

"On account of objects being presented to it, identification with modifications takes place elsewhere."

Elsewhere :—In the state of outward activity, whatever may be the modifications of the mind, the calm, the ruffled, and the forgetful, the same are the manifestations of the conscious principle as he exists in that state.

The word Sa in Sārūpya (identification) means oneness. This is the meaning. The notions, 'I am calm,' 'I am ruffled,' 'I am forgetful,' appear by fastening the modifications of the will-to-be upon the conscious principle, by taking the will-to-know and the conscious principle to be one on account of proximity, as in the case of the white crystal and the Japā flower. This happens in the same way as one looking his face reflected in a dirty mirror, becomes anxious and thinks, 'I am dim.' Although the fastening of the conscious principle upon the will-to-know, is like the knowledge of sound, etc., only a manifestation of the will-to-know, and although this manifestation must be considered to be unintelligent, having, as it does, its origin in the Prakṛti, showing forth as it does the will-to-know as the knower, the manifestation shines forth as a manifestation of consciousness. And similarly does this ātma (self) appear to possess false knowledge, although in reality he has no false knowledge. He appears as the enjoyer, although he is not the enjoyer. He appears as possessed of discriminative knowledge, and illuminated thereby although devoid of it in reality.

This will be shown further under the aphorisms :—

"Consciousness not moving, takes its form and thus the will-to-know knows itself as such."—22.4.

"Enjoyment (Bhoga) consists in the identification of the notions of the Objective Essence and the Conscious principle (puruṣa), which are quite distinct from each other."—34.3.

The Commentator now says that this is recognized by another school also.

"So is the aphorism, etc."

The aphorism "knowledge is but one; discrimination alone is knowledge," is an aphorism of the Acārya Pañcaśikhā.

But how is knowledge but one? The modifications of the will-to-be in the shape of the objects, sound, etc., and in the shape of discrimination, are to be considered Unintelligent. This is one knowledge. The intelligence of the Puruṣa is distinct from it. Its recognition also is knowledge. For this reason says, "Discrimination alone is knowledge."

It is in view of the discrimination of the world possessing the characteristics of appearance and disappearance, that it is said :

"Knowledge is but one."

As to consciousness, it is the nature of the Puruṣa, not of the discriminative faculty. This, however, is not within the range of the perceptive cognition of the world. It falls within the sphere of the inferential and verbal cognitions. This is the meaning.

While showing thus that nescience is the radical cause of mental phenomena, in the state of outgoing activity, it is also indicated that conjunction, the cause of nescience, is the cause of enjoyment, and also that there exists between the two the relation of the owner and the owned. For the purpose of establishing this the Commentator says,

"It becomes the possession of its lord."

This shows the relationship.

But the cognizer, puruṣa, can only be the lord of the mind, when it enjoys the benefit of the service rendered by the mind. And it is not possible that he should so enjoy the service without coming into relationship with the benefit rendered; but it cannot be beneficially acted upon, and there it cannot come into relationship. If, on the other hand, the enjoyment of the benefit is to be considered to be due to the conjunction thereof, then the puruṣa must be considered to be changeful.

For this reason he says, "act by mere nearness."

The mind is not conjoined to the puruṣa; it is merely placed near him. The nearness of the puruṣa is not in space, nor yet in time, on account of the absence of juxtaposition. It is defined by fitness. The puruṣa possesses the power of enjoying as subject, while the mind possesses the power of being enjoyed. This is meant by saying "Being seen, the mind becomes the possession of the lord."

The meaning is that it becomes the object of enjoyment by being transformed into the form of sound, etc. As to enjoyment, although it is a characteristic of the mind, being as it is a modification in the form of sound, etc., still it is spoken of as being a characteristic of the Puruṣa, because of his identifications, with the modifications, on account of the absence of the conception of distinctness between the mind and consciousness.

Thus is established the enjoyment by the Puruṣa of the service rendered by the mind, although he is not conjoined to it; as is also established the unchanging nature of the Puruṣa.

Well then, the relation of owner and owned which is the cause of enjoyment, has its cause in nescience. But what is the cause of nescience? There must be some cause for it, because no effect can come into existence without some cause. As they say,

"What to him doth make,
"Nescience manifest,
"Like dream and so forth."

This doubt is removed by putting the answer in the form of a summary :—"For this reason, etc."

The meaning is this. The cause of the experience of the calm, the ruffled and the forgetful forms of mental modification is the eternal conjunction caused by eternal nescience; and the relation of nescience and potentialization (vāsanā, in each being born from the other in eternal succession is without a beginning like the mutual relation of seed and sprout).

Sūtra 5

वृत्तयः पञ्चतय्यः क्लिष्टाक्लिष्टाः ॥ ५ ॥

वृत्तयः Vṛttayaḥ, modifications. पञ्चतय्यः Pañcatayyaḥ, five fold, of five kinds. क्लिष्टाः Kliṣṭāḥ, painful. अक्लिष्टाः Akliṣṭāḥ, not painful.

5. The modifications are five-fold, painful and not-painful.

ताः पुनर्निरोद्धव्या बहुत्वे सति चित्तस्य, वृत्तयः पञ्चतय्यः क्लिष्टाक्लिष्टाः। क्लेशहेतुकाः कर्माशयप्रचये क्षेत्रीभूताः क्लिष्टाः। ख्यातिविषया गुणाधिकारविरोधिन्योऽक्लिष्टाः। क्लिष्टप्रवाहपतिता अप्यक्लिष्टाः। क्लिष्टच्छिद्रेष्वप्यक्लिष्टा भवन्ति। अक्लिष्टच्छिद्रेषु क्लिष्टा इति। तथा जातीयकाः संस्कारा वृत्तिभिरेव क्रियन्ते। संस्कारैश्च वृत्तय इति। एवं वृत्तिसंस्कारचक्रमनिशमावर्तते। तदेवंभूतं चित्तमवसिताधिकारमात्मकल्पेन व्यवतिष्ठते प्रलयं वा गच्छतीति ॥ ५ ॥

Vyāsa

These then, the five-fold modifications of the mind, painful and not-painful, are to be restrained, being many. The painful are those that cause the afflictions and become the field for the growth of the vehicle of actions (karmāśaya). The not-painful are those that have discrimination for their object and which oppose the functioning of the "qualities." They remain not painful even though fallen into the stream of the painful. They are not-painful even in the intervals of the painful. The painful also remain in the intervals of the no-painful. Potencies (Faculties, of the same class are generated by the modifications themselves; and the modifications are caused by the potencies. Thus the wheel of mental modifications and potencies turns round and round. Such is the mind which when its objects have been attained, rests unmoving like the self, or disappears.

Vācaspati's Gloss

Let that be. A man is taught to do what is only possible. And it is not possible to restrain the mental modifications without knowing them. Further, no one can count them even by a thousand lives of men. Being not counted, how can they be restrained ? Having this doubt he introduces the aphorism laying down the number of these modifications. "These, the five-fold modifications of the mind, the painful and not-painful, are to be restrained, being many," Mental modifications as a class are one : real cognition and others are their five forms. For this reason, modifications having these sub-classes are five-fold, have the sub-divisions. The plural number is properly used, because these modifications are many, on account of the distinctions due to different personalities, such as those of Caitra and Maitra and others. The meaning is that whoever it may be, whether Caitra, Maitra or any other, the mental modifications of them all are five-fold and no more. The use of the singular number of the word 'mind' is for the purpose of denoting the class only. It should be understood to mean the minds.

Now the author mentions a minor classification of the same, as that is useful for the purpose of practice. "Painful and not-painful." The object is that the painful are to be restrained by the help of the not-painful, and these too by the higher desirelessness, "The painful are those, etc." This explains them.

The afflictions of egoism, etc., are the causes of certain mental modifications. The modifications of which the afflictions are the moving causes are spoken of as such, *i.e.*, painful. Or to put it another way. Of the Prakṛti, which works for the achievement of (the objects of) the Puruṣa, the manifestations of the rajas and the tamas are only the causes of the afflictions, and they alone therefore tend towards misery. Affliction being painful, the painful are those in which this affliction, the rajas and tamas manifestation, exists. Inasmuch as they come into manifestation for the purpose of supplying the afflictions only, they are for this very reason, the field for the growth of the vehicle of actions. The meaning is that the Puruṣa having become conscious of the object which is at hand by means of the manifestation of real cognition, etc., becomes attached to them, or is replied from them, and thus makes the vehicle of actions grow. Those become the painful manifestations which are fertile grounds for the growth of virtue and vice.

He describes the not-painful :—"The not-painful are those, etc." Discrimination is the illumination of the cognition of the Objective Essence of the Will-to-be, when it flows undisturbed. By speaking of it as an object, he suggests the knowledge of the distinction between the Objective essence and the Puruṣa, which is the object thereof.

And because they have for their object the knowledge of the distinction between the Objective Essence and the Puruṣa, they are for this very reason the opposers of the functionings of the qualities. The function of the qualities is the initiation of the effects. This ceases with discriminative knowledge. Thus the object of the functioning of the qualities having been fulfilled, they are said to oppose their functioning. For this reason these mental modifications of Real Cognition, etc., are not-painful.

Let that be. No one is born who has no desires. The mental modifications of all living beings are therefore painful. And it is not proper that not-painful modifications should exist in the midst of the stream of the painful modifications. Nor having fallen in the midst of opposing forces, can they be fit to perform any work, even though they do exist. Hence to say that the painful are restrained by the non-painful and the non-painful by the higher desirelessness, is only a wish. Hence the author says :—

"Fallen into the stream of the painful too they are the non-painful."

Practice and desirelessness born by the study of the Veda, induction and precept remain themselves the non-painful even though fallen into the stream of the painful. A Brāhmaṇa living in the village of Shāla which is full of the Kirātas, does not become a Kirāta.

The words "in the intervals of the non-painful" propound an analogy. Because they take their place in the intervals of the painful modifications, the non-painful ones, not suppressed by the painful, gathering strength in due course by habituation suppress the painful ones themselves. This is what the author says :—"Similar potencies are created by modifications, etc." The meaning is that by the non-painful modifications the non-painful potencies are generated. This is the wheel of mental modifications and potencies which always turns round and round, up to the ultra-cognitive Trance.

Such then is the mind, which is the state of suppression remains only in the state of residual potency and thus stands like the self; and it is said by way of an optional mode of expression that it disappears. The final meaning of the aphorism is summarized :—

"These painful and non-painful manifestations are of five descriptions." The words, "Five descriptions" give only the sense; they do not give the connotation of the word because the suffix "tayap" has never been used to connote description.

Sūtras 6 and 7

प्रमाणविपर्ययविकल्पनिद्रास्मृतयः ।। ६ ।।

प्रत्यक्षानुमानागमाः प्रमाणानि ।। ७ ।।

प्रमाण Pramāṇa, real cognition, right knowledge. विपर्यय Viparyaya, unreal cognition, indiscrimination. विकल्प Vikalpa, imagination, verbal delusion. निद्रा Nidrā, deep sleep. स्मृतयः Smṛtayaḥ, and memory.

प्रत्यक्ष Pratyakṣa, direct perception. अनुमान Anumāna, inference. आगमाः Āgamāḥ, and verbal cognition, competent evidence. प्रमाणानि Pramāṇāni, kinds of real cognition, (or proofs).

6. Real Cognition, Unreal Cognition, Imagination, Deep Sleep and Memory.
7. Perception, Verbal Cognition and Inference are real cognitions.

ताः क्लिष्टाश्चाक्लिष्टाश्च पञ्चधा वृत्तयः प्रमाणविपर्ययविकल्पनिद्रास्मृतयः। प्रत्यक्षानुमानागमाः प्रमाणानि। इन्द्रियप्रणालिकया चित्तस्य बाह्यवस्तूपरागात्तद्विषया सामान्यविशेषात्मनोऽर्थस्य विशेषावधारणप्रधाना वृत्तिः प्रत्यक्षं प्रमाणम्। फलमविशिष्टः पौरुषेयश्चित्तवृत्तिबोधः। प्रतिसंवेदी पुरुष इत्युपरिष्टादुपपादयिष्यामः। अनुमेयस्य तुल्यजातीयेष्वनुवृत्तो भिन्नजातीयेभ्यो व्यावृत्तः संबन्धो यस्तद्विषया सामान्यावधारणप्रधाना वृत्तिरनुमानम्। यथा देशान्तरप्राप्तेर्गतिमच्चन्द्रतारकं चैत्रवत्। विन्ध्यश्चाप्राप्तेरगतिः। आप्तेन दृष्टोऽनुमितो वार्थः परत्र स्वबोधसङ्क्रान्तये शब्देनोपदिश्यते शब्दात्तदर्थविषया वृत्तिः श्रोतुरागमः। यस्याश्रद्धेयार्थो वक्ता न दृष्टानुमितार्थः स आगमः प्लवते। मूलवक्तरि तु दृष्टानुमितार्थे निर्विप्लवः स्यात्।। ६-७।।

Vyāsa

These painful and non-painful modifications are of five descriptions :—Real Cognition, Unreal Cognition, Imagination, Sleep and Memory. The Real Cognitions are Perception or sense-cognition; Inference or Sequential Cognition and Verbal Cognition.

Perception is the mental modification which cognizes chiefly the specific appearance of an object, being of the nature of both the generic and the specific qualities, and which has it for its object, by means of the impression caused therein by the external object through the passage of the senses. The result is the knowledge of the modifications of the mind by the Puruṣa, as if they were not all distinguishable from himself. We shall establish further on that the Puruṣa knows by reflex conjunction with the will-to-be.

Inference or Sequential Cognition is the mental modification which cognizes the generic nature chiefly and has for its sphere the relation which exists in objects of the same class with that which is inferred, but does not exist as such in objects of different classes. For example, the moon and the stars are moving objects, because they go from one place to another like Caitra. And the Vindhyā mountain does not move, because it is not seen going from one place to another.

An object perceived or inferred by a competent man is described by him in words with the intention of transferring his knowledge to another. The mental modification which has for its sphere the meaning of words is the Verbal Cognition to the hearer. When the speaker has neither perceived nor inferred the object, and speaks of things which cannot be believed, the authority of Verbal Cognition fails. But it does not fail in the original speaker with reference to either the object of perception or of inference.

Vācaspati's Gloss

The author mentions them by their names, "Real Cognition, Unreal Cognition, Imagination, Sleep and Memory." In enumeration the different parts are understood separately as they are spoken of; and this is a copulative composition in which each word is joined to the other in the sense of the word 'ca' (and) which means the joining of the one to the other.

As in the aphorism :—

"Nescience is the taking of the non-eternal, the impure, the painful and the not-self to be the eternal, the pure, the pleasurable and the self."—5.2.

The definition does not comprehend such confused manifestations of consciousness, as the forgetfulness of directions and the unbroken circle formed by a fast-moving point of light; so even here notwithstanding that the modifications of Real Cognition, etc., are mentioned, the doubt may arise, that there are other modifications, besides those named, in existence. For the removal of this doubt, it was necessary to say Five-fold? It is thereby shown that there are so many modifications and no more.—6.

Going to divide the modification of Real Cognition, he gives the general description of the sub-heads. "The Real Cognitions are Perception, Inference and Verbal Cognitions."

Right Knowledge consists in the unknown truth, which becomes the cause of the soul's setting about to act. The means of obtaining that knowledge is the Real Cognition (the cognizing of the real). The mention of the division is for the purpose of refuting a larger or smaller number of sub-heads.

Out of these the definition of Perception is first given, because that is at the root of all other means of knowledge.

"Perception is, etc."

By using the words, "of an object" the quality of being merely fastened upon (that is, existing as an idea alone) is denied.

By using the words, 'which has it for its object' it is denied that the externality of the object is the sphere of the mental idea thereof. By using the words, 'by means of the impression therein caused by the external object,' the relation of the idea in the mind to the external object of knowledge is shown.

He gives the cause of the impression thereof, even though there be distance between (the knower and the thing known).

"Through the passage of the senses."

Some say an object is the generic quality alone. Others say, an object is the specific quality alone. Other thinkers again say that an object is *possessed* of both descriptions of qualities, the generic and the specific. For their refutation, he says :—

"Being of the nature of both the generic and the specific qualities." An object is not possessed of the generic and the specific qualities; it is of the very nature thereof. This will be shown when the question of simultaneous non-cognition is discussed.

Now he distinguishes the domain of sequential and verbal cognitions from that of perception :—'Which cognizes chiefly the specific appearance of an object.' The meaning is that although in perception, the generic quality also shines out, still it is subordinate to the specific quality. This is only suggestive of direct knowledge—Discriminative knowledge also is suggested, therefore.

He refutes the contradiction of the result of perceptive cognition.

'The result is the knowledge by the Puruṣa of the modifications of the mind.'

The question is, How can knowledge by the Puruṣa be the result of a modification of the mind? If an axe operate upon a Khadira tree, it is not a Plakṣa tree that is cut thereby.

For this reason he says, 'as if they were not at all distinguishable from himself.' It is not the cognitive modification of the mind that takes its place in the Puruṣa; it is on the contrary consciousness reflected in the mirror of the will-to-know, that appears in the form of the modification of the object, because the modification of the will-to-know takes the form of the object. This is the result of the act of perception. This consciousness thus reflected in the will-to-know is not separate from the will-to-know (Buddhi). It is of its very nature, and the modification thereof in the shape of an object is also of the nature of the will-to-know. They co-exist in the same place. It is, therefore, proper that this should be the result of the perceptive cognition. This we shall show.

For this reason the author says :—"The puruṣa knows by reflex conjunction with the will-to-know."

Because Verbal Cognition has its origin in the recognition of the relations established by the inferences of the intellect of the hearer, on account of the appearance therein of the signs of co-existence, etc., in sequence of perceptive knowledge, it is by inference that verbal knowledge becomes possible. For this reason and also because inferred knowledge is imparted thereafter by means of verbal cognition, the commentator gives the definition of inference before that of verbal cognition.

"Inference or Sequential Cognition, etc."

The inferred object is the object possessed of the characteristic desired to be known. Objects of the same class therewith are those similar objects which are placed into the same species on account of the possession of the same generic quality, which is the characteristic to be proved. By saying that it exists in objects of the same class with that which is inferred, the author does away with the presence of contrary and uncommon qualities in the antecedent. Objects of different classes are those which fall not within the same species. These are others than those which fall into the same class, are their contraries and mean their non-existence. By saying that they do not exist as such in objects of different classes, the author emphasizes the necessity of the possession of the generic qualities. Relation is that which furnishes the common bond. This is called the *liṅga,* the sign which is the common bond, the generic quality. By this he shows the characteristic nature of the thing to be proved (pakṣa, sādhya) and thus does away with non-probability.

'Has for its object', (tadviṣaya) means that to which it is bound, as the word viṣaya (object) is derived from the root *Ṣi,* to bind.

The author speaks of cognizing the generic nature, with the object of distinguishing it from the perceptive cognition. The sphere of inference is limited to the generic quality because it is dependent for its birth upon the cognition of relation, and in specific objects there can be no cognition of relationship; and for this reason the common quality alone admits of the recognition of relationship. He gives an example :—"For example." The word 'and' (ca) denotes a cause. Because the Vindhya is not a moving object, it does not change its location. Therefore when motion is removed, change of place disappears. Hence there being change of place, the moon and the stars are moving bodies; as is Caitra. This is proved.

He gives the definition of the mental modification of Verbal Cognition :—"An object perceived or inferred by a competent person, etc."

A competent person is an *Āpta.* Competence (*Āpti*) which radically means "reach," means an all-round comprehension, or the constant presence along with each other of the knowledge of the realities, mercifulness and the skilfulness in their acts of the instruments of knowledge. An *Āpta* or a competent or an authoritative person is one who is possessed of this. An object seen or inferred by him is the object of verbal cognition. The knowledge obtained by an authoritative person such as above described, by hearing is not mentioned here, because knowledge obtained through words has inferential and perceptive knowledge for its root, and therefore must be considered as having been mentioned by the mention of the two only.

"Transferring of his knowledge" consists in the production of knowledge in the mind of the hearer similar to the knowledge which exists in the mind of the authoritative person. For that object it is uttered in words, *i.e.*, is made known for causing gain to, and removing the disadvantages of the hearer. The rest is easy.

When the speaker speaks of things which cannot be believed :—such as, 'it is the ten pomegranates themselves which will become this six cakes.'

'Has neither perceived nor inferred' :—Such as one who says, 'Let him who desires heaven, worship the village tree (Caitya might mean the Buddha, the temple, etc., besides). Such an authority fails.

The question arises that if it be so, the teaching of Manu, etc., also fails because they too speak of things not seen or inferred.

Inasmuch as they say, 'whatever of the dharma of whomsoever is disclosed by Manu, all that is laid down in the Veda,' he was certainly possessed of all knowledge.

For this reason he says :—"When it has been perceived by the original speaker, etc." The original speaker is in such teachings, of course, Iśvara.

Sūtra 8

विपर्ययो मिथ्याज्ञानमतद्रूपप्रतिष्ठम् ।। ८ ।।

विपर्यय: Viparyayaḥ, unreal congnition. मिथ्या Mithyā, of the unreal. ज्ञानम् Jñānam, knowing. अतद् Atad, not its own. रूप Rūpa, form. प्रतिष्ठम् Pratiṣṭham, occupying, standing, possessing.

8. Unreal Cognition is the knowing of the unreal, possessing a form not its own.

विपर्ययो मिथ्याज्ञानमतद्रूपप्रतिष्ठम् । स कस्मान्न प्रमाणं यत: प्रमाणेन बाध्यते । भूतार्थविषयत्वात्प्रमाणस्य । तत्र प्रमाणेन बाधनमप्रमाणस्य दृष्टम् । तद्यथा द्विचन्द्रदर्शनं सद्विषयेणैकचन्द्रदर्शनेन बाध्यत इति । सेयं पञ्चपर्वा भवत्यविद्या । अविद्याऽस्मितारागद्वेषाभिनिवेशा: क्लेशा इति । एत एव स्वसंज्ञाभिस्तमो मोहो महामोहस्तामिस्रोऽन्धतामिस्र इति । एते चित्तमलप्रसङ्गेनाभिधास्यन्ते ।। ८ ।।

Vyāsa

Unreal Cognition is the knowing of the unreal, possessed of a form not its own. Why is it not the knowing of the real? Because the knowledge of the real removes it, inasmuch as Real Cognition has for its object a thing as it exists. Therein is seen the removal of the wrong knowledge by the right one; as for example, the visual knowledge of two moons is removed by the perception which has for its object the thing as it really exists, the one moon.

This it is that is the five-fold Nescience. As it is said :—Nescience, Egoism, Attachment, Aversion, and Love of life are the five afflictions.—3.2. The same are technically called respectively, darkness (tamas), forgetfulness (moha), extreme forgetfulness (mahāmoha), Excessive darkness (tāmisra) and blind darkness (andhatāmisra).

These will be described in the context of the impurities of the mind.

Vācaspati's Gloss

Unreal cognition is the knowing of the unreal, possessed of a form not its own.

Unreal cognition :—This is a statement of the thing to be defined. The knowing of the unreal, etc., is the definition. It means that it has a form which shines out as if it were real knowledge.

The words, 'possessed of a form not its own,' are equivalent to 'not possessed of the form which is its own.' As for example, the words, 'eating what is not dedicated to the Pitṛs,' mean 'not eating what is dedicated to the Pitṛs.'

Doubt also is included in this. There is, however, this much difference. In this, the unstability of the form of the notion exists in the notion itself, whereas in the case of the perception of two moons, etc., the unstability is brought home by the notion of the removal thereof.

The question arises that if it be so, then on consideration, unreal cognition shows itself in imagination also, because there also, the real object is not perceived as such. For this reason says, it is "the knowing of the unreal." This means that this cognition is contradicted by the common knowledge of all mankind. This contradiction exists in the case of unreal cognition, but not in the case of Imagination. Forms of cognition due to Imagination are in common use with mankind, and it is only to those who show the capacities of a learned man and think thereupon that the knowledge of contradiction appeals in this case.

Thus the question is raised, 'why is not that real cognition?' The meaning is that the former knowledge is not the one that is removed by the opposite knowledge acquired thereafter; but that it is the knowledge acquired thereafter that is removed by the former, which has been acquired before and nothing contrary to which has appeared.

Refutes :—'Because it is removed by right knowledge.'

It might be real cognition if the birth of the latter depended upon the former. Here, however, either cognition is given birth to by its own cause, and is not dependent upon the other knowledge. The latter knowledge thus does not take its rise by the destruction of the former and its apperance and therefore, does not consist in the removal of the former. Nor does the appearance of the former knowledge mean the removal of the latter, because this does not exist at that time. For this reason, the cause of the existence of removability is the absence of the close appearance of contrariety : and the cause of the power to remove is the close appearance of contrariety. Therefore, that which is not right knowledge, is removed by right knowledge, inasmuch as the latter has for its object, something which exists as such.

He gives an example :—'Therein is seen the removal of the wrong knowledge by the right one.'

He shows the evil nature of this unreal cognition for the purpose of removal :—'This it is that is the five-fold Nescience.' The meaning is that 'Nescience is the generic quality of all the five, Nescience, Egoism, etc.' The mistaking of the Unmanifested (Avyakta), the Manifested objective existence (Mahat), the Principle of Individuality (Ahaṅkāra), and the five atom-builders (Tanmātras)—the eight forms of the not-self, for the self, is nescience, darkness (tamas). Similarly, the mistaking by the Yogīs of the eight attainments of Aṇimā, etc., which are inauspicious, for the auspicious, is the eight-fold forgetfulness (moha) which comes after the former. And this is called Egoism (asmitā).

Similarly the idea, 'I shall enjoy sound, etc., the ten enjoyments both as seen and heard, when I have acquired by Yoga the eight attainments of Aṇimā, etc. and have thereby become a powerful man (siddha),' is the greater forgetfulness, attachment (Rāga).

Similarly, when led by such a judgment, one sets about to obtain these enjoyments, but finds that the attainments of Aṇimā, etc., are not born on account of obstacles caused by some one and that the enjoyment of the pleasures of both kinds, seen or heard about traditionally, which depend upon the attainments, is not thus obtained, anger against the cause of obstacles appears. This is aversion (dveṣa), called utter darkness.

Similarly, when the powers of Aṇimā, etc., have been attained, and the visible and heard-of objects of enjoyment have been obtained, then the fear that in the end of the Kalpa all this will be destroyed, is the love of sentient life, blind darkness (andhatāmisra or abhiniveśa).

This has been said :–

"Eight-fold is the division of darkness and so of forgetfulness; ten-fold of the greater forgetfulness. Utter darkness is eighteen-fold and so also is blind darkness."

Sūtra 9

शब्दज्ञानानुपाती वस्तुशून्यो विकल्पः ।। ९ ।।

शब्द Śabda, by verbal expression. ज्ञान Jñāna, by knowledge. अनुपाती Anupātī, followed in sequence. वस्तु Vastu, reality, an objective, substratum. शून्यः Śūnyaḥ, devoid of. विकल्पः Vikalpaḥ, imagination.

9. Imagination is followed in sequence by verbal expression and knowledge, and is devoid of object substratum.

शब्दज्ञानानुपाती वस्तुशून्यो विकल्पः । स न प्रमाणोपारोही । न विपर्ययोपारोही । वस्तुशून्यत्वेऽपि शब्दज्ञान-माहात्म्यनिबन्धनो व्यवहारो दृश्यते । तद्यथा चैतन्यं पुरुषस्य स्वरूपमिति । यदा चितिरेव पुरुषस्तदा किमत्र केन व्यपदिश्यते भवति च व्यपदेशे वृत्तिः । यथा चैत्रस्य गौरिति । तथा प्रतिषिद्धवस्तुधर्मो निष्क्रयः पुरुषस्तिष्ठति बाणः स्थास्यति स्थित इति । गतिनिवृत्तौ धात्वर्थमात्रं गम्यते । तथाऽनुत्पत्तिधर्मा पुरुष इति । उत्पत्तिधर्मस्या-भावमात्रमवगम्यते न पुरुषान्वयी धर्मः । तस्माद्विकल्पितः स धर्मस्तेन चास्ति व्यवहार इति ।। ९ ।।

Vyāsa

Imagination is followed in sequence by verbal knowledge and expression, and is devoid of objective substratum. This does not reach up to real cognition. Nor does it reach up to unreal cognition. Even in the absence of an object substratum, its action is found to be dependent upon the power of verbal expression and knowledge.

As for example :—'Puruṣa is of the nature of consciousness.' Now what is here predicated of what ? seeing that Puruṣa is consciousness itself, and that there must always be a statement of the relationship of one to another in predication; as in the phrase Citra's cow.

Similarly, the puruṣa is inactive and the characteristics of an object are denied to it."

"Bāna stands, will stand, has stood." The meaning of the root alone, is understood by (the act of) the cessation of motion.

Similarly in the sentence, "The puruṣa has the characteristics of not being born, "the mere absence of the characteristic of not being born is to be understood, and not any positive characteristic possessed by the puruṣa. That characteristic has therefore, been imagined and has come into practical usage.

Vācaspati's Gloss

"Imagination is followed in sequence by verbal expression and knowledge, and is devoid of an objective substratum." If it is followed in sequence by verbal knowledge and expression, why should not Imagination (vikalpa) fall under the heading of Real Cognition ? If, on the other hand, it is devoid of objective substratum, it must be the same as unreal cognition. For this reason, says :—'This does not reach up to Real Cognition.' Why does it not reach up to real cognition ? 'Because, in the absence of an objective substratum, etc.' This shows why it does not fall under the head of real cognition. 'Its action is found to be dependent upon the power of verbal expression and knowledge.' This shows that it does not fall under the head of Unreal Cognition.

This is the meaning. There being no differences in some particulars, it differs in others, while showing some points of similarity. There being no objective substratum for either the distinction or the absence thereof, imagination shows an unreal image of the substratum; and it is not, therefore, an act of real cognition. Nor is it Unreal Cognition, because it differs from it, in being recognised as such in practice.

Now gives illustrations taken from the sacred writings. 'As for example,' etc., which is the subject to be qualified ? What is it predicated by ? The quality and the thing qualified cannot come into relationship if they are not distinct from each other. The cow cannot be predicated of a cow; it can only be predicated of something different from itself, say Caitra.

This is what he says :—There must always be the statement of relationship of one to another in predication.' 'Predication is the relation between the predicate and the predicated.' In other words, it is the relation between the quality and the thing qualified. It is of this that the statement of a sentence consists; as in the sentence, 'This is Caitra's cow.'

Adds another illustration from the sacred writings too :—"Similarly."

He to whom the characteristics of an object (*i.e.*, the essential force which informs earth, etc.) are denied is spoken of as such. Who is he ? The inactive Puruṣa. There is of course no such characteristic of an object in the Sāṅkhya teaching as non-existence, by which the Puruṣa may be qualified.

The reading in some places is, "The characteristics of an objective substratum are denied." This means as follows :—'Are denied,' means 'are pervaded by denial,' *i.e.*, they are possessed of the quality of being denied. Or in other words, it means that the characteristics of an object are possessed of the quality of being denied. But the characteristics of an object are not possessed of the quality of the non-existence of something, because there can be no relation between existence and non-existence. They are, however, taken as such (*i.e.*, existing).

Gives illustrations from the idiom of the world :—"Bāna stands." As in the sentences, 'He cooks,' 'He breaks', the whole series of the moments of action in which some are antecedent and others subsequent, is recognized as being qualified by one affect, so also in the sentence 'He stands,' the commentator mentions the same state of antecedence and 'postcedence :—'Will stand, has stood.'

Well, suppose that the action of cessation of motion consists in antecedent and postcedent moments just like the action of cooking, and that being different from Bāna it may be predicated of him. For this reason, says :—'The meaning of the root itself is understood by the act of cessation of motion.' The cessation of motion itself is imagined to be the characteristic of an object. Then this fancied characteristic is imagined to be a form of positive existence and even there is fancied an order of the precedence and postcedence. Such is the series of astonishing fanciful conceptions. Non-existence is imagined to existence, and then it is imagined that it comes after something in succession. This fanciful conception is found in all men. It is not, however, a characteristic different from the Puruṣa, so that it might be predicated of him.

Gives another illustration :—'The Puruṣa has the characteristic of not being born.'

Many a thinker has held that the modification of imagination is not different from real and unreal cognition. The detail of these illustrations is meant to explain the matter to them.

Sūtra 10

अभावप्रत्ययालम्बना वृत्तिर्निद्रा।। १० ।।

अभाव Abhāva, of non-existence, of voidness. प्रत्यय Pratyaya, the cause, the feeling. आलम्बना Ālambanā, substratum. अलम्बन *i.e.*, having for its substratum, or support. वृत्ति: Vṛttiḥ, modification. निद्रा Nidrā, deep sleep.

10. Sleep is the mental modification which has for its objective substratum, the cause of non-existence.

अभावप्रत्ययालम्बना वृत्तिनिद्रा। सा च संप्रबोधे प्रत्यवमर्शात्प्रत्ययावशेषः। कथं सुखमहमस्वाप्सम्। प्रसन्नं मे मनः प्रज्ञां मे विशारदीकरोति। दुःखमहमस्वाप्सं स्त्यानं मे मनो भ्रमत्यनवस्थितम्। गाढं मूढोऽहमस्वाप्सम्। गुरूणि मे गात्राणि। क्लान्तं मे चित्तम्। आलसं मुषितमिव तिष्ठतीति। स खल्वयं प्रबुद्धस्य प्रत्यवमर्शो न स्यादसति प्रत्ययानुभवे। तदाश्रिताः स्मृतयश्च तद्विषया न स्युः तस्मात्प्रत्ययविशेषो निद्रा। सा च समाधावितरप्रत्ययवन्निरोद्धव्येति।। १०।।

Vyāsa

"Sleep is the mental modification which has for its objective substratum the cause of non-existence." And this is a particular kind of notion, because it is called back on awakening. How ? 'I have slept well. My mind is clear; it renders my intellect bright,' 'I have slept badly; my mind is listless; it wanders and is unsteady,' 'I have slept with great stupidity; my limbs are heavy; my mind is tired; it stands as it were lazy and absent.' This calling back would certainly not exist on awakening, if there were no recognition of the cause : and there would not be memories dependent thereupon and having that for their object. Therefore sleep is a particular kind of notion, and further it is to be checked in trance like any other modification.—10.

Vācaspati's Gloss

The word 'vṛtti' is the subject of discussion and is, therefore, understood by context. As there is no difference of opinion among rival thinkers as to Real Cognition, Unreal Cognition, Imagination and Memory being mental modifications, the word is not used in those places separately for emphasizing the distinction. In the case of sleep, however, there is difference of opinion. It has, therefore, to be specially stated that it is a modification of the mind. The understanding by context would not serve to emphasize the teaching. Therefore the word modification is repeated a second time.

The non-existence spoken of is of the modifications of the waking and dreaming states. The cause (pratyaya) thereof is the darkness (the quality of inertia) which covers the light of the intellect (the buddhi, the will-to-know). The mental modification, of which this becomes the substratum (that is the object), is spoken of as sleep. The substance of the will-to-be being possessed of the three qualities, whenever inertia appears and overpowers the qualities of essence and disturbing Energy and thus throws a veil over all the means of knowledge, then the will-to-know does not put on the shape of the object of knowledge, and the puruṣa, being conscious for the time of the overpowering darkness of inertia alone, is said to be sleeping well with consciousness turned inwards.

Why then this non-existence of the modifications should not be the modification of sleep? Why should it not be similar to the states of restraint and perfect freedom (kaivalya)? For this reason, says :—

"And that is a particular notion, because it is called back on awakening."

'Calling back' is the remembrance thereof with all its adjuncts. How? When the Tamas appears along with the Sattva, the reflection of one who has awakened after sleep, is like this :— 'I have slept well; my mind is clear and makes my intellect bright.' Bright means pure.

When the Tamas appears along with the Rajas, the reflection is similar to what is expressed by—

'I have slept painfully; my mind is unfit for work.' Why? Because it wanders, it is unsteady.

Then speaks of the reflection of one who awakes after a sleep, in which the Tamas appears, having to its utmost overpowered the Sattva and the Rajas :—

'I have slept very stupidly; my limbs are heavy; my mind is tired, lazy and as it were absent.'

The fact to be proved having been established by the canon of difference, now applies the same canon of difference to the cause thereof.

'Dependent thereupon means caused by the recognition.'

'Having that for their object,' means 'having the cause of the non-existence of the modifications for their object.'

The cause is recognized in this way, 'This is it.'

And it is recognized by him who awakens, *i.e.*, just on awakening. The meaning is that at the time of awakening, the knowledge of the notion exists along with the knowledge of the cause of the non-existence of the modifications.

The question arises : The modifications of Real Cognition, etc., show themselves in an outwardly inclined mind; they are, therefore, to be checked, being contrary to trance. Sleep, however, is similar to the modification of one-pointedness; why then should it be contrary to trance?

For this reason, says :—

'And further it is to be checked in trance like any other modification.' The meaning is that although it is similar to the modification of one-pointedness, yet it is caused by Tamas, and is, therefore, contrary to both the Cognitive and the ultra-cognitive trances.

The meaning is that, that too is to be checked.

Sūtra 11

अनुभूतविषयासंप्रमोषः स्मृतिः ।। ११ ।।

अनुभूत Anubhūta, the objective mental, perceived. विषय Viṣaya, impressions, subjects. असम्प्रमोष: Asampramoṣaḥ, not stealing away along, not slipping away. स्मृति: Smṛtiḥ, memory.

11. Memory is the not stealing away along with objective mental impressions (retained) (*i.e.*, the reproducing of not more than what has been impressed upon the mind).

अनुभूतविषयासंप्रमोषः स्मृतिः। किं प्रत्ययस्य चित्तं स्मरति। अहोस्विद्विषयस्येति। ग्राह्योपरक्तः प्रत्ययो ग्राह्यग्रहणोभयाकारनिर्भासस्तज्जातीयकं संस्कारमारभते। स संस्कारः स्वव्यञ्जकाञ्जनस्तदाकारामेव ग्राह्यग्रहणोभयात्मिकां स्मृतिं जनयति। तत्र ग्रहणाकारपूर्वा बुद्धिः। ग्राह्याकारपूर्वा स्मृतिः सा च द्वयी। भावितस्मर्तव्या चाभावितस्मर्तव्या च। स्वप्ने भावितस्मर्तव्या। जाग्रत्समये त्वभावितस्मर्तव्येति। सर्वाश्चैताः स्मृतयः प्रमाणविपर्ययविकल्पनिद्रास्मृतीनामनुभवात्प्रभवन्ति। सर्वाश्चैता वृत्तयः सुखदुःखमोहात्मिकाः। सुखदुःखमोहाश्च क्लेशेषु व्याख्येयाः। सुखानुशयी रागः। दुःखानुशयी द्वेषः। मोहः पुनरविद्येति। एताः सर्वा वृत्तयो निरोद्धव्याः। आसां निरोधे संप्रज्ञातो वा समाधिर्भवत्यसंप्रज्ञातो वेति।। ११ ।।

Vyāsa

Does the mind remember the act of knowing or the object? The notion coloured by the object of knowledge shows out both the object and the act of knowledge, and thus begins the formation of the habit of the same kind. The habit manifests its own cause, and thus generates a memory, having the same form and consisting of both the object and the act of knowledge. When the manifestation of the act of knowledge is the first of the two, the modification is the intellect (buddhi). When the appearance of the object of knowledge is the first, it is Memory.

This memory is two-fold : When the phenomenon to be remembered has become the very nature of the mind, and when it has not so become. In dream it is the former; at the time of waking the latter.

All these memories are born in sequence of the impressions of Real Cognition,

Unreal Cognition, Imagination, Sleep and Memory. Further, all these modifications are of the nature of pleasure, pain and illusion. Pleasure, pain and illusion will be described among the afflictions. 'Attachment is the sticking to pleasure as such in sequence.'—7.2. 'Aversion is the sticking to pain as such in sequence.' 8.—2. Illusion, however, is Nescience. All these modifications are to be checked. It is when these have been checked that there comes either the Cognitive or the ultra-cognitive trance.

Vācaspati's Gloss

"Memory is the not stealing away along with mental impression." Memory is the not stealing away along with an object which has come into the mind by real cognition, etc. It is only the object of knowledge which comes into consciousness by mental habit alone and which shines forth into the mind in consequence of the cognition of the cause of the habit, that is one's own. The taking of an object, however, over and above that is theft, on account of its similarity with the act. The word 'pramoṣa' is derived from the root 'muṣ,' to steal.

This is the meaning; Right cognition and others all cause the knowledge of an object unknown, either in the ordinary or in some particular way. Memory, however, does not pass over the limitation of the former knowledge. It is that former knowledge or something less than that which is its object, never something more. This is the distinction of memory from other modifications. The question, 'Does it remember the notion or the object?' starts this discussion.

It would appear that the habit generated by an act of knowledge puts into the mind the object of knowledge only, because the impression in the mind is caused by the coming in of the object of knowledge : and no mental impression can come into existence of itself. If the mental impressions itself were reproduced, it would be the mental impression alone (and not the object of knowledge).

For this reason the author comes to the final conclusion that it is a remembrance of both. Because the mental impression (the act of knowledge) takes its origin from the object of knowledge, the former is coloured by the latter. In reality, however, it manifests, *i.e.*, illuminates the form, that is the appearance of both the object, and the act of knowledge.

That which brings anything into manifestation is its cause (vyañjaka, manifester). Its manifestation is the form thereof. Hence the meaning of the original is, 'possessing the form of its cause.'

The questions arises, what is the difference between the memory and the intellect (buddhi), if they have the same form as far as their genesis is concerned?

For this reason, the author says :—"When the form of the act of knowledge is the first of the two, etc."

An act of knowledge consists in the taking in of an object; and it is not possible that there should be the taking in of an object which has already been taken in, *i.e.*, known. Hence by this is described the knowing of the yet unknown, which is intellection. It is described to be such as the form or appearance of knowledge is the first, *i.e.*, the most important factor therein. And although there is no difference in nature, the preponderance of the quality is established.

Memory is described to be that in which the form of the object of knowledge is the first or foremost appearance. By the form of the object of knowledge being the first in appearance, it is meant that the object of knowledge has already been subjected to the operation of the other mental modifications. It is said the field of memory comprises the mental impressions which have already been subjected to the operation of other mental modifications. And this is what is "not stealing along with mental impressions."

But this stealing exists in memory too. It shows in dream past phenomena impressed upon the mind at different times and places, such as the names, etc., as connected with other times and places which have not passed into the mind as such. For this reason, he says, 'It is two-fold.'

'That which has become of the very nature of mind,' means raised into being by mental potency, imagined. This is that in which the object of memory has already been made part of the mind.

The other is that which has not become of the nature of the mind, which is not raised out of mental potencies, is not imagined and is therefore real.

This is not memory, it is on the contrary unreal cognition, fitting in as it does with the definition thereof. It is called memory because it only looks like it, just as what looks like real cognition is called real cognition.

But then why is memory mentioned last of all ?

The reason is given :—'All these memories, etc.' 'Impression in sequence' means taking in. Memory is a modification preceded by this taking in. That is to say, the genesis of memory is therefrom.

The question arises that an intelligent man will only check the modifications which cause misery to the Puruṣa, and such are the afflictions, not the modifications as such. What then is the object of their suppression? For this reason, he says :—All these, etc., This is easy.

Sūtra 12

अभ्यासवैराग्याभ्यां तन्निरोधः ।। १२ ।।

अभ्यास, Abhyāsa, by practice. वैराग्याभ्याम्, Vairāgyābhyām, by desirelessness, unattachment. तद्, Tad, their. निरोधः, Nirodhaḥ, restraint, control.

12. They are restrained by practice and desirelessness.

अथासां निरोधे क उपाय इति। अभ्यासवैराग्याभ्यां तन्निरोधः। चित्तनदीनामोभयतोवाहिनी या वहति कल्याणाय वहति पापाय च। या तु कैवल्यप्राग्भारा विवेकविषयनिम्ना सा कल्याणवहा। संसारप्राग्भारा अविवेकविषयनिम्ना पापवहा। तत्र वैराग्येण विषयस्रोतः खिलीक्रियते। विवेकदर्शनाभ्यासेन विवेकस्रोत उद्घाट्यत इत्युभयाधीनश्चित्तवृत्तिनिरोधः।। १२ ।।

Vyāsa

Well then, what is the means for restraining them? "They are restrained by practice and desirelessness."

The stream of mind flows both ways; flows towards good and it flows towards evil. That which flows on to perfect independence (kaivalya) down the plane of discriminative knowledge, is named the stream of happiness. That which leads to re-birth and flows down the plane of undiscriminative ignorance, is the stream of sin.

Among these the flow of the desirables is thinned by desirelessness; the flow of discrimination is rendered visible by habituating the mind to the experience of knowldege.

Hence suppression of the mental modification is dependent upon both.

Vācaspati's Gloss

The Commentator asks the means of restraint. "Well then, what, etc." He answers by the aphorism :—'They are restrained by practice and desirelessness.' The operation of practice and desirelessness on the manifestation of restraint is collective, on account of each operating as a branch of the other. They are not optional. For this reason he says :—'The stream of mind flows both ways, etc."

'Flows towards' : The word *prāgbhārā* in the original means bank, limitation; and the idea is that the stream is so banked, *i.e.*, limited in its flow as to reach the state of perfect independence (kaivalya).

"Down the plane :" The word 'nimna' in the original means down, an inclination of the ground, such as makes it possible for water to flow in a particular direction. It also means depth, into which water would always flow.

Sūtra 13

तत्र स्थितौ यत्नोऽभ्यासः ।। १३ ।।

तत्र, Tatra, of these, there. स्थितौ Sthitau, as regards the steadiness, as regards keeping them perfectly restrained. यत्नः Yatnaḥ, the effort, continuous struggle. अभ्यासः Abhyāsaḥ (is) what is called practice.

13. Of these, practice is the effort to secure steadiness.

तत्र स्थितौ यत्नोऽभ्यासः। चित्तस्यावृत्तिकस्य प्रशान्तवाहितास्थितिस्तदर्थः प्रयत्नो वीर्यमुत्साहस्तत्संपिपादविषया तत्साधनानुष्ठानमभ्यासः।। १३ ।।

Vyāsa

Steadiness is the undisturbed calmness of the flow of the mind, when it has become free from the modifications.

Effort to secure that end is the putting out of energy to secure, and aspiration towards that.

Practice is the resort to the means thereof with the object of attaining it.

Vācaspati's Gloss

Of these, the author describes practice by stating its nature and object; 'Of these, practice is the effort to secure steadiness.'

The commentator explains the same :—'When the mind has become free from the modifications :' is separated from the modifications due to Rajas and Tamas, the flow of the modifications of the quality of Essence is established in the shape of calm one-pointedness and purity. This is steadiness.

'Effort to secure that end,' is the meaning of the locative case of the word 'sthiti' used to signify that object. As is the case in the sentence, 'Carmani dvipinam hanti,' of which the meaning is, 'Kills the tiger for the sake of the skin.'

He clears the meaning of effort by giving synonyms : energy, aspiration. He explains :—'With the object of attaining that'. 'That' here means steadiness.

He speaks of the field for the action of that energy :—'Resort to the means thereof.' The means for the attainment of steadiness are the internal and external Yogas, the restraints and observances, etc. The action of the actor is directed towards the means, not towards the fruit.

Sūtra 14

स तु दीर्घकालनैरन्तर्यसत्कारासेवितो दृढभूमिः ।। १४ ।।

सः Saḥ, that, this. तु, Tu, and. दीर्घ-काल, Dīrgha-kāla, for a long time. नैरन्तर्य Nairantarya, without interruption. सत्कार Satkāra, with devotion, आसेवितः Āsevitaḥ, being well-attended to. दृढ-भूमिः Dṛdha, bhūmiḥ, firmly rooted, of firm ground, well fixed.

14. And this is firmly rooted, being well-attended to for a long time without interruption and with devotion.

स तु दीर्घकालनैरन्तर्यसत्कारासेवितो दृढभूमिः । दीर्घकालासेवितो निरन्तरासेवितः सत्कारासेवितः । तपसा ब्रह्मचर्येण विद्यया श्रद्धया च संपादितः सत्कारवान्दृढभूमिर्भवति । व्युत्थानसंस्कारेण द्रागित्येवानभिभूतविषय इत्यर्थः ।। १४ ।।

Vyāsa

"Well attended to for a long time," "well attended to without interruption," "well attended to with devotion," *i.e.*, brought about by purificatory action (tapas), by continence, by knowledge and by faith, it becomes firmly rooted with welcome devotion. The meaning is that its operation is not then conquered all at once by the outgoing habits of the mind.

Vācaspati's Gloss

But how can practice secure steadiness, when its operations are opposed by the highway robber of outgoing habits, which are in existence from eternity ? He explains :—"And this is firmly rooted, being well attended to for a long time, without interruption and with devotion."

This practice then reaches the state of firmness, but not at once, inasmuch as being possessed of the three qualities, its domain, the appearance of calmness, is often overpowered by the habits of outgoing.

If again, having even had resort to practice of this description, one gives it up, it will be overpowered by lapse of time. Hence it should not be given up. This is the meaning.

Sūtra 15

दृष्टानुश्रविकविषयवितृष्णस्य वशीकारसंज्ञा वैराग्यम् ।। १५ ।।

दृष्ट Drṣṭa, perceptible. अनुश्रविक Anuśravika, scriptural. विषय Viṣaya, enjoyments. वितृष्णस्य Vitṛṣṇasya, in him or of him who is free from thirst for. वशीकार Vaśīkāra, supremacy. संज्ञा Sañjñā consciousness. वैराग्यम् Vairāgyam, desirelessness,

15. Desirelessness is the consciousness of supremacy in him who is free from thirst for perceptible and scriptural enjoyments.

दृष्टानुश्रविकविषयवितृष्णस्य वशीकारसंज्ञा वैराग्यम्। स्त्रियोऽन्नपानमैश्वर्यमिति दृष्टविषये विरक्तस्य स्वर्गवैदेह्यप्रकृतिलयत्वप्राप्तावानुश्राविकविषये वितृष्णस्य दिव्यादिव्यविषयसंप्रयोगेऽपि चित्तस्य विषयदोष-दर्शिनः प्रसंख्यानबलादनाभोगात्मिकाहेयोपादेयशून्यावशीकारसंज्ञावैराग्यम् ।। १५ ।।

Vyāsa

A mind free from attachment to perceptible enjoyments, such as women, foods, drinks, and power, and having no thirst for scriptural enjoyables, such as heaven and the attainment of the states of the Videha and the Prakṛtilaya, has, when it comes into contact with such divine and worldly objects, a consciousness of its supremacy, due to an understanding of the defects of the objects, brought about by virtue of intellectual illumination. This consciousness of power is the same as the consciousness of indifference to their enjoyment, and is devoid of all desirable and undesirable objects as such. This mental state is desirelessness (Vairāgya).

Vācaspati's Gloss

The author describes desirelessness :—"Desirelessness is the consciousness of supremacy in him who is freed from thirst for perceptible and scriptural enjoyments."

He describes the freedom from thirst for intelligent and non-intelligent perceptible objects :—'women, etc.'

Power is lordship. Scripture is the Veda. Those that are known from the Veda are scriptural enjoyments, such as heaven, etc. He speaks of desire for them too : such as "heaven, etc."

The Videhas are the disembodied, who live only in the vehicles which serve as instruments (of knowledge and action.) The state of the disembodied (vaidehya) is their state of existence.

Others believe the Prakṛti only to be the self. They meditate upon the Prakṛti. They are merged in the functional Prakṛti alone. (The functional Prakṛti is that in which the state of the equipoise has been disturbed, *i.e.*, not the Mūlaprakṛti). The state of the Prakṛtilaya is their state of existence.

Scriptural enjoyments consist of the attainment of these states. He who is free from thirst for scriptural objects, is the same who is free from the desire of attaining heaven etc.

The question arises that inasmuch as there is absence of desire even for objects that have never been possessed, such absence too would be desirelessness if desirelessness signified only absence of desire. Therefore the commentator says :—'when it comes into contact with such divine and worldly objects. Desirelessness is not the mere absence of desire. On the contrary, it is the consciousness of indifference to enjoyment, even though divine and worldly objects be in contact. He renders the same plainer : 'Is devoid of all desirable and undesirable objects as such.'

Consciousness of supremacy is the consciousness of indifference, freedom from attachment or aversion.

But then whence does it come? He explains :—'By virtue of intellectual illumination.'

The defect of objects is contained in their being surrounded by three-fold pain. Intellectual illumination is the full recognition of this fact with the object of removing them. By virtue thereof is the understanding of the defects brought about.

The authorities speak of four stages in the unfoldment of consciousness :—The consciousness of endeavour, the consciousness of difference, the consciousness of one faculty and the consciousness of supremacy.

Attachment, etc., are the impurities of the mind. The powers of sensation, action, and thought are led by these to work up their several objects. Endeavour is the putting in of effort for burning them, so that the powers may not incline to work upon their several objects. This is the consciousness of endeavour.

When the endeavour has begun, some of the impurities are found to be ripe; others are being ripened; and others again are going to be ripened. The consciousness of difference consists in differentiating the ripe and the ripening.

When the powers become incapable of action, the wish alone remains in the mind, so far as the ripe ones are concerned. The consciousness of this state is called 'the consciousness of the one faculty.'

When physical and ultra-physical objects of enjoyment take up the position of receding, the position of indifference even to the wish, is beyond the three stages of consciousness, and is called the consciousness of supremacy. The object of the first three having been fulfilled by this alone, they have not been mentioned separately. Thus all is plain.

Sūtra 16

तत्परं पुरुषख्यातेर्गुणवैतृष्ण्यम्।। १६।।

तत् Tat, that. परम् Param, is higher. पुरुष Puruṣa, of the Puruṣa. ख्याते: Khyāteḥ, due to the knowledge. गुण Guṇa, to the qualities. वैतृष्ण्यम् Vaitṛṣṇyam, indifference.

16. The same is Higher, when there is indifference to the knowledge of the Puruṣa.

तत्परं पुरुषख्यातेर्गुणवैतृष्ण्यम्। दृष्टानुश्रविकविषयदोषदर्शी विरक्त: पुरुषदर्शनाभ्यासात्तच्छुद्धि-

प्रविवेकाप्यायित बुद्धिर्गुणेभ्योव्यक्ताव्यक्तधर्मकेभ्यो विरक्त इति। तद्‌द्वयं वैराग्यम् तत्र यदुत्तरं तज्ज्ञानप्रसादमात्रं यस्योदये सति योगी प्रत्युदितख्यातिरेवं मन्यते। प्राप्तं प्रापणीयम्। क्षीणाः क्षेतव्याः क्लेशाः। छिन्नः शिलष्ट पर्वाभवसंक्रमो यस्या विच्छेदाज्जनित्वाम्रियते मृत्वा च जायत इति। ज्ञानस्यैव पराकाष्ठा वैराग्यम्। एतस्यैव हि नान्तरीयकं कैवल्यमिति।। १६।।

Vyāsa

He who sees the defects of the perceptible and scriptural objects of enjoyment, is indifferent (to them.)

He whose Will-to-know is saturated with the notion of the distinctive nature of the Puruṣa, brought about by the purity of the effort to know him, becomes indifferent to the 'qualities,' both in their manifested and unmanifested state.

There are two forms of desirelessness. Of these the latter is but the light of spiritual knowledge. When this light shines, discrimination arises. Then the Yogī thinks thus :— Whatever was to be obtained has been obtained. The afflictions that were to be destroyed have been destroyed. The fast-jointed chain of life which, when it is not broken, there is or occurs birth after death and death after birth, has been broken. Desirelessness is but the highest perfection of spiritual knowledge; and absolute independence (kaivalya) is nothing else.

Vācaspati's Gloss

Having described the Lower desirelessness, the author now describes the Higher : "The same is Higher when there is indifference to the 'qualities,' due to knowledge of the Puruṣa."

He shows that Lower desirelessness is the antecedent to the Higher, and that it is the entrance to that. Lower Desirelessness is shown by the words, "he who sees the defects of perceptible and scriptural objects of enjoyment, is indifferent to them."

"Brought about by the effort to know the Puruṣa;" the knowledge of the Puruṣa is his recognition by means of the Veda, by inference and by the teaching of the masters. The 'effort to know' consists in the repeated resort to the means. The purity of the knowledge consists in the steady flow of the quality of essence (sattva), due to the removal of active disturbance (rajas) and inertia (tamas). This brings about the recognition of the distinct natures of the Puruṣa and the "qualities." The Puruṣa is pure and infinite. The 'qualities' are contrary thereto. The Yogī whose intellect is saturated by the recognition, is spoken of as such. The trance known as the Cloud of Virtue is spoken of here.

Such a Yogī is entirely free from attachment to the 'qualities,' whether possessing the characteristic of the manifested or the unmanifested; so much so that he is free from attachment even to the mental phenomenon of recognition of the distinct nature of the Objective Essence and the Puruṣa, which itself is a manifestation of the qualities.

Thus there are two forms of desirelessness. The former desirelessness exists when the mental essence (sattva) has been rendered free from inertia (tamas), by the manifestation of its essential nature (the sattva), but there still remains a trace of the dirt of disturbing energy (rajas).

This view is common to the Tauṣṭikas, those who are addicted to enjoyment in the states. It is by that of course that they become Prakṛtilayas. So it has been said :—'One becomes a Prakṛtilaya by desirelessness.'

The last of the two is but the light of knowledge. By the use of the word 'but' it is indicated that in that state no objects of knowledge exist. The mental essence as it exists in that state is similar to the same, but is besides untainted by the least impurity, of Disturbing Energy (rajas). It is therefore said to be the light of knowledge. Mental Essence is by nature purity : but it puts on impurity by the taint of disturbing energy (rajas) and inertia (tamas). When the impurities of *rajas* and *tamas* have been washed away by the pure showers of desirelessness and practice, it becomes highly illuminated, and the light of spiritual knowledge is left there alone.

He shows that in that state the 'qualities' become unworthy of acceptance :—'When this light shines, discrimination arises in the Yogī'. The meaning is that the Yogī becomes possessed of the present discriminative knowledge, when other forms of knowledge have disappeared.

What was to be obtained, *i.e.*, perfect independence (kaivalya) has been obtained. As will be said, 'the wise man becomes free while living.' The meaning is that this takes place because residual potencies only remain with their root cut off. How is it that all that had to be attained, has been attained? Because the afflictions of Nescience, etc., which had to be removed, have been removed together with their residual aroma.

But then there is the store of virtue and vice which is used as a chain to bind living beings to birth and death in the universe. How then can there be absolute freedom ? For this reason, the reason, the commentator says :—'The fast-jointed chain, etc., is broken.' The 'fast-jointed chain' means that whose joints are so firmly and closely fastened together that they appear to be one whole and do not appear to have been fastened together. It is the pieces of virtue and vice stored, which, as individual pieces in the collection, are put together to make the fast joints of a chain. 'The chain of existence' implies that the living being is not freed from the bonds of birth and death. This chain is broken when the afflictions have been done away with. And so it has been said :—

'The vehicle of actions has its root in nescience.'—2.12.

'It bears fruit if there is a root.'—2.13.

It may be questioned, that in as much as restraint is the intermediate stage between the fruition of intellection and the Cloud of Virtue, what is this that is called the mere light of knowledge?

For this reason, he says :—'Desirelessness is the highest perfection of spiritual knowledge?' The Higher desirelessness is but a form of the Cloud of Virtue, nothing else. As will be said further on.

'To him who desires nothing even from intellection (prasaṅkhyāna) comes the trance known as the Cloud of Virtue, by constant manifestation of discrimination (IV. 29). and

'Then the knowable is but little, because knowledge is infinite, free as it is from all veils and impurities.'—(IV.31).

For this reason it is that absolute independence is this and nothing else.—16.

Sūtra 17

वितर्कविचारानन्दास्मितारूपानुगमात्संप्रज्ञातः ॥ १७ ॥

वितर्क Vitarka, of philosophical curiosity. विचार Vicāra, of meditation. आनन्द Ānanda, of elation. अस्मिता Asmitā, egoism. रूप Rūpa, appearances. अनुगमात् Anugamāt, by the accompaniment, by the company of, is accompanied by. संप्रज्ञातः Samprajñātaḥ, the cognitive trance.

17. The Cognitive Trance is accompanied by the appearances of philosophical curiosity, meditation, elation and egoism.

अथोपायद्वयेन निरुद्धचित्तवृत्तेः कथमुच्यते संप्रज्ञातः समाधिरिति। वितर्कविचारानन्दास्मितारूपानुगमात्संप्रज्ञातः। वितर्कश्चित्तस्यालम्बने स्थूल आभोगः। सूक्ष्मो विचारः। आनन्दो ह्लादः। एकात्मिकासंविदस्मिता। तत्र प्रथमश्चतुष्टयानुगतः समाधिः सवितर्कः द्वितीयो वितर्कविकलः सविचारस्तृतीयो विचारविकलः सानन्दः चतुर्थस्तद्विकलोऽस्मितामात्र इति। सर्व एते सालम्बनाः समाधयः।। १७।।

Vyāsa

Now then, how is the Cognitive Trance said to appear in those whose minds have been restrained by the two means? 'The Cognitive Trance is accompanied by the appearances of philosophical curiosity meditation, elation, and egoism.'

Philosophical curiosity (vitarka) is a superficial attempt of the mind to grasp any object.

Meditation is a subtle attempt. Elation is bless. Egoism is the consciousness of being one with the self.

Of these, the first is the Savitarka Trance accompanied by all the four. The second is the Meditative (Savicāra) where indistinctness ends. The third is Elative (Sānanda) where meditation ends. The fourth is the purely egoistical (Sāsmitā) where elation ends. All these trances have something to grasp (Ālambana).

Vācaspati's Gloss

Having described the means, the commentator now puts a question with the object of introducing the description of the acquisition they lead to, together with that of its various classes :—'Now then how is the Cognitive Trance, etc.' The Cognitive Trance is accompanied by the appearances of philosophical curiosity, meditation, elation, and egoism.

The Cognitive Trance is first described because it precedes the ultra-cognitive. The general nature of the Cognitive Trance is to be understood in the accompaniment of the natures, *i.e.*, the forms, of philosophical curiosity, meditation, elation and egoism.

He defines philosophical curiosity :—'A superficial attempt of the mind, etc.' Grasp (ābhoga) is the manifestation of consciousness consisting of the illumination of the nature of objects. It is called 'Superficial' because it has the gross phenomena for its sphere of action. As the new archer first aims at large objects only, and then at smaller and smaller ones by and by, so the neophyte in Yoga first learns the nature of gross objects of thought only, such as those made of the five Mahābhūtas (physical states of matter), the four-armed god, etc.; and then the subtle ones.

In this way the grasp of the objects by the mind becomes subtle. Meditation has for its sphere of action, the causes of the gross phenomena, the subtle elements, the five tanmātras, the manifested and the unmanifested essence of matter (the liṅga and the aliṅga).

Having thus shown the range of the objective phenomena, he now shows the range of the instrumental phenomena :—'Elation is, etc.' Elation is that blissful modification of consciousness, which consists in the illumination of the mind, as regards the acts of sensation, with gross phenomena for their objects. The nature of the powers of sensation is to enlighten, because they are born out of the principle of individuality, with the quality of essentiality (Sattva) predominating. Pleasure is a manifestation of the quality of Essentiality (Sattva). Acts of sensation too are therefore of the nature of pleasure. The manifestation of consciousness consisting of the illumination of this aspect is bliss.

He describes the Cognitive Trance having the subject (Gṛhitrī) for its sphere of action :—'Egoism is the consciousness of being one with the self.' Egoism is the subtle cause of the instrumental powers inasmuch as they are born out of it; and this egoism appearing as the self, the subject is the consciousness of being one with the self. This Cognitive Trance has the subject for its sphere of action, because the subject is always hidden behind egoism.

He mentions other minor differences of all the four :—'The first, etc.' The cause is always present in the effect, as its antecedent state; not so the effect in the cause, Therefore, this superficial range of consciousness is accompanied by all the four—the gross and its causes, the subtle, the instrumental and the subjective. The others have three, two and one cause, respectively as their spheres of action, and they have therefore three, two and one appearance, respectively.

He distinguishes the ultra-cognitive :—'All these, etc.'

Sūtra 18

विरामप्रत्याभ्यासपूर्वः संस्कारशेषोऽन्यः ।। १८ ।।

विराम Virāma, of cessation. प्रत्याभास pratyābhāsa, the notion. पूर्वः Pūrvaḥ, the former, the preceding, all the three together means having for its preceding the notion of cessation, preceded by the notion of cessation. संस्कार-शेषः Saṁskāra Śeṣaḥ, in which remain only the (शेष) residual potencies or impressions. (संस्कार) अन्यः Anyaḥ, the other.

18. Preceded by the constant repetition of the notion of cessation is the other; in which the residual potencies only remain.

अथासंप्रज्ञातः समाधिः किमुपायः किंस्वभावो वेति। विरामप्रत्ययाभ्यासपूर्वः संस्कारशेषोऽन्यः। सर्ववृत्तिप्रत्यस्तमये संस्कारशेषो निरोधश्चित्रस्य समाधिरसंप्रज्ञातः। तस्य परं वैराग्यमुपायः। सालम्बनो ह्यभ्यासः तत्साधनाय न कल्पत इति विरामप्रत्यया निर्वस्तुक आलम्बनी क्रियते। स चार्थशून्यः। तदभ्यासपूर्वकं हि चित्तं निरालम्बनमभावप्राप्तमिव भवतीत्येष निर्बीजः समाधिरसंप्रज्ञातः।। १८ ।।

Vyāsa

What now are the means and the nature of the ultra-cognitive trance? "Preceded by constant repetition of the notion of cessation is the other in which the residual potencies only remain."

The ultra-cognitive trance is that state of mental restraint, in which all its modifications cease from action and remain only in *posse*. Its means is the Higher desirelessness.

Inasmuch as any form of practice having an objective phenomenon for its basis, cannot become the means of achieving it, the notion of cessation which is nothing substantial, is here made the basis; and that is devoid of any objective phenomenon. By the constant repetition of this notion, the mind having no object to grasp, becomes as it were, non-existent. The trance being thus seedless, is the ultra-cognitive.

Vācaspati's Gloss

The commentator asks a question to introduce the ultra-cognitive, whose discussion is now in order :—'What now, etc.'

"Preceded by the constant repetition of the notion of cessation is the other, in which the residual potencies only remain."

The words, 'preceded by the constant repetition of the notion of cessation,' show the means; the remaining words describe the nature. The words, 'in which the residual potencies only remain,' are explained as, 'in which all its modifications cease, etc.'

The words, 'preceded by the constant repetition of the notion of cessation,' are explained by the words, 'It means is the Higher desirelessness.'

Cessation is the absence of mental modifications. Its notion is the cause. Its practice consists in its repetition over and over again. That which this repetition precedes is described as such.

Now he says why the lower desirelessness does not become the cause of restraint (nirodha) :—'Inasmuch as any form of practice having an cbjective phenomenon as its basis, etc.'

The cause must be of the same class as the effect, not of a contrary class. The desirelessness which has an objective phenomenon for its basis is contrary to the effect; the trance, that is to say, which has no object for its basis. It is therefore proper that it should be born only from a cause which has no objective phenomenon for its basis, the mere light, that is to say, of spiritual knowledge. It is only the trance known as the Cloud of Virtue, born as it is from the pure essence of the Will-to-know with the impurities of the *rajas* and the *tamas* entirely removed, and the objects thereof left behind, that is infinite, sees the defects of objects and having given them all up, stands in its own nature, that can properly become the cause, as having no object for its basis, of the seedless trance, in which the residual potencies only remain; because they are similar in nature.

'Is made the basis' :—is made dependent upon that.

Becomes as it were non-existent :—because it does not produce any effect in the shape of mental modifications.

The seedless is that which has no object for its basis. Or, it may be said that the seed consists of the vehicles of afflictions and actions. This is said to be the seedless, because the afflictions and actions have gone out of it.

Sūtra 19

भवप्रत्ययो विदेहप्रकृतिलयानाम्।। १९।।

भव Bhava, the objective existence. प्रत्ययः pratyayaḥ, the cause, *i.e.*, caused by objective existence. विदेह-प्रकृतिलयानाम् Videha-prakṛtilayānām, to the videhas (the gods) and the prakṛtilayas that merged (लय) in nature प्रकृति।

19. Is caused by Objective Existence for the Videhas and Prakṛtilayas.

स खल्वयं द्विविधः। उपायप्रत्ययो भवप्रत्ययश्च। तत्रोपायप्रत्ययो योगिनां भवति। भवप्रत्ययो विदेहप्रकृतिलयानाम्। विदेहानां देवानां भवप्रत्ययः। ते हि स्वसंस्कारमात्रोपयोगेन चित्तेन कैवल्यपदमिवानुभवन्तः स्वसंस्कारविपाकं तथाजातीयकमतिवाहयन्ति। तथा प्रकृतिलयाः साधिकारे चेतसि प्रकृतिलीने कैवल्यपदमिवानुभवन्ति। यावन्न पुनरावर्ततेऽधिकारवशाच्चित्तमिति।। १९।।

Vyāsa

This is of two descriptions :—brought about by Objective Existence and brought about by the practice of the means. In the case of Yogīs it is brought about by the practice of the means. In the case of the Videhas and the Prakṛtilayas it is caused by Objective Existence.

In the case of the Videhas, the gods, it is caused by Objective Existence, because they enjoy a state of something like absolute freedom (kaivalya) with a mind functioning only so far as its own residual potencies are capable of, and who while thus enjoying, live out the state of life, which is the fruition of their residual potencies.

Similarly do the Prakṛtilayas enjoy a state of quasi-isolation with a mind which has its work still before it, but which remains merged in the Prakṛtis, as long as it does not come back by virtue of the work still before it.

Vācaspati's Gloss

Now the author describes a sub-head of the Inhibitive Trance, being necessary as it is for deciding which is to be adopted and which to be rejected :—'This,' the inhibitive trance, 'is of two descriptions,'—caused by the practice of the means of achievement and brought about by Objective Existence.

The means are faith, etc., to be described later. That which is brought about by these means, is the inhibitive trance so spoken of.

That in which living beings are born of Objective Existence. It is Nescience. The modification of consciousness which consists in the identification of the not-self,—the forms consisting of the elements and the powers of sensation and action and the Prakṛtis, known as the Mūlaprakṛti, the Mahat, the Ahaṅkāra and the five tanmātras,—with self appears in the Tauṣṭikas who have attained the states of the lower desirelessness. This notion about the Objective Existence, becomes the antecedent of one description of the Inhibitive Trance. This is spoken of as having been brought about by Objective Existence.

Out of these two the one brought about by effort, is for the Yogīs, who work for freedom from Objective Existence. By the mention of this distinction the other is denied to those who follow the path of absolute freedom (Mokṣa).

Well then, in whom is it caused by Objective Existence ? The reply is given by the aphorism :—'Is caused by Objective Existence in the case of the Videhas and the Prakṛtilayas.'

The Videhas and the Prakṛtilayas are distinct from each other. The meaning is that this trance is so caused for both of them.

The author explains this :—'For the Videhas it is caused by, etc.'

Those who recognized either of the elements or the powers of sensation, action and thought as the self, and so constantly devote themselves to them, that their internal organ is fully saturated with that idea, remain, after separation from the body, immersed in the same elemental, sensuous and functional forms; and all that remains of their mind is the habit of their particular devotion. They are called the Videhas (the disembodied) because they are free from the physical bodies. It is they who, with a mind capable of moving only along the line marked by habit, enjoy a state of something like absolute freedom, but are without the physical body. This state resembles the state of absolute independence, because the modifications of the mind are suspended for the time being. It however differs from absolute freedom, in the possession of the power of having to perform work still to be done.

The reading in some places is "upabhoga" instead of "upayoga" in the text. Upabhoga means enjoyment. The meaning of this alternative reading would be that the residual alone are the objects of enjoyment and not the modifications.

When the limit has been reached they live out the state of life which is the fruition of their residual potencies. They come back to be born again. So says the Vāyu Purāṇa :—

"Those who devote themselves to meditation upon the powers of sensation, action and thought, live in that state for ten Manwantaras. Those who devote themselves to the elements live in that state for full one hundred Manwantaras."

Similar are Prakṛtilayas. They believe one of the Prakṛtis, the unmanifested (Mūlaprakṛti), the undifferentiated phenomenal (Mahat), and the principle of individuality, to be the self. Their internal organs are saturated with the idea of devotion to either of the Prakṛtis. They are immersed after their separation from the physical body, in the one of these Prakṛtis, which they have made the object of their devotion. But their minds have not yet fulfilled the object of their existence; they have still work before them.

The mind would fulfil the object of its existence, if while following this very course of thought, it would also manifest the discrimination of the distinct natures of the Puruṣa and objective existence. If on the other hand this consciousness be not generated in the mind, it has not fulfilled its object, and is therefore said to have its work still before it. The Prakṛtilayas having their minds merged in the Prakṛtis, with its work still undone, enjoy a state of something like absolute freedom as long as they do not come back by virtue of the work yet to be done. Although the mind has become similar to the Prakṛti, yet they come back when the limit has been reached. Then they acquire the consciousness of the distinct natures of the Puruṣa and the objective existence. As on the cessation of the rainy season, the body of the frog is assimilated to the earth, and comes back to life again on coming into contact with rain-water, (so does the mind of the Prakṛtilaya). So says Vāyu :—

"For a thousand Manwantaras, the Abhimānikas, those who identify themselves with the Prakṛtis; and for ten thousand Manwantaras the Buddhas remain without pain. Those who devote themselves to the Unmanifested remain in that state for a hundred thousand Manwantaras. The computation of time does not exist on reaching the Nirguṇa Puruṣa."

Thus this state also is given up, being subject to re-births.

Sūtra 20

श्रद्धावीर्यस्मृतिसमाधिप्रज्ञापूर्वक इतरेषाम्।। २०।।

श्रद्धा Śraddhā, faith. वीर्य Vīrya, energy. स्मृति Smṛti, memory. समाधि Samādhi, trance. प्रज्ञा Prajñā, discernment. पूर्वकः Pūrvakaḥ, having before, preceded by. इतरेषाम् itareṣām, for others.

20. For others it is preceded by faith, energy, memory, trance and discernment.

श्रद्धावीर्यस्मृतिसमाधिप्रज्ञापूर्वकं इतरेषाम्। उपायप्रत्ययो योगिनां भवति। श्रद्धा चेतसः संप्रसादः। साहि जननीव कल्याणी योगिनं पाति तस्य हि श्रद्दधानस्य विवेकार्थिनो वीर्यमुपजायते। समुपजातवीर्यस्य स्मृतिरुपतिष्ठते स्मृत्युपस्थाने च चित्तमनाकुलं समाधीयते। समाहितचित्तस्य प्रज्ञाविवेक उपावर्तते। येन यथार्थं वस्तु जानाति। तदभ्यासात्तत्द्विषयाच्च वैराग्यादसंप्रज्ञातः समाधिर्भवति।। २०।।

Vyāsa

It is brought about by the means of achievement for the Yogīs. Faith is the pleasing wishful contact of mind with the object of pursuit. It sustains the Yogī, like a mother. Energy is born in him who pursues knowledge with faith. Memory comes to help when he is possessed of energy. On the appearance of memory, the mind ceases to be disturbed and passess into trance. When the mind is entranced, discrimination appears, by which it knows an object as it is. By constant practice thereof and by desirelessness with reference to the object thereof, comes the ultra-cognitive trance.

Vācaspati's Gloss

The author describes the sequence of the means of the achievement of this trance by a Yogī :—"For others it is preceded by faith, energy, memory, trance and discernment."

But the devotees of the powers of sensation, action and thought are also possessed of faith. For this reason he says :—'Faith is the pleasing wishful contact of the mind with the object of pursuit,' and the object of the pleasing wishful pursuit of the mind here is the ultra-cognitive trance, as it comes into existence with reference thereto, after the nature of the objective world has been known by the Veda, by inference and by the teaching of the masters. There can be no wishful contact in the case of those who confound the powers of sensation, etc., with the self. In their case it is the opposite of the pleasing wishful contact, because their confusion has its origin in all-round forgetfulness. The powers of sensation, etc., cannot thus be objects of faith.

He explains why that alone is faith :—'It sustains the Yogī like a kind mother.' The meaning is that it does not let him fall down in the wrong path, leading to the destruction of its object.

It is this particular wishfulness which gives birth to energetic effort guided towards the object wished for. Therefore he says :—'Energy is born in him when he pursues knowledge with faith.'

Memory means keeping it present in the mind, thinking thereupon. 'Undisturbed' means 'not only occasionally steady, not distracted.'

"Passes into trance" :—Trance is here the trance which is described as a branch of Yoga. The restraints and observances also are indicated, inasmuch as trance is mentioned there as coming after them. Thus he who has made all the branches of Yoga his own, reaches the stage of cognitive trance. This is what he says :—"When the mind is entranced." That is to say, when the highest limit of intellection is reached.

He explains that the ultra-cognitive is born when the cognitive precedes it :—'By the constant practice thereof and by desirelessness with reference to the objects thereof at each stage comes the ultra-cognitive trance.' It is that which is the means of achieving absolute freedom. Because the suppression which comes after the manifestation of the knowledge of the distinct nature of the Puruṣa and the will to-know, is the final suppression which renders it unnecessary for the mind to go on working; inasmuch as it has now done the whole of its work and fulfilled the purpose of its existence.

Sūtra 21

तीव्रसंवेगानामासन्नः ।। २१ ।।

तीव्र Tīvra, keen. संवेग Saṁvega, the consciousness of supremacy. तीव्रसंवेगानाम् Tīvra saṁvegānām, for those having consciousness of supremacy, for the extremely energetic. आसन्नः Āsannaḥ, proximate, speedy.

21. Proximate for those whose consciousness of supremacy is keen.

ते खलु नवयोगिनो भवन्ति। मृदुमध्याधिमात्रोपाया भवन्ति। तद्यथा मृदूपायो मध्योपायोऽधिमात्रोपाय इति। तत्र मृदूपायस्त्रिविधिः। मृदुसंवेगो मध्यसंवेगस्तीव्रसंवेग इति। तथा मध्योपायस्तथाऽधिमात्रोपाय इति। तत्राधिमात्रोपायानो तीव्रसंवेगानामासन्नः समाधिलाभः समाधिफलं च भवतीति।। २१ ।।

Vyāsa

There are nine descriptions of such Yogīs. Their application to the means of achievement is mild, middling or intense. Thus some are of mild energy, others of medium energy, and others again of intense energy. Of these, the mildly energetic are three-fold, those having mild consciousness of supremacy, those having middling consciousness of supremacy, and those having keen consciousness of supremacy. Similarly, those of medium energy and those of intense energy. Of these, the attainment of trance and the fruit of trance are near to those who are intensely energetic in their application to the means of achievement and possess a keen consciousness of supremacy.

Vācaspati's Gloss

If faith, etc., are the means for the attainment of trance, then trance and its fruit would accrue to all without distinction. Attainment however is noticed in some only, non-attainment in others. In some cases attainment is distant; in others it is very distant; in other cases however it is accomplished very soon. To meet this the Commentator says :—'There are nine descriptions of such Yogīs, etc.'

The means of achievement are faith, etc. They are of mild, middling and intense energy in their application, by virtue of the habits of previous lives. The Yogīs possessed of them are spoken of as such.

Consciousness of supremacy is desirelessness. That also is mild, middling or keen by virtue of the habits of previous lives.

Among these Yogīs, the speedy attainment is shown such as it is by the Aphorism :—It is near to those who are possessed of keen consciousness of supremacy. This much is the aphorism; the rest is the commentary. The fruit of the cognitive trance is the ultra-cognitive, and of that absolute freedom.

Sūtra 22

मृदुमध्याधिमात्रत्वात्ततोऽपि विशेषः।। २२।।

मृदु Mṛdu, mild. मध्य Madhya, middling. अधिमात्र Adhimātra, intense. मृदुमध्याधिमात्रत्वात् Mṛdumadhyādhimātratvāt, by mild, middle and intense natures. ततः Tataḥ, thence, further. अपि Api, also, (further). विशेषः Viśeṣaḥ, differentiation.

22. A further also differentiation by mild, middling and intense.

मृदुमध्याधिमात्रत्वात्ततोऽपि विशेषः। मृदुतीव्रो मध्यतीव्रोऽधिमात्रतीव्र इति। ततोऽपि विशेषः। तदविशेषादप्यासन्नतरस्तीव्राधिमात्रसंवेगस्याधिमात्रोपायस्य समाधिलाभः समाधिफलंचेति।। २२।।

Vyāsa

Mild-intense middling-intense and intense-intense. There is differentiation by that too. By that differentiation too the attainment of trance and its fruit becomes the speediest in the case of one whose application is intense and whose consciousness of supremacy is keenly intense.

Vācaspati's Gloss

This has been explained by explanations already given of the commentary.

Sūtra 23

ईश्वरप्रणिधानाद् वा।। २३।।

ईश्वर Īśvara, of God. प्रणिधान Praṇidhāna, feeling omnipresence or worship, devotion. ईश्वर-प्रणिधानात् Īśvarapraṇidhānāt, by feeling the omnipresence of God. वा vā, or.

23. Or, by feeling the omnipresence of God (Īśvara).

किमेतस्मादेवासन्नतरः समाधिर्भवति। अथास्यलाभे भवत्यन्योऽपि कश्चिदुपायो न वेति। ईश्वरप्रणिधानाद्वा। प्रणिधानाद्भक्तिविशेषादावर्जित ईश्वरस्तमनुगृह्णात्यभिध्यानमात्रेण। तदभिध्यानमात्रादपि योगिन आसन्नतरः समाधिलाभः समाधिफलं च भवतीति।। २३।।

Vyāsa

Does trance become speedier of attainment in this way only ? Or, is there any other means too ? 'Or, by feeling the omnipresence of God.' Īśvara drawn towards him by the kind of devotion which consists in the feeling of His omnipresence, becomes gracious to him by merely wishing attainment. By His merely wishing the attainment, trance and its fruit become speedier of attainment for a Yogī.

Vācaspati's Gloss

The Commentator puts a question for the purpose of introducing the next aphorism :—'Does trance become speedier, etc.' The aphorism is the answer. 'Or, by feeling the omnipresence of God.'

'Feeling the omnipresence' means a particular kind of devotion of the mind, speech and body. "Drawn towards" means brought face to face. "Wish for attainment" means that any one may get something which he has not got, but which is desirable. 'Merely' signifies not by any other effort. The rest is easy.—23.

Sūtra 24

क्लेशकर्मविपाकाशयैरपरामृष्टः पुरुषविशेष ईश्वरः।। २४।।

क्लेश Kleśa, of affliction. कर्म Karma, of action. विपाक Vipāka, of fruition. आशयैः Āśayaiḥ, by the vehicles. अपरामृष्टः Aparāmṛṣṭaḥ, not touched. पुरुष-विशेषः Puruṣa, Viśeṣaḥ, a distinct Puraṣa. ईश्वरः Īśvaraḥ, God.

24. Īśvara is a distinct Puruṣa, untouched by the vehicles of affliction, action and fruition.

अथ प्रधानपुरुषव्यतिरिक्तः कोऽयमीश्वरो नामेति। क्लेशकर्मविपाकाशयैरपरामृष्टः पुरुषविशेष ईश्वरः। अविद्यादयः क्लेशाः। कुशलाऽकुशलानि कर्माणि। तत्फलं विपाकः। तदनुगुणावासना आशयास्ते च मनसि वर्तमानाः पुरुषे व्यपदिश्यन्ते। स हि तत्फलस्य भोक्तेति। यथा जयः पराजयो वा योद्धृषु वर्तमानः स्वामिनि व्यपदिश्यन्ते यो ह्यनेन भोगेनपरामृष्टः स पुरुष विशेष ईश्वरः। कैवल्यं प्राप्तास्तर्हि सन्ति च बहवः केवलिनः। ते हि त्रीणि बन्धनानि छित्वा कैवल्यं प्राप्ता ईश्वरस्य च तत्संबन्धो न भूतो न भावि। यथा मुक्तस्य पूर्वाबन्धकोटिः प्रजायते नवमीश्वरस्य। यथा वा प्रकृतिलीनस्योत्तरा बन्धकोटिः संभाव्यते नैवमीश्वरस्य। स तु सदैव मुक्तः सदैवेश्वर इति। योऽसौ प्रकृष्टसत्त्वोपादानादीश्वरस्य शाश्वतिक उत्कर्षः स किं सनिमित्त आहोस्विन्निर्निमित्त

इति। तस्य शास्त्रं निमित्तम्। शास्त्रं पुनः किं निमित्तं प्रकृष्टसत्त्वनिमित्तम्। एतयोः शास्त्रोत्कर्षयोरीश्वरसत्त्वे वर्तमानयोरनादिः संबन्धः। एतस्मादेतद्भवति सदैवेश्वरः सदैव मुक्त इति। तच्च तस्यैश्वर्यं साम्यातिशय-विनिर्मुक्तम्। न तावदैश्वर्यान्तरेण तदतिशय्यते। यदेवातिशयि स्यात्तदेव तत्स्यात्। तस्माद्यत्र काष्ठा प्राप्तिरैश्वर्यस्य स ईश्वर इति। न च तत्समानमैश्वर्यमस्ति कस्माद् द्वयोस्तुल्ययोरेकस्मिन्युगपत्कामितेऽर्थे नवमिदमस्तुपुराण-मिदमस्त्वित्येकस्य सिद्धावितरस्य प्राकाम्यविघातादूनत्वं प्रसक्तम्। द्वयोश्च तुल्ययोर्युगपत्कामितार्थप्राप्तिर्नास्ति। अर्थस्य विरुद्धत्वात्। तस्माद्यस्य साम्यातिशयैर्विनिर्मुक्तमैश्वर्यं स एवेश्वरः। स च पुरुष विशेष इति।। २४।।

Vyāsa

Now who is this called Īśvara (God) that is neither the Mūla prakṛti (the root of matter) nor the Puruṣa (the conscious principle of the human constitution)? 'Īśvara is a distinct Puruṣa, untouched by the vehicles of affliction, action and fruition.'

The afflictions are Nescience and others. The actions are good or bad. Their fruition is the effect they bring about. Habits following them in their qualifications are the vehicles. These while really existing in the mind, are attributed to the Puruṣa, as he is the enjoyer of their fruit, just as victory or defeat of the soldiers is attributed to their master. He who is not touched by this experience, is the distinct Puruṣa, Īśvara.

Are all those then who have reached the state of absolute freedom Īśvaras and there are many such for they have reached the state of absolute freedom after cutting the three bonds? No, Īśvara never had, nor will have, any relation to these bonds. As former bondage is known in the case of the emancipated, not so in the case of Īśvara. Or, as future bondage is possible in the case of the Prakṛtilayas, not so in the case of Īśvara. He is ever free, ever the Lord.

Is there any, or, is there no reason for this supremacy of the Lord, unlimited by time, and due to His taking up the Universal Supreme Essence? The reason for that is the sacred teaching. What then is the authority of the teaching? The authority is the supremacy of His Universal Essence. These two, the supremacy and the sacred teaching, exist in the Universal Essence of Īśvara eternally related to each other. For this reason does it become possible that He is ever free, and ever the Lord.

And this divinity of His is free from excess or equality. It is not exceeded by another divinity. Whichever is the Highest, must be the divinity Īśvara. For this reason wherever there is the culmination of this divinity that is Īśvara.

Nor is there any divinity equal to that. Because, in the case of equality, if one of the two equals says with reference to a common object of their attention, 'let this be new,' and the other says, 'let this be old,' then one thing only necessarily happening, unrestrained fulfilment of the wish is interfered with, and one becomes less than the other. Further it cannot be that two equals should at once possess an object desired by both. Because the wishes are contradictory. Hence he alone is Īśvara whose divinity is free from equality or excess, and He is a distinct Puruṣa.—24.

Vācaspati's Gloss

The word is made of the conscious and the unconscious principles only. There is none else that goes to make it, If Īśvara is unconscious, He must be the Mūlaprakṛti, comprehending as it does all the non-intelligent modifications. If this be so, then there can be no such thing, by reason of his being non-intelligent that he should be brought face to face with the devotee. If, on the other hand, he is intelligent then too it is impossible that he should be brought face to face with the devotee, because the power of consciousness is by nature indifferent, and because Īśvara is not like other Puruṣas in evolution, on account of the absence of any connection with the principles of egoism, etc. Furthermore how is it possible that he should possess a wish for the attainment (of trance by the devotee)?

This is the meaning of the question, now who is this Īśvara, etc.? The answer to the question is given by the aphorism :—'Īśvara is a distinct Puruṣa untouched by the vehicles of affliction, action and fruition.'

Nescience (avidyā) and others are the affliction (kleśas), so called, because they afflict the Puruṣa in evolution with various painful blows. Good and bad actions are virtue and vice. They are called actions metaphorically because they are born from actions. Their fruition consists in life-state, life-period and life-experience. The vehicles are so called, because by their means the residue which show themselves as fruitions, are embedded as potencies in the substance of the mind.

As long as the karma which brings about the manifestation of the life-state of a camel does not bring into play the potencies of the experience which having been generated by previous existence, are suited to the life-state of a camel, the experience suited to the life-ṣtate of a camel cannot be caused. Therefore there must be a potency causing the subsequent experience of the life-state of a camel, and it must be possessed of qualities similar to the experience of the life-state of a camel.

Another question arises. What is the use of adding the words, untouched 'by the vehicles of affliction, action and fruition' in the aphorism, seeing that afflictions, etc., are the characteristics of the Will-to-be, and that they never touch the Puruṣa and therefore the mere use of the word Puruṣa would have implied that he was untouched by them? For this reason, he says :—'These while really existing in the mind are attributed to the Puruṣa' in evolution. Why? Because he is the enjoyer, the intelligent agent of their fruit. Hence it is possible that Īśvara being a Puruṣa might come to be considered as having some relation to these. For this reason their special denial of Him is proper. Therefore he says that the distinct Puruṣa who is not touched by the experience present in the Will-to-be even, is Īśvara.

'Distinct' is that which is distinguishable. He is differentiated from the other Puruṣas. With the object of showing those who are taken out of the conception of the word Īśvara by the use of the word 'distinct,' he first states an objection and then replies :—'All those then who have reached the state of absolute freedom. There are three kinds of bondages,—the bondage of the Prākṛtic modifications in the case of the Videhas, the bondage of the Prakṛtis in the case of the Prakṛtilayas, and the bondage of honour, etc., in the case of those who experience the divine and worldly enjoyments. Those whose mind are saturated with devoted thought of the Prakṛtis, reach the state of submersion into the Prakṛtis immediately after separation from the physical body. For this reason the others are spoken of as being bound at the previous end (of the chain of life) and the Prakṛtilayas are spoken of as being bound only at the next, the future end only; the previous and the second bondages being denied to them. Thus he shows the distinction in brief :—'He is always free, always the Lord.'

Divinity consists in the possession of knowledge and the power of action (Kriyā Śakti). In this connection he puts the question :—'Has this supremacy of the Lord, unlimited by time, etc.' The reason for the question is that knowledge and power of action are not possible to the unchanging constant power of consciousness. It has been said that they live in the purified mental essence, when the rajas and the tamas have been removed. Further, it is not proper that Īśvara who is ever free should become related even to the Highest Mental Essence, which after all has its origin in Nescience, as an owner to the thing owned.

For this reason it is said that it is due 'to his taking the Universal Supreme Essence in hand.' The relation of Īśvara to the Essence of the mind is not due to Nescience like that of ordinary Puruṣas; and there is therefore no sense of ownership in it. On the other hand he takes the Universal Mental Essence in hand thinking that he will thus give freedom to men surrounded by the three sorts of pain, and rescue them, being drowned as they are in the great ocean of birth after death, by teaching them virtue and giving them knowledge; and that this teaching is not possible without the possession of highest power of action and knowledge; and that this cannot be possible without taking in hand the mental Essence, pure and freed from the dirt of the disturbing energy (rajas) and inertia (tamas). The Lord even though untouched by Nescience, and conscious of knowledge, assumes the nature of Nescience, and becomes the possessor thereof. He does not devote Himself to Nescience as Nescience. A mimic personating Rāma shows all his actions but all the while does not forget himself. This form of his is assumed, not real.

Let it be so. Inasmuch, however, as Īśvara has to take up the Mental Essence (sattva), on account of the wish of helping the afflicted, and the wish to help is caused by the taking up of Mental Essence, because the wish itself is a modification of the Mūlaprakṛti, the relation of mutual support is evident. To remove this misconception he says that he is unlimited by time. It might be so if creation came first and the wish to help manifested afterwards. But the arrangement of successive creation and dissolution being eternal, Īśvara draws the world inwards, having first made up his mind that he will take up the Highest Universal Essence, when the time comes for the wish, arising out of an interior manifestation, to reach the limit of its operation. This divine Mental Essence potent with the residuum of this determination even though it passes into a state similar to that of noumenal matter (Mūlaparakṛti) comes to manifestation again in the same state as Mental Essence, by virtue of the potency of that determination, when the ulterior limit of the Mahāpralayas, the Great Latency, is reached. This happens in the same way as in the case of Caitra who goes to sleep, having made a determination that he must rise early next morning, and awakes at the same time by virtue of the potency of the determination. Hence because the determination of the Lord and the taking in hand of the Universal Essence are eternal and thus ever present, their relation to each other cannot be that of interdependence.

Further, it should not be said that the divine Mental Essence does not pass into the state of the noumenal root-matter, the equipoise of the Mūlaprakṛti, even at the time of the Great Latency. That which never passes into the state of the Mūlaprakṛti, can never be the effect thereof. Nor can this Universal Mental Essence be the power of consciousness, because it is non-intelligent by its own nature. If it be not both these, then, it would come to this that it must be another class of substance, for which there is no authority. This is not proper. There is no substance existing independently of the noumenon of matter (Prakṛti) and consciousness (Puruṣa).

Such is the greatness of the Lord unlimited by time. Is there any reason, any authority for it? Or, is it without reason, without authority? The answer is 'Its authority lies in the sacred teaching,' the Vedas, the Smṛtis, the Itihāsas and the Purāṇas.

The author introduces the consideration of the Sacred Teaching :—"What then is the reason of the Teaching ? The Sacred Teaching is based upon observation and inference. The Universal Mental Essence of the Lord cannot depend upon anybody's observation and inference. Nor is the Sacred Teaching based upon the observation of the Lord. Some one may, therefore, think that the proper reason for the existence of the Sacred Teaching is that Īśvara desires to manifest his own divinity.

He refutes this by saying that the Sacred Teaching has its reason in the Divine Universal Essence. The meaning is this. Evidently the *mantras* and the science of life are proved to be the works of the Lord by the virtue they show in action and by the certainty of the things mentioned therein, being never found to be otherwise. Further, it is not possible that any one possessed only of the ordinary means of knowledge of the world should be able, even in a thousand human lives, to note the agreements and differences of various medicinal agents, their various compositions, and those of the mantras, by throwing them into and taking them out of the various classes. It cannot evidently be said on the ground of the existence of the relation of eternal interdependence, that the agreements and differences are known from authority, and that authority is again based upon the canons of agreement and difference. Because during the Great Latency, the Mahāpralaya, both these manifestations cease to exist.

Further, it is not the case that there is not authority for their existence. It will be shown that the universe is a modification of noumenal matter, the Mūlaprakṛti, not different from it. It has been observed that things of the same class change into different forms, as in the case of the modifications of curds and sugar, etc., from milk and cane-juice. It has also been observed that different modifications have the same form in their antecedent state. Similarly the noumenal root-matter having different modifications in the forms of the Great Will-to-be, the principle of individuality and others, must have a form common to all in the antecedent state. This common antecedent state of the noumenal matter is the state of equipoise, and that is the state of the Great Latency, the Mahāpralaya. Hence the Universal Essence of the will-to-be of the Lord, shining all round by reason of the absence of the veil of the impurities of disturbing energy (rajas) and inertia (tamas), must be considered as established by at least the promulgation by Him of the Mantras and the science of life. And similarly that collection of the Vedic knowledge too, which has for its object the teaching of how to attain worldly progress and divine freedom, can be a divine production only by virtue of the Universal supremacy of His Spiritual and Mental Essence. It is not possible to have confusion and falsehood, the products of disturbing energy and inertia (rajas and tamas), the face of the culmination of Universal Essence. Hence it is established that the authority of the sacred teaching lies in the divinity of the Universal Essence.

Let it be so. The teaching has its origin in the supreme manifestation of the divine Mental Essence, and therefore it shows the highest knowledge. This is an instance of inference by the canon of residue, not of the authority of verbal cognition. To meet this objection he says :—'The relation of these two, the Teaching and the Highest manifestation of divine Mental Essence, etc.' The meaning is that the Teaching does not give the highest knowledge because it is the product of the Highest Universal Essence, but that it teaches because of the existence of an eternal relation of the explainer and the explained. Supremacy exists in the Universal Essence of the divine mind, and the Teaching which promulgates it, is also present there as such.

The author states the final conclusion :—Hence by it, *i.e.*, the teaching which promulgates the Highest Universal Divine Mental Essence, is it known, in the same way that the differentiating qualities of the signified are known by the sign, that He is ever free, ever the Lord.

Having thus distinguished Him from other Puruṣas he now distinguishes Him from other lords also :—'This divinity of His is free, etc.' and explains freedom excess :—'There is no other divinity, etc.' Why? 'Wherever there is the highest, etc.' For what reason is His divinity free from the defect of being exceeded by any other divinities? He gives the reason :—'Wherever there is the highest perfection of this divinity, etc.' The meaning is that the divinity of those in whom it has not reached the highest perfection, is unreal.

Now he explains freedom equality :—'Nor is there divinity equal, etc.' Unrestrained fulfilment of wishes means the removal of obstacles from the path thereof. When wishes are checked in their fulfilment, it means weakness. Even if it do not mean weakness, it means equality. For that reason he says that in both cases the unrestrained fulfilment of desires is interfered with. The desired effect is not produced, or if it is produced then the same thing is found to possess contradictory qualities (which is absurd). With this object, he says : 'In the case of two equals, etc.' If the wishes of more divinities than one be considered as never being contradictory, then each must be an Īśvara. But then what is the use of having more Īśvaras than one? The purpose of divine rule is fulfilled by One only. Or, if it be supposed that they perform the work of divine government by common consent, then there would be no supreme Lord, just as in a republic. Further in the case of those who believe in the eternal possession of divinity, the succession of divinity is improper. Furthermore there is the defect of cumbersomeness (positing more agents than is necessary for the purpose of bringing about an effect). Thus everything is plain.—24.

Sūtra 25

तत्र निरतिशयं सर्वज्ञबीजम् ।। २५ ।।

तत्र Tatra, in Him. निरतिशयम् Niratiśayam, such as is not exceeded. सर्वज्ञ Sarvajña, of the omniscient. बीजम् Bījam, the seed.

25. In Him the seed of the omniscient is not exceeded.

किं च तत्र निरतिशयं सर्वज्ञबीजम् । यदिदमतीतानागतप्रत्युत्पन्नप्रत्येकसमुच्चयातीन्द्रियग्रहणमल्पं बह्विति सर्वज्ञबीजमेतद्विवर्द्धमानं यत्र निरतिशयं स सर्वज्ञः । अस्ति काष्ठाप्राप्तिः सर्वज्ञबीजस्य सातिशयत्वात्परिणाम-वदिति । यत्र काष्ठाप्राप्तिर्ज्ञानस्य स सर्वज्ञः स च पुरुषविशेष इति । सामान्यमात्रोपसंहारे च कृतोपक्षयमनुमानं न विशेषप्रतिपत्तौ समर्थमिति । तस्य संज्ञादिविशेषप्रतिपत्तिरागमतः पर्यन्वेष्या । तस्यात्मानुग्रहाभावेपि भूतानुग्रहः

प्रयोगजनम्। ज्ञानधर्मोपदेशेन कल्पप्रलयमहाप्रलयेषु संसारिणः पुरुषानुद्धरिष्यामीति तथा चोक्तम्। आदिविद्वान्निर्माणचित्तमधिष्ठाय कारुण्याद्भगवान्परमर्षिरासुरये जिज्ञासमानाय तन्त्रं प्रोवाचेति।। २५।।

Vyāsa

The seed of the omniscient is the larger or smaller knowledge of the individual, the collective or the ultra-sensuous arising out of the past or the future. Whenever this reaches a point in expansion, beyond which there is nothing, it is the omniscient. There must be the highest limit of the expansion of the seed of omniscience, inasmuch as there is larger or smaller manifestation of intelligence, just as it is in the case of dimension. Wherever knowledge reaches the highest limit that is the omniscient and that is a distinct Puruṣa. Inference is of service only in establishing the general idea. It has not the power of giving the special qualities. The knowledge of His distinctive names, etc., is to be sought out of the Veda.

Although Īśvara has no purpose of His own to fulfil by His (creation), His (creation) is purposed by compassion for other beings. 'I shall lift the Puruṣa in evolution out of the world by teaching them knowledge and virtue, throughout the manifestations (Kalpas), the Latencies (Pralayas) and the Great Latencies (Mahāpralays).' This is what he proposes to Himself. And so it has been said :—'The first Wise Being, the revered Great Sage, informed a self-made mental vehicle out of compassion, and gave the teaching to Āsuri who wished to know.—25.

Vācaspati's Gloss

Having thus established the authority of the Sacred Teaching for His powers of action and knowledge, he now puts forward the authority of inference for His power of knowledge :— 'In Him the seed of the Omniscient is not exceeded. He explains :—'The seed of the Omniscient, etc.

The knowledge of things beyond the range of the senses, existing either individually or collectively, and caused, by the appearance of the past and future forms, is qualified by the attributes of largeness and smallness, on account of the veil of darkness covering more or less of the essence of the will-to-be. The meaning is that this knowledge is the seed, the cause of the omniscient. One takes in a little of the past, etc., another more than that, another the most of all. Knowledge is spoken of as being more or less with reference to the thing known. Wherever this knowledge expands so much that it passes beyond the limit of being further exceeded, that is the omniscient.

This describes only the thing to be known. Now he speaks of the means of knowledge :— 'The seed of the omniscient must reach the highest limit, etc.' This is the statement of the proposition to be proved. The 'highest limit' means the state of intensity which cannot be exceeded. It is not, therefore, by fixing a limit only that the proposition can be established.

'Inasmuch as there is larger or smaller manifestation of intelligence :' This is the statement of the reason. Every thing which possesses the quality of being more or less, has a limit beyond which there is no manifestation of the kind; as is the case with the lotus, the emblic fruit and the

Bel tree. The quality of largeness exists in these more or less. In the self (Ātma), however, the largeness is such that there is no largeness more than that. He shows the pervasion (Vyāpti). 'As in dimension.' This means that the conclusion does not fail by the qualities of largeness, etc., being exceptions to the rule. Thus the proposition is established.

It is not necessary that the largeness of the parts only should be contributed to the largeness of the whole. The fact is that dimension is known to expand by the putting together of as many largenesses of individual factors as there may be, consisting of infinitesimal wholes reaching down to the atoms themselves. In the case of knowledge too this rule is not violated : and knowledge can, therefore, be more or less by having one, two or more objects of knowledge. Thus there is no exception to the rule, (or technically speaking, there is no exclusion of the middle term, which is marked by the pervasion).

He summarizes :—'Wherever knowledge reaches, etc.'

The question arises that there are many Tīrthaṅkaras, such as the Buddha, the Arhats and the seer Kapila; why should not they be considered to be omniscient by this inference ? For this reason, he says :—'Inference is of service only.'

How then is the knowledge of his specific qualities to be acquired ? Says :—'The knowledge of his special names, etc.'

Further, teaching of the Buddha, etc., is not properly speaking authority; it only looks like authority. The reason is that it teaches things against all reasoning, such as the momentary nature of all objects and the non-existence of the self, etc. It is, therefore, all misleading. Hence that which comes into the mind from the Veda, the Smṛti, the Itihāsa and the Purāṇa is the only true verbal cognition, the real authority; and is for this reason the only true means of worldly progress and the Highest Good. With this object the knowledge of special names, etc., should be obtained. Special names, such as Śiva, Īśvara, etc., are well known in the Vedas, etc.

By the mention of the word "etc." it is understood that He is possessed of the six accessories and the ten unchangeables. As says the Vāyu Purāṇa :—

'Omniscience, satisfaction, eternal knowledge, independence, constant presence of power, infinity of power—these six are said to be the accessories (aṅgas) of the Great Lord by those who know the law. Similarly, knowledge, desirelessness, power of control, purificatory action, truth, forgiveness, endurance, creation, the knowledge of the self, and being the substratum of all activities—these ten unchangeable qualities (avyayas) always live in the Great source of all Good.'

Well let that be. But the Lord is ever satisfied and possessed of the Highest desirelessness. It is not possible that He should have any wish for the fulfilment of any objects of His own. Further, being compassionate He should be given to the creation of men possessed of undisturbed pleasure. It cannot, therefore, be that He should create a world, full of pain of all sorts. Further, a wise being cannot be considered as undertaking a useless task. He, therefore, has not created the world, although He is possessed of Kriyā Śakti, the power of creation.

For this reason, he says :—'Although Īśvara has no purpose of His own, etc.' compassionate help of living objects is His object. The individual mind fulfils its object, when it has caused the experience of sound, etc., and the manifestation of the consciousness of the distinct nature of the self and the not-self. Its activity ceases when it has done so, and the Puruṣa then becomes absolutely independent of objective existence (kevali). With that object the compassionate Lord informs men of the means of obtaining knowledge of the distinct nature of the self and the not-self; because thereby the object of the existence of the mind is fulfilled. Īśvara, therefore, helping man as He does with reference to the performance of pure and impure works by them, is not cruel, even though He sees their pleasures and pains and feels for them.

Now he speaks of the entrance into the region of compassion, for the sake of explaining the means of obtaining the knowledge of the distinct natures of the self and not-self :—'By teaching them knowledge and virtue, etc.' Knowledge and virtue are both to be understood together. They manifest the knowledge of the distinct natures of the self and the not-self.

Latency (pralaya) means the end of the day of Brahmā. In this state, the whole world except the Satyaloka becomes latent. The Mahāpralaya, the Great Latency, is that in which the Satyaloka and Brahmā himself come to an end. Then the Puruṣas in evolution go back to their causes and hence are subject to the pain of death. The word Kalpa is only suggestive here. The meaning is that the Lord's determination to help the Puruṣas refers to the other Puruṣas also, who by virtue of the fruition of their action have to undergo births and deaths, and who become free from pain on reaching the state of absolute independence. This is the meaning.

This theory that the compassionate Lord teaches knowledge and virtue is also common to the teaching of Kapila :—So has it been said by Pañca Śikha. 'The first wise man, etc.' This is a quotation from Pañcaśikhācārya. The first wise man means the teacher who was the first emancipated being of his school. It does not mean the Highest Teacher who is ever free. The reference is to Kapila who was the founder of the school, and who was the first of those emancipated ones who had gone before among the followers of the school. The tradition is that Kapila got the knowledge by the grace of Maheśwara just as he was born, and he is known as such as a particular kind of Viṣṇu's incarnations. Svayambhū is Hiraṇyagarbha. It is learnt from the Veda that he too got the knowledge of the Sāṅkhya Yoga. The same Īśvara, the self-existence Viṣṇu, was the first Wise man, Kapila. The meaning is that he is the Īśvara of those who proceeded from Svayambhū and others.—25.

Sūtra 26

स एष पूर्वेषामपि गुरुः कालेनानवच्छेदात् ।। २६ ।।

सः Saḥ, that, He. एषः Eṣaḥ, this, here. पूर्वेषाम् Pūrveṣām, of the ancients. अपि Api, too. गुरुः Guruḥ, the teacher. कालेन Kālena, by time. अनवच्छेदात् Anavacchedāt, owing to the non-limitation, not being limited by.

26. He is the Teacher of the Ancients too, not being limited by time.

स एष पूर्वेषामपि गुरुः कालेनानवच्छेदात्। पूर्वे हि गुरवः कालेनावच्छिद्यन्ते यत्रावच्छेदार्थेन कालो नोपावर्तते स एष पूर्वेषामपि गुरुः यथास्य सर्गस्यादौ प्रकर्षगत्यासिद्धस्तथातिक्रान्तसर्गादिष्वपि प्रत्येतव्यः ।। २६ ।।

Vyāsa

The ancient teachers were conditioned by time. Wherever time does not exist as condition, that is Īśvara, the teacher of the ancient teachers too. As the knowledge of

His supreme power as existing in the beginning of the creation is obtained, so also is it obtained about His existence as such in other creations and other times.

Vācaspati's Gloss

Now he shows the distinction of the Lord from Brahmā, etc., 'He,' *i.e.*, the one described formerly, 'is (the real aphorism begins here) the teacher of the ancients too.'

He explains—'The ancients, etc.' Time means a century, etc.

'Does not exist as a condition' means time does not approach as a condition.

The supremacy of power means the manifestation thereof. Its knowledge is to be obtained from the Veda. By this arrangement the Lord Īśvara is described.—26.

Sūtra 27

तस्य वाचकः प्रणवः ।। २७ ।।

तस्य Tasya, Him. वाचकः Vācakaḥ, connoting. प्रणवः: Praṇavaḥ, the Sacred word—ओम् Om.

27. The Sacred word connotes Him.

तस्य वाचकः प्रणवः। वाच्य ईश्वरः प्रणवस्य। किमस्य संकेतकृतं वाच्यवाचकत्वमथ प्रदीपप्रकाशवदवस्थितिमिति। स्थितोऽस्य वाच्यस्य वाचकेन सह संबन्धः। संकेतस्त्वीश्वरस्य स्थितमेवार्थमभिनयति। यथावस्थितः पितापुत्रयोः संबन्धः संकेतेनावद्योत्यते अयमस्य पिता। अयमस्य पुत्र इति। सर्गान्तरेष्वपि वाच्यवाचकशक्त्यपेक्षस्तथैव सङ्केतः क्रियते ।। २७ ।।

Vyāsa

The sacred word connotes 'Him.' He is denominated by the sacred word, the Praṇava (AUM). Is the relation of the sign and the thing signified between these conventional, or inherent as between flame and light? His relation with the sign is inherent and thus ever present. Further, the convention of God shows only an object which exists (that which is inherent). As the relation already existing between father and son, is only expressed by convention, this is the father, this the son. In other creations too the same convention is adopted on account of the dependence upon the connotative powers of the sign and the thing signified.

Vācaspati's Gloss

Now he speaks of His sign (indicator, Vācaka) in order to explain the meaning of his devotion. 'The sacred word connotes Him.' Explains :—He is denoted by Praṇava, etc. Introduces the opposite theory by putting a question. Is the relation, etc. Signifying is laying down, expressing.

Others, of course, hold that if the relation of word and meaning is inherent, and that it is manifested by a convention that such and such a meaning is to be denoted by such and such a

word, then in the absence of any relation between word and meaning, the meaning would not be conveyed even by a hundred conventions. If no jar exists which may be shown by a lamp, even a hundred lamps would not reveal one. It is, however, observed that the word 'elephant' will signify a camel if a convention is made that this word will be used to signify an animal of that class. Hence the power to signify is conventional.

Having thus stated their position, he explains his own teaching :—'Its relation is inherent.' This is the meaning. All words have the capability of meaning objects of all forms. Their relation with objects of all forms must, therefore, be inherent. And the convention of Īśvara is the determining factor and the shower thereof. The division of the sign signifying and not-signifying something is also made by Īśvara's convention or non-convention. This is what he says : 'Further the convention of God, etc.' He gives an illustration :—"already existing between, etc."

The question arises. Sound is a manifestation of the Prakṛti. At the time of the Great Latency it passes back into the state of the Prakṛti. Its power also thereby disappears. 'Then a particular verbal sign is born again through the successive states of Mahat, etc. But then the power of signification having disappeared, its manifestation does not remain possible. For this reason, he says :—'In other creations also, etc.'

Although a word does become one with the Prakṛti along with the power it comes back into manifestation along with the power. As earth-born creatures becoming one with the earth on the cessation of the rains, come back to life on being wetted by showers of rain water. Thus God makes a convention similar to the convention which indicated the former relation. Hence on account of the eternity of the succession of similar usage, due to simultaneous knowledge, the relation of word and meaning is eternal. Independent eternity is not meant. So say the Āgamis. Without the authority of the Āgama (the Veda) it is not possible to ascertain that in other creations also the convention is the same. This is the meaning.—27.

Sūtra 28

तज्जपस्तदर्थभावनम् ।। २८ ।।

तद् Tad, its. जप: Japaḥ, repetition. तद् Tad, its. अर्थ Artha, meaning. भावनम् Bhāvanam, the understanding of.

28. Its repetition and the understanding of its meaning.

संप्रतिपत्ति नित्यतया नित्य: शब्दार्थ सबन्ध इत्यागमिन: प्रतिजानते विज्ञातवाच्यवाचकत्वस्य योगिन:। तज्जपस्तदर्थभावनम्। प्रणवस्य जप: प्रणवाभिधेयस्य चेश्वरस्य भावनम्। तदस्य योगिन: प्रणवं जपत: प्रणवार्थं च भावयतश्चित्तमेकाग्रं संपद्यते। तथा चोक्तम्। स्वाध्यायाद्योगमासीत योगात्स्वाध्यायमासते। स्वाध्याययोगसंपत्त्या परमात्मा प्रकाशत इति ।। २८।।

Vyāsa

The Vedic teachers hold that the relation of word and meaning is eternal, inasmuch as one co-exists with the other. The Yogī who has come to know well the relation between word and meaning must constantly repeat it, and habituate the mind to the manifestation therein of its meaning. The constant repetition is to be of the Praṇava (AUM) and the habitual mental manifestation is to be of what it signifies, Īśvara. The mind of the Yogī who constantly repeats the Praṇava and habituates the mind to the constant manifestation of the idea it carries, becomes one-pointed. Are so it has been said :—

'Let the Yoga be practised through study, and let study be effected through Yoga. By Yoga and study together the Highest Self shines'.—28.

Vācaspati's Gloss

Having described the sign, he now describes the devotion, praṇidhāna, the means of feeling the presence of the Lord everywhere, in all circumstances and phenomena :—'Its constant repetition and the repeated understanding of its meaning.' Explains :—'The constant repetition of the Praṇava, etc.'

Repeated understanding (Bhāvanā) means making it to enter the mind over and over again until it becomes the very substance of the mental existence.

What attainment does he acquire thereby ? Says :—'The mind of the Yogī who constantly repeats the Praṇava, etc.' The mind feels bliss in the One Lord alone. Quotes a verse of Vyāsa in this connection :—And so it has been said :—The Lord then becomes gracious to him up to his attaining the faculty of trance (Samādhi) and its fruit.—28.

Sūtra 29

ततः प्रत्यक्चेतनाधिगमोऽप्यन्तरायाभावश्च ।। २९ ।।

ततः Tataḥ, thence. प्रत्यक् Pratyak, the individual. चेतन Cetana, Soul. अधिगमः Adhigamaḥ, understanding. अपि Api, also, too. अन्तराय Antarāya, of obstacles. अभावः Abhāvaḥ, absence. च Ca, and.

29. Thence the understanding of the individual self and the absence of obstacles too.

किं चास्य भवति। ततः प्रत्यक्चेतनाधिगमोऽप्यन्तरायाभावश्च। ये तावदन्तराया व्याधिप्रभृतयस्ते तावदीश्वरप्रणिधानान्न भवन्ति स्वरूप दर्शनमप्यस्य भवति यथैवेश्वरः पुरुषः शुद्धः प्रसन्नः केवलोऽनुपसर्गस्तथायमपि बुद्धेः प्रतिसंवेदी यः पुरुषस्तमधिगच्छति।। २९ ।।

Vyāsa

And what else comes to him ? "The understanding of the individual self and the absence of obstacles." Whatever obstacles there may be—diseases, etc.—cease to be by feeling the omnipresence of the Lord; and the true nature of himself is also seen. It is known that just as Īśvara is a Puruṣa, pure, calm, free and without appendants, such is this Puruṣa also, the self underlying the individual manifestation of the Will-to-be.

Vācaspati's Gloss

What more than this? 'Thence the understanding of the individual self, and the absence of obstacles.' The individual self is the Pratyakcetana, the conscious principle whose cognitions are contradictory of the real, that is to say, the ignorant Puruṣa. In the case of the Wise this turns back on account of the possession of the eternal divine essence. He gets the understanding of the individual self as it really is.

The obstacle will be described and their absence too.

'Whatever obstacles there may be :' These words contemplate their description. The nature of a thing is its own self. By speaking of the nature of the self, the characteristics fastened on to the self by Nescience (avidyā) are denied.

The question arises. Since Īśvara is the object of devotion, how is it that the Individual unit of consciousness will be known by feeling His omnipresence? It is evidently going beyond the mark. In reply to this, he says :—'As is Īśvara, etc.'

Pure :—free from rise and fall on account of constant eternity.

Calm :—undisturbed by afflictions.

Free :—he from whom virtue and vice keep aloof. For this very reason He is without appendants. The 'appendants' are life-state, life-period, and life-experience.'

A similarity must necessarily mean some distinction. Therefore now he distinguishes the Individual self from Īśvara. The 'self underlying the individual manifestation of the Will-to-be.' This explains why the word 'Individual' has been added.

When there are two contradictory objects, the understanding of the one does not conduce to the understanding of the other. The understanding of similars, however, conduces to the understanding of the other objects possessed of similar qualities. This happens in the same way as the understanding of one science contributes to the better understanding of an allied science. The effect of the analogy is in the understanding of one's own self, not of the Highest self. Thus all is plain.—29.

Sūtra 30

व्याधिस्त्यानसंशयप्रमादालस्याविरतिभ्रान्तिदर्शनालब्धभूमिकत्वानवस्थितत्वानि चित्तविक्षेपास्तेऽन्तरायाः ।। ३० ।।

व्याधि Vyādhi, disease. स्त्यान Styāna, langour. संशय Saṁśaya, indecision. प्रमाद Pramāda, carelessness. आलस्य Ālasya, sloth. अविरति Avirati, sensuality, want of non-attachment. भ्रान्ति Bhrānti, mistaken notion. दर्शन-अलब्ध-भूमिकत्व Darśana-alabdha-bhūmikatva, missing the point, not being able to see a place which is just seen. अनवस्थितत्व Anavasthitatva, instability. चित्तविक्षेपाः Citta-vikṣepāḥ, causing distractions, or divertion of the mind. ते Te, these are. अन्तरायाः Antarāyāḥ, the obstacles.

30. Disease, langour, indecsion, carelessenss, sloth, sensuality, mistaken notion, missing the point, instability,—these causing distractions are the obstacles.

अथ केऽन्तराया ये चित्तस्य विक्षेपाः। पुनस्ते कियन्तो वेति। व्याधिस्त्यानसंशयप्रमादालस्याविरति-भ्रान्तिदर्शनालब्धभूमिकत्वानवस्थितत्वानि चित्तविक्षेपास्तेऽन्तरायाः। नवान्तरायाश्चित्तस्य विक्षेपाः। सहैते चित्तवृत्तिभिर्भवन्ति। एतेषामभावे न भवन्ति पूर्वोक्ताश्चित्तवृत्तयः। तत्र व्याधिर्धातुरसकरणवैषम्यम्। स्त्यानमकर्मण्यता चित्तस्य। संशय उभयकोटिस्पृग्विज्ञानं स्यादिदमेवं नैवं स्यादिति प्रमादः समाधिसाधनानामभावनम्। आलस्यं कायस्य चित्तस्य च गुरुत्वादप्रवृत्तिः। अविरतिश्चित्तस्य विषयसंप्रयोगात्मगर्द्धः। भ्रान्तिदर्शनं विपर्ययज्ञानम्। अलब्धभूमिकत्वं समाधिभूमेरलाभः। अनवस्थितत्वं यल्लब्धायां भूमौ चित्तस्याप्रतिष्ठा समाधिप्रतिलम्भे हि सति तदवस्थितं स्यादिति। एते चित्तविक्षेपा नवयोगमला योगप्रतिपक्षायोगान्तराया इत्यभिधीयन्ते।। ३०।।

Vyāsa

Now what are the obstacles that distract the mind? How many are they and what is their nature ? 'Disease, etc.' There are nine obstacles causing distraction to the mind. These exist with mental modifications. In their absence they do not exist. The mental modifications have been described before.

Disease is the disturbance of the equilibrium of the humours, chyle and the organs of the body.

Languor is the indisposition of the mind to work.

Indecision is the notion touching both sides of a question : It might be thus or thus.

Carelessness is want of resort to the means of trance.

Sloth is the inertia of mind and body consequent upon heaviness.

Sensuality is the desire consequent upon objects of sense having taken possession of the mind.

Mistaken notion is False knowledge.

Missing the point, is the non-attainment of the state of trance.

Instability is the incapacity of the mind to keep in any state that has been attained, because it becomes stable only when the state of trance has been reached.

These distractions of the mind are designated the enemies and the obstacles of Yoga.

Vācaspati's Gloss

He puts a questions :—'Now what are the obstacles ?' The answer consists of the words, "distractions of the mind." Again he asks for the specific enumeration :—'How many, etc.' The answer is 'Disease, etc.' the whole aphorism. The nine obstacles are mental manifestations which stand in the way of Yoga. They are contrary to Yoga and disturb the mind. They are called obstacles, because they turn the aspirant away from the direct path of Yoga.

He gives the cause of their being the antagonists of Yoga :—'They manifest with mental modifications.' Indecision and False knowledge are antagonistic to the inhibition mind, because they are mental modifications. The others, however, which are not mental of the modifications such as disease, etc., likewise antagonistic, because mental modifications manifest themselves along with them.

He explains the meaning of the words :—'Disease, etc.'

The humours are bile, mucus and gas, called *Dhātus,* because they keep up the body. Chyle (rasa) is a particular modification of foods and drinks. The organs of the body are the organs of sensation and action. Disturbance of equilibrium means one of these becoming more and the other less than what is necessary. The indisposition of the mind to work means incapacity to work. Indecision or doubt is knowledge touching both sides of a question. Although the basis of doubt is the knowing of a thing to be what it is not and therefore doubt and False knowledge do not differ from each other, yet doubt is separately mentioned here, because it is especially intended to bring out here the special characteristic of doubt, the touching and giving up of both sides of a question, which makes a sub-head of False knowing.

'Want of resort, to the means of trance' means the absence of these means, the want of effort. The heaviness of the body is caused by phlegm, etc. The heaviness of the mind is caused by inertia, *tamas.* Desire means thirst for an object. The states of trance are *Madhumatī,* etc. If one has reached a particular state of progress in trance and is satisfied with it, then he will not reach the higher state and will lose the one already attained. Therefore, when a state of trance has been reached, effort must always be made to retain it.—30.

Sūtra 31

दुःखदौर्मनस्याङ्गमेजयत्वश्वासप्रश्वासा विक्षेपसहभुवः ।। ३१ ।।

दुःख Duḥkha, pain. दौर्मनस्य Daurmanasya, dispair, dejection. अङ्गमेजयत्व Aṅgamejayatva, shakiness. श्वास Śvāsa, inspiration. प्रश्वासाः Praśvāsāḥ, and expiration. विक्षेप Vikṣepa, of distraction. सहभुवः Saha-bhuvaḥ, companions.

31. Pain, despair, shakiness, inspiration and expiration are the companions of these distractions.

दुःखदौर्मनस्याङ्गमेजयत्वश्वासप्रश्वासा विक्षेपसहभुवः। दुःखमाध्यात्मिकमाधिभौतिकमाधिदैविकं च येनाभिहताः प्राणिनस्तदपघाताय पयतन्ते तद्दुःखम्। दौर्मनस्यमिच्छाविघाताच्चेतसः क्षोभः यदङ्गान्येजयति कम्पयति तदङ्गमेजयत्वम्। प्राणो यद् बाह्यं वायुमाचामति स श्वासः। यत्कौष्ठ्यं वायुं निःसारयति स प्रश्वासः। एते विक्षेपसहभुवो विक्षिप्तचित्तस्यैते भवन्ति। समाहितचित्तस्यैते न भवन्ति।। ३१ ।।

Vyāsa

Pain is either from one's self, or from external terrestrial objects, or from the powers of nature. Pain is that affected by which people try to do away with it.

Despair is the condition of the mind consequent upon the non-fulfilment of some desire.

Shakiness is that which causes the organs to shake.

Inspiration is the action of the life-force drinking in external air.

Expiration is that which throws out the internal gas.

These are the companions of the distractions of the mind. They appear in him whose mind is distracted. They do not exist in him whose mind is entranced.

Vācaspati's Gloss

Now he says that it is not only the nine obstacles, but that pain, etc., too appearing as their companions, act similarly :—'Pain, etc.'

Pain is that which is cognized as being contrary to the mind for the time. It is from one's self, when it is either bodily such as caused by disease, or, mental, such as caused by desire, etc. It is from external causes when it is caused by a tiger, etc. It comes from the powers of nature when it is caused by such things as the planetary influences. All this pain is cognized by every living creature as contrary to one's being. It is, therefore, to be removed. This is what he says :—'Affected by which, etc.' When physical life drinks in, *i.e.*, takes in external air contrary to one's wish, the act of in-breathing becomes contrary to the branch of Yoga known as the Recaka, the conscious out-breathing). When physical life expels the internal air against wish, the act of out-breathing is contrary to the branch of Yoga known as Pūraka, the (conscious in-breathing).—31.

Sūtra 32

तत्प्रतिषेधार्थमेकतत्त्वाभ्यासः ।। ३२ ।।

तत् Tat, their. प्रतिषेध Pratiṣedha, preventions. अर्थम् Artham, for. एक Eka, of one. तत्त्व Tattva, truth or subject. अभ्यासः Abhyāsaḥ, habituation.

32. For their prevention, habituation to one Truth.

अथैते विक्षेपाः समाधिप्रतिपक्षास्ताभ्यामेवाभ्यासवैराग्याभ्यां निरोद्धव्याः। तत्राभ्यासस्य विषयमुपसंहरन्निदमाह। तत्प्रतिषेधार्थमेकतत्त्वाभ्यासः। विक्षेपप्रतिषेधार्थमेकतत्त्वावलम्बनं चित्तमभ्यसेत्। यस्य तु प्रत्यर्थनियतं प्रत्ययमात्रं क्षणिकं च चित्तं तस्य सर्वमेव चित्तमेकाग्रं नास्त्येव विक्षिप्तम्। यदि पुनरिदं सर्वतः प्रत्याहृत्यैकस्मिन्नर्थे समाधीयते तदा भवत्येकाग्रमित्यतो न प्रत्यर्थनियतम्। योऽपि सदृशप्रत्ययप्रवाहेन चित्तमेकाग्रं मन्यते तस्यैकाग्रता यदि प्रवाहचित्तस्य धर्मस्तदैकं नास्ति प्रवाहचित्तं क्षणिकत्वात्। अथ प्रवाहांशस्यैव प्रत्ययस्य धर्मः स सर्वः सदृशप्रत्ययप्रवाही वा विसदृशप्रत्ययप्रवाही वा प्रत्यर्थनियतत्वादेकाग्र एवेति विक्षिप्तचित्तानुपपत्तिः। तस्मादेकमनेकार्थमवस्थितं चित्तमिति। यदि च चित्तनैकेनानन्विताः स्वभावभिन्नाः प्रत्यया जायेरन्नथ कथमन्यप्रत्ययदृष्टस्यान्यः स्मर्ता भवेत्। अन्यप्रत्ययोपचित्तस्य च कर्माशयस्यान्यः प्रत्युपभोक्ता भवेत्। कथंचित्समाधीयमानमप्येतदगोमयपायसीयन्यायमाक्षिपति। किं च स्वात्मानुभवापह्नवश्चित्तस्यान्यत्वे प्राप्नोति। कथं यदहमद्राक्षं तत्स्पृशामि यच्चास्प्राक्षं तत्पश्याम्यहमितिप्रत्ययः सर्वस्य प्रत्ययस्य भेदे सति प्रत्ययिन्यभेदेनोपस्थितः। एक प्रत्ययिविषयोपमभेदात्मा अहमिति प्रत्ययः। कथमत्यन्तभिन्नेषु चित्तेषु वर्तमानं सामान्यमेकं प्रत्ययिनमाश्रयेत्। स्वानुभवग्राह्यश्चायमभेदात्मा अहमितिप्रत्ययः। न च प्रत्यक्षस्य माहात्म्यं प्रमाणान्तरेणाभिभूयते। प्रमाणान्तरं च प्रत्यक्षबलेनैव व्यवहारं लभते तस्मादेकमनेकार्थमवस्थितं च चित्तम् ।। ३२ ।।

Vyāsa

Now these distractions, the antagonists of trance, are to be checked by the same practice and desirelessness. It is to finish the subject of practice that he says :—'For the prevention thereof, habituation to **One Truth.**' For the prevention of distractions, let the mind take to *One Truth* and make itself habitually familiar with it.

To him who believes in a mind separate and distinct for every cognized object, in fact a bundle of notions only, and but momentary (in existence) all mind, are one-pointed (ekāgra) only. There is no distracted mind.

If, however, the mind is concentrated on one object, only when, having been drawn away from all other objects, it turns away to one object, then it is not separate and distinct for every cognized object.

He who believes the mind to be one-pointed if it flows along similar notions, might opine that one-pointedness is a characteristic of the flowing mind. If so, then the flowing would not be one, because it is said to be momentary.

If, however, it is the characteristic of a notion which is only a portion of the entire stream (of flowing mental phenomena), then it is always one-pointed, whether it flows along similar or dissimilar notions; because in this case it is separate and distinct for every object. Thus we would fall upon the non-existence of a distracted mind. Hence the mind is one, has many objects, and is not momentary, but stable.

Further, if it be thought that the notions are born, each separate from the other in nature, and are not linked (by the common basis of) one single mind, then how would one mind remember a notion cognized by another. And how would any one enjoy the vehicle of action brought into being by the notions of another?

Howsoever the matter is examined, it illustrates the story of the milk and the cowdung.

Further, if the mind be separate and distinct for every cognized object, then the notion of the identity of the self is destroyed. How can such notions as, 'I touch what I saw,' and 'I see what I touched previously,' point to a common knower, when all the notions are separate and distinct?

The notion of the 'I am' is always identical with itself and points out to but one cognizer. But there can be no single cognizer as a common basis, if it manifest itself in entirely distinct minds every moment. The notion of 'I am' as one undifferentiated continuous self is cognized by internal perception; and the authority of perception is not to be defeated by any other means of knowledge. Other means of knowledge work only by the power of perception. Hence the mind is one and has many objects and it changes not every moment.—32.

Vācaspati's Gloss

Introduces the aphorism which finishes the subject under discussion :—'Now these distractions, etc.'

Now it is on account of the context that this aphorism is spoken of as finishing only half the subject under discussion. These distractions are spoken of as antagonists of the trance to explain the object with which they are to be checked.

Although in the aphorism, 'By feeling the omnipresence of the Lord' the process of mental habituation only is described, yet desirelessness also is to be understood, because it is a help to habituation. With this in mind, he says :—'They are to be checked by the same practice *and desirelessness.'*

'This is said to finish the subject of practice' :—This sentence is spoken because the subject of practice immediately precedes. The **One Truth** is God, because that is the context.

To the Vaināṣikas all minds are one-pointed only; there is no distracted mind. Hence their teachings and the acts they inculcate, are all useless. With this object he says :—"To him who believes, etc." The theory is that the mind is separate and distinct for every object whether it to be a single one in itself, or one out of many. It remains in being only so long as the object shines in consciousness and then disappears at once, not going to another object.

Why does not the mind take in another object after having taken in one before that? Because it is said to be momentary. This means that existence before and after, cannot be posited of a mind, which cannot be spoken of as remaining the same in more than one successive moment of time.

According to our teaching the mind is not momentary in existence, and remains constant, whether the objects of thought be one or manifold. It is not confined to one single object seeing that it takes in and gives up objects every moment and can so far be called distracted, and also that it can cultivate one-pointedness when the modification of distractedness has been removed. This teaching and the acts recommended on its strength are not useless. With this object, he says :—'And if it becomes concentrated, etc.' Concludes :—'Thus it is not distinct and separate for every object.'

Again he introduces the Vaināṣika :—'He who believes the mind to be one-pointed if it flows along similar notions, etc.' His meaning is stated to be as follows :—'Let it be granted that the cultivation of one-pointedness is not possible in a mind confined to one moment only and that therefore it is useless to put forth effort with that object. The continuous succession of minds, however, is unending and not momentary in its nature; it is possible in the succession that distraction may be removed and one-pointedness cultivated.'

He shows the defects of the theory in the case of either of the two statements thereof. If in the philosophy of the Vaināṣika one-pointedness is a characteristic of the flowing mind, *i.e.*, of the un-ending succession of minds, then, there being successive mental births for succeeding mental impressions, there does not exist one flowing mind common to all the successive impressions. But why should it not be so? Because in your philosophy, whatever exists for as long a time as it may be, must be momentary; there is nothing that is not momentary.

Takes the other form of the theory :—'If however it is, etc.' If in the successive flow of mental phenomena a notion having the Highest Good appears at a single point, one-pointedness with reference to this particular notion may be secured by effort.

Shows the defects of this theory. The whole of this successive flow of mental phenomena may be a flow of either similar or dissimilar notions. It is, therefore, separate and distinct for every distinct object, and as such takes the form of the Highest Good simply for the expression of it, and therefore it is destroyed on the disappearance of the mind. Such a mind is always one-pointed. There can, therefore, be no distracted mind. It cannot, therefore, be that one-pointedness may be cultivated by and after the removal of distractedness. Concludes :—'Hence the mind is, etc.'

Further says, that for another reason too the mind is one having many objects, and is constant not momentary :—'And if it be so, etc.' As the Teaching studied by Maitra is not remembered by Caitra, and as the fruit of the vehicle of action grown by Maitra in not enjoyed by Caitra, in the shape of virtue and vice, inasmuch as Caitra is not related to it, so one notion cannot remember the object of another notion; nor can one notion enjoy the fruit of the vehicle of action grown by another notion.

But, says the questioner, this line of reasoning will not be violated, if the relation of cause and effect exists; and it is on account of the existence of that differentia, that in the *Śrāddha* and *Vaiśvānara* sacrifice, etc., the fruit is seen reaching father, mother, and son, who are not the performers thereof; and also because the sweetness of the mango, seeds, etc., always appears in due course in the fruits thereof.

For this reason, says :—'However is the matter examined, etc.' This is the meaning. What is the difference between notions falling into one succession and those falling into another, so that a notion falling into one succession may remember and enjoy the notions, experience and the vehicle of action grown by the notions of the same succession but not by the notions of another succession ? Succession is not an independently existing substabce, so that one succession may be differentiated from another succession. And it is not proper that a fanciful differentia may be fastened upon an action. No one can cook if he only fancies the existence of fire anywhere. Further, the relation of cause and effect also is not real. In the case of simultaneous existence there can be no such relation, as for example, between the right and left horns. In the case of objects which do not exist simultaneously, no relation of cause and effect necessarily exists; because it may be that none of them can be predicated of a phenomenon appearing in the immediate present. The past and the future cannot exist together as being related to a phenomenon appearing independently in the present. Therefore, being independent real objects as they are, they do not differ from each other whether they fall in their own or in independent successions. The reason is that they do not come into contact with each other, not being related to each other by either natural causation or by succession. This logic is like that of the milk and cow-dung cakes.

"All that is produced from the cow is milk,
Cow-dung cakes are produced from the cow.
Therefore cow-dung cakes are milk."

This illustrates the story, which means that it surpasses in fallacy even the logic of the milk and the cow-dung.

Furthermore, the destruction of that which has been done, and the appearance of that which has not been done, should not be mentioned here as an argument. Because the mind alone is the doer of actions, and the mind alone is associated with the pleasures and pains born out of them. It is because the mind enjoys pleasure and pain on account of the presence therein of the reflection of consciousness, and because the consciousness and the mind in which it is present are taken to be one, that they are attributed to the Puruṣa. The notions born in the mind, when the notion of its being the self has already come in there, are of such a nature that they alone remember and enjoy their own fruits, not others. And it is not reasonable to say that the nature of a thing may be separated from it, and then joined to it again. It cannot be said of the said of the nature of a thing that it might or might not be so, or why is it not so?

He speaks to those who are satisfied with the above :—'Further, if the mind be separate and distinct for every object, etc., mental impressions and their memories have the characteristics of manifestation and latency. They are many and yet the mind in which they live, *i.e.,* the notion of the 'I am,' is one and not different for each. This one notion of the 'I am' unites all those separate notions into one. How can this one hold all the extremely different notions into itself? Inasmuch as there is difference in the causes of the phenomena of cognition and memory and also on account of the presence in them of the contradictory qualities of manifestation and latency, there can be no single notion of reflex condition by virtue of which the mind, in which all the different and contradictory notions are generated, may be considered to be a single entity.

For this reason, he says :—'It is cognised by internal perception.'

But it may be said that the difference of causes and the possession of contradictory qualities refute the truth of this perception. In answer to this objection, he says :—'and the authority of perception, etc.'

It is on the basis of perception alone that the unity of material and the contradictory nature of the characteristics of latency and manifestation have been established in the Nyāyakanikā; and the action of objections in a permanent mind is established in the Nyāyakanikā and the Brahmatattva-samīkṣā. Thus all is plain.—32.

Sūtra 33

मैत्रीकरुणामुदितोपेक्षाणां सुखदुःखपुण्यापुण्यविषयाणां भावनातश्चित्त-प्रसादनम्।। ३३।।

मैत्री Maitrī, friendliness. **करुणा** Karuṇā, compassion, mercy. **मुदिता** Muditā, gladness complacency. **उपेक्षा** Upekṣā, indifference of all these. **सुख** Sukha, happiness. **दुःख** Duḥkha. misery. **पुण्य** Puṇya, virtue. **अपुण्य** Apuṇya, vice. **विषयाणाम्** Viṣayāṇām, regarding the subjects, towards the subjects (respectively). **भावनात:** Bhāvanātaḥ, by cultivating habits, by constant thinking. **चित्त** Citta, of the mind. **प्रसादनम्** Prasādanam, purification.

33. By cultivating habits of friendliness, compassion, complacency and indifference towards happiness, misery, virtue and vice (respectively) the mind becomes pure.

यस्य चित्तस्यावस्थितस्येदं शास्त्रेण परिकर्म निर्दिश्यते तत्कथम्। मैत्री करुणामुदितोपेक्षाणां सुखदुःखपुण्यापुण्यविषयाणां भावनातश्चित्तप्रसादनम्। तत्र सर्वप्राणिषु सुखसंभोगापन्नेषु मैत्रीं भावयेत्। दुःखितेषु करुणाम्। पुण्यात्मकेषु मुदिताम्। अपुण्यशीलेषूपेक्षाम्। एवमस्य भावयतः शुक्लो धर्म उपजायते। ततश्च चित्तं प्रसीदति। प्रसन्नमेकाग्रं स्थितिपदं लभते।। ३३।।

Vyāsa

How is the embellishment of the permanent mind taught by this science, secured? 'The mind becomes pure by cultivating habits of friendliness, compassion, complacency and indifference towards happiness, misery, virtue and vice.' Let him cultivate in his mind the habit of friendliness towards all those who are found in the enjoyment of pleasure; compassion towards those who are suffering from pain; complacency towards those who are virtuous; indifference towards the vicious. By thus habituating the mind to these notions, the white characteristic makes appearance. Thence the mind becomes pure. Having become pure, it becomes one-pointed and attains the state of steadiness.—33.

Vācaspati's Gloss

Now the author begins to lay down the means of purifying the mind, which are contrary to such vices as jealousy, because trance and the means of its achievement cannot appear in a mind, unembellished and full of jealousy, etc. :—'How is the embellishment, etc.'

Whoever shows friendliness, *i.e.*, a heart ready to help, towards the happy, the dirt of envy leaves him. When the mind shows compassion, *i.e.*, the wish to remove the miseries of others as if they were his own, towards those who are suffering, the dirt of the desire to do evil by others is removed. Whoever shows complacency, *i.e.*, pleasure towards virtuously inclined beings, the dirt of envy is removed from his mind. Whoever shows indifference, *i.e.*, the taking of the middle path and not taking sides, towards the viciously inclined, the dirt of impatience is removed from his mind.

By this removal of the characteristics of the qualities of disturbing energy (rajas) and inertia (tamas), the white characteristic of essential purity (sattva) manifests itself. He becomes possessed of a very high manifestation of essential purity. His mind becomes inclined to the side of the restraint of mental modifications, because this enlightenment is natural to that state. When the mind becomes pure, it attains the state of steadiness and becomes one-pointed by the means to be described. If friendliness, etc., are not cultivated, the means cannot lead to steadiness.—33.

Sūtra 34

प्रच्छर्दनविधारणाभ्यां वा प्राणस्य।। ३४।।

प्रच्छर्दन Pracchardana, by the expulsion. विधारणाभ्याम् Vidhāraṇābhyām, and by the retentions. वा Vā, optionally. प्राणस्य Prāṇasya, of breath.

34. Optionally, by the expulsion and retention of breath.

प्रच्छर्दनविधारणाभ्यां वा प्राणस्य। कौष्ठ्यस्य वायोर्नासिकापुटाभ्यां प्रयत्नविशेषाद्वमनं प्रच्छर्दनं विधारणं प्राणायामास्ताभ्यां वा मनसः स्थितिं संपादयेत्।। ३४।।

Vyāsa

Expulsion is the throwing out of the air in the lungs through the nostrils by special effort. Retention is the Prāṇāyāma, the lengthening of the dùration of the stay of the air outside the lungs. Let mental steadiness be optionally cultivated by these.—34.

Vācaspati's Gloss

Now then he describes the means of steadiness :—'Optionally by the expulsion and retention of breath'. The word optionally refers to the succeeding means. The option is not given with reference to the cultivation of friendliness, etc., because they must be present along with all (the means).

Now he explains expulsion :—'The throwing out of the air in the lungs, etc.' "By special efforts" means such an effort as is laid down in the science of Yoga, by which the air is thrown out of the lungs slowly.

Now he describes retention :—Retention is Prāṇāyāma. It means the keeping out of the air which has been expired, lengthening the duration of its stay outside, not drawing in all at once. By thus expiring and inspiring air the body becomes light, and the mind thence attains the state of steadiness. The words 'let it be cultivated' have been taken from the sense of the words 'causes mental steadiness, (sthitinibandhinī) in the next aphorism.

Sūtra 35

विषयवती वा प्रवृत्तिरुत्पन्ना मनसः स्थितिनिबन्धिनी।। ३५।।

विषयवती Viṣayavatī, of the sense, of the objects of senses, bringing sense perceptions. वा Vā, or. प्रवृत्तिः Pravṛttiḥ, higher activity. उत्पन्ना Utpannā, appearing. मनसः Manasaḥ, of the mind, mental. स्थिति Sthiti, steadiness. निबन्धनी Nibandhanī, causing.

35. Or, Higher sense-activity appearing causes mental steadiness.

विषयवती वा प्रवृत्तिरुत्पन्ना मनसः स्थितिनिबन्धिनी। नासिकाग्रे धारयतोऽस्य या दिव्यगन्धसंवित्सा गन्धप्रवृत्तिः। जिह्वाग्रे रससंवित्। तालुनि रूपसंवित्। जिह्वामध्येस्पर्शसंवित्। जिह्वामूले शब्दसंविदित्येता वृत्तय उत्पन्नाश्चित्तं स्थितौ निबध्नन्ति संशयं विधमन्ति समाधिप्रज्ञायां च द्वारीभवन्तीति। एतेन चन्द्रादित्य-ग्रहमणिप्रदीपरश्म्यादिषु प्रवृत्तिरुत्पन्ना विषयवत्येव वेदितव्या। यद्यपि हि तत्तच्छास्त्रानुमानाचार्यो-पदेशैरवगतमर्थतत्वं सद्भूतमेव भवति। एतेषां यथाभूतार्थप्रतिपादनसामर्थ्यात्तथापि यावदेकदेशोऽपि कश्चिन्न स्वकरणसंवेद्यो भवति तावत्सर्वं परोक्षमिवापवर्गादिषु सूक्ष्मेष्वर्थेषु न दृढां बुद्धिमुत्पादयन्ति। तस्माच्छास्त्रा-नुमानाचार्योपदेशोपोद्बलनार्थमेवावश्यं कश्चिदर्थविशेषः प्रत्यक्षीकर्तव्यः। तत्र तदुपदिष्टार्थैकदेशप्रत्यक्षत्वे सति सर्वं सूक्ष्मविषयमपि आ अपवर्गाच्छ्रद्धीयते। एतदर्थमेवेदं चित्तपरिकर्म निर्दिश्यते। अनियतासु वृत्तिषु तद्विषयायां वशीकारसंज्ञायामुपजातायां समर्थं स्यात्तस्य तस्यार्थस्य प्रत्यक्षीकरणायेति। तथा च सति श्रद्धावीर्यस्मृतिसमाधयोऽस्याप्रतिबन्धेन भविष्यन्तीति।। ३५।।

Vyāsa

The power to cognize superphysical (divya) smell, which one gets by concentrating upon the fore-part of the nose (the olfactory organ) is the higher olfactory sense-activity. By concentration upon the fore-part of the tongue, the power to cognize taste; over the palate, cognition of colour; in the middle of the tongue, cognition of touch; in the root of the tongue, cognition of the sound.

The Higher sense-activities appearing cause the steadiness of mind, destroy doubt and become the entrance to that state of cognitive power which is called trance (Samādhi).

By this the Higher sense-activity, which is caused by concentrating upon the moon, the sun, the planets, jewels, the lamp and precious stones, etc., is also to be understood to have that name.

Although whatever of the nature of an object is known by any science, by inference, or by the instruction of a teacher, is of course true, because they are capable of establishing the truth by teaching, yet, as long as even as portion is not known by one's own senses, everything remains as it were unknown. The knowledge of such subtle matters as the state of absolute freedom does not obtain firm ground in the mind. Therefore even if it were for the purpose of giving fuller light to what has been learnt from any science, by inference, or by the instruction of a teacher, it is necessary that some particular object be perceived by one's self. When one portion of what has been taught is perceived, the subtlest remaining portions are easily believed. It is for this very reason that mental embellishment is taught; so that when consciousness of power over the unrestrained mental modifications shows itself, the Yogī becomes capable of perceiving the objects of all such modifications. And when this happens, he gets faith, energy, memory and trance without any obstacle.—35.

Vācaspati's Gloss

The author now mentions another means of steadiness :—'Or, Higher sense-activity appearing, causes mental steadiness.' Explains :—'By concentration upon the fore-part of the nose, etc.' The power is acquired by the performance of concentration, contemplation and trance. The cognition of superphysical smell means that the smell lies revealed to his sense. In the other Higher sense-activities, also it should be understood in the same way. This is to be believed on authority, not by contact with one's self.

Let it be so. But what is the use of these Higher sense-activities? They do not help in the attainment of the state of absolute freedom. For this reason, he says :—These mental modifications appearing, in but a short time, incline the mind to steadiness either with reference to God, or with reference to discriminative knowledge.

But the question is, how can a mental modification having one object, become steady with reference to other object also? For this reason, he says :—They destroy, *i.e.,* they remove, doubts and for this very reason become the entrance to trance consciousness.

Teaches that other modifications also which are taught by the Veda consist in Higher sense-activity :—'By this, etc.'

Then the question arises, wherefore should there be doubt with reference to objects known by authority, etc.? For this reason, he says :—'Although whatever...... of course, etc.' The root of Yoga is of course in faith. Arising from that, it reaches up to contemplation, etc., without obstacles. This is the meaning.—35.

Sūtra 36

विशोका वा ज्योतिष्मती ।। ३६ ।।

विशोका Viśokā, the painless state, the concentration on the painless. वा Vā, or. ज्योतिष्मती Jyotiṣmatī, the bright effulgent state, the state of lucidity, the concentration on luminous objects.

36. Or, the state of painless lucidity.

विशोका वा ज्योतिष्मती। प्रवृत्तिरुत्पन्ना मनसः स्थितिनिबन्धिन्यनुवर्तते। हृदयपुण्डरीके धारयतो या बुद्धिसंविद्ऽबुद्धिसत्त्वं हि भास्वरमाकाशकल्पं तत्र स्थितिवैशारद्यात्प्रवृत्तिः सूर्येन्दुग्रहमणि प्रभारूपाकारेण विकल्पते। तथास्मितायां समापन्नं चित्तं निस्तरङ्गमहोदधिकल्पं शान्तमनन्तमस्मितामात्रं भवति। यत्रेदमुक्तम्। तमणुमात्रमात्मानमनुविद्यास्मीति। एवं तावत्संप्रतिजानीत इत्येषा द्वयी विशोकविषयवती अस्मितामात्रा च प्रवृत्तिर्ज्योतिष्मतीत्युच्यते। यया योगिनश्चित्तं स्थितिपदं लभत इति।। ३६ ।।

Vyāsa

'Or, the state of painless lucidity' *appearing as a Higher Activity, causes the steadiness of the mind.* These words (italicised) are to be taken from the previous aphorism. This is the consciousness of thought-forms, which comes to him who concentrates upon the lotus of the heart. The essence of the Will-to-know is shining in substance. It acts like the Ākāśa (space, giving room to, or transforming easily into any form). By diligent perseverance in that, the Higher Activity appears, taking optionally the shapes of the lights of the sun, moon, planets and precious stones. Similarly the mind concentrating itself upon the notion of the 'I am' becomes like a waveless ocean calm, infinite, pure egoism. The following has been said in this connection :—

"Knowing that self, small as an atom, his consciousness manifests as 'I am' only."

This two-fold Higher Activity, the painless sensuous and the Purely Egoistic, is called the lucidity. By this the Yogī's mind reaches the state of steadiness.—36.

Vācaspati's Gloss

'Or, state of the painless lucidity.' Painless lucidity means that which is devoid of pain. The state of lucidity is the light shining in the lotus of the heart. Let the mind be concentrated upon the lotus which is located between the chest and the abdomen. It has eight petals and is placed with its face downwards. Its face has first to be turned upwards by the process of the expirative control of breath. In the middle thereof is the sphere of the sun, the place of waking consciousness, and is called A. Above that is the sphere of the moon, the place of dreaming consciousness, the U. Above that is the sphere of the fire, the place of dreamless sleep, the M. Above that is the Higher space, the Sound of Brahma Itself, the fourth state of ultra-consciousness, which the knowers of Brahma call the half-measure (the ardha mātrā). In the stalk thereof is the Artery of Brahma (the Brahmanāḍī), with its face upwards. This passes through the spheres of the sun, etc. Beginning above that, is the channel known as *Suṣumnā.* That runs through the external spheres of the sun, etc., too. That is the place of the mind. Performing concentration upon that, the Yogī obtains consciousness of thought-forms.

He now shows the form of the mental essence with the reason thereof :—'The essence of the Will-to-be, etc.' By saying that it acts like the Ākāśa, it is intended to be shown that it pervades all forms. The lights of the sun, etc., appear as different forms; and they putting on different forms optionally, appear as such (forms). The text understands here by the word Will-to-be, the mind and not the Mahattattva; and it is intended to state here that the mind is of the shape of light appearing as such from its position in the Suṣumnā channel, inasmuch as it takes its birth from the Vaikārika (the essential sāttvic) form of the principle of Individuality (Ahaṅkāra), and is therefore full of the essence thereof. Its possession of the quality of pervasion too is established by its action upon various objects.

Having spoken of concentration upon the mind, which is evolved out of the principle of Individuality (Asmitā, the basis of the 'I am'), now he describes the nature of the concentration upon the principle of Individuality or egoism :—Similarly, etc.

'Calm' means that which is free from the waves of disturbing energy (rajas) and inertia (tamas).

Infinite means all-pervading.

'Pure Egoism' signifies that which does not show more colours than one.

He supports his theory by another's authority :—The following has been said in this connection, by Pañcaśikhā.

'Small as an atom,' because it is difficult to know.

'That self,' which is the basis of the principle of Individuality.

'Knowing' means having pondered upon it and having come to know only this much, 'I am.'

Well then the lucidity might appear as various forms of light; but how can it be pure egoism only? In answer to this, he says :—'This two-fold, etc.' The meaning is that the principle of Individuality remains essential light itself when the dirt of disturbing energy (rajas) and inertia (tamas) has been washed away.

He describes the result of both form of lucidity :—'By this, etc.'—36.

Sūtra 37

वीतरागविषयं वा चित्तम् ।। ३७ ।।

वीत-राग Vīta-rāga, one who is desireless. **विषय** Viṣaya, an object. **वीतरागविषयम्** Vītarāgaviṣayam, having the desireless for its object. **वा** Vā, or. **चित्तम्** Cittam, the mind.

37. Or, the mind having the desireless, for its object.

वीतरागविषयं वा चित्तम् । वीतरागचित्तालम्बनोपरक्तं वा योगिनश्चित्तं स्थितिपदं लभत इति ।। ३७ ।।

Vyāsa

The mind of the Yogī tinged by the colour of the mind of the desireless, which it takes up for study, reaches the position of steadiness.—37.

Vācaspati's Gloss

The desireless are such personages as Dvaipāyana and others, their minds become the objects of concentration, and the colour thereof is imparted to the mind of the Yogī.—37.

Sūtra 38

स्वप्ननिद्राज्ञानालम्बनं वा ।। ३८ ।।

स्वप्न Svapna, of dream. निद्रा Nidrā, of deep sleep, sleeps. ज्ञान Jñāna, the knowledge study. आलम्बनम् Ālambanam, taking for tis objects, resorting to, meditating on. वा Vā, or.

38. Or, having the knowledge of dream and sleep as its object of study.

स्वप्ननिद्राज्ञानालम्बनं वा। स्वप्नज्ञानालम्बनं वा निद्राज्ञानालम्बनं वा तदाकारं योगिनश्चित्तं स्थितिपदं लभत इति ।। ३८ ।।

Vyāsa

By making the knowledge of dreams and the knowledge of sleep an object of study, the mind of the Yogī determines towards the shape and attains the position of steadiness.—38.

Vācaspati's Gloss

When the time comes that this Yogī, in his dream state, worships the Lord Maheśvara's form, enrapturing the mind by its beauty, placed in a secluded spot of some lonely forest, appearing as if arising out of the sphere of the light of the moon, the limbs large and small of the shape appearing as soft as the stalks of the lotus, the form seen as if made of shining moon-stones, encircled with garlands of sweet-smelling Mālatī and Mallikā; then on awakening he is full of elation, and then remembering the same form which was the object of dream consciousness, his mind determines towards the unity of that one form and attains the position of steadiness.

The sleep to be understood here is the one in which the light of the quality of essentiality appears. (This is the sāttvic sleep). It is the same, on awakening from which the remembrance is, 'I have slept pleasurably.' This explains that the mind in that state becomes one-pointed. It is this that the knowers of Brahma define to be of the nature of Brahma (Brahmarūpa).

In the dream state it is not possible to bring mere knowledge without an object, within the range; therefore, the object also is brought within the range.—38.

Sūtra 39

यथाभिमतध्यानाद्वा ।। ३९ ।।

यथा-भिमत Yathā abhimata, according to one's own choice, or what appeals one, according to one's predilection. ध्यानात् Dhyānāt, by meditating on. वा Vā, or.

33. Or, by meditating according to one's predilection.

यथाभिमतध्यानाद्वा। यदेवाभिमतं तदेव ध्यायेत्। तत्र लब्धस्थितिकमन्यत्रापि स्थितिपदं लभत इति।। ३९।।

Vyāsa

Let him meditate upon whatever he wishes. Becoming steady in that instance, it reaches the position of steadiness in other matters also.—39.

Vācaspati's Gloss

What more? Whatever is desired by one, the same has the form of his deity.—39.

Sūtra 40

परमाणुपरममहत्त्वान्तोऽस्य वशीकारः।। ४०।।

परमाणु Parmāṇu, the minutest atom. परम Parama, greatest. महत्त्वः Mahattva, infinity. अन्तः Antaḥ, end. परमाणुपरममहत्त्वान्तः Reaching down to the minutest and up to the largest. अस्य Asya, of this Yogī. वशीकारः Vaśīkāraḥ, power.

40. His power reaches down to the minutest, and up to the largest.

परमाणुपरममहत्त्वान्तोऽस्य वशीकारः। सूक्ष्मे निविशमानस्य परात्परमाण्वन्तं स्थितिपदं लभत इति। स्थूले निविशमानस्य परममहत्त्वान्तं स्थितिपदं चित्तस्य। एवं तामुभयीं कोटिमनुधावतो योऽस्याः प्रतीघातः स परो वशीकारस्मद्वशीकारात्परिपूर्णं योगिनश्चित्तं न पुनरभ्यासकृतं परिकर्मापेक्ष्यत इति।। ४०।।

Vyāsa

Entering into the subtle it attains the position of steadiness upon the smallest of the small, down to an atom. Entering into the large, the position of mental steadiness reaches up to the largest of the large. His great power consists in not being turned back by any check while running along both these lines. The mind of the Yogī, full of this power, does not again stand in need of the mental embellishment due to habitual practice.—40.

Vācaspati's Gloss

He shows how the nature of the self is to be reached as a point of steady concentration :—'His power reaches down to the minutest and up to the largest.' Explains :—'Entering into the subtle, etc.'

Summarizing what has, already been said, he describes the connotation of the word 'power'. 'While running along, etc.' Now describes a subsidiary result of the power. 'Full of this power, etc.'

Thus the means of obtaining mental steadiness have been described. The power too obtained by the steady mind has been shown.—40.

Sūtra 41

क्षीणवृत्तेरभिजातस्येव मणेर्ग्रहीतृग्रहणग्राह्येषु तत्स्थतदञ्जनता समापत्तिः ।। ४१ ।।

क्षीण Kṣīṇa, disappearing, powerless. वृत्ति Vṛtti, modification of the mind. क्षीणवृत्तेः Kṣīṇa, Vṛtteḥ, of that (mind) whose modifications have become powerless, have disappeared. अभिजातस्य Abhijātasya, of a transparent. इव Iva, like. मणेः Maṇeḥ, of a crystal, ग्रहीतृ Grahītṛ, the knower. ग्रहण Grahaṇa, knowing. ग्राह्य Grāhya, the knowable all these three. तत्स्थ Tat-stha, remaining in it, what is presented to it. तदञ्जनता Tad añjanatā, taking the tinge of that object, being coloured by that object, the power of appearing in the shape of any object. समापत्तिः Samāpatiḥ, the power of thought—transformation, concentration and oneness.

41. Becoming like a transparent crystal on the modifications disappearing, (the mind acquires) the power of thought-transformation (samāpatti), the power of appearing in the shape of whatever object is presented to it, be it the knower, the knowable or the act of knowing.

अथ लब्धस्थितिकस्य चेतसः किंस्वरूपा किं विषया वा समापत्तिरिति तदुच्यते। क्षीणवृत्तेरभिजातस्येव मणेर्ग्रहीतृग्रहणग्राह्येषु तत्स्थतदञ्जनता समापत्तिः। क्षीणवृत्तेरिति प्रत्यस्तमितप्रत्ययस्येत्यर्थः। अभिजातस्येव मणेरिति दृष्टान्तोपादानम्। यथा स्फटिक उपाश्रयभेदात्तत्तद्रूपोपरक्त उपाश्रयरूपाकारेण निर्भासते तथा ग्राह्यलम्बनोपरक्तं चित्तं ग्राह्यं समापन्नं ग्राह्यस्वरूपाकारेण निर्भासते। तथा भूतसूक्ष्मोपरक्तं भूतसूक्ष्मसमापन्नं भूतसूक्ष्मस्वरूपाभासं भवति। तथा स्थूलालम्बनोपरक्तं स्थूलरूपसमापन्नं स्थूलरूपाभासं भवति। तथा विश्वभेदोपरक्तं विश्वभेदसमापन्नं विश्वरूपाभासं भवति। तथा ग्रहणेष्वपीन्द्रियेष्वपि द्रष्टव्यम्। ग्रहणालम्बनोपरक्तं ग्रहणसमापन्नं ग्रहणस्वरूपाकारेण निर्भासते। तथा ग्रहीतृपुरुषालम्बनोपरक्तं ग्रहीतृपुरुषसमापन्नं ग्रहीतृपुरुषस्वरूपाकारेण निर्भासते। तथा मुक्तपुरुषालम्बनोपरक्तं मुक्तपुरुषसमापन्नं मुक्तपुरुषस्वरूपाकारेण निर्भासत इति। तदेवमभिजातमणिकल्पस्य चेतसो ग्रहीतृग्रहणग्राह्येषु पुरुषेन्द्रियभूतेषु या तत्स्थतदञ्जनता तेषु स्थितस्य तदाकारापत्तिः सा समापत्तिरित्युच्यते।। ४१ ।।

Vyāsa

Now what is the nature of the power of thought-transformation which the mind acquires, when it has thus obtained rest ? This is described :—'Becoming like a transparent crystal on the modifications disappearing, the mind acquires the power of thought-transformation,—the power of appearing in the shape of whatever is presented to it, be it the knower, the knowable, or the act of knowing.'

'On the modifications disappearing' :—When the notions are at rest, (not in active work).

'Like a transparent crystal' :—This is the statement of an analogy. As the crystal becomes coloured by the colour of the object placed beside it, and then shines according to the form of the object, so the mind is coloured by the colour of the object presented to it and then appears in the form of the object.

Coloured by subtle elements placed in contact, it becomes of the nature of the subtle elements and shines out in the shape of the subtle elements.

Similarly, coloured by the distinctions of the world coming into contact with it, it becomes of the nature of those distinctions, and shines out in the form of the world.

Similarly, is this to be understood in the case of the acts of knowing, *i.e.*, the powers of sensation. Coloured by the acts of knowing taken as objects of thought, it becomes of the nature of the acts of knowing, and shines out in forms which show the nature of the acts of knowing.

Similarly, coloured by the enjoying Puruṣa, taken as the object of thought, it puts on the nature of the enjoying Puruṣa, and shines out in the form which shows the nature of the enjoying Puruṣa.

Similarly, coloured by the released Puruṣa taken as object of thought, it becomes of the nature of the released Puruṣa, and shines out in the form which shows the nature of the released Puruṣa.

This then is Samāpatti, thought-transformation,—the mind showing itself like a transparent crystal, in the form of the object it comes in contact with, be it the knower, the knowable, or the acts of knowledge.

Vācaspati's Gloss

Now the question is what is the nature and what are the object of the Cognitive trance, when the mind has thus obtained rest? The Commentator introduces the next aphorism :—"This is described, etc." Reads the aphorism :—'Becoming like a transparent crystal, etc.' Explains it :—The words, 'when the notions are at rest,' describe the mind as existing in the state, in which that class of mental modifications which have their origin in the qualities of disturbing energy and inertia (rajas and tamas) have been destroyed by habitual practice and desirelessness. By this it is meant to be explained that Mental Essence (sattva) being by nature pure, is not overpowered at the time, by disturbing energy (rajas) and inertia (tamas).

He explains the analogy :—'As the crystal, etc.'

'The object placed beside it' is the upādhi, the attributive substance such as the Japā flower, etc.

'Coloured by proximity,' taking up the light thereof.

The form of the object placed beside, 'is the red, blue or other colour of its own.'

'Shines out,' means, 'shows the qualities of that form.'

He applies the analogy :—'Similarly, coloured by the object, etc.'

The object of knowledge (grāhya) is the same to which the mind is at the time turned (ālambana). It is coloured thereby when the object passes into it. Thus is the knowable distinguished from the knower and the act of knowing.

'Becomes of the nature of the object,' means, 'as if it has put on the quality of knowability having thus covered up its own mental form. For this reason shines out in the form of the knowable object itself.'

The subtle and the gross are colours from the objective world only. The commentator divides them therefore into two :—'Coloured by the subtle, etc.' The distinctions of the world consist in its being self-conscious and not self-conscious, and of the differences of objects, such as the animals, cows, etc., and the mineral substances, such as the jar, etc. By this the two trances which are accompanied by philosophical curiosity and meditation are shown.

Similar is the case with the acts, the means of knowledge, the powers of sensation (indriyas). They are so called because knowledge is obtained through their instrumentality.

The commentator renders the same plainer :—'Coloured by the acts of knowledge, etc.' Being an act of knowledge, but taken as an object of knowledge, it is here mentioned as having both these qualities at the same time.

'Coloured by that,' *i.e.*, pierced through and through by that, and having covered up its own mental form it appears as if it were the means, the external instrument of knowledge.

By this has been described the Cognitive trance which is accompanied by elation.

The one which is accompanied by egoism is now alluded to. 'Coloured by the Enjoying Puruṣa, etc.' The Enjoying Puruṣa means, he in whom the notion of the 'I am' resides.

Because the quality of being a Puruṣa is common to the released Puruṣa, such as Śuka and Prahlāda too, they too have to be taken hère as objects of trance. For this reason, the commentator says :—'Similarly, coloured by the released Puruṣa, etc.'

Coming to the end, he explains the words 'tastha tadañjnatāt,' appearing in the form of the object it comes into contact with.

The thought-transformation called the Cognitive Trance consists in the assumption by the Mental Essence of the forms of the knower, the knowable and the act of knowledge, and the consequent showing of itself in the shape of the phenomenon which has entered therein, when the dirt of the *rajas* and the *tamas* has been removed by the increased power of contemplation, and when it is directed towards, *i.e.*, fixed upon, these objects of knowledge.

Here the order of the reading of the words, 'the knower, the act of knowledge and the knowable,' in the aphorism is not to be regarded, because it is contrary to the natural succession of the objects of knowledge. Similarly in the Commentary too the mentioning of the subtle elements first in order, is not to be regarded. All is thus beautiful.—41.

Sūtra 42

तत्र शब्दार्थज्ञानविकल्पैः सङ्कीर्णा सवितर्का समापत्तिः ।। ४२ ।।

तत्र, Tatra, there. **शब्द**, Śabda, of words. **अर्थ** Artha, of meaning. **ज्ञान**, Jñāna, of idea. **विकल्पैः**, Vikalpaiḥ, with options. **सङ्कीर्णा**, Saṅkīrṇā, mixed up. **सवितर्का**, Savitarkā, indistinct. **समापत्तिः** Samāpattiḥ, the thought transformation.

42. There, the thought-transformation in which the options of word, meaning and idea are mixed up, is called Indistinct, (verbal).

तत्र शब्दार्थज्ञानविकल्पैः सङ्कीर्णा सवितर्का समापत्तिः। तद्यथा गौरितिशब्दो गौरित्यर्थो गौरिति ज्ञानमित्यविभागेन विभक्तानामपि ग्रहणं दृष्टम्। विभज्यमानाश्चान्ये शब्दधर्मा अन्येऽर्थधर्मा अन्ये विज्ञानधर्मा

इत्येषां विभक्तः पन्थाः। तत्र समापन्नस्य योगिनो यो गवाद्यर्थः समाधिप्रज्ञायां समारूढः स चेच्छब्दार्थज्ञान-विकल्पानुविद्ध उपावर्तते सा सङ्कीर्णा समापत्तिः सवितर्केत्युच्यते। यदा पुनः शब्दसङ्केतस्मृतिपरिशुद्धौ श्रुतानुमानज्ञानविकल्पशून्यायां समाधिप्रज्ञायां स्वरूपमात्रेणावस्थितोऽर्थस्तत्स्वरूपाकारमात्रतयैवावच्छिद्यते सा च निर्वितर्का समापत्तिस्तत्परं प्रत्यक्षम्। तच्च श्रुतानुमानयोर्बीजम्। ततः श्रुतानुमाने प्रभवतः। न च श्रुतानुमानस-ज्ञानसहभूतं तद्दर्शनम्। तस्मादसङ्कीर्णं प्रमाणान्तरेण योगिनो निर्वितर्कसमाधिजं दर्शनमिति ।। ४२ ।।

Vyāsa

And that as follows :—The cow as a word, the cow as an object and the cow as an idea, although different from one another, are cognized as indistinct. Being analyzed, the characteristics of the word are different; and the characteristics of an idea are different; and the characteristics of an object, too are different. Thus their lines of existence are distinct. 'There,' among the various descriptions of thought-transformation, if an object such as a cow, is present in the trance-consciousness of the Yogī, who has reached this state of thought-transformation, being pierced through by the indeterminate notions of word, meaning and idea, then the thought-transformation is mixed up and is called Indistinct.

When, however, the mind becomes free from the memories of verbal convention, and the trance-consciousness is devoid of the options of inferential and verbal cognitions, the object makes its appearance in the mind in its own distinct nature (unmixed up with word and meaning), the thought-transformation is called Distinct (nirvitarka). This is Higher Perception. This further becomes the seed of verbal and inferential knowledge are born therefrom. It does not go along with verbal and inferential knowledge. Verbal and inferential knowledge. Hence the knowledge obtained by a Yogī through the stage of trance, called Distinct thought-transformation, is not confused by any other cognition.—42.

Vācaspati's Gloss

Thought-transformation in general has been described. By subsidiary classification it is four-fold. Thus : Indistinct or verbal, Distinct or wordless, Meditative and Ultra-meditative. Out of these the description of the Indistinct thought-transformation is given :—'There, etc.' Out of these thought-transformations the Indistinct thought-transformation is to be known. How? The notion of word, meaning and idea consists in this. The faculty of imagination (vikalpa) raises distinctions in the same thing and shows sameness in different things. Thus the word, meaning and idea are confused together, although in reality they are different from one another. Therefore is this thought-transformation confused, *i.e.*, mixed up with the notions of word, meaning and idea :—'And that as follows. The word cow, etc.' The first phrase, 'the word cow' shows the unreal cognition of the word being fancied as confused with meaning and idea.

The second phrase, 'the meaning cow,' shows the notion of indistinctness from the meaning, when word and idea are taken in.

The third phrase, 'the cow as an idea' shows the notion of indistinctness from the idea when word and meaning are taken in. It is in this way that the world is seen taking in these three without making any distinction among them, although in reality they are all distinct from one another.

Well, but if they are taken in as not distinct from one another, whence does the distinction come in ? For this reason, the commentator says :—"Analyzed, etc." Being examined by philosophers in accordance with the canons of agreement and difference, the characteristics of a word are found to be, that it is a modification of sound only, and that it possesses the qualifications of intensity, etc. The characteristics of the object are different, being absence of intelligence and form, etc. The characteristics of an idea are different, such as illumination and the absence of fixity in form, etc. Therefore their lines of existence are different, the lines, that is to say, along which their natural distinctions show themselves.

When the Yogī is in the state of thought-transformation with reference to 'this cow, etc., taken in optionally, etc.' This describes the Yogī's lower perception (the ordinary perception). The rest is easy. To connect this with the next aphorism he first describes the Distinct Thought-transformation :—'When however, etc.'

Freedom from memories, etc., means their absence. Verbal and inferential cognitions become possible only when preceded by the memory of verbal conventions. Convention consists in the mutual super-imposition of word, meaning and idea, in the phrase, 'This is a cow.' By these become possible the real and imaginative cognitions, traditional teaching and inference. For this reason the trance consciousness preceded by these is Indistinct.

When, however, the mind is full of the object only and favouring the object only, constantly habituates itself to the cognition of the object alone, the memory of the convention does no longer interfere and is therefore given up. Further the options of verbal and inferential cognitions too, in which it has its origin, are also given up. Then in the trance-consciousness, void of these descriptions of knowledge, the object takes its place in its own distinct nature, and the mind is confined to the manifestation of the nature of the object alone. It does not show any of the mixed up percepts of the word and the idea. This is the Distinct Thought-transformation. That is the Higher Perception of the Yogīs, because there is not in this, even a trace of untrue knowledge, the unreal fastening thereupon of other notions.

Well let this be. The Yogīs lay down and teach the truths which they have learnt by Higher perception. And how do they do that, but by promulgating and teaching the truths by means of the processes of verbal and inferential knowledge resorted to for the sake of others. Hence verbal and inferential knowledge have the Higher Perceptive knowledge for their object. And verbal and inferential knowledge are subject to the interference of imaginatio (vikalpa). For this reason the Higher Perception also is but a modification of imagination.

Therefore he says :—'That is the seed of verbal and inferential knowledge.' If Higher Perception went along with verbal and inferential knowledge in the same way as is the case with Indistinct thought-transformation, *i.e.*, if the perception were confused on account of the percepts being mixed up, then it would be a modification of imagination only. This, however, is their seed. Verbal and inferential knoweldge are born therefrom; and it is not possible that the cause of a thing may also be the sphere of its manifestation and be co-extensive with it. It is not that the fire lives in smoke, because the knowledge of the existence of smoke becomes the cause of the knowledge of the existence of fire. Therefore, the Yogīs take in objects by non-fictitious (real and distinct) perception, and only teach it and promulgate it by means subject to fiction (mixing up, confusion).

Summarizes :—'For this reason, etc.'

Sūtra 43

स्मृतिपरिशुद्धौ स्वरूपशून्येवार्थमात्रनिर्भासा निर्वितर्का ।। ४३ ।।

स्मृति, Smrti, of memory. परिशुद्धौ, Pariśuddhau, on the purification, or cessation. स्वरूप, Svarūpa, its own nature. शून्या Śūnyā, devoid of. इव Iva, as it were. अर्थ Artha, as the object. मात्र Mātra, alone. निर्भासा Nirbhāsa, shining. निर्वितर्का Nirvitarkā, distinctive (wordless).

43. Distinctive (wordless) thought-transformation is that in which the mind shines out as the object alone on the cessation of memory, and is as it were devoid of its own nature.

निर्वितर्कायाः समापत्तेरस्याः सूत्रेणः लक्षणं द्योत्यते। स्मृतिपरिशुद्धौ स्वरूपशून्येवार्थमात्रनिर्भासा निर्वितर्का या शब्दसङ्केतश्रुतानुमानज्ञानविकल्पस्मृतिपरिशुद्धौ ग्राह्यस्वरूपोपरोक्ता स्वमिव प्रज्ञास्वरूपं ग्रहणात्मकं त्यक्त्वा पदार्थमात्रस्वरूपा ग्राह्यस्वरूपापन्नेव भवति सा तदा निर्वितर्का समापत्तिः। तथा च व्याख्यातम्। तस्या एकबुद्ध्युपक्रमो ह्यर्थात्मा अणुप्रचयविशेषात्मा गवादिर्घटादिर्वा लोकः। स च संस्थानविशेषो भूतसूक्ष्माणां साधारणो धर्म आत्मभूतः फलेन व्यक्तेनानुमितः स्वव्यञ्जकाञ्जनः प्रादुर्भूतो भवति। धर्मान्तरस्य कपालादिरुदये च तिरोभवति। स एष धर्मोऽवयवीत्युच्यते। योऽसावेकश्च महांश्चाणीयांश्च स्पर्शवांश्च क्रियाधर्मकश्चानित्यश्च तेनावयविना व्यवहाराः क्रियन्ते। यस्य पुनरवस्तुकः स प्रचयविशेषः सूक्ष्मं च कारणमनुपलभ्यं तस्यावय-व्यभावादतद्रूपप्रतिष्ठं मिथ्याज्ञानमिति। प्रायेण सर्वमेव प्राप्तं मिथ्याज्ञानमिति। तदा च सम्यग्ज्ञानमपि किं स्याद्विषयाभावात्। यद्यदुपलभ्यते तत्तदवयवित्वेनाम्नातम्। तस्मादस्त्ववयवी यो महत्तत्त्वादिव्यवहारापन्नः समापत्तेर्निर्वितर्काया विषयीभवति।। ४३ ।।

Vyāsa

The description of this Distinctive Thought-transformation is given by the aphorism :—"It is Distinctive, when on the cessation of memory, the mind shines out as the object alone and is, as it were, devoid of its own nature." The thought-transformation becomes Distinctive at the time when the memory of the fictions of verbal convention, verbal and inferential knowledge, ceases; when the mind is coloured by the nature of the object; when it, as it were, gives up its own nature of conscious cognition; and when, therefore, it only shows out the nature of the object, and has, as it were, transformed into the shape of the object itself. And so it has been explained.

The object itself is but a single output of the effort of that (thought-transformation of the mind).

The visible world, the cow, etc., or the jar, etc., consists each in its own nature, of different collections of atoms. Each of these collections is a particular arrangement of the subtle elements. It is a generic quality and constitutes the very nature of the object. It is inferred by its visible effect. It has the form of its cause. It shows itself and exists. When other characteristics, such as those of the half-jar, etc., arise, it disappears. This characteristic is called the substratum (the independent Whole, the avayavī). It is this substratum which is spoken of as being one, or large, or small, or tangible, or possessing the quality of action or transitory.

To him, however, who does not believe this particular collection to be an independent reality and for whom the subtle cause does not admit of perception, there is of course no substratum; and therefore nearly all knowledge is false, being untrue knowledge and not possessing the form of the real. And then what would Real Cognition be, when there was no real object? Hence there is a substratum (independent of the constituent parts) which being spoken of as being large, etc., is the object of Distinctive Thought-transformation.—43.

Vācaspati's Gloss

Connects the aphorism to be explained :—'The description of this Distinctive Thought-transformation, etc.'

'It is Distinct, etc.' :—this is the aphorism. Imagination affects the knowledge of word-convention, verbal and inferential cognitions only. Cessation of the memory born therefrom, is spoken of here.

Here, the cessation of the memory of the convention is the cause. The cessation of the memory of the verbal and inferential cognitions is caused thereby. The words 'inferential cognition,' denote here the thing to be inferred by means of the process of induction. The words 'as it were' used in the text after 'own nature' are to be taken as qualifying the words 'give up.'

He refutes the contrary theories about the object of (this thought-transformation) :—"The object itself is but a single, etc." 'A single output of the mind,' consists in what puts out the mental act but singly. This means that the atoms which go to make up an object being naturally many are not the objects for the Distinctive Thought-transformation. The reason is that although the atom may otherwise well be the object of this thought-transformation, it cannot be so on account of its extreme subtlety, and because many of them being joined together to make a single whole large object, each cannot singly shine out in the mind and make as such as single notion.

If so, why then it may be supposed that really existing atoms possess the characteristic of shining out in the mind by virtue of existing as derivative qualities of the single whole, *i.e.*, by showing out (what might be called a) derivative grossness. For this reason, he says : 'The object itself (*i.e.*, not the constituent parts).' The meaning is that the grossness of an object being provable by perception, is impossible to conceal in the absence of any defect.

To those who say that the objects cow, etc., and jar, etc., are formed by the successive formations of diatoms, etc., he says that these objects 'consist, each in its own nature, of different collections of atoms.'

A collection of atoms is a modification showing a gross form, and it differs from another such modification. Each particular modification of collectivity is of the very nature of the object, its own form. The description applies equally whether it be an object such as a cow which is capable of enjoying, or, an object such as a jar which is capable of being enjoyed. Both these classes of objects fall within the connotation of the word 'world' (loka, that which is visible).

Now the questions arises : Is this collection appearing as a gross form different from the subtle atoms, or, is it the same with them? If different, how could they live in it as such and how could it have that form? A jar is different from a cloth. A jar cannot therefore take the form of a cloth; nor can the qualities which go to make a jar, live in a cloth.

If, on the other hand, the whole in its collective form were the same with the parts (the atoms), it would likewise be subtle and independent (asādhāraṇa).

For this reason, he says :—'Each of these collections is a particular arrangement, etc.' This is the meaning. A jar and other such objects are not entirely different from atoms; nor are they entirely of the same nature. In the case of their being like the horse and the cow, the existence of the relation of the characteristic and the characterized could not be predicated. If, however, they were not different they would be of the nature of the characterized object itself, and this is not proper. Hence the substratum (the characterized object, the Whole) should be considered to be in some respects different and in others similar to its constituent parts, the subtle atoms. In this way everything becomes proper.

By placing the words 'subtle elements' in the genitive case, he shows partial difference; and the words, 'constitutes the very nature of the object,' etc., show the absence of difference.

'It is inferred by its visible effect' :—'Visible effect' means its perception as such and its being dealt with as such.

'It has the form of its cause' :—This is intended to show that in so far as it is not different from its cause, it is in the nature of things that it should possess the form of the cause.

Is this characteristic which is of the nature of the characterized object itself, permanent ? The commentator answers in the negative :—"when other characteristics such as those of the half-jar appear, etc."

Now he shows that the form of the characterized object, the whole as such, is different from the atoms :—'This characteristic is called the substratum, etc.' The meaning is that its function is the possession of qualities like the sweetness of water, etc., which are quite different from the functions to be performed by atoms.

It is not only by inference that the independent existence of a substratum (the *avayavī,* the Whole as such) is established; but by the fact as well of the whole world treating it as such, inasmuch as the business of the world depends upon that. For this reason, he says :—'By this, etc.'

Well, but the mental conception of the percept as an individual existence independent of its parts, may only avail if there is no contradiction. There is, however, contradiction. Thus, whatever exists has no parts, such as consciousness (vijñāna); and the cow and the jar, etc., do exist. This is a reason taken from the very nature of the things. Existence is qualified by the absence of the touch of such characteristics as are contradictory thereof. It is contradicted by the touch of contradictory qualities.

The touch of contraductory qualities being found in an object possessed of parts, contradicts the pervading quality (excludes the middle term). It, therefore, disproves even the existence of the object.

In the substratum there exists the touch of contradictory characteristic, such as occupying the same space or not occupying the same space, not being covered or uncovered, redness and not-redness, movability and immovability, etc.

For this reason, he says :—'To him however, etc.' This is the meaning. The proof of the existence by perception is given as the reason. But the pole perceived as a limb of a bedstead may also become the pole of a plough, or something else different from what it has been proved to be by perception. As to its becoming something else, that is no reason, because the something else is not so proved. As to the existence of the jar, etc., being proved by perception, why this existence consists of the capacity of performing certain functions; and that capacity is not different from grossness (sthūlatva). The reasoning which does away with grossness, does away with the nature of thing itself.

But the objection may still arise that the grossness of a thing is not its existence itself. Existence is the absence of non-existence. Grossness is the absence of non-grossness. The absences differ on account of the difference of the objects whose absences are contemplated. Therefore existence is not destroyed, even though grossness may be absent, because the two are different. Or, it might be said that there is difference in the objects to be determined on account of the difference of their absences. If with a view to determine the nature of the object of perception, which being true cognition and free from the taint of imagination, precedes the determination of the nature of the object as such, you say that it is made up of the visible atoms, being incessantly born without there being any internal between them, and without their having put on the nature of extreme subtlety; then, it is to be noted that the atoms of odour, taste and touch fall into the intervals of the visual atoms and that they do not exist without them.

Besides, the notion of a grove, as a single whole, comes into the mind, because the intervals among the trees thereof is not perceived, (although it does exist). The theory, therefore, which speaks of the atoms as being visible and gross in themselves and as having no intervals, is false. How can the fancies based upon such a theory have anything to do with the realities of things, even on the strength of the conception of a causal chain (pāramparya)? How can it be accepted as establishing the nature of the existence to the effect that they do not exist as parts but are wholes themselves.

Therefore he who believes in the authority of perception free from the taint of fancy, must grant that grossness itself, being as it is the object of such perception, does exist as such. This is determined for certain without the taint of the fancy, and must be admitted even by one who has no desire left for such things. And further, if existence as such were to contradict and thus exclude grossness, why, it would exclude itself too as a necessary consequence.

The very highly subtle atoms have, therefore, their intervals filled up with atoms of another class, and the theory of their being the objects of perception is shorn of admissibility. This is meant by saying, 'To him, however, who does not believe this particular collection to be an independent reality, etc.' But the particular collection although independently existing is still the object of certain (nirvikalpa) perception.

Well then the subtle atoms may be the objects of certain perception. For this reason, he says :—'And the subtle object does not admit of perception,' Perception here means that which is free from the taint of imagination, is certain.

'To him who has such a chief,' there is of course no substratum and for this reason, all knowledge is false, being defined as it is "to be untrue knowledge, not possessing the form thereof." The knowledge, that is to say, which has grossness for its object, and that again on which this rests, the knowledge of existence, is all false to him.

Well, even so, the knowledge of self would not be untrue, inasmuch as the self does not exist as a whole consisting of parts. How then should it be said that all knowledge would become false ? For this reason, he says :—"Nearly all knowledge."

The question now arises, 'What even if it were so?' In answer he says :—'And then what would Right Cognitions be, etc.' If the knowledge of existence (sattva), etc., be false then the knowledge of things which have their origin in Satta, etc., such as the knowledge of there being no substratum, independent of parts, must also be false. For what is the object of this knowledge but the grossness which is the object of certain perception? And inasmuch as this grossness does not exist, its knowledge would certainly be false. But how is it that the object itself does not as such exist? For this reason, he says :—"Whatever is perceived, etc."

As to contradiction (virodha) that is to be explained in accordance with the aforesaid method of knowledge, by means of the variety of modifications, and by differentiation and non-differentiation. Thus all is beautiful.—43.

Sūtra 44

एतयैव सविचारा निर्विचारा च सूक्ष्मविषया व्याख्याता ।। ४४ ।।

एतया Etayā, by this. एव Eva, also. सविचारा Savicārā, this meditative. निर्विचारा Nirvicārā, the ultrameditative. च Ca, and. सूक्ष्मविषया Sūkṣma-viṣayā, having the subtle for their or its objects. व्याख्याता Vyākhyātā, are described.

44. By this the meditative and the ultra-meditative, having the subtle for their objects, are also described.

एतयैव सविचारा निर्विचारा च सूक्ष्मविषया व्याख्याता। तत्र भूतसूक्ष्मकेष्वभिव्यक्तधर्मकेषु देशकाल-निमित्तानुभवावच्छिन्नेषु या समापत्तिः सा सविचारेत्युच्यते। तत्राप्येकबुद्धिनिर्ग्राह्यमेवोदितधर्मविशिष्टं भूतसूक्ष्ममालम्बनीभूतं समाधिप्रज्ञायामुपतिष्ठते। या पुनः सर्वथा सर्वतः शान्तोदिताव्यपदेश्यधर्मानवच्छिन्नेषु सर्वधर्मानुपातिषु सर्वधर्मात्मकेषु समापत्तिः सा निर्विचारेत्युच्यते। एवंस्वरूपं हि तद्भूतसूक्ष्मम्। एतेनैव स्वरूपेणालम्बनीभूतमेव समाधिप्रज्ञास्वरूपमुपरञ्जयति। प्रज्ञा च स्वरूपशून्येवार्थमात्रा यदा भवति तदा निर्विचारेत्युच्यते। तत्र महद्वस्तु विषया सवितर्का निर्वितर्का च सूक्ष्मवस्तुविषया सविचारा निर्विचारा च। एवमुभयोरेतयैव निर्वितर्कया विकल्पहानिर्व्याख्यातेति।। ४४।।

Vyāsa

Of these the thought-transformation into subtle element is called Meditative, when their characteristics are in manifestation and when the limitations of consciousness in space, time and operative cause are present. In this state too the subtle element comes into the trance-consciousness as qualified only by the present characteristics; and is taken in only by a single effort of consciousness; and it is this much alone of an object that comes into contact with the faculty of Meditative Thought-transformation.

That, however, is the ultra-meditative thought-transformation, which operates with reference to subtle objects unlimited in all ways, all round by the past, the present and the unpredictable characteristics, but running after all the characteristics possessing as they do in fact a nature common to all of them. This in fact is the nature of the subtle element. It presents itself to the trance-consciousness as such and colours it similarly by contact. As to the cognition it is called ultra-meditative, when it becomes the object itself, and thus as it were, becomes void of its own nature.

Of these the Indistinctive and Distinctive thought-transformations have to operate upon things extended in time and space; the Meditative and the Ultra-meditative operate upon the subtle elements. It is thus that the absence of uncertainty in both these is described by the description of the Indistinctive alone.—44.

Vācaspati's Gloss

Those that have manifested the characteristics of the jar, etc., are said to 'have their characteristics in manifestation.' It means those that already taken up the characteristics of the jar, etc.

Space is indicated by above, below and the directions, etc. Time here is the present. 'Operative cause' : The earthly atom is born from the five classes of ultimate atoms (tanmātras), with a prevalence of the odoriferous minima. Similarly the liquid atom (apas tattva) is born from the four classes of ultimate atoms except the odoriferous minima with the prevalence of the gustiferous minima. Similarly, the fiery atom is made of the three minima besides the odoriferous and the gustiferous minima, with a prevalence of the luminiferous minima. Similarly, the gaseous atom is born from the tangiferous and soniferous minima without an admixture of the other three classes of minima, with a prevalence of the tangiferous minima. Similarly, the birth of Ākāśa us from the one class of soniferous minima alone. This is the operative cause of the subtle elements.

The subtle elements in this state are qualified by the limitations of space, time and their causes such as those specified. It means that, being limited by the consciousness of time, space and causes as they are, the cognition of these qualified objects is not independent of the cognition of their qualities.

The question is, what is the similarity of the Indistinctive to the Meditative Thought-transformation ? For this reason, he says :—'Further in that state, etc.' The earthy atom perceives its individuality from the five classes of ultimate atoms (tanmātras) grouping together and is taken in by a single effort of consciousness as a single whole. Similarly are the liquid atoms, etc., to be understood as coming into consciousness as single substances, receiving as they do their individuality by groupings of three, two and one class of ultimate atoms (tanmātras), respectively.

The present characteristic is that which at is present rising. By saying that 'it is qualified only by the present characteristics,' it is indicated that in this state of consciousness are present along with the object the optional operations of the memory of convention and of verbal and inferential cognitions. Perception, while it congizes the gross state, does not reveal the atoms.

They are revealed by verbal and inferential cognitions. Hence it is proper that it (the Meditative Thought-transformation) should be mixed up with the operations of verbal and inferential cognitions.

Now explains the Ultra-meditative :—'That however, etc.'

'In all ways' means in all modes of manifestation, as blue, yellow etc. All round means by the consciousness of all the conditions of time, space, and causation. By describing them thus, it is shown that the atoms are not limited by time. Further, he says that they are neither limited by the characteristics which are brought into operation by time :—'Unlimited by the past characteristic, *i.e.*, those which have had their operation; by rising characteristics, *i.e.*, those that are to be found in the present; by the unpredicable characteristics, *i.e.*, the future ones.

The question arises that if the atoms are not conditioned by any of these characteristics, are they then quite fortuitous? For this reason he says :—'but running after all the characteristics.' By what connection then do the atoms run after the characteristics ? For this reason, he says :—'Possessing as they do in fact a nature common to all the characteristics.' The meaning is that characteristics differ in some respects from, and are identical in others to, the atoms.

Now he says why this thought-transformation has this nature of the atoms as its object :—This in fact is the nature of the subtle element! The power which gives the knowledge of reality does not operate upon the unreal.

Having described the object of that state of consciousness, now he describes its nature :—'As to the cognition, etc.'

Summarising he makes a statement which shows the differences of their natures—'Of these, etc.' Finishes :—'It is thus, etc.'

In both these :—in itself and the ultra-meditative.—44.

Sūtra 45

सूक्ष्मविषयत्वं चालिङ्गपर्यवसानम् ।। ४५ ।।

सूक्ष्म Sūkṣma, of the subtle. विशयत्वम् Viṣayatvam, province both mean the quality of having the subtle for its object. च Ca, and. आ Ā, up to. लिङ्ग Liṅga, the noumenal. पर्यवसानम् Paryavasānam, ending, extremity. आलिङ्गपर्यवसानम् Āliṅgaparyavasānam, Reaching up to the noumenal.

45. And the province of the subtle reaches up to the noumenal.

सूक्ष्मविषयत्वं चालिङ्गपर्यवसानम्। पार्थिवस्याणोर्गन्धतन्मात्रं सूक्ष्मो विषयः। आप्यस्यापि रसतन्मात्रम्। तैजसस्यं रूपतन्मात्रम्। वायवीयस्य स्पर्शतन्मात्रम्। आकाशस्य शब्दतन्मात्रमिति। तेषामहङ्कारः। अस्यापि लिङ्गतन्मात्रं सूक्ष्मो विषयः। लिङ्गमात्रस्याप्यलिङ्गं सूक्ष्मो विषयः। न चालिङ्गात्परं सूक्ष्ममस्ति। नन्वस्ति पुरुषः सूक्ष्म इति। सत्यम्। यथा लिङ्गात्परमलिङ्गस्य सौक्ष्म्यं न चैवं पुरुषस्य। किंतु लिङ्गस्यान्वयि कारणं पुरुषो न भवति। हेतुस्तु भवतीति। अतः प्रधाने सौक्ष्म्यं निरतिशयं व्याख्यातम् ।। ४५ ।।

Vyāsa

The odoriferous ether (gandha tanmātra) is the subtle object in relation to the atoms of the earthly class (pṛthvī); the gustiferous (rasa tanmātra) to the liquid (āpas) atom; the lumniferous ether (rūpa tanmātra of the fiery (taijas) atom; the tangiferous ether (sparśa tanmātra) of the gaseous (vāyu) atom; the soniferous ether (śabda tanmātra) of the Ākāśic atom. Of these the principle of individuality (ahaṅkāra) is the subtler cause. Subtler than this too is the purely Phenomenal Objective Existence. The principal subtler than this too is the Noumenal (Aliṅga). There is nothing subtler than the Noumenal.

But it might be said that there is the Puruṣa who is also subtle. True. As however is the subtlety of the noumenal in comparison with the purely phenomenal, such is not the subtlety of the Puruṣa. On the other hand, the Puruṣa is not the material cause of the Purely Phenomenal. It is only the instrumental cause. For this reason the subtlety of the Mūlaprakṛti is described as not liable to be exceeded.

Vācaspati's Gloss

Does the range of thought-transformation with reference to objective appearances extend up to the subtle elements only ? No. 'And the province of subtle reaches up to the noumenal.

The characteristic of the odoriferous ultimate atom (gandha tanmātra) is in relation to the atom of the earthy class (Pṛthvī) the subtle object of the faculty of thought-transformation. In other places it should be construed in the same way.

The purely Phenomenal is the Great Principle (Mahāttattva), because it is that which immediately passes into latency (liṅga) into the Mūlaprakṛti. The noumenal is the Mūlaprakṛti, because it does not pass into latency (aliṅga), into any other state.

He describes the reaching up to the noumenal :—'There is nothing subtler, etc.'

States an objection :—'But it may be, etc.' Replies :—'True, etc.' The meaning is that as a material cause subtlety exists in the noumenal only, nowhere else.

But the Mahat and the principle of individuality exist for fulfilling the objects of the Puruṣa. The Puruṣa also is, therefore, a cause of the noumenal. Why should it be said that stublety exists only in the noumenal? For this reason, he says :—It is certainly a cause but not the material cause. As Mūlaprakṛti evolves into the phenomenon of Mahat and onwards, not so the Puruṣa.

Finishes :—'For this reason the sublety of the Mūlaprakṛti is described as not capable of being exceeded.—45.

Sūtra 46

ता एव सबीजः समाधिः ।। ४६ ।।

ताः Tāḥ, they. एव Eva, only. सबीजः Sabījaḥ, seeded. समाधिः, Samādhiḥ, trance.

46. They are the seeded trance only.

ता एव सबीजः समाधिः। ताश्चतस्रः समापत्तयो बहिर्वस्तुबीजा इति समाधिरपि सबीजः। तत्र स्थूलेऽर्थे सवितर्कः। निर्वितर्कः सूक्ष्मेऽर्थे सविचारो निर्विचार इति। स चतुर्धोपसङ्ख्यातः समाधिरिति।। ४६ ।।

Vyāsa

These four descriptions of thought-transformation have their origin (seed) in external objects. Therefore is the trance too 'seeded.' In the case of the gross objects it is the Indistinctive and the Distinctive. In the subtle objects it is the Meditative and the Ultra-meditative. Thus is trance described to be four-fold.—46.

Vācaspati's Gloss

Says that the four states of thought-transformation have the objective for their sphere of operation, constitute the cognitive trance :—'They are the seeded trance only.' The word 'only' is to be taken as qualifying the word 'seeded.' By this the four descriptions of thought-transformation, having the objective state of existence as their sphere, are limited by being qualified as seeded.

The quality of being seeded, however, is not restricted to these. It applies to the thought-transformations which have the subjective and the instrumental modifications also for their sphere of operation, in both its descriptions of Uncertain (savikalpa) and Certain (nirvikalpa). For this reason there are said to be four descriptions of thought-transformation in the case of the objective and the instrumental phenomena. Thus there are eight descriptions in all. The meaning of the commentary has been explained.—46.

Sūtra 47

निर्विचारवैशारद्येऽध्यात्मप्रसादः ।। ४७ ।।

निर्विचार Nirvicāra, of the ultra-meditative. वैशारद्ये Vaiśāradye, when there is the undisturbed, pure flow. अध्यात्म Adhyātma, subjective, spiritual. प्रसादः Prasādaḥ, luminosity, the fixedness of the mind.

47. The undisturbed flow of the ultra-meditative causes Subjective Luminosity.

निर्विचारवैशारद्येऽध्यात्मप्रसादः। अशुद्ध्यावरणमलापेतस्य प्रकाशात्मनो बुद्धिसत्त्वस्य रजस्तमोभ्या-मनभिभूतः स्वच्छः स्थितिप्रवाहो वैशारद्यम्। यदा निर्विचारस्य समाधेर्वैशारद्यमिदं जायते तदा योगिनो भवत्यध्यात्मप्रसादः। भूतार्थविषयः क्रमाननुरोधी स्फुटः प्रज्ञालोकः। तथा चोक्तम्। प्रज्ञाप्रसादमारुह्य अशोच्यः शोचतो जनान्। भूमिष्ठानिव शैलस्थः सर्वान्प्राज्ञोऽनुपश्यति।। ४७।।

Vyāsa

'Undisturbed flow' is the pure and constant flow, not overpowered by disturbing energy (rajas) and inertia (tamas), of the essence (sattva) of the Will-to-know, the very self of light, with the veil of impurity covering it removed. When this undisturbed flow is secured for the Ultra-meditative trance, the Yogī attains Subjective Luminosity. His intellectual vision becomes clear with regard to objects as they exist, irrespective of all sequence. And so it has been said :—'Having reached the stage of intellectual luminosity, the wise man is no longer an object of compassion; he looks upon and compassionates others, as one upon a height looks down upon those in the plains.'

Vācaspati's Gloss

Now he describes the beauty of the ultra-meditative among the four descriptions of thought-transformation, which have the objective as their sphere of operation :—The undisturbed flow of the ultra-meditative causes Subjective Luminosity.' Describes the meaning of the words, 'undisturbed flow' :—'The pure, etc.' 'Impurity' is the adhesion of disturbing energy (rajas) and inertia (tamas). The same is a sort of dirt having the quality of a veil. When the veil is removed from the essence of the Will-to-know, it shines out as the very self of light, and is therefore said to be not overpowered by them.

But then, if the sphere of thought-transformation is the objective modification of existence, how can it secure Subjective Luminosity? For this reason, he says :—'With regard to objects as they exist.' The subjective is not its object. It is only that in which the subjective self lives, that becomes its object as such.

'Without regard to all sequence' means simultaneously.

Quotes on this subject the Gāthā of the Great Seer :—'And so it has been said.' Finding himself above all, on having reached the highest point of the vision of knowledge, he is sorry to see the men of the world suffering from the three descriptions of pain.—47.

Sūtra 48

ऋतंभरा तत्र प्रज्ञा ।। ४८ ।।

ऋतंभरा Ṛtambharā, full of truth, full of essence, essential cognition. तत्र Tatra, there in. प्रज्ञा Prajñā, the faculty of cognition.

48. Therein the faculty of Essential Cognition.

ऋतंभरा तत्र प्रज्ञा । तस्मिन्त्समाहितचित्तस्य या प्रज्ञा जायते तस्या ऋतंभरेति संज्ञा भवति । अन्वर्था च सा सत्यमेव बिभर्ति । न च तत्र विपर्यासज्ञानगन्धोऽप्यस्तीति । तथा चोक्तम् । आगमेनानुमानेन ध्यानाभ्यासरसेन च । त्रिधा प्रकल्पयन्प्रज्ञां लभते योगमुत्तममिति ।। ४८ ।।

Vyāsa

The cognitive faculty which shows itself in that state in the mind of the wise, bears the name of Essential Cognition (Ṛtambharā). The term itself expresses the defintion. It always cognizes the essence, the truth. There is not even a trace of false knowledge.

And so it has been said :—'Cultivating the mind in the three ways of verbal and inferential cognitions and the practice of contemplation with tastefulness, one gets the highest Yoga.'—48.

Vācaspati's Gloss

Expresses the concurrence of the Yogis by mentioning a technical term well-known among them and defining its own meaning :—'Therein, the faculty of essential cognition.' The Commentary is easy. 'Cultivation by verbal cognition' means the hearing of the Vedas.

'Cultivation by inferential cognition' means thinking.

Contemplation means keeping in mind. Practice means over and over again. Contemplation with tastefulness means welcome contemplation.—48.

Sūtra 49

श्रुतानुमानप्रज्ञाभ्यामन्यविषया विशेषार्थत्वात् ।। ४९ ।।

श्रुत Śruta, heard, verbal. अनुमान Anumāna, inferential. प्रज्ञाभ्याम् Prajñābhyām, from those of cognition. अन्य Anya, different. विषय Viṣaya, object. अन्यविषया Anya viṣayā, having objects different from. विशेषार्थत्वात् Viśeṣa-arthatvāt, because it refers to particulars (विशेष).

49. It has different objects from those of verbal and inferential cognition, as it refers to particulars.

सा पुनः । श्रुतानुमानप्रज्ञाभ्यामन्यविषया विशेषार्थत्वात् । श्रुतमागमविज्ञानं तत्सामान्यविषयम् । न ह्यागमेन शक्योविशेषोऽभिधातुम् । कस्मात्? न हि विशेषेण कृतसङ्केतः शब्द इति । तथानुमानं सामान्यविषयमेव । यत्र प्राप्तिस्तत्र गतिर्यत्राप्राप्तिस्तत्र न भवति गतिरित्युक्तम् । अनुमानेन च सामान्ये नोपसंहारः । तस्माच्छ्रुतानुमानविषयो न विशेषः कश्चिदस्तीति । न चास्य सूक्ष्मव्यवहितविप्रकृष्टस्य वस्तुनो लोकप्रत्यक्षेण ग्रहणमस्ति । न सास्य विशेषस्याप्रमाणस्याभावोऽस्तीति । समाधिप्रज्ञानिर्ग्राह्य एव स विशेषो भवति । भूतसूक्ष्मगतो वा पुरुषगतो वा तस्माच्छ्रुतानुमानप्रज्ञाभ्यामन्यविषया सा प्रज्ञा विशेषार्थत्वादिति ।। ४९ ।।

Vyāsa

And that, moreover, 'has different objects from those of verbal and inferential cognitions, as it refers to particulars.'

Verbal cognition refers to knowledge received from another. It has the generals for its objects. It is not possible to describe the particulars by words. Why? Because there is no conventional denotation of the particular in words.

Similarly, inferential cognition has the generals for its objects. Wherever there is approach there is motion; wherever there is no approach there is no motion in existence. This has been said. Further inference arrives at conclusions by means of the generic qualities. Therefore there is no particular which can be made the object of induction and verbal cognition.

Ordinary perception does not cognize the subtle, the distant and the intercepted. Nor can it be said that this particular does not exist for want of authority. This particular can only be cognized by the trance cognition, whether it be present in the subtle elements or in the Puruṣa. Hence this cognition has different objects from those of inferential and verbal cognitions, because it has the particulars for its objects.

Vācaspati's Gloss

Very well, the ultra-meditative has for its sphere of action the objects cognizable by verbal and inferential cognition and is the culmination of these faculties. It can therefore operate upon the objects of verbal and inferential cognitions only. Because it is not certainly possible that a mental potency born out of practice with reference to one object of thought, should be capable of causing the knowledge of another object. This would mean going beyond the proper limits. Therefore if the essential cognition is the same as the ultra-meditative, its objects must be the same as those of verbal and inferential cognitions. For this reason, he says :—'It has different objects.'

Mental Essence is luminous by nature, and has the power of knowing all objects. When veiled by inertia (tamas) it cognizes only upon the veil being removed by energy (rajas). When, however, upon the impurities of inertia and disturbing energy being removed by practice and desirelessness, the pure light shines forth, then, light passes beyond the limits of all measures and all finite objects, and becomes infinite; what then is there that does not fall within the sphere of its action?

Explains :—'Verbal cognition is the knowledge received from another.' Its sphere of action consists of the universal. Why? Words cannot connote particulars. Why? Because of their not being limited and because of overlapping (vyabhicāra).

'There is no conventional denotation of the particular in words,' because the relation of the sign and the thing signified is not found existing between a word and the particular. Nor is such particular possible of being expressed by the meaning of sentence.

The same is the case with inference, whose operation depends upon the relation existing between the sign and the thing signified (the liṅga and the liṅgi) :—'Similarly, has induction, etc.' The words 'wherever' and 'there' denote the pervader and the pervaded, by a change of places. For this reason the conclusion is arrived at here by virtue of the common property. Concludes—'therefore there is, etc.'

Well, then, let it be the ordinary perception which does not depend for its operation upon the knowledge of any relationship. For this reason, he says :—'Nor can it be said, etc.' Ordinary perception may not depend for its operation upon the recognition of relationship. It does certainly depend upon the senses, and the senses are not in their sphere here (*i.e.*, in the essential cognition). This is the meaning.

Well, but, if the particulars are not such objects as can be known by verbal, inferential and perceptive cognitions, then, there is no authority for their existence. For this reason, he says :—'Nor can it be said that the particular does not exist for want of authority.' The meaning is that a means of knowledge (pramāṇa) is neither co-existent with nor the cause of the thing known. It is not therefore necessary that the reality to be known should cease to exist, because there is no means or power of knowing it. Those who rely upon the ordinary means of knowledge, do not doubt the existence of a deer-like mark in the moon at a time when only certain phases of hers are visible. For this reason it is said that it is capable of being known by the trance cognition alone.

Here the atoms and the Puruṣas which are the subjects of discussion, are each of the nature of independent particularities, because, being substances, they are all separate from each other. All those that are separate from one another, being substances, are of the nature of independent particularities, as, say, sugar and a hair-shorn mendicant. Thus by this inference and by authority the special province of the essential cognition is defined, because otherwise there would remain a doubt as to its real nature, brought about by ordinary reasoning. Still, the attempt to define it is not complete, and its existence is brought within the sphere of consciousness with difficulty, on account of its being far removed from ordinary objects, by inference and authority. The knowledge although thus brought about with difficulty is not so plain and well-defined as the knowledge of collectivity, etc., obtained by words denoting them along with the proper accessories of enumeration of signs (signifying the particular object). Thus it is that its object is different from the objects of verbal and inferential cognitions.—49.

Sūtra 50

तज्जः संस्कारोऽन्यसंस्कारप्रतिबन्धी ।। ५० ।।

तज्जः Tajjaḥ, born thereform. संस्कारः Saṁskāraḥ, residual potencies, impressions. अन्य Anya, other. संस्कार Saṁskāra, residual potencies, impressions. प्रतिबन्धी Pratibandhī, impeding.

50. Residual potencies born therefrom impede other residual potencies.

समाधिप्रज्ञाप्रतिलम्भे योगिनः प्रज्ञाकृतः संस्कारो नवो नवो जायते तज्जः । संस्कारोऽन्यसंस्कारप्रतिबन्धी । समाधिप्रभवः संस्कारो व्युत्थानसंस्काराशयं बाधते । व्युत्थानसंस्काराभिभवात्तत्प्रभवाः प्रत्यया न भवन्ति प्रत्ययनिरोधे समाधिरुपतिष्ठते । ततः समाधिजा प्रज्ञा ततः प्रज्ञाकृतः संस्कारा इति नवो नवः संस्काराशयो जायते । ततश्च प्रज्ञा ततश्च संस्कारा इति कथमसौ संस्काराशयश्चित्तं साधिकारं न करिष्यतीति । न ते प्रज्ञाकृताः संस्काराः क्लेशक्षयहेतुत्वाच्चित्तमधिकारविशिष्टं कुर्वन्ति । चित्तं हि ते स्वकार्यादवसादयन्ति । ख्यातिपर्यवसानं हि चित्तचेष्ठितमिति ।। ५० ।।

Vyāsa

When the trance cognition has been reached, the Yogī acquires by the exercise of that cognition, newer and newer residual potencies. 'The residual potencies born therefrom impede other residual potencies.' The potency born of trance impedes the outgoing vehicle of potencies. By overpowering the outgoing tendencies, notions due to them cease to exist. On the suppression of these notions the trance faculty gains in power. Then again the activity of trance cognition. Then again residual caused by the act of cognition. In this way the vehicle of potencies is being constantly renewed.

Well the act of cognition is caused by the potency and the potency is caused by the act. How is it then possible that the mind may not be given by this vehicle of potencies an object in itself? The potencies born out of the trance cognition do not give the mind a duty to perform with reference to themselves, because they are the cause of the removal of the afflictions. They bring about the finishing of the duty which the mind has to perform. It is only up to the attainment of discriminative knowledge that the activity of the mind has to last.

Vācaspati's Gloss

Let that be. The cognitive trance has the reality of an object for its sphere of operation. Practice and the other means of restraint as described, are however outgoing potencies. The trance cognition is known to be firmly bound up with them. They must therefore be obstacles to the full realization of that state of consciousness, shine as it would like atomic twinkles of light in the midst of a hurricane. To remove this doubt the commentator introduces the aphorism :—'When the trance cognition has been reached, etc.' Reads the aphorism :—'Residual potencies born therefrom impede other residual potencies.

The word, 'there' in 'therefrom' signifies the ultra-meditative thought-transformation. 'Other' means the outgoing. Inclination towards the realities of objects is of the very nature of the mind. It is unsteady and wanders only so long as it does not reach the reality. When that is reached it takes up a steady position, and turns round and in the way of the wheel of potency, bent upon purification (*i.e.*, upon acquiring that potency). Doing this it must certainly impede the mutual succession of the power and act of the cognition of unrealities, although the succession has had no beginning. The outsiders also say the same :—'Unreal cognitions do not contradict the nature of the objects as they do exist in reality, free from defects, even though the unrealities have existed from eternity; because the mind is naturally inclined towards the realities.'

Very well, grant that the outgoing potencies are restrained by the operations of the trance cognition. But the first manifestation of the trance cognition has for its final object the ever-increasing unchecked manifestation of the potency of trance cognition. Thus it is lain that the mind even in that state, has the same old quality of having still a function to perform. (The attainment of the trance cognition too does not take it any nearer to the fulfilment of its object). This is the question raised 'How is it then that the mind, etc.' Refutes :—'The potencies born out of, etc.' There are but two objects of the mind, the enjoyment of sound, etc., and the attainment of Discrinative knowledge. Of these the enjoyment of sound etc., comes into operation with the existence of the vehicles of affliction and action. When, however, the power which springs from the manifestation of trance cognition, entirely roots out the vehicles of action and affliction and the mind for that reason exists in the state of having mostly fulfilled its objects, the only object that then remains for it to achieve, is the attainment of Discriminative knowledge. Therefore the potencies of the mind due to the practice of the trance cognition cannot generate the habits of returning to that duties of enjoyment. They must check their forward march. They bring about the end of its duty of enjoyment, *i.e.*, render it impotent to enjoy them. How? The action of the mind lasts only up to the attainment of discriminative knowledge. The mind only works for enjoyment as long as it does not experience discriminative knowledge. When, however, discriminative knowledge is born, the afflictions are removed, and the duty of causing enjoyment is over. This is the meaning.—50.

Sūtra 51

तस्यापि निरोधे सर्वनिरोधान्निर्बीजः समाधिः ।। ५१ ।।

तस्य Tasya, of that. अपि Api, too. निरोधे Nirodhe, by the suppression. सर्व Sarva, of all. निरोधात् Nirodhāt, owing to the supression. निर्बीजः Nirbījaḥ, seedless. समाधिः Samādhiḥ, trance.

51. All being suppressed, by the supression of that too comes the seedless trance.

किं चास्य भवति। तस्यापि निरोधे सर्वनिरोधान्निर्बीजः समाधिः। स न केवलं समाधिप्रज्ञाविरोधी। प्रज्ञाकृतानामपि संस्काराणां प्रतिबन्धी भवति। कस्मान्निरोधजः संस्कार समाधिजान्संस्कारान्बाधत इति। निरोधस्थितिकालक्रमानुभवेन निरोधचित्तकृतसंस्कारास्तित्वमनुमेयम्। व्युत्थाननिरोधसमाधिप्रभवैः सह कैवल्यभागीयैः संस्कारैश्चित्तं स्वस्यां प्रकृतावविस्थतायां प्रविलीयते। तस्मात् संस्काराश्चित्तस्याधिकारविरोधिनो न स्थितिहेतवो भवन्तीति। यस्मादवसिताधिकारं सहकैवल्यभागीयैः संस्कारैश्चित्तं निवर्तते। तस्मिन्निवृत्ते पुरुषः स्वरूपमात्रप्रतिष्ठोऽतः शुद्धः केवलो मुक्त इत्युच्यत इति।। ५१।।

इति श्रीपातञ्जले सांख्यप्रवचने योगशास्त्रे प्रथमः समाधिपादः समाप्तः।। १।।

Vyāsa

And what more comes to the mind? 'All being suppressed by the supression of that too comes the seedless trance.' This opposes not only the trance cognition, but cheeks also the operation of the potencies generated by that cognition. Why? The potency of the habit of suppression that is acquired, removes the potencies of the habit of trance cognition. That there exists the potency of the habit of suppression, generated by the acts of mental control, is to be inferred by the mental experience of the succession in time of the act of suppression and the consequent rest. The mind disappears into its own inactive cause, along with the potencies which operate to lead to absolute freedom, and which are born of the trance cognition operating to suppress the outgoing potencies. These potencies, therefore, being opposed to the continuance of the duty of the mind, do not become the cause of its further existence as such. And it is for this reason that the mind which has achieved its purpose, and along with it the potencies which operate to lead to absolute freedom, ceased to act further. When the mind ceases to act further, the Puruṣa remains in its own true self, and is therefore pure, absolutely free, and released (mukta) as he is called.—51.

This finishes the first chapter, on trance, of the Sāṅkhyapravacana Commentary of the Yogaśāstra of Patañjali by Vyāsa.

Vācaspati's Gloss

It has been said that the cessation of the function of enjoyment is the reason for acquiring the potencies of the trance cognition. Now he puts a question : 'And what more comes to the mind ?' The meaning is that inasmuch as the mind possessing the potencies of the trance cognition, generates the flow of these potencies (into activity) the mind has still a duty to perform as before; because something else is necessary to remove the necessity of the performance of this function too. The answer is given by the aphorism :—'All being suppressed, by the suppression of that too comes the seedless trance.' The meaning of the word 'too' is that not only the trance cognition, but the potencies generated by the cognition are also suppressed by means of generating side by side with these the potency of higher desirelessness, defined to be the light of knowledge alone. The stream of the potency and the act of cognition which are being constantly generated one from the other, having been checked, the effect is not born without the cause; and this is the seedless trance. Explains :—'That' seedless trance, being brought about by the higher desirelessness, which opposes the trance cognition, does by means of its cause, not only because the opposer of the trance cognition, but at the same time obstructs the flow of the potencies generated by that cognition also.

Well, the knowledge born of desirelessness may very well destroy the cognition alone, because it exists as a cause. How can it destroy the potency, which in fact is no knowledge? Memory is seen operating even in a waking man with reference to objects seen in dreams. With this object he puts the question : 'Why?' The answer is : 'The potency of the habit of suppressing, etc., 'Supression' is that by which the cognition is suppressed, that is the Higher desirelessness. It is from that, that the potency of the habit of suppression is born. The meaning is that it is not by the cognition but by the potency born of higher desirelessness, long, uninterruptedly and devotedly practised, that the potency of the cognition is destroyed. Well, let that be. But what authority is there for the existence of the potency of the habit of suppression ? It can either be known by perception, or inferred by its effect, the memory thereof. But the Yogī can have no perception when all the mental modifications have been suppressed. Nor can he have memory, because the act of suppression operating upon the act of modification as such can leave no memory behind. For this reason, he says :—'The existence of the potency is to be inferred, etc.' The 'rest' in suppression means the state of suppression.

The succession in time of that state means a *muhūrta,* an hour and a half, day and night, etc. The experience is to be of this succession. This is the meaning. The intensity of suppression is in accordance with the intensity of desirelessness and practice; and this intensity is taken note of by its extension over the periods of time known as *muhūrta,* an hour-and-a-half, etc., by the Yogī. And inasmuch as the moments of desirelessness do not exist together on account of a fixed order in the appearance, and on account of their extending over their own special periods of time, they cannot be adequate to bring about the intensity of suppression; it is therefore the store of the potential energy thereof, born of the collective effect of the moments of desirelessness, indulfed now and again, that is desired to be understood here.

Well the potencies of cognition may be destroyed. But how can the potencies of suppression be destroyed? For if they be not destroyed, the mind has still a duty, left to perform. For this reason, he says :—'The mind disappears, etc.'

The trance cognition which suppresses the outgoing tendencies is the cognitive trance. It is the potencies born from that, that are here spoken of. The potencies which operate to lead to absolute freedom are the potencies born from the acts of suppression. Because the potencies of the outgoing acts of cognition have become embedded in the mind, it is said to be the possessor of the potency of outgoing cognition. The potency of suppression, however, is but newly born in the mind. The mind has therefore no duty to perform, even though the potency of suppression exists. The mind which has the duty of achieving the purposes of the Puruṣa, is said to have the duty of achieving those objects. The purposes it has to achieve are the enjoyments of sound, etc., and the attainment of discriminative knowledge.

When however the potency of suppression only remains, the Puruṣa is no longer the substratum of the reflex consciousness of the Will-to-be (buddhi). Hence the potency of suppression cannot be an object of the Puruṣa to be fulfilled by the mind. The minds of the Videhas and the Prakṛtilayas do not consist of a balance of suppressive potencies alone; they have therefore still a duty to perform. Also because they are possessed of the aroma of afflictions.

With this in mind, says the commentator :—'And it is for this reason, etc.' The rest is easy.—51.

The object and explanation of Yoga, the meaning of the modifications for the purpose of the performance thereof, the means of Yoga and its kinds are described in this chapter.

Here ends the first chapter of Vācaspati's Gloss the Vācaspatya, on the commentary of Vyāsa on the Aphorisms of Patañjali.

2
The Practice of Yoga

Sūtra 1

तपःस्वाध्यायेश्वरप्रणिधानानि क्रियायोगः ।। १ ।।

तपः Tapaḥ purificatory action. स्वाध्याय Svādhyāya, study. ईश्वर-प्रणिधान Īśvara-praṇidhāna, worship of God, making God the motive of action. क्रिया Kriyā, of action. योगः Yogaḥ, the Yoga.

1. Purificatory action, study and making God the motive of action, Is the Yoga of action.[1]—52

उद्दिष्टः समाहितचित्तस्य योगः। कथं व्युत्थितचित्तोऽपि योगयुक्तः स्यादित्येतदारभ्यते। तपः स्वाध्यायेश्वरप्रणिधानानि क्रियायोगः। नातपस्विनो योगः सिध्यति। अनादिकर्म क्लेशवासना चित्रा प्रत्युपस्थित-विषयजाला चाशुद्धिर्नान्तरेण तपः संभेदमापद्यत इत्रि तपस उपादानम्। तच्च चित्तप्रसादनमबाध्य-मानमनेनासेव्यमिति। मन्यते। स्वाध्यायः प्रणवादिपवित्राणां जपो मोक्षशास्त्राध्ययनं वा। ईश्वरप्रणिधानं सर्वक्रियाणां परमगुरावर्पणम्। तत्फलसंन्यासो वा।। १।।

Vyāsa

The Yoga for him whose mind is already inclined towards trance cognition, has been described. How may one with an out-going mind become also possessed of Yoga, is now considered. 'The Yoga of action is purificatory action, study and the devotion to God and making Him the motive of action.'

---

1. The word 'tapas' has been translated as purificatory action, because 'tapas' means that which burns up impurities.
The word 'Īśvarapraṇidhāna' has been translated as the devotion to God being the motive of action. The same word in the first chapter (I. 23) has been translated as feeling the omnipresence of the Lord. The root meaning of the word 'praṇidhāna' is the placing of anything under another to the fullest extent (pra=fullness, Ni=under and dhāna=placing). In the chapter on trance the word can only mean the contemplation of Him as the substratum of all phenomena. Hence 'Īśvarapraṇidhāna' as a means of achieving trance can only mean the habituating of the mind to feel the omnipresence of the divine principle. In a chapter on the Yoga of action however the word cannot be interpreted as carrying the same meaning. As a branch of the Yoga of action 'praṇidhāna' must have special reference to action which would be out of place in contemplation. It has, therefore, been translated here as above. The root meaning, it is easy to see, runs through both these meanings.

Yoga is not attained by one not given to purificatory action. Impurity is variegated by the eternal in-dwelling of the aroma of action and affliction, and is ever in contact with the network of enjoyables. It cannot be dispersed without purificatory action (tapas). For this reason purificatory action has been taken up (as a factor of the Yoga of action). This is considered an action worthy of performance, as it purifies the mind when not impeded.

Study is the repeated utterance of purifying words, like the AUM and others; or, the reading of the teachings about absolute spiritual freedom (Mokṣa).

'The devotion to God and making Him the motive of all actions' means the dedicating of all actions to the Highest Teacher, or the renunciation of its fruit.—52.

Vācaspati's Gloss

The question is that the fruit of Yoga and the means thereof, having been described in the first chapter along with their sub-heads, what is the necessity of writing a second chapter? The answer is given :—'The Yoga for him, etc.'

It is only practice and desirelessness that have been mentioned in the first chapter to be the means of Yoga. They are, however, not possible for the out-going mind also at once. The means, therefore, to be taught in the second chapter are necessary in order to achieve the required purity of mental essence. It is only thereafter that the essence of the Will-to-know, becoming strong enough to preserve itself in that state, daily shows forth the powers of practice and desirelessness.

'Already inclined towards the trance cognition' means not only occasionally steady. The meaning is how may the out-going mind also become possessed of Yoga by the practice of the means to be taught ?

The author of the aphorisms first takes up some of these means as of first rate importance and usefulness, and describes them as the Yoga of action 'Purificatory action, etc.'

It is the action itself that is the Yoga in the Yoga of action. It is for this reason that in the Viṣṇupurāṇa in the dialogue between Keśidhvaja and Khāṇḍikya it is said :—

'When the Yogī first comes into contact with the Yoga, he is called the Yuñjamāna, the Neophyte, the Beginner.' And beginning with this are mentioned purificatory action and study, etc.

Now the comment shows by the canon of difference that purificatory action must be a means of Yoga :—'Yoga is not attained by one who is not given to purificatory action.'

He shows a subsidiary result of the purificatory action, justifying its nature as a means of Yoga :—'Impurity, etc.' The impurity which is variegated by the aroma of eternal action and affliction, and which is for this very reason in contact with, *i.e.*, approached by the network of enjoyables, consists in the intensity of disturbing energy (rajas) and inertia (tamas), and cannot come to dispersion without purificatory action. Dispersion means the entire separation of objects in thick cohesion.

But the question is what purificatory action may be inimical to Yoga, inasmuch as being taken up as a means of Yoga, it may become the cause of the disturbance of the physiological equilibrium of the forces of the body. How then can it be a means of Yoga ? For this reason the commentator says :—'This is considered an action, etc.' The meaning is that so much of a purificatory action only is to be performed as does not cause the disturbance of the equilibrium of physiological forces.

The words AUM, etc., include such portions of the Veda as the Puruṣa Sūkta, the Rudra Maṇḍala and the Brāhmaṇas, etc., as also the portions of the Purāṇas such as the Brahmapāra, etc. Highest Teacher is Īśvara. To him are actions to be dedicated. It is on this subject that the following has been said :—'Whatever I am doing, beautiful or ugly, with desire or without desire, I renounce all that on thy account; I do all things with submission to thee.'

The renunciation of fruit means the doing of an action without thinking in connection with it of the fruit to be obtained thereby. The following has been said in this connection :—It is in the doing of action alone that thy duty lies, never in its fruits. Never make the fruit of action its motive; never become attached to inaction.—1.

Sūtra 2

समाधिभावनार्थः क्लेशतनूकरणार्थश्च ।। २ ।।

समाधि Samādhi, trance. भावन Bhāvana, bringing about. अर्थः Arthaḥ, for the purpose of. क्लेश Kleśa, afflictions. तनू-करणार्थः Tanū-karaṇārthaḥ, for the purpose of attenuating. च: Caḥ, and.

2. For the purpose of bringing about trance and for the purpose of attenuating affliction.—53.

सहि क्रियायोगः। समाधिभावनार्थः क्लेशतनूकरणार्थश्च। स ह्यासेव्यमानः समाधिं भावयति। क्लेशांश्च प्रतनूकरोति। प्रतनूकृतान्क्लेशान्प्रसंख्यानाग्निना दग्धबीजकल्पान् प्रसवधर्मिणः करिष्यतीति तेषां तनूकरणात्पुनः क्लेशैरपरामृष्टः सत्त्वपुरुषान्यतामात्राख्यातिः सूक्ष्मा प्रज्ञा समाप्ताधिकाराप्रतिप्रसवाय कल्पयिष्यत इति।। २।।

Vyāsa

The Yoga of action is certainly to be performed, 'for the purpose of bringing about trance and for the purpose of attenuating the afflictions.' It is that which being performed, brings about trance and attenuates the afflictions. The afflictions thus attenuated become characterized by unproductiveness. When their seed power has, as it were, been signed by the fire of High Intellection; and for this reason the mind after their attenuation, is never again touched by the affliction; and having by subtle cognition come up to the discrimination of the distinct natures of the Puruṣa and Objective Essence, has the whole of its duty fulfilled and can only resolve into its cause.—53.

Vācaspati's Gloss

The aphorism defining its object is introduced :—'The Yoga of action is certainly, etc.' The aphorism is :—'For the purpose of bringing about trance and for the purpose of attenuating the afflictions.'

The question arises that if the Yoga of action alone be competent to attenuate the afflictions, there remains no use at all in High Intellection. For this reason the commentator says :—"The afflictions thus attenuated become, etc." The action of the Yoga of action operates only in attenuating them; it does not render the afflictions barren. High Intellection, however, operates to render them barren.

Let that be granted. But if High Intellection alone is competent to render the affliction non-productive, what is the use of attenuating them ? For this reason he says :—'On account of their attenuation, etc.' If the afflictions are not attenuated, the discrimination of the distinct natures of the Puruṣa and the Objective Essence, remaining overpowered by a powerful enemy, does not even show the energy to rise and render them barren, from the very first. When, however, the afflictions have been dispersed and rendered weak, even then, though inimical to them, it only arises by practice and desirelessness. When it has thus been born, it is not again touched by them, it is not overpowered so long as it is not touched by them. The discrimination of the distinct natures of the Puruṣa and Objective Essence is a subtle faculty, because its object is subtle.

"Can only resolve into its cause" means can only disappear.—2.

Sūtra 3

अविद्यास्मितारागद्वेषाभिनिवेशाः क्लेशाः ।। ३ ।।

अविद्या Avidyā, nescience. अस्मिता Asmitā, egoism. राग Rāga, attachment. द्वेष Dveṣa, aversion. अभिनिवेश Abhiniveśa, love of life, all these. क्लेशाः Kelśāḥ, afflictions.

3. The afflictions are Nescience, Egoism, Attachment, Aversion and Love of Life.—54.

अथ के क्लेशाः कियन्तो वेति। अविद्यास्मितारागद्वेषाभिनिवेशाः क्लेशाः। क्लेशा इति पञ्चविपर्यया इत्यर्थः। ते स्पन्दमाना गुणाधिकारं द्रढयन्ति परिणाममवस्थापयन्ति कार्यकारणस्त्रोत उन्नमयन्ति परस्परानुग्रहणतन्त्रीभूत्वा कर्मविपाकं चाभिनिर्हरन्ति।। ३ ।।

Vyāsa

What then are the afflictions and how many? 'The afflictions are Nescience, Egoism, Attachment, Aversion and Love of Life.'

'The afflictions' are the five forms of Unreal Cognition. When quick with life, they render the rule of the "qualities" firm, establish change, send out the stream of cause and effect, bring about the fructification of action by coming to depend upon one another for mutual support.—3.

Vācaspati's Gloss

How is its duty fulfilled? It can only be so said to have fulfilled its duty, when it has caused the cessation of the action of the "qualities" inasmuch as the duty is noting else but the bringing about of an effect by the "qualities." For this reason the commentator puts the question, 'What are the afflictions, etc.' And he answers by the aphorism :—"Nescience, etc." Nescience and the others are the afflictions. He explains :—'The five forms of Unreal Cognition, etc.'

Nescience is Unreal Cognition itself. Egoism and the others also carry nescience with them and cannot exist without it. They too are therefore unreal cognitions. The meaning is that for this reason, they are destroyed with the destruction of Nescience.

He says now that the reason for their destructibility exists in their being the cause of repeated births :—'When quick with life,' *i.e.*, when they are in operation, they render the rule of the qualities firm, *i.e.*, strong. For this very reason they establish change. They send out, *i.e.*, show forth the stream of cause and effect in the shape of the Unmanifested, the Mahattattva (the great principle) and the principle of individuality.

Now he shows the object for which all this is done by them :—'Being about, etc... for mutual support.' Fructification of action consists in life-state, life-period and life-experience. This is the object of the Puruṣa. It is these that the afflictions bring about. Does each of them do this by itself? No he says :—'By mutual support!' The actions are supported by the afflictions and the afflictions by the actions.—3.

Sūtra 4

अविद्याक्षेत्रमुत्तरेषां प्रसुप्ततनुविच्छिन्नोदाराणाम्॥ ४॥

अविद्या: Avidyā, nescience. क्षेत्रम् Kṣetram, field. उत्तरेषाम् Uttareṣām, for the others. प्रसुप्त: Prasupta, dormant. तनु Tanu, tenuous. विच्छिन्न: Vicchinna, alternated. उदाराणाम् Udārāṇām, or fully operative, for all these.

4. Nescience is the field for the others, whether dormant, tenuous, alternated or fully operative.—55.

अविद्याक्षेत्रमुत्तरेषां प्रसुप्ततनुविच्छिन्नोदाराणाम्। अत्राविद्याक्षेत्रं प्रसवभूमिरुत्तरेषामस्मितादीनां चतुर्विधविकल्पानां प्रसुप्ततनुविच्छिन्नोदाराणाम्। तत्र का प्रसुप्ति:। चेतसि शक्तिमात्रप्रतिष्ठानां बीजभावोपगम:। तस्य प्रबोध आलम्बने सम्मुखीभाव: प्रसंख्यानवतो दग्धक्लेशबीजस्य सम्मुखीभूतेप्यालम्बने नासौ पुनरस्ति। दग्धबीजस्य कुत: प्ररोह इति अत: क्षीणक्लेश: कुशलश्चरमदेह इत्युच्यते। तत्रैव सा दग्धबीजभावा पञ्चमी क्लेशावस्था नान्यत्रेति। सतां क्लेशानां तदा बीजसामर्थ्यं दग्धमिति। विषयस्य सम्मुखीभावेऽपि सति न भवत्येषां प्रबोध इत्युक्ता प्रसुप्तिर्दग्धबीजानां चाप्ररोहश्च तनुत्वमुच्यते प्रतिपक्षभावनोपहता: क्लेशास्तनवो भवन्ति। तथा विच्छिद्य विच्छिद्य तेन तेनात्मना पुन: पुन: समुदाचरन्तीति विच्छिन्ना: कथं रागकाले क्रोधस्यादर्शनात्। नहि रागकाले क्रोध: समुदाचरति रागश्च क्वचिद् दृश्यमानो न विषयान्तरे नास्ति। नैकस्यां स्त्रियां चैत्रो रक्त इत्यन्यासु स्त्रीषु विरक्त: किंतु तत्र रागो लब्धवृत्तिरन्यत्र तु भविष्यद्वृत्तिरिति। स हि तदा प्रसुप्ततनुविच्छिन्नो भवति। विषयो यो लब्धवृत्ति: स उदार:। सर्व एवैते क्लेशविषयत्वं नातिक्रामन्ति। कस्तर्हि विच्छिन्न: प्रसुप्तस्तनुरुदारो वा क्लेश इत्युच्यते सत्यमेवैतत्। किंतु विशिष्टानामेवैतेषां विच्छिन्नादित्वम्। यथैव प्रतिपक्षभावनातो निवृत्तस्तथैव स्वव्यञ्जकाञ्जनेनाभिव्यक्त: सर्व इति सर्व एवामी क्लेशा अविद्याभेदा:।

कस्मात्सर्वेष्वविद्यैवाभिप्लवते यदविद्ययावस्त्वाकार्यते तदेवानुशेरते क्लेशा विपर्यासप्रत्ययकाल उपलभ्यन्ते क्षीयमाणां चाविद्यामनुक्षीयन्त इति ।। ४ ।।

Vyāsa

Of these, Nescience is the field, the breeding ground for the others that follow, the Egoism, etc., having a four-fold possible mode of their existence, as the dormant, the tenuous, the alternated and the fully operative.

What is dormancy ? It is the existence in the mind as power alone in the germinal state. It is awake when it turns its face towards its objects. In the case of him who possesses discriminative knowledge, the germs of the afflictions are singed, and therefore even on the object coming in front, they do not come into operation. How can the burned up seed sprout ? Hence, the wise man whose affliction are gone, is said to have had his last birth. It is in him alone that the afflictions pass into the fifth state, that of the seed being burnt up; inasmuch as the afflictions do exist in that state, although their seed-power has been burnt up. It is for this reason that they do not awaken even when an object comes in front of them. This is the dormancy of those whose seed-power has been burnt up.

Tenuity is now described. The afflictions become tenuous on being cut down by habituation to contraries.

And they are alternated, inasmuch as they disappear and appear over and over again in the same condition. Anger is not observed to be in operation at the time of attachment. Anger does not arise when attachment has its play. Nor does it happen that attachment, while manifesting with reference to another object. Because Caitra is attached to one woman, it does not follow that he is averse to others. The fact is that in the one his attachment has manifested itself, while in others it can be active in the future. It is this that becomes either dormant, tenuous or alternated.

The fully operative is that which has found manifestation in the object.

All these do not pass beyond the sphere of affliction. What is it then that is called an affliction, whether it be the dormant, the alternated or the fully operative ? This is true. But they becomes either alternated or any one else, only when they appear as so qualified. As all are removed by habituation to contraries, all are manifested by the operation of competent causes.

All these afflictions are the modifications of Nescience only. How ? It is Nescience alone that is the quickness of their life. The afflictions appear only in the form which is put upon an object by Nescience. They are found existing simultaneously with the cognition of the unreal; and they disappear when Nescience disappears.—55.

Vācaspati's Gloss

The commentator shows that the afflictions which are to be overcome as being painful have their root in Nesciense. "Nescience is the field for the others, whether dormant, tenuous, alternated or fully operative."

What of these is dormancy ? The meaning of the questioner is that there is no authority for the existence of the afflictions at a time when they are not in operation with reference to object. The answer is :—'In the mind, etc.' The afflictions of the Videhas and the Prakṛtilayas do not operate with reference to their proper objects; they have gone to the germinal state, and as such do exist only *in posse,* as curds exist in milk. There is no other means of making them barren besides discriminative knowledge. It is for this reason that the Videhas and the Prakṛtilayas are understood as not possessed of discriminative knowledge. Their afflictions are dormant so long as they do not reach the limit of their time. When they do reach the limit, the afflictions come round again into manifestation and turn towards their various objects. They have existed in the potential state alone. This potency means the power of manifesting. The approach to the germinal state indicates the power of producing the effect.

How is it that the afflictions of him who is possessed of discriminative knowledge are not also dormant? To show this the commentator says :—'To him who is possessed of discriminative knowledge.'

'Last birth' means that he will not be born in another body. There will be no birth after the present one.

'Now where else' means in the disembodied (the Videhas), etc. But inasmuch as that which is, cannot be entirely destroyed, there is no use in the power of Yoga; the afflictions arise when their objects come in front. For this reason the commentator says :—'The afflictions do exist, etc.' The meaning is that although the affliction exist, yet their seed-power is burnt up.

The contraries of the afflictions are the practices of the Yoga of action. The afflictions become tenuous when they are put down by the Yoga of action. Or, Right knowledge is the contrary of Nescience : the recognition of the distinction is the contrary of egoism : justice is the contrary of attachment and aversion; the removal of the idea of dependence upon the body, *i.e.,* that the body is the necessary adjunct of the soul, is the opposite of the love of life.

Now he describes alternation :—'Similarly, etc.' The afflictions are overpowered by another affliction being in operation for the time; or they arise and manifest themselves after alternate cessations on account of excessive enjoyment. Its difference from the dormant is explained by its being dependent for manifestation upon the seed-power and the organs of enjoyment; or by its repeated manifestation and cessation on account of the weakness of other manifestations which tend to overpower it; or by reiterated manifestations. Further attachment *in esse* may overpower anger, which belongs to a different class of afflictions. Or, an affliction of the same class, such as attachment to one object may overpower attachment to a different object. For this reason he says :—'Attachment, etc.'

Now he says that the affliction which is to manifest in the future must be understood to possess a three-fold line of action, whichever it may be at any time :—'It is at that time, etc.' The word 'that' points only to the affliction which is to manifest in the future, not to the attachment of Caitra, because that is of one of the three classes, *i.e.,* the alternated.

Now he describes the one in full operation :—'That which is, etc.' The question is that it is the one in full operation alone that afflicts, and it is therefore proper to call it an affliction; but how is it proper to call the others afflictions? They do not afflict, not being in operation. For this reason he says :—'All these afflictions, etc.' The meaning is that they do not pass beyond the sphere of afflictions, and may well be called by that name, because they tend to operation, and for this very reason are to be removed.

Well inasmuch as they are all afflictions, they are one only. Why then are they described as being more than one? The answer is :—'It is true, etc.'

The question now arises that although it may be that the afflictions take their rise in Nescience, yet why should it be that they should cease to exist when Nescience is destroyed? The cloth is not destroyed with the destruction of the weaver. For this reason he says :—"All these are the forms, etc." All these are the modifications.

This means that they are different modifications only in appearance, not in reality; because they do not exist as separate from it. Why? The answer is :—'In all these nescience, etc.' He explains the same. 'Whenever, etc.' The rest is easy. The following is a brief statement. In those that are merged in some principle, the afflictions are dormant. In the Yogīs they are tenuous. In those who are given to enjoyment (the ordinary mortals), they are alternative operative.

Sūtra 5

अनित्याशुचिदुःखानात्मसु नित्यशुचिसुखात्मख्यातिरविद्या ।। ५ ।।

अनित्य Anitya, the non-eternal. अशुचि Aśuci, the impure. दुःख Duḥkha, the painful. अनात्मन् Anātman, the not self, all these. नित्य Nitya, the eternal. शुचिः Śuciḥ, the pure. सुख Sukha, the pleasureable. आत्मन् Ātman, soul. ख्यातिः Khyātiḥ, supposing, taking to be. अविद्या Avidyā, nescience.

5. Nescience is the taking of the non-eternal, the impure, the painful and the not-self to be the eternal, the pure, the pleasurable and the self.—56.

तत्राविद्यास्वरूपमुच्यते। अनित्याशुचिदुःखानात्मसु नित्यशुचिसुखात्मख्यातिरविद्या। अनित्ये कार्ये नित्यख्यातिस्तद्यथा ध्रुवा पृथिवी ध्रुवा सचन्द्रतारका द्यौः अमृता दिवौकस इति। तथाशुचौ परमबीभत्से काये शुचिख्यातिः। उक्तं च। स्थानाद् बीजादुपष्टम्भान्निःस्पन्दान्निधनादपि। कायमाधेयशौचत्वात्पण्डिता ह्यशुचिं विदुरिति। अशुचौ शुचिख्यातिर्दृश्यते। नववे शशाङ्क–लेखा कमनीयेयं कन्या मध्वमृतावयवनिर्मितेव चन्द्रं भित्वा निःसृतेव ज्ञायते। नीलोत्पलपत्रायताक्षीहावगर्भाभ्यां लोचनाभ्यां जीवलोकमाश्वासयन्तीवेति कस्य केनाभिसंबन्धः। भवति चेयमशुचौ शुचिविपर्यासप्रत्यय इति। एतेनापुण्ये पुण्यप्रत्ययस्तथैवानर्थे चार्थप्रत्ययो व्याख्यातः। तद्यथा दुःखे सुखख्यातिं वक्ष्यति परिणामतापसंस्कारदुःखैर्गुणवृत्तिविरोधाच्च दुःखमेव सर्वं विवेकिन इति। तत्र सुखख्यातिरविद्या तथानात्मन्यात्मख्यातिर्बाह्योपकरणेषु चेतनाचेतनेषु भोगाधिष्ठाने वा शरीरे पुरुषोपकारणे वा मनस्यनात्मन्यात्मख्यातिरिति। तथैतदत्रोक्तम्। व्यक्तमव्यक्तं वा सत्त्वमात्मत्वेनाभिप्रतीत्य तस्य संपदमनुनन्दत्यात्मसंपदं मन्वानस्तस्य। व्यापदमनुशोचत्यात्मव्यापदं मन्वानः स सर्वोऽप्रतिबुद्ध इत्येषा चतुष्पदा भवत्यविद्या मूलमस्य क्लेशसन्तानस्य कर्माशयस्य च सविपाकस्येति तस्याश्चामित्रागोष्पदवद्वस्तुसतत्त्वं विज्ञेयम्। यथा नामित्रो मित्राभावो न मित्रमात्रं किंतु तद्विरुद्धः सपत्नः। यथा चागोष्पदं न गोष्पदाभावो न

गोष्पदमात्रं किंतु देश एव ताभ्यामन्यद्वस्त्वन्तरम्। एवमविद्या न प्रमाणं न प्रमाणाभावः। किंतु विद्याविपरीतं ज्ञानान्तरमविद्येति॥५॥

Vyāsa

Out of these the nature of Nescience is described :—"Nescience is the taking of the non-eternal, the impure, the painful, and the not-self to be the eternal, the pure, the pleasurable and the self."

The taking of the non-eternal to be eternal is the possession of such notions as that the earth is permanent, the firmament with the moon and the stars is permanent, the gods are immortal, etc.

Similar is the seeing of purity in the body, which is impure and highly disgusting. And it has been said :—'The wise know the body to be impure on account of its position, its origin, its process of up-keep, its perspiration and destruction and also on account of the necessity of keeping it constantly clean.' Thus is purity seen in the impure. 'The girl is attractive like the new moon. Her limbs are, as it were, made of honey and nectar. She looks, as it were, she has emerged from the moon. Her eyes are large like the leaves of the blue lotus. With playful flashes of her eyes she imparts life to the world of men.' Now what is in this connected to what? This unreal cognition, however, of the pure in the impure is daily seen. By this is described the cognition of the sacred in the profane, the cognition of purposeless. As here so will the cognition of pleasure in pain be later described.

"All is pain to the discriminating because of the end, the remorse, the residual potency, and the mutual contrariety of the manifestations of the 'qualities.'" II.15.

The cognition of pleasure under these circumstances is Nescience.

Similar is the cognition of the self in the not-self. The external accessories, whether sentient or not sentient, the body which is the vehicle for enjoyments, the mind which is only a vehicle for the Puruṣa, are all manifestations of the not-self. The notion that any one of these is the self is Nescience. On this subject the following has been said :—

'Those who believing the sentient or insentient objective essence to be the self, rejoice in their increase believing it the prosperity of the self, and are anxious when they decrease, believing it to be the adversity of the self have not awakened.'

This nescience is thus possessed of four locations. It is the root of all this overgrowth of afflictions, the vehicle of action together with the vehicle of fruition. This nescience should be understood as being a real substance, like the word Amitra (a, not, and mitra, friend, the compound meaning an enemy) and the word Agoṣpada (a, not, and goṣpada, cow's foot, the compound meaning a particular place). As the word Amitra does not mean the absence of a friend nor a particular friend, but something opposite to a friend, an enemy; and as the word Agoṣpada, does not mean the absence of a Goṣpada, nor a particular Goṣpada, but a particular place distinct from both, another substance;

so is nescience neither Real Cognition nor the absence of Real Cognition. On the contrary, Nescience is another form of cognition, which is contrary to real knowledge (the cognition of the real).—56.

Vācaspati's Gloss

Nescience is not-eternal and impure. It is, that is to say, an effect which is ever qualified by the presence of non-eternity. There are some, it is well-known, who believe the elements to be eternal, and meditate upon them devotedly with the object of assimilating their natures. Similarly do others meditate with devotion upon the heavens, the sun, moon, and stars as stages of the path of Smoke (the Pitṛyāna), with the object of reaching them in the belief of their eternity. Similarly do people drink the Soma juice for attaining the state of the denizens of heaven, the gods, believing them to be eternal and immortal, inasmuch as the Veda says :—'Drink we the Soma so that we may become immortal.' This is the Nescience which is described as the cognition of the eternal in the non-eternal.

Similarly with reference to the impure and highly disgusting body. Having said this much, he stops in the middle to quote a verse of Vyāsa, describing the disgusting nature of the body.

'The wise, etc.'

The 'position of the body' in the mother's womb close to urine, etc. The 'origin' is the germ and sperm cells of parents. 'The process of upkeep of the body' is the transformation of the foods and drinks into chyle, etc. It is by this that the body is supported. Perspiration means sweating. Destruction or death renders the body of even a man learned in the Veda, impure, inasmuch as a bath is ordained after it has been touched.

The question is that if the body is by nature impure, what then is the use of washing it with earths and water? For this reason he says : 'On account of the necessity, etc.' This means that although by nature impure, the body admits of being purified by external applications; as, for example, take the bodies of women by means of sweet smelling applications.

He finishes the sentence :—The body which is impure is cognised to be pure in the way now described. 'Like the new moon, etc.'

"Playful flashes denote the frolicsomeness of love."

'Now what is here connected with what?' The first 'what' stands for the body of a woman which is by nature so impure and therefore disgusting. By what poor similitude is the body related to the new moon?

By this illustration of the cognition of the pure in the impure body of a woman, is also described the cognition of virtue in the vices of causing pain to others under the impression of their being released from the world.

Similarly are described the notions of usefulness in wealth, etc., which on account of the troubles incident upon collection and preservation, etc., are really things which contradict the real purpose of life. They are all impure on account of their being causes of disgust.

Similar is the case of the cognition of pleasure in pain. This is easy.

'Similar is the cognition of self, etc.' This also is easy.

Similarly has it been said on this subject by Pañcaśikhā.

'The sentient' are the intelligent objects of enjoyment, such as wife, etc., and animals.

'The insentient' are the non-intelligent objects, such as seats and couches, etc.

All such have not awakened, means they are forgetful.

This nescience is said to possess four locations, *i.e.*, places where it manifests.

Upon this the question arises that nescience being really located in an infinity of places, such for example, as the forgetfulness of directions and the appearance of a complete circle in the case of a rapidly rotating point of light, etc., why should it be described as being located in four places only? For this reason he says :—'It is the root, etc.' There be other forms of nescience; that however, which is the root of repeated births is only four-fold.

Now another question :—The word 'nescience' is a compound of 'ne' (न=not) and science (विद्या=Science). Now is the prohibitive Ne (a), the effective word of the compound, thus signifying the mere absence of the thing signified by the second word, as in the word Amakṣika, one meaning of which is the absence of bees. Or, is the second word of the compound the effective portion thereof, in which case it would mean a particular form of knowledge, as in the case of the word Arājapuruṣa, Not-public servant. Or, is it that the word denotes something which is neither the meaning of the first word nor of the second, but something different from both ? Such a word would be the word Amakṣika, beeless place. This meaning is different from the meaning of both the factors of the compound.

Now the meaning of the word Nescience would be the absence of knowledge already existing, if the first word of the compound were the effective one. This, however, cannot be the cause of the afflictions. It the second word of the compound be the effective one, then the meaning of the compound would be a science qualified by the absence of something (particular) the science of the negation, (A, of something). Science, however, can only be the opposite of the afflictions, etc., not their seed. It is not proper that the destroyer of a thing should be a quality thereof.

If it be considered that it means something different from both, then it can only mean the Will-to-know (buddhi) with the knowledge absent there from, *i.e.*, something in which there is no knowledge. Now the Will-to-know can never be the cause of afflictions, etc., even though knowledge be absent therefrom. Whatever thus be the meaning given to Nescience, it can never be the root of afflictions, etc.

For this reason he says :—'It is to be considered, etc.' It is possessed of substantiality. This means cannot be the absence of something existing as such. Neither is Nescience a particular form of science; nor is it the Will-to-know devoid of knowledge. It is, as has been said, a cognition contrary to the Real Cognition; it is the cognition of the unreal (or briefly, unreal cognition).

The relation of word and meaning depends upon how the world begins to understand it. In the world it is often seen that in words compounded with deprivative prefixes, the deprivative prefix, while denying the existence of the last word of the compound, signifies something which is the contrary thereof. Similar is the meaning here. He gives analogies :—'As the word Amitra.' It does not mean the absence of a friend; nor does it mean a particular friend (a friend called A). On the contrary, it means the opposite of a friend, as enemy.

Similarly, the word Agoṣpada does not mean the absence of a cow-shed (goṣpada); nor does it mean a particular cow-shed (styled A). On the other hand, it means a particular country where king are not found. It is a substance different from both. He applies the analogy to the thing illustrated :—'In the same way, etc.'

Sūtra 6

दृग्दर्शनशक्त्योरेकात्मतेवास्मिता ।। ६ ।।

दृग् **Dṛg, the subjective, power of consciousness. दर्शन Darśana, the instrumental power of seeing. शक्त्योः Śaktyoḥ, of (both these) powers. एकात्मता Ekātmatā, identity. इव Iva, appearance. अस्मिता Asmitā, egoism.**

6. Egoism is the appearance of identity in the natures of the subjective power of consciousness and the instrumental power of seeing.—57.

दृग्दर्शनशक्त्योरेकात्मतेवास्मिता । पुरुषो दृक्शक्तिर्बुद्धिर्दर्शन–शक्तिरित्येतयोरेकस्वरूपापत्तिरिवास्मिता क्लेश उच्यते । भोक्तृभोग्यशक्त्योरत्यन्तविभक्तयोरत्यन्तासङ्कीर्णयोरविभागप्राप्ताविव सत्यां भोगः कल्पते । स्वरूप–प्रतिलम्भे तु तयोः कैवल्यमेव भवति कुतो भोग इति । तथा चोक्तम् । बुद्धितः परं पुरुषमाकारशीलविद्यादि–भिर्विभक्तमपश्यन्कुर्यात्तत्रात्मबुद्धिं मोहेनेति ।। ६ ।।

Vyāsa

The Puruṣa is the subjective power of consciousness, and the Will-to-know is the instrumental power of seeing. The appearance of these two powers as if they were identical, is the affliction known as Egoism. Enjoyment is rendered possible when the power of enjoyment in the enjoyer and the capacity of being enjoyed in the Objective Existence, which are quite distinct and different from each other, are looked upon as, as it were, identical. When, however, their natures have been understood they become isolated; and how then can there be enjoyment? And so it has been said :—'Not knowing the Puruṣa beyond the Will-to-know to be different therefrom in nature, character and knowledge, etc., a man has by forgetfulness the notion of self therein.—57.

Vācaspati's Gloss

Having described Nescience, now he describes Egoism, which is quite as dear to the heart of man as attachment and the others :—'Egoism is the appearance of identity in the natures of the subjective power of consciousness and the objective power of seeing.'

Consciousness and seeing are two distinct powers. They are, respectively, the self and the not-self. The particular Nescience which is responsible for the cognition of this not-self as the self, and which is only a delusion and not a reality is Egoism. Although it was sufficient only to say "consciousness" and "seeing" the word power is added to bring out their mutual relation of fitness as the enjoyer and the enjoyed. He explains the aphorism :—'The Puruṣa, etc.'

The question arises, why should they not in fact be considered as one when in fact they are taken in as such? How is it that their unity afflicts the Puruṣa? For this reason he says :—'Enjoyment, etc.' The capacity of being enjoyed means the Will-to-be. The power of enjoyment in the enjoyer means Puruṣa. They are quite distinct from each other. Why? The reason is given to be that they are seen to be quite distinct from each other. The Puruṣa possesses the characteristics of unchangeability, etc., the Will-to-know has the characteristics of chageability, etc. They are, therefore, quite distinct from each other. It is meant to be said by this that although they appear to be identical they are not in reality the same. 'Are looked upon, as it were, to be one with each other.' This explains that this notion is an affliction. This employs the canon of agreement.

The cannon of difference is now applied :—'When, however, their natures are understood, etc.' Understood means when the consciousness of discrimination has been attained.

Now he shows that is conceded by others also :—'And so it has been said' by Pañcaśikhā. 'Knowing the Puruṣa beyond the Will-to-know, etc.' Its nature is constant purity, its character is indifference, its knowledge means intelligence. The Will-to-know is impure, not indifferent and non-intelligent. The notion of self therein is Egoism and it is Nescience. Forgetfulness is the potency generated by former nescience. Or it may be the darkness of inertia (tamas), because Nescience is born of the quality of inertia (tamas).—6.

Sūtra 7

सुखानुशयी रागः ।। ७ ।।

सुख Sukha, pleasure. अनुशयी Anuśayī, the sequential attraction to. रागः Rāgaḥ, attachment.

7. Attachment is the sequential attraction to pleasure.—58.

सुखानुशयी रागः । सुखाभिज्ञस्य सुखानुस्मृतिपूर्वः सुखे तत्साधने वा योगर्द्धस्तृष्णा लोभः स राग इति ।। ७ ।।

Vyāsa

The desire to possess, the thirst for and the hankering after pleasure or the means thereof, preceded by a remembrance of the pleasure in one who has enjoyed it, is attachment.—68.

Vācaspati's Gloss

On the attainment of discriminative knowledge, attachment, etc., are removed, Egoism, brought about by nescience, is the root of attachment, etc. For this reason he describes attachment, etc., after egoism. Attachment is the sequential attraction to pleasure.

Memory is not possible to one who has not cognized. Hence is it said :—'In one who has enjoyed.' When pleasure is remembered, attachment is preceded by the remembrance of the pleasure in consequence of the enjoyment thereof. When pleasure is being enjoyed there is no necessity of the remembrance. The attachment, however, to the means thereof, whether remembered or actually present, is also preceded by the remembrance of the pleasure. As a matter of course when a means of pleasure is perceived, it is remembered as a cause of the pleasure of the same class. Or it is inferred that it will cause a pleasure similar to what has been before caused by an object of the same class. The means of pleasure is, therefore desired.

He describes the meaning of the word attraction :—'The desire to possess, etc.'—7.

Sūtra 8

दुःखानुशयी द्वेषः ।। ८ ।।

दुःख Duḥkha, pain. अनुशयी Anuśayī, the sequential repulsion. द्वेषः Dveṣaḥ, aversion.

8. Aversion is the sequential repulsion from pain.—59.

दुःखानुशयी द्वेषः । दुःखाभिज्ञस्य दुःखानुस्मृतिपूर्वो दुःखे तत्साधने वा यः प्रतिघो मन्युर्जिघांसा क्रोधः स द्वेषः ।। ८ ।।

Vyāsa

The repulsion, the anxiety, the wish for removal and the anger at pain and the means thereof, which stick in the mind in consequence of the feeling of pain, in the case of him who has felt the pain, preceded by a remembrance of the pain, is aversion.—59.

Vācaspati's Gloss

'Aversion is the sequential repulsion from pain.' "One who has felt pain, etc." This is to be explained as before. Describes the meaning of the words sequential repulsion from pain :—'The repulsion, etc.' Repulsion is the force which repels. Amplifies the same by stating synonyms :—'The anxiety, etc.'—8.

Sūtra 9

स्वरसवाही विदुषोऽपि तथारूढोऽभिनिवेशः ।। ९ ।।

स्व-रस Sva-rasa, by its own potency. वही Vāhī, flowing. विदुषः Viduṣaḥ, in the wise. अपि Api, even. तथा Tathā, all the same. रूढः Rūḍhaḥ, established. अभिनिवेशः Abhiniveśaḥ, love of life.

9. Flowing on by its own potency, established all the same even in the wise, is Love of Life.—60.

स्वरसवाही विदुषोऽपि तथारूढोऽभिनिवेशः । सर्वस्य प्राणिन इयमात्माशीर्नित्या भवति मानभूवं भूयासमिति । न चाननुभूतमरणधर्मकस्यैषा भवत्यात्माशीः । एतया च पूर्वजन्मानुभवः प्रतीयते स चायमभिनिवेशः क्लेशः । स्वरसवाही कृमेरपि जातमात्रस्य प्रत्यक्षानुमानागमैरसंभावितो मरणत्रास उच्छेददृष्ट्यात्मकः पूर्वजन्मानुभूतं मरणदुःखमनुपयति । यथाचायमत्यन्तमूढेषु दृश्यते क्लेशस्तथा विदुषोऽपि विज्ञातपूर्वापरान्तस्य रूढः कस्मात् । समाना हि तयोः कुशलाकुशलयोर्मरणदुःखानुभवादियं वासना ।। ९ ।।

Vyāsa

In all living beings exists the self-benediction, 'would that I were never to cease. May I live on.' And this self-benediction cannot exist in him who has not experienced the nature of death. And by this the experience of a former life is inferred. This is the affliction of Love of Life, which flows by its own potency.

That even a worm just born should know the fear of death, which is the same as the knowledge of annihilation, and that this fear cannot be explained by perceptive, verbal and inferential knowledge, leads to the inference that the pain of death has been experienced in a former life. And as this affliction is found existing in the extremely ignorant, so also is it established even in the wise, who have come to know both the starting and finishing ends of life. Why? The residual potency having been brought about by an experience of the pain of death, is necessarily common to both of them, the knowing and the ignorant.—60.

Vācaspati's Gloss

Explains the meaning of the words, Love of Life (abhiniveśa). 'In all living beings, etc.' This self-benediction, this desire with reference to one's self is constant. 'Would that I were never to cease to be', *i.e.*, May I never become extinct. 'May I live on, *i.e.*, May I retain life.' And this self-benediction, this love of life, this fear of death is not possible in a living being who has not experienced his liabilities to die. The unbeliever denies the fact of a previous life. The author, therefore, takes the opportunity to refute him :—'And by this the experience of a former life, etc.' The experience of a former life is inferred, because the present body is being maintained. Birth means the coming into relationship with the experiences of a body, senses and mind which are new and which are specialized by a new coming together. Its experience means coming into contact therewith. That is inferred, How? Explains :—'This the love of life, etc.' Without completing the sentence says that is an affliction : 'this affliction.' It is this love of life which through evil deeds, etc., afflicts, *i.e.*, gives pain to living beings. It is, therefore, called an affliction. Finishes the sentence, 'which flows on, etc.'

The meaning is that it flows on by its own potency brought about by habituation, and is not external. Gives the reason, why it is not external even in the case of a worm which is just born, is full of pain and is of a very low type of intelligence. 'That even a worm just born, etc.' 'Can not be experienced' means cannot be caused. This is the meaning. A child just born begins to shake when he sees a death-dealing object. The knowledge of death is inferred by his peculiar trembling. It is thereby found that he is afraid. Fear is seen as being caused by pain or the cause of pain. He has not experienced death in this life. Neither has inferred or heard about it. The knowledge of the peculiar pain and of the particular cause thereof which is causing pain at any moment is therefore a previous possession of his. All other means of the knowledge being excluded, the only one that remains by the canon of residues, is memory. And this memory cannot exist without the residual potency of a former experience. And inasmuch as there is no experience in this birth, the experience of a former birth only remains as the cause proved to exist by the canon of residues. For this reason there was certainly contact with a former birth. The word 'even' necessitates a contact with something. Hence completes the meaning of the sentence by saying, 'And as, etc.'

The extremely ignorant are those whose intelligence is very low. Explains wisdom :—'Who have come to know both the starting and finishing ends of life.' The end means the point.

The world of experience is the first of the life of the Puruṣa. The final one is absolute freedom (kaivalya). The wise are so called because they have come to know of this by verbal and inferential knowledge.

The fear of death is then established in the worm on the one side and in the wise man on the other. The question arises that although the fear of death might well exist in an ignorant man, it is not proper that it should exist in the wise, inasmuch as in the latter's case it must have been uprooted by knowledge. And if it be said that it is not uprooted in this case, then the highest manifestation of the quality of essentiality (sattva) must be absent from him. With this object puts the question, 'Why?' Gives the answer. 'This residual potency, etc.... is common, etc.'

The meaning is that the wise man is not he who has reached the state of the Cognitive trance, but only he who can discriminate by inference and verbal knowledge.—9.

Sūtra 10

ते प्रतिप्रसवहेयाः सूक्ष्माः ।। १० ।।

ते Te, these. प्रति-प्रसव Prati-prasava, along with the passing out of activity. हेयाः Heyāḥ, that are destroyed. सूक्ष्माः Sūkṣmāḥ, (when but) potential.

10. These when but potential, are destroyed along with the passing out of activity.—61.

ते प्रतिप्रसवहेयाः सूक्ष्माः। ते पञ्च क्लेशा दग्धबीजकल्पा योगिनश्चरिताधिकारे चेतसि प्रलीने सह तेनैवास्तं गच्छन्ति ।। १० ।।

Vyāsa

These five afflictions, when their seed-power has, as it were, been burnt up, disappear of themselves along with that Yogī's mind, when having fulfilled the purpose of its existence, it becomes latent.—61.

Vācaspati's Gloss

The afflictions have been defined and they have been shown to be possessed of four states—the dormant, the tenuous, the alternated and the fully operative—all of which are to be destroyed. How is it that the author of the aphorism has not mentioned the fifth state of the afflictions, the potential, in which the seed-power is, as it were, burnt up ? For this reason says :—'They when but potential are destroyed along with the passing out of activity.' That which falls within the sphere of man's effort is of course taught. The destruction of the potential state is not within the sphere of man's effort. It is, on the contrary, to be destroyed by the passing out of activity; that is, by the mind passing back into its cause, the principle of egoism.

Explains :—'These five, etc.' This is easy.—10.

Sūtra 11

ध्यानहेयास्तद्वृत्तयः ।। ११ ।।

ध्यान Dhyāna, by meditation. हेयाः Heyāḥ, that are destroyed. तद् Tad, their. वृत्तयः Vṛttyaḥ, modification.

11. Their modifications are destroyed by meditation.—62.

स्थितानां तु बीजभावोपगतानाम्। ध्यानहेयास्तद्वृत्तयः। क्लेशानां या वृत्तयः स्थूलास्ताः क्रियायोगेन तनूकृताः सत्यः प्रसंख्यानेन ध्यानेन हातव्या यावत्सूक्ष्मीकृता यावद्दग्धबीजकल्पा इति। यथा च वस्त्राणां स्थूलो मलः पूर्वं निर्धूयते पश्चात्सूक्ष्मो यत्नेनोपायेन वा अपनीयते तथा स्वल्पप्रतिपक्षाः स्थूलावृत्तयः क्लेशानां सूक्ष्मास्तु महाप्रतिपक्षा इति।। ११ ।।

Vyāsa

When, however, they exist as retaining their seed-power, their modifications are destroyed by meditation. The modifications of the afflictions which are essential are attenuated by the Yoga of action; and having been so attenuated, are destroyed by the high intellection of meditation, so that they are rendered potential, *i.e.*, their seed-power is, as it were, burnt up. As the gross dirt of clothes is at first shaken off, and then the fine dirt is washed off by effort and appliance, so the gross essential modifications need but small antagonistic efforts, whereas the potential ones need very powerful antagonists.—62.

Vācaspati's Gloss

Well then, when the afflictions have been attenuated by the Yoga of action, to what sphere should the effort of the Puruṣa be directed, in order that they may be destroyed? For this reason says :—'When, however, they exist as retaining their seed-power, etc.

Differentiates them from the barren ones and reads the aphorism :—'Their modifications are destroyed by meditation.' Explains :—'The modifications of the afflictions, etc.' They are called essential, because even though attenuated by the Yoga of actions, they are further capable of destruction by being rendered incapable of producing effects and losing their very nature by means of the mind resolving back into its cause.

Mentions the limit of the effort of the Puruṣa in the sphere of intellection :—'So that they are rendered potential.'

Explains potentiality :—'Their seed-power has, as it were, been burnt up.' Gives an illustration of the same :—'As the gross dirt of clothes, etc.'

Effort means washing, etc. Appliance means the use of washing ingredients. The illustration and the illustrated are analogous only so far as they possess grosser and finer dirt, and not in their removability by effort, because it is impossible in the potential afflictions, which disappear along with the mind resolving back into its cause.

Those that require but little effort for their removal are said to need small antagonistic ingredients. Those that require the agency of very powerful causes for removal, are said to need very powerful antagonists. High intellection is described as small, because it is lower in comparison with the resolving the mind into its own cause.—11.

Sūtra 12

क्लेशमूलः कर्माशयो दृष्टादृष्टजन्मवेदनीयः ।। १२ ।।

क्लेश Kleśa, afflictions. मूल Mūla, origin. क्लेशमूलः Kleśamūlaḥ, Having its origin in afflictions. कर्म Karma, of actions. आशयः Āśayaḥ, the vehicle. दृष्ट Dṛṣṭa, visible. अदृष्ट Adṛṣṭa, invisible. जन्म Janma, in births. वेदनीयः Vedanīyaḥ, to be experienced.

12. The vehicle of actions has its origin in afflictions, and is experienced in visible and invisible births.—63.

क्लेशमूलः कर्माशयो दृष्टादृष्टजन्मवेदनीयः। तत्र पुण्यापुण्यकर्माशयः कामलोभमोहक्रोधप्रभवः। स दृष्ट जन्मवेदनीयश्चादृष्टजन्मवेदनीयश्च। तत्र तीव्रसंवेगेन मन्त्रतपः समाधिभिर्निर्वर्तित ईश्वरदेवतामहर्षिमहानुभावा-नामाराधनाद्वा यः परिनिष्पन्नः स सद्यः परिपच्यते पुण्यकर्माशय इति। यथा तीव्रक्लेशेन भीतव्याधितकृपणेषु विश्वासोपगतेषु वा महानुभावेषु वा तपस्विषु कृतः पुनः पुनरपकारः स चापि पापकर्माशयः सद्य एव परिपच्यते। यथा नन्दीश्वरः कुमारो मनुष्यपरिणामं हित्वा देवत्वेन परिणतः। तथा नहुषोऽपि देवानामिन्द्रः स्वकं परिणामं हित्वा तिर्यक्त्वेन परिणत इति। तत्र नारकाणां नास्ति दृष्टजन्मवेदनीयः कर्माशयः। क्षीणक्लेशानामपि नास्त्यदृष्टजन्मवेदनीयः कर्माशय इति।। १२।।

Vyāsa

The vehicle of actions has its origin in afflictions, and is experienced in visible and invisible births.

Here the vehicle of good and bad actions is born of lust, avarice, forgetfulness and anger. Its operation is felt in the visible as well as in the invisible birth. Of these, the vehicle of good actions, which is supplemented by intense energy in the shape of purificatory action, trance and repetition of *mantras,* or, which is accompanied by devotion to the Lord, the devas, the great seers and other possessors of great power, ripens into fruit at once. This happens in the same way in which, in the event of repeated evil done to men who are suffering the extreme misery of fear, disease and helplessness, or to those who place confidence in the evil-doer, or to those who are high-minded and perform *tapas,* the vehicle of evil-actions also ripens into fruit at once. As for example, the youth Nandīśvara passed out of the human form and was transformed into a god. As also Nahuṣa, the ruler of the gods, passed out of his own form and was transformed into an animal. Of the vehicles of action, that which culminates into the life of hell, is said to be experienced in the invisible birth.

As to those whose afflictions have been destroyed, the vehicle of actions is not experienced in the invisible births.—63.

Vācaspati's Gloss

Very well, what afflicts the Puruṣa by causing life-time, life-state and life-experience may be called an affliction. But it is the vehicle of actions that brings these about, not Nescience and the others. Why then are Nescience, etc., called afflictions ? For this reason says :—'The vehicle of actions has its origin in afflictions, and is experienced in visible and invisible births.' It is so called because the afflictions are the roots out of which it is born and which bring out its operation. The meaning is that inasmuch as the vehicle of action has its origin in Nescience, etc., and is for the reason the cause of life-state, life-time and life-experience, they are called afflictions. Explains :—'The vehicle of good and bad actions, etc.' That in which something lives is its vehicle. Here the Puruṣas in evolution are to be understood as living in the vehicle of actions (which is for the reason called a vehicle). Virtue and vice are the vehicles of actions. Virtue becomes the cause of the enjoyment of heaven, etc., when desirable actions are performed with desire. Similarly, vice manifests when such actions as the taking away of other people's property are performed through avarice. The vice for which forgetfulness is responsible is such as the taking of the life of others in the belief that it is a virtue.

The question arises that there is such a thing as virtue caused by forgetfulness and virtue caused by anger. An illustration may be taken from the fact of Dhruva having been given the highest position in the starry world on account of the pure vehicle of action, brought about by the desire to conquer his father, due to anger born of his ill-treatment. As to vice caused by anger, why that is well known, as it becomes the cause of people dealing death to Brāhmaṇas and others.

Says that it is of two descriptions :—'It is experienced either in the visible, etc.' Describes that which is experienced in the visible life :—'That which is brought about by, etc.' Gives illustrations, respectively :—'As the youth Nandīśvara, etc.'

'Of the vehicle of action which culminates in the life of hell :' The makers of the vehicle of action which takes to the hells known as *Kumbhīpāka,* etc., are spoken of as 'leading to the lifre of hell.' The vehicle of action formed thereby is not experienced in the visible life. It is not possible that by means of the human body which is the consequent form thereof, residua like that should be lived out, even by the constant suffering of thousands of years. The rest is easy.—12.

Sūtra 13

सति मूले तद्विपाको जात्यायुर्भोगाः ।। १३ ।।

सति Sati, if existing. मूले Mūle, be the root. तद् Tad, its. विपाकः Vipākaḥ, ripening. जाति Jāti, life-state. आयुः Āyuḥ, life-time. भोगाः Bhogāḥ, life-experience, all these three.

13. It ripens into life-state, life-experience and life-time, if the root exists.—64.

सति मूले तद्विपाको जात्यायुर्भोगाः। सत्सु क्लेशेषु कर्माशयो विपाकारम्भी भवति नोच्छिन्नक्लेशमूलः। यथा तुषावनाद्धाः शालितण्डुला अदग्धबीजभावाः प्ररोहसमर्था भवन्ति नापनीततुषा दग्धबीजभावा वा तथा

क्लेशावनद्धः कर्माशयो विपाकप्ररोही भवति नापनीतक्लेशो न प्रसंख्यानदग्धक्लेशबीजभावो वेति। स च विपाकस्त्रिविधो जातिरायुर्भोग इति। तत्रेदं विचार्यते। किमेकं कर्म एकस्य जन्मनः कारणमथैकं कर्मानेकं जन्माक्षिपतीति। द्वितीया विचारणा किमनेकं कर्मानेकं जन्म निर्वर्तयति अथानेकं कर्मैकं जन्म निर्वर्तयतीति। न तावदेकं कर्मैकस्य जन्मनः कारणम्। कस्मादनादिकाल प्रचितस्यासंख्येयस्यावशिष्टस्य कर्मणः सांप्रतिकस्य च फलक्रमानियमादनाश्वासो लोकस्य प्रसक्तः। स चानिष्ट इति। न चैकं कर्मानेकस्य जन्मनः कारणम्। कस्मादनेकेषु कर्मसु एकैकमेव कर्मानेकस्य जन्मनः कारणमित्यवशिष्टस्य विपाककालाभावः प्रसक्तः स चाप्यनिष्ट इति। न चानेकं कर्मानेकस्य जन्मनः कारणं कस्मात्तदनेकं जन्म युगपन्न संभवतीति क्रमेणैव वाच्यम्। तथा च पूर्वदोषानुषङ्गः। तस्माज्जन्मप्रायणान्तरे कृतः पुण्यापुण्यकर्माशयप्रचयो विचित्रः प्रधानोपसर्जनभावेनावस्थितः प्रायेणाभिव्यक्त एकप्रघट्टकेन मरणं प्रसाध्य संमूर्छित एकमेव जन्म करोति तच्च जन्मतेनैव कर्मणा लब्धायुष्कं भवति। तस्मिन्नायुषि तेनैव कर्मणा भोगः संपद्यत इति। असौ कर्माशयो जन्मायुर्भोग हेतुत्वाच्च त्रिविपाकोऽभिधीयत इति। अत एकभविकः कर्माशय उक्त इति। दृष्टजन्मवेदनीयस्त्वेक-विपाकारम्भी भोगहेतुत्वाद्द्विविपाकारम्भी वा जन्मभोगायुर्हेतुत्वान्नन्दीश्वरवन्नहुषवद्वेति। क्लेशकर्मविपाकानुभव-निर्वर्तिताभिस्तु वासनाभिरनादिकालसंमूर्छितमिदं चित्तं विचित्रीकृतमिव सर्वतो मत्स्यजालं ग्रन्थिभिरिवाततमित्येता अनेकभवपूर्विका वासनाः। यस्त्वयं कर्माशय एष एवैकभविक उक्त इति। ये संस्काराः स्मृतिहेतवो वासनास्ताश्चानादिकालीना इति। यस्त्वसावेकभविककर्माशयः स नियतविपाकश्चानियतविपाकश्च। तत्र दृष्टजन्मवेदनीयस्य नियतविपाकस्यैवायं नियमो नत्वदृष्टजन्मवेदनीयस्यानियतविपाकस्यैव। कस्मात्। यो ह्यदृष्टजन्मवेदनीयोऽनियतविपाकस्तस्य त्रयी गतिः। कृतस्याविपाकस्य विनाशः प्रधानकर्मण्यावापगमनं वा नियतविपाकप्रधानकर्मणाभिभूतस्य वा चिरमवस्थानमिति। तत्र कृतस्याविपाककस्य नाशो यथा शुक्लकर्मोदयादिहैव नाशः कृष्णस्य। यत्रेदमुक्तम्। द्वे द्वे ह वै कर्मणी वेदितव्ये पापकस्यैको राशिः पुण्यकृतोऽपहन्ति तदिच्छस्व कर्माणि सुकृतानि कर्तुमिहैव ते कर्म कवयो वेदयन्ते। प्रधानकर्मण्यावापगमनम्। यत्रेदमुक्तं स्यात्स्वल्पः सङ्करः सपरिहारः सप्रत्यवमर्शः कुशलस्य नापकर्षायालम्। कस्मात्कुशलं हि मे बह्वन्यदस्ति यत्रायमावापं गतः स्वर्गेऽप्यपकर्षं करिष्यतीति नियतविपाकप्रधानकर्मणाभिभूतस्य वा चिरमवस्थानं कथमित्यदृष्टजन्मवेदनीयस्यैव नियतविपाकस्य कर्मणः समानं मरणमभिव्यक्तिकारणमुक्तम्। नत्वदृष्टजन्म-वेदनीयस्यानियतविपाकस्य वा। यत्त्वदृष्टजन्मवेदनीयं कर्मानियतविपाकं तन्नश्येदावापं वा गच्छेदभिभूतं वा चिरमप्युपासीत। यावत्समानं कर्माभिव्यञ्जकं निमित्तमस्य न विपाकाभिमुखं करोतीति। तद्विपाकस्यैव देशकालनिमित्तानवधारणादियं कर्मगतिश्चित्रा दुर्विज्ञाना चेति। न चोत्सर्गस्यापवादान्निवृत्ति- रित्येकभविकः कर्माशयोऽनुज्ञायत इति।। १३।।

Vyāsa

The vehicle of actions begins to ripen into fruit when the afflictions exist; not when the afflictions have been rooted out. As the rice in the paddy has the power to grow only so long as the chaff remains attached thereto and their seed-power is not burnt up, not when the chaff has been removed; so also does the vehicle of actions grow into ripeness, when the afflictions are attached to it, and when is seed-power has not been burnt up by intellection; not when the afflictions have been removed.

The fruition is of three descriptions, life-state, life-time and life-experience. The following has to be considered in this connection. Is one action the cause of one life? Or, does it bring about more lives than one? The second question is this. Do more actions than one bring about more lives than one; or do they bring about one life only?

It is not that one action only is the cause of one life only. Why? Because in that case there would be no regularity of succession in the fruition of present actions and those that are being heaped up eternally and some of which still remain unconsumed; and thus the world would lose all patience. This, however, is not the desired end.

Nor is one action the cause of more lives than one. Why? There being more actions than one, it would necessarily follow that one action requiring more lives than one for fruition, there would remain no time for the fruition of the remainder. That also is not a desirable end.

Nor again are more actions than one, the cause of more lives than one. Why? It is impossible that all of them should exist at once, and it must, therefore, be said that if such a thing be possible it can only be is succession that so many lives can manifest. And in this latter case the defect already stated is apparent.

For this reason, the vehicle of the entire collection of good and bad actions done in the interval between birth and death, stands in all its variety with every action attached to one ruling factor of one life. This is brought into manifestation by death, is joined together by one link which at the time brings about death and thus causes but one life.

The period of this life is limited by this very action. During the life-period all experience is also caused by that very action alone. This vehicle of actions is said to possess a three-fold fruition, causing as it does the manifestation of life-state, life-period and life-experience.

For this reason the vehicle of actions is termed uni-genital (Ekabhāvika), causing one birth only.

That, however, which is experienced in the visible life only, may bring about but a single fruition, as causing life-experience; or, double fruition as causing life-experience and life-period; or, a triple fruition as causing life-experience, life-period and life-state. It may be like Nandīśvara or like Nahuṣa.

This mind, however, is as it were, variously coloured, all through on account of its becoming pervaded from eternity by the residua of the experiences of afflictions, actions and fruitions; and as such looks like a fishing net pervaded all over with knots. These, therefore, must have been brought about by more (previous) lives than one.

It is this vehicle of actions which has been termed *uni-genital* (Ekabhāvika), causing one birth only; and the potencies which as residua cause memory, exist from eternity.

Further the *uni-genital* (Ekabhāvika) vehicle of actions is either of appointed or of unappointed fruition. The rule applies to that portion only which has to be experienced in the visible life and whose fruition has been appointed. It does not apply to that which has to be experienced in an invisible life and whose fruition has not been appointed.

Why? Because, that which has to be experienced in an invisible life and whose fruition has not been appointed, has a three-fold end. It may be destroyed without fruition. It may become merged in the ruling action. It may live on for a long time overpowered by the ruling action whose fruition has been appointed.

Of these, the destruction of an action done takes place without fruition in this way that the black actions are destroyed by the rise of the white actions. The following has been said on this subject :—

'Two and two the actions, know,
'Of him that evil does
One heap of virtue kills;
To do good actions therefore tend;
The wise such actions tell.'

As to emergence in the ruling action, the following has been said on the subject :— 'A little mixture of evil may be easily removed or borne; it cannot do away with the good.' Why? 'There is much of the good for me, mixed wherewith it may cause some insignificant diminution even in heaven.'

And now how may it live on for a long time, overpowered by the ruling action whose fruition has been appointed? Death is said to be the cause of the simultaneous appearance of the actions whose fruition has been appointed and which are to be experienced in the invisible birth, not that of the actions which although to be experienced in the invisible birth, yet whose fruition has not been appointed. The actions whose fruition has not been determined upon, may either be destroyed or get mixed up, or stand unfructified for a long time, overpowered so long as similar actions competent to bring the cause of manifestation into play, do not incline it towards fruition. It is because the time, the place and the cause of manifestation are not determined that the working of karma is variegated and difficult to know. Inasmuch as the rule is not abolished by the exception, the vehicle of actions is recognized as causing one birth only.—64.

Vācaspati's Gloss

Let it be so, seeing that the vehicle of actions has its origin in Nescience. Let it also be granted that on the destruction of Nescience being brought about by the birth of knowledge, there should not come into existence another vehicle of actions. But the old vehicles of action which have been laid by in an eternal succession of innumerable lives, and the times of whose fruition have not been appointed, are impossible to finish off by experience and thus the chain of repeated births becomes interminable. For this reason he says :—'It ripens into life-state, life-experience and life-period if the root exists.' The meaning is this. The vehicle of actions fructifies into pleasure and pain only. Life-sate and life-period also are meant to fulfil that object and not to put in an obstacle thereto. Pleasure and pain follow in the wake of attachment and aversion, never exist in separation from them and cannot exist without them. And it is not possible that if any one is attached or averse to anything, he will not feel pleasure and pain respectively in contact with that thing. For this reason the mental plane becomes a field for the production of the fruit of actions only when it is watered by the stream of the afflictions. Hence the afflictions help the vehicle of actions in the production of their fruits also. It is for this reason that when the afflictions are destroyed, the power which helps to bring about the manifestation also disappears; and on that account, the vehicle of actions although existing, being innumerable and having no time for its fruition appointed, does not possess the power of producing fruit, because its seed-power has been destroyed by high intellection.

The Commentary makes the same subject clear :—'The vehicle of actions begins to ripen when the afflictions exist.' Illustrates the same :—'As the rice in the paddy, etc.' even though covered by the chaff, their seed-power should not have been burnt up by heat, etc., before they can sprout. Applies the illustration to the illustrated :—'So also, etc.'

The question arises that the afflictions can never be destroyed, because nothing that exists can be destroyed. For this reason says :—'And not when the seed-power has been burnt up by intellection.'

Mentions three descriptions of fruition :—'This fruition is, etc.' Fruit is that into which the actions ripen.

The first discussion relates to the unity or multiplicity of lives as the result of a single action taken as the starting point. The second discussion refers to the unity or multiplicity of lives caused by more actions than one taken as the starting point. Thus there are four options. Refutes the first of these options :—'One actions is not the cause of one life.' Question :—'Why ?' The answer is this. Actions have been laid by from eternity in each life. They are for this very reason innumerable. If a single life exhausts one action only, many a one remains unexhausted. To this are to be added the actions of the present life. There will thus be no rule for the successive fruition of actions. As a necessary result there will be no comfort for the world, and this is not desirable. The meaning is that when the actions that are exhausted are only isolated ones, and those that are being born are many, the vehicles of action will run into each other in confusion. They will keep being constantly born in uninterrupted succession, but there being no law for their fruition, there will be no comfort for men. It will be impossible for intelligent people to determine the order of their fruition, and thus there will be no satisfaction in the performance of virtuous actions.

He refutes the second alternative :—'Nor is one the cause of more lives than one.' Question :—'Why?' The answer is this :—If one action out of those that have been laid by in many lives, becomes the cause of bringing about many lives, then the actions that remain unexhausted will be many more, and the result will be that there will be no time available for their fruition. That also is useless, because the performance of actions having thus become useless, no one will attend to them. When on account of there being no rule for the succession of fruition, satisfaction disappears in case of one action only being considered exhaustible in one life, what mention is to be made of the option in which one action is considered as exhaustible in more lives than one. In this case there will be no opportunity and no time available for the fruition of any present actions that may be done.

He refutes the third alternative :—'Nor again are more actions than one the cause of more lives than one.' He gives the reason thereof. These many lives cannot be lived all at once in the case of one who is not a Yogī. It must, therefore, be said that such a thing is possible only in succession, if at all. It is only if a thousand lives were simultaneously caused by a thousand actions, that the thousand actions becoming thus exhausted, time would become available for the fruition of the remaining ones, and a law for the succession of fruition becomes possible. But more lives than one cannot be possible all at once. The same defect, therefore, that was found in the first alternative becomes apparent here also.

Three alternatives having thus been refuted, the only one that remains available by the canon of residues, is the last :—'More actions than one are the cause of one life.' For this reason he says :—'The vehicle, etc.'

'The interval between birth and death' is the period of life which falls between the two events, birth and death on either side.

'In all its variety' means variegated by the presentation of the fruits of actions in the shape of pleasure and pain.

The ruling factor of life is that which is in evidence above all and which fructifies in immediate succession.

'The action merged into' is that which fructifies sometime along with it. Death means passing beyond the present life. It is by that, that the vehicle of actions is brought into manifestation. This means that it is inclined towards the bringing about of its effects.

'Is joined together by one link' :—Is brought into the state of one active force, working towards the bringing about of its effects in the shape of birth, etc. It thus causes one birth only, not more than one. This birth is as man, etc. The period of each such life is determined by that very karma. Each life has its appointed limit, with difference in time. During that life-period the enjoyment of pleasure and pain is brought about by that very karma, being as it is related thereto. For this reason the vehicle of actions is said to cause three fruitions, causing as it does life-state, life-period and life-experience. The author summarizes the general rule :—'For this reason the vehicle of actions is termed uni-natāl' or unigenetal (ekabhāvika). The meaning is that its manifestation is limited to one birth only.

Having thus described the three-fold fruition of the one-birth vehicle as being the general rule, he now differentiates the three-fold fruition of the present karma, the one that is experienced in the visible life :—'That, however, which is experienced in the visible life only, etc.' In the case of Nandīśvara, whose human life was broken off at the age of eight, the special virtue which on account of high energy and intense application, became the cause thereof, resulted in the double fruition of life-state and life-experience. In the case of Nahuṣa, however, the period of life being already determined by the karma which determined his attainment of the position of Indra, his antagonistic action of kicking Agastya, resulted only in his experience of the result of the vice.

The question arises, Have the residua of afflictions and the residua brought about by the experiences of the fruitions of actions causing similar enjoyments, their fruition in one life only, just as the one-birth vehicle of actions has ? For if it be so, a man passing into the animal state of life would not have the experiences which are suited to that state of life alone. For this reason he says :—'The mind however, is as it were variously coloured, etc.'

'Pervaded from eternity' means unified into a single manifestation of energy.

Now he describes the nature of residua in order to differentiate virtue from vice. And the potencies which as residua, etc.

The author introduces now the discussion of occasional exceptions to the general rule of the vehicle of actions causing one-birth only. 'The vehicle of actions, however, etc.' The word 'however' differentiates it from the residual potencies. The rule of causing one birth only applies only to the vehicle whose fruition is to be experienced in the visible life only, and whose fruition has been appointed. It does not apply to that which has to be experienced in an invisible life, and whose fruition has not yet been appointed. He asks the reason therefore :—

'Why ?' and mention the reason :—'Because that which has to be experienced, etc.'

The author mentions now one of the three ends :—'It may be destroyed without fruition.' Mentions the second :—'It may be merged in, etc.' Mentions the third :—'It may live on for a very long time, etc."

Of these, he divides the first :—'Of these the destruction of an action done without fruition, etc.'

There are only three kinds of actions, the white, the black and the white-black, besides the actions of a Sannyāsī, which are neither whiten or black. Now here the white vehicle of actions brought about by purificatory action and study, etc., becomes, as soon as it arises, the destroyer of the black one, which has not begun to fructify.

It should also be understood that it destroys the white-black one too, there being similarity on account of the presence of the black one in that. His reverence quotes the Veda on this very subject :—'The following has been said, etc.' 'Two and two the actions, etc.'

The two and two actions are the white and the white-black. This is related to the verb 'kills.' The word 'two' is used twice to indicate manifoldness. Of whom are these two-fold actions ? Of the man who does the evil. What is that which kills? The answer is :—'The heap of the good actions of him who does good deeds.' He speaks of a heap because a heap can be managed by a heap only. This makes out the white vehicle of actions to be the third one. The meaning is that the white vehicle of actions which is brought into being by the performance of such actions as avoid causing pain to others, is of such a nature that although one, it destroys the contrary vehicles of black and white-black actions, although they may be many. For this reason they tend, *i.e.*, incline towards good actions, such as the wise men teach. Here it is a very high class virtue, this rise of white actions, that destroys others.

It is not by the pain consequent upon study, etc., that they are destroyed. It is not pain *qua* pain that is contrary to vice. It is contrary to that pain only which is brought about by vice itself. The pain which accompanies study, etc., is not brought about by vice. If it were so, the ordinances of study, etc., would be useless, because in that case vice would be born out of the very strength of the study, etc., ordained. Further the pain which accompanies study, etc., is not caused by them. If it were caused by them, the recommendation of study, etc., would become useless, because the more intense the application to study, etc., the more would thus be the pain caused thereby. If no pain be caused by the application to study, etc., thus recommended, why then the hellish states of Kumbhīpāka, etc., may also be recommended as desirable, because in that case it would appear to be only on account of their not being recommended as desirable that pain would not be produced. Everything, therefore, runs into all four corners (*i.e.*, nothing is well established in its own right place and is therefore absurd).

The author divides now the second end (of actions) :—In the ruling action such as the sacrifice of Jyotiṣṭoma, etc., its minor actions such as the killing of animals, etc., are merged as parts in the whole.

The killing of animals, etc., has two effects. The first is that being ordained as part of the principal action, it helps in its fulfilment. The second is that the causing of pain to all living beings being forbidden, it results in undesirable consequences. Of these when it is performed only as subsidiary to the principal action, then, for that very reason, it does not manifest its result all at once independently of the principal action. On the contrary it keeps its position of an accessory only and manifests only when the fruition of the principal ruling action begins. It is said to be tacked on to the ruling action, when, while helping the ruling action, it exists only as the seed of its own proper effect. Pañcaśikhā has said the following on the subject :—'A little mixture.'

When the ruling factor of the present karma born from the sacrifice of Jyotiṣṭoma, etc., is mixed up with the present cause of evil, it may be easily removed. It is possible of removal by a small expiatory sacrifice. Even if an expiatory sacrifice be not performed by carelessness, the subsidiary action would ripen at the time of the ripening of the principal only, and in that case the evil generated thereby would be easy to bear. The wise who are taking their baths in the great lake of the nectar of pleasure brought about by a collection of good actions, put up easily with a small piece of the fire of pain produced by a small evil. It is not, therefore, capable of diminishing, *i.e.*, appreciably lessening the effect, of the good, *i.e.*, of his large virtues.

He puts the question :—'Why?' The answer is put into the mouth of the virtuous man :—'There is much other good for me,' which stands apart as a consequence of the fruition of the principal factor of action beginning with the taking of the vow of sacrifice and ending with the distribution of charities. With that there will be a little of the admixture of evil. Even in heaven which is considered as free from all pain, the enjoyment is the result of virtue mixed up with a little of vice and there will, therefore, be a somewhat inappreciable diminution of enjoyment only.

He divides the third alternative :—'How may it optionally live on, etc.' The ruling action here means the most powerful one, not the whole consisting of many parts. 'The most powerful' is that whose fruition has been appointed with regard to time, because there remains no other opportunity for its fruition. That whose fruition has not been appointed is considered weak, inasmuch as there is opportunity for its fruition at other times. 'Living on for a very long time' is in the seed state only, not as helper of the principal action, that being independent.

The question arises. It has been said that the vehicle of actions manifests at once at the time of death. It is now said that it lives on for a very long time overpowered. How is it that the former is not contrary to the latter? With this object he puts the question :—'How may it, etc.' The answer is :—'Death is said to be the cause of the simultaneous appearance, etc.' The singular denotes the class.

Now he lays down that what has been said applies to the other as well. 'Not that of the action, etc.' The rest is easy.—13.

Sūtra 14

ते ह्लादपरितापफलाः पुण्यापुण्यहेतुत्वात् ।। १४ ।।

ते Te, they. ह्लाद Hlāda, pleasure. परिताप Paritāpa, pain. फलाः Phalāḥ, fruits. ह्लाद-परिताप-फलाः Hlādaparitāpaphalāḥ, Having pleasure and pain as fruits. पुण्य Puṇya, virtue. अपुण्य Apuṇya, vice. हेतु Hetu, reason. पुण्यापुण्यहेतुत्वात् Puṇyāpuṇyahetutvāt, Because virtue and vice are their causes.

14. They have pleasure or pain as the fruit, by reason of virtue or vice.—65.

ते ह्लादपरितापफलाः पुण्यापुण्यहेतुत्वात् । ते जन्मायुर्भोगाः पुण्यहेतुकाः सुखफला अपुण्यहेतुका दुःखफला इति । यथा चेदं दुःखं प्रतिकूलात्मकमेवं विषयसुखकालेऽपि दुःखमस्त्येव प्रतिकूलात्मकं योगिनः ।। १४ ।।

Vyāsa

They, *i.e.*, life-state, life-period and life-experience, have pleasure for their fruit, when caused by virtue, and have pain for their fruit when caused by vice.

As pain consists in what is contrary to the prevalent mental tendencies at a time, there must be pain to the Yogī's mind even at the time of the enjoyment of pleasurable objects.—65.

Vācaspati's Gloss

It has been said that karma has its origin in afflictions. It has also been said that the fruitions have their origin in actions (karma). Now the question is of what are the fruitions the origin, so that they too have to be given up? For this reason he says :—'They have pleasure or pain as their fruit, by reason of virtue and vice.' Explains :—'They, *i.e.*, life-state, etc.'

Although life-state and life-period only have pleasure and pain as their fruit, inasmuch as those come before these, and not so life-experience, inasmuch as that comes after pleasure and pain have arisen, and inasmuch as it consists in the very experience thereof, yet that too is spoken of as the fruit of enjoyment, because being perceivable and enjoyable, it is an object of the action of enjoyment.

The question arises that although the life-state, life-experience and life-period caused by vice and causing pain may well be regarded as removable, being found to be contrary, why should those be given up which have been caused by virtue and cause pleasure? They are seen to be moving along the proper line. It is impossible that even a thousand inferences and so-called authoritative statements should do away with the fact of their moving along the line of every individual mind. Nor are pleasure and pain possible of existence the one without the other, inasmuch as when pleasure is taken up, pain too is there as not to be given up, as they have different causes and different appearances. For this reason he says :—'And as this pain, etc.'—14.

Sūtra 15

परिणामतापसंस्कारदुःखैर्गुणवृत्तिविरोधाच्च दुःखमेव सर्वं विवेकिनः ।। १५ ।।

परिणाम Pariṇāma, of change. ताप Tāpa, anxiety. संस्कार Saṁskāra, habituation. दुःखैः Duḥkhaiḥ, by reason of the pains. गुण Guṇa, of the qualities. वृत्तिः Vṛttiḥ, of the functionings. विरोधात् Virodhāt, by reason of the contrariety. च Ca, and. दुःखम् Duḥkham, pain. एव Eva, indeed. सर्वम् Sarvam, all. विवेकिनः Vivekinaḥ, to the discriminating.

15. By reason of the pains of change, anxiety and habituation and by reason of the contrariety of the fuctionings of the 'qualities,' all indeed is pain to the discriminating.—66.

कथं तदुपपद्यते। परिणामतापसंस्कारदुःखैर्गुणवृत्तिविरोधाच्च दुःखमेव सर्वं विवेकिनः। सर्वस्यायं रागानुविद्धश्चेतनाचेतनसाधनाधीनः सुखानुभव इति। तत्रास्ति रागजः कर्माशयस्तथा च द्वेष्टि दुःखसाधनानि मुह्यति चेति। द्वेषमोहकृतोऽप्यस्ति कर्माशयः। तथाचोक्तम्। नानुपहत्य भूतान्युपभोगः संभवतीति। हिंसाकृतोऽप्यस्ति शारीरः कर्माशय इति। विषयसुखं चाविद्येत्युक्तम्। या भोगेष्विन्द्रियाणां तृप्तेरुपशान्ति-स्तत्सुखम् या लौल्यादनुपशान्तिस्तद्दुःखम्। न चेन्द्रियाणां भोगाभ्यासेन वैतृष्ण्यं कर्त्तुंशक्यम्। कस्माद्यतो भोगाभ्यासमनुविवर्धन्ते रागाः कौशलानि चेन्द्रियाणामिति। तस्मादनुपायः सुखस्य भोगाभ्यास इति। स खल्वयं वृश्चिकविषभीत इवाशीविषेण दष्टो यः सुखार्थी विषयानुवासितो महति दुःखपङ्के निमग्न इति। एषा परिणामदुःखता नाम प्रतिकूला सुखावस्थायामपि योगिनमेव क्लिश्नाति। अथ का तापदुःखता सर्वस्य द्वेषानुविद्धश्चेतनाचेतनसाधनाधीनस्तापानुभव इति। तत्रास्ति द्वेषजः कर्माशयः सुखसाधनानि च प्रार्थयमानः कायेन वाचा मनसा च परिस्पन्दते ततः परमनुगृह्णात्युपहन्ति चेति परानुग्रहपीडाभ्यां धर्माधर्मावुपचिनोति स कर्माशया लाभान्मोहाच्च भवतीत्येषा परितापदुःखतोच्यते। का पुनः संस्कारदुःखता सुखानुभवात्सुखसंस्काराशयो दुःखानुभवादपि दुःखसंस्काराशय इति। एवं कर्मभ्यो विपाकेऽनुभूयमाने सुखे दुःखे वा पुनः कर्माशयप्रचय इति। एवमिदमनादिदुःखस्रोतो विप्रसृतं योगिनमेव प्रतिकूलात्मकत्वादुद्वेजयति। कस्मादक्षिपात्रकल्पो हि विद्वानिति। यथोर्णातन्तुरक्षिपात्रे न्यस्तः स्पर्शेन दुःखयति न चान्येषु गात्रावयवेषु। एवमेतानि दुःखान्यक्षिपात्रकल्पं योगिनमेव क्लिश्नन्ति नेतरं प्रतिपत्तारम्। इतरं तु स्वकर्मोपहृतं दुःखमुपात्तमुपात्तं त्यजन्तं त्यक्तं त्यक्तमुपाददानमनादिवासनाविचित्रया चित्तवृत्तया समन्ततोऽनुविद्धमिवाविद्यया हातव्य एवाहङ्कारममकारानु-पातिनं जातं जातं बाह्याध्यात्मिकोभयनिमित्तास्त्रिपर्वाणस्तापा अनुप्लवन्ते। तदेवमनादिना दुःखस्रोतसा व्यूह्यमानमात्मानं भूतग्रामं च दृष्ट्वा योगी सर्वदुःखक्षयकारणं सम्यग्दर्शनं शरणं प्रपद्यत इति गुणवृत्तिविरोधाच्च दुःखमेव सर्वं विवेकिनः। प्रख्या प्रवृत्तिस्थितिरूपा बुद्धिगुणाः परस्परानुग्रहतंत्रीभूत्वा शान्तं घोरं मूढं वा प्रत्ययं त्रिगुणमेवारभन्ते। चलं च गुणवृत्तमिति क्षिप्रपरिणामि चित्तमुक्तम्। रूपातिशया वृत्त्यतिशयाश्च परस्परेण विरुध्यन्ते सामान्यानि त्वतिशयैः सह प्रवर्तन्ते। एवमेते गुणा इतरेतराश्रयेणोपार्जितसुखदुःखमोहप्रत्ययाः सर्वे सर्वरूपा भवन्तीति गुणप्रधानभावकृतस्त्वेषां विशेष इति। तस्माद्दुःखमेव सर्वं विवेकिन इति तदस्य महतो दुःखसमुदायस्य प्रभवबीजमविद्या। तस्याश्च सम्यग्दर्शनमभावहेतुः। यथा चिकित्साशास्त्रं चतुर्व्यूहम। रो·गो

रोगहेतुरारोग्यं भैषज्यमिति। एवमिदमपि शास्त्रं चतुर्व्यूहमेव। तद्यथा संसारः संसारहेतुर्मोक्षो मोक्षोपाय एवेति। तत्र दुःखबहुलः संसारो हेयः। प्रधानपुरुषयोः संयोगो हेयहेतुः। संयोगस्यात्यन्तिकी निवृत्तिर्हानम्। हानोपायः सम्यग्दर्शनम्। तत्र हातुः स्वरूपमुपादेयं वा हेयं वा न भवितुमर्हतीति। हाने तस्योच्छेदवादप्रसङ्गः। उपादाने च हेतुवादः। उभयप्रत्याख्याने शाश्वतवाद इत्येतत्सम्यग्दर्शनम्। तदेतच्छास्त्रं चतुर्व्यूहमित्यभिधीयते।। १५।।

Vyāsa

How is that possible ? 'By reason of the pains, etc.' The feeling of pleasure depending upon the enjoyment of intelligent and non-intelligent objects, is in the case of every one followed by attachment. Here the vehicle of actions is born out of attachment. Further inasmuch as there is aversion to the causes of pain and also delusion, there exists also the vehicle of actions brought about by aversion and delusion. And so it has been said :— 'Enjoyment is not possible without giving pain to beings.' There is also the physical vehicle of actions caused by giving pain to others.

It has been said that the pleasure of enjoyment is Nescience. The calming down of the powers of action, sensation and thought, which comes in consequence of the satisfaction derived from enjoyment of their objects, is pleasure. The activity in consequence of want of satisfaction is pain.

Further, it is not possible to make the powers of action, etc., free from desire by the frequent repetition of enjoyments, because attachment increases in consequence of the repetition of enjoyments, and so also does the dexterity of the powers. The repetition of enjoyment is, therefore, no cause of pleasure. Whoever desiring pleasure enjoys certain objects and thus becomes addicted to them, in consequence, and having become addicted thus becomes entangled in the morass of pain, is like one who being afraid of the bite of a scorpion, is bitten by a serpent.

This is the pain of change. In the state of pleasure even, it produces a contrary effect and thus afflicts a Yogī alone.

Well, what is the painfulness of anxiety? The feeling of pain in depending upon intelligent and non-intelligent objects is in the case of every one followed by aversion. Here the vehicle of action is born out of aversion. Whoever desires objects of pleasure, acts with his mind, body and speech and thereby favours some and disfavours others. He thus lays by virtue and vice by favours and disfavours shown to others. This is a vehicle of actions brought about by avarice and delusion. This is termed the painfulness of consequent suffering (tāpa).

What again is the painfulness of habituation ? By the enjoyment of pleasure comes into being the vehicle of the potency of pleasure. By the feeling of pain comes the vehicle of the potency of pain. By thus experiencing the fruition of actions in the shape of pleasures and pains, the vehicle of actions grows.

This is the eternal stream of painfulness which thus flowing on frightens the Yogī alone. Why the Yogī alone? Because the wise have in this case a similarity to the eye-ball. As a thread of wool thrown into the eye pains by mere touch, but not so by coming into contact with any other organ, so do these pains afflict the Yogī tender as the eye-ball, but not anyone else whom they reach.

As to others, however, who give up the pain they have again and again taken up as the consequence of their own karma, and who again take it up after having repeatedly given it up; who are all round as it were pierced through by Nescience, possessed as they are of a mind full of afflictions, variegated by eternal residua; who follow in the wake of the 'I' and the 'Mine', in relation to things that should be left apart,—the three-fold pain caused by both external and internal means, run after them as they are repeatedly born. The Yogī then seeing himself and the world of living beings thus surrounded by the eternal flow of pain, turns for refuge to right knowledge, the cause of the destruction of all pains.

Further, by reason of the contrariety of the functionings of the qualities, 'all is indeed pain to the discriminating'. The qualities of the Will-to-know being of the nature of essentiality, activity and inactivity, become dependent upon mutual help, and set the formation of either a quiescent, a disturbed or a delusive notion possessed of the three qualities themselves. And the functioning of the qualities being changeful, the mind is said to possess the nature of changing quickly. The intensities of their natures and the intensities of their functionings are contradictory to one another. The ordinary, however, function together with the intense. Thus do these qualities bring about the notions of pleasure, pain and delusion by each subserving the others, and all thus enter into the formations of the others. It is by the quality which is the leading factor, that the difference is introduced. It is for this reason that all is pain to the discriminating.

The seed out of which this large heap of pains grows is Nescience, and of that the means of destruction is right knowledge.

As the Science of Medicine has four Departments, Disease, the Cause of Disease, the Absence of Disease, and Medicine or the Means of Removal, so also this Science has four Departments. It is thus divided : the Universe in Evolution, the Cause of the Universe in Evolution, Liberation, the Means of Liberation. Of these, the Universe in Evolution being full of troubles is the pain to be avoided; the conjunction of the Puruṣa (the conscious principle) and the Prakṛti is the cause of pain; the final cessation of the conjunction is the removal of pain. Right knowledge is the cause of the removal of the pain. Here the individuality of the remover is not to be considered the pain to be avoided; nor is to be considered as an object of desire to be aimed at. In the case of avoidability, the theory of their destructibility would come in. In the case of its being considered an object of desire to be aimed at, the theory of its being the effect of some preceding cause would come in. When both these positions have been given up, the theory of eternal immutability only remains. This is the Right knowledge.

Thus is the Science said to possess four Departments.—66.

Vācaspati's Gloss

The author introduces the aphorism by putting a question with the object of explaining in the sequence, that although ordinary people do not at the time of feeling pleasure, have the sense of its contrariety to the mind, and do not, therefore, feel the pain thereof, the Yogī has the sense of pain therein :—'How is that possible?' 'By means, etc.' This is the aphorism. The consequential change, the suffering (tāpa) and the habituation are themselves pains. It is by means of these, etc.

He describes the painfulness of an object on account of the painfulness of sequential change :— 'This feeling of pleasure....in the case of every one, etc.' It is plain that pleasure is not possible without the consequent bond of attachment. Where there is no co-existence there is no pleasure. It is in that that the feeling of pleasure consists. Attachment causes activity. Activity is responsible for the heaping up of virtues and vices. Of these consists the vehicle of actions born out of attachments, because nothing that does not exist cannot be born. He who enjoys pleasure and is at the time even devoted to it, goes on at the same time hating the causes of pain, by means of the mental modifications of aversion which exists distinct and independent. When one becomes incapable of removing the causes of pain, he becomes deluded forgetting as he does the true nature of things. Thus a vehicle of actions is brought into being by aversion also, and like aversion by delusion also. This is but another name of Unreal Cognition. There is, therefore, nothing contradictory in its being the cause of the vehicle of action coming into existence.

The question arises : How can one who is attached, be at the same time averse and deluded? Aversion and delusion are not seen at the time of attachment. For this reason he says :—'And so it has been said :' by us when speaking of the characteristic of alternation in the afflictions. The virtue and vice which have their origin in the activity of speech and mind have both been described by what has been said so far, because the incident of their being born out of attachment etc., is common to both, inasmuch as there is no difference in this matter between a mental and verbal expression of desire. As they say :—'The mental modification of desire differs not from its verbal expression.'

Now he shows that there is a physical vehicle of actions also :—'Enjoyment is not possible without giving pain to others.' It is for this reason that the writers of the Dharmaśāstras speak of the five sins of householders.

It may be so. But it is not proper that the pleasure derived from an object of enjoyment should be denied on account of this contrariety to the feeling of Yogīs. For this reason he says :—'It has been said that the pleasure of enjoyment is Nescience,' when describing Nescience as consisting of the four-fold unreality of cognition. The elders do not look with favour upon mere consequential conditions. There is, of course, no feeling of pleasure caused to anyone by the enjoyment of honey mixed up with poison, even though he may use it. On the contrary, there is a feeling of pain in the sequence. So also has it been said by the Lord :—'The pleasure which is felt by the contact of the senses with their objects, that which is like nectar in the beginning and like poison in the end is *Rājasic* pleasure.'—(Gītā).

He introduces this :—'The calming down, etc.' We do not hold that pleasure consists in the enjoyment of an object. On the contrary, the greatest pain of man consists in the desire for objects, of men, who being satisfied by objects are pained by the wish to possess them. This does not calm down without the enjoyment of the object. Further, its calming down does not come about, being followed as it is by attachment, etc. Why then should it not be considered as the pain of consequence? This is the meaning. Satisfaction is caused by the cessation of the thirst for an object. The calming down thus caused consists in the cessation of the powers from their work. The author shows this very meaning by means of the canon of difference :—'The restlessness in consequence of absence of satisfaction is pain.'

He refutes :—'Further it is not possible, etc.' It is true that the cessation of desire is the faultless pleasure. It is not the repetition of enjoyments, however, that brings this about. The repetition of enjoyment, on the contrary, brings about the manifestation of desire, which is the opposite of the cessation thereof. As they have said :—'The desire for enjoyments is not calmed down by their enjoyment. It gathers strength like fire by oblations.'—(Manu). The rest is not difficult.

Now he questions about the pain of anxiety :—'Well, what is the painfulness of anxiety?' He gives the answer :—'The feeling of pain, etc.' The full description of its nature has not been undertaken, because it is well known to all men. It is similar to the pain of consequence or sequential change. The details of this are the same as those of the other.

He now questions about the painfulness of habituation :—'What again, etc.' Answers :—'By the enjoyment of pleasure, etc.' The feeling of pleasure nourishes its residual potency. That brings about the memory of pleasure. That again causes attachment. From this follow the movements of mind, body and speech. These cause virtue and vice. Thence comes the enjoyment of their fruition. Thence again is the mind habituated to it. This is the meaning of eternity, absence of beginning. And here again memory comes in by the intensity of the potencies of pleasure and pain. Thereby come attachment and aversion. Thence come actions. From actions proceeds fruition. Thus should this be understood. Following thus this stream of pain troubles the Yogī alone, not any one else. For this reason he says :—'This is the eternal stream, etc.' As to others the three-fold pain runs after them....this is the construction. The pains caused by other beings and the powers of nature are described by one common characteristic, the external. The modifications variegated by the eternal residua are described as the Nescience. It is the Nescience which causes modifications in the mind; they are, in fact, Nescience itself. It is by this that the feelings of 'This is myself' and 'This is mine' are generated in the Will-to-be the senses and the body, etc., and in wife and children, etc. These are the lines along which the ordinary Puruṣa moves.

Under these circumstances there is no rescue at all except in right knowledge. For this reason he says :—'The Yogī then, etc.'

Having thus shown the painfulness of pleasurable enjoyments, on account of the surrounding circumstances of sequential change, habituation and anxiety, he now shows the painfulness due to the very nature of their being :—'Further by reason of the contrariety of the functionings of the qualities, etc.' He explains :—'The qualities of Essence (Sattva), disturbing energy (Rajas) and inertia (Tamas) evolved as essentiality, activity and inactivity in their transformation as the Will-to-be, being dependent for support upon each other, bring about every notion, even though it be the notion of pleasurable enjoyments, as necessarily possessed of the three qualities, being as it is as such, either quiescent, that is pleasurable, disturbed, i.e,. painful or inert, *i.e.*, seedy (a feeling which is neither of active pleasure nor yet of pain). And even such a modification in the form of a notion of this Will-to-be is not permanent. So says he :—'And the functioning of the qualities being changeful, etc.' The mind has been said to be of a quickly changing nature.

But how can one notion become possessed of the opposite qualities of quiescence, disturbance and seediness at one time? For this reason he says :—'The intensities of their nature and the intensities of their functionings are contradictory to one another.'

Natures differ from natures, that is, the eight modes of mental being characterization, etc. Their functionings are pleasure and pain. Thus characteristic (*i.e.*, virtue) differs when ripening into fruit, from Vice (that which is non-characteristic), when that ripens into fruit. Similarly, knowledge, desirelessness and power as also pleasure, etc., differ from contradictory characteristics of the same classes. The ordinary manifestations, *i.e.*, when their natures are not intensified, do not contradict their intense manifestations, *i.e.*, when they are in the height of their manifestation. They, therefore, do manifest along with them.

Well, we understand this. But how can the enjoyment of pleasurable objects be painful by nature? For this reason he says :—'Thus do these, etc.' The meaning is that they are both the same inasmuch as there is no difference in their material causes and the material cause and the effect thereof are the same in nature.

What, is it then a case of absolute identity of nature ? If so, there would be no difference among mental conceptions as they do exist. For this reason he says :—'It is by the quality which is the leading factor, etc.' The presence of the qualities is in their ordinary nature. The leading factor is that which is intense. For this reason, all is but pain to the discriminating, by nature as well as on account of surrounding circumstances. And pain has to be removed by the wise. And pain cannot be removed unless its root is removed. Further, the root cannot be removed unless it is known. For this reason shows the root thereof :—'The seed out of which grows, etc.' The meaning is that the seed is that out of which the heap of pains grows, *i.e.*, from which it takes its birth.

He mentions the means of its eradication :—'And of that the means of destruction, etc.'

Now he explains that this science, which is taught for the welfare of all, is similar to another science of the same class :—'As the science of medicine, etc.' That science which has four branches of discussion, is said to be a science of four departments. The question now arises that inasmuch as pain was ere now described as the thing which has to be removed and the universe in evolution is now described as the thing to be removed, is there not an evident contradiction in this? For this reason he says :—'The universe in evolution being full of pain, etc.'

Now he describes the minor operation of Nescience, whereby the evolution of the universe is set in :—'The conjunction of the Prakṛti and the Puruṣa etc.'

He describes the means of liberation :—'Right knowledge is the means, etc.'

Some are of opinion that liberation consists in the destruction of the very being of him who does away with pain. As they say :—'The salvation of the mind is like the extinguishment of a lamp.' Others say that liberation consists in the appearance of pure knowledge by the destruction of the afflictions together with their potencies. He says to them :—'Here the individuality of the remover is not to be considered the pain, etc.'

He points out the defect in the theory of removal :—'In the case of avoidabiltiy, etc.' No wise man ever works for self-destruction. It is, however, seen that men who carry a body full of intense pain, do attempt to destroy themselves. True. But it is only a few who do so.

Further, if this were so, there would remain no object of existence for the Puruṣa, inasmuch as there are spirits in evolution who enjoy different kinds of pleasure as gods, etc.., and they too reach the state of liberation. Hence, liberation is not to be considered to be the anihilation of the very being of him who removes the pain.

Well, then, let us suppose that the mind in the state of liberation takes up another nature. For this reason he says :—'In the case of it being supposed that another nature is put on, the theory of there being another cause for it, etc.' It means that if it is something which comes into existence, it is an effect and is, therefore, impermanent. Being impermanent it cannot be considered liberation (Mokṣa). Mokṣa consists in immortality. The expression of pure knowledge is not immortal. It is not possible that expression (santana) should exist as separate from the thing expressed, and as an independent existence. The things that are expressed are, of course, impermanent. For this reason we should try to find out a theory which would make it possible that Mokṣa should be permanent. Is is only thus that it would be possible to make Mokṣa an object for the Puruṣa to achieve. For this reason he says :—'When both these positions, etc.' Hence Mokṣa is only the establishment of the self in its own nature. This alone is Right Knowledge. Thus is this science said to possess four Departments.—15.

Sūtra 16

हेयं दुःखमनागतम् ।। १६ ।।

हेयम् Heyaṁ, the avoidable. दुःखम् Duḥkham, pain. अनागतम् Anāgatam, not-yet-come.

16. Pain not-yet-come is the avoidable.—67.

हेयं दुःखमनागतम् । दुःखमतीतमुपभोगेनातिवाहितं न हेयपक्षे वर्तते । वर्तमानं च स्वक्षणोपभोगारूढमिति न तत्क्षणान्तरे हेयतामापद्यते । तस्माद्यदेवानागतं दुःखं तदेवाक्षिपात्रकल्पं योगिनं क्लिश्नाति नतेरं प्रतिपत्तारं तदेव हेयतामापद्यते । तस्माद्यदेव हेयमित्युच्यते तस्यैव कारणं प्रतिनिर्दिश्यते ।। १६ ।।

Vyāsa

The pain which has passed away has been spent up by experience. It cannot, therefore, fall within the sphere of the avoidable. And that which is present, is being experienced at the time of its existence; it cannot, therefore, be considered as the avoidable with reference to the future moment of time. Hence that pain alone which has not yet been experienced, troubles the Yogī who is sensitive as the eye-ball; it does not trouble any other knower. Hence that alone is the avoidable pain. It is that cause of this avoidable pain only that is to be discussed.—67.

Vācaspati's Gloss

By the use of the words 'not yet come', the past and the present have been taken out of the purview. He shows the propriety thereof :—'The pain that has passed away, etc.'

But why should pain which is present, *i.e.*, in the process of being suffered, be not considered as falling within the sphere of the avoidable, seeing that it has not been spent up by suffering? For this reason he says :—'And that which is present, etc.' The rest is easy.—16.

Sūtra 17

द्रष्टृदृश्ययोः संयोगो हेयहेतुः ।। १७ ।।

द्रष्टृ Draṣṭṛ, of the knower. दृश्ययोः Dṛśyayoḥ, and of the knowable. संयोगः Saṁyogaḥ, conjunction. हेय Heya, of the avoidable pain. हेतुः Hetuḥ, the cause.

17. The Conjunction of the knower and the knowable is the cause of the avoidable pain.—68.

द्रष्टृदृश्ययोः संयोगे हेयहेतुः। द्रष्टा बुद्धेः प्रतिसंवेदी पुरुषः। दृश्या बुद्धिसत्त्वोपारूढाः सर्वे धर्माः। तदेतद्दृश्यमयस्कान्तमणिकल्पं सन्निधिमात्रोपकारी दृश्यत्वेन स्वं भवति पुरुषस्य दृशिरूपस्य स्वामिनः। अनुभवकर्मविषयतामापन्नं यतोऽन्यस्वरूपेण प्रतिपन्नमन्यस्वरूपप्रतिलब्धात्मकं स्वतन्त्रमपि परार्थत्वात्परतन्त्रम्। तयोर्दृग्दर्शनशक्त्योरनादिरर्थकृतः संयोगो हेयहेतुर्दुःखस्य कारणमित्यर्थः। तथा चोक्तम्। तत्संयोगहेतु-विवर्जनात्स्यादयमात्यन्तिको दुःखप्रतीकारः। कस्माद्दुःखहेतोः परिहार्यस्य प्रतीकारदर्शनात्। तद्यथा पादतलस्य भेद्यता कण्टकस्य भेत्तृत्त्वं परिहारः कण्टकस्य पादानधिष्ठानं पादत्राणव्यवहितेन वाधिष्ठानमेतत्त्रयं यो वेद लोके स तत्र प्रतीकारमारभमाणो भेदजं दुःखं नाप्नोति। कस्मात्त्रित्वोपलब्धिसामर्थ्यादिति। अत्रापि तापकस्य रजसः सत्त्वमेव तप्यम्। कस्मात्तपि क्रियायाः कर्मस्थत्वात्सत्त्वे कर्मणि तपिक्रिया नापरिणामिनि निष्क्रिये क्षेत्रज्ञे दर्शितविषयत्वात्। सत्त्वे तु तप्यमाने तदाकारानुरोधी पुरुषोऽनुतप्यत इति।। १७।।

Vyāsa

The knower is the Puruṣa (the conscious principle) who cognizes the reflection from the Will-to-know by conjunction. The knowable consists of all the characteristics present in the essence of the Will-to-know. This then, the knowable behaves like a magnet. It is useful only when placed here. On account of its capacity of knowability, it becomes the possession of the lord, the Puruṣa, who is of the nature of the power of knowing. It becomes the object of the act of enjoyment, inasmuch as although by nature independent, it becomes dependent upon another, existing as it does for fulfilling the object of that other. It is different in nature from the power of knowing (consciousness), but puts on that nature by taking it up from another. The eternal conjunction of the power of knowing and the capacity of being known, brought about by the purpose of existence, is the cause of the avoidable pain. And so it has been said :—'The conjunction therewith is the cause; by giving that up is secured the complete remedy of pain, inasmuch as that is found to be the cause of the removal of the real thing, the cause of pain. As, for example, the soles of the feet possess the capacity of being pierced, and the thorn possesses the power of piercing. The remedy consists in not putting the foot on the thorn, or putting it with a shoe on. Whoever in the world knows these three things, secures the remedy and does not suffer the pain caused by the prick. By what means? By the power of the three-fold knowledge.

And here, too, it is the quality of the disturbing motion (rājas) that brings about the pain; and it is the quality of the Essence (sattva) which is pained. Why? Because the act of pain must live in an object, and it can, therefore, live in the Objective Essence alone. It cannot live in the unchaning actionless knower of the field. Because consciousness (Puruṣa) has the Objective Essence for its field it follows along the lines of the Phenomena of the Essence, and when the Objective Essence is pained, the Puruṣa also is pained by reflex action.—68.

Vācaspati's Gloss

The avoidable pain has been described. Its cause is now discussed. 'The conjunction of the knower and the knowable is the cause of the avoidable pain.'

Now he describes the nature of the knower :—'The knower, etc.' The cognition by conjunction of the reflection from the Will-to-know (Buddhi) is the same as the reflection of consciousness into the Will-to-know. This is present even in the Puruṣas who are indifferent (Udāsina).

Well, but if this is all, it is the Will-to-know alone that can thus be visible to him, not sound, etc., which are not thus in contact with him (the Puruṣa). For this reason he says :—'The knowable consists of all the characteristics the Will-to-be.' By means of the passage of the senses of the Will-to-be transforms as sound, etc. Sound, etc., thus becomes the characteristics of the knowable. This is the meaning. Well, but it is the Will-to-be that transforms as sound, etc., and thereby puts on these appearances. As to the Puruṣa however, the change takes place in him when his relation with the Will-to-be is perceived. If this relation is not recognised, how can sound, etc., be perceived even though they have entered the essence of the Will-to-be? The knowable cannot be cognized without being in contact with the power of consciousness. For this reason he says :—'This then, the knowable behaves like, etc.' We have discussed in the first chapter that the essence of Will-to-be, being touched by consciousness, takes in the reflection of consciousness on account of its extreme purity, and being thus as it were tranformed into consciousness cognizes sound, etc., in sequence. And it is for this reason that the seer enjoying sound, etc., presented to it by the essence of the Will-to-be having transformed into the sound, etc., becomes the master, and the essence of the Will-to-be standing to it in that relation becomes its possession. This is the essence of the Will-to-be, which possessed of forms behaves as a magnet and becomes a possession of the Puruṣa, who is the lord, as the power of consciousness. Why? Because it becomes the object of the act of cognition in sequence. The cognition in sequence is the experience of the Puruṣa. This means the action of the Puruṣa with the object in view. Becoming the object thereof means becoming enjoyable. It is spoken of as his possession, because it becomes enjoyable by him.

The question again arises that the essence of the Will-to-be being self-illuminated, how can it be the object of cognition? For this reason he says :—'It is different in nature from, etc.' The essence of the Will-to-be can be self-illuminating only, if it is reality of the nature of consciousness. Its nature, however, is different from that of consciousness, being as it is of the nature of the non-intelligent. It takes up the nature of consciousness by borrowing it from the other. It is for this reason an object of cognition.

The question now is that inasmuch as anything is said to be dependent upon another when something constituting it rests in that other, the Will-to-be cannot be dependent upon the Puruṣa, because nothing that belongs to the Will-to-be rests upon the Puruṣa, who is by nature indifferent. It further follows from this that the Puruṣa can have no action of his own. For this reason the author says :—'Although independent by nature, it becomes dependent upon another etc. The purpose of its existence being the fulfilment of the object of another, *i.e.*, of the Puruṣa, it becomes dependent upon the other, *i.e.*, the Puruṣa.

Well then this relation of the power of seeing and the capacity of being seen can either be innate or accidental. If it be innate, then both the related objects must always remain as such. The relation cannot cease to exist, because both of them are indestructible. The relation being thus impossible of cessation, there can never be an end of births and deaths. If it be incidental (naimittika), then because the afflictions, the actions and their potencies are the modifications of the internal organ, they can exist only when the internal organ exists. And the internal organ is brought into existence by means of them. Thus each comes to depend for its existence upon the existence of the other. Inasmuch as there cannot be this eternity of succession in the beginning of creation, the very setting in of evolution thus becomes impossible, and in fact non-existent. And so it has been said :—"Action is brought about by the 'qualities' even according to those who believe that the Puruṣa is not the actor. But how can that be brought about ? Karma does not exist then ? Nor is there untrue knowledge, nor attachment, nor aversion, etc. Nor is the mind born then, nor can any mental modifications exist at all in the case of any one." To remove this doubt the author says :—'The eternal conjunction of the power of knowing and the capacity of being known, brought about by the purpose of existence, etc.'

True, the relation is not innate; it is incidental. And although it is thus incidental, it has no beginning, because its existence has been caused by an eternal cause. And this succession of afflictions, actions and potencies is eternal. In each creation they become merged into the Prakṛti together with the internal organ, and manifest again in the beginning of another creation in the same state in which they were before. The illustration has been mentioned more than once before of how certain creatures of the earth are reduced to earth on the cessation of the rains, but come back to life again when the rains return.

Nescience is the cause of the conjunction by antecedence. The fulfilment of the object of the Puruṣa is the cause of keeping it on. It is by virtue of that that the conjunction lasts. For this reason is it said to have been caused by the purpose of the Puruṣa.

"And so it has been said" by Pañcaśikhā :—'Conjunction with that' means the conjunction with the Will-to-be (buddhi). It is this conjunction which is the cause of pain. By the cessation of that is secured the absolute remedy of pain. It is implied that pain lives on as long as the conjunction does not cease. The author repeats a well known illustration of the same :—'As the soles of the feet, etc.'

Well let that be so. But when it is said that the conjunction with 'qualities' is the cause of pain, it becomes admitted that the 'qualities' are the pain-givers. Further the action of the verb 'to pain' does not terminate in the actor alone, like that of the verb 'Is' and others of the same class. There must be another object in its case which is pained. The Puruṣa cannot be the object in which this pain may reside, because the Puruṣa being immutable it cannot possess the nature of being affected by the fruit of action. Therefore, it being necessary for pain that there should be something pained, we infer its non-existence when no object of pain exists, just as we see that no smoke exists when there is no fire. For this reason the author says :—"And here too the quality of essentiality is pained, etc." It is the qualities which are either the pain-givers or the pained. Of these the Sattva being delicate like the soles of the feet, is pained; the Rajas being sharp is the pain-giver.

The author now puts a question :—"Why is it the Sattva alone that is pained ? and not the Puruṣa." The answer is :—"On account of the action of pain, etc."

Well, then, does not the Puruṣa get pain? And further if it is only the non-intelligent Sattva that is pained, what loss is thereby caused to us? For this reason he says :—'The Puruṣa is pained by reflex action.'—17.

Sūtra 18

प्रकाशक्रियास्थितिशीलं भूतेन्द्रियात्मकं भोगापवर्गार्थं दृश्यम् ।। १८ ।।

प्रकाश Prakāśa, of illumination. क्रिया Kriyā, of activity. स्थिति Sthiti, inertia. शीलं Śīlam, nature. प्रकाशक्रियास्थितिशीलम् Prakāśakriyāsthitiśīlam, Having the nature of illumination, activity and inertia. भूत Bhūta, the elements. इन्द्रिय Indriya, the powers of sensation. आत्मकम् Ātmakam, consisting of. भोग Bhoga, experience. अपवर्ग Apavarga, emancipation. अर्थम् Artham, object. दृश्यम् Dṛśyam, knowable.

18. The knowable is of the nature of illumination, activity and inertia; it consists of the elements and the powers of sensation, action and thought; its objects are emancipation and experience.—69.

दृश्यस्वरूपमुच्यते। प्रकाशक्रियास्थितिशीलं भूतेन्द्रियात्मकं भोगापवर्गार्थं दृश्यम्। प्रकाशशीलं सत्त्वम्। क्रियाशीलं रजःस्थितिशीलं तम इति। तएे गुणाः परस्परोपरक्तप्रविभागाः परिणामिनः संयोगवियोगधर्माण इतरेतरोपाश्रयेणोपार्जितमूर्तयः परस्पराङ्गाङ्गित्वेऽप्यसंभिन्नशक्तिप्रविभागास्तुल्यजातीयातुल्यजातीय-शक्तिभेदानुपातिनः प्रधानवेलायामुपदर्शितसन्निधानानुगुणत्वेऽपि व्यापारमात्रेण च प्रधानान्तरणीतानुमिताऽस्तिताः पुरुषार्थकर्तव्यतया प्रयुक्तसामर्थ्याः सन्निधिमात्रोपकारिणोऽयस्यकान्तमणिकल्पाः प्रत्ययमन्तरेणैकतमस्य वृत्तिमनुवर्तमानाः प्रधानशब्दवाच्या भवन्ति। एतदृश्यमित्युच्यते। तदेतद्भूतेन्द्रियात्मकं भूतभावेन पृथिव्यादिना सूक्ष्मस्थूलेन परिणमते। तथेन्द्रियभावेन श्रोत्रादिना सूक्ष्मस्थूलेन परिणमत इति। तत्तु नाप्रयोजनं प्रयोजनमुररीकृत्य प्रवर्तत इति। भोगापवर्गार्थं हि तद् दृश्यं पुरुषस्येति। तत्रेष्टा निष्टगुणस्वरूपावधारणमविभागापन्नं भोगो भोक्तुः स्वरूपावधारणमपवर्ग इति। द्वयोरतिरिक्तमन्यद्दर्शनं नास्ति। तथा चोक्तम्। अयं तु खलु त्रिषु गुणेषु कर्तृष्वकर्तरि च पुरुषे तुल्यातुल्यजातीये चतुर्थे तत्क्रियासाक्षिण्युपनीयमानान्सर्वभावानुपपन्नाननु-पश्यन्नदर्शनमन्यच्छङ्कत इति। तावेतौ भोगापवर्गौ बुद्धिकृतौ बुद्धावेव वर्तमानौ कथं पुरुषे व्यपदिश्येते इति। यथा च जयः पराजयो वा योद्धिषु वर्तमानः स्वामिनि व्यपदिश्यते स हि तत्फलस्य भोक्तेति। एवं बन्धमोक्षौ बुद्धावेव वर्तमानौ पुरुषे व्यपदिश्येते स हि तत्फलस्य भोक्तेति। बुद्धेरेव पुरुषार्था परिसमाप्तिर्बन्धस्तदर्थावसायो

मोक्ष इति। एतेन ग्रहणधारणोहापोहतत्त्वज्ञानाभिनिवेशा बुद्धौ वर्तमानाः पुरुषेऽध्यारोपितसद्भावाः स हि तत्फलस्य भोक्तेति॥ १८॥

Vyāsa

The nature of the knowable is now described :—'The knowable is of the nature of, etc.' The quality of essentiality (Sattva) is of the nature of illumination. Energy (Rajas) is of the nature of activity. Inertia is of the nature of inactivity. These 'qualities' are capable of being coloured more or less by proximity to one another. They are ever evolving. They have the characteristics of conjunction and separation. They manifest forms by each lending support to the others by proximity. None of these loses its distinct power into those of the others, even though each may exist as the principal factor of a phenomenon, with the others as subsidiary thereto. They take to the lines of different manifestations of power in objects of the same or of different classes. When anyone of them is the principal factor of any phenomenon, the others show their presence in close contact. Their existence as subsidiary energies of the principal factor is inferred by their distinct and independent functioning, even though it be as subsidiary qualities. Their powers come into manifestation by virtue of the objects of the Puruṣa having to be fulfilled. They bring about the fulfilment by mere proximity, acting in the same way as loadstone. They follow along the line of the manifestation of one of them independently of any disposing cause. They are called by the name of Pradhāna (primordial matter). This is styled the knowable. This it is that consists of the elements and the powers of action, sensation and thought. It evolves as the elements, the subtle and the gross *Pṛthvī,* etc. Similarly does it evolve as the powers of sensation, action and thought, the subtle and gross auditory and other powers. And this evolution is not purposeless, beginning as it does with a set purpose before it. The object of the "knowable" is of course the fulfilment of the objects of the Puruṣa, experience and emancipation. Of these, experience consists in obtaining the knowledge of the nature of the desirable and undesirable phenomena of the qualities; which knowledge, however, does not recognize them as only the modifications of the qualities. Emancipation is the ascertainment of the nature of the enjoyer the Puruṣa. Beyond the knowledge of these two there is no wisdom. And so it has been said :—"And this one, however, having come to know the three 'qualities' to be the actors and the fourth Puruṣa to be the actionless knower of their action, and knowing also the outputs of the qualities, not yet known, that are being presented to the Puruṣa, who is of the same and not yet of the same class with them, no longer suspects the existence of any other wisdom."

Well, but how can either experience or emancipation, which being both of them the works of the Will-to-be live in the Will-to-be alone, be predicated of the Puruṣa? As victory and defeat existing in the soldiers are predicated of their master, because it is he who enjoys the fruit thereof, so are bondage and freedom existing in the Will-to-be alone predicated of the Puruṣa, because he is the enjoyer of their fruit. It is of the Will-to-be alone that the bondage exists until the object of the Puruṣa is fulfilled; and it is the fulfilment of the object that is emancipation (Mokṣa). Similarly have perception, retention, judgment, rejection knowledge of realities and the distinction of unrealities their existence fastened on to the Puruṣa although they have their existence in the Will-to-be, because he is the enjoyer of their fruit.—69.

Vācaspati's Gloss

The presentation of objectivity is the cause of pain, and that has been described before. The author now describes the knowable :—'The knowable is of the nature of illumination, etc.' It is a quantum of essence (Sattva) as luminosity that is coloured by a quantum of inertia (Tamas) as weakness and by a quantum of disturbing energy (Rajas) as pain. Similarly may this be illustrated in the case of existences in which Rajas, etc., prevail. It is this that is intended to be said by,

'These qualities are capable of being coloured more or less by proximity to one another.'

They have the characteristics of conjunction and separation 'with and from the Puruṣa.' As it is said in the Veda :—'One unborn is there who is red, white and black; she goes on giving birth to many similar children. One unborn Puruṣa follows her enjoying; another unborn (Puruṣa) gives her up, having enjoyed all her enjoyables.—(Śvetāśvatara Upaniṣad)

It is said of them that they manifest forms, by lending support to one another, inasmuch as it is thus that the *pṛthvī* and other *tattvas* are evolved. Grant that. But inasmuch as Disturbing Energy (rājas) and Inertia (tāmas) subserve the quality of Essentiality (sattva), when the latter brings about the production of the quiescent notion (śānta pratyaya), they too are the causes of the production and must as such possess the virtues (that bring about the production and must as such possess the notion must be manifest even when the rājas and the tāmas are the principal factors as is manifested in the case of the equality of Essentiality being the principal factor, and not the disturbed and forgetful notions. For this reason the author says :—'None of these loses its distinct power into those of the others, even though each may exist as the principal factor of a phenomenon, with others as subservient thereto.' It may be that Rājas and Tāmas exist as subservient factors when the quiescent notion has to be manifested, but their energies are not merged into that of the other. The fact the energies are not merged is to be inferred from the fact of the effects thereof not disappearing into each other. Inasmuch as the quiescent, disturbed and forgetful effects are found along with the intensified manifestation of the several 'qualities', not being merged into the others, it is proved that the separate qualities of their energies are not destroyed by conjunction.

Let that be granted. But if these energies are separate from one another and cannot be merged into the others, that it cannot be said of the 'qualities' that they can come together with the object of bringing about a single effect. Different energies are never found coming together to bring about a single effect. It never happens that thread, earth and straw should come together to produce a jar and such other things. To this he says in answer :—'They take to the lines of different manifestations of power in objects of the same and of different classes.' Although the power of forming the material cause exists with reference to objects of the same class only and not with respect to others, the power of helping the cause to manifest as a particular effect does certainly exist in objects of different classes also. As to a cloth, straw does not possess the power of even helping the material cause in the manifestation thereof. It, therefore, cannot come together with thread to bring about a cloth. They are spoken of as taking to the lines of different energies in objects of the same and different classes, because it is their nature to do so.

'At the time of their being the principal factors' :—When a divine body has to be generated, the quality of essentiality becomes the principal factor, and the qualities of disturbing energy (rājas) and inertia (tāmas) are subservient. It is for this reason that these qualities show their antecedent closeness at the time of their not being the principal factors, *i.e.*, their modifications tend towards the immediate manifestation of the intended effects.

The words 'principal factors' are intended chiefly to signify the state of being. As in the aphorism of Pāṇini, 'The dual and the singular in case of two and one,' the meaning is that in case of duality and unity, the dual and singular are to be used; for were it not so, the words used would be 'twos' and 'ones' (in the plural number).

Well, but the question arises, that in the case of their being the principal factors of any phenomenon it is possible to posit their existence because they are then in manifestation; not so however when they are not in manifestation. What reason is then there to suppose that they do exist, when they are not in manifestation? For this reason he says :—'Their existence as subservient energies, etc.' Even though they are not in manifestation, yet their existence as substances subserving the principal factor is helping it to bring about a particular effect is inferred by their functioning alone, inasmuch as they do not possess the power of discriminating intelligently, the one from the other, and they do not possess the power of discriminating intelligently, the one from the other, and have the capacity of causing effect by coming together. They are, therefore, thus described.

Well but granting that the qualities have the power of bringing about the manifestation of effects by coming together, how is it that they do bring about the effects. It is not necessary that whoever has the power must use it also. To show that this power does not stop in its action of causing the manifestation of effects, he says :—'Their powers come into manifestation by virtue, etc.' The meaning is that the 'qualities' cease to act only when all the objects of the Puruṣa have been fulfilled. It is only then that they do not produce effects.

The question arises that inasmuch as the qualities do not confer any benefit upon the Puruṣa, how can it be said that the fulfilment of the objects of the Puruṣa sets them into actions. For this reason he says :—'They bring about the fulfilment by mere proximity.'

But the question arises that virtue and vice being the evident disposing causes of the action of the 'qualities' why is it said that their powers come into manifestation by virtue of the objects of the Puruṣa having to be fulfilled? In answer to this he says :—'They follow in the line of the manifestation of one of them, etc.' Whichever of the three, whether the Sattva, the Rājas or the Tāmas functions as the principal factor to manifest its effect, the others follow along its line without the existence of a disposing cause in the shape of virtue and vice. The same will be said :—

"No disposing cause sets the Prakṛtis in motion; it removes the obstacles only, like the husbandman."—3.28.

"These qualities" are called by the name of Pradhāna—this is the construction. They are called by the name of Pradhāna, derived as the word is from the root √DHā 'to maintain,' meaning those by which the whole world is maintained. This is called 'the knowable.'

Having thus described the nature of the qualities, now the author describes their effects :—'This it is that consists, etc.' When it is proved that the effects exist in reality, it is apparent that everything evolves according to its own nature. Now he explains how it is of the nature of the elements and the powers of sensation, etc. 'It evolves as the elements, etc.' Now he introduces the portion of the aphorism. Its objects are experience and emancipation. And this evolution is not purposeless, inasmuch as it sets in with a fixed purpose before it.

The author explains experience (bhoga) :—'Of these, experience, etc.' Pleasure and pain are the phenomena of the Will-to-be which is of the nature of the three qualities. It is the Will-to-be that modifies as these. Experience, however, does not consist in determining their nature as qualities. For this reason he says :—'Which knowledge, however, does not recognize them as only modifications of the qualities.' This has often been discussed.

The author explains emancipation. 'The ascertainment of the nature of the enjoyer.' The radical meaning is that by which it is separated from something (Apa vṛj, varga).

Now he explains the non-existence of any other purpose :—'Beyond the knowledge of these two there is no other wisdom. And so it has been said by Pañcśikhā :—'And this one however, etc.'

The question now arises that experience and emancipation being both the modifications of the Will-to-be and as such having their being in the Will-to-be, how is it that they are predicated of the Puruṣa, who is not their cause and in whom they do not live? For this reasons he says :—"Well but how can either, etc." It has ben said that the Puruṣa is the enjoyer, and the subject will be discussed further besides. In reality, however, it is by the Will-to-be alone that the object of the Puruṣa is fulfilled. It is by this description of the nature of the relationship of the Puruṣa to experience and emancipation, that the nature of the relationship of the Puruṣa to perception, etc., should also be known. But of these perception is the knowledge of an object such as it is. The memory thereof is retention. Judgement consists in discovering the particular differential of the precepts. Rejection means the removal by reasoning of the untrue facts that have entered the mind. The knowledge of realities consists in coming to a conclusion by judgement and rejection. The knowledge of the things to be rejected and accepted, preceded by the knowledge of the realities is the distinguishing of the unrealities.—18.

Sūtra 19

विशेषाविशेषलिङ्गमात्रालिङ्गानि गुणपर्वाणि।। १९।।

विशेष Viśeṣa, specialised. अविशेष Aviśeṣa, unspecialised. लिङ्गमात्र Liṅga-mātra, undifferentiated phenomenal. आलिङ्गानि Āliṅgāni, and the noumenal. गुण Guṇa, of the qualities. पर्वाणि Parvāṇi, stages.

19. The Specialised, the Unspecialised the Undifferentiated phenomenal and the noumenal are the stages of "the qualities"—70.

दृश्यानां तु गुणानां स्वरूपभेदावधारणार्थमिदमारभ्यते। विशेषाविशेषलिङ्गमात्रालिङ्गानि गुणपर्वाणि। तत्राकाशवाय्वग्न्युदकभूमयो भूतानि शब्दस्पर्शरूपरसगन्धतन्मात्राणामविशेषाणां विशेषाः। तथा श्रोत्रत्वक्चक्षु-

जिह्वाघ्राणानि बुद्धीन्द्रियाणि। वाक्पाणिपादपायूपस्थानि कर्मेन्द्रियाणि। एकादशं मनः सर्वार्थमित्येतान्यस्मिता-लक्षणस्याविशेषस्य विशेषाः। गुणानामेष षोडशको विशेषपरिणामः। षडविशेषाः तद्यथा शब्दतन्मात्रं स्पर्शतन्मात्रं रूपतन्मात्रं रसतन्मात्रं गन्धतन्मात्रं चेति। एकद्वित्रिचतुष्पञ्चलक्षणाः शब्दादयः पञ्चाविशेषाः। षष्ठश्चाविशेषो-ऽस्मितामात्र इति। एते सत्तामात्रस्यात्मनो महतः षडविशेषपरिणामाः। यत्तत्परमविशेषेभ्यो लिङ्गमात्रं महत्तत्त्वं तस्मिन्नेते सत्तामात्रे महत्यात्मन्यवस्थाय विवृद्धिकाष्ठामनुभवन्ति। प्रतिसंसृज्यमानाश्च तस्मिन्नेव सत्तामात्रे महत्यात्मन्यवस्थाय यत्तान्निःसत्तासत्तं निःसदसन्निरसदव्यक्तमलिङ्गं प्रधानं तत्प्रतियन्ति। एष तेषां लिङ्गमात्रः परिणामो निःसत्तासत्तं चालिङ्गपरिणाम इति। अलिङ्गावस्थायां न पुरुषार्थो हेतुर्नालिङ्गावस्थायामादौ पुरुषार्थता कारणं भवतीति। न तस्याः पुरुषार्थताकारणं भवतीति। नासौ पुरुषार्थकृतेतिनित्याख्यायते। त्रयाणां त्ववस्थाविशेषाणामादौ पुरुषार्थता कारणं भवति। स चार्थे हेतुर्निमित्तकारणं भवतीत्यनित्याख्यायते। गुणास्तु सर्वधर्मानुपातिनो न प्रत्यस्तमयं तेनोपजायन्ते। व्यक्तिभिरेवातीतानागतव्ययागमवतोभिर्गुणान्वयिनीभिरुपजनना-पायधर्मका इव प्रत्यवभासन्ते। यथा देवदत्तो दरिद्राति। कस्मात्। यतोऽस्य म्रियन्ते गाव इति। गवामेव मरणात्तस्य दरिद्राणं न स्वरूपहानादिति। समः समाधिर्लिङ्गमात्रमलिङ्गस्य प्रत्यासन्नं तत्र तत्संसृष्टं विविच्यते क्रमानतिवृत्तेः। तथा षडविशेषा लिङ्गमात्रे संसृष्टा विविच्यन्ते परिणामक्रमनियमात्। तथा तेष्वविशेषेषु भूतेन्द्रियाणि संसृष्टानि विविच्यन्ते। तथाचोक्तं पुरस्तान्न विशेषेभ्यः परं तत्त्वान्तरमस्तीति विशेषाणां नास्ति तत्त्वान्तरपरिणामः। तेषां तु धर्मलक्षणावस्था परिणामा व्याख्यायिष्यन्ते।। १९।।

Vyāsa

This is composed for the purpose of ascertaining the differences of nature shown by 'the qualities' which constitute the 'knowable.' The Specialized, the Unspecialized, the Undifferentiated Phenomenal and the Noumenal are the stages of 'the qualities.'

Here the elements known as Ākāśa (ether), Vāyu (Invisible gas), Tejas (Steam or visible gas), Aps (liquid) and Pṛthvī (solid) are the specialized modifications of the unspecialized soniferous, tangiferous, lumniferous, gustiferous and odoriferous measures thereof (the tanmātras, the subtle elements).

Similarly are the powers of sensation (hearing, touch, sight, taste and smell), the powers of action (speech, grasp, position, execution and generation), the eleventh Manas, which has all these as its sphere, the specialized modification of the unspecialized modification of the principle of egoism. Thus sixteen-fold is the specialized modifications of the qualities. Six are the unspecialized modifications and these are soniferous, the tangiferous, the luminferous, the gustiferous and the odoriferous 'ultimates' the tanmātras. These five unspecialized modifications, the soniferous and the others, possess respectively one, two, three, four and five of the qualities of sound, etc. The sixth unspecialized modification is the Pure Egoism.

These six are the unspecialized modifications of Pure Be-ness, the Great Principle, the Mahā Ātmā. This Great Reality is the Undifferentiated Phenomenal Stage beyond the Unspecialized. In the Great Principle of Pure Be-ness do these live and grow up to their highest capacity. On involution they pass back into that state of Pure Be-ness, the great principle; and these they pass into the state which neither **Is,** nor yet **Is Not,** that in which it exists and yet does not; that which is **Real,** the Unmanifested, the noumenon, the background of all. This is their undifferentiated phenomenal modification; and that which neither **Is** nor yet **Is Not,** is the noumenal modification. The objects of the Puruṣa are no cause of the noumenal state. That is to say, the fulfilment of the objects of the Puruṣa does not act as the cause of manifestation with reference to the noumenal state, in the beginning. The fulfilment of the objects of the Puruṣa is not, therefore, the reason of the existence of the cause. For the reason that it is not brought into existence by the Puruṣa's objects it is said to be eternal. As to the three specialized states, the fulfilment of the objects of the Puruṣa becomes the cause of their manifestation in the beginning. And because the objects of the Puruṣa become the cause of their manifestation, they are said to be non-eternal. The 'qualities,' however follow, up all these characteristics. They are, therefore, neither born nor disappear at each stage. They only appear as it were possessed of the characteristics of birth and death, because their individual phenomena in which they of course are present, are possessed and present, etc. As (when we say) "Devadatta has become poor," Why? Because all his cattle are dead. The death of his cattle has caused his poverty and not the destruction of his own substance. This is an analogous conception.

The Undifferentiated phenomenal (Liṅga) is the next after the Noumenal (Aliṅga). It exists therein as the same substance, and is distinguished from that, because the law of the order of appearance is invisible.

Similarly, the six unspecialised modifications have their being in the undifferentiated phenomenal and are distinguished from that by the order of evolution being inviolable.

Similarly are the elements and the power of sensation having their being in these unspecialized modifications, distinguished from them. And it has been said before that there is no other tattva appearing in succession after specialized modifications. Their modifications consist of the characteristic (dharma) the secondary quality (lakṣaṇa) and condition (avasthā, accident). They will be described.—70.

Vācaspati's Gloss

It is for ascertaining the different modifications of the 'qualities' that go to make up the knowable that this is composed :—

"The specialized, the unspecialized, the undifferentiated phenomenal and the noumenal are the stages of qualities."

"The specialized" :—The unspecialized modifications are those that are free from the specialities which may be described as the quiscent, the disturbed and the forgetful. The specialized modifications are their outcomes only. They do not evolve further tattvas.

He describes them :—"Here the elements found, etc." They are enumerated here in the order of their manifestation.

The powers of sensation and thought are the specialized modifications of the unspecialized principle of egoism, with the quality of essentiality (sattva) as the principal factor. The powers of action are the modifications of the Rājasic form of that principle. The Manas is of the nature of both and should be considered as possessing both of these as the principal factors. Here the five tanmātras are the effects of the Will-to-be (buddhi), because they are the unspecialized modifications, just like the principle of egoism. Non-specialization consists in being the cause of further modifications.

Having enumerated the tanmātras and the principle of the egoism as the unspecialized modifications, now he enumerates the specialized :—'This is the sixteenfold, etc.' Then he enumerates the unspecialized :—"Six, etc." Next he illustrates by putting them together :— "And these are, etc." The latter is in each case qualified by the former. The 'smell vibration' has by nature five secondary qualities. The taste vibration has by nature four; the luminiferous three, the tangiferous two, and the soniferous has but one secondary quality, namely, the sound.

Well of what are these six modifications or effects? He says :—'They are the modifications of **Pure Be-Ness.**' That which is capable of fulfilling the objects of the Puruṣa **Is.** Its state is signified by **Be-Ness.** Pure means limited by that alone. This is the Great Principle, the Mahattattva. The meaning is that whatever of work is there for fulfilling the objects of the Puruṣa, whether it appears in the shape of the enjoyables of sound, etc., or in the shape of the discrimination of the distinction between the Puruṣa and Sattva (consciousness and the Essence of Objective matter), all has its end in the shape of the discrimination of the distinction between the Puruṣa and Sattva (consciousness and the Essence of Objective matter), all has its end in the Great Principle of the Will-to-be. This is described as the Ātmā, with the object of denying its smallness by showing that it constitutes the very nature, the very being of all modifications. This is the first modification of the Prakṛti. It is a real modification, not a mere unfoldment thereof.

"Beyond the undifferentiated means divided off from it in time with reference to the other objects which are nearer to it in time, *i.e.*, the unspecialized. This is the Mahattattva, the Great Principle of the undifferentiated Phenomenal. In the Great Principle of Pure Be-ness lives the determining energy of all further phenomenal modifications, that is the unspecialized phenomena, because it is proved that they possess the capacity of effecting the fulfilment of the objects of the Puruṣa, possessed as they are of real existence. There they grow to their highest capacity of growth, *i.e.*, reach that state. As to the modifications in succession of the specialized modifications of the unspecialized ones, these further modifications are characteristic secondary quality and condition. This is the end of their growth, *i.e.*, of their further modifications.

Having thus described the order of evolution, now he describes the order of involution.

Involution means passing into latency into the antecedent modification, the determining cause of its existence, its Ātmā (self). The Unspecialized modifications into which the Specialized ones have already become latent, pass back in their turn into the Pure Be-ness, the Great Mahattattva. Thence the Unspecialized modifications along with their Mahat modification pass back into the Unmanifested. It is called Aliṅga, the Noumenal, because beyond this do the phenomena pass into latency. This is the final state of latency of the phenomenal world. "That which neither **Is** nor yet **Is Not**" is a description of this state. Its existence consists in its possessing the capacity of effecting the fulfilment of the objects of the Puruṣa. Non-existence means want of capacity to be taken into account, to force itself upon attention. It is so described, as, being beyond both these states of existence and non-existence. This is the meaning. The state of the equipoise of the three qualities of Essence, Inertia, and Energy is nowhere of use in fulfilling the objects of the Puruṣa. It, therefore, does not exist as such. On the other hand, it does not admit of being rejected as non-existent, like the lotus of the sky. It is, therefore, not non-existent.

Grant that. But the principles of Mahat, etc., exist as such in the state of the unmanifested also, because nothing that exists can be destroyed; and if it is destroyed it cannot be born again, because nothing that does not exist can be born. It follows, therefore, that the principles of Mahat, etc., existing in the state of the unmanifested, that state also can effect the fulfilment of the objects of the Puruṣa. How then can it be said that the unmanifested is not possessed of existence? For this reason he says :—'That in which it exists and yet does not exist.' This means that the cause exists in that state but not the effect as such. Although the effect exists in the cause *in posse,* yet it is incapable of performing its function of fulfilling the object of the Puruṣa. It is, therefore, said to be non-existent as such.

Further he says that this cause is not of the nature of a hare's horn :—"That which is real (not asat, non-existent)." It is beyond the state of non-existence, that is, of the existence of the effect only as such. If it were like that, then it would be like the lotus of the sky and no effect would follow from that.

Having described what takes place in the case of every manifestation, now he summarizes :—'This is their undifferentiated, etc.' 'This' refers to what has gone immediately before. The states of existence from the undifferentiated Phenomenal downwards are impermanent, because they have been brought into manifestation by virtue of the objects of the Puruṣa having to be fulfilled. The noumenon, however, is permanent, because it has not been brought into being by the objects of the Puruṣa. The author describes the cause :—'The objects of the Puruṣa are no cause, etc.'

How is it, however, that the objects of the Puruṣa are no cause ? He says :—'That is to say, etc.' By using the words, 'does not act as the cause,' he indicates, the knowledge of the nature of the principle under discussion. This is the meaning. The fulfilment of the objects of the Puruṣa may be understood to be the cause with reference to the noumenal state, if that state bring about the enjoyment of sound, etc., or manifest the discrimination of the distinction between consciousness and Objective Existence. If, however, it did that there would be no equipoise. For this reason the objects of the Puruṣa are not understood to be the cause of the noumenal state. Hence the fulfilment of the object of the Puruṣa is not the cause of the noumenal state. This he summarizes :—'For the reason that it is not brought into existence, etc.' The word ITI in the text means, 'for the reason that.' He describes non-eternity :—"As the three states, *i.e.*, the undifferentiated phenomenal, the unspecialized and the specialized."

Having described the nature of the stages, now he describes the nature of the 'qualities,' :—'The qualities, however, etc.' Then he gives an illustration :—'As for example, Devadatta becomes poor.'

The meaning is that when the entirely different phenomena of the rise, increase and decrease of his bovine wealth cause the rise and fall of Devadatta to be inferred, what need then be said of the appearance and disappearance of individual phenomena which although different from the "qualified" themselves, are yet of their very nature and not altogether different from them.

The question now is whether the order of manifestation is alterable. The answer is, 'It is not.' 'The undifferentiated phenomenal is the next after, etc.' The seeds of Nyagrodha are not certainly capable of putting forth at once the full-grown, thickly set tree of Nyagrodha capable of protecting from the fierce heat of the sun with the thick setting of its leaves, twigs, branches and body. The tree comes out only gradually in the ordered appearance of shoots, leaves, body and branches, brought about by contact with earth, water and heat. Here too must, therefore, be established an order of appearance proved to exist both by reason and authority.

How have the elements and the powers of sensation and action their origin in the unspecialised modifications? It has been said before in the Commentary to this very aphorism.

Now he says why the further modification of the specialized modifications into other principles has not been spoken of. 'There is no other appearance in succession after, etc.' Are the specialized modifications then quite unchangeable ? If so, they must be permanent. For this reason he says :—'Their modifications consist of the characteristic, etc.'—19.

Sūtra 20

द्रष्टा दृशिमात्रः शुद्धोऽपि प्रत्ययानुपश्यः ।। २० ।।

द्रष्टा Draṣṭā, the seer. दृशिमात्रः Dṛśi-mātraḥ, consciousness only. शुद्धः Śuddhaḥ, pure. अपि Api, even though. प्रत्यय Pratyaya, by imitation. अनुपश्यः Anupaśyaḥ, cognizing ideas.

20. The seer is consciousness only; even though pure, he cognizes ideas by imitation.—71.

व्याख्यातं दृश्यमथ द्रष्टुः स्वरूपावधारणार्थमिदरमारभ्यते। द्रष्टा दृशिमात्रः शुद्धोऽपि प्रत्ययानुपश्यः। दृशिमात्र इति दृक्शक्तिरेव विशेषणापरामृष्टेत्यर्थः। स पुरुषो बुद्धेः प्रतिसंवेदी स बुद्धेर्न सरूपो नात्यन्तं विरूप इति। न तावत्सरूपः। कस्मात्। ज्ञाताज्ञातविषयत्वात्परिणामिनीहि बुद्धिस्तस्याश्च विषयो गवादिर्घटादिश्च ज्ञाताज्ञातश्चेति परिणामित्वं दर्शयति। सदाज्ञातविषयत्वं तु पुरुषस्यापरिणामित्वं परिदीपयति। कस्मान्नहि बुद्धिश्च नाम पुरुषविषयश्च स्यादगृहीता गृहीता चेति सिद्धं पुरुषस्य सदाज्ञातविषयत्वं ततश्चापरिणामित्वमिति। किंच परार्था बुद्धिः संहत्यकारित्वात्स्वार्थः पुरुष इति। तथा सर्वार्थाध्यवसायकत्वात्रिगुणाबुद्धिस्त्रिगुण-त्वादचेतनेति। गुणानां तूपद्रष्टा पुरुष इत्यतो न सरूपः। अस्तु तर्हि विरूप इति नात्यन्तं विरूपः कस्माच्छुद्धोऽप्यसौ प्रत्यानुपश्यो यतः प्रत्ययं बौद्धमनुपश्यति तमनुपश्यन्न तदात्मापि तदात्मक इव प्रत्यवभासते। तथाचोक्तम्। अपरिणामिनी हि भोक्तशक्तिरप्रतिसङ्क्रमा च परिणामिन्यर्थे प्रतिसङ्क्रान्तेव तद्वृत्तिमनुपतति। तस्याश्च प्राप्तचैतन्योपग्रहरूपाया बुद्धिवृत्तेरनुकारमात्रतया बुद्धिवृत्त्याऽविशिष्टा हि ज्ञानवृत्तिरित्याख्यायते ।। २० ।।

Vyāsa

The knowable has been described. Discussion is now begun with the object of describing and ascertaining the nature of the seer (knower). 'The seer is consciousness only : even though pure, he cognizes ideas by imitation.'

'Consciousness only' : This means that he is nothing other than the power of becoming conscious; that is to say, he is not touched by the qualities. This Puruṣa cognizes the Will-to-be by reflex action. He is neither quite similar nor quite dissimilar to the Will-to-be (buddhi). 'He is not quite similar.' Why? The Will-to-be having for its sphere of action objects known, and not yet known, is of course changeful. The changefulness is shown by its objects, such as the cow and the jar, etc., being both known and unknown. The fact, however, that the sphere of consciousness is always *the Known,* renders it plain that consciousness is not changeful. How? It never happens that the Will-to-know becomes the sphere of consciousness both when it takes in some notion and when it does not. Hence it is proved that the Known is always the sphere of the Puruṣa. Thence the unchangeability of the Puruṣa is shown. Further the Will-to-be exists to fulfil another's object, bringing as it does more than one phenomenon together into itself, for the purpose of presenting them to the Puruṣa. The Puruṣa, however, has his own object before it.

Besides the Will-to-be is the underlying determinative energy of all objective phenomena, and is as such of the nature of the qualities. It is, therefore, non-intelligent. The Puruṣa, however, is the seer of the qualities by proximity. For these reasons he is not similar.

Well then let him be dissimilar. To meet this he says :—'He is not quite dissimilar.' Why? 'Even though pure, he sees the ideas after they have come into the mind.' Inasmuch as the Puruṣa cognizes the ideas as the Will-to-be seized of consciousness is transformed into them, he appears by the act of cognition to be as it were the very self of the Will-to-be, although in reality he is not so. As it has been said :—'The power of the enjoyer is certainly unchangeable, and it does not run after every object. In connection with a changeful object it looks as it were being transferred to every object, and imitates its modifications.'

And when that modification of the Will-to-be assumes the form of consciousness by which it is coloured, it imitates it and looks as if it were a manifestation of consciousness unqualified by the modifications of the Will-to-be. It is accordingly so spoken of.—71.

Vācaspati's Gloss

The knowable has been described; the discussion for the ascertainment of the nature of the seer is now begun :—'The seer is consciousness alone; even though pure, he cognizes ideas by imitation.' He explains it :—'Consciousness alone, not touched by modifying characteristics.' By this the object of using the word only or alone is shown.

Well, if it be so, if the power of the seer be free from all the attributes of sound, etc., they would not be known. Nothing that is not touched by the act of seeing, can be knowable. For this reason he says :—'That Puruṣa, etc.' The passing of the reflection of the Puruṣa into the mirror of the Will-to-be is the knowing of the Will-to-be by the Puruṣa by reflex action. It is thus that sound and touch, etc., are known by the Will-to-be which has received into itself the reflection of the Puruṣa. And it is thus that they become the knowable.

Well, if this be so, why should not consciousness and the Will-to-be considered to be really one in nature? What is the use of this reflection of the Puruṣa into the Will-to-be? For this reason he says :—'He is not similar to the Will-to-be'. Inasmuch as in the case of dissimilarity it would be difficult to account for reflection, it is further said :—'Nor is he quite dissimilar.' Of these he denies similarity :—'He is not quite similar, etc.' Then he asks the question :—'Why?' He gives the answer with grounds :—'The Will-to-be having for the sphere of its action, etc.' Inasmuch as the Will-to-be is changeful it is dissimilar. When it assumes the shapes of sound, etc., then its sphere becomes instinct with sound, etc., and thus becomes known. If it has not taken up the forms of sound, etc., then they remain unknown. Hence the Will-to-be which takes up the form of sound, etc., only sometimes is changeful. And the statement is so made :—'The Will-to-be is changeful because it is the sphere of both the known and the yet unknown, like the sense of hearing, etc.'

As to the dissimilarity of the Puruṣa with the Will-to-be, it is proved by the opposite reasoning :—'The fact, however, that the sphere of consciousness is always the known, etc.'

Well, but if the known is always the sphere of the Puruṣa, then he can never be absolutely free (kevaīl.) With this in view he puts the question :—'How ?' The answer is :—'It never happens that the Will-to-be becomes, etc.'

Inasmuch as it is possible that in the state of the restraint of mental faculties, the Will-to-be and the absence of actual cognition might co-exist it is said with the object of indicating contrariety :—'because the sphere of consciousness both when, etc.'

The first copulative signifies that the Will-to-be must be the sphere and the other shows the contrary state. The statement of the reasoning will stand thus :—The Puruṣa never changes, because he is the constant factor in the phenomena of knowledge, in the outgoing mental state and the state of the Cognitive trance. That which is changeful cannot be the constant factor in the phenomena of knowledge, as the power of hearing, etc. This inference is by the canon of difference.

He mentions another contrary characteristic also :—'The Will-to-be fulfilling as it does the objects of the Puruṣa by means of the residua of the afflictions and actions and the objects and powers of sensation, etc., coming together into it, exists for the purpose of another.' The statement of the reasoning is thus :—The Will-to-be exists for the purpose of another, because its work is fulfilled by bringing together into itself various objects such as beds, seats and toilet powers, etc.

He says that the Puruṣa is not like that :—'The Puruṣa, however, has its own object before it.' All is made for the Puruṣa. The Puruṣa is not designed for any other. This is the meaning.

He states another contrary characteristic :—'Because the Will-to-be is the underlying characteristic, etc.' The Will-to-be determines the nature of all objects, as it is being transformed into their respective forms. Further, all these are the modifications of the three qualities of Essence, Energy and Inertia. For this reason the Will-to-be is proved to possess the three qualities by nature. He says that 'the Puruṣa is not such.' 'The Puruṣa, however, is the seer, etc.' The meaning is that he sees by reflection into it, not by being transformed into the forms of the objects (like the Will-to-be). He summarizes :—'For these reasons, etc.' The result of the reasoning being that he must be dissimilar, it is added that he is not altogether dissimilar. Why? Because (heaving been reflected into the mind) he sees the ideas by imitating the modifications of the Will-to-be. The way in which this happens, has been described in the aphorism : "Identification with modifications elsewhere,"—I.4.

So also has it been said by Pañcaśikha :—'The power of the knower is certainly unchangeable. The power of the knower means the self (Ātmā.) And although for this very reason it does not in reality change with the modifications of the Will-to-be, it as it were follows the modifications of the Will-to-be, resting as it does in each object that comes into the changeful mind.

The question arises, How is it that it looks as it were running after every object, although it, as a matter of fact, does not do so. Further how does it follow the modifications of the mind, when it does not modify itself? For this reason he says :—'Inasmuch as the Puruṣa cognizes, etc.'

"Seized of consciousness" :—This means having been coloured by contiguity. Whatever form the Will-to-be is transformed into, is as such coloured by consciousness. The Will-to-be is said to be 'seized of consciousness' when each transformation of it is as such coloured by consciousness. This is the meaning. Although the moon is not as a matter of fact transferred into pure water, yet inasmuch as its reflection passes into water it is as it were transferred into it. So also, the power of consciousness, although not actually transferred into the Buddhi, yet it is, as it were, transferred into it, because it is reflected into it. By that fact consciousness becomes, as it were, of the very nature of the Will-to-be. It accordingly follows the modifications of the Will-to-be. This explains the words 'by imitation.' It is said it cognizes by imitation as it cognizes by following the modifications of the Will-to-be.—20.

Sūtra 21

तदर्थ एव दृश्यस्यात्मा ।। २१ ।।

तद् Tad, his. अर्थ: Arthaḥ, purpose. तदर्थ: Tadarthaḥ, for his purpose. दृश्यस्य Dṛśyasya, of the knowable. आत्मा Ātmā, being, existence.

21. For his purpose only in the being of the 'knowable.'—72.

तदर्थ एव दृश्यस्यात्मा । दृशिरूपस्य पुरुषस्य कर्मरूपतामापन्नं दृश्यमिति तदर्थ एव दृश्यस्यात्मा भवति । स्वरूपं भवतीत्यर्थः । तत्स्वरूपं तु पररूपेण प्रतिलब्धात्मकं भोगापवर्गार्थतायां कृतायां पुरुषेण न दृश्यत इति । स्वरूपहानादस्य नाशः प्राप्तो न तु विनश्यति ।। २१ ।।

Vyāsa

The knowable comes out as the object of the Puruṣa appearing as an act of consciousness. For this purpose only, therefore, is the being of the knowable. The meaning is that it possesses the nature it does, for that purpose. Its nature, however, depending as it does upon another for its existence as such, is not cognized by the Puruṣa when the objects of achieving the purposes of enjoyment and emancipation are over. This would seem to imply that it is destroyed, because what constitutes its very being is thus done away with. But it is not destroyed.—72.

Vācaspati's Gloss

Having described the nature of the knower and the knowable, now he says that the knowable exists for the knower, showing as this does in part the relationship existing between the two, the relation, that is to say, of the lord to his possessions. 'For this purpose only is the being of the knowable.' He explains it :—'The knowable comes out as the object of, *i.e.*, being enjoyable by the enjoyer, the Puruṣa, appearing as an act of consciousness.' For this reason the existence of the knowable is for his purpose only, *i.e.*, for the purpose of the knower alone, and not for the purpose of the knowable.

(The word translated here as the *being* is in the original Ātmā, the self. Hence arises the question, How can the *self,* exist for the self?) For this reason he says :—Possesses the nature it does for that purpose. This is the meaning :—The knowable being of the very nature of pleasure and pain, is the enjoyable. Pleasure and pain which consist in being of the same class with the then prevailing mental habit, are in reality put up as such for his purpose only. The objects also such as sound, etc., cause pleasure and pain only because they also are of the nature of the knowable. And it is not themselves that are to be pleased or pained, because in that case these modifications would act as contrary to themselves. By the canon of residues, therefore, the power of consciousness only can be opposed or favoured. Therefore the being of the knowable is for the purpose of the Puruṣa only and not for the purpose of the knowable itself.

It is because the being of the knowable is for the purpose of the Puruṣa and not for the purpose of the knowable itself, that its nature acts to that purpose until that purpose of the Puruṣa is achieved; and ceases to act when that purpose has been achieved. For this reason he says :—'Its nature, however, etc.' In itself the knowable is unintelligent. It is ensouled by another, by consciousness which is the nature of the self. "Ensouled by consciousness" means that its nature as such is informed thereby. When enjoyment and emancipation have been achieved, it is no longer seen by the Puruṣa. Enjoyment is the experience of sound, etc., as pleasure and pain, etc. Emancipation is the direct knowledge of the distinction between the Puruṣa and Objective Existence (Sattva). The Will-to-be is unintelligent and by itself does not know either. It is only by the reflection of the Puruṣa into itself that it does so. The enjoyment and the direct knowledge of the distinct nature of the Puruṣa and Objective Existence, belong therefore to the Puruṣa Himself. Thus when the enjoyment and emancipation of the Puruṣa have been achieved, the purpose of the existence of the knowable no longer remains. The enjoyment and emancipation have no longer to be achieved. Hence it has been said :—'When the object of achieving enjoyment and emancipation has been achieved, etc.'

In this connection he raises a doubt :—'It would follow, etc.' and refutes it :—'But it is not destroyed.'—72.

Sūtra 22

कृतार्थं प्रति नष्टमप्यनष्टं तदन्यसाधारणत्वात्॥ २२॥

कृतार्थम् Kṛta-artham, whose objects have been achieved. प्रति Prati, to him. नष्टम् Naṣṭam, destroyed. अपि Api, although. अनष्टम् Anaṣṭam, not destroyed. तद् Tad, from that. अन्य Anya, to others. साधारणत्वात् Sādhāraṇatvāt, being common, owing to commonness.

22. Although destroyed in relation to him whose objects have been achieved, it is not destroyed, being common to others.—73.

कस्मात्। कृतार्थं प्रति नष्टमप्यनष्टं तदन्यसाधारणत्वात्। कृतार्थमेकं पुरुषं प्रति दृश्यं नष्टमपि नाशं प्राप्तमप्यनष्टं तदन्यपुरुषसाधारणत्वात्। कुशलं पुरुषं प्रति नाशं प्राप्तमप्यकुशलान्पुरुषान्प्रति न कृतार्थमिति तेषां दृशेः कर्मविषयतामापन्नं लभत एव पररूपेणानात्मरूपमिति। अतश्च दृग्दर्शनशक्त्योर्नित्यत्वादनादिः संयोगो व्याख्यान इति। तथा चोक्तम्। धर्मिणामनादिसंयोगाद्धर्ममात्राणामप्यनादिः संयोग इति।। २२।।

Vyāsa

Why is it not destroyed ? "Although destroyed in relation to him whose objects have been achieved, it is not destroyed, being common to others" than him. Even though destroyed, *i.e.*, passed into annihilation, in relation to one Puruṣa, whose objects have been achieved, it is not destroyed in reality, because it is common to other Puruṣas beside him. Although it is destroyed to the Puruṣa who has attained wisdom, it is not destroyed in relation to the Puruṣas who have not attained wisdom, as it has not done its duty by them yet. It is, therefore, still related to them, as an object of the act of consciousness, and is as such of course, ensouled by them into form.

This further explains the eternal conjunction of the indestructible energies of the knower and the knowable. As has been said :—The characterised being eternally conjoined, there is eternal conjunction of mere characteristics also.—73.

Vācaspati's Gloss

But becoming altogether unperceivable as it does, how is it that it is not destroyed? Forestalling this objection, he asks the question, 'Why is it not destroyed?' and answers by the aphorism :—'Although destroyed in relation to him whose objects have been achieved, etc.' The Puruṣa whose objects have been achieved, is so spoken of here. Even though destroyed in relation to him, it, the knowable, is not really destroyed, because it is common to all the other Puruṣas, whether they be the wise ones or the unwise ones. He explains :—'Even though destroyed, in relation, etc.' Destruction means disappearance. The knowable, however, is not destroyed, being common to all the other Puruṣas. Consciousness is the nature of the self which is beyond the knowable. It is by that, that the knowable is ensouled. That is known in the Śruti, Smṛti, Purāṇas and Itihāsa as the Unmanifested, One without parts, not dependent upon anything else, pervading, eternal, possessing the energy of all the effects in the world. It does not become the object of knowledge to the wise man the act being contrary to his nature. It is, however, seen by the unwise, and is not therefore non-existent. Colour is not seen by the blind man; it does not, therefore, cease to exist, being visible to a man with eyes. Further, there is not one Puruṣa only like the Prakṛti. That there are more Puruṣas than one is proved by differences of life, death, pleasure and pain and evolution and emancipation. As to the Vedic texts which speak of the unity of the Puruṣas, they are contrary to other authoritative knowledge; they also can somehow be reconciled by the absence of difference of time and place and by devotion. Further, the Vedic texts themselves lay down clearly that the Prakṛti is one and that the Puruṣas are many. Thus the text :—"One unborn is there, who is red, black and white; she goes one giving birth to many children. One unborn Puruṣa follows her enjoying; another unborn Puruṣa gives her up, having enjoyed all her enjoyables."—(Śvetāśvatara Upaniṣad). The aphorism under discussion explains only the meaning of this text.

Inasmuch as the knowable, although destroyed in relation to one, exists in relation to another Puruṣa, the powers of seeing (consciousness) and being seen (the knowable) are permanent, and the eternity of their conjunction is hereby explained. The author states the concurrence of the Āgamis with this position :—'As it has been said.' The 'characterized,' *i.e.*, the qualities are in eternal conjunction with the selves (the ātmās). Hence their conjunction with the characteristics, *i.e.*, the phenomenal state of Mahat, etc., is also eternal. Although the conjunction of the Mahat, etc., with each one of the Puruṣas has an end, notwithstanding its having has no beginning, yet the conjunction of all of them with the Mahat, etc., has no end, as these are common to all. It is for this reason that the words used are 'characteristics only.' The author shows the generic qualities pervading all the phenomena of that class by using the word "only." It is for this reason that although the conjunction of *one* Puruṣa with one manifestation of the principle of Mahat has ceased to exist, the conjunction of another Puruṣa with another manifestation of the Mahat has not become a thing of the past. It has, therefore, been spoken of as ever-present (Nitya).—22.

Sūtra 23

स्वस्वामिशक्त्योः स्वरूपोपलब्धिहेतुः संयोगः ।। २३ ।।

स्व- Sva, of being owned. स्वामि Svāmi, of owning. शक्त्योः Śaktyoḥ, of the powers of both. स्वरूप- Svarūpa, of the natures. उपलब्धि Upalabdhi, the recognition. हेतुः Hetuḥ, that brings about. संयोगः Saṁyogaḥ, conjunction.

23. Conjunction is that which brings about the recognition of the natures of the power of owning and the capacity of being owned.—74.

संयोगस्वरूपाभिधित्सयेदं सूत्रं प्रववृते। स्वस्वामिशक्त्योः स्वरूपोपलब्धिहेतुः संयोगः। पुरुषः स्वामी दृश्येन स्वेन दर्शनार्थं संयुक्तस्तस्मात्संयोगाद् दृश्यस्योपलब्धिर्या स भोगः। या तु द्रष्टुः स्वरूपोपलब्धिः सोऽपवर्गो दर्शनकार्यावसानः संयोग इति। दर्शनं वियोगस्य कारणमुक्तम्। दर्शनमदर्शनस्य प्रतिद्वन्द्वीत्यदर्शनं संयोगनिमित्तमुक्तम्। नात्र दर्शनं मोक्षकारणमदर्शनाभावादेव बन्धाभावः स मोक्ष इति। दर्शनस्य भावे बन्धकारणस्यादर्शनस्य नाश इत्यतो दर्शनं ज्ञानं कैवल्यकारणमुक्तम्। किंचेदमदर्शनं नाम किं गुणानामधिकार आहोस्विद् दृशिरूपस्य स्वामिनो दर्शितविषयस्य प्रधानचित्तस्यानुत्पादः स्वस्मिन्दृश्ये विद्यमाने यो दर्शनाभावः किमर्थवत्तागुणानामथाविद्या स्वचित्तेन सहनिरुद्धा स्वचित्तस्योत्पत्तिबीजम्। किं स्थितिसंस्कारक्षये गतिसंस्काराभिव्यक्तिः। यत्रेदमुक्तं प्रधानं स्थित्यैव वर्तमानं विकाराकरणादप्रधानं स्यात्। तथा गत्यैव वर्तमानं विकारनित्यत्वादप्रधानं स्यात्। उभयथा चास्य वृत्तिः प्रधानव्यवहारं लभते नान्यथा। कारणान्तरेष्वपि कल्पितेष्वेव समानश्चर्च्चः। दर्शनशक्तिरेवादर्शनमित्येके प्रधानस्यात्मख्यापनार्था प्रवृत्तिरिति श्रुतेः। सर्वबोध्याबोधसमर्थः प्राक्प्रवृत्तेः पुरुषो न पश्यति सर्वकार्यकरणसमर्थं दृश्यं तदा न दृश्यत इत्युभयस्याप्यदर्शनं धर्म इत्येके। तत्रेदं दृश्यस्य स्वात्मभूतमपि पुरुषप्रत्ययापेक्षं दर्शनं दृश्यधर्मत्वेन भवति। तथा पुरुषस्यानात्मभूतमपि दृश्यप्रत्ययापेक्षं

पुरुषधर्मत्वेनेवादर्शनमवभासते। दर्शनं ज्ञानमेवादर्शनमिति केचिदभिदधति। इत्येते शास्त्रगता विकल्पाः। तत्र विकल्पबहुत्वमेतत्सर्वपुरुषाणां गुणानां-संयोगे साधारणविषयम्।। २३।।

Vyāsa

This aphorism was composed for the purpose of explaining the nature of conjunction. 'Conjunction is that which brings about the recognition of the natures of the power of owning and the capacity of being owned.' The Puruṣa is the owner. 'The knowable' is whatever is owned. The former is conjoined to the latter for the purpose of knowing. The cognition of the knowable which follows from that conjunction is enjoyment. The knowable which follows from that conjunction is enjoyment. The knowledge, however, of the nature of the knower is emancipation. Conjunction, therefore, ends when it has caused knowledge. Knowledge is, therefore, called the cause of separation. Knowledge is the contradictory of ignorance. Therefore, ignorance is said to be the reason for conjunction. Her knowledge is not the cause of freedom (Mokṣa); because the absence of Ignorance itself, meaning as it does the absence of bondage, is freedom (Mokṣa). When knowledge comes into existence, ignorance which is the cause of bondage disappears, and with it the bondage which is caused thereby. It is for this reason that knowledge, the seeing of the true nature of things, is said to be the cause of Kaivalya (absolute independence, standing alone).

And now what is this Ignorance (adarśana), this absence of knowledge? Is it a function of the qualities? Or, is it the non-reproduction of the mind which after having shown all the objects to the Puruṣa has become latent? That there should be absence of knowledge notwithstanding the presence of the knowable or the thing owned, is also unreasonable. Is it again the purposefulness of the qualities? Or, is it Nescience which has passed into the state of latency with its own appropriate mental state, and has become the seed which produces the mind appropriate to its own manifestation? Is it again the manifestation of the potency of motion, on the potency of rest having expended itself. It has been said on this subject, that the Pradhāna, the material cause of all manifestation, would become what it is not, if it tended only to rest, because in that case there would not be any manifestation into phenomena; nor would it be what it is, if it were to remain in constant motion, because in that case, the phenomena would become eternal and never disappear. It is only when it tends to both these states, that it can be called the Pradhāna (the cause of manifestation) not otherwise. The same considerations apply to any other causes that might be imagined.

Some say that Ignorance (adarśana) is nothing but the power which manifests as knowing (darśana). As the text says, 'The activity of the Pradhāna is for the sake of showing herself.'

Others say that Ignorance (adarśana) is the characteristic of both the knower (Puruṣa) and he knowable, because the Puruṣa possesses only the power of knowing all that may be known, but does not know, before the setting in of manifestation; and the knowable possesses only the capacity of causing all effects, but is not known at the time. Here this knowledge, though of the very nature of the knowable, stands in need of the incoming of the Puruṣa for its achievement, and is therefore a characteristic of the knowable. Again although it is not of the nature of the Puruṣa, yet depending as it does for its completion upon the illumination of the knowable, Ignorance looks as if it were a characteristic of the Puruṣa.

Some again say that Ignorance is seeing or knowing (darśana) only.

These are alternative conceptions of the teaching only. This manifoldness of alternative conceptions is the common ground for the conjunction of the qualities with all the Puruṣas.—74.

Vācaspati's Gloss

Thus then having described the cause of conjunction to be the achievement of the objects of the Puruṣa and having further described the concomitant eternity of the Pradhāna as well as the cause of the conjunction common to all the Puruṣas, this aphorism was composed to explain the nature of the conjunction which is not common to all the Puruṣas but pertains only to the individual :—'Conjunction is the cause of the recognition of the nature of the power of owning and the capacity of being owned.' Inasmuch as the knowledge is for his sake, the Puruṣa enjoying the benefits conferred by it, becomes its owner, and the knowable becomes its own (possession). This correlation of theirs being determined as it is by the nature of the powers themselves, becomes the cause of the recognition of their natures. It is this that is illuminated by the Commentary :—"The Puruṣa is the owner." On account of fitness only as such, he is conjoined with the knowable as its own by virtue of its fitness again. The rest is easy.

Very well. The recognition of the nature of the seer is called emancipation (Apavarga) because by the instrumentality thereof one is drawn away from the conjunction. Perfect freedom (Mokṣa), however, is not a thing which can be brought about by means of anything. It would, therefore, certainly fall short of perfect freedom. For this reason he says :—Conjunction, therefore, ends when it has caused knowledge; the conjunction, that is to say, of the individual Puruṣa with the individual Will-to-be. Therefore, knowledge is called the cause of separation.

But then how is it that the conjunction ceases with the attainment of knowledge. He says that :—'Knowledge is the contradictory of ignorance, etc.' What then? For this reason the says :—'Ignorance, *i.e.*, Nescience is said to be the reason for conjunction.' Further he illuminates the same meaning :—'Here knowledge is not the cause of freedom (Mokṣa), etc.'

Well, but knowledge may remove ignorance being contradictory thereto; how çan bondage be removed? For this reason he says :—'When knowledge comes into existence etc.' The meaning is that perfect freedom (Mokṣa) is the establishment of the self in its own nature, quite independent as he is of the Will-to-be; and that the means whereby it is brought about is not knowledge, but the removal of ignorance.

In order to establish the particular ignorance which is the cause of the conjunction to all the Puruṣas, he now sets out the alternative forms of ignorance as such :—'And now what is, etc.' He suggests a theory :—'Is it a function of the qualities, etc.' The function of the qualities is their power of bringing about effects. It is by virtue of that that conjunction becomes the cause of creation (Saṁsāra).

Taking up the form of denying what seems to be implied, he states the second alternative :—'Or is it, etc.' The meaning is that the mind by whom the objects, such as sound, etc., and the mental manifestation of the distinction between the Puruṣa and the Objective Existence are shown, is not born along with these states. He explains the same :—'In its own knowability, that is, sound, etc., and the manifestation in the mind of the distinctive natures of the Puruṣa and the essence of matter, the Pradhāna is active only so long as the two-fold knowledge has not been brought about. When the two-fold knowledge has been brought about it ceases to act.' This is another suggestion thrown out.

Now he mentions the third alternative :—'Is it again the purposefulness of the qualities.' The meaning is that inasmuch as the effect always exists, enjoyment and emancipation which have to manifest in the future, exist though not predicable in the present.

He suggests the fourth alternative in the same form of suggestive interrogation :—'Or is it Nescience, etc.' The suggestion is that it may be Nescience which at the time of every creation goes into the state of latency of the Pradhāna having been drawn in along with its own mind and then becomes the seed for the production of the same mind by its own potentiality. For this reason it is the residual potency of Nescience which is different from knowledge that is called Ignorance.

He states the fifth alternative in the same form of a suggestive question :—'Is it that the potency of motion of the Pradhāna, the potency, that is to say, which is responsible for inclining the Pradhāna, towards the manifestation of effects, is essentialized on the potentiality of rest which lives in the Pradhāna and which consists in the continued successive manifestation of the modification of equipoise, coming to an end? He states the teaching of another school in support of the existence of both these potencies :—'It has been said on this subject,' by those who deny the existence of the one only. The *Pradhāna* is that by which the world of modifications is created. If that *Pradhāna* always tend towards rest and never towards motion, then it cannot create any modification and must, therefore, become the contradiction of itself. If again it go on always moving and never tend to rest, then he says :—'If it were to remain in constant motion, etc.'

In some places the reading of both the words 'sthiti' and 'gati', is in the dative case. In that case the dative case and the word 'eva' are to be read as meaning the same thing. If it did not go into the state of rest, then no modification would disappear; and if a thing which exists does not disappear, it can never also re-appear; and thus there would be no modifications. In this view nothing would ever be created, and thus there would be no Pradhāna. It is by motion and rest, both alternating, that this cause becomes Pradhāna, not otherwise, if only one of these alternative states were admitted then not only in the case of Pradhāna, but in the case of other first Causes, such as Parabrahma, Māyā, atoms, etc., also the same discussion would be relevant. These causes too would be no causes, if they were to remain in constant rest, because in that case they would not reduce effects. They would similarly be no causes, if they were to remain in constant motion, because in that case, the modifications themselves becoming eternal, no necessity would remain for a cause.

He states the sixth alternative again as a suggestive interrogation. "Some say that ignorance is nothing but the power which manifests as knowing (darśana). It is said in the case of the Prajāpati vow, 'Do not see the rising sun.' This signifies the mental mood which co-exists with and is responsible for the act of seeing not. So also in the case of ignorance too the denial of knowledge means that, co-existent with the absence of knowledge, there is a power which takes its origin therein and which with the object of bringing about the knowledge termed enjoyment, etc., joins the knower to the knowable.

He cites a Vedic text in support of the same subject :—'The activity of the Pradhāna is etc.' Grant that the Pradhāna becomes active for the purpose of showing herself as the Vedic text says; but it is not the power of knowing the nature of the self that becomes active. For this reason he says :—'The Puruṣa possessing the power of knowing all that may be known, etc.' It is not the object of showing herself that only sets the Pradhāna into activity, because before the setting in of activity, it could not be said whether it possessed the power of being seen. Hence it is the capacity of being seen that sets in activity. This the Vedic text says by implication.

This is the sixth alternative, that the power of seeing (knowing) depends upon the Pradhāna. Now he states the seventh alternative, which takes up the position that the power of knowing depends upon both. 'Ignorance depends upon both, etc.' Ignorance, *i.e.*, the power of seeing is the characteristic of both the Puruṣa and the knowable. Such is the position of some (thinkers).

This may be allowed with regard to the knowable, because all the powers have it as their substratum. We cannot, however, allow it with regard to the Puruṣa. The power of knowing has not the Puruṣa for its substratum, because knowledge does not enter into the Puruṣa to make a part of him. If it did, the Puruṣa would become changeable. (He would not remain the constant factor which he is always found to be in all mental phenomena). For this reason he says :—'Here this knowledge, etc.'

Let it then be of the nature of the 'knowable.' In that case knowledge, being a modification of the constituent energy of the 'knowable' must also be un-intelligent by nature. It could not, therefore, perform the function of the knowing as a characteristic of the knowable. The non-intelligent is not self-illuminating. For this reason knowledge becomes a characteristic of the 'knowable,' only with reference to the incoming of the knower, the self, the reflection of consciousness therein. This is known by the act indicating the actor.

Well but this too makes knowledge to be a characteristic of the knowable, not at the same time a characteristic of the Puruṣa too. For this reason he says :—'Again although it is not of the nature of the Puruṣa, etc.' The essence of matter is certainly not of the nature of the Puruṣa. Still the incoming of the Puruṣa, *i.e.*, the reflection of consciousness on which the act of knowing the knowable essence of the Will-to-be depends, makes it possible that the act of knowing be spoken of as it were to be an act of the Puruṣa, although not really so. This is the meaning. The characteristics of the Will-to-be shine forth as the characteristics of consciousness, because consciousness and the Will-to-be appear to be one, on account of the Will-to-be always carrying reflection of consciousness along with itself.

He now mentions the eighth alternative :—'Some say that the seeing, *i.e.*, the knowing of sound, etc., is itself ignorance, not that of the distinction between the Puruṣa and the Objective Essence. This is the same as that the power of seeing, although an authority for the perception of colour, is no authority for the perception of taste, etc. This is the meaning. The cognitions of sound, etc., as pleasurable appearances, etc., point to the conjunction of knower and the knowable, because it is necessary for their achievement.

All the alternative theories have been described. In order to accept the fourth alternative, he rejects all the others, because all the other alternative conceptions of the teaching of the Sāṅkhya, being common to all the Puruṣas lead to the absence of variety of experience :—"These are the alternative concepions of the teaching, etc."—23.

Sūtra 24

तस्य हेतुरविद्या ।। २४ ।।

तस्य Tasya, its. हेतुः Hetuḥ, effective cause. अविद्या Avidyā, nescience.

24. Nescience is its effective cause.—75.

यस्तु प्रत्यक्चेतनस्य स्वबुद्धिसंयोगः। तस्य हेतुरविद्या। विपर्ययज्ञानवासनेत्यर्थः। विपर्ययज्ञानवासनावासिता च न कार्यनिष्ठां पुरुषख्यातिं बुद्धिः प्राप्नोति साधिकारा पुनरावर्तते। सा तु पुरुषख्यातिपर्यवसानां कार्यनिष्ठां प्राप्नोति। चरिताधिकारा निवृत्तादर्शना बन्धकारणाभावान्न पुनरावर्तते। अत्र कश्चित्पण्डकोपाख्यानेनोद्घाटयति। मुग्धया भार्ययाभिधीयते। पण्डक आर्यपुत्र अपत्यवती मे भगिनी किमर्थं नाम नाहमिति स तामाह मृतस्तेऽहमपत्यमुत्पादयिष्यामीति। तथेदं विद्यमानं ज्ञानं चित्तनिवृत्तिं न करोति। विनष्टं करिष्यतीति का प्रत्याशा। तत्राचार्यदेशीयो वक्ति। ननु बुद्धिनिवृत्तिरेव मोक्षोऽदर्शनकारणाभावाद् बुद्धिनिवृत्तिः। तच्चादर्शनं बन्धकारणं दर्शनान्निवर्तते। तत्र चित्तनिवृत्तिरेव मोक्षः किमर्थमस्थान एवास्य मतिविभ्रमः।। २४।।

Vyāsa

The effective cause, however, of the conjunction of the individual consciousness with its own Will-to-be is Nescience, which means the potency of the habit of unreal cognition. The Will-to-know, possessed as it is of the aroma of the habits of unreal cognition, does not culminate into the knowledge of the self, which is the end of its work, and thus having still a duty to perform, comes back. When, however, it reaches the culmination of its work, which is the attainment of the knowledge of the Puruṣa, its work is achieved, ignorance is gone, the cause of bondage no longer remains, and it does no longer come back.

Someone ridicules this position by the story of the impotent husband. A foolish wife thus addressed her husband :—"My dear, my sister has got children. Wherefore have I none?" He said to her :—"I shall beget children unto thee when I am dead." Similarly, this knowledge while in existence, does not cause the mind to cease from action; what hope is there that it will cause cessation when suppressed? Says on this subject a teacher very nearly perfect :—"Is not Mokṣa (freedom) the cessation of the Will-to-be itself and nothing else? The Will-to-be ceases to act when the cause of ignorance no longer remains. The Ignorance which is the cause of bondage is removed by knowledge. Mokṣa (perfect freedom) then is only the cessation of the mind from its work. Wherefore then this mental confusion out of place ?"—75.

Vācaspati's Gloss

In order to establish the fourth alternative the introduces the aphorism :—'The effective cause, however, of the conjunction, etc.' 'Individual consciousness' :—The word Pratyak-cetana in the text means consciousness which cognizes by reflex action, and as the conjunction which makes it possible is not common to all the Puruṣas, and is the conjunction of one Puruṣa with his won independent Will-to-be, variety of experience is effected. (Hence the translation Individual Consciousness).

He reads the aphorism :—'Nescience is its effective cause.' But Nescience is Unreal Cognition. It is due to the conjunction of consciousness with the individualized Will-to-be just as other experiences and emancipation are due to it. If the Will-to-be is not conjoined to consciousness, there can be no existence for unreal cognition. How is it then that Nescience is the cause of any kind of cognition? For this reason he says :—'Which means the residual potency of Unreal cognition.' The Nescience of other creations drawn in with the mind in which it manifested, live in the Pradhāna in the shape of potential energy. The Pradhāna, possessed as it is of the aroma of this potential energy, evolves out of itself, the Will-to-be of a particular Puruṣa, just as it was before. Similarly in the regular order of each creation preceding another. The order of creation being eternal no defect arises in the theory. It is for this reason that the Puruṣa is not free at the time of each creation. For this reason he says :—'The Will-to-be possessed as it is, etc.'

When, however, the knowledge of the Puruṣa reaches its end, then the cause of bondage in the shape of the residua of unreal cognition no longer exists, and it does not come back. For this reason he says :—'When, however, it reaches its culmination, etc.'

Here some nihilists ridicule this state of absolute independence (Kaivalya) by relating the story of the impotent husband. The author tells the story of the impotent husband :—"A foolish wife, etc." "Wherefore" in the translation stands for "with what object" in the original. Object here stands for reason. The object of an act is the reason of the action.

The author shows the similarity with the story of the impotent :—'Similarly, etc.' This existing knowledge of the distinction between consciousness and the 'qualities' does not cause mental cessation; what reason is there that higher desirelessness, the light of knowledge alone will make the mind to disappear after having restrained it along with its residual potency? The effect of something exists only so long as the cause itself exists. It does not remain in existence when the cause ceases to exist. He refutes this by quoting the reasoning of a teacher who agrees on this point :—'Says on this subject a teacher, etc.'

A teacher very nearly perfect though not altogether, is called *Ācāryadeśa.* As to a perfect teacher Vāyu has described his qualities thus :—'One is called an Ācārya because he understands the meaning of the teaching (Śāstra) well, establishes one in right conduct also, and also himself keeps the right line of action.'

Mokṣa (absolute freedom) is only the cessation of the Will-to-be after it has achieved experience and the discrimination of the distinction between the Puruṣa and Objective Existence. It is not that the Will-to-be itself ceases to exist. This ceasing of the Will-to-knowfrom its work of causing experience and emancipation, although the Will-to-know itself lives on, follows immediately upon its establishment in the state of the Cloud of Virtue (Dharma Megha) which is the culmination of discriminative knowledge. He illuminates the same :—'The Will-to-know ceases to act when ignorance, which is the cause of bondage, is removed by knowledge. The removal of knowledge (the cessation of the act of knowing) is brought about by higher desirelessness. The meaning is that perfect freedom (Mokṣa) exists even though the Will-to-know itself lives on.' Having described the opinion of the teacher, he now gives his own :—'Mokṣa then is only the cessation of the mind from its work.'

But it has been said that when the act of knowing ceases the mind itself very soon ceases to exist. How is it then this brought about by knowledge? For this reason he says :—'Wherefore then this mental confusion quite out of place?' The construction is as follows :—We may be taunted thus if we believe that knowledge is the direct cause of the cessation of the mind. We, however, lay down that discriminative knowledge becomes useful in establishing the Puruṣa in its own nature, when having reached the highest point, by the successive appearances of the higher and higher stages of the inhibitive trance, it comes to co-exist with the state of mental cessation. How then have we laid ourselves out for a taunt?—24.

Sūtra 25

तदभावात्संयोगाभावो हानं तद्दृशेः कैवल्यम्।। २५ ।।

तद् Tad, its. **अभावात्** Abhāvāt, on account of disappearance. **संयोगाभावः** Saṁyogābhāvaḥ, the disappearance. **अभावः** Abhāvaḥ, of conjunction. (**संयोग**). **हानम्** Hānam, removal. **तद्** Tad, that. **दृशेः** Dṛśeḥ, of the knower. **कैवल्यम्** Kaivalyam, absolute freedom.

25. Removal is the disappearance of conjunction on account of its disappearance that is the absolute freedom of the knower.—76.

हेयं दुःखं हेयकारणं च संयोगाख्यं सनिमित्तमुक्तमतः परं हानं वक्तव्यम्। तदभावात्संयोगाभावो हानं तद्दृशेः कैवल्यम्। तस्यादर्शनस्याभावाद् बुद्धिपुरुषसंयोगाभाव आत्यन्तिको बन्धनोपरम इत्यर्थः। एतद्धानं तद्दृशेः कैवल्यं पुरुषस्यामिश्रीभावः पुनरसंयोगो गुणैरित्यर्थः।। २५ ।।

Vyāsa

The pain that has to be removed has been described, as also what is called conjunction, the cause of the pain to be removed, together with the reason of its existence. Removal has to be discussed henceforward. 'Removal is the disappearance of conjunction brought about by its disappearance; that is, the absolute freedom of the knower. The meaning is that on the disappearance of the conjunction of the Puruṣa and the Will-to-be being brought about by the disappearance of ignorance, bondage is for ever removed. This is removal. This is the freedom of the seer (Puruṣa). It means his not getting mixed up again, *i.e.*, not being conjoined again with the 'qualities.'—76.

Vācaspati's Gloss

Having thus described two departments of the science, now he introduces the aphorism for describing the third :—'The pain that has been removed is the future pain. Removal is the disappearance, etc.' Explains :—'The meaning is etc.' Because there is disappearance of conjunction even in the state of the Great Latency (Mahāpralaya), the words 'for ever' have been used. The removal is the cessation of pain. This shows that the object of the removal is the fulfilment of the objects of the Puruṣa. The rest is easy.—25.

Sūtra 26

विवेकख्यातिरविप्लवा हानोपायः ।। २६ ।।

विवेक Viveka, of discrimination. ख्याति: Khyātiḥ, knowledge, अविप्लवा Aviplavā, undisturbed. हान Hāna, of the removal. उपायः Upāyaḥ, the means.

26. The means of the removal is discriminative knowledge undisturbed.—77.

दुःखकारणनिवृत्तौ दुःखो परमो हानं तदा स्वरूपप्रतिष्ठः पुरुष इत्युक्तमथ हानस्य कः प्राप्त्युपाय इति। विवेकख्यातिरविप्लवा हानोपायः। सत्त्वपुरुषान्यताप्रत्ययो विवेकख्यातिः। सा त्वनिवृत्तमिथ्याज्ञाना प्लवते। यदा मिथ्याज्ञानं दग्धबीजभावं बन्ध्यप्रसवं संपद्यते तदा विधूतक्लेशरजसः सत्त्वस्व परे वैशारद्ये परस्यां वशीकारसंज्ञायां वर्तमानस्य विवेकप्रत्ययप्रवाहो निर्मलो भवति सा विवेकख्यातिरविप्लवा हानोपायः। ततो मिथ्याज्ञानस्य दग्धबीजभावोपगमः पुनश्चाप्रसव इत्येष मोक्षस्य मार्गो हानस्योपाय इति।। २६ ।।

Vyāsa

Pain is removed on the removal of the cause of pain. In the removal of pain consists the establishment of the Puruṣa in its own nature. What them is the means of attaining the state of this removal of pain? 'Discriminative knowledge undisturbed is the means of the removal.'

Discriminative knowledge is the recognition of the distinct natures of the Puruṣa and the Essence of matter (Sattva). This, however, remains shaky as long as false knowledge has not been removed. When false knowledge has its seed burnt up and thus becomes incapable of fruition, then the dirt of disturbing energy (Rajas) being removed, mental essence is in that state of the highest purity and possesses the consciousness of the highest power; and in the state flows on the stream of the notion of discrimination, free from impurity. It is this discriminative knowledge undisturbed, that is the means of the removal. By this it is clear that the means of removal, the path of Mokṣa (absolute freedom), is the burning of the seed of false knowledge, so that it may not sprout again. 77.

Vācaspati's Gloss

The author introduces the aphorism, in order to describe the means of removal, the fourth branch of the science :—'What then, etc.' "Discriminative knowledge, undisturbed is the means of removal." Discriminative knowledge comes into existence by verbal and inferential cognition also. The knowledge so obtained does not remove the actual or potential outgoing energies of the mind. In the case of such discriminative knowledge they always return to action. It is with the object of excluding the discriminative knowledge thus acquired, that the word 'Undisturbed' is used. Undisturbed means 'free from false knowledge.' Disturbance is false knowledge. This is the meaning. Discriminative knowledge should be obtained by the teaching which consists of verbal knowledge. It should then be established in the mind by reasoning. It should be carried to its highest limit of illumination by devoted attention for a long time without interruption and with reverence. Then does discriminative knowledge become direct. False knowledge is removed together with its residua. It becomes undisturbed. This is the means of removal. The rest of the Commentary is easy.—26.

Sūtra 27

तस्य सप्तधा प्रान्तभूमिः प्रज्ञा।। २७।।

तस्य Tasya, his. सप्तधा Saptadhā, is sevenfold. प्रान्त-भूमिः Prānta-bhūmiḥ, final at each stage. प्रज्ञा Prajñā, discrimination.

27. His discrimination becoming final at each stage, sevenfold.—78.

तस्य सप्तधा प्रान्तभूमिः प्रज्ञा। तस्येति प्रत्युदितख्यातेः प्रत्याम्नायः सप्तधेति। अशुद्ध्यावरण-मलापगमाच्चित्तस्य प्रत्ययान्तरानुत्पादे सति सप्तधैव सप्तप्रकारैव प्रज्ञा विवेकिनो भवति। तद्यथा परिज्ञातं हेयं नास्य पुनः परिज्ञेयमस्ति। क्षीणा हेयहेतवो न पुनरेतेषां क्षेतव्यमस्ति। साक्षात्मकृतं निरोधसमाधिना हानम्। भावितो विवेकख्यातिरूपो हानोपाय इत्येषा चतुष्टयी कार्याविमुक्तिः प्रज्ञायाः। चित्तविमुक्तिस्तु त्रयीचरिताधिकारा बुद्धिः। गुणा गिरिशिखरतटच्युता इव ग्रावाणो निरवस्थानाः स्वकारणे प्रलयाभिमुखाः सह तेनास्तं गच्छन्ति। न चैषां प्रविलीनानां पुनरस्त्युत्पादः प्रयोजनाभावादिति। एतस्यामवस्थायां गुणसंबन्धातीतः स्वरूपमात्रज्योतिरमलः केवली पुरुष इत्येतां सप्तविधां प्रान्तभूमिप्रज्ञामनुपश्यन्पुरुषः कुशल इत्याख्यायते। प्रतिप्रसवेऽपि च चित्तस्य मुक्तः कुशल इत्येव भवति गुणातीतत्वादिति।। २७।।

Vyāsa

"His" in whom discrimination has come up into consciousness, consideration of attainments is sevenfold. "Sevenfold," *i.e.*, of seven descriptions only is the conscious discrimination of the thinker when at each stage the mental notion is not further produced, on account of the removal from the mind of the dirt which constitutes the veil of impurity. This is as follows :—(1) The pain to be removed is known. Nothing further remains to be known of it. (2) The causes of pain to be removed have been done away with. (3) Removal has become a fact of direct cognition by means of inhibitive trance. (4) The means of knowledge in the shape of discriminative knowledge has been understood.

This is the four-fold freedom of conscious discrimination from external phenomena. The freedom from the mind itself is three-fold. The Will-to-be has done its duty. The 'qualities' tending to become latent into their cause, disappear along with it, finding no support as they do, like stones rolled down from the edge of a hill-top. Nor once passed into latency, do they come back to life again, there being no object for it. In this state the Puruṣa, having passed beyond the limits of the relation with the 'qualities,' remains only the light of his own pure nature and is free.

The Puruṣa who has seen successively these seven stages of discrimination is called 'adept' (kuśala). He remains free and wise even when the mind is resolved into its cause, because he has passed beyond the sphere of the 'qualities'.—78.

Vācaspati's Gloss

The author describes by the aphorism the nature of the finality of the perfection of discriminative knowledge :—'His discrimination becoming final at each stage is sevenfold.' Explains :—'His, etc.'

He in whom the discrimination has just up into consciousness, is the Yogī, in whom the mental phenomenon is present at the time.

His 'consideration of attainments,' means the sending back of his thought over the whole ground that has already been passed over.

The veil of impurity of the mental essence is the same as dirt. When that is removed, and when consequently, 'the mental notion is not further produced,' *i.e.*, the outgoing energy of the notions due to the qualities of disturbance (rajas) and inertia (tamas) is no longer active, he reaches the final point in a stage of undisturbed discriminative knowledge. This consciousness of discrimination of his is seven-fold, *i.e.*, of seven descriptions only. The difference of descriptions of consciousness is due to the difference of its objects.

The stages, *i.e.*, the states are spoken of as each becoming final, because each as such reaches its ultimate and highest point. The ultimate and highest point is that beyond which there is no point of its culmination. The stages of consciousness, *i.e.*, of discriminative knowledge, each of which reaches its culmination, are spoken of as becoming final at each stage.

Now he describes these even stages, each reaching its own culmination :—'That as follows, etc.'

Out of the four stages which are brought about by the effort of man, he illustrates the first :—'The pain to be removed has been known.' Whatever has its origin in the Pradhāna is certainly pain, by reason of the pains of consequence, anxiety and habituation, and by reason of the contrariety of the modifications of the qualities.' It has, therefore, to be removed. It is that which has been known. He shows its finality :—'nothing further remains to be known of it.'

He mentions the second stage :—'The causes.... have been done away with.' He speaks of the finality :—'Nothing more of them, etc.'

He mentions the third :—'The removal which is brought about by inhibitive trance, has been made by me a fact of direct cognition, ascertained by internal perception, while I am in the state of Cognitive trance only. It is to be understood that nothing further of it remains to be ascertained."

He mentions the fourth :—"The means of removal in the shape of discriminative knowledge has been understood, *i.e.*, has been brought into existence. It is to be understood that there is nothing more of it to be brought into being. This is the four-fold freedom of consciousness from external phenomena. Freedom means their ending. The fact of their being the objects of human effort has been shown by their being external phenomena."

Now he speaks of the freedom from the mind, which is brought about after the states brought about by human effort and which does not depend upon effort :—'The freedom from the mind is, however, three-fold.' He mentions the first :—'The Will-to-be has done its duty.' The meaning is that it has achieved experience and emancipation. He mentions the second :—'The qualities, etc.' He shows their finality :—'Nor once passed into latency, etc.'

He mentions the third :—'In this state, etc. In this state the Puruṣa even while in life, is called free and wise; because this is his last birth. He says this :—'The Puruṣa who has seen in succession these, etc.' He says that this state is not dependent upon the mind :—'He remains free and wise even when the mind is resolved into its cause, because he has passed beyond the sphere of the qualities.'—27.

Sūtra 28

योगाङ्गानुष्ठानादशुद्धिक्षये ज्ञानदीप्तिराविवेकख्यातेः।। २८।।

योग Yoga, of yoga. अङ्ग Aṅga, of the accessories. अनुष्ठानाद् Anuṣṭhānād, by the sustained practice. अशुद्धि Aśuddhi, of impurity. क्षये Kṣaye, on the destruction. ज्ञान Jñāna, of wisdom. दीप्तिः Dīptiḥ, the light. आ Ā, reaching up to. विवेक Viveka, of discrimination. ख्यातेः Khyāteḥ, the knowledge.

28. On the destruction of impurity by the sustained practice of the accessories of Yoga, the light of wisdom reaches up to discriminative knoweldge.—79.

सिद्धा भवति विवेकख्यातिर्हानोपाय इति न च सिद्धिरन्तरेण साधनमित्येतदारभ्यते। योगाङ्गानुष्ठनदशुद्धिक्षये ज्ञानदीप्तिराविवेकख्यातेः। योगाङ्गान्यष्टावभिधायिष्यमाणानि तेषामनुष्ठानात्पञ्चपर्वणो विपर्ययस्याशुद्धिरूपस्य क्षयो नाशस्तत्क्षाये सम्यग्ज्ञानस्याभिव्यक्तिः। यथा यथा च साधनान्यनुष्ठीयन्ते तथा तथा तनुत्वमशुद्धिरापद्यते। यथा यथा च क्षीयते तथा तथा च क्षयक्रमानुरोधिनी ज्ञानस्यापि दीप्तिर्विवर्धते। सा खल्वेषा विवृद्धिः प्रकर्षमनुभवत्याविवेकख्यातेः। आगुणपुरुषस्वरूपविज्ञानादित्यर्थः। योगाङ्गानुष्ठानमशुद्धेर्वियोगकारणम्। यथा परशुश्छेद्यस्य। विवेकख्यातेस्तु प्राप्तिकारणं यथा धर्मः सुखस्य नान्यथा कारणम्। कति चैतानि कारणानि शास्त्रे भवन्ति। नवैवेत्याह। तद्यथा उत्पत्तिस्थित्यभिव्यक्तिविकारप्रत्ययाप्तयः। वियोगान्यत्वधृतयः कारणं नवधास्मृतमिति। तत्रोत्पत्तिकारणं मनो भवति ज्ञानस्य स्थितिकारणं मनसः पुरुषार्थता शरीरस्येवाहार इति अभिव्यक्तिकारणं यथा रूपस्यालोकस्तथा रूपज्ञानं विकारकारणं मनसोविषयान्तरम्। यथाग्निः पाक्यस्य। प्रत्ययकारणं धूमज्ञानमग्निज्ञानस्य। प्राप्तिकारणं योगाङ्गानुष्ठानं विवेकख्यातेः। वियोगकारणं तदेवाशुद्धेः। अन्यत्वकारणं यथा सुवर्णस्य सुवर्णकारः। एवमेकस्य स्त्रीप्रत्ययस्याविद्या मूढत्वे द्वेषो दुःखत्व रागः सुखत्वे तत्त्वज्ञानं माध्यस्थ्ये धृतिकारणं शरीरमिन्द्रियाणाम्। तानि च तस्य महाभूतानि शरीराणां तानि च परस्परं सर्वेषां तैर्यग्योनमानुषदैवतानि च परस्परार्थत्वादित्येवं नव कारणानि। तानि च यथासम्भवं पदार्थान्तरेष्वपि योज्यानि योगाङ्गानुष्ठानं तु द्विधैव कारणत्वं लभत इति।। २८।।

Vyāsa

Discriminative knowledge becomes the means of removal, when achieved. There can be no achievement without the adoption of the means thereof. This, therefore, is taken up. "By the sustained practice of the accessories of Yoga is impurity destroyed and then the light of wisdom shines up to discriminative knowledge.' "

The accessories of Yoga are eight, to be further named. By their sustained practice is destroyed the five-fold unreal cognition, which is of the nature of impurity. Destruction means disappearance. When that is destroyed, real knowledge is manifested. As the means of achievement are being practised more and more, so is the impurity being attenuated more and more. And as more and more of it is being destroyed, so also goes on increasing more and more the light of wisdom following in the wake of destruction. This increase reaches its culmination in discriminative knowledge. This means that its highest culmination is in the knowledge of the nature of consciousness and the 'qualities.'

The practice of the accessories of Yoga is the cause of the separation of impurity, as the axe is the cause of the separation of the piece of wood cut off thereby. It is, however, the cause of the attainment of discriminative knowledge, as virtue is the cause of happiness. It is not a cause otherwise.

Well, how many of these causes are there in the Teaching? They have been said to be nine only as follows :—'A cause is said to operate in nine ways :—As the cause of birth, of preservation, of manifestation, of modification, of sequential cognition, of attainment, of separation, of differentiation, of upholding.'

Of these the cause of birth : the mind is of knowledge.

The sustaining cause : the achievement of the objects of the Puruṣa is of the mind, as food is of the body.

The cause of manifestation is as light is the cause of the manifestation of colour; as also the knowledge of colour.

The cause of change or modification is, as for example, a different object of the mind. Or fire of the food that is cooked.

The cause of sequential cognition is as the knowledge of smoke is of the knowledge of fire.

The cause of attainment is as the practice of the accessories of Yoga of the attainment of discriminative knowledge.

The cause of separation is as the same of impurities.

The cause of differentiation is as the goldsmith is of gold. Similarly, as in the case of the one notion of the same woman, Nescience causes forgetfulness; anger makes it painful; desire makes it pleasurable; the knowledge of realities makes it indifferent, neither pleasurable nor painful.

The cause of upholding is as the body is of the organs of sensation and action and *vice versa;* the elements of the bodies and each of these mutually of all the others. So also the animals, men and gods each of the others. Thus there are nine descriptions of the causal operations. These are to be applied to other objects also as may be. As to the practice of the accessories of Yoga they operate as causes in two ways only.—79.

Vācaspati's Gloss

Now then having described the four departments of the science, and seeing that the discriminative knowledge which as the means of removal falls within these departments, has not been achieved like cow's milk, etc., (which although existing in the udders, is not obtained until it is drawn out) and further seeing that this cannot be achieved without employing some means, he goes on to describe the means :—'Discriminative knowledge becomes the means, etc.'

Here shows by the aphorism in what way does the means of knowledge operate as a cause of discriminative knowledge. 'On the destruction of impurity, etc.' The accessories of Yoga destroy impurity by operating as may be along visible and invisible lines. It should be understood that the five branches of Untrue cognition are spoken of here as indicative of virtue and vice also, because they too are of the nature of impurities, being as they are the causes of life-state, life-experience and life-period. The rest is easy.

A cause is seen operating in more ways than one. In what does the practice of Yoga operate as the cause? For this reason he says :—

'The practice of the accessories of Yoga, etc.' The cause of impurity being removed, means that it separates impurity from the essence of the Will-to-be. He gives an illustration :—'As the axe, etc.' The hatchet separates the tree to be cut from the root.

Further, having separated the essence of the Will-to-be from impurity, it leads it to the attainment of discriminative knowledge, as obedience to law is the means of the attainment of happiness. Similarly is the practice of Yoga accessories the means of the attainment of discriminative knowledge. There is no other ways in which the cause operates. He says this :— 'It is the cause of attainment. etc.' Inasmuch as it is said that there is no other way in which it operates, he puts the question, How many are the ways of operation altogether? He answers : 'They are nine only.' He enumerates them by a verse :—'Birth, preservation, etc.' Now he illustrates them : 'The cause of birth, etc.' The mind operates to bring knowledge from the state of being unpredicable into the state of present existence; it is, therefore, the cause of the birth of knowledge. The fulfilment of the purpose of the Puruṣa is the cause of the preservation of the mind. Born of the principle of egoism, the mind is preserved as long as it has not fulfilled both the objects of the Puruṣa. When, however, both the objects of the Puruṣa have been fulfilled, it is no longer preserved as such. For this reason the non-achievement of the objects of the Puruṣa is the cause of the preservation of the mind, after it has been born out of its cause. He gives an illustration :—'As food of the body.'

Manifestation means the placing of an object under certain conditions so that they may help in the act of perception either by means of the senses or by the act of the mind itself; as light is the cause of the manifestation of colour.

The cause of change or modification of the mind is an object other than that which has possession of the mind at the time. So goes the story. Mṛkaṇḍu was sitting with his mind entranced. He heard the fifth note of the musical scale emitted by a creeper that was ripening.

He at once opened his eyes, and what did he see? The fair and youthful nymph Pramlocā. The sight of her beauty drew away his mind from the object of his then mental application. and his mind became attached to her. He gives an illustration of this :—'As fire is of the things cooked.' When raw, the particles of rice, etc., are so close as to make them hard to be separated. By cooking a change is introduced. The particles become loose. Fire operates as the cause of change, that is, of the introduction of softness instead of hardness.

It is only the knowledge of an existing object that is brought about by sequential cognition. The knowledge of smoke is the cause of the knowledge of fire. Knowledge is that which is known. The knowledge of fire here means the knowledge which is the same as fire, the mental idea of fire. This is the meaning. It is by sequential cognition that it operates as the cause of the knowledge of fire existing in the present as the thing to be known.

It is natural with causes to pass into effects; but for some reason they sometimes do not pass into that state. Take, for example, water. It is the nature of water to flow downwards when poured on a higher level. But an embankment may be made to check its downword flow. The same is the case here. The essence of the Will-to-be is by nature pleasing and luminous. It is natural for it to reach the state of happiness and discriminative knowledge. It, however, does not reach that state somehow by reason of being checked in its operations by vice (adharma) or by inertia (tamas). That check is removed by virtue or by the practice of the accessories of Yoga. Its operations thus become unhampered; it reaches that state, being its natural producer. As will be said :—There is no operative cause to set the Prakṛtis into action; but it pierces through the impediments like the husbandman.'—iv.3. It is thus that the practice of the accessories of Yoga is said to operate as the cause of the attainment of discriminative knowledge. With reference, however, to another effect lower down, it is described as the cause of separation. Thus he says :—'The cause of separation is as, etc.'

Now he describes the cause of differentiation :—'The cause of differentiation is as the goldsmith of the gold.' Gold is both different and not different from wristlets, ear-rings and armlets. It is different when it is necessary to point out the difference; not different when it is not desired to point out the difference. Thus is it different from the ear-rings. The goldsmith, however, who makes wristlets, makes them from gold which is not other than the gold of the ear-rings. He, therefore, becomes the cause of introducing another differential altogether into the otherwise quite identical gold. He is, therefore, the cause of differentiation.

Similarly is fire the cause of the differentiation of things that are cooked. It is, however, described above as the cause of modification. What is intended to be said there is that the difference between cooked and raw rice, as the characteristics of the same qualified thing, is not intended to be conveyed; and therefore even though the two characteristics are born and disappear respectively, the thing qualified remains the same in both conditions. It is not possible to say that the thing qualified has become quite another thing. It is for these considerations that fire is only spoken of as the cause of modification. There is no overlapping.

The meaning is not to be understood to be that different arrangement is the cause of differentiation, because in that case the goldsmith in the text will be quite out of place.

Having in the beginning described the cause of differentiation in the outside world, now he describes the operation of the same with reference to the mind :—Similarly as in the case of a single notion about one woman, etc. Nescience consists in the cognition of lovability, etc., in a damsel. When this nesceience is coupled with forgetfulness (moha) one becomes stupid, that is full of stupid imaginings. 'Maitra is a very fortunate man to possess such a jewel of a wife. I am unfortunate not to possess her. In the same way the notion of the same woman in the mind of a co-wife causes aversion and consequent pain. Similarly, the notion of the same woman in the mind of the husband Maitra causes attachment and consequent pleasure. The knowledge of the realities thereof consists in the recognition of the fact that the body of the woman is after all nothing but skin, muscle, fat, bone and mucus; and that it is naturally impure on account of the place of its foundation and seed which grows into it. This knowledge in the mind of the wise becomes the cause of the idea that it is neither pleasurable nor painful; and thus it becomes the cause of desirelessness.

The cause of upholding :—The body is the upholder of the power of sensation and action. These powers again are the upholders of the body. The five forces of Prāṇa, etc., are the manifestations of the common energy of these powers. The body dies in their absence. Similarly, muscle and the other portions of the body support each other in life. Similarly, are the elements of Pṛthvī, etc., the supporters of the bodies of men, of Varuṇa, Sun, Vāyu and those that live in the Candraloka. The elements further support each other in life. The Pṛthvī having the five qualities of odour, taste, colour, touch and sound, all the five elements are present therein supporting and supported by each other; as also four in the Apas, three in the Tejas, two in the Vāyu. The animals, men and gods also exist supporting each other in life. But how can they be the supporters of each other, seeing that they are not related to each other as the container and the contained. For this reason he says :—'They live for each other, etc.' The body of man is sustained by the materials supplied by the bodies of beasts, bird, deer, snakes and vegetables. Similarly, the bodies of tigers and others of the same class are supported by the bodies of men, beasts, and deer, etc. Similarly, the bodies of beasts and deer, etc., are supported by vegetables, etc. Similarly, the bodies of gods are supported by the sacrifices of goats, deer, clarified butter and Puroḍāśa, etc., offered by men as also by means of the accessories of sacrifice, branches and stone, etc., Similarly, the gods also support men by giving them the objects of their desires and by causing rain, etc. Therefore do they live for each other. The rest is easy.—28.

Sūtra 29

यमनियमासनप्राणायामप्रत्याहारधारणाध्यानसमाधयोऽष्टावङ्गानि ।। २९ ।।

यम Yama, restraint. नियम Niyama, observance. आसन Āsana, posture. प्राणायाम Prāṇāyāma, regulation of breath. प्रत्याहार Pratyāhāra, abstraction. धारणा Dhāraṇā, concentration. ध्यान Dhyāna, meditation. समाधि Samādhi, trance. (All these). अष्टौ Aṣṭau, eight. अङ्गानि Aṅgāni, the accessories.

29. Restraint, Observance, Posture, Regulation of breath (Prāṇāyāma), Abstraction, Concentration, Meditation and Trance are the eight accessories of Yoga.—80.

तत्र योगाङ्गान्यवधार्यन्ते । यमनियमासनप्राणायामप्रत्याहारधारणाध्यानसमाधयोऽष्टावङ्गानि । यथाक्रममेषामनुष्ठानं स्वरूपं च वक्ष्यामः ।। २९ ।।

Vyāsa

The accessories of Yoga are now determined. "Restraint, etc." We shall now describe their nature and practice in order.—80.

Vācaspati's Gloss

Now the author determines the accessories of Yoga with the object of determining their number more or less. 'The accessories of Yoga, etc.'

'Restraint, etc.' Practice, desirelessness, faith, energy, etc., are by their very nature to be understood as falling under these wherever they may properly fall, not as independent means.—29.

Sūtra 30

तत्राहिंसासत्यास्तेयब्रह्मचर्यापरिग्रहा यमाः ।। ३० ।।

तत्र Tatra, there. अहिंसा Ahiṁsā, Abstinence from injury. सत्य Satya, veracity. अस्तेय Asteya, abstinence from theft. ब्रह्मचर्य Brahmacarya, continence. अपरिग्रह Aparigraha, Abstinence from avariciousness, all these. यमाः Yamāḥ, are the restraints.

30. Of these the restraints are : Abstinence from injury (Ahiṁsā); Veracity; Abstinence from theft; Continence; Abstinence from avariciousness.—81.

तत्राहिंसासत्यास्तेयब्रह्मचर्यापरिग्रहा यमाः। तत्राहिंसा सर्वथा सर्वदा सर्वभूतानामनभिद्रोहः। उत्तरे च यमनियमास्तन्मूलास्तात्सद्धिपरतयैव तत्प्रतिपादन्नाय प्रतिपाद्यन्ते। तदवदातरूपकरणायैवोपादीयन्ते। तथा चोक्तम्। स खल्वयं ब्राह्मणो यथा यथा व्रतानि बहूनि समादित्सते तथा तथा प्रमादकृतेभ्यो हिंसानिदानेभ्यो निवर्तमानस्ता–मेवावदातरूंपामहिंसां करोति। सत्यं यथार्थे वाङ्मनसे। यथादृष्टं यथानुमितं यथाश्रुतं तथा वाङ्मनश्चेति परत्र स्वबोधसङ्क्रान्तये वागुक्ता सा यदि न वञ्चिता भ्रान्ता वा प्रतिपत्तिवन्ध्या वा भवेदित्येषा सर्वभूतोपकारार्थंप्रवृत्ता न भूतोपघाताय यदि चैवमप्यभिधीयमानाभूतोपघातपरैव स्यान्न सत्यं भवेत्पापमेव भवेत्तेन पुण्याभासेन पुण्यप्रतिरूपकेण कष्टं तमः प्राप्नुयात्तस्मात्परीक्ष्य सर्वभूतहितं सत्यं ब्रूयात्। स्तेयमशास्त्रपूर्वकं द्रव्याणां परतः स्वीकरण तत्प्रतिषेधः पुनरस्पृहारूपमस्तेयमिति। ब्रह्मचर्यं गुप्तेन्द्रियस्योपस्थस्य संयमः। विषयाणामर्जनरक्षणक्षयसङ्गहिंसादोषदर्शनादस्वीकरणमपरिग्रह इत्येते यमाः।। ३०।।

Vyāsa

Of these, abstinence from injury is the not causing of pain any living creation in any way at any time. The restraints and observances that follow have their origin in it. They are meant to achieve it. They are taught with the object of teaching it. They are taken up with the object of rendering the light of its appearance purer. And so it has been said :—As the Brāhmaṇa goes on undertaking many a vow of restraint and observance, he goes on turning away from the sins committed on account of forgetfulness, and having their origin in injury caused to others (Hiṁsā); and by so doing he goes on rendering the Ahiṁsā itself purer and purer.

Veractiy consists in word and thought being in accord with facts. Speech and mind corresponds to what has been seen, heard and inferred as such. Speech is uttered for the purpose of transferring one's knowledge to another. It can only be said to have been employed for the good of others and not for their injury, if it is not deceptive, confused or barren in knowledge. If, however, it proves to be injurious to living beings even though uttered as such, it is not truth; it is a sin only. By this outward appearance, this is a facsimile of virtue, and one gets into painful darkness. Therefore, let every one examine well and then utter truth for the benefit of all living beings.

Theft is the making one's own unlawfully of things belonging to others. Abstinence from theft consists in the absence of the desire thereof.

Continence is the restraint of the hidden power, the power of generation.

Absence of avariciousness is the non-appropriation of things not one's own, consequent upon seeing the defects of attachment and of the injury caused by the collection, preservation and destruction of goods. These are the restraints.—81.

Vācaspati's Gloss

Having enumerated the accessories of Yoga as the restraints and observances, etc., now he enumerates the restraints by introducing the aphorism :—'Of these abstinence from injury, etc.' The restraints are abstinence from injury, etc. Now describes abstinence from injury as an accessory of Yoga :—'Not causing of pain, etc.' Qualifies such Ahiṁsā : 'The restraints and observances that follow, etc.'

'Have their origin in it' :—the other restraints and observances when performed without observing the vow of causing no pain are, as it were, not performed; because in that case they are quite useless. The practice is resorted to only for the purpose of achieving Ahiṁsā.

If Ahiṁsā is the root of all those that follow, how is it that they are meant for achieving it? For this reason he says :—'They are taught with the object of teaching it.' The meaning is that achievement here refers to knowledge, not to birth.

Let that be. But if the following restraints and observances are for the purpose of giving a knowledge of Ahiṁsā, then they are of no use; because that knowledge is obtained from the other sources. For this reason he says :—'For the purpose of rendering the light of its appearance purer.' The meaning is that if the following ones are not practised, Ahiṁsā would remain impure on account of the existence of untruth, etc.

He mentions the concurrence of the Āgamis with this :—'And so it has been said.'

Now he describes the nature of truth :—'Word and thought being in accord with facts.' Next he describes the nature of the facts :—'What has been heard, seen and inferred as such.'

Otherwise it would not be truth. He describes this with reasoning. Speech is uttered with the object of transferring one's thoughts to another; that is, for the purpose of creating in the other minds a knowledge similar to the knowledge existing in the mind of the speaker. For this reason, if it is not deceptive, etc. For example, Yudhiṣṭhira was questioned by Droṇācārya with reference to the death of his son "My dear, your wealth is truth, is Aśvatthāmā dead"? His answer was, "It is true that Aśvattāmā is dead," but he thought at the time of the death of Aśvattāmā, the elephant, and not the son of Droṇa. This was merely a reply in the terms of the question. It did not transfer to the mind of Droṇa what was in the mind of Yudhiṣṭhira. The knowledge in Yudhiṣṭhira's mind was that the elephant was dead, and this he had obtained by the sense of his sight. The knowledge, however, that was transferred to the mind of Droṇa was that his son was dead. This is deceptive knowledge.

'Confused speeches' is that which is born from confusion. The confusion may exist at the time of speaking, or, at the time of ascertaining the object of knowledge.

Barren in knowledge is that which carries no information. As, for example, the knowledge of barbarians carries no impression of the objects of knowledge to the mind. It also means the speech which may be objectless. Such speech is not desirable to utter. In this case, even though the knowledge of the speaker is transferred to the mind of the hearer, yet it is not as it were transferred, because it is useless.

Such speech also must be uttered for the good of others. It not so uttered, it is only the semblance of truth, not truth. For this reason he says :—'It can only be said to be employed, etc.'

'If, however, it proves injurious to living beings, etc.' Take, for example, the case of a man who has taken the vow of truth, being asked by a gang of robbers if the caravan they be in pursui of had passed that way. He has been it passing that way and says so. This utterance of his, even though technically truth, is not so in reality, as it tends to the injury of others. The rest is easy.

He now describes theft, because the abstinence from any act depends upon the understanding of the nature of the act. 'Theft is the making of things, etc.' The object is to indicate the general by the particular.

Inasmuch as the functioning of speech and body depends upon the mind, the mental modification is mentioned here as the principal factor :—'Absence of the desire thereof.'

Next he describes the nature of continence :—'The restraint of the hidden power :' The words "hidden power," are used to signify that the mere non-use of the organ is not continence. The desire of seeing and speaking to women and embracing them as the seats of Cupid is also incontinence. The meaning is that the other sensations tending towards that are to be checked.

He describes the nature of abstinence from avariciousness :—'Absence of avariciousness, etc.' Here the defect of attachment has been described. Attachment increases in consequence of the repetition of enjoyment, as also the deftness of the powers in their functioning.

The defect of injury also has been described. No enjoyment is possible without causing injury to others.

Absence of avariciousness is the not making one's own of objects, inasmuch as their possession originates in undesirable means if they are not sanctioned by the Śāstras and are obtainable without effort even; and because there is evil done even in the preservation of possessions, that are obtained even in accordance with the Śāstras.—30.

Sūtra 31

जातिदेशकालसमयानवच्छिन्ना: सार्वभौमा महाव्रतम् ।। ३१ ।।

जाति Jāti, life-state. देश Deśa, space. काल Kāla, time. समय Samaya, and circumstance.

अनवच्छिन्नाः, Anvacchinnāḥ, not limited by. सार्वभौमाः Sārva-bhaumāḥ, universal. महाव्रतम् Mahāvratam, the great vow.

31. They are the Great Vow, universal, and not-limited by life-state, space, time, and circumstance. (Samaya).—82.

ते तु। जातिदेशकालसमयानवच्छिन्नाः सार्वभौमा महाव्रतम्। तत्राहिंसाजात्यवच्छिन्ना मत्स्यवधकस्य मत्स्येष्वेव नान्यत्र हिंसा सैव देशावच्छिन्ना न तीर्थे हनिष्यामीति सैव कालावच्छिन्ना न चतुर्दश्यां न पुण्येऽहनि हनिष्यामीति। सैव त्रिभिरुपरतस्य समयावच्छिन्ना देवब्राह्मणार्थे नान्यथा हनिष्यामीति। यथा च क्षत्रियाणां युद्ध एव हिंसा नान्यत्रेति। एभिर्जातिदेशकालसमयैरनवच्छिन्ना अहिंसादयः सर्वथैव परिपालनीयाः। सर्वभूमिषु सर्वविषयेषु सर्वथैवाविदितव्यभिचाराः सार्वभौमा महाव्रतमित्युच्यन्ते।। ३१।।

Vyāsa

And these are 'the great vow, universal, not-limited by life-state, space, time and circumstance.'

Of these, abstinence from injury is limited to life-state, as for example, the injury inflicted by a fisherman is limited to fish alone, and to none else. The same is limited to space, as for example, in the case of a man who says to himself, "I shall not injure at a sacred place." The same is limited to time, as for example, in the case of a man who says to himself, "I shall not cause injury on the sacred day of the Caturdaśī, (the fourteenth) of the lunar fortnight."

The same in the case of a man who has given up the three injuries is limited by circumstance, as for example, when a man says so himself, "I shall cause injury only for the sake of gods and Brāhmaṇas and not in any other way." Or, as for example, injury is caused by soldiers in battle alone and nowhere else. The restraints of Ahiṁsā and the others are always practised without being limited by life-state, time, space and circumstance. Universal is that which pervades all conditions of life, everywhere, always; and is nowhere out of place. They are called the Great Vow.—82.

Vācaspati's Gloss

They have been described in general. Now he introduces the aphorism in order to describe how they are to be observed by the Yogīs. 'And these, etc.' They are called Universal, because they are known in all states, described as life-state, etc.' Inasmuch as it is said that the restraint of Ahiṁsā and the others are to be practised, the same limitations are to be considered as applicable in the case of other restraints also.—31.

Sūtra 32

शौचसन्तोषतपःस्वाध्यायेश्वरप्रणिधानानि नियमाः।। ३२।।

शौच, Śauca, cleanliness. सन्तोष Santoṣa, contentment. तपः Tapaḥ, purifactory action.

स्वाध्याय Svādhyāya, study. ईश्वरप्रणिधानानि, Īśvara-praṇidhāna, the making of God, the motive of all action, all these नियमा: Niyamāḥ, the observances.

32. The observances are Cleanliness, Contentment, Purificatory action, study and the making of the Lord the motive of all action.—83.

शौचसंतोषतपः स्वाध्यायेश्वरप्रणिधानानि नियमाः। तत्र शौचं मृज्जलादिजनितं मेध्याभ्यवहरणादि च बाह्यम्। आभ्यन्तरं चित्तमलानामाक्षालनम्। संतोषः सन्निहितसाधनादधिकस्यानुपादित्सा। तपो द्वन्द्वसहनम्। द्वन्द्वं च जिघत्सापिपासे शीतोष्णे स्थानासने काष्ठमौनाकारमौने च। व्रतानि चैषां यथायोगं कृच्छ्रचान्द्रायण-सान्तपनादीनि स्वाध्यायो मोक्षशास्त्राणामध्ययनं प्रणवजपो वा। ईश्वरप्रणिधानं तस्मिन्परमगुरौ सर्वकर्मार्पणम्। शय्यासनस्थोऽथ पथि व्रजन्वा स्वस्थः परिक्षीणवितर्कजालः। संसारबीजक्षयमीक्षमाणः स्यान्नित्ययुक्तो-ऽमृतभोगभागी। यत्रेदमुक्तं ततः प्रत्यक्चेतनाधिगमोऽप्यन्तरायाभावश्चेति।। ३२।।

Vyāsa

Cleanliness, Contentment, Purificatory Action, Study and the making of Īśvara the motive of all actions, are the observances.

Of these Cleanliness is external when brought about by earths and water, etc., and consists in the eating of pure things, etc. It is internal when it consists in the washing away of impurities of the mind.

Contentment is the absence of desire to secure more of the necessaries of life than one already possesses.

Purificatory action consists in the endurance of the pairs of opposites. The pairs of opposites are such as the desire to eat and the desire to drink; heat and cold; standing and sitting; the absence of speech (Kāṣṭha Mauna) and the absence of facial indications (Ākāra Mauna). It also includes such vows as the fasts of Cāndrāyana and Śantapana, etc., so far as necessary.

Study is the reading of the sciences of liberation (Mokṣa), or the repetition of the Praṇava, the syllable Aum.

The making of Īśvara the motive of all actions, means the doing of all actions to fulfil the purpose of that Great Teacher. It is with reference to this state that the following has been said :—'Lying down on a bed or seated or wandering along a road, ever given to Yoga, with the network of the sins to be restrained, removed, conscious of the destruction of the seed of repeated births, he shares the joys of immortality."

Then is the understanding of the individual self and the absence of obstacles.—83.

Vācaspati's Gloss

He describes the observances of Cleanliness, etc.

"Cleanliness, Contentment, Purificatory Action, Study and the making of God the motive of all actions are the observances......." He explains these :—"Cleanliness is etc., The first 'et cetera' means such things as cowdung plaster and other similar thing. Pure things are such as the urine of the cow, and barley, etc., which purify the body by removing impurities. The word 'et cetera' in connection with the eating of purifying things means the limitation of mouthfuls in size and number, etc.' Instead of speaking of the purity caused by eating, etc., of purifying things, the words used here are only eating, etc., things. It is to be understood that the effect is meant by the mention of the cause.

Mental impurities are pride, jealousy, vanity, etc. Mental purity consists in their removal.

Contentment is the absence of desire to possess more than is necessary for the preservation of life. It should be added that this is because the appropriation of things not one's own has already been given up.

The absence of facial indications which let into the secret of one's mind, is the control of one's self, so as not to transfer the thought at random. Absence of speech is the ordinary holding of the tongue.

The sins to be restrained are the causing of injury to others, lying, etc., which will be described later. They also include doubt and Untrue cognition. Next is described the sequence, on becoming purified by this much.

Further these restraints and observances are described in the Viṣṇu Purāṇa :—"Let the Yogī practise continence, harmlessness, truthfulness, abstinence from theft and non-covetousness without desire of fruit; and let him make his mind gradually fit for progress. He should also apply himself to study, cleanliness and purificatory actions and contentment; and let his mind rest upon the Parabrahma. These are the restraints and observances five each. When practised with desire they secure special fruit. To those who have no desire for fruit, they secure liberation."—32.

Sūtra 33

वितर्कवाधने पतिपक्षभावनम्।। ३३।।

वितर्क Vitarka, of the thoughts of sin. बाधने Bādhane, on the troubling of. प्रतिपक्ष Pratipakṣa, to the contrary. भावनम् Bhāvanam, habituation.

33. Upon thoughts of sin troubling, habituation to the contrary.—84.

एतेषां यमनियमानाम्। वितर्कबाधने प्रतिपक्षभावनम्। यदास्य ब्राह्मणस्य हिंसादयो वितर्का जायेरन् हनिष्याम्यहमपकारिणमनृतमपि वक्ष्यामि द्रव्यमप्यस्य स्वीकरिष्यामि दारेषु चास्यव्यवायी भविष्यामि परिग्रहेषु चास्य स्वामी भविष्यामीति। एवमुन्मार्ग प्रवणवितर्कज्वरेणातिदीप्तेन बाध्यमानस्तत्प्रतिपक्षान्भावयेत्। घोरेषु संसाराङ्गारेषु पच्यमानेन मया शरणमुपगतः सर्वभूताभयप्रदानेन योगधर्मः। स खल्वहं त्यक्त्वा वितर्कान्पुनस्ताना ददानस्तुल्यः श्ववृत्तेनेति भावयेत्। यथा श्वा वान्तावलेही तथा त्यक्तस्य पुनराददान इति एवमादि सूत्रान्तरेश्वपि योज्यम्।। ३३।।

Vyāsa

When during the practice of the restraints and observances sinful thoughts give trouble, the mind is to be habituated to the contrary ideas. When thoughts of the sins of causing injury to others and other sins appear in the mind of this devotee of wisdom, such as, 'I shall kill the evil-doer,' 'I shall tell lies,' 'I shall appropriate this man's wealth,' 'I shall spoil this man's wife,' 'Why should I not possess the things which this man possesses.' When he is touched by the high fever of these sins, which tend to push him along the wrong path, he should habituate himself to think upon the contraries of such sins. He should entertain such ideas as these :—Being burnt up as I am in the fires of the world, I have taken refuge in the practice of Yoga, giving as it does protection to all living beings. Were I to take up the sins, having once given them up, I should certainly be a dog in my conduct. As the dog licks up his own vomit, so should I be acting, if I were to take up again what I have once given up.' This should be applied to other aphorisms also.—84.

Vācaspati's Gloss

There are many obstacles in the way to good things. Thus obstruction being possible, the aphorism teaching the remedy thereof is introduced :—When these restraints and observances, etc.' The aphorism is, 'Upon thoughts of sin troubling, habituation to the contrary.' In the Commentary explaining the sins there is nothing difficult to understand.—33.

Sūtra 34

वितर्का हिंसादयः कृतकारितानुमोदितालोभक्रोधमोहपूर्वका मृदुमध्याधिमात्रा दुःखाज्ञानानन्तफला इति प्रतिपक्षभावनम् ।। ३४ ।।

वितर्काः Vitarkāḥ, the thoughts of sin are. हिंसादयः Hiṁsādayaḥ, the causing of injury to others and the rest. कृत Kṛta, done. कारित Kārita, caused to be done. अनुमोदिताः Anumoditāḥ, and permitted to be done. लोभ Lobha, desire. क्रोध Krodha, anger. मोह Moha, ignorance. पूर्वका Pūrvakāḥ, preceded by. मृदु Mṛdu, slight. मध्य Madhya, middling. अधिमात्राः Adhimātrāḥ, and intense. दुःख Duḥkha, pain. अज्ञान Ajñāna, unwisdom. अनन्त Ananta, infinite. फल Phala, result, fruit. दुःखाज्ञानानन्तफलाः Resulting in an infinity of pain and unwisdom. इति Iti, thus. प्रतिपक्ष Pratipakṣa, to the contrary. भावनम् Bhāvanam, thinking.

34. The sins are the causing of injury to others and the rest. They are done, caused to be done and permitted to be done; they are preceded by desire, anger and ignorance; they are slight, middling and intense; their result is an infinity of pain and unwisdom; thus comes the habit-of-thinking to the contrary.—85.

वितर्का हिंसादयः कृतकारितानुमोदितालोभक्रोधमोहपूर्वका मृदुमध्याधिमात्रा दुःखाज्ञानानन्तफला इति प्रतिपक्षभावनम् । तत्र हिंसा तावत् । कृतकारितानुमोदितेति त्रिधा । एकैका पुनस्त्रिविधा । लोभेन मांसचर्मार्थेन क्रोधेनापकृतमनेनेति मोहेन धर्मो भविष्यतीति । लोभक्रोधमोहाः पुनस्त्रिविधाः मृदुमध्याधिमात्रा इत्येवं

सप्तविंशतिर्भेदा भवन्ति हिंसायाः। मृदुमध्याधिमात्राः पुनस्त्रिविधाः। मृदुमृदुर्मध्यमृदुस्तीव्रमृदुरिति। तथा मृदुमध्यो मध्यमध्यस्तीव्रमध्य इति। तथा मृदुतीव्रो मध्यतीव्रोऽधिमात्रतीव्र इति। एवमेकाशीतिभेदा हिंसा भवति। सा पुनर्नियमविकल्पसमुच्चयभेदादसंख्येया। प्राणभृद्भेदस्यापरिसंख्येयत्वादिति एवमनृतादिष्वपि योज्यम्। ते खल्वमी वितर्का दुःखाज्ञानानन्तफला इति। प्रतिपक्षभावनम्। दुःखमज्ञानं चानन्तं फलं येषामिति प्रतिपक्षभावनम्। तथा च हिंसकस्तावत्प्रथमं वध्यस्य वीर्यमाक्षिपति। ततश्च शस्त्रादिनिपातेन दुःखयति ततो जीवितादपि मोचयतीति। ततो वीर्यक्षेपादस्य चेतनाचेतनमुपकरणं क्षीणवीर्यं भवति। दुःखोत्पादान्नरकतिर्यक्प्रेतादिषु दुःखमनुभवति जीवितव्यपरोपणात्प्रतिक्षणं च जीवितात्यये वर्तमानो मरणमिच्छन्नपि दुःखविपाकस्य नियतविपाकवेदनीयत्वात्। कथंचिदेवोच्छ्वसिति यदि च कथंचित्पुण्यावापगता हिंसा भवेत्तत्र सुखप्राप्तौ भवेदल्पायुरिति। एवमनृतादिष्वपि योज्यं यथासंभवम्। एवं वितर्काणां चामुमेवानुगतं विपाकमनिष्टं भावयन्न वितर्केषु मनः प्रणिदधीत। प्रतिपक्षभावनाहेतोर्हेया वितर्काः। यदास्य स्युरप्रसवधर्माणस्तदा तत्कृतमैश्वर्यं योगिनः सिद्धिसूचकं भवति॥ ३४॥

Vyāsa

Of these the causing of injury to others :—It is of three descriptions, that which is done, that which is caused to be done and that which is permitted to be done. Each again is three-fold. Prompted by desire of gain, as in the case of one who desires to obtain flesh and skin; prompted by anger as in the case of a man who has received some injury; done through ignorance of the real nature of an act, under the impression that the act proposed is a virtue.

Desire, anger and ignorance are again three-fold, slight, middling and intense. Thus there are twenty-seven modifications of injury caused to others.

Mild, middling and intense are again three-fold each; Mild-mild, Middling-mild, and Mild-intense. Also Middling-mild, Middling-middling, and Middling-intense. Also Intense-mild, Intense-middling, and Intense-intense. Thus injury is of eighty-one descriptions.

This again becomes infinite on account of rule (niyama), option (vikalpa) and conjunction (samuccaya). Similarly should this be applied to untruthfulness, etc.

The contrary tendency consists in the notion that these immoral tendencies cause an infinity of pain and nature cognition. This means that pain and unwisdom are the unending fruits of these immoralities, and that in this idea lies the power which causes the habit of the contrary trend of thought.

Further more the injurer first overpowers the strengths of the victim; then gives him by blows from weapons; then takes his life even.

Now as a consequence of overpowering strength, his intelligent and non-intelligent means of enjoyment lose the power of causing enjoyment. By causing pain he suffers pain among animals, earth-bound disembodied spirits, etc., and in hell. By taking life he lives every moment in a state of waning life. He is so much troubled that he prefers and longs for death; and yet, inasmuch as the effects of pain must run their course, he somehow lives on. And if somehow these acts of injury be mixed up with virtue, he is full of enjoyment but short-lived.

These observations may also be applied to untruthfulness, etc., as far as may be. Thus making himself familiar with the undesirable consequences of these sins, he no longer allows his mind to rest over evil acts. The habituation to the contrary tendencies becomes the cause of removing the sins. When these become characterised by non-productivity, then power caused by them becomes, to the Yogī, the indication of his success.—85.

Vācaspati's Gloss

These sins having different natures, modes, characteristics and fruits, and each of these being an object of habituation to the contrary tendency, he now describes them by the aphorism, with the object of describing the nature of the contrary tendency :—'The sins are the causing of injury to others, etc.' Explains :—'Now as the injury, etc.' Rule (niyama) and untrue cognition and their combinations co-exist with the sins of injury, etc., on account of the infinity of differentiation among living beings. Then, vice causing the intensification of inertia, arises unwisdom also, which is nothing more than the four classes of untrue cognition. For this reason they fructify as unwisdom also. Thus the thought of their fruition as an immensity of pain and unwisdom is also an habituation to the contrary tendency. The author renders the same contrary tendency clearer. 'First overpowers the strength, *i.e.*, his activity, the free motions of the body of the victim, that is the animal, etc., to be killed.' By binding to the sacrificial pillar the animal loses the light of his life. The rest is very plain.

The restraints and observances have been described. The removal of their tendencies by means of the habituation to the contrary tendency has also been described. There being thus no obstacles left, now he describes the indications of the success of these practices. By knowing these the Yogī having attained what he has undertaken, turns towards the work which is yet to be done. For this reason he says :—'When these become characterized, etc.'—34.

Sūtra 35

अहिंसाप्रतिष्ठायां तत्सन्निधौ वैरत्यागः ।। ३५ ।।

अहिंसा Ahiṁsā, of (the habit of) not causing injury. **प्रतिष्ठायाम्** Pratiṣṭhāyām, on the confirmation of. **तत्** Tat, his. **सन्निधौ** Sannidhau, in presence. **वैरत्यागः** Vairatyāgaḥ, giving up of hostilities (**त्याग**) (**वैर**).

35. (The habit of) not-causing-injury being confirmed, hostilities are given-up in his presence.—86.

तद्यथा । अहिंसाप्रतिष्ठायां तत्सन्निधौ वैरत्यागः । सर्वप्राणिनां भवति ।। ३५ ।।

Vyāsa

As for example all living beings give up their hostilities in his presence.—86.

Vācaspati's Gloss

Horse and buffalo, rat and cat, snake and mongoose, and others being natural enemies of each other, give up their animosities, by following the tendencies of the mind of the revered one, whose habit of not causing injury is confirmed.—35.

Sūtra 36

सत्यप्रतिष्ठायां क्रियाफलाश्रयत्वम् ।। ३६ ।।

सत्य Satya, of veracity. प्रतिष्ठायाम् Pratiṣṭhāyām, in the confirmation. क्रिया Kriyā, of action. फल Phala, of fruition. आश्रयत्वम् Āśrayatvam, the dependence of.

36. Veracity being confirmed, action and fruition become dependents.—87.

सत्यप्रतिष्ठायां क्रियाफलाश्रयत्वम् । धार्मिको भूया इति भवति धार्मिकः स्वर्गं प्राप्नुहीति स्वर्गं प्राप्नोति । अमोघास्य वाग्भवति ।। ३६ ।।

Vyāsa

'Be virtuous.' This being said the object of the benediction becomes virtuous. 'Go to heaven,' he attains the heavenly state. His speech becomes effective.—87.

Vācaspati's Gloss

Action signifies virtue and vice which are the results thereof and their fruition consists in heaven and hell. They become dependents upon him : they come to live in him. They come into existence by the speech of the master. He illustrates the dependence of action :—'Be virtruous.' Illustrates the dependence of fruition :—'Go to heaven.' "Effective" means "unchecked."—36.

Sūtra 37

अस्तेयप्रतिष्ठायां सर्वरत्नोपस्थानम् ।। ३७ ।।

अस्तेय Asteya, of not stealing. प्रतिष्ठायाम् Pratiṣṭhāyām, in the confirmation of. सर्व Sarva, of all. रत्न Ratna, of jewels उपस्थानम् Upasthānam, the approaching him of.

37. (The habit of) not-stealing being confirmed, all, jewels, approach him. 88.

अस्तेयप्रतिष्ठायां सर्वरत्नोपस्थानम् । सर्वदिक्कान्यस्योपतिष्ठन्ते रत्नानि ।। ३७ ।।

Vyāsa

Jewels approach him from all quarters.—88.

Vācaspati's Gloss

This is easy.—37

Sūtra 38

ब्रह्मचर्यप्रतिष्ठायां वीर्यलाभः ।। ३८ ।।

ब्रह्मचर्य Brahmacarya, of Brahmacarya; continence. प्रतिष्ठायाम् Pratiṣṭhāyām, in the confirmation. वीर्य Vīrya, vigour. लाभः Lābhaḥ, gaining; obtaining.

38. Continence being confirmed, vigour is obtained.—89.

ब्रह्मचर्यप्रतिष्ठायां वीर्यलाभः । यस्य लाभादप्रतिघान्गुणानुत्कर्षयति । सिद्धश्च विनेयेषु ज्ञानमाधातुं समर्थो भवतीति ।। ३८ ।।

Vyāsa

By whose atainment, the Yogī perfects his attainments unchecked, and having attained the power becomes capable of imparting knowledge to learners.—89.

Vācaspati's Gloss

Vigour is power by attaining which, being unchecked, *i.e.*, without giving way to obstacles, the Yogī perfects, that is, lays by the store of Aṇimā, etc.

Having attained the power :—When he is possessed of the eight attainments known as Tāra, etc., and having other names as Uha, etc.

Learners are the disciples of the Yogī. Knowledge means the Yoga which is an accessory of the Yoga. He becomes capable of teaching Yoga.—38.

Sūtra 39

अपरिग्रहस्थैर्ये जन्मकथंता संबोधः ।। ३९ ।।

अपरिग्रह Aparigraha, of non-covetousness. स्थैर्ये Sthairye, in the confirmation. जन्म-कथंता Janma-kathaṁtā, of the how of births. संबोध: Saṁbodhaḥ, the knowledge.

39. Non-convetousness being confirmed, the knowledge of-the-how of births.—90.

अपरिग्रहस्थैर्ये जन्मकथंता संबोधः। अस्य भवति कोऽहमासं कथमहमासं किंस्विदिदं कथंस्विदिदं के वा भविष्यामः कथं वा भविष्याम इत्येवमस्य पूर्वान्तापरान्तमध्येष्वात्मभावजिज्ञासा स्वरूपेणोपावर्तते। एता यमस्थैर्ये सिद्धयो नियमेषु वक्ष्यामः ।। ३९ ।।

Vyāsa

Non-covetousness being confirmed, the knowledge of the how-of-births comes to

him. Who was I? How was I? What is this? How is this? What shall we be? Or, How shall we be? In this shape comes to him the desire of knowing the nature of his own existence in the past, the present and the future.

These are attainments due to the confirmation of the restraints. We shall now speak of those that are caused by observances.—90.

Vācaspati's Gloss

Non-covetousness being confirmed, the knowledge of the 'how-of-births.' Birth means coming into relationship with the physical body and powers of sensation, etc., together. The how-of-birth means its modality. Its knowledge means its direct consciousness. It means the perfect knowledge of the past, the present and of all that is beyond ken, together with their modes.

Questions about the past :—'Who was I?' Questions about the different modes of the birth and preservation of the same :—'How was I?' Wishes to know the nature of the present birth :—'What is this ?' Is the physical body the mere collection of the physical elements or something different therefrom? Here too the words 'How is this?' are to be understood. In some books they actually appear.

Questions about the future :—'What shall we be?' Here too the how must be understood. Thus comes to him the desire to know of his existence, *i.e.*, the coming into relationship with the body, etc., in the past, the present and the future. From the desire comes the knowledge, the rule being that one does whatever he desires.—39.

Sūtra 40

शौचात्स्वाङ्गजुगुप्सापरैरसंसर्गः ।। ४० ।।

शौचात् Śaucāt, by cleanliness. स्वाङ्ग Sva-aṅga, to one's own body. जुगुप्सा Jugupsā, disinclination. परैः Pariaḥ, with others. असंसर्गः Asaṁsargaḥ, cessation of contact.

40. By cleanliness, disinclination to-one's-body, and cessation-of-contact with-others.—91.

शौचात्स्वाङ्गजुगुप्सा परैरसंसर्गः। स्वाङ्गे जुगुप्सायां शौचमारभमाणः कायावद्यदर्शी कायानभिष्वङ्गी यतिर्भवति। किंच परैरसंसर्गः कायस्वभावालोकी स्वमपि कायं जिहासुर्मृज्जलादिभिराक्षालयन्नपि कायशुद्धिमपश्यन्कथं परकायैरत्यन्तमेवाप्रयतैः संसृज्यत ।। ४० ।।

Vyāsa

One begins to clean himself, being disgusted with the dirt of his body. Then he sees the defects of the body. He loses his attachment to the body, and becomes restrained in himself. Furthermore, he ceases to come into contact with others. He sees the nature of the body. He wishes to give up his own body, seeing that it is never pure, even though it is being constantly washed by water, etc. How should he come into contact with the body of others which are all the more impure?—91.

Vācaspati's Gloss

This shows the external cleanliness to be the indicator of attainments.—40.

Sūtra 41

सत्त्वशुद्धौ सौमनस्यैकाग्र्येन्द्रियजयात्मदर्शनयोग्यत्वानि च ।। ४१ ।।

सत्त्व Sattva, of the essence. शुद्धौ Śuddhau, on the purification. सौमनस्य Saumanasya, high-mindedness. एकाग्र्य Ekāgrya, one-pointedness. इन्द्रिय Indriya of the senses. जय Jaya, control. आत्म Ātma, of the self. दर्शन Darśana, the knowledge. योग्यत्व Yogyatva, fitness for all these. च Ca, and.

41. And upon-the-essence becoming-pure, come high-mindedness, one-pointedness, control of the senses and fitness for the knowledge of the self.—92.

किं च। सत्त्वशुद्धौ सौमनस्यैकाग्र्येन्द्रियजयात्मदर्शनयोग्यत्वानि च। भवन्तीतिवाक्यशेषः। शुचेः सत्त्वशुद्धिस्ततः सौमनस्यं तत ऐकाग्र्यं तत इन्द्रियजयस्ततश्चात्मदर्शनयोग्यत्वं बुद्धिसत्त्वस्य भवतीत्येतच्छौच-स्थैर्यादधिगम्यत इति ।। ४१ ।।

Vyāsa

Further, high-mindedness, control of the senses and fitenss for self-knowledge, come upon the essence becoming pure. By cleanliness comes the purity of the essence. Thence high-mindedness, thence one-pointedness, thence control of the senses and thence fitness for self-knowledge, of the essence of the mind. This it is that comes to the Yogī by cleanliness being confirmed.—92.

Vācaspati's Gloss

Now he describes the attainments indicated by internal cleanliness :—'Further, etc.' By washing off the impurities of the mind the essence of the mind shows itself in its purity. By the removal of dirt comes high-mindedness which is an index of purity. That which is pure becomes one-pointed. The mind having been thus controlled, the senses too are controlled, being dependent as they are upon the mind. Thence the essence of the mind becomes fit for self-knowledge.—41.

Sūtra 42

संतोषादनुत्तमः सुखलाभः ।। ४२ ।।

सन्तोषाद् Santoṣād, by contentment. अनुत्तमः Anuttamaḥ, excellent, extreme. सुख Sukha, of happiness. लाभः Lābhaḥ, acquisition.

42. By contentment the acquisition of extreme happiness.—93.

संतोषादनुत्तमः सुखलाभः तथा चोक्तम्। यच्च कामसुखं लोके यच्च दिव्यं महत्सुखम्। तृष्णाक्षयसुखस्यैते नार्हतः षोडशीं कलामिति ।। ४२ ।।

Vyāsa

And so it has been said :—'Whatever of pleasure is there in the world of desires, and whatever of larger happiness is there in the world of heaven, they do not come to the sixteenth part of the joy due to the suppression of desires.'—93.

Vācaspati's Gloss

Extreme means that than which there is nothing higher in existence. As was said by Yayāti to Puru when he was begging his youth from him :—'The wise man who gives up desire so difficult to give up by the ignorant and never becoming old with age is full bliss.' Shows this by 'whatever is there, etc.'—42.

Sūtra 43

कायेन्द्रियसिद्धिरशुद्धिक्षयात्तपसः ।। ४३ ।।

काय Kāya, of the physical body. इन्द्रिय Indriya, of the senses. सिद्धिः Siddhiḥ, the attainment. अशुद्धि Aśuddhi, of impurity. क्षयात् Kṣayāt, owing to the removal. तपसः Tapasaḥ, through purificatory actions.

43. By-purificatory-actions, the removal of impurity and the attainments of the physical-body and the senses.—94.

कायेन्द्रियसिद्धिरशुद्धिक्षयात्तपसः। निर्वर्त्यमानमेव तपो हिनस्त्यशुद्ध्यावरणमलं तदावरणमलापगमात्कायसिद्धिरणिमाद्या। तथेन्द्रियसिद्धिर्दूराच्छ्रवणमननाद्येति ।। ४३ ।।

Vyāsa

Purificatory actions, as they are being done, destroy the dirt of the veil of impurity. By the destruction of the dirt of this veil, come the attainments of the physical body, Aṇimā and others. So also the attainments of the sense, chair audience and thought-reading from a distance, etc.—94.

Vācaspati's Gloss

Mentions the indications of the attainment of the Purificatory action. By Purificatory action, etc. The veil which is described as impurity consists of vice, etc., due to inertia. Aṇimā and others, such as Mahimā, Laghimā and Prāpti. It is all easy.—43.

Sūtra 44

स्वाध्यायादिष्टदेवतासंप्रयोगः ।। ४४ ।।

स्वाध्यायाद् Svādhyāyāt, by study. इष्ट देवता Iṣṭa-devatā, with the desired deity. संप्रयोगः Samprayogaḥ, communion.

44. By-study comes communion with the desired deity.—95.

स्वाध्यायादिष्टदेवतासंप्रयोगः। देवा ऋषयः सिद्धाश्च स्वाध्यायशीलस्य दर्शनं गच्छन्ति कार्ये चास्य वर्तन्त इति।। ४४।।

Vyāsa

The gods, the Ṛṣis and the Siddhas become visible to him who is given to study, and they do take part in his work.—95.

Vācaspati's Gloss

Mentions the attainments indicated by the perfection of study :—'By study communion with the desired deity.' This is easy.—44.

Sūtra 45

समाधिसिद्धिरीश्वरप्रणिधानात्।। ४५।।

समाधि Samādhi, of trance. सिद्धिः Siddhiḥ, the attainment. ईश्वर-प्रणिधानात् Īśvara-praṇidhānāt, by making Īśvara the motive of all actions.

45. The attainment of trance by making Īśvara the-motive-of-all-actions.—96.

समाधिसिद्धिरीश्वरप्रणिधानात्। ईश्वरार्पितसर्वभावस्य समाधिसिद्धिर्यया सर्वमीप्सितमवितथं जानाति देशान्तरे देहान्तरे कालान्तरे च। ततोऽस्य प्रज्ञा यथाभूतं प्रजानातीति।। ४५।।

Vyāsa

The faculty of trance (samādhi) becomes perfect in him who dedicates all his powers to Īśvara. By this he knows all that he desires to know, just as it is in reality, in another place, in another body or at another time. Then his intellect knows everything as it is.—96.

Vācaspati's Gloss

'The attainment of trance by making Īśvara the motive of all actions.' It should not be said that inasmuch as the Cognitive trance is attained by making Īśvara the motive of all actions, the remaining seven accessories are useless. These accessories are useful in the attainment of that mental mood which devotes all action to he purposes of Īśvara, by known and unknown subsidiary methods. They are also useful in the attainment of the Cognitive trance, by a separate combination of accessories. Thus the same curds serve the purpose of a man and are useful for he purposes of a sacrifice.

In this case the accessories of concentration, meditation and trance would not be the internal accessories of the Cognitive trance. The Cognitive trance would thus become a cause equal in degree with them. Its directness (internality) is perceived by the other accessories not being directly turned towards it. The observance of making Īśvara the motive of all action has Īśvara only for its direct object. Its direct object is not the object of Cognitive trance. Therefore this is an external, indirect means . Thus all is plain.

The word Prajanāti = 'knows,' shows the radical meaning of Prajñā, intellect.—45.

Sūtra 46

स्थिरसुखमासनम्।। ४६ ।।

स्थिर Sthira, steady. सुखम् Sukha, easy. आसनम् Āsanam, posture.

46. Posture is steadily easy.—97.

उक्ताः सहसिद्धिभिर्यमनियमाः। आसनादीनि वक्ष्यामस्तत्र। स्थिरसुखमासनम्। तद्यथा पद्मासनं वीरासनं भद्रासनं स्वस्तिकं दण्डासनं सोपाश्रयं पर्यङ्कं क्रौञ्चनिषदनं हस्तिनिषदनमुष्ट्रनिषदनं समसंस्थानं स्थिरसुखं यथासुखं चेत्येवमादीनि।। ४६ ।।

Vyāsa

The restraints and observances have been described with attainments. We shall now describe the posture, etc. Of these, posture is steadily easy. Thus, for example, the Padmāsana, the Vīrāsana, the Bhadrāsana, the Svastika, the Daṇḍāsana, the Sopāśraya, the Paryaṅka, the Krauñcniṣādana, the Hastiniṣādana, the Uṣṭraniṣādana, the Samasaṁsthāna, the Sthirasukha, the Yathāsukha and such others.—97.

Vācaspati's Gloss

Introduces the next aphorism :—'The restraints and observances, etc.' 'Of these, posture is steadily easy.' Steadiness means absence of motion. The same must be easy. It must not cause trouble. Such should be the posture. This is the meaning of the aphorism. Postures is the way in which one sits. He mentions different postures :—As for example :—The Padmāsana is well-known. The Vīrāsana is that in which a sitting man has one foot in contact with the ground, and places the other over the partially inclined other knee.

The Bhadrāsana is that in which the sitting man places the soles of both feet joined together below the testicles, and places both hands with the fingers interlaced over that region.

The Svastika is that in which the left foot is placed, a little downward inclined between the right thigh and shank, and the right foot is placed in a similar position between the left thigh and shank.

The Daṇḍāsana is practised by sitting with thighs, shanks and feet stretched straight along the ground with the ankles joined together, but the toes kept apart.

The Paryaṅka is that in which the knees are extended and the arms are used to lie upon.

The Sopāśraya is that in which the tiger's skin or the deer skin or some cloth is used to sit upon.

The Krauñcaniṣādana and others of the same class are to be imitated from the sitting postures of the Krauñca, the elephant, the camel.

The Samasaṁsthāna is that in which the feet are so placed that the heels and foreparts of both are joined together with the feet a little bent.

The Sthirasukha is whatever posture may secure steadiness and ease. This is approved by the writer of the aphorisms. It is also described as Yathāsukha. This means any position that may secure ease.—46.

Sūtra 47

प्रयत्नशैथिल्यानन्तसमापत्तिभ्याम् ।। ४७ ।।

प्रयत्न Prayatna, of effort. शैथिल्य Śaithilya, by slackening. अनन्त Ananta, as in the infinite. समापत्तिभ्याम् Samāpattibhyām, and by thought transformation.

47. By-slackening of effort and by thought-transformation as infinite.—98.

प्रयत्नशैथिल्यानन्तसमापत्तिभ्याम् । भवतीति वाक्यशेषः । प्रयत्नोपरमात्सिध्यत्यासनं येन नाङ्गमेजयो भवति । अनन्ते वा समापन्नं चित्तमासनं निर्वर्तयतीति ।। ४७ ।।

Vyāsa

The sentence is completed by adding the word, 'is secured.' Posture becomes perfect when effort to that end ceases, so that there may be no more movement of the body. Or, when the mind is transformed into the infinite, that is, makes the idea of infinity its own, it brings about the perfection of posture.—98.

Vācaspati's Gloss

Having described the nature of posture, he describes the means thereof :—'By slackening of effort and by thought-transforming as infinite.' The effort which is directed towards the accomplishment of a certain posture helps to keep the body in a particular position. It is not the cause of the posture which as an accessory of Yoga is meant to be taught here. If that were its cause, thé teaching would be useless, inasmuch as in that case the posture would be achieved by its own operation. Therefore this natural effort of the body does not bring about the posture that is meant to be taught. It is in fact its antagonistic. Further this natural effort being the antecendent of the posture that may at any time be desired, does away with the very object of posture. Therefore, he who practises posture as an observance taught here, should employ an effort which consists in suppressing the natural efforts of the body. Otherwise the posture taught here will not be accomplished. It is for this reason that the slackening of the natural efforts of the body is said to be the means of accomplishing posture.

Or, the mind transformed into the idea of the infinite, the Great Serpent, who upholds the sphere of the earth by means of his very steady thousand heads, brings about steadiness.—47.

Sūtra 48

ततो द्वन्द्वानभिघात: ।। ४८ ।।

तत: Tath, then. द्वंद्व Dvandva, from the pairs of opposite. अनभिघात: Anabhighātaḥ, cessation of disturbance.

48. Thence cessation-of-disturbance from-the-pairs-of-opposites.—99.

ततो द्वन्द्वानभिघात: । शीतोष्णादिभिर्द्वन्द्वैरासनजयान्नाभिभूयते ।। ४८ ।।

Vyāsa

When posture has been mastered he is not disturbed by the pairs of opposites such as heat and cold.—99.

Vācaspati's Gloss

Mentions the indications of the achievement of posture.
"Thence the cessation of disturbance from the pairs of opposite."
The Commentary has been explained by what has already been said.—48.

Sūtra 49

तस्मिन्सति श्वासप्रश्वासयोर्गतिविच्छेद: प्राणायाम: ।। ४९ ।।

तस्मिन् Tasmin, that (the posture). सति Sati, being. श्वास Śvāsa, of the inspiratory breath. प्रश्वासयो: Praśvāsayoḥ, of the expiratory breath. गति Gati, of the movements. विच्छेद: Vicchedaḥ, stoppage. प्राणायाम: Prāṇāyāmaḥ, regulation of breath.

49. Regulation-of-breath (Prāṇāyāma) is the stoppage of the inspiratory and expiratory movements (of breath) which follows, when that has-been-secured.—100.

तस्मिन्सति श्वासप्रश्वासयोर्गतिविच्छेद: प्राणायाम: । सत्यासनजये बाह्यस्य वायोराचमनं श्वास: । कौष्ठ्यस्य वायोर्नि:सारणप्रश्वास: । तयोर्गतिविच्छेद उभयाभाव: प्राणायाम: ।। ४९ ।।

Vyāsa

When posture has been achieved the cessation of the movements of both inspiration, the drinking in of external air, and expiration, the throwing out of the internal air, is the regulation of breath (Prāṇāyāma).—100.

Vācaspati's Gloss

Posture also has been described in the Viṣṇu Purāṇa :—'Having thus practised the Bhadrāsana, etc., and being full of their qualities, etc.' After posture describes the Prāṇāyāma, at the same time showing that posture must precede it :—'Prāṇāyāma is the cessation of the

inspiratory and expiratory movements of breath which follows when that has been secured.' The cessation of the movements of expiration and inspiration exists in the Recaka, Kumbhaka and Pūraka branches of the regulation of breath. This, therefore, is a description of the ordinary Prāṇāyāma. This means that where in the Pūraka the external air having been expelled is retained inside, the cessation of the movements of inspiration and expiration takes place. Similarly, where in the Recaka, the external air having been expelled is restrained outside, the cessation of the movements of inspiration and expiration takes place. Similarly, in the Kumbhaka too. This is what the commentary says :—'When posture has been, etc.'—49.

Sūtra 50

बाह्याभ्यन्तरस्तम्भवृत्तिर्देशकालसंख्याभि: परिदृष्टो दीर्घसूक्ष्म: ।। ५० ।।

बाह्य Bāhya, external. आभ्यन्तर Ābhyantara, internal. स्तम्भ Stambha, total restraint. वृत्ति: Vṛttiḥ, manifestation. देश Deśa, place. काल Kāla, time. संख्या Saṅkhyā, number, by these three. परिदृष्ट: Paridṛṣṭaḥ, regulated. दीर्घ Dīrgha, long. सूक्ष्म: Sūkṣmaḥ, and subtle.

50. Manifestation as external, internal and total restraint is regualted by place, time and number; and thus it becomes long-induration and subtle.—101.

स तु । बाह्याभ्यन्तरस्तम्भवृत्तिर्देशकालसङ्ख्याभि: परिदृष्टो दीर्घसूक्ष्म: । यत्र प्रश्वासपूर्वको गत्यभाव: स बाह्य: । यत्र श्वासपूर्वको गत्यभाव: स आभ्यन्तर: । तृतीयस्तम्भवृत्तिर्यत्रोभयाभाव: सकृत्प्रयत्नाद्भवति । यथा तप्ते न्यस्तमुपले जलं सर्वत: संकोचमापद्येत तथा द्वयोर्युगपद्गत्यभाव इति । त्रयोऽप्येते देशेन परिदृष्टा इयानस्य विषयो देश इति । कालेन परिदृष्टा: क्षणानामियत्तावधारणेनावच्छिन्ना इत्यर्थ: । सङ्ख्याभि: परिदृष्टा एतावद्भि: श्वासप्रश्वासै: प्रथम उद्घातस्तद्वन्निगृहीतस्यैतावद्भिर्द्वितीय उद्घात एवं तृतीय: । एवं मृदुरेवं मध्य एवं तीव्र इति सङ्ख्यापरिदृष्ट: स खल्वयमेवमभ्यस्तो दीर्घसूक्ष्म: ।। ५० ।।

Vyāsa

And that manifests as external, internal and total restraints, is regulated by time, place and number; is of long duration and subtle. The cessation of the motion of breath which precedes expiration is external. The cessation of the motion of breath which precedes inspiration is internal. The third manifests total restraint where cessation of both these motions takes place by a single effort. As water thrown on a heated stone shrivels up from all sides, so do both cease simultaneously. All these three are regulated by place. So much of space is occupied by it. Also are they regulated by time. The meaning is that they are measured by ascertaining the seconds of their duration. They are also regulated by number. The first cessation is for so many, the second for so many, and similarly the third. Similarly it is thus mild, thus middling and thus intense. Thus it is regulated by number. This verily thus practised becomes long induration and subtle.—101.

Vāçaspati's Gloss

He introduces the aphorism by describing the three descriptions of Prāṇāyāma :—'And that manifests as external, internal and total restraint; is regulated by time, place and number; is of long duration and subtle.' The word Vṛtti 'manifestation' is related to all the three. He describes the Recaka :—'That which precedes expiration.' Describes the Pūraka :—'That which precedes inspiration.' Describes the Kumbhaka :—'The third, etc.' Renders the same plainer :—'Where the cessation of both inspiration and expiration takes place simultaneously by a single effort of restraint, not that it stands in need of restraining effort which is the culmination of the effort of inspiration, nor that it stands in need of the restraining effort which culminates in the effort of expiration. On the other hand, as water thrown on a heated stone shrivels upon all sides as it is being dried up, so also the air running in or out ceases its action by a strong effort of restraint, and stays in the body reduced to a state of greater than ordinary tenuity. It does not fill in and is not, therefore, Pūraka. Nor does it go and is not therefore Recaka.

In the external the limit of space is measured in a place free from wind by the effect upon straw or a piece of cotton wool, by a yard or foot-rule or by the hand. Similarly, in the internal it is measured by the sensation of touch at the soles of feet or at the forehead, slight like the touch of an ant.

A 'second' (kṣaṇa) is the fourth part of the period of time taken by the act of shutting the eyes. It is measured by ascertaining the seconds of duration.

A 'mātrā' (measure) is the time which is taken up by thrice turning up one's hand over one's knee and then snapping the fingers once.

Measured by thirty-six such mātrās is the first attempt (udghāta) which is mild Twice that is the second, which is middling. Thrice that is the third which is intense. This is the Prāṇāyāma as measured by number. It is describe :—Thus is it measured by number, etc.

The time taken by the inspiration and expiration of a healthy man is the same as that which is measured by snapping the fingers, as described, after turning the hand thrice over the knee.

The first attempt when carried to its completion is said to be conquered or mastered. The time is intended to be described by so many inspirations and expirations. They are practically the same.

This prāṇāyāma becomes of long duration when it takes up greater space and time, beings daily practised and being increased in succession of a fortnight, a day, etc. It is subtle, because it is known by very subtle trance (samādhi) not because it becomes weak.—50.

Sūtra 51

बाह्याभ्यन्तरविषयाक्षेपी चतुर्थः ।। ५१ ।।

बाह्य Bāhya, the external. आभ्यन्तर Ābhyantara, the internal. विषय Viṣaya, region, spheres. आक्षेपी Ākṣepī, passing over, going beyond. चतुर्थः Catūrthaḥ, the fourth.

51. The fourth is that which follows when the spheres of the external and internal have-been-passed.—102.

बाह्याभ्यन्तरविषयाक्षेपी चतुर्थः। देशकालसङ्ख्याभिर्बाह्यविषयपरिदृष्ट आक्षिप्तः तथाभ्यन्तरविषयपरिदृष्ट

आक्षिप्तः। उभयथा दीर्घसूक्ष्मः। तत्पूर्वको भूमिजयात्क्रमेणोभयोर्गत्यभावश्चतुर्थः प्राणायामः। तृतीयस्तु विषयानालोचितो गत्यभावः सकृदारब्ध एव देशकालसङ्ख्याभिः परिदृष्टो दीर्घसूक्ष्मः। चतुर्थस्तु श्वासप्रश्वासयोर्विषयानवधरणात्क्रमेण भूमिजयादुभयाक्षेपूर्वको गत्यभावश्चतुर्थः प्राणायाम इत्ययं विशेष इति।।५१।।

Vyāsa

The sphere of the external, having been mastered by the measurements of time, space and number, is left behind. Similarly is the sphere of the internal thus measured, left behind. In the case of both, it becomes long and subtle. The cessation of the movements of both, in sequence of the attainment of that state, by gradual mastery over the different states, is the fourth. In the third the sphere is not considered; the cessation of motion takes place with one single effort, and is then measured by space, time and number; and thus becomes long and subtle. In the fourth, however, the spheres of inspiration and expiration are ascertained, the different states are mastered by and by, and it follows the perfection of both. Thus comes about the cessation of the movements of both. This is the fourth Prāṇāyāma and is thus distinguished.—102.

Vācaspati's Gloss

Thus three descriptions of Prāṇāyāma have been described. Now the describes he fourth :—'The fourth is that, etc.' Explains :—'The shpere of the external, etc.'

'Left behind' :—dethroned from its position, which has been mastered by practice. That also is protracted and subtle.

'In sequence of' :—The external and internal Prāṇāyāmas preceded by a calculation of time, space and number. And this fourth one is not brought about all at once, by a single effort like the third one.

On the other hand it reaches different states of perfection, as it is being practised; and as one state has been mastered it goes on to the higher stage in succession, and it is thus acquired. This is said :—'By gradual mastery over the different states.'

The question is that the cessation of the motion of both the Prāṇāyāmas takes place in the third Prāṇāyāma also, which is described as the total restraint; what then is the distinction between the third and the fourth. For this reason he says :—'In the third, etc.' The third is brought about by a single effort and is not preceded by the thought of measurements. The fourth, however, is preceded by the knowledge of the measurements, and is brought about by much effort. This is the difference. The meaning is that the spheres of the Pūraka and the Recaka are not considered, but this is measured by time, space and number.—51.

Sūtra 52

ततः क्षीयते प्रकाशावरणम्।।५२।।

ततः Tataḥ, then. क्षीयते Kṣīyate, is destroyed. प्रकाश Prakāśa, of light. आवरणम् Āvaraṇam, the cover.

52. Thence the cover of light is destroyed.—103.

ततः क्षीयते प्रकाशावरणम्। प्राणायामानभ्यस्यतोऽस्य योगिनः क्षीयते विवेकज्ञानावरणीयं कर्म यत्तदाचक्षते। महामोहमयेनेन्द्रियजालेन प्रकाशशीलं सत्त्वमावृत्य तदेवाकार्ये नियुक्तमिति। तदस्य प्रकाशावरणं कर्म संसारनिबन्धनं प्राणायामाभ्यासाद् दुर्बलं भवति प्रतिक्षणं च क्षीयते। तथा चोक्तम्। तपो न परं प्राणायामात्ततो विशुद्धिर्मलानां दीप्तिश्च ज्ञानस्येति।। ५२।।

Vyāsa

The karma of the Yogī which covers up the discriminative knowledge is destroyed as he practises the Prāṇāyāma. This is what they say :—'By the magic panorama of desire, the Essence, which is luminous by nature, is covered up, and the same is directed towards vice.' This karma of the Yogī which covers up the light and binds him to repeated births, becomes weak by the practice of Prāṇāyāma every moment, and is then destroyed. And so it has been said :—'There is no purificatory action higher than Prāṇāyāma; purity is secured by that, through the destruction of impurity; and the light of knowledge shines.—103.

Vācaspati's Gloss

He describes the object of Prāṇāyāma :—'Thence the cover of light is destroyed.' The cover is that which covers up the light of Mental Essence. It means the afflictions and sin. He explains :—'The karma of Yogī....as he practices Prāṇāyāma.' Knowledge is that by which anything is known. It is the light of the Mental Essence. Discriminative knowledge is the knowledge of the distinction (between the Objective Essence and consciousness). That which covers up discriminative knowledge 'is the karma which covers up.' Karma means the vice which is brought about by action so called, and the afflictions caused thereby. He says that the Āgamis agree in this matter :—'This is what they say.' Desire is spoken of as the Great Forgetfulness. By the mention of desire is to be understood Nescience also which is found inseparably joined to it.

Vice is that which should not be done.

The question arises that if Prāṇāyāma alone does away with vice what is the use of purificatory action ? (Tapas). For this reason he says :—"Becomes weak" and not altogether destroyed by it. Therefore, purificatory action is necessary for its destruction. In this too the Āgamis agree :—'And so it has been said.'

Manu also says :—'Let the defects be burnt up by Prāṇāyāma.'

The Viṣṇu Purāṇa speaks of the Prāṇāyāma as an accessory of Yoga :—'He who masters the air known as Prāṇa by practice, is said to have secured Prāṇāyāma.' It is either seeded or seedless. When the powers known as Prāṇa and Apāna are mastered one by the other, it is two-fold. The third is that when both are checked.—52.

Sūtra 53

धारणासु च योग्यता मनसः ।। ५३ ।।

धारणासु Dhāraṇāsu, for concentration. च Ca, and. योग्यता Yogyatā, the fitness. मनसः Manasaḥ, of the mind.

53. And the fitness of the mind for concentration.—104.

किंच। धारणासु च योग्यता मनसः। प्राणायामाभ्यासादेव प्रच्छर्दनविधारणाभ्यां वा प्राणस्येति वचनात् ।। ५३ ।।

Vyāsa

Further, the fitness of the mind for concentration. By the practice itself of Prāṇāyāma is this secured. As laid down :—

"By the expulsion and retention of breath optionally."—I.34.—104.

Vācaspati's Gloss

Prāṇāyāma renders the mind fit for concentration, by making it steady.—53.

Sūtra 54

स्वविषयासंप्रयोगे चित्तस्य स्वरूपानुकार इवेन्द्रियाणां प्रत्याहारः ।। ५४ ।।

स्व Sva, their own. विषय Viṣaya, objects. असंप्रयोगे Asaṁprayoge, on not coming into contact with. चित्तस्य Cittasya, of the mind. स्वरूप Svarūpa, the nature. अनुकारः Anukāraḥ, the following of. इव Iva, as it were. इन्द्रियाणाम् Indriyāṇām, of the senses of the part of the senses. प्रत्याहारः Pratyāhāraḥ, is abstraction.

54. Abstraction (Pratyāhāra) is that by which the senses do not-comes-into-contact with their objects and follow at-it-were the nature of the mind.—105.

अथ कः प्रत्याहारः। स्वविषयासंप्रयोगे चित्तस्य स्वरूपानुकार इवेन्द्रियाणां प्रत्याहारः। स्वविषयसंप्रयोगाभावे चित्तस्वरूपानुकार इवेति। चित्तनिरोधे चित्तवन्निरुद्धानीन्द्रियाणि नेतरेन्द्रियजयवदुपायान्तरमपेक्षन्ते। यथा मधुकरराजानं मक्षिका उत्पतन्तमनूत्पतन्ति निविशमानमनुनिविशन्ते तथेन्द्रियाणि चित्तनिरोधे निरुद्धानीत्येष प्रत्याहारः ।। ५४ ।।

Vyāsa

Now what is Pratyāhāra? 'Pratyāhāra is that by which the senses do not come into contact with their objects and, as it were, follow the nature of the mind.' The meaning is that in the absence of contact with their objects, they initiate, as it were, the nature of the mind. The senses are restrained, like the mind, when the mind is restrained. They do not stand in need of other means like the control of the other organs. Just as the bees fly, as the queen flies; and sit as the queen sits down; so the sense becomes restrained, as the mind is restrained. This is Pratyāhāra.—105.

Vācaspati's Gloss

Thus then having been purified by the restraints, etc., begins the practice of Pratyāhāra with a view to secure Saṁyama. The author puts a question to introduce the aphorism describing it :—'Now what, etc.' Pratyāhāra is that by which the senses do not come into contact with their objects, and as it were, follow the nature of the mind.' The meaning is that inasmuch as the mind does not come into contact with objective sounds, etc., as cause of forgetfulness, attachment and aversion, the senses of sight etc., too do not, on account of the absence of that contact, incline towards their objects. This is the imitation of the mind by the senses. Inasmuch however, as the senses do not imitate the mind in the fact of the taking in the realities of the objects, because their field of operation is the external world alone, it is said that they, *as it were,* imitate the mind. By using the locative case it is shown that the ordinary quality of non-contact with their objects is the operative cause of the senses imitating the mind. 'In the absence of contact with their, etc.' Explains the imitation :—'The senses are restrained like the mind, etc.' The similarity is that the cause of the restraint of both is and the restraint of both is due to, the same effort. Illustrates the same :—'Just as the bees etc.' Applies the illustration to the object to be illustrated :—'So, etc.'

In this connection also says the Viṣṇu Purāṇa :—'The Yogī who is devoted to the practice of Pratyāhāra should restrain the senses which are attached to the objects of sound, etc., and make them imitate the mind.'

Its object is shown even there. "Those of undisturbed mind have thereby the highest possible control of the senses. If the senses are uncontrolled, the Yogī cannot achieve Yoga."—54.

Sūtra 55

ततः परमावश्यतेन्द्रियाणाम् ।। ५५ ।।

ततः Tataḥ, thence. **परमा** Parmā, the highest. **वश्यता** Vaśyatā, control. **इन्द्रियाणाम्** Indriyāṇām, of the senses.

55. Thence the senses are under the highest control.—106.

ततः परमावश्यतेन्द्रियाणाम्। शब्दादिष्वव्यसनमिन्द्रियजय इति केचित्। सक्तिर्व्यसनं व्यस्यत्येनं श्रेयस इति। अविरुद्धप्रतिपत्तिर्न्याय्या। शब्दादिसंप्रयोगः स्वेच्छयेत्यन्ये। रागद्वेषाभावे सुखदुःखशून्यं शब्दादिज्ञानमिन्द्रियजय इति केचित्। चित्तैकाग्र्यादप्रतिपत्तिरेवेति जैगीषव्यः। ततश्च परमा त्वियं वश्यता यच्चित्तनिरोधे निरुद्धानीन्द्रियाणि नेतरेन्द्रियजयवत्प्रयत्नकृतमुपायान्तरमपेक्षन्ते योगिन इति।। ५५ ।।

।। इति श्रीपातञ्जले सांख्यप्रवचने योगशास्त्रे साधननिर्देशो नाम द्वितीयः पादः समाप्तः ।। २ ।।

Vyāsa

Some say that the conquest of the senses is their non-attachment to sound, etc.

Attachment is a defect which draws them away from the good. Others say that inasmuch as the enjoyment of unprohibited objects is proper, it should be said that contact with sound, etc., subject to one's wishes, is the conquest of the senses. Others again say that the conquest of the senses is the obtaining of knowledge of sound, etc., without their causing pleasure and pain, in the absence of attachment and aversion. Jaugiṣavya says that it is only the want of action of the senses, on account of the one-pointedness of the mind. For this reason it is then that this control is the very highest, the restraint, that is to say, of the senses along with the restraint of the mind; and also for the reason that the Yogīs, being thus restrained, do not stand in need of employing other means, like those employed in the conquest of other organs.—106.

Vācaspati's Gloss

'Thence the senses come under the highest control.' Are there any controls of the senses which may be said not to be the highest, so that it is said here that the highest control is secured? Shows them :—'Some say that the conquest, etc.' Explains this :—Attachment is desire. The word in the original is Vyasana, which is described as meaning that which removes away from the good. The absence of this attachment which draws one away from the good, is the control. Describes another control :—The enjoyment of such sound, etc., as is not forbidden by Śruti, etc., and the avoidance of those that are forbidden, is proper, that is, in accordance with propriety.

He describes another control :—'Contact with sound, etc.' The contact of the senses with sound, etc., depends upon one's wishes. Man is free to enjoy whatever he likes. He is not dependent upon the enjoyment.

He mentions another control also :—'The knowledge of sound, etc., without pleasure and pain, etc.'

He mentions the control which is preferred by the author of the aphorism, and with which a great Ṛṣi is in accord. Jaigīṣavya says that it is the non-inclination of the senses towards their objects, the sounds, etc., along with the mind which has become one-pointed. Now the says that this is the highest control :—'For this reason is it then, etc.' The word 'then' (TU in the original) differentiates this control from other controls. The other controls do not remove the possibility of contact with the poison of afflictions, because they are of the nature of the conjunction between the serpent and the poison. Even the greatest professor of the science of poisons who has controlled a serpent, sleeps not with the serpent in his arms, without fear. This control, however, which is free from contact with all poisons, leaves no fear, and is, therefore, called the Highest.

'Like the control of the other organs' :—In the state of the Yatātma Yogī, when one sense has been controlled, the Yogī stands in need of further effort for controlling the remaining senses. Not so is there need of other effort to control the external senses, when the mind is restrained. This is the meaning.—55.

Five objects have been treated in this chapter : The Kriyā Yoga, the Afflictions, Fruitage of actions, the consequent Pain, and the four branches of the science of Sorrow.

Here finishes the Gloss of Vācaspati on the second Chapter of the Commentary of Vyāsa on Patañjali's Yoga Philosopy. The chapter describing 'The means of Yoga.'

3
Attainments (Vibhūtis or Siddhis)

Sūtra 1

देशबन्धश्चित्तस्य धारणा ।। १ ।।

देश-बन्धः (देश), Deśa-bandhaḥ, fixity in one place. Steadfastness. चित्तस्य Cittasya, of the mind. धारणा Dhāraṇā, concentration.

1. Concentration is the steadfastness of the mind.—107.

उक्तानि पञ्च बहिरङ्गानि साधनानि । धारणा वक्तव्या । देशबन्धश्चित्तस्य धारणा । नाभिचक्रे हृदयपुण्डरीके मूर्ध्नि ज्योतिषि नासिकाग्रे जिह्वाग्र इत्येवमादिषु देशेषु बाह्ये वा विषये चित्तस्य वृत्तिमात्रेण बन्ध इति धारणा ।। १ ।।

Vyāsa

The five external means of attainment have been described. Concentration (Dhāraṇā) is now discussed. 'Concentration is the steadfastness of the mind.' Concentration means the mind becoming fast in such places as the sphere of the navel, the lotus of the heart, the light in the brain, the fore-part of the nose, the fore-part of the tongue, and such like parts of the body; or by means of the modifications only in any other external object only.—107.

Vācaspati's Gloss

Trance (Samādhi) and the means of its attainment have been described in the first and second chapters. In the third chapter are to be described the attainments which follow in their wake and which are means of generating faith. The attainments are achieved by *Saṁyama.* consists of concentration, meditation and trance together. As means for the achievement of attainments, these three accessories are more intimate than the five external ones, and thus being internal, they are described here, in order that they may be specifically mastered. Among these too, concentration, meditation and trance are related to one another as cause and effect consecutively, and their order of causation is fixed. The order is respected here in the enumeration. Therefore concentration is described first. Thus the Bhāṣyakāra says :—'The five external means, etc.' 'Concentration is the steadfastness of the mind.' He enumerates the places for concentration in the body :—'The sphere of the navel, etc.' 'Such like parts of the body' indicate the palate, etc. He describes the external objects :—'Or any other external object.' It is not possible for the mind to come into relationship with the external objects bodily; hence is it said : 'By means of the modifications only.'

On this subject also says the Purāṇa :—

"Having mastered the breath by means of controlling the processes of breathing, and having likewise subjected the senses to the mind by the practice of making their activity dependent upon the process of thought, he should let his mind rest upon some auspicious object." The external auspicious objects are the Golden Foetus (Hiraṇyagarbha), Indra and Prajāpati, etc.

Further the following is said there :—

"The personified appearance of the Lord leaves no room for the desire to possess any other object of concentration. The fact of the mind being held fast there is what is called concentration. And, O king, hear what that personified appearance of the Lord is that should be meditated upon; there can be no concentration without something upon which the mind may rest. The face is cheerful and pleasing to the mind, the eyes are full of freshness and depth like lotus-leaves, the cheeks are beautiful, the forehead is bright and high, the ears are symmetrical and well-adorned by drops, the neck is long-like the shell of a conch; the auspicious sign of fortune, the Śrīvatsa, marks his chest; with a deep navel and deep furrows appearing in the abdomen; with eight or four arms hanging from his body; sitting with thighs and shanks evenly placed, and feet placed in the form of a *Svaṣṭika.* Such is the appearance of Viṣṇu clad in clean yellow garb, adorned with beautiful head-dress, armlet, bracelet, etc.; carrying his bow, the Śārṅga, his discus, his club, his sword, his conch-shell and his rosary of Rudrākṣa. He has become Brahma. With mind merged in Him, let the Yogī devote himself to meditating upon Him. Let him apply his mind to him so long as his concentration becomes well established. Practising this concentration or doing some other work in accordance with his own wishes, so long as the mind learns not to get away from the object of concentration, the Yogī should in that state consider his concentration achieved.—1.

Sūtra 2

तत्र प्रत्ययैकतानता ध्यानम्।। २।।

तत्र Tatra, there. प्रत्यय Pratyaya, of the mental effort. एकतानता Ekatānatā, continuation. ध्यानम् Dhyānam, meditation.

2. The continuation there of the mental-effort (to understand) is meditation (dhyāna).—108.

तत्र प्रत्ययैकतानता ध्यानम्। तस्मिन्देशे ध्येयालम्बनस्य प्रत्ययस्यैकतानता सदृशः प्रवाहः प्रत्ययान्तरेणापरामृष्टो ध्यानम्।। २।।

Vyāsa

Meditation is the continuance, *i.e.*, the unchanging flow, of the mental effort to understand the object of meditation, untouched by any other effort of the understanding.—108.

Vācaspati's Gloss

The author describes the meditation which is brought about by concentration :—'Continuance of the mental effort to understand it is meditation.' Continuance of the mental effort means one-pointedness. The Commentary is easy. Here too says the Purāṇa : 'Meditation is the continuance of one-pointedness with reference to the effort of understanding directed to any object, there being absence of desire to understand anything else at the time. This is brought about, O King, by the foregoing accessories"—2.

Sūtra 3

तदेवार्थमात्रनिर्भासं स्वरूपशून्यमिव समाधिः ।। ३ ।।

तद् Tad, the same. एव Eva, the same. अर्थ Artha, object, the light of the object. मात्र Mātra, alone. निर्भासम् Nirbhāsam, shining with. स्वरूप Svarūpa, itself. शून्यम् Śūnyam, devoid of. इव Iva, as it were. समाधि: Samādhiḥ, trance, contemplation.

3. The same when shining with the light of the object alone, and devoid, as-it-were, of itself, is trance (or contemplation, Samādhi).—109.

तदेवार्थमात्रनिर्भासं स्वरूपशून्यमिव समाधिः। ध्यानमेव ध्येयाकारनिर्भासं प्रत्ययात्मकेन स्वरूपेण शून्यमिव यदा भवति ध्येयस्वभावावेशात्तदा समाधिरित्युच्यते ।। ३ ।।

Vyāsa

When on account of the object of contemplation taking entire possession of the mind, contemplation shows forth only the light of the form of the contemplated object, and is devoid, as it were, of its nature of self-cognition, then it is called trance (or contemplation).—109.

Vācaspati's Gloss

The author describes trance which is brought about by meditation :—

"The same when it shines by the light of the object alone, and is devoid, as it were of itself, is trance." The Bhāṣyakāra explains :—'When on account of contemplation, etc.'; Shows forth only the form of the object of contemplation : 'Devoid, etc.' Inasmuch as the question arises that if it is devoid of the nature of self-cognition, how can it illuminate the object, he adds :—'As it were.' He mentions its cause :—'On account of the object of contemplation taking entire possession of the mind.'

The Purāṇa has on this too : "Trance is that in which the mind takes in the nature of the object of thought free from 'Fancy' (kalpanā). It is brought about by meditation." Fancy (kalpanā) consists in the perception of the act and the object of meditation as distinct from each other. The Trance-Cognition is free from this fancy.

Having described the eight accessories of Yoga to Khāṇḍikya, Kuśīdhvaja thus summarized :—'The knower of the field is the employer of the field is the employer of the means. The means is knowledge, that is not intelligent. Having achieved the work of salvation, it has nothing of its duty left to do, and turns back."—3.

Sūtra 4

त्रयमेकत्र संयमः ।। ४ ।।

त्रयम् Trayam, the three. एकत्र Ekatra, together. संयमः Saṁyamaḥ, Saṁyama.

4. The three together are Saṁyama.—110.

त्रयमेकत्र संयमः । तदेतद्धारणाध्यानसमाधित्रयमेकत्र संयमः । एकविषयाणि त्रीणि साधनानि संयम इत्युच्यते । तदस्य त्रयस्य तान्त्रिकी परिभाषा संयम इति ।। ४ ।।

Vyāsa

These three together, concentration, meditation and trance are Saṁyama. The practice of all the three accessories with reference to one object of thought is Saṁyama. This word Saṁyama is a technical term of the science meant to denote the three.—110.

Vācaspati's Gloss

Inasmuch as the mention of concentration, meditation and trance, all three, each by its own separate name at every place, would be very lengthy, this aphorism is introduced with the object of laying down a technical term for the sake of brevity :—'The three together are Saṁyama.' The Bhāṣyakāra explains :—'With reference to one object, etc.' He moves the possible doubt that the word has the radical meaning of these three :—"The word is a technical term, etc." (The word Tantra in the original means the science of Yoga. Hence 'Tāntrika' means a technical term of the science.) The province of Saṁyama is the 'Three changes' and such other places.—4.

Sūtra 5

तज्जयात्प्रज्ञालोकः ।। ५ ।।

तद् Tad, of that. जयात् Jayāt, by the achievement. प्रज्ञा Prajñā, of the cognition. लोकः Lokaḥ, the visibility.

5. By achievement thereof comes the visibility of the Cognition.—111.

तज्जयात्प्रज्ञालोकः । तस्य संयमस्य ज़यात्समाधिप्रज्ञाया भवत्यालोको यथा यथा संयमः स्थिरपदो भवति तथा तथा समाधिप्रज्ञा विशारदी भवति ।। ५ ।।

Vyāsa

By the achievement of this 'Saṁyama' comes the visibility of the Trance-Cognition.

As Saṁyama becomes firmer and firmer so does the Trance-Cognition become more and more lucid.—111.

Vācaspati's Gloss

The author mentions the fruit of the practice for the achievement of Saṁyama :—'By achievement thereof comes the visibility of the Cognition.' Visibility consists in the maintenance of its flow free from impurity and unimpeded by any other effort of cognition. The Commentary is easy.—5.

Sūtra 6

तस्य भूमिषु विनियोगः ।। ६ ।।

तस्य Tasya, its. भूमिषु Bhūmiṣu, to the planes, regions. विनियोगः Viniyogaḥ, application.

6. Its application is to the planes.—112.

तस्य भूमिषु विनियोगः । तस्य संयमस्य जितभूमेर्यानन्तराभूमिस्तत्र विनियोगः । नह्यजिताधरभूमिरनन्तरभूमिं विलङ्घ्य प्रान्तभूमिषु संयमं लभते । तदभावाच्च कुतस्तस्य प्रज्ञालोक ईश्वरप्रणिधानाज्जितोत्तरभूमिकस्य च नाधरभूमिषु परचित्तज्ञानादिषु संयमो युक्तः । कस्मात्तदर्थस्यान्यथैवावगतत्वाद् भूमेरस्या इयमनन्तरा भूमिरित्यत्र योग एवोपाध्यायः । कथम् । एवं ह्युक्तम् । योगेन योगो ज्ञातव्यो योगो योगात्प्रवर्तते । योऽप्रमत्तस्तु योगेन स योगे रमते चिरमिति ।। ६ ।।

Vyāsa

When one plane has been conquered by Saṁyama, it is applied to the next immediately following. No one who has not conquered the lower plane, can jump over the plane immediately following, and then achieve Saṁyama with reference to the plane further off. And if this Saṁyama cannot be achieved, how can the visibility of the Cognition come? For him, however, who has conquered the higher planes by making Īśvara the motive of all actions it is not proper to perform Saṁyama with reference to the lower planes, such as thought-reading, etc. Why? Because the object thereof has already been achieved by means other than this. As to which is the next immediate plane after a certain plane, it is the practice of Yoga alone that will teach this. How? It has been so said :—'The Yoga is to be known by the Yoga; the Yoga becomes manifest by the Yoga; whoever is not confused, enjoys the Yoga for long by the Yoga.'—112.

Vācaspati's Gloss

But whereto is this Saṁyama to be applied in order to achieve this fruit? For this reason the author says :—'Its application is to be to the planes.' The Commentator specifies the planes. 'When one plane, etc.' The application is to the unconquered plane immediately following the plane, that is, the mental state, which has been conquered.

When the Indistinct Trance Cognition, having the gross world for its sphere, has been achieved by Saṁyama, the application of the Saṁyama is to be to the yet unconquered Distinct Trance. When that has been conquered, the application is to be to the Meditative Transformation. Similar is the application to the Ultra-meditative.

For this very reason the Purāṇa introduces the trance with reference to the subtle objects, after the thought-transformation into gross objects has been achieved, and all the arms and ornaments have been put off one after the other :—'Then let the wise man meditate upon the form of the Lord as devoid of the conch, the club, the discus and the bow, calm and possessing only the rosary of Rudrākṣa. When concentration has become well-established hereupon, then let the Yogī meditate upon (Him as devoid of the ornaments of head-dress, armlet, etc. Then should he devote himself to Him as possessed of the limbs alone; and then should he think of himself as **His Self.** 'I am **He.**' Then should he devote himself to the thought of the 'I am' alone.

But then why is it that one conquers the higher plane only after having conquered the lower one? Why does he not conquer in the reverse order? For this reason the Bhāṣyakāra says :— 'No one who has not conquered the lower plane, etc.' No one who starts to the Ganges from the Śilāhrada, reaches the Ganges without first reaching the Meghavāna.

"For him who has conquered the higher planes by making Īśvara the motive of all actions, etc." Why? Because the object, *i.e.*, the conquest of the higher planes, has been achieved by another very proximate means, that is, devotion to God. When an object has been achieved, then the employment of a means for its achievement which does not introduce something new in the expected result, oversteps the propriety of the rule of practice.

Well, let that be. But the sub-planes are known by authority. Their order, however, is not so known. How is that order to be known? For this reason he says :—'As to which is the next, etc.' When the preceding state of Yoga is conquered it becomes the cause of the knowledge of the nature and activity of the next. This is to be understood by seeing that the state is intended to be spoken of as being identical with the object of which the state is named.

Sūtra 7

त्रयमन्तरङ्गं पूर्वेभ्यः ।। ७ ।।

त्रयम् Trayam, the three, अंतरङ्गम् Antaraṅgam, forming an internal part more than, more intimate. पूर्वेभ्य: Pūrvebhyah, than the preceding.

7. The three are more-intimate than-the-preceding.—113.

त्रयमन्तरङ्गं पूर्वेभ्यः । तदेतद्धारणाध्यानसमाधित्रयमन्तरङ्गं संप्रज्ञा तस्य समाधेः पूर्वेभ्यो यमादिभ्यः पञ्चभ्यः साधनेभ्य इति ।। ७ ।।

Vyāsa

The three, concentration, meditation and trance are more intimate means of the Cognitive Trance than the preceding five, the restraints, etc.—113.

Vācaspati's Gloss

How is it that Saṁyama alone is to be employed in all places here and there, and not the other five, although both are the accessories of Yoga equally? For this reason the author says :— 'The three are more intimate than the preceding ones.' This three-fold means has the object to be achieved as its direct sphere of operation; it is, therefore, called intimate. The restraints, etc., are not such; they are, therefore, called non-intimate. This is the meaning.—7.

Sūtra 8

तदपि बहिरङ्गं निर्बीजस्य ।। ८ ।।

तद् Tad, that. अपि Api, even. बहिरङ्गम् Bahiraṅgam, the external part, non-intimate. निर्बीजस्य Nirbījasya, to the seedless.

8. Even that is non-intimate to the seedless.—114.

तदपि बहिरङ्गं निर्बीजस्य। तदप्यन्तरङ्गं साधनत्रयं निर्बीजस्य योगस्यं बहिरङ्ग भवति कस्मात्तदभावे भावादिति ।। ८ ।।

Vyāsa

This intimate triad of means too becomes an external accessory of the seedless trance. Why? Because it comes into existence upon its cessation.—114.

Vācaspati's Gloss

The triad of means is intimate only to the Cognitive Trance, not to the Ultra-Cognitive. The Ultra-Cognitive Trance being seedless, there is no similarity between the spheres of their operation and also because the seedless, trance is born when the triad of means has long been under restraint, and the Cognitive Trance has reached its highest culmination, or which is the same thing, when the state of the higher desirelessness consisting as it does of the purity of knowledge, is reached. 'The triad of means, etc.' 'Even that is non-intimate to the seedless.'

'Intimacy' consists in having a common sphere of operation. Then, however, does not exist here. There is no immediate sequence here. What it is said that the non-intimate means of devotion to the Lord brings about that state and that therefore there is overlapping, it is meant that although the definition of the intimate overlaps, including as it does the means of devotion to the Lord, it does not possess the characteristic of following in immediate sequence and thus differs from the non-intimate. For this reason, in order to show that in the case of the Ultra-Cognitive the Saṁyama is rather a remote cause, it is said that it comes into existence upon the cessation thereof.—8.

Sūtra 9

व्युत्थाननिरोधसंस्कारयोरभिभवप्रादुर्भावौ
निरोधक्षणचित्तान्वयो निरोधपरिणामः ।। ९ ।।

व्युत्थान Vyutthāna, of outgoing. निरोध Nirodha, of suppressing. संस्कारयो: SAṁskārayoḥ, of the potencies. अभिभव Abhibhava, the disappearance. प्रादुर्भावौ Prādurbhāvau, and the

appearance. निरोध Nirodha, of the suppression. क्षण Kṣaṇa, with the moment. चित्त Citta, of the mind. अन्वय: Anvayaḥ, the conjunction. निरोध Nirodha, of the suppression, suppressive. परिणाम: Pariṇāmaḥ, Modification.

9. The suppressive modification is the conjunction of the mind with the moment of suppression (nirodha), when the outgoing and suppressive potencies disappear and appear respectively.—115.

अथ निरोधचित्तक्षणेषु चलं गुणवृत्तमिति कीदृशस्तदा चित्तपरिणामः। व्युत्थाननिरोध- संस्कारयोरभिभवप्रादुर्भावौ निरोधक्षणचित्तान्वयो निरोधपरिणामः। व्युत्थानसंस्काराश्चित्तधर्मा न ते प्रत्ययात्मका इति प्रत्ययनिरोधेन निरुद्धा निरोधसंस्कारा अपि चित्तधर्मास्तयोरभिभवप्रादुर्भावौ व्युत्थानसंस्काराश्चित्तधर्मा हीयन्ते निरोधसंस्कारा आधीयन्ते निरोधक्षणं चित्तमन्वेति तदेकस्य चित्तस्य प्रतिक्षणमिदं संस्कारान्यथात्वं निरोधपरिणामस्तदा संस्कारशेषं चित्तमिति निरोधसमाधौ व्याख्यातम्।। ९।।

Vyāsa

Change is of the very nature of the functioning of 'the qualities.' What sort of change does, therefore, take place at the time of this functioning in the moments of mental suppression? 'The suppressive modification is the conjunction of the mind with the moment of suppression, when the outgoing and suppressive potencies disappear and appear respectively.'

The outgoing potencies are the characteristics of the mind. It is not that they are suppressed by the restraints of the acts of cognition, being of the nature of the acts of cognition, (as they are not of the nature of the acts of cognition). The potencies of suppression too are characteristics of the mind. The respective suppression and appearance of these two, when the characteristics of the outgoing potencies are destroyed and the potencies of suppression acquired, is the moment of suppression which the mind appears in conjunction with. This acquiring of different potencies by the one mind every moment is the suppressive change. In that state the potencies alone are left in the mind. This has been described as the Suppressive Trance.—115.

Vācaspati's Gloss

The three changes are to be utilized in 'By Saṁyama over the three changes, etc.' (P. III, 16).

It is desirable to explain them. Hence the question in connection with the seedless trance mentioned in the last aphorism : 'What sort of a change, etc.' In the states of outgoing mental activity and trance (Cognitive), the heaping up of different evident changes is a matter of direct knowledge. No change is, however, perceived in the Suppressive Trance. It is not, however, that it does not exist because it is not directly perceived, inasmuch as the mind is changeable on account of its being made up of the three qualities, and because it is impossible that the 'qualities' should not change even for a moment. This is the meaning of the question. The aphorism is the answer to the question :—'The suppressive change is the conjunction of the mind with the moment of suppression, when the outgoing and suppressive potencies appear and disappear respectively.' In relation to the Ultra-Cognitive the cognitive too is an outgoing. Suppression is that by which this is suppressed,—the illumination of knowledge, the higher desirelessness. The disappearance and appearance (mentioned here) are of these outgoing and suppressive potencies respectively. This being the case, the disappearance of the outgoing and the appearance of the suppressive potency consists in the conjunction of the mind, the characterized, with the moment of suppression. This conjunction in time with the suppression is the conjunction with both these states. The mind as an individualized phenomenon capable of possessing characteristics, does not, either in the Cognitive or the Ultra-Cognitive states, differ in nature from the states of the suppression and manifestation of potencies.

Well, but the afflictions following Nescience, which have their root in Nescience, are removed on the removal of Nescience, and do not after the removal of Nescience stand in need of any other effort distinct therefrom to remove them. In the same way, seeing that the potencies having their origin in the outgoing acts of the mind are removed by the removal of the outgoing activity itself, the potency of suppression should not be needed further for their removal. For this reason the Bhāṣyakāra says :—'The potencies of the outgoing, etc.' It is not necessary that the effect should be removed by the mere removal of the cause. The cloth is not destroyed by the removal of the weaver. The fact is that the effect which is of the nature of the cause itself, is only removed upon the removal of that cause.

The afflictions which have been described as following Nescience have been said to be of the nature of Nescience itself. It is, therefore, very proper that they should be removed on the removal of Nescience. It is not in this way that potencies are of the nature of the acts of Cognition; because it is seen that memory exists even though the acts of Cognition have been suppressed for a very long time. For this reason although the acts of Cognition may have ceased for a long time, it is necessary that the storage of potencies of suppression be attended to for the removal of the potencies originating in the acts. Therest is easy.—9.

Sūtra 10

तस्य प्रशान्तवाहिता संस्कारात् ।। १० ।।

तस्य Tasya, its. प्रशान्त-वाहिता Praśānta-vāhitā, undisturbed (प्रशान्त) Flow (वाहिता) संस्कारात् Saṁskārāt, by potency.

10. By potency comes its undisturbed flow.—116.

तस्य प्रशान्तवाहिता संस्कारात् । निरोधसंस्काराभ्यासपाटवापेक्षा प्रशान्तवाहिता चित्तस्य भवति तत्संस्कार-मान्द्ये व्युत्थानधर्मिणा संस्कारेण निरोधधर्मः संस्कारोऽभिभूयत्र इति ।। १० ।।

Vyāsa

Undisturbed flow comes to the mind by the deftness of practice in the generating of the mental potencies of suppression. In case the potencies are weak, the potency characterized by suppression is overpowered by the potency characterized by outgoing activity.—116.

Vācaspati's Gloss

Of what sort is the change of the mind brought about by means of the powerful suppressive tendency, when the potencies of outgoing activity have been altogether overpowered? In answer to the question the author says :—'By potency comes its undisturbed flow.'

"Undisturbed flow" means the flow in uninterrupted succession of the suppressive potencies alone, free from the impurity of the outgoing potencies.

But then why does it stand in need of the deftness in generating potencies? Why not potency alone? For this reason the Bhāṣyakāra says :—'In case the potencies are weak, etc.' The potencies referred to are those of suppression. Those however who read a 'not' before 'overpowered,' explain the potencies to be those of the outgoing activities.—10.

Sūtra 11

सर्वार्थतैकाग्रतयोः क्षयोदयौ चित्तस्य समाधिपरिणामः ।। ११ ।।

सर्वार्थता Sarvārthatā, of all pointedness. एकाग्रता Ekāgratā, one pointedness, of these two. क्षय Ksaya, the destruction (of all pointedness). उदय Udaya, the rise (of one pointedness) these two respectively of the previous two. चित्तस्य Cittasya, of the mind, समाधिपरिणामः Samādhi-pariṇāmaḥ, the trance modification.

11. The trance modification of the mind is the destruction and rise of all-pointedness and one-pointedness, respectively.—117.

सर्वार्थतैकाग्रतयोः क्षयोदयौ चित्तस्य समाधिपरिणामः। सर्वार्थता चित्तधर्मः। एकाग्रतापि चित्तधर्मः। सर्वार्थतायाः क्षयस्तिरोभाव इत्यर्थः। एकाग्रताया उदय आविर्भाव इत्यर्थः। तयोर्धर्मित्वेनानुगतं चित्तं तदिदं चित्तमपायोपजननयोः स्वात्मभूतयोर्धर्मयोरनुगतं समाधीयते स चित्तस्य समाधिपरिणामः ।। ११ ।।

Vyāsa

All-pointedness is a characteristic of the mind. One-pointedness is also a characteristic of the mind. The destruction of all-pointedness is its disappearance. The rise of one-pointedness is its appearance. The mind; puts on both these characteristics. This mind then following along both these characteristics of destruction and manifestation which make its very nature, inclines towards contemplation. This is the trance modification of the mind.—117.

Vācaspati's Gloss

Now the author shows the state of the mental change towards Cognitive trance. 'The trance modification of the mind is the disappearance and rise of all-pointedness and one-pointedness respectively.'

All-pointedness means distractedness. It cannot be destroyed; hence its destruction is only its disappearance. Nothing which exists is destroyed. Rise is appearance. The disappearance and birth of the characteristics of all-pointedness and one-pointedness which are of the very nature of the mind, means that the disappearance is to be of all-pointedness and the appearance is to be of one-pointedness. The mind following these too becomes inclined towards trance. The meaning is that it becomes qualified by the trance condition which is achieved gradually by the latter condition becoming the former.—11.

Sūtra 12

ततः पुनः शान्तोदितौ तुल्यप्रत्ययौ चित्तस्यैकाग्रतापरिणामः ।। १२ ।।

ततः Tataḥ, thence. पुनः Punaḥ, again. शान्ता-उदितौ Śānta-uditau, the subsiding and rising. (शान्त) (उदित) तुल्य-प्रत्ययौ Tulya-pratyayau, having similar. (तुल्य) Cognitive, acts. (प्रत्यय) चित्तस्य; Cittasya, of the mind, mental. एकाग्रता Ekāgratā, of the one-pointedness, परिणामः Pariṇāmaḥ, modification.

12. Thence again comes the mental modification of one-pointedness, when the subsiding and rising cognitive acts are similar.—118.

ततः पुनः शान्तोदितौ तुल्यप्रत्ययौ चित्तस्यैकाग्रतापरिणामः। समाहितचित्तस्य पूर्वप्रत्ययः शान्त उत्तरस्तत्सदृश उदितः समाधिचित्तमुभयोरनुगतं पुनस्तथैवासमाधिभ्रेषादिति। स खल्वयं धर्मिणश्चित्तस्यैकाग्रता-परिणामः।। १२ ।।

Vyāsa

Of him whose mind is inclined towards the trance modification, the former cognitive act subsides; and the later that rises is similar thereto. The mind inclined towards trance is common to both. The same happens again and again up to the end of trance.

This of course is the modification of the one-pointedness of the mind which exists as an individualized unit independent of the characteristics.—118.

Vācaspati's Gloss

'Thence again comes the mental modification of one-pointedness, when subsiding and cognitive acts are similar.'

Again, when trance having been achieved, the later state of trance becomes the former, the former subsides and the later cognitive trance modification arises. That is to say, one becomes the past and the other the present. When both these cognitive acts of him who has become inclined towards trance, become similar to each other, it becomes one-pointed. This shows the achievement of trance, and also of one-pointedness itself. The Bhāṣyakāra shows the limit :— 'Up to the end of trance.'—12.

Sūtra 13

एतेन भूतेन्द्रियेषु धर्मलक्षणावस्थापरिणामा व्याख्याताः।। १३।।

एतेन Etena, by this. भूत Bhūta, in the objective phenomena. इन्द्रियेषु Indriyeṣu, and in the instrumental phenomena. धर्म Dharma, the characteristic quality. लक्षण Lakṣana, the secondary quality. अवस्था Avasthā, condition of all these three. परिणामा: Pariṇāmāḥ, the changes. व्याख्याता: Vyākhyātāḥ, are described.

13. By this are described the changes of characteristic (dharma), secondary quality (lakṣaṇa), and condition (avasthā) in the objective and instrumental phenomena.—119.

एतेन भूतेन्द्रियेषु धर्मलक्षणावस्थापरिणामा व्याख्याताः। एतेन पूर्वोक्तेन चित्तपरिणामेन धर्मलक्षणावस्थारूपेण भूतेन्द्रियेषु धर्मपरिणामो लक्षणपरिणामोऽवस्थापरिणामश्चोक्तो वेदितव्यः। तत्र व्युत्थाननिरोधयोर्धर्मयोरभिभवप्रादुर्भावौ धर्मिणि धर्मपरिणामो लक्षणपरिणामश्च। निरोधस्त्रिलक्षणस्त्रिभिरध्वभिर्युक्तः। स खल्वनागतलक्षणमध्वानं प्रथमं हित्वा धर्मत्वमनतिक्रान्तो वर्तमानलक्षणं प्रतिपन्न। यत्रास्य स्वरूपेणाभिव्यक्तिरेषोऽस्य द्वितीयोऽध्वा। न चातीतानागताभ्यां लक्षणाभ्यां विमुक्तः तथा व्युत्थानं त्रिलक्षणं त्रिभिरध्वभिर्युक्तं वर्तमानलक्षणं हित्वा धर्मत्वमनतिक्रान्तमतीतलक्षणं प्रतिपन्नमेषोऽस्य तृतीयोऽध्वा। न चानागतवर्तमानाभ्यां लक्षणाभ्यां विमुक्तः। एवं पुनर्व्युत्थानमुप संपद्यमानमनागतलक्षणं हित्वा धर्मत्वमनतिक्रान्तं वर्तमानलक्षणं प्रतिपन्नं यत्रास्य स्वरूपाभिव्यक्तौ सत्यां व्यापार एषोऽस्य द्वितीयोऽध्वा। न चातीतानागताभ्यां लक्षणाभ्यां विमुक्तमित्येवं पुनर्निरोध एवं पुनर्व्युत्थानमिति। तथावस्थापरिणामः। निरोधक्षणेषु निरोधसंस्कारा बलवन्तो भवन्ति दुर्बला व्युत्थानसंस्कारा इति। एष धर्माणामवस्थापरिणामस्तत्र धर्मिणो धर्मैः परिणामो धर्माणां त्र्यध्वनां लक्षणैः परिणामो लक्षणानामप्यवस्थाभिः परिणाम इत्येवं धर्मलक्षणावस्थापरिणामैः शून्यं न क्षणमपि गुणवृत्तमवतिष्ठते। चलं च गुणवृत्तम्। गुणस्वाभाव्यं तु प्रवृत्तिकारणमुक्तं गुणानामिति। एतेन भूतेन्द्रियेषु धर्मधर्मिभेदात्त्रिविधः परिणामो वेदितव्यः। परमार्थतस्त्वेक एव परिणामो धर्मिस्वरूप मात्रा हि धर्मो धर्मिविक्रियैवैषा धर्मद्वारा प्रपञ्च्यत इति। तत्र धर्मस्य धर्मिणि वर्तमानस्यैवाध्वस्वतीतानागतवर्तमानेषु भावान्यथात्वं भवति न तु द्रव्यान्यथात्वम्। यथा सुवर्णभाजनस्य भित्वान्यथ क्रियमाणस्य भावान्यथात्वं भवति न सुवर्णान्यथात्वमिति। अपर आह। धर्मानभ्यधिको धर्मी पूर्वतत्त्वानतिक्रमात्। पूर्वापरावस्थाभेदमनुपतितः कौटस्थ्येनैव परिवर्तेत यद्यन्वयी स्यादिति। अयमदोषः। कस्मात्। एकान्ततानभ्युपगमात्तदेतत्त्रैलोक्यं व्यक्तेरपैति नित्यत्वप्रतिषेधात्। अपेतमप्यस्ति विनाशप्रतिषेधात्। संसर्गाच्चास्य सौक्ष्म्यं सौक्ष्म्याच्चानुपलब्धिरिति। लक्षणपरिणामो धर्मोऽध्वसु वर्तमानोऽतीतलक्षणयुक्तोऽनागतवर्तमानाभ्यां लक्षणाभ्यामविमुक्तः। तथा वर्तमानो वर्तमानलक्षणयुक्तोऽतीतानागताभ्यां लक्षणाभ्यामविमुक्त इति। तथानागतोऽनागतलक्षणयुक्तो वर्तमानातीताभ्यां लक्षणाभ्यामविमुक्त इति। यथा पुरुष एकस्यां स्त्रियां रक्तो न शेषासु विरक्तो भवतीति। अत्र लक्षणपरिणामे सर्वस्य सर्वलक्षणयोगादध्वसङ्करः प्राप्नोतीति परैर्दोषश्चोद्यत इति तस्य परिहारः। धर्माणां धर्मत्वमप्रसाध्यम्। सति च धर्मत्वे लक्षणभेदोऽपि वाच्यो न वर्तमानसमय एवास्य धर्मत्वम्। एवं हि न चित्तं रागधर्मकं स्यात्।

क्रोधकाले रागस्यासमुदाचारादिति। किंच त्रयाणां लक्षणानां युगपदेकस्यां व्यक्तौ नास्ति सम्भवः। क्रमेण तु स्वव्यञ्जकाञ्जनस्य भावो भवेदिति। उक्तं च रूपातिशया वृत्त्यतिशयाश्च विरुध्यन्ते। सामान्यानि त्वतिशयैः सह प्रवर्तन्ते तस्मादसङ्करः। यथा रागस्यैव क्वचित्समुदाचार इति न तदानीमन्यत्राभावः किंतु केवलं सामान्येन समन्वागत इत्यस्ति तदा तत्र तस्य भावः। तथा लक्षणस्येति न धर्मी त्र्यध्वा। धर्मास्तु त्र्यध्वानस्ते लक्षिता अलक्षितास्तत्र लक्षितास्तां तामवस्थां प्राप्नुवन्तोऽन्यत्वेन प्रतिनिर्दिश्यन्ते। अवस्थांन्तरतो न द्रव्यान्तरतः। यथैका रेखा शतस्थाने शतं दशस्थाने दश एका चैकस्थाने। यथा चैकत्वेऽपि स्त्री माता चोच्यते दुहिता च स्वसा चेति। अवस्थापरिणामे कौटस्थ्यप्रसङ्गदोषः कैश्चिदुक्तः। कथम्। अध्वनो व्यापारेण व्यवहितत्वाद्यदा धर्मः स्वव्यापारं न करोति तदानागतो यदा करोति तदा वर्तमानो यदा कृत्वा निवृत्तस्तदातीत इत्येवं धर्मधर्मिणोर्लक्षणानामवस्थानां च कौटस्थ्यं प्राप्नोतीति परैर्दोष उच्यते। नासौ दोषः। कस्माद् गुणिनित्यत्वेऽपि गुणानां विमर्दवैचित्र्यात्। यथा संस्थानमादिमद्धर्ममात्रं शब्दादीनां गुणानां विनाश्यविनाशिनामेवं लिङ्गमादिमद्धर्ममात्रं सत्त्वादीनां गुणानां विनाश्यविनाशिनां तस्मिन्विकारसंज्ञेति। तत्रेदमुदाहरणं मृद्धर्मी पिण्डाकाराद्धर्माद्धर्मान्तरमुपसम्पद्यमानो धर्मतः परिणमते घटाकारमिति। घटाकाराऽनागतं लक्षणं हित्वा वर्तमानलक्षणं प्रतिपद्यत इति लक्षणतः परिणमते। घटो नवपुराणतां प्रतिक्षणमनुभवन्नवस्थापरिणामं प्रतिपद्यत इति। धर्मिणोऽपि धर्मान्तरमवस्था धर्मस्यापि लक्षणान्तरमवस्थेत्येक एव द्रव्यपरिणामो भेदेनोपदर्शित इति। एवं पदार्थान्तरेष्वपि योज्यमिति। त एते धर्मलक्षणावस्थापरिणामा धर्मिस्वरूपमनतिक्रान्ता इत्येक एव परिणामः सर्वानमून्विशेषानभिप्लवते। अथ कोऽयं परिणामोऽवस्थितस्य द्रव्यस्य पूर्वधर्मनिवृत्तौ धर्मान्तरोत्पत्तिः परिणाम इति।। १३।।

Vyāsa

It must be understood that by describing as above the changes of characteristic, secondary quality and condition with reference to the mind, the change of characteristic, the change of secondary quality and the change of condition with reference to the objective forms of matter and instruments of action and sensation have also been described.

There, the disappearance and appearance of the characteristics of the outgoing activity and suppression were the modifications of characteristic (primary quality) in the characterized (the object as existing independently of the quality); also the modification of secondary quality. Suppression has three secondary qualities; it is connected with three paths of being (adhvā).

Having given up the first path of being which consist of the secondary quality not yet manifested, it takes it up as a secondary quality existing in the present, although it has not thereby overstepped its primary quality. It is in this secondary quality which manifests in the present that its true nature is manifested. This is its second path of being. It is not devoid of the past and the yet-unmanifested qualities (lakṣaṇa).

Similarly is the outgoing activity possessed of three secondary qualities and is connected with three paths of being. Having given up the present secondary quality, but not having given up its characteristic, it puts it on as the second quality of the past. This is its third path of being, and it is not devoid of the secondary qualities of the future and the present.

Similarly, inclining again to outward activity, it gives up the yet-unmanifested secondary quality; but not having given up its characteristic of existence as such, it gets on to it as the secondary quality of the present, where manifesting its true nature, it acts as such. This is its second path of being. And it is not devoid of the past and the future secondary qualities.

Similarly, suppression again and outgoing activity again.

Similar is the modification of condition. During moment of suppression, the suppressive potencies are being strengthened; and the potencies of the outgoing activities are being weakened. This is the modification of the conditions of the characteristics.

Thus the objective changes by means of the characteristics; the characteristics possessed of three paths of being are changed by means of secondary qualities; the secondary qualities too are modified into conditions.

Thus is it that the functioning of the "qualities" is never devoid even for a moment of the changes of the characteristics, secondary qualities and conditions; and the functioning of the qualities consists in ceaseless activity. It has further been said that the cause of the activity of the 'qualities' is their very nature.

By this must be understood the three-fold change in the objective and instrumental phenomena, due to the conception of a distinction between the characteristic and the characterized. In reality, however, there is but one change, because the characteristic is the very being itself of the characterized; and it is the change of the characterized alone that is detailed by means of the characteristic. It is only the characteristic present in the characterized object that changes states in the past, the present and future, the substance is not changed. Thus when a vessel of gold is broken to be made into something else, it is only the condition that changes, not the gold.

Another says :—The characterized is nothing more than the characteristic, inasmuch as the reality of the former does not overstep the latter. If it were something co-existent, it would change as an independent existence only, simply changing into distinct anterior and posterior conditions.

This is no defect. Why? Because constancy is not found therein. Thus the three worlds give up their individual appearances, because eternity has been denied to them. Yet they exist in the case of disappearance also, because destruction has been denied to them.

Further its subtlety is due to conjunctive existence; and it is not perceived on account of its subtlety.

The change of secondary quality is the moving of the characteristic along the paths of being. The past characteristic joined to the past secondary quality, is not devoid of the future and the present secondary quality.

Similarly, the present (characteristic) joined to the present secondary quality is not devoid of the past and the future secondary quality. Similarly, the future joined to the future secondary quality is not devoid of the present and past secondary qualities. For example, a man who is attached to one woman, does not hate all the others.

Others find a fault in this change of secondary qualities. They say that all the qualities being in simultaneous existence, their paths of being must be confused, (and thus overlapping one another cannot be considered as distinct and different).

This is thus met with. That the characteristics do exist as such requires no proof. When there is such a thing as a characteristic, the differences of the secondary qualities also must be posited. It is not only in the present time that the characteristic characterizes. If it were so the mind would not possess the characteristic of attachment, seeing that attachment is not in manifestation at the time of anger. Further the three secondary qualities are not possible of existence in one individual simultaneously. They may however appear in succession by virtue of the operation of their several causes. And so it has been said :—'The intensities of nature and those of function are opposed to each other; but the ordinary manifestations co-exist with the intense ones.' Therefore, there is no confusion. For example, attachment being in the height of manifestation with reference to some object, it does not for that reason cease to exist with reference to all other objects. On the contrary it is then ordinarily in existence with reference to them.

Similar is the case with the secondary qualities. It is not the characterized object that is possessed of the three paths of being. It is the characteristics that are possessed of the three paths. They may be visible or latent. Of these the visible ones assume different conditions, and are termed accordingly differently because the conditions are different and not the substance. This is in the same way as the figure of 1 means ten in the place of ten, hundred in the place of hundred, and one in the place of unity. Or again a woman, although one, is called a mother, a daughter and a sister.

Some make the theory of change of condition defective as rendering independent existence necessary. How? There being intervals between the operations of the paths of being a characteristic is the future one, when it does not perform its function; it is the present one when it does; it has become he past when it has ceased to operate.

Now the defect that the opponents find is that in this way, the characteristic and the characterized object, as also the secondary quality and the condition must necessarily be considered as independent existences.

This is no defect. Why? On account of the variety due to the interaction of the 'qualities' even in case of the 'qualified' being permanent. As the coming together of the indestructible qualities of sound, etc., is only a characteristic having a beginning and is destructible, so also is the undifferentiated phenomenal state of matter with a beginning, and is only a characteristic of the indestructible 'qualities' of Essentiality, etc., and is as such destructible. It is for this reason that it is termed a 'Vikāra,' a product. Here is an illustration in this connection. Clay is an object possessed of characteristics. Its existence in the shape of a sod is a characteristic thereof. Given up this particular characteristic it takes up another; and thus takes up another characteristic when it takes up the form of a jar. In the form of jar its secondary quality gives up its futurity and comes to possess the secondary quality as manifested in the present. It thus changes its secondary quality. The jar changes, showing comparative oldness and newness every moment. This is change of condition.

Another characteristic taken up by the characterized substratum is but a change of condition. Of the characteristic too another secondary quality is a change of condition. It is, therefore, the change of one substance only that is thus shown by differentiation. In this way this may be applied to other things also. Thus it is that the change of characteristic, secondary quality and condition do not overstep the being of the characterized substratum, and it is for this reason that there is but one change which runs through all these specializations thereof.

Well what is this change? Change is the manifestation of another characteristic on the removal of the previous characteristic of a substance which remains constant.—119.

Vācaspati's Gloss

The author classifies the changes of the objective and instrumental phenomena of matter, whose use will be described later, but whose occasion has come now :—'By this the changes of characteristic, secondary quality and condition in the objective and instrumental phenomena have been described.'

The Commentator explains :—'It must be understood, etc.' The question is that it is the fact only of mental change that has been mentioned, not its modes in the shape of characteristic secondary quality and condition. How is it then that they are spoken of here over and above that? For this reason he says :—'There the disappearance and appearance of the characteristics of outgoing and suppression, etc.' The brief meaning is that the words of characteristic, secondary quality and condition have no doubt not been used, but it is not that for that reason the changes themselves of characteristic, secondary quality and condition have not been described. Thus in the aphorism :—'The suppressive modifications' etc. (III. 9), the change of characteristic, is spoken, of.

Further he says that by showing this change of characteristic, the change of secondary quality also in the characteristic taken as substratum indicated :—'So also the change of secondary quality.'

Secondary quality stands for 'Lakṣaṇa.' It means that by which something is indicated. This quality is due to difference in time. It is by time that a thing is given certain qualities by means of which it is differentiated from certain things standing in a different relationship to time.

Suppression has three different secondary qualities. It is but another mode of saying that it is related to three paths of being. The word 'adhvā,' path of being, implies time.

"Having given up the first path of being, which consists of the secondary quality not yet manifested."

The question arises, 'Does this suppression, while giving up the first path of being, overstep the nature of the characteristic too in the same way as it gives up the path of being ?' The Commentator says that it does not :—'Although it has not overstepped its primary quality too.'

It does not overstep its characteristic, but takes up the secondary quality as existing in the present. The same suppression which had not manifested yet, has now come into present existence, not that suppression has become non-suppression.

The meaning of the nature of a thing existing in the present is now described :—'It is in this secondary quality which manifests in the present that its true nature is manifested.'

'True nature' is that which performs the function proper to its existence as such.

Manifestation means its essentialization as such.

With reference to the yet unmanifested first path of being this is its second path of being.

Well if it be so that it gives up the yet unmanifested path of being and takes up he present, and that having given up the present state, it will pass on to the past path of being, then, it necessarily follows that paths of being are subject to birth and destruction. This however is not proper, because nothing is born that exists not, nor is anything that exists destroyed. For this reason the Commentator says :—'And it is not devoid of the past and the yet unmanifested secondary quality,' which go on existing in their generic unspecialized state.

Having shown the secondary quality of the present existence of the yet unmanifested suppression, the Commentator now shows the third path of being, the passing on to the past of the present outgoing activity :—

"Similar is the outgoing activity, etc."

Well then does suppression alone exist in the yet unmanifested state, not outgoing activity? The Commentator says No : —'Similarly inclining again to outward activity, etc.'

This repeated manifestation of the outgoing activity is not the manifestation of any individual output thereof. It is a manifestation of the same class only. That which has passed cannot comeback.

"The manifestation of true nature is the essentialization of the object as possessing the capacity of performing its proper function."

It is this change of secondary quality thus described, which appears with reference to objects of the same class over and over again. For this reason the Commentator says :—'Similarly, suppression again, etc.'

Now he describes the changes of condition which is indicated by the change of characteristic :—'Similar is the modification, etc.'

The strength and weakness of the characteristics in their present path of being, are their conditions. The increase or decrease of weakness and strength every moment is the change of condition.

He summarizes :—'This is the modification of the conditions of the characteristics.'

Now he determines the different relation of the different changes :—'Thus the object changes, etc.'

Is then this change of the 'qualities' only occasional? He says No :—'Thus it is that the functioning of the qualities is never, etc.'

But then why is this change ever-existent? He says :—'The functioning of the qualities consists in ceaseless activity.' The word 'and' in this sentence means a cause.

Functioning means action. But whence this functioning itself? He says :—'It is of their very nature.' 'It has been said' here in before.

This three-fold change of the mind is taught by the author of the Aphorisms to be existing in the objective and instrumental phenomena of matter. He says :—'By this must be understood, etc.'

'This' means the distinction between the characteristic and the characterized. When the distinction between the characteristic and the characterized is kept in sight, the physical elements of Pṛthvī etc., are the objects characterized, and the bodies of cow, etc., or the jar, etc., are the changes of the characteristic thereof. The forms which the characteristics put on in the past and the yet unmanifested and the present ones constitute the change of their secondary quality. When the cow, etc., have taken up the secondary qualities as existing in the present, their change of condition consists in their taking up the states of the newly-born calf, a little advanced in age, youth and old age. In the case of the jar, etc., too, their newness and oldness are their changes of condition.

Similarly are the instrumental phenomena the characterized objects. The taking in of this or that blue, etc., is the change of characteristic of the sense of sight. The change of secondary quality consists in the assumption by the characteristic of the qualities due to the existence in the present, etc., as such. The present sensation of a jewel, etc., may be distinct or indistinct. This is its change of condition.

The change of the objective and instrumental phenomena is described, looking upon the characteristic, the secondary quality and condition as distinct from the characterized.

Now the Commentator speaks of them when they are looked upon as the same :—'In reality, however, there is but one change, etc.' The word 'however' turns away from the other view according to which the characteristic and the characterized are looked upon as distinct. Its reality is made known here, not that the nature of change is denied to the other. For what reason ? Because the characteristic is the very being of the characterized.'

The question is that if the characteristic is only a modification of the characterized, how is it that people do not confuse the notions of the changes ? For this reason he says :—'And it is the change of the characterized alone that is detailed through the characteristic.' By the word 'characteristic' here are understood all the three things, namely, characteristic, secondary quality and condition. All this is the modification of the characterized alone by means of them. There is, therefore, but one change of the characteristic, etc., one not confused with the others, because there is no real distinction between them, the characterized objects themselves do not overlap one another.

The question arises that inasmuch as the characteristic and the characterized are not different from each other, and because the paths of being of the characteristic objects are different, the characteristic also must in this case behave as the characterized object, on account of the characteristic and the characterized object being the same. For this reason he says :—'It is only the characteristic present in the characterized, etc.'

'That changes states' :—The word 'state' here means a different arrangement of the thing, a different appearance. Thus when vessels of gold are styled differently as a Rucaka and Svastika, they differ only so far; not that the substance gold becomes not-gold. The reason is evident. They do not differ entirely. This will be stated further on.

The Commentator brings forward the example of the Bauddha, who holds that the characteristic only is what exists :—"Another says :—It is only the characteristics of the Rucaka, etc., that are being thus born, which are the realities. There is no such thing as gold which might be looked upon as a substance remaining the same among more changes than one. If there be such a thing as substance which remains constant even though the characteristics are being changed, then that thing would be immutable like the power of consciousness. It would become an independent reality; independent, that is to say, of the change which is of the very nature of the thing appearing to change. As the power of consciousness does not give up its nature even though the 'qualities' are constantly putting on different appearances, and is therefore independently eternal, so also would gold, etc., become independently eternal. This, however, is not desirable. Therefore the characteristic is not different from the characterized; the substance is not different from the qualities."

The Commentator refutes this argument :—'This is no defect. Why? Because constancy is not found therein.'

We might admit this if we found that as a matter of fact the substance was constant in its so-called eternity like unto the power of consciousness. We, however, do not find this constancy of eternity. On the other hand the whole of this world, to say nothing of one substance only, is seen giving up its individual appearances; the appearances, that is to say, that are meant to perform certain functions.

How is this? On account of eternity being denied to them by the authority of reasoning. If a jar of earth did not give up its individuality of appearance, it would plainly be seen as a jar even when it existed in the condition of a half-jar or in that of powdered clay, etc.; and it would go on performing its function too all the same as before. Hence the three worlds are non-eternal.

Well then let it be non-eternal alone, being practically quite non-existent as it is like the lotus of the sky, on account of its universality and the non-performance of any function. For this reason he says :—'It exists in the case of non-appearance also, because destruction has been denied to it.'

The meaning is that it is not so very insignificant as to be altogether non-eternal and therefore to be classed as non-existent. Why ? Because destruction has been denied to it by reason.

Thus stands the reasoning :—

That which is non-existent is never visible and does not perform any function, as the lotus of the sky.

The three worlds, however, sometime have some functions and are visible.

So are the following causes proving its existence to be mentioned. A thing is seen being born; characteristic secondary quality and conditions are over found appearing therein. For this reason they are out of the category of such non-existent things as the lotus of the sky and the horns of a man.

It is not, therefore, constant in its eternity, so that it may be classed with the independent reality of consciousness. On the contrary it is only in a way eternal. This also proves that it is changeful. It is eternal in its change.

By this it must be understood that in a piece of clay exist its effects that the states of the jar, etc., which have not yet expressed themselves. Well, let that be. But if it exist even if removed, how is it that it is not perceived as before ? For this reason the Commentator says :—'It becomes subtle on account of conjunctive existence, that is, on account of its emergence into the casual state. It becomes unperceivable on account of its subtlety and is not, therefore, perceived.'

Having thus explained the change of characteristic the Commentator now explains the change of secondary qualities also as such secondary qualities.

'The change of secondary qualities, etc.'

The meaning is that each secondary quality is followed by others along with itself. The question is that inasmuch as at the time of conjunction with one secondary quality, the others are not perceived, how can it be said that the others also are present along with it? For this reason the Commentator says :—'For example, a man who is attached to one woman, etc.' The non-existence of perception does not disprove the existence of anything, proved to exist by other means of knowledge. The birth itself of a thing at different places is a reason for its existence. Nothing that exists not, can be born. As for example, the horn of a man.

The Commentator states a defect suggested by another :—'Others find a fault in this change of secondary quality.' If the past the present, exist at the time when the present characteristic is in existence in the present, then the three paths of being must overlap one another. If, however, the paths come into being one after the other, then it comes to this that the non-existent comes into existence. This is the meaning.

He refutes the argument :—'This is thus met with, etc.' The existence of the characteristics in the present is only proved by perception. It also gives the knowledge of its existence in the past and in the future as related to the present. It is plain that the non-existing does not come into existence and the existing is not destroyed. He says the same :—'If it were so the mind would not possess, etc.' The mind is found possessing the characteristic of attachment after the time of anger has passed away. If it be that attachment did not exist at the time of anger as capable of manifestation in the future, how could it be born? And if not born, how could it be perceived?

It may be so. Even then, however, how is it proved that paths of being do not overlap? He gives the answer :—'Further the three secondary qualities, etc.' The three secondary qualities are impossible of existence simultaneously. Where? In one mental modification. In succession, however, one of the qualities does come into manifestation by virtue of its manifesting cause. The ascertainment of the secondary qualities being dependent upon the thing qualified thereby, it is along with the form of the thing qualified that the mind becomes possessed of the qualities. He quotes Pañcaśikhā Ācārya on this very subject :—'And so it has been said, etc.' This has been explained before. He summarizes :—'Therefore there is, etc.' On account of the contrary characteristics of manifestation and disappearance remaining merged in the cause, the paths of being do not overlap. He gives an illustration :—'For example, attachment to, etc.' The knowledge of the existence of attachment with anger was explained before. Now, however, is explained the existence of relationship existing between attachment with respect to one object and attachment with reference to another. He applies the illustration to the subject to be illustrated :—'Similar is the case with secondary qualities etc.'

The question is that inasmuch as identity can exist even though the identical object may not be perceived as such altogether, it follows that characteristic, secondary quality and condition being distinct phenomena, the characterized object which is nothing separate from them, should also be considered to be distinct from itself under each and every one of these varying states. He says that this view is not desirable, because it is contradicted by the perception of the identical substance remaining the same under all varying states. 'It is not the characterized object that is possessed of the three paths of being,' because the characteristics which are not distinct from it, are possessed of the three paths of being. The fact of the taking up of the three paths of being of the characteristics is further elucidated :—They are either visible, *i.e.*, essential, present, or latent, that is not is *esse*. These are the past and the future. Of these, visible ones assume different states of strength and weakness, etc., and are termed accordingly differently, because the states are different, not the substance. By the word state are to the understood here all the three things, namely, characteristic, secondary quality and condition. This is the meaning. It is only perception as such that establishes the distinction from, or the identity of the characterized object with the characteristic, the secondary quality or the condition. If there were unqualified identity between the characterized object and the characteristic, etc., then characteristics, etc., would no longer be what they are. They would not qualify, characterize and condition, as does not the very substance of the characterized object itself. Nor would they qualify the characterized object in case of unqualified distinction; as the horse and the cow can in no way become the characteristic, secondary quality and condition, each of the other. Perception establishes that the characteristic and the secondary quality are neither totally distinct nor completely identical with the characterized object, and it also shows that the characteristics, etc., have all of them the properties of appearance and disappearance, and that during these changes the object remains the same; and it also shows that the characteristics are not mutually exclusive. This is so perceived by every individual self. We follow this common perception. It is not competent to us to leave that aside and establish some theory of the perception of characteristics which may please ourselves.

The Commentator gives on this very subject an illustration from the world :—'This is in the same way as figure of 1 etc.'

As the nature of unity remains the same, although with reference to its relative position it is styled as hundred, etc., so also the nature of the characterized object remains the same but it is styled differently on account of the differences brought about by the distinctions of distinct characteristics, secondary qualities and conditions. This is the meaning.

He gives another illustration to elucidate the subject to be illustrated :—'Or again a woman, although one, etc.'

In this connection he introduces the discussion of a defect considered as existing in this by others :—'Some make the theory of the change of conditions, etc.'

In the change of condition, *i.e.*, the change of condition, of characteristic and secondary quality all the three, the defect of the imminence, of the independent existence of the characterized, the characteristic, the secondary quality and the condition is pointed out.

He puts the questions :—How ? The answer is :—'There being intervals between the operations of the paths of being, etc.' The existence of milk as such in the present is the operation of the yet unmanifested path of being of curds. When on account of being intercepted thereby, the characteristic of changing into curds does not operate notwithstanding its presence in milk, then it is said to be yet unmanifested. When it does come into manifestation, it is said to be in present operation. When having achieved the change, it ceases from the operation of setting in the formation of curds, etc., then it is said to exist in the past. Thus the characterized, the characteristic, the secondary quality and condition existing as they do all of them in all the three times, must be recognized as independent existences. Eternity is but existence for ever. Further, there being existence for ever, all the four are never born. And this much and no more is the description of independent eternity (Kūṭastha nityatā). The meaning is that the independent eternity of the power of consciousness too has no other speciality.

He refutes the argument :—'This is no defect.' Why? On account of the variety due to the inter-action of the 'qualities' even in the case of the qualified being permanent. Inter-action means the relation of overpowering and being overpowered by each other. The variety is of the inter-action. This is the meaning. Although the qualified and the qualities, all the four always exist, the eternity does not consist in being independent of phenomenal changes, because the nature of their change consists in he appearance and disappearance of their modifications, which modifications although brought about by the variety of the inter-action of the qualities, are of the very being of the thing modified.

The power of consciousness, however, does not put forth any such modifications of its own being as periodical appearance and disappearance. Its eternity, therefore, is independent of phenomenal change. As they say :—'He whose nature is not destroyed, the wise call constant in eternity.'

Now he shows that the variety of inter-action is the cause of the variety of modification in the substratum (Prakṛti) and the Vikāras, the phenomena thereof. As the coming together, which may be described as the change into Pṛthvī, etc., has a beginning and is destructive, that is a disappearing characteristic only of sound, etc., *i.e.*, of the five tanmātras of sound, touch, form, taste and smell, which in relation to their effects are indestructible, *i.e.*, do not pass into latency.

He shows the same in the case of Parkṛti :—'So also the undifferentiated phenomenal state of matter, etc.' That is termed a product. Not however subject to such changes is the power of consciousness. This is the substance.

Having illustrated the Prakṛti and the product (Vikṛti), which are proved by philosophers, he new takes an illustration from the product itself well known in the world, in order to show the variety due to the inter-action of the qualities which is the cause of the changes of the characteristic, the secondary quality and condition : 'Here is an illustration of this connection, etc.'

It is not necessary that there should be change of condition in the case of secondary qualities only. The characteristic, the secondary quality and the condition are all implied here by the word condition (avasthā) in the text. All, therefore, is a change of conditions. For this reason he says :—'Another characteristic taken up by an object, etc.'

He gives the definition of Change (Pariṇāma), which covers the whole connotation of the word :—'Change is the assumption by an existing object, etc.'—13.

Sūtra 14

शान्तोदिताव्यपदेश्यधर्मानुपाती धर्मी: ।। १४ ।।

शान्त Śānta, to the latent. उदित Udita, to the rising. अव्यपदेश्य Avyapadeśya, the unpredicable. धर्म Dharma, characteristics. अनुपाती Anupātī, common, closely following. धर्मी Dharmī, the object characterised.

14. "The object characterized" is that which is common to the latent, the rising and unpredicable characteristics.—120.

तत्र। शान्तोदिताव्यपदेश्यधर्मानुपाती धर्मी। योग्यतावच्छिन्ना धर्मिणः शक्तिरेव धर्मः स च फलप्रसवभेदानुमितसद्भाव एकस्यान्योऽन्यस्यान्यश्च परिदृष्टः। तत्र वर्तमानः स्वव्यापारमनुभवन्धर्मी धर्मान्तरेभ्यः शान्तेभ्यश्चाव्यपदेश्येभ्यश्च भिद्यते। यदा तु सामान्येन समन्वागतो भवति तदा धर्मिस्वरूपमात्रत्वात्कोऽसौ केन भिद्येत। तत्र ये खलु धर्मिणो धर्माः शान्ता उदिता अव्यपदेश्याश्चेति। तत्र शान्ता ये कृत्वा व्यापारानुपरताः सव्यापारा उदितास्ते चानागतस्य लक्षणस्य समनन्तरा वर्तमानस्यानन्तरा अतीताः। कमर्थमतीतस्यानन्तरा न भवन्ति वर्तमानाः पूर्वपश्चिमताया अभावात्। यथानागतवर्तमानयोः पूर्वपश्चिमता नैवमतीतस्य तस्मान्नातीतस्यास्ति समनन्तरः। तस्मादनागत एव समनन्तरो भवति वर्तमानस्येति। अथाव्यपदेश्याः के सर्वं सर्वात्मकमिति। यत्रोक्तम्। जलभूम्योः परिणामिकं रसादिवैश्वरूप्यं स्थावरेषु दृष्टम्। तथा स्थावराणां जङ्गमेषु जङ्गमानां स्थावरेष्वित्येवं जात्यनुच्छेदेन सर्वं सर्वात्मकमिति। देशकालाकारनिमित्तोपबन्धात्। न खुल समानकालमात्मनामभिव्यक्तिरिति। य एतेष्वभिव्यक्तानभिव्यक्तेषु धर्मेष्वनुपाती सामान्यविशेषात्मा सोऽन्वयी धर्मी। यस्य तु धर्ममात्रमेवेदं निरन्वयं तस्य भोगाभावः। कस्मादन्येन विज्ञानेन कृतस्य कर्मणोऽन्यत्कथं भोक्तृत्वेनाधिक्रियेत। तत्स्मृत्यभावश्च नान्यदृष्टस्य स्मरणमन्यस्यास्तीति वस्तुप्रत्यभिज्ञानाच्च स्थितोऽन्वयी धर्मी यो धर्मान्यथात्वमभ्युपगतः प्रत्यभिज्ञायते। तस्मान्नेदं धर्ममात्रं निरन्वयमिति।। १४।।

Vyāsa

Characteristic is the virtue (or power) of an object differentiated by fitness. The existence of this fit and proper virtue of an object is inferred by the production of specific results thereof, as found to be of one sort in one and of another sort in another (object). Of these characteristics the present is that which is showing itself in operation; and it differentiates between those that have become latent and those that are unpredicable yet. When, however, it coincides with the generic quality common to all these states, then it becomes of the very nature of the object alone; then what is it in itself, and by what does it differ?

Now of the characteristics of an object that are either latent, rising or unpredicable, the latent are those that have been in operation and ceased. The rising characteristics are those that are in operation. They are immediate postcedents of the yet unmanifested secondary quality. Those that have passed are the postcedents of the present ones. Why are not the present ones the immediate consequents of the past? On account of the absence of the relation of antecedence and postcedence (between the two). As the relation of antecedence and postcedence exists between the present and the future, not so between it and the past. It is not, therefore, the immediate antecedent of the past. For this reason it is only the yet unmanifested that is the antecedent of the present.

What then are the unpredicable? All are of the nature of all. With regard to this it has been said :—The variety of all forms of juice, etc., due to the changes of earth and water, is seen in stationary objects. So also of the stationary in the self-moving and of the self-moving in the stationary. Thus all is of the nature of all without the destruction of species. This is subject to the limitations of time, space, form and disposing cause. Their natures certainly do not manifest simultaneously.

'The characterized object' is that constant nature thereof which remains common to all these manifested and unmanifested characteristics and which is the substratum of both the generic and the specific. In the case of him, however, to who this is a characteristic only without a substratum, there must be absence of experience. How is it possible to adopt one cognition as the enjoyer of the action done by another? Further there would be no memory thereof, because no one can remember what has been seen by another. Further a substratum common to changing states does exist, because objects are called back to memory and recognized as such. It is this constant substratum that is identified as such even when it has taken up a different characteristic. For this reason it is not a mere characteristic, not common to different states.—120.

Vācaspati's Gloss

The word 'characteristics' is used here to denoted characteristic, secondary quality and condition, because that is the basic quality. The Commentator describes the characterized object which is subject to this three-fold change, by the aphorism :—"The 'characterized object' is that which is common to the latent, the rising and the unpredicable characteristics." The characterized object is that which is possessed of a characteristic. It is not possible of being known without the characteristic being known. He explains the characteristic :—'Differentiated by fitness, etc.' The characteristic is the virtue of a substance, such as clay, etc. That is the power of its producing a powder, a kneaded lump, a jar, etc. All these exist therein in a state of latency (non-manifestation).

If the characteristics exist in a state of latency in an object, they have to manifest themselves. But they do not manifest without the help of such adjuncts as water, etc. Water, etc., do not however exist in the causal states of the objects that are produced. Whence then do they come? For this reason he says :—'Differentiated by fitness. The power producing jars, etc., is differentiated by the fitness (capacity) of being dependent for action upon the action of water, etc. Hence jars, etc., derive the capacity of being helped into manifestation by water, etc., from their causes themselves. They are not accidental. This is the meaning.

Or, it might be that the words, "characterized by fitness" are an answer to the question. 'What is a characteristic?' It is the virtue (power) of an object. The meaning is that it is their fitness alone that is the characteristic. Hence it is proved that the characterized object is what is possessed of that. He mentions authority for its existence :—'The existence of this fit and proper virtue of an object is inferred by the production of specific results thereof, as found to be this or that, that is, the different appearances as powder, kneaded lump, a jar, etc. The meaning is that it is seen to be distinct in different objects by the observation of its effects, and the difference that is apparent in its effects. 'Found' means observed.

He now describes how a lump of kneaded clay which is perceived as existing in the present, differs from the state of its existence as powder which has now become latent and the state of its existence as a jar which is yet unpredicable :—'Of these characteristics the present is that, etc.' The meaning is that if they did not differ, the operations of the powder and the jar would also become similar to those of the kneaded lump, and overlapping be the result.

He now says that the distinction described is not possible in the case of a lump which is yet in the state of latency :—'When however it coincides with the generic quality, etc.' What is it in itself and by what distinguishing trait should it differ.?

Having thus described the distinguishing traits of characteristics, he now divides them :—'Now of these characteristics of an object, etc.'

The rising characteristics are those that exist in the present.

Now he explains the antecedence and postcedence of the pathways of being :—'They are the immediate postcedents, etc.' He asks the reason :—Why are not the present ones the immediate consequents of the past ? He states the reason :—On account of the absence of the relation of antecedence and postcedence between the two. He explains the non-perception of a thing by the object in which it exists :—He also shows the non-perception of the existence by being the opposite of the perception thereof :—'As the relation of antecedents and postcedence between the yet-unmanifested and the present, etc.' He summarizes :—For this reason the yet-unmanifested is the only immediate antecedent of the present, because the yet-unmanifested precedes the present. The past cannot be the antecedent of the present. The present precedes the past and is therefore its antecedent, not unpredicable of it. Hence is it established that the past is the least important of the pathways of being.

Well, let that be. It is possible to distinguish the present and the past as being and having been perceived respectively. The unpredicable characteristics, however, from the very fact of their being unpredicable, are incapable of being distinguished. With this in mind he puts the question :—'What are then the unpredicables ? And in what objects are we to examine them ?' He answers the question :—'All are of the nature of all.' With regard to this it has been said :—(He establishes the same). 'The variety of all forms of juice, etc., due to the changes of earth and water, etc.' The liquid is possessed of the soniferous, tangiferous, luminiferous and gustiferous ultimate atoms. The earth (solid) is possessed of the soniferous, the tangiferous, the luminiferous, the gustiferous and the odoriferous ultimate atoms. A modification of all these is seen in the variety of all the forms of juice, etc., found in the roots, fruits, flowers, leaves, etc., of tree, creeper and cane-plant, etc. All these cannot be the modifications either of the solids or of the liquids different in nature from themselves. It has of course been shown that nothing can come out of nothing.

Similarly the modifications of unmoving objects are seen in moving objects in the shape of a variety of chyle, etc. It is of course the use of these fruits, etc., that brings about the wealth of the variety of forms, etc.

Similarly is seen the modification of animals into plants. It is well-known that pomegranates become as big as the fruits of Tāla by obtaining a suck of blood.

He concludes :—'Thus all is of the nature of all, etc.' Thus all, *i.e.*, liquid and solid, etc., is of the nature of all, *i.e.*, juice, etc. He gives the reason thereof :—'Without destruction of species.' The liquidity and solidity (earthiness), the generic qualities of these, are recognized as existing everywhere, and they are not therefore destroyed.

Well, but if all this is of the nature of all, then everything being present everywhere always and in all possible modes, even those results which do not exist simultaneously should manifest at once. For certainly, when all the necessary causes of an effect are present, it would not delay in its appearance. For this reason he says :—This is subject to the limitations of time, space, etc. Although everything can of course become the cause of everything, yet the operation of the cause is limited by space. Thus Kāśmīra (Cashmere) being the country of saffron, it will not grow in the Pāñcāla country, even though the other causes of its growth were all present there. Hence saffron does not grow in the Pāñcāla and other countries.

Similarly there are no rains in the summer season; therefore no growth of rice is possible in that season. Similarly a deer does not give birth to a man; the form of man cannot arise out of that of a deer. Similarly, a man who is not virtuous, does not enjoy the nature of pleasure; the disposing cause of virtue does not operate in him. Therefore it is that on account of the limitations of space, time, form and disposing cause, the nature, *i.e.*, existing objects, are not produced simultaneously.

Having thus divided the characteristics, he now describes the substratum as being common to all these states :—'The characterized object is that common, etc.' The generic is the nature of the characterized, the substratum; and the specific is the characteristic. The substratum is of the nature of both these. This is the meaning.

Having shown that the substratum, the characterized object, appearing in all the states thereof, is proved by direct knowledge, he now calls to mind the undesirable consequences of the theory of the Vainaṣika philosophers, who say that no independent substratum exists, and that the mind is but a momentary act of cognition :—'In the case however, etc.'

Further the object is called back to memory and recognized as such. Yajñadatta does not call back to mind what has been seen by Devadatta. For this reason whoever has been the seer must be the recogniser.—14.

Sūtra 15

क्रमान्यत्वं परिणामान्यत्वे हेतुः ॥ १५ ॥

क्रम Krama, of succession. अन्यत्वं Anyatvam, the distinctness. परिणाम Pariṇāma, of modifications. अन्यत्वे Anyatve, for the distinctness. हेतुः Hetuḥ, the reason.

15. The distinctness of succesion is the reason for the distinctness of modifications.—121.

क्रमान्यत्वं परिणामान्यत्वे हेतुः। एकस्य धर्मिण एक एव परिणाम इति प्रसक्ते: क्रमान्यत्वं परिणामान्यत्वे हेतुर्भवतीति। तद्यथा चूर्णमृत्पिण्डमृद्घटमृत्कणमृदिति च क्रमः। यो यस्य धर्मस्य समनन्तरो धर्मः स तस्य क्रमः। पिण्डः प्रच्यवते घट उपजायत इति धर्मपरिणामक्रमः। लक्षणपरिणामक्रमो घटस्यानागतभावाद्वर्तमानभावः क्रमः। तथा पिण्डस्य वर्तमानभावादतीतभावः क्रमो नातीतस्यास्ति क्रमः। कस्मात्पूर्वपरतायां सत्यां समनन्तरत्वं सा तु नास्त्यतीतस्य तस्माद् द्वयोरेव लक्षणयोः क्रमः। तथावस्थापरिणामक्रमोऽपि घटस्याभिनवस्य प्रान्ते पुराणता दृश्यते। सा च क्षणपरम्परानुपातिना क्रमेणाभिव्यज्यमाना परां व्यक्तिमापद्यत इति। धर्मलक्षणाभ्यां च

विशिष्टोऽयं तृतीयः परिणाम इति। त एते क्रमा धर्मधर्मिभेदे सति प्रतिलब्धस्वरूपाः। धर्मोऽपि धर्मी भवत्यन्यधर्मस्वरूपापेक्षयेति। यदा तु परमार्थतो धर्मिणोऽभेदोपचारस्तद्द्वारेण स एवाभिधीयते। धर्मस्तदायमेकत्वेनैव क्रमः प्रत्यवभासते। चित्तस्य द्वये धर्माः परिद्रष्टाश्चापरिदृष्टाश्च। तत्र प्रत्ययात्मकाः परिदृष्टां। वस्तु मात्रात्मका अपरिद्रष्टास्ते च सप्तैव भवन्त्यनुमानेन प्रापितवस्तुमात्रसद्भावाः। निरोधधर्मसंस्काराः परिणामोऽथ जीवनम्। चेष्टाशक्तिश्च चित्त्स्य धर्मादर्शनवर्जिता इति।। अतो योगिन उपात्तसर्वसाधनस्य बुभुत्सितार्थप्रतिपत्तये संयमस्य विषय उपक्षिप्यते।। १५।।

Vyāsa

It then coming to this that can be but one modification for one substratum, it is said that the distinctness of succession becomes the cause of the distinctness of modifications. This takes place as follows :—The order of causation is : the clay as powder, the clay kneaded into a lump, the clay appearing as a jar, the clay appearing as a half-jar, the clay appearing as a potsherd.

The succession of a characteristic is that characteristic, which comes before it immediately. The kneaded lump of clay disappears and the jar appear in close sequence. This is the order of the sequence of the changes of the characteristic. The order of the change of secondary qualities is the sequential appearance of the present state of a jar out of its yet-unmanifested state of existence. Similarly is there a succession for the passing into its past state, of the present state of the kneaded lump of clay. There is no succession for the past. Why? Immediate sequence exists only where there is a relation of antecedence and postcedence. That does not exist in the case of the past. Hence succession exists in the case of two secondary qualities only.

Such is also the succession in the case of the change of condition. A new jar begins to become old in immediate sequence of its appearance as a new one. This oldness is found being manifested in succession which follows the sequence of the moments of time, until it reaches the last stage. And this third change is distinct from the changes of characteristic and secondary quality. All these successions find their being in the conception of there being a distinction between the characteristic and the characterized object, because the characteristic also becomes sometimes the characterized, in its relation to the nature of another characteristic.

When, however, the characterized object is spoken of as being what it really is, as not distinct from the characteristic, then by virtue of that conception, the object itself is described as a characteristic; and then the succession appears to be one only.

The characteristics of the mind are two-fold, the conscious (or patent Paridrṣta) and the unconscious (or latent, A-paridrṣta). Of these the patent are those that appear in consciousness as notions. The latent are those that are but the substance itself. They are seven only and it is by inference that their existence itself has been established. 'Suppression, characterization, potentialization, constant change, physical life, movements, power are the characteristics of the mind, besides consciousness.'

Hereafter is introduced the subject of Saṁyama to be performed by a Yogī with the object of obtaining the knowledge of any desirable subject, when he has mastered all the means of obtaining knowledge as described.—121.

Vācaspati's Gloss

'The distinctness of succession is the reason for distinctness of modifications.' Is one substratum subject only to one change, which may be described as characteristic, secondary quality, or condition, as the case may be? Or, are the changes of characteristic, secondary quality and condition more than one? What does it come to then? It comes to this that the change must be one because the substratum is one. A cause which has but one form, cannot produce a variety of effects, because the variety in that case would be causeless.

This being the suggestion, it is said :—Distinct changes are posited, because the orders of succession are different.

Observers of the world have plainly observed that an order obtains in the succession of the changes of one clay into dust, kneaded lump, jar, half-jar and sherds. It is also seen that the sequence between powdered clay and kneaded lump is independent of the sequence between kneaded clay and jar : the sequence between a jar and a half-jar is quite another. The sequence between a half-jar and pot-sherds is again quite different. In each of these one of the elements precedes another. The difference of order existing in one succession of changes establishes the distinctness of the changes. Although the substratum of clay is one, it puts on a succession of changes, whose order is established by allied characteristics appearing in succession to each other in due order. The appearance is not, therefore, causeless. This is the meaning.

As is the case with the changes of characteristics, so also is the distinctness of the succession the reason for the distinctness of the changes of secondary qualities and the changes of condition.

The same is illuminated by the Commentary :—'It comes to this that there can be but one modification for one substratum, etc.'

'The succession of characteristic, etc.' :—The word 'succession' is used here to denote that which succeeds, looking upon the one to be nothing distinct from the order.

'Such is also the succession in the case of the change of condition.' And so it happens that the barley grain, even though kept with great care by a cultivator in a grain-pit is, on the lapse of a large number of years, reduced to a condition, such that the cohesion of its particles gives way to the mere touch of hand, *i.e.*, of being reduced to an atomic condition. This is not possible to take place all at once causelessly in the case of new grain. It is, therefore, by a succession of different states appearing one after the other in moments of time as being small, smaller and smallest on the one side, and large, larger and largest on the other, that the specific condition appears.

This distinctness of succession exists only in the case of distinctness being conceived as between the characteristic and the substratum. So he says :—'All these successions find their being, etc.'

The sate of the characterized and the characteristic are relative down from the undifferentiated phenomenal to the products, and *vice versa,* inasmuch as the solids, clay, etc., are also characteristics in correlation with the ultimate atoms (the tanmātras, or divine measures). So he says :—'The characteristic also sometimes becomes the characterized object is relation to the nature of another characteristic.'

When, however, the conception of the unity of the substratum and the characteristic is entertained with reference to the real substratum, the noumenal, *i.e.*, when 'by virtue of that conception,' of the substratum being common to all its states, the characterized object itself is considered as the characteristic, then there is but one change, the change, that is to say, of the characterized object alone. Characteristic, secondary quality and condition enter then into the very being of the characterized.

It is to be considered as having been said by this that the substratum is far removed from the state of constant independent eternity (Kūṭastha nityatā).

Speaking of the change of characteristic, the Commentator takes up in the context, the distinctions of the modality of the characteristics of the mind :—'The characteristics of the mind, etc.'

The conscious (patent) characteristics are those that come into our consciousness, of which we are conscious. The latent are those of which we have no direct knowledge. Those that appear, in consciousness as notions are the real cognitions, etc. Suppression, etc., are those that are but the substance itself. This explains that they are not of the nature of illumination.

Well, but if characteristics are latent, they certainly do not exist at all. For this reason he says :—'And it is by inference that their existence as substance itself is established.' The knowledge that comes through authority is also spoken of here as inference by the similarity of their coming into existence after other knowledge. He mentions the seven characteristics by a verse :—'Suppression, etc.'

Suppression is the ultra-cognitive state of mental modifications. It is known by authority as well as by inference to be a state of residual potency.

By the word 'characterization' the author suggests virtue and vice. The reading in some places is 'Karma' (action) instead of 'Dharma' (characterization). There too virtue and vice caused by action are to be understood. Virtuous and vicious tendencies of the mind (or, which is the same thing, good and bad character) are known by authority or inferred by the existence of pleasure and pain.

Potentialization or the power which generates mental potencies, is inferred by memory.

Similarly is the constant change of the mind in evolution inferred from the fact of the mind being made up of the three 'qualities' and of the function of the qualities being changeful.

Similarly physical life, the specific action of the mind which sustains physical life, is inferred as a characteristic of the unconscious mind by expiration and inspiration.

Similarly are the movements of the mind, *i.e.*, the acts which set the different organs and parts of the body into motion, inferred by these very movements following thought in that direction.

Similarly is power the subtle state of all the effects of thought which manifest in action (It is the idea of all actions). That this also as a characteristic of the mind, is inferred by seeing the gross appearances due to the mental images therefore.—15.

Sūtra 16

परिणामत्रयसंयमादतीतानागतज्ञानम् ।। १६ ।।

परिणाम-त्रय Pariṇāma-traya, the three fold change. संयमात् Saṁyamāt, by Saṁyama over. अतीत Atīta, of the past. अनागत Anāgata, of the future. ज्ञानम् Jñānam, knowledge.

16. By *Saṁyama* over the three-fold change, comes the knowledge of the past and the future.—122.

परिणामत्रयसंयमादतीतानागतज्ञानम्। धर्मलक्षणावस्थापरिणामेषु संयमाद्योगिनां भवत्यतीतानागतज्ञानम्। धारणाध्यानसमाधित्रयमेकत्र संयम उक्तस्तेन परिणामत्रयं साक्षात्क्रियमाणमतीतानागतज्ञानं तेषु सम्पादयति।। १६।।

Vyāsa

By *Saṁyama* over the changes of characteristic, secondary quality and condition, comes to the Yogīs the knowledge of the past and the future. The triad of concentration, medition and trance together has been termed *Saṁyama.* When direct knowledge of the three-fold change is obtained by means of *Saṁyama,* knowledge of their past and present is obtaiend.—122.

Vācaspati's Gloss

Henceforward up to the end of the chapter, the objects of *Saṁyama* and the attainments which indicate mastery over them, are discussed. Of these, the first object of the *Saṁyama* of a Yogī, familiar with all the accessories of Yoga, that is introduced, is the triad of changes itself, whose modality has already been described :—'By *Saṁyama* over the three-fold changes, comes the knowledge of the past and the future.'

The question is that inasmuch as direct knowledge is obtained only of the object with reference to which *saṁyama* is performed, how is it that the *Saṁyama* on the triad of changes will become the cause of the direct knowledge of the past and the future? For this reason the Commentator says :—When direct knowledge of the three-fold change has been obtained by means of *Saṁyama*, the knowledge of the past and the future, having as they do the relation of co-existence with these changes, is also brought about. The direct knowledge of the triad of changes itself, is the direct knowledge of the past and the present which it comprehends. The very essence of the one being the essence of the other, the object of *Saṁyama* and direct knowledge are not different (in the aphorism). This is the meaning.—16.

Sūtra 17

शब्दार्थप्रत्ययानामितरेतराध्यासात्सङ्करस्तत्प्रविभागसंयमात्सर्वभूतरुतज्ञानम्।। १७।।

शब्द Śabda, the word. अर्थ Artha, the meaning, the object. प्रत्यय Pratyaya, the idea of all these. इतरेतर Itaretara, of each with the other. अध्यासात् Adhyāsāt, because of the coinciding. सङ्करः Saṅkaraḥ, becoming one, appearing as one. तत् Tat, their. प्रविभाग Pravibhāga, distinctions. संयमात् Saṁyamāt, by Saṁyama over. सर्व Sarva, all. भूत Bhūta, of living being. रुत Ruta, of the sounds. ज्ञानम् Jñānam, knowledge.

17. The word, the object and the idea appear as one, because each coincides

with the other; by Saṁyama over their distinctions comes the knowledge of the sounds of all-living-beings.—123.

शब्दार्थप्रत्ययानामितरेतराध्यासात्सङ्करस्तत्प्रविभागसंयमात्सर्वभूतारुतज्ञानम्। तत्र वाग्वर्णेष्वेवार्थवती। श्रोत्रं च ध्वनिपरिणाममात्रविषयम्। पदं पुनर्नादानुसंहारबुद्धिनिर्ग्राह्यमिति। वर्णा एकसमयासम्भवित्वात्परनिरनुग्रहात्मानस्ते पदमसंस्पृश्यानुपस्थाप्याविर्भूतास्तिरोभूताश्चेति प्रत्येकमपदस्वरूपा उच्यन्ते। वर्णः पुनरेकैकः पदात्मा सर्वाभिधानशक्तिप्रचितः सहकारिवर्णान्तरप्रतियोगित्वाद्वैश्वरूप्यमिवापन्नः। पूर्वश्चोत्तरेणोत्तरश्च पूर्वेण विशेषेऽवस्थापित इत्येवं बहवो वर्णाः क्रमानुरोधिनोऽर्थसङ्केतेनावच्छिन्ना इयं त एते सर्वाभिधानशक्तिपरिवृत्ता गकारौकारविसर्जनीयाः सास्नादिमन्तमर्थं द्योतयन्तोति। तदेतेषामर्थसङ्केतेनावच्छिन्नानामुपसंहृतध्वनीक्रमाणां य एको बुद्धिनिर्भासस्तत्पदं वाचकं वाच्यस्य सङ्केत्यते। तदेकं पदमेकबुद्धिविषयमेकप्रयत्नाक्षिप्तमभागमक्रममवर्णं बौद्धमन्त्यवर्णप्रत्ययव्यापारोपस्थापितं परत्र प्रतिपिपादयिषया वर्णैरेवाभिधीयमानैरुच्चार्यमाणैः श्रूयमाणैश्च श्रोतृभिरनादिवाग्व्यवहारवासनानुविद्धया लोकबुद्ध्या सिद्धवत्संप्रतिपत्त्या प्रतीयते तस्य सङ्केतबुद्धितः प्रविभागः। एतावतामेवं जातीयकोऽनुसंहार एतस्यार्थस्य वाचक इति। सङ्केतस्तु पदपदार्थयोरितरेतराध्यासरूपः स्मृत्यात्मकः। योऽयं शब्दः सोऽयमर्थो योऽयमर्थः सोऽयं शब्द इत्येवमितरेतराध्यासरूपः सङ्केतो भवतीति। एवमेते शब्दार्थप्रत्यया इतरेतराध्यासात्सङ्कीर्णाः। तद्यथा गौरितिशब्दो गौरित्यर्थो गौरिति ज्ञानं य एषां प्रविभागज्ञः स सर्ववित्। सर्वपदेषु चास्ति वाक्यशक्तिर्वृक्ष इत्युक्तेऽस्तीति गम्यते न सत्तां पदार्थो व्यभिचरतीति। तथा नह्यसाधना क्रियास्तीति। तथा च पचतीत्युक्ते सर्वकारकाणामाक्षेपो नियमार्थोऽनुवादः कर्तृकरणकर्मणां चैत्राग्नितण्ड्डलानामिति। दृष्टं च वाक्यार्थे पदरचनं श्रोत्रियंश्छन्दोऽधीते। जीवति प्राणान्धारयति। तत्र वाक्ये पदपदार्थाभिव्यक्तिस्ततः पदं प्रविभज्य व्याकरणीयं क्रियावाचकं वा कारकवाचकं वा। अन्यथा भवत्यश्वोऽजापय इत्येवमादिषु नामाख्यातसारूप्यादनिर्ज्ञातं कथं क्रियायां कारके वा व्याक्रियेतेति। तेषां शब्दार्थप्रत्ययानां प्रविभागः। तद्यथा श्वेतते प्रासाद इति क्रियार्थः श्वेतः प्रासाद इति कारकार्थः शब्दः क्रियाकारकात्मा तदर्थः प्रत्ययश्च। कस्मात्। सोऽयमित्यभिसंबन्धादेकाकार एव प्रत्ययः सङ्केत इति। यस्तु श्वेतोऽर्थः स शब्दप्रत्ययोरालम्बनीभूतः स हि स्वाभिरवस्थाभिविक्रियमाणो न शब्दसहगतो न बुद्धिसहगतः। एवं शब्द एवं प्रत्ययो नेतरेतरसहगत इत्यन्यथार्थोऽन्यथाशब्दोऽन्यथा प्रत्यय इति विभागः। एवं तत्प्रविभागसंयमाद्योगिनः सर्वभूतरुतज्ञानं सम्पद्यत इति।। १७।।

Vyāsa

Now the power of speech functions in the manifestation of literal sounds only. The auditory power is the substratum for the changes of sound alone. A word, however, is taken in by the will-to-know (buddhi, understanding) all at once, having taken up a unified appearance just as the last literal sound ceases. Literal sounds, from the impossibility of being expressed simultaneously, have not the nature of giving support to each other. They appear and disappear showing no connection with the particular word, nor bringing it into consciousness. It is, therefore, said that each of them is not the word (itself).

The letter, however, is singly a constituent of the word; it has the potentiality of supplying a name for all objects; it is, as it were, of universal application, inasmuch as it appears in combination with every conjoined letter, it takes different places in different combinations, sometimes being placed before and sometimes after another letter. Thus there are many literal sounds, which being placed in different orders, help in denoting, by convention, certain different sounds according to the difference in the order of their positions. For example, the literal sound of g, au, and ḥ, possessed as they are of the potentiality of giving names to all objects, denote in this particular order (gauḥ) the particular object which is possessed of udders, etc., (a cow).

A word is that single manifestation of consciousness, which appears just as the succession of literal sounds limited to a particular conventional meaning ceases; it is a conventional sign for the thing signified.

Thus a single word is perceived as a single manifestation of consciousness; it is brought into existence by a single effort; it has no parts and no order; it is not a whole of separate and distinct literal sounds. It is a phenomenon of the will-to-be (buddhi); it is brought into consciousness by the operation of the notion of the last literal sound; it is understood by the mind of the world, as having come into existence by conjunction of letters) on account of the eternal habit brought about by its ever having been with the help of literal sounds, separately named, uttered and heard, that the power of speech has functioned for the purpose of transferring the complete verbal thought signs from one mind to another. (And this being so), the ordinary mind distinguishes a word from another by conventional meaning, saying that such and such a succession of so many letters, so ending, denotes such and such an object.

Convention, however, is a manifestation of memory showing the mutual correlation of word and meaning, in the shape of coincidence. 'This object is the same as this word, and this word is the same as this object'—such is the convention showing the one correlated to the other.

Thus do word, meaning and idea run into each other on account of mutual correlation of coincidence. Take, for example, the word cow the object cow and the idea cow. Whoever knows their distinction knows all.

And in all words lies the power of a sentence. If you say "A tree," the word 'is' is understood, inasmuch as he object signified by a word never fails of existence.

Similarly no action is possible without its means. Thus on pronouncing the word 'cooks,' all the appliances necessary for the act of cooking are meant to be understood. It is only for the purpose of specialization that the object, the subject and the instrument such as Caitra, fire and rice are expressly mentioned.

Then is also seen the combination of words in sentences for expressing meanings by the entire sentences. 'The Vedic student reads the hymns, lives, bears life.' In a sentence like this the words and the meanings of words are both expressed in consciousness. Hence should words be etymologically divided as expressing actions or nominal cases. Otherwise how would it be possible to construe a word, noun or a verb, when one cannot be known from the other on account of external similarity. For example, take the words Bhavati, Aśvaḥ, Ajapāyāḥ.

The words, the meaning and the idea of the sentence are distinct from each other. Thus *svetate prāsādaḥ* (The mansion shines white) means an action. The words *svetaḥ prāsādaḥ* (A white mansion), signify a noun.

Both forms of speech denote both a noun and an affirmation of an action and also the meaning and the idea thereof. How? By the correlation, 'this is that.' The notion puts on but one appearance, the same as the conventional sign. As to the white object, it is the support for both the word and the idea. It changes its state, but goes neither with the word nor with the idea. Such is a word and such an idea; none goes with the other. Another is a word, another its meaning and another the idea. By performing Saṁyama in this way on their mutual distinction, a Yogī obtains knowledge of the sounds of all living beings.—123.

Vācaspati's Gloss

This is another subject for Saṁyama, here discussed :—'The word, the object and the idea appear as one, because each coincides with the other; by Saṁyama on their distinctions comes knowledge of the sounds of all living beings.'

Here with the object of explaining the sound (verbal) which denotes a meaning, the commentator first mentions the province of the operation of the power of speech (Vāk). Now the power of speech, Vāk, manifests literal sounds in eight places. As it is said :—'There are eight seats of literal sounds, the chest, the throat, and the head, and also the root of the tongue, the teeth, the nose, the lips and the palate.'

This Vāk, the power of speech, is purposed to operate in literal sounds only, such as they have come into existence by the recognition of the world. It does not operate to express the sign as such of a thing signified. This is the meaning.

He ascertains the sphere of the operation of the power of hearing :—The auditory power, again, operates to change itself into the particular form of a literal sound, which is a distinct modification of the manifested inarticulate sound striking against the organs of speech. Its operation is limited to that much; it does not as such signify the thing signified. This is the meaning.

He distinguishes the verbal sign signifying an object as such, from literal sounds as they have come into existence by the recognition of the world :—'A word, however, (that is to say, the sign signifying a thing) is taken by the understanding all at once, having assumed a unified appearance, just as the last literal sound disappears.' Each of the literal sounds is first taken in according as the sounds are familiar to the world; and after they have been taken into the mind, they are brought together into a single manifestation of consciousness, and thus as a sign signifying an object it is taken in by the understanding all at once. The single verbal sound 'cow' is a word, and is taken in as such by the understanding. Although each of the preceding sounds of component letters tends to bring into the field of consciousness the sound of the whole verbal sign, yet until the last literal sound is added to the sound-image that is being formed, the whole is not made distinct and clear. When the last literal cognition has, however, come into operation, the entire sound-image constituting the world becomes clear. For this reason it is said that 'a word is taken in by the understanding all at once, having assumed a unified appearance, just as the last sound ceases.'

'Literal sounds from the impossibility, etc.' This is said in reply to him who does no recognize on account of the distinctions obtaining among the different classes of letters, that words are taken in as entire single concepts all at once, but establishes on the contrary that the letters themselves singly have the power of signifying the object.

It may be in one of two ways that the literal sounds may generate the mental impression of the signified object as each is being pronounced as a part of a complete word. They may carry the capacity of signifying the object, each of them, either as pegs which give support to a basket hung therefrom; (Thus whenever the peg goes, the basket would go too) or, they may give support to the meaning as several stones places together and made into a platrom give support to a stool.

The first theory does not hold. The pronouncement of one letter only does not carry the object to the mind, for if it did, the uttering of the other letters would be quite useless. When a work has been completed, the employment of an effort for its achievement, such as is not calculated to give the completed work any extra quality, would take the effort out of the category of the means of achievement.

If this does not hold, the other remains. It is certainly possible in this case, as was not possible in the case of many pegs placed separately, that stones placed together to make a single platform should hold a stool because in this case the capacity of giving support to the stool is being employed at one and he same time. Letters however, cannot all be pronounced simultaneously, and for this reason they cannot carry the meaning to the mind even when brought together, because each of them does not take after the other, and the pronouncement of the one does not sugest the other. They do not attach to the form of one word only as if they were of its very nature. They, therefore, do not suggest the word, as each is being pronounced and passing into latency. Each maintains itself in separate and independent existence like a rod of steel. It is, therefore, said that each of them is not of the nature of a word.

Inasmuch as this defect would not arise, if the letters forming parts of a word constituted as such the word itself, he says :—'Each letter, however, singly is a necessary constituent of a word : it has the potentiality of supplying a name for all objects.' All the potentialities of making all names are present in it. Thus the letter, G, is found to exist in the words GAU, GAṆA, GAURA, NĀGA, etc., which signify different objects (a cow and others respectively). It has, therefore, the potency of supplying names for each and all of these objects. Similarly is the letter, O, found in the words, SOMA, ŚOCI, etc., which means God and other things, and that too has, therefore, the capacity of naming all these objects. Similarly should it be understood everywhere else. Each of these letters G, etc., appears in combination with, *i.e.*, in contact with other conjoined letters, such as, O, etc. On account of there being such contact, it becomes, as it were, of universal application, *i.e.*, each of these letters becomes, at it were many, and does not remain, as it is, one only. It does not of course, actually become many. Therefore the words, 'as it were,' have been added. The letter, of course, remains the same.

The letter, G, placed before and the letter, O, placed thereafter distinguish the consequent sonorous impression from the words GANA, etc. Similarly does the letter, O, placed after G, distinguish it from the words ŚOCI, etc. A specific sonorous impression is thus established in the mind as the succession of literal sounds appearing in the word ceases. This specific mental impression is the single image of the word, GAU, as manifested in the mind (sphoṭa). It is this sonorous image that denotes the specific quality of the species COW.

This is the meaning. It is impossible that the notion of an object be caused by literal sounds on account of there being a fixed order of their succession in a word : because they do not come into existence simultaneously. Nor is it proper to hold that notwithstanding the order of the succession of literal sounds in a word being fixed they come together to manifest the notion of an object by the operation of their residual potencies, in the same way as there is absence of antecedence and postcedence in the purificatory potencies brought about by oblations of combustibles, etc.; or in the same way as the heavenly state of existence is brought about. This is so, because option is inadmissible.

Knowledge of an object is not, therefore, caused by literal sounds. It is necessary that there should be perception of a single word as the means of calling it forth.

This, however, is not the case with a word. A word is expressed by sounds which differ from each other in the effort which is put forth in pronouncing them (prayatna). These constituent sounds which go to form this and that word, each differing from the other, are similar to each other in having their place of formation in the mouth and the effort requisite for their pronouncement, always the same. For this reason they make up a word similar to the others in some respect, although dissimilar in reality. The similarities here and there differ from each other by the difference caused by the relative positions of the letters. It is by this complacement that words appear as possessing different parts and composite natures, although in reality they are single and without parts. This happens in the same way as a face possessing a constant tinge of colour and fixed features and dimensions show more reflections than one, each possessed of different colour, dimensions and features, when placed differently with respect to a mirror, a dagger and a jewel. The difference is not real.

A verbal sign is single and partless. The letters are taken to be its parts by virtue of the difference of the contiguity of similar letters in different words. The difference of words being thus due to the conception of there being constituted by letters conceived as such a single and partless sonorous image (sphoṭa). Having no distinctions in itself, it is kept up in the mind, as it were, distinct and possessed of parts. It is for this reason that the specific sonorous image of the word GAU is not determined by its part G, because therein it is similar to the sonorous images of such other words as GAURA, etc. It, however, determines the whole verbal image when qualities by the literal sound O. Similarly the letter O is not competent to determine the single whole, the sonorous image of the word GAU, on account of its similarity therein with the words ŚOCI, etc. It, however, does so, being qualified by the literal sound G. Although they do not co-exist, yet one can be qualified by the other by means of residual potencies coming to co-exist. And the two residual potencies have not different spheres of action, because two percepts of two different parts and the potencies born thereform, have one word as the sphere of their operation. By the perception of the parts alone, the whole word is not manifested; but it is manifested as the succession of literal sounds ceases : and it should be added that the consciousness of the cessation of this succession manifests by virtue of the residual potencies of the perceptions of the different parts. It is a matter of observation that the past unmanifested impressions strengthen the present manifested impression by means of the successive storage of their residual potencies. Thus the notion of the existence of a tree at a distance is at first dim, but by and by becomes distinct. It is not, however, possible that this may be the method of the literal sounds bringing about the perception of the object. Because the rule of dimness and clearness applies only to perceptive cognitions; and it is not by perceptions that literal sounds bring about the consciousness of an object. It cannot, of course, be that each of the constituent literal sounds of a word should produce an indistinct image of the object which becomes distinct only in the end. If the image is raised by the letters it must be quite distinct. Or, it may be said that it is never born at all. It can never be said that it remains indistinct and dim (asphuṭa). The dissimilarity is that in the case of the sonorous image the distinctness and indistinctness are fancied after the perceptibility is established. Thus when the notion of the cessation of literal sounds takes its place in the mind through the auditory sense, along with the residual potencies left therein by the perception of each literal sound in succession, the literal sounds come together into the manifested sonorous image of a single word. This manifestation is brought about by a specific output of energy. The speciality of this energy depends upon the fixity of a particular order of the succession of literal sounds. When, therefore, the order of the succession changes, the specific energy which is competent to bring about the particular verbal manifestation no longer exists, and the particular manifestation is not brought about. Literal sounds are thus limited to the expression of a particular meaning by their dependence upon the order of their succession. They, therefore, show the conventional limitation as it appears in the world, to be the sphere of the operation of a word having more parts than one. So many as two, three, four, five or six literal sounds possessing the power of naming all objects denote the particular object which is possessed of udders, etc., when they appear as G, AU and the aspirate Ḥ.

Well, then, is it the letters alone which by virtue of distinct orders of succession denote an object? Is not a word independent of its constituent letters? For this reason he says :—'Thus a single word, etc.'

'The succession of literal sounds' is the succession brought about by literal sound.

'The succession of literal sounds limited to a particular object ceases' :—Such are the letters of a word at the time when the successive pronouncement of the literal sounds is over.

'Manifestation of consciousness' means the shining out of the Will-to-know (the buddhi) in the shape of a particular image.

'Limited to a particular conventional meaning' :—The literal sounds limited to a particular conventional meaning are, as has been said, the sounds of G, AU and Ḥ, in accordance with the conceptions of superficial observers. The meaning is that G, etc., are also taken to be the signifiers of an object, being as they are the parts of a word and thus its necessary constituents. In reality, however, it is a single mental phenomenon which, as a word, signifies an object. He renders the same plainer :—'Thus a single word is a single manifestation of consciousness, etc. All this related to it is understood by the mind of the world, etc.'

But why a single manifestation of consciousness ? For this reason he says :—'It is the object of a single effort of consciousness.' A cow : This single word is the object of a single phenomenon of consciousness; it is, therefore spoken of as a single manifestation.

He mentions the cause of its manifestation :—'It is brought into existence by a single effort.' The effort which manifests the word RASA is different from the effort which manifests the word SĀRA. And it is single, inasmuch as it is possessed of the quality of the individuality of the word RASA from the beginning, is differentiated by the fruit thereof, and has a determinate order of the antecedent and postcedent (literal sounds thereof). The different parts of the word which are understood to be existing as such by differences in similarity and order of contiguity, do not exist as such in reality, and a word is, therefore, said to be without parts. For this reason it has no order, because there is no existence in it of parts which may exist either before or after each other.

The question arises, that literal sounds appearing in order before and after one another in a word and being therefore its parts, how is it said under the circumstances that a word has no order and no parts? For this reason he says :—'It is not a whole made of separate and distinct literal sounds.' Literal sounds are not parts of a word; but by means of differences in similarity and order of contiguity, the word puts on of itself different forms and appears as it is in reality. The faces appearing in a jewel, a dagger, a mirror, etc., are not parts of the real face. 'It is a manifestation of the Will-to-know (buddhi). This means that the collective appearance at the cessation of a succession is known by the *buddhi,* is found in the *buddhi.* The operation of the notion of the last literal sound means the residual potency of the cognition of that sound. This residual potency when it is thrown in with the residual potencies of the cognitions of the previous literal sounds, brings the whole word into consciousness, that is, renders it to the object of cognition. And it is shown below that the residual potencies left in the mind by the cognitions of sounds, coincide in space with the sphere of the word they make up.

Well; but if a word has no parts, no order and no constituent literal sounds, why does it never appear as such? A white crystal may appear to be red when be smeared with molten shellac; but it is not that it will not appear pure white even when the colour has been removed. Literal sounds are, therefore, parts of a word. For this reason he says :—'It is understood by the mind of the world, etc.' The eternal functioning of the power of speech has gone on through the articulation into words of different literal sounds. This has been carried on with the help of literal sounds, separately named uttered and heard by the hearers for the purpose of transferring them from one to other minds. Eternal habit is secured by the operation.

'On account of eternal habit' means that the mind which has perceived thus, is possessed of the habit thus acquired; the habit, that is to say, of understanding the whole word as coloured by separate literal sounds. 'As having come into existence' (Siddhavat) means 'as it were, having a real and independent existence.'

By 'conjunction of letters' he means the speech of the older people which has always been so achieved. 'Thus is the word known.' The meaning is this. There is a certain application (upādhi) which may either be applied to anything or separated form it. Take for example lac or something similar. If it is separated from the crystal it shines out in its white purity. This is proper. As to the notion of a word, however, it is never produced except by a particular sound which is brought about by a particular effort. Further a word is always marred by similarity, and its notion is generated in the mind only as being made up of literal sounds. How then is it possible that a word may also be spoken or known as pure and independent of literal sounds ? As they say :—'Sounds being similar in their nature becomes causes of wrong impressions. The cause of wrong impression takes them in as such; in the sight of those who know the word, it is fixed with reference to its means of production. This certain confusion in the world is but the contradiction of knowledge.' Because the body of a word shows itself as always made up of articulated sounds; the world being superficial observers, believe that the literal sounds themselves are words; and they think that the literal sound only appearing in different combinations give different meanings. He says this :—'Distinguished by conventional meaning, etc.' The meaning is that for the benefit sounds by an act of the mind which is called convention. He describes the division into article sounds :—'Of so many letters,' neither more nor less.

'Such and such a succession' means one having a particular order of uninterrupted succession. 'Succession so ending,' is that which is taken in by a single act of the understanding. He illustrates such and such an object :—'Such as the generic quality of a cow, etc.'

'Well, but if convention means that a particular word is to denote a particular object, then there is no confusion between word and meaning. For this reason he says :—'Convention, however, etc.'

'A manifestation of memory' :—The existence of this conventional relation is due to the function of memory. The convention which determines the meaning is not only this, that such and such a meaning has been given to such and such a sound; it is also that such and such a sound is remembered as correlated to such and such a meaning. This is the meaning.

'Whoever knows their distinction performs Saṁyama thereon and thereby knows all,' that is, understands the sounds of all living beings. The genitive case used, 'their distinction' is used only with reference to convention in which the forms are not distinct.

A word has thus been established to be a single partless and jointless output of sound in which the literal sounds are only fancied to be articulations. Now he establishes that a sentence also is a single complete notion in the mind and that the words are simply fancied to be parts thereof. So he says :—'And in all words lives the power of a sentence.' This is the explaination. A word is used to convey information to another. It is only what they are intended to convey that is conveyed to the other. The same is intended to be conveyed by them which is the field of any action, etc., with reference to them. It is not the object alone that is signified by them, but the entire meaning of a sentence. All words are meant to complete the meaning of a complete sentence. Hence the same is their meaning. For this reason, where even a single word is used, even there the meaning is understood to be what it would be, if it were used together with another word. The whole meaning is not conveyed by one word alone. Why? Because that such alone has not the power to convey the whole meaning. Therefore in such places it is the sentence alone that conveys the meaning not the separate words. Because however the words are parts of a sentence, they too have the power of denoting the meaning of a sentence, in the same way as literal sounds have the power of conveying the meaning of a word on account of appearing as articulations thereof. For this reason just as every literal sound is possessed of the power of forming all means, so every word also is as such possessed of the power of forming all sentences and thus denoting the meaning intended to be conveyed by all sentences. This is what is meant by saying, 'And in all words lives the power of a sentence.' When some one says, 'A tree,' it is understood, that a tree exists. The word, 'tree', together with the word, 'is', understood, give the meaning of a sentence, and hence the word, tree, exists as part of a sentence.

But then how is it that the word, 'is', is understood? For this reason he says :—'The object signified by a word never fails of existence.' In the world, words are the means of ascertaining the existence of objects; and a word, always joining the object signified to the word 'is,' everywhere gives the meaning of a sentence. This is the meaning of an object never failing of existence. It is for this reason the practice of those who know the usage of words, that wherever there is no other verb, word 'is' and 'becomes' are to be considered understood, and are to be supplied.

Having described the nominal bases as never falling of a particular action he now shows that a particular-action never fails of a noun :—Thus on pronouncing the word 'Cooks' the appropriate agents of the action signified are always understood. And the word excludes other inappropriate agents. It is thus that the meaning of a sentence is differentiated.

Similarly are words found existing in a sentence although they are not required there : and for this reason all the more is it that words possess the power of giving the meaning of a sentence. For this reason he says :—'Then is also seen the combination of words in a sentence.' Not even thus the words 'Vedic student,' etc., used independently would convey such a meaning if they were not understood as conjoined to the words 'is,' etc. Thus the meaning is that this too has been fancied to be a part of a sentence.

Let that be. But if the words themselves have the power of conveying the meaning of a sentence, there is no use of making sentences. The meaning intended to be conveyed by a sentence is conveyed by the words themselves. For this reason he says :—'In a sentence like this, etc.' It has been said that the meaning intended to be conveyed by a word is not conveyed by a word alone, until it is conjoined to another word understood. Hence are words separated from a sentence and fancied as separate from them; and hence also are words separated from the meaning of a sentence, and are distinguished as either verbs or nominal bases. Thus are words to be etymologically explained by introducing the divisions of cases.

But then why should so much trouble be taken to explain them? For this reason he says :—'Otherwise how, etc.'

In the sentence *GHAṬO BHAVATI, BHAVATI BHIKṢĀM DEHI, BHAVATĪ TIṢṬHATI,* the nouns and verbs appear to be similar in external shape. The word *BHAVATI* in the first sentence is a verb and means 'exists.' In the other two sentences it is a noun and might be translated as 'Your ladyship.'

Similarly in the sentences, Āśvastvaṁ and Aśvas Yśti, the former Āśvas is a verb and means 'be appeased.' The second Āśvas in a noun and means a horse.

Similarly in the sentences, Ajāpayaḥ Piva and Marayajapaya Śhat-rūn. In the former sentence it means the milk of a she-goat, and in the second it means 'kill.'

Thus names and verbs being similar in external appearance, they would not be known as nouns and verbs if they were not to be separated from the sentence. How could they otherwise be explained as either verbs or nominal bases? Hence words should be separated from a sentence and explaiend. It is not that, merely by thus explaining words after having taken them out of the sentence, they would really become different in nature.

Having thus ascertained the nature of words, he now begins the discussion of the absence of real confusion (saṅkara) among word, meaning and idea, upon which confusion has been fastened by convention :—'These are the word, the meaning and the idea among which obtains a distinction.'

Thus, Śvetate Prāsādaḥ, (white shines the mansion) means an action. It is very plain here that the action of looking white which has to be established, comes first, and then arises the consciousness of the purpose of the action having been established. The word 'Śveta' is a separate thing. Even where the word and meaning have their forms established, there exists a difference between word and meaning. He says this :—'Śvetaḥ Prāsādaḥ iti' (the palace is white). The word here has the meaning of a noun. The absence of the case-ending is because the word is intended to express its own meaning. He divides the meaning :—'These are words denoting both a noun and an action. The meaning of both these words is both of the nature of a noun and an action.' He divides the idea :—'And also the meaning and the idea thereof.' It is the word 'CA' in the original which gives the meaning of the words, 'the meaning of the idea thereof.' The relation shown here is with another object which is signified.

The question is that if word, meaning and notion are known as single on account of confusion (saṅkara, coming together) where does the distinction come? He puts the question with this object :—'How?' He gives the answer :—'By the correlation, this is that, etc.'

The meaning is that the cause of the notion of unity is the qualification of the convention; it is not real, however. The use of words 'In the conventional sign' in the locative case shows that convention is the cause thereof. He shows the reality :—'And the white object, etc.' The 'states' are newness and oldness. 'Goes with' means becomes confused.

By performing Saṁyama in this way with reference to the distinctions of word, meaning and idea, the sounds of all animals, insects, etc., become distinctly intelligible to the Yogī. The Saṁyama performed with respect to the speech of man is equally performed with respect to their sounds also, inasmuch as both are of the same class. The Yogī knows their different sounds, their different meanings and their notions. Thus is it proved.—17.

Sūtra 18

संस्कारसाक्षात्करणात्पूर्वजातिज्ञानम् ।। १८ ।।

संस्कार Saṁskāra, of residual potencies. साक्षात्करणात् Sākṣāt Karaṇāt, by the bringing of into consciousness. पूर्व Pūrva, of previous. जाति Jāti, life : status. ज्ञानम् Jñānam, knowledge.

18. By bringing residual-potencies into consciousness, the knowledge of previous life-states (Jāti)—124.

संस्कारसाक्षात्करणात्पूर्वजातिज्ञानम् । द्वये खल्वमी संस्कारा: । स्मृतिक्लेशहेतवो वासनारूपा विपाकहेतवो धर्माधर्मरूपास्ते पूर्वभवाभिसंस्कृता: । परिणामचेष्टानिरोधशक्तिजीवनधर्मवदपरिदृष्टाश्चित्तधर्मास्तेषु संयम: संस्कारसाक्षात्क्रियायै समर्थ: । न च देशकालनिमित्तानुभवैर्विना तेषामस्ति साक्षात्करणम् । तदित्थं संस्कारसाक्षात्करणात्पूर्वजातिज्ञानमुत्पद्यते योगिन: । परत्राप्येवमेव संस्कारसाक्षात्करणात्परजातिसंवेदनम् । अत्रेदमाख्यानं श्रूयते । भगवतो जैगीषव्यस्य संस्कारसाक्षात्करणाद्दशसु महासर्गेषु जन्मपरिणामक्रममनुपश्यतो विवेकजं ज्ञानं प्रादुरभूत् । अथ भगवानावट्यस्तनुधरस्तमुवाच । दशसु महासर्गेषु भव्यत्वादनभिभूतबुद्धिसत्त्वेन त्वया नरकतिर्यग्गर्भसंभवं दु:खं सम्पश्यता देवमनुष्येषु पुन: पुनरुत्पद्यमानेन सुखदु:खयो: किमधिकमुपलब्धमिति । भगवन्तमावट्यं जैगीषव्य उवाच । दशसु महासर्गेषु भव्यत्वादनभिभूतबुद्धिसत्त्वेन मया नरकतिर्यग्भवं दु:खं संपश्यता देवमनुष्येषु पुन: पुनरुत्पद्यमानेन यत्किंचिदनुभूतं तत्सर्वं दु:खमेव प्रत्यवैमि । भगवानावट्य

उवाच। येदिदमायुष्मतः प्रधानवशित्वमनुत्तमं च संतोषसुखं किमिदमपि दुःखपक्षे निःक्षिप्तमिति। भगवान् जैगीषव्य उवाच। विषयसुखापेक्षयैवेदमनुत्तमं संतोषसुखमुक्तम्। कैवल्यसुखापेक्षया दुःखमेव। बुद्धिसत्त्वस्यायं धर्मस्त्रिगुणस्त्रिगुणश्च प्रत्ययो हेयपक्षे न्यस्त इति दुःखरूपस्तृष्णातन्तुः तृष्णादुःखसन्तापापगमात्तुप्रसन्नमबाधं सर्वानुकूलं सुखमिदमुक्तमिति।। १८।।

Vyāsa

Residual potencies are two-fold,—those appearing as habits and causing memories and afflictions; and those appearing as virtue and vice and causing fruition. These are the unconscious characteristics of the mind-change (pariṇāma), activity (ceṣṭā), suppression (nirodha), ideation in action (śakti), physical life (Jīvana), characterization (dharma), now appearing along with them as they have been potentialized in previous births. Saṁyama over these has the power achieving the direct knowledge of the residual potencies. And their direct knowledge is not possible without the knowledge of space, time and operative cause. Thus is it that a Yogī brings into consciousness the previous life-states by obtaining direct knowledge of residual potencies. Similarly is obtained the knowledge of the life-states of others by obtaining direct knowledge of their residual potencies.

The following story is heard in this connection :—Bhagavān Jaigiṣavya obtained the knowledge of the distinction between the real and the unreal after he had seen the direct succession of live-changes during ten great creations by having obtained direct knowledge of his residual potencies. The holy Āvaṭya, having taken a body asked him : 'You have lived and thereby become chastened through ten Great Kalpas. The essence of your Will-to-know has not been overpowered. You have experienced by troubles of life in hells, among animals and in wombs. You have been born again and again among men and gods. Have you through all this life experienced the greater quantity of pleasure or of pain,—which?

Jaigīṣavya replied to Bhagavān Āvaṭya :—'I have lived through ten great creations. My mental essence has not been overpowered. I have experienced the troubles of hell and animal life. I have been born again and again among men and gods. I consider all that I have experienced as pain only.'

Said the revered Āvaṭya :—'This mastery of your reverence over the First Cause and this invaluable joy of contentment of yours,—do you place these too to the credit of pain?

The revered Jaigiṣavya said—'The joy of contentment is invaluable only in comparison with the pleasures of sensation. Compared to the bliss of absolute freedom (Kaivalya) it is pain only. The possession of the three qualities is of the nature of the essence of the Will-to-know and whatever is possessed of three qualities is thrown to the side of avoidable pain. The chain of desire is of the nature of pain. It has been said that when the anxiety of the pain of desire is removed, then comes joy, calm, undisturbed, all-embracing.'—124.

Vācaspati's Gloss

The residual potencies born of cognitions are the causes of memories. The potencies of Nescience, etc., are the causes of the fruition of the afflictions of Nescience, etc. Fruition has the form of life-state, life-experience and life-period. The causes have the forms of virtue and vice.

'Potentialized in previous births' :—Brought about their causes in previous life-states. The characteristics of the mind are change, activity, suppression, active ideation, physical life and characterization. Like them are these potentializations too unconscious. The characteristics have been heard about and inferred. Saṁyama performed over these along with their sub-heads has the power of producing the direct knowledge of both the residual potencies.

Well; if this be so, the two residual potencies may be directly known. But how can the previous life-states be known in this way? For this reason the Commentator says :—'And their direct knowledge is not possible without the knowledge of space, time and operative cause.' Operative cause is the former body and the organs of the powers of sensation and action. The meaning is that the knowledge of the residual potencies together with the circumstances of their fruition, is not different at all from the direct knowledge of life-state, etc. Now he says that the Saṁyama over one's own potencies applies to others also :—'Similarly is obtained the knowledge, etc.'

For the purpose of creating faith in this he relates the story of the dialogue between the revered Āvaṭya and Jaigiṣavya :—'The following story, etc.' The great Kalpa is the Great Creation.

'Having taken a body' :—This means possessed of the glory of a Nirmānkāya. 'Chastened' denotes the state from which the dirt of Rajas and Tamas has been removed.

'Mastery over the First Cause' is godhead. It is by the possession of that, that he sets the Pradhāna, the First Cause, into motion and gives to whomsoever he pleases such powers of body and sense as he wishes; and having made for himself thousands of bodies and powers he goes about as he pleases in heaven, midheaven and earth.

Contentment is the destruction of desire, the characteristic of calmness of the essence of the Will-to-be.

Sūtra 19

प्रत्ययस्य परचित्तज्ञानम्।। १९।।

प्रत्ययस्य Pratyayasya, of the notions. पर Para, of other (minds). चित्त Citta, of minds. ज्ञानम् Jñānam, knowledge.

19. Of the notions, the knowledge of other minds.—125.

प्रत्ययस्य परचित्तज्ञानम्। प्रत्यये संयमात्प्रत्ययस्य साक्षात्करणात्ततः। परचित्तज्ञानम् न च तत्सालम्बनं

तस्याविषयीभूतत्वात्। रक्तं प्रत्ययं जानात्यमुष्मिन्नालम्बने रक्तमिति न जानाति। परचित्तस्य प्रत्ययस्य यदालम्बनं तद्योगिचित्तेन नालम्बनीकृतं परप्रत्ययमात्रं तु योगिचित्तस्यालम्बनीभूतमिति।। १९।।

Vyāsa

By Saṁyama over the notions and thus by obtaining the direct knowledge of the notions, comes the knowledge of other minds. But not of its object, that not being the direct object of the Yogī's mind. He knows the mental emotion of love, but does not know the object of love. Because that which has been the object of the other man's mind has not been the object of the Yogī's mind. It is only the other's mental state that has been the object of the Yogīs Saṁyama.

Vācaspati's Gloss

Of the notions, the knowledge of other minds.

Because the mind of the other only becomes directly known, the notion only is known.

As the direct knowledge of the potencies brings about the knowledge of the previous life-states also, by causing the direct knowledge of the environments, so also it follows that when the mind of another is known, the object which is responsible for the existence of any particular state of the mind should also become known. This being the suggestion, the Commentator says :—'But not along with its object.' The former Saṁyama was with reference to all the environments : this is with reference to the mind of the other only. This is the meaning.

Sūtra 20

कायरूपसंयमात्तद्ग्राह्यशक्तिस्तम्भे चक्षुःप्रकाशासंप्रयोगेऽन्तर्धानम्।। २०।।

काय Kāya, of the body. रूप Rūpa, over the form. संयमात् Saṁyamāt, by Saṁyama. तद् Tad, that (form). ग्राह्य Grāhya, capable of receiving (that). शक्ति Śakti, the power. तद्ग्राह्यशक्ति Tad Grāhya Śakti, Of perceptibility. स्तम्भे Stambhe, on the checking of. चक्षुः Cakṣuḥ, of the eye. प्रकाश Prakāśa, with the light. असंप्रयोगे Asaṁprayoge, there being no contact. अन्तर्धानम् Antardhānam, disappearance.

20. By Saṁyama over the form of the body, on perceptibility being checked, and thus there being no-contact with the light of eye, comes disappearance.—126.

कायरूपसंयमात्तद्ग्राह्यशक्तिस्तम्भे चक्षुःप्रकाशासंप्रयोगेऽन्तर्धानम्। कायस्य रूपे संयमाद्रूपस्य या ग्राह्या शक्तिस्तां प्रतिष्टभ्नाति। ग्राह्यशक्तिस्तम्भे सति चक्षुःप्रकाशासंप्रयोगेऽन्तर्धानमुत्पद्यते योगिनः। एतेन शब्दाद्यन्तर्धानमुक्तं वेदितव्यम्।। २०।।

Vyāsa

By Saṁyama over the form of the body, he checks the perceptibility of the form.

On perceptibility being checked, and thus there no longer being contact with the light which carries it to the eye, disappearance of the Yogī is brought about. By this the cessation of the perception of sound, etc., must be understood as explained.—126.

Vācaspati's Gloss

'By Saṁyama over the form of the body, on perceptibility being checked, and thus there being no contact with the light of the eye, comes disappearance.'

The body is made of the five tattvas. It becomes an object of perception to the eye on account of its possession of colour (for form). It is by colour that the body and its form becomes objects of perception. When the Yogī performs Saṁyama with reference to the form of the body, then is checked the operation of the perceptibility of colour, which is responsible for causing the ocular perception of the body. For this reason when the power of being perceived is checked, the Yogī is no longer visible. Thereby the light of sensation which is born in the eye of another, does not come into contact with the body that has disappeared. The meaning is that the body of the Yogī does not become the object of the other's knowledge. Disappearance is to be brought about when it is desired that the Yogī should not be seen by anybody. By this should also be understood another aphorism to the following effect :—By Saṁyama over the sounds, touches, tastes, smells of the body, their perceptibility being checked, there is no contact with the tymnanum skin, tongue and nose; and hence these disappear.

Sūtra 21

सोपक्रमं निरुपक्रमं च कर्म तत्संयमादपरान्तज्ञानमरिष्टेभ्यो वा।। २१।।

सोपक्रमम् Sopakramam, fast in fruition. निरुपक्रमम् Nirupakramam, slow. च Ca, and, or. कर्म Karma, action, Karma. तत् Tat, over these. संयमात् Saṁyamāt, by Saṁyama. अपरान्त Aparānta, of death. ज्ञानम् Jñānam, the knowledge. अरिष्टेभ्य: Ariṣṭebhyaḥ, by portents. वा Vā, or.

21. Karma is either fast-in-fruition or slow; by Saṁyama over these comes knowledge of death; or, by portents.—127.

सोपक्रमं निरुपक्रमं च कर्म तत्संयमादपरान्तज्ञानमरिष्टेभ्यो वा। आयुर्विपाकं कर्म द्विविधं सोपक्रमं निरुपक्रमं च। तत्र यथार्द्रं वस्त्रं वितानितं रूसीयसा कालेन शुष्येत्तथा सोपक्रमम्। यथा च तदेवं सम्पिण्डितं चिरेण संशुष्येदेवं निरुपक्रमम्। यथा वाग्नि: शुष्के कक्षे मुक्तो वातेन समन्ततो युक्त: क्षेपीयसा कालेन दहेत्तथा सौपक्रमम्। यथा वा स एवाग्निस्तृणराशौ क्रमशोऽवयवेषु न्यस्तश्चिरेण दहेत्तथा निरुपक्रमम्। तदैकभविकमायुष्करं कर्म द्विविधं सोपक्रमं निरुपक्रमं च। तत्संयमादपरान्तस्य प्रायणस्य ज्ञानमरिष्टेभ्यां वेति त्रिविधमरिष्टंमाध्यात्मिकमाधिभौतिकमाधिदैविकं च। तत्राव्यात्मिकं घोषं स्वदेहे पिहितकर्णो न श्रृणोति ज्योतिर्वा नेत्रेऽवष्टब्धे न पश्यति। तथाधिभौतिकं यमपुरुषान्पश्यति पितृनतीतानागतानकस्मात्पश्यति। तथाधिदैविकं स्वर्गमकस्मात्सिद्धान्वा पश्यति। विपरीतं वा सर्वमित्यनेन वा जानात्यपरान्तमुपस्थितमिति।। २१।।

Vyāsa

The Karma which fructifies as life-period is two-fold, that which is fast-in-fruition and that which is show-in-fruition. Thus, for example, a wet piece of cloth, well spread, dries in a short time. Similarly the fast-in-fruition.

The same cloth when gathered up, however, will take a long time to dry. Similar is the slow-in-fruition.

Further fire, thrown into dry hay and accompanied by wind in every direction, burns it in a short time; such is the fast-in-fruition. The same fire, however, applied to detached pieces of straw out of a heap, burns them in a very long time. Similarly the slow-in-fruition.

Thus the one-birth Karma which is responsible for the period of life is two-fold, the fast-in-fruition and the slow-in-fruition. By Saṁyama over these comes the knowledge of death, the smaller end of life.

'Or, by the portents' :—A portent is three-fold :—Personal (ādhyātmika), elemental (ādhibhautika) and divine (ādhidaivika). Of these, the personal :—He hears not the sound in his own body on stopping the passage of the ears. He sees not the light in the eyes on pressing them.

And the elemental :—He sees the messengers of Yama. He sees suddenly and without thought the ancestors that have passed away.

Similarly the divine :—He sees the heavenly worlds and the Siddhas suddenly. Or, he sees everything contrary to what he has been seeing the whole of his life.

It is by these that a Yogī may optionally know the proximity of death.

Vācaspati's Gloss

'Karma is either fast-in-fruition or slow; by Saṁyama over these comes the knowledge of death; or, by portents.'

The Karma which fructifies into life-time is two-fold, the fast-in-fruition and the slow-in-fruition. The one-birth Karma certainly which is the cause of life-time, life-state and life-experience, fructifies into life-period. The fast-fructifying Karma is that which is going on fructifying without any reference to what time it may take to finish by causing experience, of which more has been over and a little only remains, whose operation is going on but whose fruitage is impossible to enjoy during life by one body and which, therefore, delays the Yogī, keeping him in the bondage of births.

The same when but a small portion of the fruit has been enjoyed and which is operating to produce the remaining fruit with reference to the time that has been taken by the enjoyment of the past, works but slowly and, now and then, is slow to fructify.

The Commentator renders this plain by two illustrations :—'As for example.' He gives an illustration to return the same plainer still :—'Or, as fire.'

The words 'smaller end of life' (aparānta) mean death with reference to the Great Latency which is the ultimate end. By Saṁyama over that Karma, that is, over virtue and vice, accrues the knowledge of death. By this the Yogī knows his fast-fructifying Karma, and then makes many bodies for himself and thereby enjoys the fruit thereof as fast as he likes and dies whenever he pleases.

He takes up the context :—'Or by portents.' The indications are three-fold. They are called portents (ariṣṭas), because they frighten like an enemy.

'Or sees everything contrary, etc.' :—This excludes the trick of jugglers. But otherwise he begins to see heaven in villages and towns; he begins to see also that the world of men only is the world of gods.—21.

Sūtra 22

मैत्र्यादिषु बलानि।। २२।।

मैत्र्यादिषु Maitrī ādiṣu, over friendliness, etc. बलानि Balāni, the powers.

22. Over frinedliness, etc., the powers.—128.

मैत्र्यादिषु बलानि। मैत्रीकरुणामुदितेति तिस्रो भावनास्तत्र भूतेषु सुखितेषु मैत्रीं भावयित्वा मैत्री बलं लभते। दुःखितेषु करुणां भावयित्वा करुणाबलं लभते। पुण्यशीलेषु मुदितां भावयित्वा मुदिताबलं लभते। भावनातः समाधिर्यः स संयमस्ततो बलान्यवन्ध्यवीर्याणि जायन्ते। पापशीलेषूपेक्षा नतु भावना। ततश्च तस्यां नास्ति समाधिरित्यतो न बलमुपेक्षातस्तत्र संयमाभावादिति।। २२।।

Vyāsa

Friendliness, compassion and complaisance are three feelings. Of these he gets the power of friendliness by habituating the mind through conscious volition to sympathy towards happy beings. He gets the power of compassion by habituating the mind to compassion towards sufferers. He gets the power of complaisance by habituating the mind to complaisance towards the virtuous. By conscious habituating volition comes trance which is Saṁyama. Thereby are born the powers which know of no obstacle in their working.

It is indifference that is practised towards the sinful, not conscious habitual volition. Hence there is no trance here; and hence by reason of there being no Saṁyama, there is no power of indifference.—128.

Vācaspati's Gloss

'Over friendliness, etc., the powers.' By the performance of Saṁyama over friendliness, etc., the powers of friendliness, etc., come to him. Of these the power which comes by the practice of the feeling of friendliness, is that by which he can make the whole living world happy, and hence becomes the well-wisher of all.

Similarly, by the power of compassion he lifts suffering creatures out of pain and the causes of pain.

Similarly, by the power of complaisance he becomes just to all the world.

Now the Commentator describes that the conscious practice of habituating volition is the cause of trance, as this will be of use further.

'By conscious habituating volition comes trance which is Saṁyama.'

Although Saṁyama means concentration, meditation and trance, and not only trance, still because trance is their immediate effect and is, therefore, the chief of the three, therefore the word is used here as applying to the same.

In some places the reading is—

'Conscious habituating volition is trance.' There conscious habituating volition and trance would become the causes, *i.e.*, the limbs of Saṁyama taken as whole.

Power (vīrya) is effort. For this reason the man who possesses the power of friendliness, etc., puts forth an effort to render people happy, etc., and his effort is not checked. Indifference, however, means absence of effort. There can be no volition with respect to that; nor does there exist anything such as happiness, etc., which might thereby be brought into existence.—22.

Sūtra 23

बलेषु हस्तिबलादीनि ।। २३ ।।

बलेषु Baleṣu, over the powers. हस्ति Hasti, elephants. बल Bala, power. आदीनि Ādīni, and the others.

23. Over the powers, the powers of elephant, etc.—129.

बलेषु हस्तिबलादीनि । हस्तिबले संयमाद्धस्तिबलो भवति । वैनतेयबले संयमाद्वैनतेयबलो भवति । वायुबले संयमाद्वायुबलो भवतीत्येवमादि ।। २३ ।।

Vyāsa

By Saṁyama with reference to the strength of an elephant he comes to possess the strength of an elephant.

By Saṁyama over the power of the king of birds, one gets the power of the king of birds.

By Saṁyama over the powers of Vāyu, one gets the power of Vāyu.—129.

Vācaspati's Gloss

'Over the powers, the powers of elephant, etc. He gets the strength of whomsoever he performs Saṁyama over.—23.

Sūtra 24

प्रवृत्त्या लोकन्यासात्सूक्ष्मव्यवहितविप्रकृष्टज्ञानम् ।। २४ ।।

प्रवृत्त्या Pravṛttyāḥ, of the higher sense-activity. लोक Loka, of the light. न्यासात् Nyāsāt, by the directing. सूक्ष्म Sūkṣma, of the subtler. व्यवहित Vyavahita, of the veiled. विप्रकृष्ट Viprakṛṣṭa, of the remote. ज्ञानम् Jñānam, the knowledge.

24. The knowledge of the subtle, the veiled, the remote, by directing the light of higher sense-activity towards them.—130.

प्रवृत्त्या लोकन्यासात्सूक्ष्मव्यवहितविप्रकृष्टज्ञानम्। ज्योतिष्मती प्रवृत्तिरुक्ता मनसस्तस्यां य आलोकस्तं योगी सूक्ष्मे वा व्यवहिते वा विप्रकृष्टे वार्थे विन्यस्य तमर्थमधिगच्छति।। २४।।

Vyāsa

The higher sense-activity of lucidity has been described. It is that higher sight which the Yogī's mind directs towards the suble, the vieled or the remote and thereby knows the object.—130.

Vācaspati's Gloss

Throwing that sight by Saṁyama over the subtle, the veiled and the remote, the Yogī thereby knows the object.—24.

Sūtra 25

भुवनज्ञानं सूर्ये संयमात्।। २५।।

भुवन-ज्ञानम् Bhuvana-Jñānam, the knowledge of the regions. सूर्ये Sūrye, on the sun. संयमात् Saṁyamāt, by Saṁyama.

25. By Saṁyama on the sun, knowledge of the regions.—131.

भुवनज्ञानं सूर्ये संयमात्। तत्प्रस्तारः सप्तलोकास्तत्रावीचेः प्रभृति मेरुपृष्ठं यावदित्येवं भूर्लोकः मेरुपृष्ठादारभ्य आध्रुवाद् ग्रहनक्षत्रताराविचित्रोऽन्तरिक्षलोकः। ततः परः स्वर्लोकः पञ्चविधो माहेन्द्रस्तृतीयो लोकः। चतुर्थः प्राजापत्यो महर्लोक स्त्रिविधो ब्राह्मः। तद्यथा जनलोकस्तपो लोकः सत्यलोक इति। ब्राह्मस्त्रिभूमिको लोकः प्राजापत्यस्ततो महान्। माहेन्द्रश्च स्वरित्युक्तो दिवि तारा भुवि प्रजा इति संग्रहश्लोकः। तत्रावीचेरुपर्युपरि निविष्टाः षण्महानरकभूमयो घनसलिलानलानिलाकाशतमःप्रतिष्ठा महाकालाम्बरीषरौरव-महारौरवकालसूत्रान्धतामिस्राः। यत्र स्वकर्मोपार्जितदुःखवेदनाः प्राणिनः कष्टमायुदीर्घकालमाक्षिप्य जायन्ते। ततो महातलरसा तलातलसुतलवितललातलपातालाख्यानि सप्त पातालानि। भूमिरियमष्टमी सप्तद्वीपावसुमती यस्याः सुमेरुर्मध्ये पर्वतराजः काञ्चनस्तस्य राजतवैदूर्यस्फटिकहेममणिमयानि शृङ्गाणि। तत्र वैदूर्यप्रभानु-रागान्नीलोत्पलपत्रश्यामो नभसो दक्षिणभागः श्वेतेः पूर्वः स्वच्छः पश्चिमः कुरण्टकाभ उत्तरो दक्षिणपार्श्वे चास्य जम्बूर्यतोऽयं जम्बूद्वीपस्तस्य सूर्यप्रचाराद्रात्रिंदिवं लग्नमिव वर्तते। तस्य नीलश्वेतशृङ्गवन्त उदीचीनास्त्रयः पर्वता द्विसाहस्रायामास्तदन्तरेषु त्रीणि वर्षाणि नवनवयोजनसाहस्राणि रमणकं हिरण्मयमुत्तराः कुरव इति। निषधहेमकूटशैला दक्षिणतो द्विसाहस्रायामास्तदन्तरेषु त्रीणि वर्षाणि नवनवयोजनसाहस्राणि हरिवर्षं किंपुरुषं भारतमिति। सुमेरोः प्राचीना भद्राश्वमाल्यवत्सीमानः प्रतीचीनाः केतुमालगन्धमादनसीमानः मध्ये वर्षमिलावृतम्। तदेतद्योजनशतसाहस्रं सुमेरोर्दिशि दिशि तदर्धेन व्यूढम्। स खल्वयं शतसाहस्रायामो जम्बूद्वीपस्ततो द्विगुणेन लवणोदधिना वलयाकृतिना वेष्टितः। ततश्च द्विगुणा द्विगुणाः शाककुशक्रौञ्चशाल्मलगोमेधपुष्करद्वीपाः सप्त

समुद्राश्च सर्षपराशिकल्पाः सविचित्रशैलावतंसा इक्षुरससुरासर्पिर्दधिमण्डक्षीरस्वादूदकसप्तसमुद्रपरिवेष्टिता वलयाकृतयो लोकालोकपर्वतपरिवाराः पञ्चाशद्योजनकोटिपरिसङ्ख्याताः। तदेतत्सर्वं सुप्रतिष्ठितसंस्थान-मण्डमध्ये व्यूढम्। अण्डं च प्रधानस्याणुरवयवो यथाकाशे खद्योत इति। तत्र पाताले जलधौ पर्वतेष्वेतेषु देवनिकाया सुरगन्धर्वकिन्नरकिंपुरुषयक्षराक्षसभूतप्रेतपिशाचापस्मारकाप्सरो ब्रह्मराक्षसकूष्माण्डविनायकाः प्रतिवसन्ति। सर्वेषु द्वीपेषु पुण्यात्मानो देवमनुष्याः। सुमेरुस्त्रिदशानामुद्यानभूमिः। तत्र मिश्रवनं नन्दनं चैत्ररथं सुमानसमित्युद्यानानि। सुधर्मा देवसभा। सुदर्शनं पुरम्। वैजयन्तः प्रासादः। ग्रहनक्षत्रतारकास्तु ध्रुवे निबद्धाः। वायुविक्षेपनियमेनोपलक्षितप्रचाराः। सुमेरोरुपर्युपरि सन्निविष्टा दिवि विपरिवर्तन्ते। माहेन्द्रनिवासिनः षडेव देवनिकायाः। त्रिदशा अग्निष्वात्तायामास्तुषिता अपरिनिर्मितवशवर्तिनः परिनिर्मितवशवर्तिनश्चेति। ते सर्वे सङ्कल्पसिद्धाः। अणिमाद्यैश्वर्योपपन्नाः कल्पायुषो वृन्दारकाः कामभोगिन औपपादिकदेहा उत्तमानुकूला-भिरप्सरोभिः कृतपरिचारा महति लोके प्राजापत्ये पञ्चविधा देवनिकाया। कुमुदा ऋभवः प्रतर्दना अञ्जनाभा प्रचित्ताभा इत्येते महाभूतवशिनो ध्यानाहाराः कल्पसहस्रायुषः। प्रथमे ब्रह्मणो जनलोके चतुर्विधो देवनिकायो ब्रह्मपुरोहिता ब्रह्मकायिका ब्रह्ममहाकायिका अजरा अमरा इति। ते भूतेन्द्रियवशिनो द्विगुणा द्विगुणोत्तरायुषः। द्वितीये तपसि लोके त्रिविधो देवनिकायः। आभास्वरा महाभास्वराः सत्यमहाभास्वरा इति। ते भूतेन्द्रियप्रकृतिवशिनो द्विगुणद्विगुणोत्तरायुषः सर्वेध्यानाहारा कल्पसहस्रायुष ऊर्ध्वरेतस ऊर्ध्वमप्रतिहतज्ञाना अधरभूमिष्वनावृतज्ञानविषयाः। तृतीये ब्रह्मणः सत्यलोके चत्वारो देवनिकाया अच्युताः शुद्धनिवासाः सत्याभाः संज्ञासंज्ञिनश्चेति। अकृतभवनन्यासाः स्वप्रतिष्ठा उपर्युपरिस्थिताः प्रधानवशिनो यावत्सर्गायुषः। तत्राच्युताः सवितर्कध्यानसुखाः शुद्धत्रयीनिवासाः सविचारध्यानसुखाः सत्याभा आनन्दमात्रध्यानसुखाः संज्ञासंज्ञिनश्चा-स्मितामात्रध्यानसुखास्तेऽपि त्रैलोक्यमध्ये प्रतिष्ठन्ते। त एते सप्तलोकाः सर्वे सब्रह्मकाः। विदेहप्रकृति लयास्तु मोक्षपदे वर्तन्ते इति न लोकमध्ये न्यस्ता इत्येतद्योगिना साक्षात्करणीयम्। सूर्यद्वारे संयमं कृत्वा ततोऽन्यत्रापि। एवं तावदभ्यसेद्यावदिदं सर्वं दृष्टमिति।। २५।।

Vyāsa

Their detail :—There are seven regions. Of these beginning from Avīci up to the back of the Meru, is the region called Bhur.

Beginning from the back of the Meru up to the pole-star adorned with planets, asterisms and stars, is the starry region, the Antarikṣa.

Beyond this is the region Svar, having five planes. The third is Mahendra; the fourth is the Maharloka of the lords of creation; after this is the three-fold Brāhma region. These are the Janaloka, the Tapoloka and the Satyaloka.

> 'First comes the triple plane
> of Brahmā's region high;
> Creation's lords have then
> Their region; and then,

Cometh Indra's region—
Know all these as Heaven;
Then come the stars above,
And the last cometh Bhur.'

This verse puts all these together.

Then up to the Avīci, one placed above the other, are the six great hells : (1) the Mahākāla, (2) the Ambarīṣa, (3) the Raurava, (4) the Mahāraurava, (5) the Kālasūtra, and (6) the Andhatāmisra, in which are the excesses of earth, air, fire, ākāśa, and darkness respectively. Here are born beings who are to suffer from the consequences of their stored up Karma.

Then are the seven Pātālas, the nether worlds, Sutala, Vitala, Talātala, Mahātala, Rasātala, Atala and Pātāla.

The eighth is this earth, having seven dvīpas and known as Vasumatī. In the middle thereof is the golden king of mountains, the Sumeru. Its peaks are of silver, coral, crystal, gold and pearl. Here, blue like the leaf of the blue lotus, on account of the sheen of the emerald, is the southern region of the heaven; the eastern is white, the western bright, and the northern yellow.

And on its right side is the Jambu (tree), whence is this called the Jambudvīpa. Its night and day take their round of existence from the motion of the sun.

This has three northern mountain chains having blue and white peaks. Their length is 2,000 yojanas. Surrounded by these mountains are three continents, 9,000 yojanas each. They are Ramaṇaka, Hiraṇmaya, and Uttarakuru.

To the south are the three mountain chains, Niṣāda, Hemakūṭa, and Hemaśṛṅga, 2,000 yojanas in extension each. Among these are continents, Harivarṣa, Kimpuruṣa and Bhārata. The eastern regions of Sumeru are bounded by Bhadrāśva and Malayavat, the western by Ketumāla and Gandhamādana.

In the middle is the continent of Ilāvṛta. All this is one hundred thousand yojanas of Sumeru, each side being half that dimension.

It is to be known that this Jambudvīpa is 100,000 yojanas in dimension. It is surrounded by double its extent of salt ocean.

Each twice as large as the preceding one are the other dvīpas : Śaka, Kuśa, Krauñca, Śālmala, Gomedha, and Puṣkara. So are the seven oceans. There are beautiful mountains looking like mustard seed. The seven oceans which surround these like bracelets, taste as sugar-cane, wine, clarified butter, curds, gruel and milk (besides the salt one). They reach up to the real horizon. They measure fifty crores of yojanas (500,000,000). All this is well arranged in the sphere of phenomenal world.

Here then in the Pātālas, the oceans and the mountains are the habitations of the elementals. The *asuras, gandharvas, the kinnaras, yakṣas, rākṣasas, bhūtas, pretas, piśācas, apasmārakas, apsarās, brahmarākṣasas, kuṣmāṇḍas,* and *vināyakas,* live there.

In the dvīpas live good men and gods. Sumera is the garden of the gods. The gardens are Miśravana Nandana, Caitrāratha, and Sumānasa. Sudharmā is the council of the gods. Sudarśana is their city; Vaijayanta their palace.

Above the Sumeru is the astral region, in which the planets, asterisms and stars move round the pole-star, carried on in their courses by certain motive forces (Vāyus).

In the Mahendraloka live six classes of devas, the tridaśas, agniṣvāttās, yāmyas, tuṣitas, aparanirmitavaśavartinas, and parinirmitavaśavartinas. All of them have the power of fulfilment of desires by mere thoughts, and are possessed of the attainments known Aṇimā, etc. Their life-times are measured by a Kalpa. They are very beautiful. They enjoy their desires. Their bodies come into existence without parents, by the mere force of their good actions. They have good and obedient nymphs in their families.

In the great Prājāpatya regions there are five descriptions of gods; Kumudas, Ṛbhus, Pratardanas, Añjanābhas, and Pracitābhas. They have the Mahābhūtas in their power. Contemplation is their food. They live on for a thousand Kalpas.

In the first sphere of Brahmā, the Janaloka, there are four classes of gods, the Brahmapurohitas, the Brahmakāyikas, the Brahmamahākāyikas, and the Amaras. They have power over the elements and the powers of sensation and action. Each lives twice as long as the preceding one.

In the second, the Tapoloka, there are three classes of gods, the Abhāsvaras, the Mahābhāsvaras, and the Satyamahāsvaras. They have power over the source of elements and powers, the tanmātras. Each lives twice as long as the preceding one.

All of them are nourished by contemplation. Their knowledge is not checked in the region above them. There is nothing which is hidden from them on the lower planes.

In the third sphere of Brahmā, the Satyaloka, live four classes of gods, the Acyutas, the Suddhanivāsa, the Satyābhās and the Saṁjñāsaṁjñinas. They do not build habitations. They live in themselves, one above the other. They have their power over the Mūlaprakṛti. They live on till the end of creations. Of these, the Acyutas enjoy the bliss of the Indistinctive trance (savitarka samādhi); the Suddhanivāsas enjoy the bliss of the Meditative trance. The Satyābhās revel in pure bliss, (ānanda). The Saṁjñā-saṁjñinas are happy in the Egoistic trance. They live within the three regions (trilokī).

These are seven regions including the Brahmalokas. The Videhas and the Pakṛtilayas have reached the state of quasi-freedom, they have therefore not been placed in the phenomenal world.

All this, the yet unseen, the Yogī must see by performing Saṁyama over the solar entrance and thence over the connected objects. Let him practise until all becomes clear.—131.

Vācaspati's Gloss

'Knowledge of the regions by Saṁyama over the sun.'

First, the Commentator describes the seven regions briefly up the end of the verse which puts them together. Then he takes up in detailed description :—'Then up from Avīci, etc.' The word 'ghana' is used for Pṛthivī (earth). These great regions are to be understood as having many sub-divisions. He gives their other names :—'The Mahākāla, etc.' 'Its night and day take their round of existence from the the motion of the sun.' Whichever portion the sun leaves, there is night. Whichever the sun adorns there is day.

He gives the dimensions of the whole of the Jambudvīpa. This is a hundred thousand yojanas. How is this hundred thousand arranged? Half of it, that is fifty thousand, is placed on either side of the Meru. It is for this reason that the Meru is the middle thereof. The oceans are twice each. They are like heaps of mustrad seed. As the heap of mustrad seed is neither above the ground like a heap of barley, nor yet level with the surface of the earth, so are the oceans also. They are adorned by mountains as with ornaments. Such are the dvīpas. All this sphere of the earth is very well arranged in the body of Brahmā's Egg together with the seven dvīpas and all its forests and mountains, cities, ocean, which surround it like a necklace.

Now he shows who live there in different places :—'Here then in the Pātālas, etc.'

He mentions the arragement of the Sumeru :—'Sumeru is the garden of the gods.'

Having described the Bhurloka with its various details, he now describes the Antarikṣaloka as well with details :—'Above the Sumeru is the astral region, etc.'

'Operation of motive forces,' means the working of the forces.

He describes the heaven world :—'In the Mahendra loka, etc.'

'Classes of gods' means species of gods. He describes the highest of powers of all the six :—'All of them have the power of fulfilment, etc.' Desirable objects come to them by the mere force of wishing for them. They are very beautiful, adorable. 'They enjoy their desires :' This means that they are fond of the sex-passion.

He describes the Maharloka :—'In the great, etc.' 'They have the Mahābhūtas in their power.' Whatever they like, the Mahābhūtas supply them with. The Mahābhūtas take this and that form in obedience to and in accordance with their wishes.

'Contemplation is their food' :—They are satisfied by mere contemplation and grow thereby.

He describes the Janaloka :—'In the first of the Brahmalokas, etc.' 'They have power over the elements and the powers of sensation, etc.' The elements are the Pṛthvī, etc. The powers are the senses of hearing, etc. Howsoever they desire to employ these, they do so employ them.

Following the order of the above description he now takes up the second region of Brahmā :—'In the second, etc., they have power over the source, etc.' The source is the five tanmātras. They have power over them. The Āgamīs say that by their wish the tanmātras take the form of any body they desire.

'Each lives twice as much as the preceding one' :—The Mahābhāsvaras have twice the limit of the age of the Abhāsvaras; the Satyamahāsvaras have double their age. This is the meaning.

'Their knowledge is not checked in the region above them' :—'Above' means in the Satyaloka. From the Avīci up to the Tapaloka whatever is there of the subtle and remote, they know.

He describes the third region of Brahmā, the Satyaloka :—'In the third shphere of Brahmā, etc.' 'They do not build habitations, houses.' Because they have no place where to support themselves, they live in themselves independent of any support in space.

They have power over the Mūlaprakṛti. The three qualities, the Sattva, the Rajas and the Tamas, function in accordance with their wishes. They live up to the end of creation. And so it is heard :—Having reached the performance of a function similar to that of Brahmā, their spirits are prepared for that, and they accordingly reach the highest state.

Having described the generic function of the gods, he now takes their names and describes the specific functions of each :—'Of these the Acyutas, etc.' The gods named Acyutas derive their happiness by the contemplation of gross objects. They are satisfied thereby. The gods known as Suddhanivāsinas find happiness in the contemplation of subtle objects; they are pleased thereby. The gods named Satyābhās derive happiness from the contemplation of the objects of the senses. The Saṁjñāsaṁjñinas derive their happiness fórm the contemplation of egoism alone, and are pleased thereby. All these take up the Cognitive trance.

Why are the performers of the ultra-cognitive trance, the Videhas and the Prakṛtilayas, not laced within the lokas? Those whose Will-to-be is active and shows objects to the Puruṣa, carry on the evolution of the universe and are, therefore, within the world. Not so the Videhas and the Prakṛtilayas, even though their minds have still their duty to fulfil. All this up to the Satyaloka and down to the Avīci, the Yogī should know in the solar entrance, *i.e.*, the tube called Suṣumnā.

Even by this much all is not known. For this reason he says :—'And thence on other objects besides the Suṣumnā, wherever the teacher of Yoga points out, until all this world becomes visible.

The essence of the Will-to-know is by its very nature possessed of the power of illuminating the universe. Being however covered by darkness it illuminates only those regions from which the cover is removed by Rajas. When the solar entrance is uncovered, the regions are illuminated. This rule does not apply elsewhere. The Saṁyama performed elsewhere has only the power of unveiling as much of the Buddhic essence, as the Saṁyama is performed with reference to. Thus all is plain.—25.

Sūtra 26

चन्द्रे ताराव्यूहज्ञानम् ।। २६ ।।

चन्द्रे Candre, on the moon. तारा Tārā, of the stars, starry. व्यूह Vyūha, of the systems. ज्ञानम् Jñānam, the knowledge.

26. On the moon, the knowledge of the starry systems.—132.

चन्द्रे ताराव्यूहज्ञानम् । चन्द्रं संयमं कृत्वा ताराणां व्यूहं विजानीयात् ।। २६ ।।

Vyāsa

Let him know the starry systems by performing Saṁyama with reference to the moon.—132.

Sūtra 27

ध्रुवे तद्गतिज्ञानम्।। २७।।

ध्रुवे Dhruve, on the pole-star. **तद्** Tad, of their. **गति** Gati, movement. **ज्ञानम्** Jñānam, the knowledge.

27. On the pole-star the knowledge of their movements.—133.

ध्रुवे तद्गतिज्ञानम्। ततो ध्रुवे संयमं कृत्वा ताराणां गतिं विजानीयात्। ऊर्ध्वविमानेषु संयमं कृत्वा तानि विजानीयात्।। २७।।

Vyāsa

Then let him know the movements of the stars by performing Saṁyama with reference to the pole-star.—133.

Sūtra 28

नाभिचक्रे कायव्यूहज्ञानम्।। २८।।

नाभि Nābhi, of the navel. **चक्रे** Cakre, on the plexus. **काय** Kāya, of the body. **व्यूह** Vyūha, of the system. **ज्ञानम्** Jñānam, the knowledge.

28. On the plexus of the navel, the knowledge of the system of the body.—134.

नाभिचक्रे कायव्यूहज्ञानम्। नाभिचक्रे संयमं कृत्वा कायव्यूहं विजानीयात्। वातपित्तश्लेष्माणस्त्रयो दोषाः। धातवः सप्त त्वग्लोहितमांसस्नाय्वस्थिमज्जाशुक्राणि। पूर्वं पूर्वमेषां बाह्यमित्येष विन्यासः।। २८।।

Vyāsa

Let him know the system of the body by performing Saṁyama over the plexus of the navel. There are three humours, gas, bile and phelgm. There are seven substances, skin, blood, muscle, tendon, bone fat and semen. The previous in order among these is external to the next following. Such is their comparative position.—134.

Sūtra 29

कण्ठकूपे क्षुत्पिपासानिवृत्तिः।। २९।।

कण्ठ Kaṇṭha, of the throat, कूपे Kūpe, in the pit. क्षुत् Kṣut, of hunger. पिपासा Pipāsā, thirst. निवृत्तिः Nivṛttiḥ, the subdual.

29. In the pit of the throat, subdual of hunger and thirst.—135.

कण्ठकूपे क्षुत्पिपासानिवृत्तिः। जिह्वाया अधस्तात्तन्तुस्ततोऽधस्तात्कण्ठस्ततोऽधस्तात्कूपस्तत्र संयमात्क्षुत्पिपासे न बाधेते।। २९।।

Vyāsa

Below the tongue is the throat; below that the gullet; below that the pit (stomach). By Saṁyaam there, hunger and thirst tease not.—135.

Sūtra 30

कूर्मनाड्यां स्थैर्यम् ।। ३० ।।

कूर्मनाड्याम् Kūrma-nāḍyām, tortoise tube, स्थैर्यम् Sthairyam, steadiness.

30. On the tortoise tube (kūrmanāḍī), steadiness.—136.

कूर्मनाड्यां स्थैर्यम् । कूपादध उरसि कूर्माकारा नाडी तस्यां कृतसंयमः स्थिरपदं लभते । यथा सर्पो गोधा चेति ।। ३० ।।

Vyāsa

Below the throat pit in the chest is a tube of the shape of a tortoise. By performance over that, the Yogī gets firmness of position as that of snake, alligator, etc. (*i.e.*, the power of hibernation).—136.

Vācaspati's Gloss

26, 27, 28, 29 and 30.

Whatever the Yogī wishes to know, he must perform Saṁyama with reference to that. Thus Saṁyama tending to bring about the cessation of hunger and thrist and steadiness have been taught by the words of the aphorism and have been explained by the words of the Commentary already explaiend.—30.

Sūtra 31

मूर्धज्योतिषि सिद्धदर्शनम् ।। ३१ ।।

मूर्ध Mūrdha, of the head, the coronal. ज्योतिषि Jyotiṣi, on the light सिद्ध Siddha, of the perfected ones. दर्शनम् Darśanam, the vision.

31. In the coronal light, vision of the Perfected-Ones.—137.

मूर्धज्योतिषि सिद्धदर्शनम् । शिरः कपालेऽन्तश्छिद्रं प्रभास्वरं ज्योतिस्तत्र संयमं कृत्वा सिद्धानां द्यावापृथिव्योरन्तरालचारिणां दर्शनम् ।। ३१ ।।

Vyāsa

In the skull there is a bright light in the hole. By Saṁyama thereupon comes vision of the perfected ones, he Siddhās, moving in space between earth and heaven.—137.

Vācaspati's Gloss

By the word 'coronal' the Suṣumnā tube is indicated The Saṁyama is to be there.—31.

Sūtra 32

प्रातिभाद्वा सर्वम्।। ३२।।

प्रातिभाद् Prātibhād, by prescience. वा Vā, or. सर्वम् Sarvam, all.

32. Or, all knowledge by prescience (prātibha).—138.

प्रातिभाद्वा सर्वम्। प्रातिभं नाम तारकं तद्विवेकजस्य ज्ञानस्य पूर्वरूपम्। यथोदये प्रभा भास्करस्य तेन वा सर्वमेव जानाति योगी प्रातिभस्य ज्ञानस्योत्पत्ताविति।। ३२।।

Vyāsa

Prescience is also named Tāraka. It is the fore-runner of discriminative knowledge, as light is the fore-runner of the sun at sunrise. The Yogī may also may also know everything by that, (as an alternative means) after the birth of knowledge, called prescience.—138.

Vācaspati's Gloss

Prātibha, prescience, is the same as self-suggestion (Uha), the coming into consciousness without external aid of anything unknown. When Saṁyama is performed with the object of attaining the Highest Intellection, then at the time of the height of practice, there takes its rise a power which, as it were, draws in all knowledge. The Yogī knows everything by that. It is called Tāraka, (from tri to swim, to cross over), because by bringing about the Higest Intellection it helps in crossing over the world of life and death.—32.

Sūtra 33

हृदये चित्तसंवित्।। ३३।।

हृदये Hṛdaye, in the heart. चित्त Citta, of the mind. संवित् Saṁvit, the knowledge.

33. In the heart, the knowledge of the mind.—139.

हृदये चित्तसंवित्। यदिदमस्मिन्ब्रह्मपुरे दहरं पुण्डरीकं वेश्म तत्र विज्ञानं तस्मिन्संयमाच्चित्तसंवित्।। ३३।।

Vyāsa

In the lotus-like cavity, the temple in the city of Brahmā, lives the Intelligence. By performing Saṁyama with reference to that, comes the power of knowing the (Citta).—139.

Vācaspati's Gloss

The Commentator describes the word heart (Hṛdaya). The self is called Brahma, being largest of all. His city is that in which he is housed, knowing it as he does to be his own. Cavity means hollow. The same is the lotus too with its face downwards. The same is the temple.

He gives the reason for the mind knowing mind (the Manas knowing the Citta) : 'Intelligence lives there.' By Saṁyama over that, the Yogī knows the Citta with its modifications.—33.

Sūtra 34

सत्त्वपुरुषयोरत्यन्तासङ्कीर्णयोः प्रत्ययाविशेषो
भोगः परार्थत्वात्स्वार्थसंयमात्पुरुषज्ञानम्।। ३४।।

सत्त्व Sattva, of the objective essence. पुरुषयोः Puruṣayoḥ, and of the Puruṣa. अत्यन्त Atyanta, quite. असङ्कीर्णयोः Asankīrṇayoḥ, distinct from each other. प्रत्यय Pratyaya, the notion of distinction. अविशेषः Aviśeṣaḥ, the absence. भोगः Bhogaḥ, is experience. परार्थत्वात् Parārthatvāt, because it exists for another. स्वार्थ Svārtha, on his own object. संयमात् Saṁyamāt, by Saṁyama. पुरुष-ज्ञानम् Puruṣa-Jñānam, the knowledge of the Puruṣa.

34. Experience consists in the absence of the notion of distinction between the Puruṣa and Objective-Essence, which are really quite distinct-form-each-other, becasue it exists for another. By Saṁyama on his own object, comes the knowledge of the Puruṣa.—140.

सत्त्वपुरुषयोरत्यन्तासङ्कीर्णयोः प्रत्ययाविशेषो भोगः परार्थत्वात्स्वार्थसंयमात्पुरुषज्ञानम्। बुद्धिसत्त्वं प्रख्याशीलम्। समानसत्त्वोपनिबन्धनेरजस्तमसी वशीकृत्य सत्त्वपुरुषान्यताप्रत्ययेन परिणतम्। तस्माच्च सत्त्वात्परिणामिनोऽत्यन्तविधर्मा विशुद्धोऽन्यश्चितिमात्ररूपः पुरुषस्तयोरत्यन्तासङ्कीर्णयोः प्रत्ययाविशेषो भोगः। पुरुषस्य दर्शितविषयत्वात्। स भोगप्रत्ययः सत्त्वस्य परार्थत्वाद् दृश्यः। यस्तु तस्माद्विशिष्टश्चितिमात्ररूपोऽन्यः पौरुषेयः प्रत्ययस्तत्र संयमात्पुरुषविषया प्रज्ञा जायते। न च पुरुषप्रत्ययेन बुद्धिसत्त्वात्मना पुरुषो दृश्यते। पुरुष एव तं प्रत्ययं स्वात्मावलम्बनं पश्यति। तथा ह्युक्तम्। विज्ञातारमरे केन विजानीया- दिति।। ३४।।

Vyāsa

The essence of the Will-to-be is of the nature of illumination; and when it overpowers the qualities of Disturbing energy (Rajas) and Inertia (Tamas), which are equally related to it by co-existence, it takes up the form of the notion of the distinction between the Puruṣa and Objective Essence. Widely different from that changing Objective Existence also in characteristic is the Puruṣa who appears as pure consciousness. They are quite distinct from each other. Experience consists in the notions of the two not being taken as distinct, because the objects are shown to him. The notion of enjoyment is the knowable, because the Essence of matter exists for another. There is another notion, however, the notion of the Puruṣa, which is quite distinct from this, and which appears as pure consciousness.

By Saṁyama with reference to this notion is born the knowledge of the Puruṣa. The Puruṣa is not known by that notion of itself, which is the self-same as the Objective Buddhi. The Puruṣa only sees that notion of self by himself. And so it has been said :—'By what, Oh! is the knower to be known?—140.

Vācaspati's Gloss

When the Essence of the Will-to-be, which is of the very nature of the luminous essence of things, which is extremely pure, and which is on account of the utter suppression of the Rajas and Tamas modified into the phenomenon of the distinction between the Puruṣa and the Objective Essence, is entirely different from the Puruṣa, what to speak of the Rajas and the Tamas? It is with this in his mind that the author of the aphorisms says, 'Distinction between the Puruṣa and the Objective Essence.'

Having the same in mind the author of the Commentary too says :—'The essence of the Will-to-be, etc.' Not only possessing the nature of illumination, but modified too at the same time as the discriminative knowledge, and therefore extremely pure and luminous, it therefore bears extreme resemblance to consciousness. This would mean confusion. For this reason he says :—'Which are equally related to it by co-existence.' Co-existence is the relation of one not existing without the other. Those which bear the relation of co-existence equally, are the qualities of Disturbing Energy (Rajas) and Inertia (Tamas), 'Overpowering' means controlling. He describes the absence of confusion :—'Widely different from the Changing Objective, etc.'

The word 'also' signifies that it is not only different from the Sattva, but from the Rajas and Tamas also. 'Changing Objective existence' is used to indicate the distinction of the unchanging Puruṣa.

'The notion of these two not being taken as distinctive' :—The Will-to-be is of the nature of either the quiescent, the disturbed, or the forgetful notions. When consciousness is reflected into it, then the quiescence, the disturbance and the forgetfulness are fastened on to the consciousness. (This happens in the same way) as the moon reflected into pure water, looks as if trembling on account of the unsteadiness of the water.

He mentions the cause of experience :—'Because the objects are shown to the Puruṣa.' This has been explained often.

Well ; let the essence of the Will-to-be different from the Puruṣa. But how can experience be different from the Puruṣa? For this reason he says :—'The notion of enjoyment,' *i.e.*, the notion consisting of enjoyment, 'is of the Objective Essence and therefore existing for the sake of another.' And that is enjoyable is of the nature of the knowable. Objective Essence is for the sake of another, because it consists of many things brought together; and because experience is a characteristic. That also is for the sake of another. It becomes the enjoyable of that particular enjoyer for whose sake soever it may be in existence.

Or, it may be said that experience is the feeling of pleasure and pain as being in consonance or dissonance with the prevailing mental trend at any time. This cannot be in consonance or dissonance with itself. No self-contradictory manifestation can exist in itself. Hence it must be the objects that are either in consonance or dissonance; and it is this that constitutes experience. The self is the enjoyer; the knowable is that which he enjoys.

'Which is quite distinct from this' :—The words 'on account of existence for the sake of another' are to be supplied here as understood to explain the distinction.

Well ; let that be. But if the Puruṣa is thus the object of knowledge, then there must be posited another intelligence, which this intelligence knows, and so on and on and thus there would be no stability of thought. For this reason he says :—'The Puruṣa is not known by that notion of itself, etc.' This is the construction : The non-intelligent is illuminated by consciousness, not consciousness by the non-intelligent. How could the notion of the Puruṣa (being non-intelligent, as being a modification of the Will-to-be illuminate the conscious self? It has, however, been said that the conscious self, not depending for illumination upon another, illuminates the non-intelligent. By saying that the notion of the Puruṣa is of the nature of the essence of the Will-to-be, it is meant to be stated that it is of the nature of the non-intelligent, and is therefore unconscious as such, What looks like the objective appearance of the Puruṣa, and becomes as such an object of knowledge, is the reflection of the Puruṣa into the essence of the Will-to-be. This reflection depends upon the Puruṣa as the reflection of the face into the mirror depends upon the face. The Will-to-be becomes the object of the Puruṣa by that reflection and not in its own nature of illumination. The notion of self-knowledge.consists in making the object of knowledge, the reflection of the Puruṣa into the Buddhi. He Illustrates the same by a Vedic text (Br. Up. II. 4-14 :—) 'And so it has been said' by Īśvara :—'By what Oh! is the knower to be known?' That is, by nothing.—34.

Sūtra 35

ततः प्रातिभश्रावणवेदनादर्शास्वादवार्ता जायन्ते।। ३५।।

ततः Tataḥ, thence. प्रातिभः Prātibhaḥ, prescience. श्रावण Śrāvaṇa, higher hearing. वेदन Vedana, higher touch. आदर्श Ādarśa, higher vision. आस्वाद Āsvāda, higher taste. वार्ता Vārtā, higher smell. जायन्ते Jāyante, proceed.

35. Thence proceed prescience, higher hearing, touch, vision, taste, and smell.—141.

ततः प्रातिभश्रवणवेदनादर्शास्वादवार्ता जायन्ते। प्रातिभात्सूक्ष्मव्यवहितविप्रकृष्टातीतानागतज्ञानम्। श्रावणाद्दिव्यशब्दश्रवमणम्। वेदनाद्दिव्यस्पर्शाधगमः। आदर्शाद्दिव्यरूपसंवित्। आस्वादाद्दिव्यरससंवित्। वार्तातो दिव्यगन्धविज्ञानमित्येतानि नित्यं जायन्ते।। ३५।।

Vyāsa

By prescience comes the knowledge of the subtle, the intercepted, the remote and the past and future. By higher hearing comes the hearing of divine sounds; by touch, the knowledge of divine touch; by the vision comes the knowledge of heavenly colour; by smell, the cognition of higher odours; by taste comes the cognition of divine tastes. These are born constantly.—141.

Vācaspati's Gloss

Saṁyama over self-illumination is impossible until the Pradhāna has fulfilled its object of making the whole of herself known to the Puruṣa. Therefore, the author shows all the attainments which precede it :—'Thence proceed prescience, higher hearing, touch, vision, taste, and smell.' By this it is also said that mind, hearing, skin, eye, tongue and nose favourably strengthened with the virtues resulting from the practice of Yoga, are the invisible causes respectively of prescience and higher hearing, etc.

The words Śrāvaṇa, etc., used in the text are technical terms for denoting the hearing of divine sounds, etc. The Commentary is easy.—35.

Sūtra 36

ते समाधावुपसर्गा व्युत्थाने सिद्धयः ।। ३६ ।।

ते Te, they. समाधौ Samādhau, to trance. उपसर्गाः Upasargāḥ, obstacles. व्युत्थाने Vyutthāne, to the outgoing of the mind. सिद्धयः Siddhayaḥ, perfections.

36. They are obstacles to trance, but perfections to the out-going mind.—142.

ते समाधावुपसर्गा व्युत्थाने सिद्धयः। ते प्रातिभादयः समाहितचित्तस्योत्पद्यमाना उपसर्गास्तद्दर्शन-प्रत्यनीकत्वात्। व्यूत्थितचित्तस्योत्पद्यमानाः सिद्धयः।। ३६ ।।

Vyāsa

They, the powers of prescience etc., prove to be obstacles when they appear in a mind which has reached the state of trance; because they oppose the knowledge obtained in that state. When, however, they appear in a mind which is active in going out, they are attainments.—142.

Vācaspati's Gloss

As it may be that one who has been performing Saṁyama with reference to the self, may on the appearance of these attainments think that the has achieved what had to be achieved, and thus give up further effort, the author says :—'They are obstacles to trance, but perfections to the out-going mind.'

It is only he whose mind is active in going out that becomes proud of the possession of these as attainments. A beggar in life may think that the possession of a little wealth is the fullness of riches. The Yogī, however, who is inclined to the attainment of trance must reject them whenever they come. He has vowed the removal of all the three descriptions of pain to their utmost limit. That being the object of the Puruṣa, how can he take pleasure in the attainments which are the opponents of that state of being ? This is the meaning of the aphorism and the commentary.—36.

Sūtra 37

बन्धकारणशैथिल्यात्प्रचारसंवेदनाच्च चित्तस्य परशरीरावेशः।। ३७।।

बन्ध Bandha, of bondage. कारण Kārana, of the cause. शैथिल्यात् Śaithilyāt, on relaxation. प्रचार Pracāra, of the passages. संवेदनात् Saṁvedanāt, by knowledge. च Ca, and. चित्तस्य Cittasya, of the mind. पर Para, other's. शरीर Śarīra, body. आवेशः Āveśaḥ, entering into.

37. The mind may enter another body, on relaxation of the cause of bondage, and by knowledge of the passages of the mind.—143.

बन्धकारणशैथिल्यात्प्रचारसंवेदनाच्च चित्तस्य परशरीरावेशः। लोलीभूतस्य मनसोऽप्रतिष्ठस्य शरीरे कर्माशयवशाद् बन्धः प्रतिष्ठेत्यर्थः। तस्य कर्मणो बन्धकारणस्य शैथिल्यं समाधिबलाद्भवति। प्रचारसंवेदनं च चित्तस्य समाधिजमेव कर्मबन्धक्षयात्स्वचित्तस्य प्रचारसंवेदनाच्च योगी चित्तं स्वशरीरान्निष्कृष्य शरीरान्तरेषु निःक्षिपति निःक्षिप्तं चित्तं चेन्द्रियाण्यनुपतन्ति। यथा मधुकरराजानं मक्षिका उत्पतन्तमनूत्पतन्ति निविशमानमनुनिविशन्ति तथेन्द्रियाणि परशरीरावेशे चित्तमनुविधीयन्त इति।। ३७।।

Vyāsa

The mind (citta) which by nature passes into new states of life and never remains fixed in one state, is bound down to, *i.e.*, comes to stay in a body, because of the power of the vehicle of action. By the force of trance, the vehicle of action which chains it down, slackens its operation. And the consciousness of how the mind acts in the body is also the fruit of trance. By the destruction of the bonds imposed by Karma, and by knowing the method of the mind acting upon the body, the Yogī withdraws his mind from his own body and throws it into the body of another. As the mind is thus thrown into another body, the powers of sensation, etc., follow it. Even as bees follow their king, as he goes on resting or moving on, so do the powers follow the mind as it enters another body.—143.

Vācaspati's Gloss

Having described the power of knowledge, which has its culmination in the knowledge of the Puruṣa, as being the result of Saṁyama, the author now describes the result of Saṁyama which takes the shape of the power of action :—'The mind may enter a other body on relaxation of the cause of bondage, and by knowledge of the passages of the mind.' 'By the force of trance' :—This means the performance of Saṁyama on the cause of bondage. Trance alone is mentioned because that is the principal factor of the three. By 'passages of the mind' are understood the passages through which and the modes according to which the mind acts in the body. There are nerves in the body by which the mind travels in the body to perform its functions. From the performance of Saṁyama on the passage of the mind along these nerves, accrues the consciousness thereof, which slackens the bond. Then by destruction of the cause of bondage he no longer remains confined to the body. But it may be that even though he may no longer be confined to the body, he may not know how to get out of the body by the proper passage, and he may thus not be able to go out of the body without injury, and may not also be else to enter another body. For this reason the passages and modes of movement also must be known. As the powers of sensation, etc., follow the mind they take their proper places in the body, as the mind enters therein.—37.

Sūtra 38

उदानजयाज्जलपङ्ककण्टकादिष्वसङ्ग उत्क्रान्तिश्च।। ३८।।

उदान Udāna, over Udāna. जयात् Jayāt, by mastery. जल Jala, water. पङ्क Paṅka, mud. कण्टक Kaṇṭaka, thorns, with these. आदिषु Ādiṣu, and with the others. असङ्गः Asaṣgaḥ, non-contact. उत्क्रान्तिः Utkrāntiḥ, ascension. च Ca, and.

38. By mastery over Udāna, ascension and non-contact with water, mud, thorns, etc.—144.

उदानजयाज्जलपङ्ककण्टकादिष्वसङ्ग उत्क्रान्तिश्च। समस्तेन्द्रियवृत्तिः प्राणादिलक्षणा जीवनं तस्य क्रिया पञ्चतयी प्राणो मुखनासिकागतिराहृदयवृत्तिः। समं नयनात्समानश्चानाभिवृत्तिः। अपनयनादपान आपादतलवृत्तिः। उन्नयनादुदान आशिरोवृत्तिः व्यापी व्यान इति। एषां प्रधानं प्राणः। उदानजयाज्जलपङ्ककण्टकादिष्वसङ्ग उत्क्रान्तिश्च प्रायणकाले भवति तां वशित्वेन प्रतिपद्यते।। ३८।।

Vyāsa

Life which shows itself as the operations of Prāna and others, is the manifestation of all the powers of sensation and action. Its action is five-fold. The Prāṇa moves through the mouth and the nose, and manifests itself within the chest.

The Samāna manifests up to the navel. It is so called because it carries equally (Sama) (to all parts of the body, the juice of food, etc.) Manifesting down to the soles of feet (all over) is the Apāna, so called because it carries away (apa). Manifesting up to the head is the Udāna, so called because it carries upward (ut). The Vyāna is so called because it pervades the whole body in every direction. Of these, the Prāṇa is the chief.

'By mastery over Udāna is secured non-contact with water, mud, thorns, etc., and ascension comes at the time of death. He secures that because he has the power.'—144.

Vācaspati's Gloss

By mastery over Udāna is secured non-contact with water, mud, thorns, etc. 'Life is the manifestation of the functions of all the powers of sensation, etc.' It functions as Prāṇa etc. Prāṇa and others are indications thereof. The functioning of the indriyas is two-fold, external and internal. The external is indicated by the cognition of colour, etc. The internal function is life. It is a particular effort, which is the common property of all the indriyas (powers of action and sensation) and the cause of the different actions of the Vāyu Tattva, the motive power of the body. As they say :—'Prāṇa and other motive forces, the functions of the Vāyu Tattva, are the five modifications of the Vāyu Tattva. They are the five modifications of the Indriyas (powers of action and sensation) in common. Because they point to this that 'its action is five-fold', the action of that effort (prayatna) is five-fold.

The Prāṇa has its sphere from the fore-part of the nose down to the heart. The Samāna is that which carries equally, that is, to places where it is properly required and inasmuch as is required, the chyle which is made of foods and drinks. Its sphere of action is down from the heart to the navel. The Apāna is the cause of sending out of the body urine, faeces, foetus, etc. Its sphere of action is up to the navel and also down to the soles of feet. The Udāna is so called because it carries upwards chyle, etc. Its function is from the fore-part of the nose up to the head. The Vyāna is all-pervading. The Prāṇa is the chief of all these that have been described, because the Vedic text speaks of all these going out when Prāṇa goes out.

Having thus described the differences of Prāṇa etc., with reference to their functions and the places of their location, the Commentator now introduces the aphorism :—'By mastery over Udāna, etc.' When Udāna is mastered by the performance of Saṁyama thereupon, he is no longer checked by water, etc.

As to ascension, that takes place by the path which has its beginning in the flame (the Arcirādi, northern path), after death. Having mastered that path, he ascends by that path.

By the performance over Prāṇa, etc., and by the acquirement of mastery over these, come appropriate attainments too. They should be understood according to the differences of their function, place of manifestation, and mastery, etc.—38.

Sūtra 39

समानजयाज्ज्वलनम् ।। ३९ ।।

समान Samāna, over Samāna. जयात् Jayāt, by mastery. ज्वलनम् Jvalanam, efflugence.

39. By mastery over Samāna comes effulgence.—145.

समानजयाज्ज्वलनम् । जितसमानस्तेजस उपध्मानं कृत्वा ज्वलयति ।। ३९ ।।

Vyāsa

He who has obtained mastery over the Samāna blows the fire into flame and thus shines.—145.

Vācaspati's Gloss

The fire is of the body. The blowing it into flame means rendering it brighter.—39.

Sūtra 40

श्रोत्राकाशयोः संबन्धसंयमाद्दिव्यं श्रोत्रम् ।। ४० ।।

श्रोत्र Śrotra, the power of hearing. आकाश Ākāśa between these two. सम्बन्ध Sambandha, over the relation. संयमात् Saṁyamāt, by Saṁyama. दिव्यम् Divyam, higher. श्रोत्रम् Śrotram, power of hearing.

40. By Saṁyama over the relation between Ākāśa and the power-of-hearing, comes the higher power-of-hearing.—146.

श्रोत्राकाशयोः संबन्धसंयमाद्दिव्यं श्रोत्रम्। सर्वश्रोत्राणामाकाशं प्रतिष्ठा सर्वशब्दानां च। यथोक्तम्। तुल्यदेशश्रवणानामेकदेशश्रुतित्वं सर्वेषां भवतीति। तच्चैतदाकाशस्य लिङ्गम्। अनावरणं चोक्तम्। तथामूर्तस्याप्यन्यत्रानावरणदर्शनाद्विभुत्वमपि प्रख्यातमाकाशस्य शब्दग्रहणनिमित्तं श्रोत्रम्। बधिराबधिरयोरेकः शब्दं गृह्णात्यपरो न गृह्णातीति तस्माच्छ्रोत्रमेव शब्दविषयम्। श्रोत्राकाशयोः संबन्धे कृतसंयमस्य योगिनो दिव्यं श्रोत्रं प्रवर्तते ।। ४० ।।

Vyāsa

In Ākāśa abide all powers of hearing and all sounds. As has been said :—'To all those whose organs of hearing are similarly situated, the situation of hearing comes to be the same.'

And this is a reason for (the existence of Ākāśa). Absence of obstruction also has been so spoken of. The Ākāśa is also described as all-pervading, seeing that there is absence of obstructions in other places also than where a form may be.

The power of hearing is the means of perceiving sound. Of a deaf and a not-deaf, one senses sound and the other does not. Therefore, the power of hearing only is the sphere for action of sound. Whoever performs Saṁyama with reference to the relation between the power of hearing and the Ākāśa, evolves the power of higher audition.—146.

Vācaspati's Gloss

It has been said that the power of higher audition comes to the Yogī who is performing Saṁyama with reference to the purpose of the self, because there yet remains something of the Pradhānȧ to be seen. Now the author says that the powers of higher audition and other sense powers come by the performance of Saṁyama with reference to the powers themselves. :—

'By Saṁyama on the relation between the power of hearing and Ākāśa (the soniferous ether) comes the higher power of audition.' He describes the sphere of Saṁyama :—'The relation between the power of hearing and Ākāśa,' the relation being that of the thing supporting and the thing supported.

All powers of hearing, even though they have their origin in the principle of egoism, reside in Ākāśa, placed in the hollow of the earth. It is this where the power of hearing is located. When soundness or defect is noticed therein, soundness of defect, as the case may be, is noticed in the power of hearing also.

Further, when of the sounds working in unison with the power of hearing, the sounds of solids, etc., are to be taken in, then the power of hearing located in the hollow of the ear, stands in need of the capacity of resonance residing in the substratum, the Ākāśa of the ear.

In the perception of the external smells of solids, etc., by the senses of smell, etc., working in unison with the qualities of odour, etc., the operation is seen to be that the senses of smell, taste, touch, sight and hearing are located in physical vehicles only because the powers of smell, etc., are seen to be working soundly or defectively when the physical vehicles are sound or injured respectively,.

This sense of hearing then, having its origin in the principal of egoism, acts like iron, drawn as it is by sound originating and located in the mouth of the speaker, acting as loadstone, transforms them into its own modifications in sequence of the sounds of the speaker, and thus senses them. And it is for this reason that for every living creature, the perception of sound in external space is in the absence of defects, never void of authority. So says the quotation from Pañcaśikha :—'To all those whose organs of hearing are similarly situated, the situation of hearing is the same.' All those are Caitras and other organs of hearing are similarly situated in space. The meaning is that the powers of hearing of all are located in Ākāśa. Further the Ākāśa in which the power of hearing is located is born out of the soniferous Tanmātra, and has therefore the quality of sound inherent in itself. It is by this sound acting in unison that it takes the sounds of external solids, etc. Hence the hearing *i.e.*, the sound of all is of the same class. (The class is determined by the relative situation in space).

This them establishes that the Ākāśa is the substratum of the power of hearing, and also possesses quality of sound. And this sameness of the situation of sound is an indication of the existence of Ākāśa. That which is the substratum of the auditory power (Śruti) which manifests as sound of the same class, is Ākāśa. Such a manifestation of sound cannot be without such an auditory power. Nor is such an auditory power a quality of Pṛthvī, etc., because it cannot be in its own self both the manifester and manifested (vyaṅgya and vyañjaka).

Further the absence of obstruction is an indication of Ākāśa. If there were no Ākāśa, the forms would be in such close contact with one another that even a needle-point would not find room between them. Everything would thus be obstructed by everything. It cannot be said that the absence of obstruction is the result only of the non-existence of things possessed of form, because non-existence depends upon existence, inasmuch as there can be no cessation of existence in the absence of existence. Further the power of consciousness cannot be its substratum, because it is immutable and cannot, therefore, be limited. And further space and time, etc., are nothing different from the Pṛthvī and other substances. Therefore such a kind of change can only be of the Ākāśa. Thus all is plain.

When it is shown that absence of obstruction is an indication of the existence of Ākāśa, then it is clear that wherever absence of obstruction is found, there must be Ākāśa in existence, and hence the Ākāśa is proved to be all-pervading also. For this reason, the Commentator says :—'Therefore although having no form, etc.'

He mentions authority for the existence of the power of hearing :—'The power of hearing is the means, etc.' Action is found to be capable of performance by means of an instrument only. As a hole can be made by a gimlet only, so here too the action of hearing sound can only be performed by means of some instrument only. Whatever is the instrument of hearing, is the power of hearing. But then why should not the eye and other organs be the instruments of hearing also? For this reason he says :—'A deaf and a not-deaf, etc.' The proof is given by the canons of agreement and difference both.

Further this is suggestive of other powers. By Saṁyama over the relations between the skin and Vāyu, the eye and the light, the taste and the Apas, the nose and Pṛthvī, the attainment of the higher powers of touch, etc., is also to be understood.—40.

Sūtra 41

कायाकाशयोः संबन्धसंयमाल्लघुतूलसमापत्तेश्चाकाशगमनम् ।। ४१ ।।

कायाकाशयो: Kāyākāśayoḥ, between the body (काय) and the Ākāśa. सम्बन्ध Sambandha, over the relation. संयमात् Saṁyamāt, by Saṁyama. लघु Laghu, light. तूल Tūla, cotton. समापत्तेः Samāpatteḥ, by atatining to. च Ca, and. आकाश Ākāśa, through space. गमनम् Gamanam, passage.

41. By Saṁyama on the relation between the body and the Ākāśa, or by attaining to (the state of thought transforming as) the lightness of cotton, etc., passage through space (Ākāśa).—147.

कायाकाशयो: संबन्धसंयमाल्लघुतूलसमापत्तेश्चाकाशगमनम् । यत्र कायस्तत्राकाशं तस्यावकाशदानात्कायस्य तेन संबन्धावाप्तिस्तत्र कृतसंयमो जित्वा तत्संबन्धं लघुषु वा तूलादिष्वापरमाणुसमापत्तिं लब्ध्वा जितसंबन्धा लघुर्भवति लघुत्वाच्च जले पादाभ्यां विहरति ततस्तूर्णनाभितन्तुमात्रे विहृत्य रश्मिषु विहरति ततो यथेष्टमाकाशगतिरस्य भवतीति ।। ४१ ।।

Vyāsa

Wherever there is the body, there is the Ākāśa. The body becomes related to the Ākāśa, because the latter gives room to the former. Having mastered the relation by the attainment of the state of thought transforming into light things such as cotton, etc., down to the atom, the Yogī becomes light. Thence does he get the power of roaming through space and walking over water with his feet. He walks ovei a spider's web, and then walks over the rays of light. Then does he get the power of roaming through space at will.—147.

Vācaspati's Gloss

By performance of Saṁyama on the relation between the body and the Ākāśa, or having attained by Saṁyama on cotton, etc., the state of the mind transforming itself as such, it becomes the cause of manifesting the qualities present therein. The Commentator mentions the stage of the attainments :—'Move over water, etc.'—41.

Sūtra 42

बहिरकल्पिता वृत्तिर्महाविदेहा ततः प्रकाशावरणक्षयः ।। ४२ ।।

बहिः Bahiḥ, actual passing out. अकल्पिता Akalpitā, outside the body. वृत्तिः Vṛttiḥ, acting. महा-विदेहा Mahā-videhā, the great ex-corporeal. ततः Tataḥ, by that. प्रकाश Prakāśa, of light. आवरण Āvaraṇa, of the veil. क्षयः Kṣayaḥ, the destruction.

42. Actual-passing-out and acting outside the body is the Great Excorporeal; by that is destroyed the veil of light.—148.

बहिरकल्पितावृत्तिर्महाविदेहा ततः प्रकाशावरणक्षयः। शरीराद् बहिर्मनसो वृत्तिलाभो विदेहा नाम धारणा सा यदि शरीरप्रतिष्ठस्य मनसो बहिर्वृत्तिमात्रेण भवति सा कल्पितेत्युच्यते। या तु शरीरनिरपेक्षा बहिर्भूतस्यैव मनसो बहिर्वृत्तिः सा खल्वकल्पिता तत्र कल्पितया साधयन्त्यकल्पितां महाविदेहामिति। यया परशरीराण्याविशन्ति योगिनः। ततश्च धारणातः प्रकाशात्मनो बुद्धिसत्त्वस्य यदावरणं क्लेशकर्मविपाकत्रयं रजस्तमोमूलं तस्य च क्षयो भवति।। ४२।।

Vyāsa

That form of concentration in which the mind acts upon something outside the body, is named excorporeal concentration.

This excorporeal concentration, if taking place by merely the mind functioning, while yet staying in the body, is called Fancied (kalpita) Excorporeal.

That, however, in which the mind has no need of the body left and passes out of the body and then functions outside the body, is called the Actual Excorporeal concentration.

Of these, the Actual Excorporeal, which is also called the Great Excorporeal, is attained by means of the Fancied Excorporeal. It is by this that the Yogīs effect their entrance into other bodies. By this concentration the veil of the luminous essence of the Will-to-be, in the shape of the three vehicles of affliction, action and fruition, which has its origin in the Rajas and Tamas, is destroyed.—148.

Vācaspati's Gloss

The author describes another Saṁyama too, which becomes the means of entering into another body, and also the means of destruction of afflictions, actions and fruitions :—'Actual passing out of the body and then acting there, is the Great Excorporeal; by this the veil of light is destroyed.'

The Commentator describes the Excorporeal :—'That form of concentration in which the mind functions outside the body, etc.' In order to describe the nature of the Actual Excorporeal and for explaining its means, he describes the Fancied Excorporeal :—'If that, etc.' 'By merely the mind functioning outside the body.' Fancy means that the presence outside the body has been fancied, although the mind is still in the body and has been acting outside only functionally and not by actual presence.

He describes the Great Excorporeal :—'That however,.' Now he says that the relation between the Fancied and the Actual Excorporeal is that the former is the means of attaining the other.' 'By that concentration.'—By means of that concentration the mental modification of the Great Excorporeal is achieved. The afflictions, the actions and the three-fold fruition thereof in the shape of life-state, life-time and life-experience have all their origin in the Rajas and the Tamas; because when the Rajas and the Tamas are destroyed, the manifestation of the discrimination takes place by the quality of essentiality (Sattva) alone. This three-fold fruition having its origin in the Rajas and the Tamas, is of their nature and covers the essence of the Will-to-be therewith. It is destroyed with its destruction, and the mind of the Yogī goes about at will and similarly knows also.—42.

Sūtra 43

स्थूलस्वरूपसूक्ष्मान्वयार्थवत्त्वसंयमाद् भूतजयः।। ४३।।

स्थूल Sthūla, the gross. **स्वरूप** Svarūpa, the substantive. **सूक्ष्म** Sūkṣma, the astral. **अन्वय** Anvaya, conjunction. **अर्थवत्त्व** Arthavattva, purposefulness. **संयमाद्** Saṁyamād, by Saṁyama. **भूतजयः** Bhūta-jayaḥ, mastery over the elements.

43. By Saṁyama on the gross (sthūla), the substantive (svarūpa), the astral (sūkṣma), conjunction (anvaya) and purposefulness (arthavattva), is obtained mastery over the elements (bhūtas).—149.

स्थूलस्वरूपसूक्ष्मान्वयार्थवत्त्वसंयमाद्भूतजयः। तत्र पार्थिवाद्याः शब्दादयो विशेषाः सहकारादिभिर्धर्मैः स्थूलशब्देन परिभाषिताः। एतद्भूतानां प्रथमं रूपम्। द्वितीयं रूपं स्वसामान्यं मूर्तिर्भूमिः। स्नेहो जलं बह्निरुष्णता वायुः प्रणामी सर्वतो गतिराकाश इत्येतत्स्वरूपशब्देनोच्यते। अस्य सामान्यस्य शब्दादयो विशेषाः। तथा चोक्तम्। एकजातिसमन्वितानामेषां धर्ममात्रव्यावृत्तिरिति। सामान्यविशेषसमुदायोऽत्र द्रव्यं द्रष्टव्यम्। द्विष्ठो हि समूहः प्रत्यस्तमितभेदावयवानुगतः शरीरं वृक्षो यूथं वनमितिशब्देनोपात्तभेदावयवानुगतः समूहः। उभये देवमनुष्याः। समूहस्य देवा एव एको भागो मनुष्या द्वितीयो भागस्ताभ्यामेवाभिधीयते समूहः। स च भेदाभेदविवक्षितः। आम्राणां वनं ब्राह्मणानां सङ्घ इति। आम्रवणं ब्राह्मणसङ्घ इति। स पुनर्द्विविधो युतसिद्धावयवोऽयुतसिद्धावयवश्च। युतसिद्धावयवः समूहो वनं सङ्घ इति। अयुतसिद्धावयवः सङ्घातः शरीरं वृक्षः परमाणुरिति। अयुतसिद्धावयवभेदानुगतः समूहो द्रव्यमितिपतञ्जलिः। एतत्स्वरूपमित्युक्तम्। अथ किमेषां सूक्ष्मरूपं तन्मात्रं भूतकारणं तस्यैकोऽवयवः परमाणुः सामान्यविशेषात्मा अयुतसिद्धावयवभेदानुगतः समुदाय इत्येवं सर्वं तन्मात्राण्येतत्तृतीयम्। अथ भूतानां चतुर्थं रूपं ख्यातिक्रियास्थितिशीला गुणाः कायस्वभावानुपातिनोऽन्वयशब्देनोक्ताः। अथैषां पञ्चमं रूपमर्थवत्त्वं भोगापवर्गार्थता गुणेष्वेवान्वयिनी। गुणास्तन्मात्रभूतभौतिकेष्विति सर्वमर्थवत्। तेष्विदानीं भूतेषु पञ्चसु पञ्चरूपेषु रूपे संयमात्तस्य तस्य रूपस्य स्वरूपदर्शनं जयश्च प्रादुर्भवति। तत्र पञ्चभूतस्वरूपाणि जित्वा भूतजयीभवति। तज्जयाद्वत्सानुसारिण्य इव गावोऽस्य सङ्कल्पानुविधायिन्यो भूतप्रकृतयो भवन्ति।। ४३।।

Vyāsa

Here the word Sthūla, gross, is used to denote the specific forms of Pṛthvī, Apas, Tejas, Vāyu and Ākāśa, which appear as sound, colour, taste and odour, and have the qualities of conjoint action, etc. This is the first appearance of the elements.

The second appearance is that which is common to the others too. The Pṛthvī has forms, the Apas smoothness, the Tejas heat, the Vāyu impulsion, the Ākāśa motion in every direction. This is denoted by the word substantive appearance (svarūpa), sounds, touches, tastes, colours are the specific manifestations of these common qualities. And so it has been said :—'These manifested together in one species manifest their own distinguishing characteristics.' A group of the generic and specific qualities is here considered a substance (dravya).

A group is of two descriptions. The first is that in which the distinction of individuals disappears in the whole, such as the body, the tree, the herd, the forest. The second is where the word shows the distinction between different individuals of the same group, as for example, a group of both gods and men. Of this group the gods are one portion, and the men the other. Both make one group. In this the distinction of individuals may or may not be mentioned; as in a grove of mangoes, a crowd of Brahmaṇas; a mango grove, the Brāhmaṇa class.

This again is of two descriptions; where the parts of the whole are separate from each other and where they are not. A forest and a class are groups where the parts are separate from each other. A body, a tree, an atom are all groups whose parts are not separable from each other. Substance, according to Patañjali, is a group whose parts are not meant to be distinguished from each other, and cannot be separated from each other. This has been called the etheric or substrantive appearance (svarūpa).

And now what is their subtle appearance? It is the Tanmāntra (the astral atom), the cause of the elements. The atom is one part thereof. It is a group, a composite substance, which consists of generic and specific qualities, and whose parts are not distinguished from each other, and which cannot be separated from one another. All the Tanmātrās are similar to this. This is the third appearance of the elements.

Now as to the fourth appearance of the elements. These are the 'qualities' whose characteristics are essence, activity and inertia, and which follow the nature of effects. These are denoted by the word conjunction (anvaya).

And now the fifth appearance of purposefulness (arthavattva). The purpose of experience and emancipation is apparent in conjunction with the qualities. The qualities are to be found in Tanmātrās, in the elements and in things made of elements. Hence all these are full of purpose. Now by Saṁyama over the five elements, with their five appearances, the nature of every appearance over which Saṁyama is performed, becomes apparent and conquest over it is obtained. Having obtained conquest over the five appearances he becomes the Lord of elements. The powers of the elements begin by this conquest to follow his thought, as the cow follow their calves.—149.

Vācaspati's Gloss

'By Saṁyama on gross, the substantive appearance, the subtle, the conjunction and purposefulness, is obtained mastery over elements.' Mastery is obtained by Saṁyama over each separately, the gross, the substantive, the subtle, the conjunction and purposefulness. The Commentator describes the gross :—'The word Sthūla here, etc.' The sounds, the touches, the colours, the tastes, and the odours of Ākāśa, Vāyu, Tejas, Apas, and Pṛthivī are their specific forms so far as may be.

The notes of the gamud, DO and MA, etc., cold and heat, etc., blue and yellow, etc., sweet-smelling, etc., all these differ from each other in name, appearance and object. For this reason they are specific. Of the qualities, five are the specific forms of the Pṛthvī; four (except smell) of the Apas; three (besides odour and taste) of the Tejas; two (besides odour, taste and colour) of the Vāyu and only one of the Ākāśa. These specific forms together with the characteristics of conjoint action, etc., are termed Gross in this philosophy.

Among those, the characteristics of the Pṛthvī are :—Form, heaviness, roughness, obstruction, stability, manifestation (vṛtti), difference, support, turbidity, hardness, enjoyability by all.

The characteristics of the Apas are :—Smoothness, subtlety, clearness, whiteness, softness heaviness, coolness, preservation, purification, cementation.

The characteristics of the Tejas are :—Going upward, cooking, bruning, lightness, shining, destruction, power; possessed of such qualities is the Tejas different from the previous ones.

The qualities of the Vāyu are :—transverse motion, purification, throwing, pushing, strength, movability, throwing no shadow, roughness; these are the various characteristics of the Vāyu.

The characteristics of the Ākāśa :—Motion in all directions, non-agglomeration, and non-obstruction : these three are said to be the characteristics of Ākāśa, different from the characteristics of the preceding ones.

It is together with these characteristics that they are called gross.

Form (mūrti) is hardness brought about (samsiddhikam), stability of the lines of action and manifestation.

Tejas is heat, stomachic, solar, terrestrial; everywhere heat exists along with Tejas.

The whole of this terminology makes no distinction between the characteristic and the characterized.

The Vāyu is changing ; has the nature of constant motion. By movements of straw, etc., and by the movements of the body, the Vāyu is inferred to be everywhere possessed of the quality of motion.

The Ākāśa is motion in all directions, because the perception of sound is found everywhere. It has been established above that the sounds of terrestrial objects, etc., are only perceived on account of the sound-quality of Ākāśa, which resides in the power of hearing.

This is meant by the word Svarūpa, substantive appearance. It is of this generic form that the sounds of the notes DO, etc. heat, etc., Whiteness, etc., astringent and sweet smell, etc., are the specializations. The generic qualities of form, etc., too, such as Jambīra, Panas and emblic fruit, etc., differ from each other on account of the differences of taste, etc. For this reason these tastes, etc., are specific modifications of these. And so it has been said :—Of those that fall under a common genus, *i.e.*, those each of which possesses one generic quality of form, smoothness or flow, etc., the differences are due to the characteristics possessed by the individual appearances of DO, etc.

Thus the generic qualities of form, etc., and the specific qualities of sound, etc., have been described.

Now he speaks to those who says that a substance (dravya) is the substratum of the generic and the specific : 'In this philosophy a substance is a collection (samudāya) of the generic and specific qualities.' Even those who desire to establish that substratum of the qualities, cannot possibly conceal the fact of their existence in one group together. And if they do conceal it, it cannot be that a substratum of theirs may be possible of existence as substance. Hence let even that be the substance. We, however, do not find a substratum separate from the collection of qualities, and existing as substance.

As a collection of stones differs from the stones, and as further a different kind of their collection in the shape of a mountain is called a substance, the doubt arises that a mere collection is a substance. For the purpose of removing that doubt and for establishing that it is only a particular kind of collection that is called a substance, he now describes the variety of groupings :—"A collection is of two descriptions." Because of this a substance is not a mere collections. This is the meaning. 'Two descriptions' mean two different sorts of collection. He describes the first mode :—'The first is that in which the distinction of individuals disappears altogether in the whole.' They are so called because the distinction between the different parts has disappeared. It is so called because the separation has disappeared. This is the meaning : A collection is understood by the words body, tree, herd, forest. These words denote a collection, but do not denote the different parts of the collections. That is no word denoting these individual parts is used. Hence it is the collection that is understood. Four illustrations are given with reference to the parts being joined or separate and with reference to intelligence and non-inelligence. The meaning of the joined and separate parts will be described further on.

He describes the second mode :—'A collection, the distinction of whose parts is understood by the words as both gods and men.'

'Gods and men' : This collection signifies an account of the parts being indicated by separate words, the two separate parts of the group.

But the question is that inasmuch as the disctinction of parts is not conveyed by using the word *both*, how is it said that the idea of the collection carries with it the idea of the distinction of parts? For this reason he says :—And it is by these two parts that a collection is signified. The word 'both' together with the words signifying the different parts forms the collection, since the sentence as such denotes the meaning to be conveyed by it. This is the meaning.

Again he says that they are two-fold :—'This again, etc.' With reference to whether the distinction is or is not intended to be conveyed. He describes where the distinction is intended to be conveyed :—'A grove of mangoes, a crowd of Brāhmaṇas.' There must be distinction because the genitive case is actually used (not only implied). As in the case of the phrase, 'the cow of the Gargas.'

He describes where the distinction is not intended to be conveyed :—'Mango grove, Brāhmaṇa class.' The meaning is that the mangoes are the same as the grove; it is not intended that there should be difference understood between the collection and the individuals that go to make up the collection. They both imply a common object.

He mentions another division :—'That again is twofold. Where the parts of the whole are separate from each other.' This means that there is space between the individuals that go to make up the collection. Such groups are signified by the words, a herd, a forest.

Their parts have spaces between them, the trees and the kine.

The groups whose parts are not separate from each other are such as a tree, a cow, an atom. Their parts have no space between them. Whether they are taken to be the generic or the specific qualities, or the udders, etc., they have no spaces between.

Now he establishes which of these collections is what is called a substance :—'Whose parts are not meant to be distinguished from each other, etc.'

Having thus described a substance as the context demanded, he now comes to the subject in hand :—'This has been called the substantive appearance.'

He puts a question with the object of describing the third appearance :—'And what is their subtle appearance ?' and gives the answer :—'It is the Tanmātra, etc.' One of its parts is an atom possessing dimension. The generic quality thereof is form (mūrti). Sound, etc., are its specific qualities. It consists of the generic and specific qualities. It is a group which follows the difference of the generic and specific qualities, its parts existing without any intervening space. Further as an atom has subtlety in appearance, so are the Tanmātras subtle in appearance. He summarizes :—'This is the third.'

Now the fourth appearance of the elements consists of the qualities which have respectively the characteristics of illumination, activity and inertia and whose characteristics too follow the nature of effects. For this reason are they describes by the word Conjunction (anvaya). Now he describes their fifth appearance, purposefulness :—'The purpose of enjoyment and emancipation is apparent in conjunction with the qualities.'

Well, even if it be so, if the qualities be purposeful, how are the effects of the qualities purposeful? For this reason he says :—'The qualities are to be found, etc.,' The things made of elements are such as a cow or a jar.

Having thus described the Saṁyama and that upon which the Saṁyama is to be performed, he now describes the Saṁyama and its fruit :—'Now by Saṁyama over the elements, etc." The powers (prakṛtis) of the elements are their natures.—43.

Sūtra 44

ततोऽणिमादिप्रादुर्भावः कायसम्पत्तद्धर्मानभिघातश्च ।। ४४ ।।

ततः Tataḥ, thence. अणिमादि Aṇimā-ādi, of attenuation and the other powers. प्रादुर्भावः Prādurbhāvaḥ, the manifestation of. काय Kāya, of the body. सम्पद् Sampad, perfecton. तद् Tad, their. धर्म Dharma, characteristics. अनभिघातः Anabhighātaḥ, non-resistance by. च Ca, and.

44. Thence the manifestation of attenuation (aṇimā) and the other (powers); as also the perfection of the body and non-resistance by their characteristics.—150.

ततोऽणिमादिप्रादुर्भावः कायसम्पत्तद्धर्मानभिघातश्च। तत्राणिमा भवत्यणुः। लघिमा लघुर्भवति। महिमा महान्भवति। प्राप्तिरङ्गुल्यग्रेणापि स्पृशति चन्द्रमसम्। प्राकाम्यमिच्छानभिघातः। भूमावुन्मज्जति निमज्जति यथोदके। वशित्वं भूतभौतिकेषु वशीभवत्यवश्यश्चान्येषाम्। ईशितृत्वं तेषां प्रभवाप्ययव्यूहानामीष्टे। यत्र कामावसायित्वं सत्यसङ्कल्पता यथा सङ्कल्पस्तथा भूतप्रकृतीनामवस्थानम्। न च शक्तोऽपि पदार्थविपर्यासं करोति। कस्मात्। अन्यस्य यत्र कामावसायिनः पूर्वसिद्धस्य तथा भूतेषु सङ्कल्पादिति। एतान्यष्टावैश्वर्याणि कायसम्पद्वक्ष्यमाणा तद्धर्मानभिघातश्च पृथ्वी मूर्त्या न निरुणद्धि योगिनः शरीरादिक्रियाशीलामप्यनुविशतीति। नापः स्निग्धाः क्लेदयन्ति। नाग्निरुष्णो दहति। न वायुः प्रणामी वहत्यनावरणात्मकेऽप्याकाशे भवत्यावृत्तकायः सिद्धानामप्यदृश्यो भवति।। ४४।।

Vyāsa

Of these, attenuation (Aṇimā) : becomes atomical. Buoyancy becomes light. Enlargement : becomes large. Approach (Prāpti) : touches even the moon by the tip of his finger. Unrestrained will (Prākāmya) : absence of restraint to his will : merges into earth just as he plunges into water.

Control (Vaśītva) :—Obtains power over the elements and objects made thereof, and controls others.

Creative Power (Īśitṛtva) :—Controls appearance and disappearance and aggregations.

Fulfilment of desires is the objective reality of one's determination, *i.e.*, the natures of the elements assume such appearances as he thinks of.

Although he possesses the power, he does not interfere to set the objects of the world topsy-turvy. Why not? Because his desire with reference to them is the same always which another Siddha of the same power has formerly willed. These are the eight attainments. The perfection of the body will be described. 'Non-resistance by their characteristics' :—The Pṛthvī does not by cohesion interfere with the action of a Yogī's body. He might even enter a stone in virtue of the use of his powers. The waters with their viscidity do not wet him. The fire does not burn him by its heat. The air moves him not by its motion. Even in Ākāśa, which naturally offers no obstruction, his body might become obstructed to sight. Even the Siddhas may fail to see him.—150.

Vācaspati's Gloss

Now the author describes what the Yogī attains, when the elements begin to follow his thoughts :—'Thence the manifestation of Attenuation (Aṇimā) as also the perfection of the body, and non-resistance by their characteristics.

The Commentator says that by Saṁyama over the gross states of the elements and thereby mastering them come four attainments. Of these, attenuation is the power of the body's becoming small even though it is large. Buoyancy means the power of its becoming light, even though it is heavy. Having become light it moves in space like a straw or a piece of cotton wool. Enlargement is the power of its becoming large like a mountain or the sky, even though it is small. Approach is the power by which all existences come within the reach of the Yogī; thus he can touch the moon with the tip of this finger, though standing on the earth.

He describes the attainments obtained by the performance of Saṁyama over substantive appearance (svarūpa). Unrestrained will is the absence of restraint to his will. His form is not resisted by the substantive qualities of form, etc. He merges into and emerges out of earth, as if it were water.

He describes the attainment to be obtained by Saṁyama and consequent mastery over the subtile form :—'Control :—The elements are Pṛthvī etc.' Objects made thereof are such as a cow and a jar. 'Obtains power over them' : acts with reference to them just as he wishes.

As to the objects made of the elements, it is necessary that when their causes, the tanmātras, and the atoms of Pṛthvī, etc., are controlled, their effects also should come under control, because they remain in whatever condition or arrangement he places them.

Now he describes the attainments to be obtained by Saṁyama over and mastery of the conjunction (anvaya) :—Creative Power :—Having mastered the Mūlaprakṛti he can control the birth, destruction, and present existence, as it is for the time being of the elements and things made of them.

He describes the attainments due to the performance of Saṁyama over purposefulness. 'Fulfilment of desires' means the objective reality of one's desires. The Yogī who has become the master of the purpose of the qualities, makes everything according to the purpose he thinks they should fulfil. Even if he conceives that poison should act upon the body as Amṛta, it would act so, and having taken poison he would still live.

Well, let that be, but if he possessed these powers he would interfere with the order of nature in the world, but why does he not do so? He may transform the moon into the sun : or he may make the day from which the moon is totally absent, one from which she is not at all absent. For this reason he says :—Although he possesses the power, etc., these worshipful ones who have obtained the power of ordering as they desire, do not like to act against the will of Īśvara. As to the powers of objects they are changeable according to the difference of class, space, time and condition, and their natures are not for that reason permanent. It is, therefore, proper that they should act in accordance with their desire. These are the eight attainments.

'Non-resistance by their characteristics' :—The mention of non-resistance of these elements after the attainment of attenuation, etc., even though this is the result of the attainments themselves, is similar to the mention of the perfection of the body even though that is achieved by this very attainment. The reason is that the object of Saṁyama mentioned in this aphorism may be easily understood together with the fruit to be obtained by the performance of the Saṁyamas mentioned in the aphorism. The rest is easy.—44.

Sūtra 45

रूपलावण्यबलवज्रसंहननत्वानि कायसम्पत् ।। ४५ ।।

रूप Rūpa, beauty. लावण्य Lāvaṇya, grace. बल Bala, strength. वज्र Vajra, of adamant, adamantine. संहनन Saṁhanana, the power of striking or of bearing the strokes, hardness, all these embody. कायसम्पत् Kāya-Sampat, perfection of the body.

45. The perfection of the body consists in beauty, grace, strength and adamantine hardness.—151.

रूपलावण्यबलवज्रसंहननत्वानि कायसम्पत्। दर्शनीयः कान्तिमानतिशयबलो वज्रसंहननश्चेति ।। ४५ ।।

Vyāsa

Fit to be seen, lovely, possessed of great strength, a body hard as adament.—151.

Vācaspati's Gloss

The body is said to be adamantine when its build is as hard as that of adamant.

Sūtra 46

ग्रहणस्वरूपास्मितान्वयार्थवत्त्वसंयमादिन्द्रियजयः ।। ४६ ।।

ग्रहण Grahaṇa, the act. स्वरूप Svarūpa, the substantive appearance. अस्मिता Asmitā, egoism. अन्वय Anvaya, conjunction. अर्थवत्त्व Arthavattva, purposefulness (of sensation). संयमाद् Saṁyamād, by Saṁyama over. इन्द्रिय-जयः Indriya-jayaḥ, mastery over the senses.

46. By Saṁyama over the act, the substantive appearance, the egoism, the conjunction and the purposefulness (of sensation) comes mastery over them.—152.

ग्रहणस्वरूपास्मितान्वयार्थवत्त्वसंयमादिन्द्रियजयः। सामान्यविशेषात्मा शब्दादिर्विषयः। तेष्विन्द्रियाणां वृत्तिर्ग्रहणम्। न च तत्सामान्यमात्रग्रहणाकारं कथमनालोचितः स विषयविशेष इन्द्रियेण मनसा वानुव्यवसीयेतेति। स्वरूपं पुनः प्रकाशात्मनो बुद्धिसत्त्वस्य सामान्यविशेशयोरयुतसिद्धावयवभेदानुगतः समूहो द्रव्यमिन्द्रियम्। तेषां तृतीयं रूपमस्मितालक्षणोऽहङ्कारः तस्य सामान्यस्येन्द्रियाणि विशेषाश्चतुर्थं रूपं व्यवसायात्मकाः प्रकाशक्रियास्थितिशीला गुणा येषामिन्द्रियाणि साहङ्काराणि परिणामः। पञ्चमं रूपं गुणेषु यदनुगतं पुरुषार्थवत्त्व-मिति। पञ्चस्वेवैतेष्विन्द्रियरूपेषु यथाक्रमं संयमस्तत्र तत्र जयं कृत्वा पञ्चस्वरूपजयादिन्द्रियजयः प्रादुर्भवति योगिनः।। ४६।

Vyāsa

Sound, etc., possessed of generic qualities are objects. The act of sensation consists in the functioning of the senses with reference to the objects. And this functioning is not merely the taking in of the generic qualities of an object, because if also the specific qualities of an object were not thus taken in, how would they otherwise be perceived by the mind?

As to their substantive appearance, a sense is a substance; it is a collection of generic and specific qualities whose parts are not possessed of intervening space and are not distinguishable as being separate from each other. These generic and specific qualities are of the essence of the Will-to-be whose very nature is illumination.

Their third appearance is the principle of individuality characterized by egoism. The senses are the specialized appearances of that generic appearance.

The fourth appearance consists of the qualities which are of the nature of illumination, activity and inertia and which determine the nature of phenomena. The senses together with the principle of individuality are their manifestations.

The fifth appearance is that of their having the purpose of the Puruṣa to fulfil. This is inherent in the qualities. Saṁyama is to be performed over the five appearances of sensation, respectively, one after the other. When all the five appearances have been mastered, then the power of over-mastering sensation is manifested in the Yogī.—152.

Vācaspati's Gloss

The author describes the means of conquering the senses for the Yogī who has mastered the elements :—'By Saṁyama over the act, the substantive appearance, the egoism, the conjunction and the purposefulness (of sensation), comes mastery ever the senses.' The meaning is that Saṁyama is to be performed with reference to the act, the substantive appearance, the egoism, the conjunction and the purposefulness, separately, one after another. The act of sensation consists in the taking in of objects, and this depends upon the object to be taken in. Hence the determination of the nature of the act depends upon the determination of the nature of the objects to be taken in.

The Commentator describes the nature of the object to be taken in :—'Sounds, etc., are possessed of the generic and specific qualities.'

Having described the objects to be taken in he now describes the act of taking in :—'And the functioning, etc.' This functioning consists of sensing, *i.e.*, the sense being modified into the form of the object. As to those who hold that the sphere of the function of the senses is the generic qualities alone, he says to them :—'And it does not consist in taking in only the form of the generic qualities.' That which is taken in is not only co-existence with the generic qualities of the object. The mind is dependent for its action upon external senses, and works upon the external objects and depends upon them. If this were not so, there would be no blind and deaf people. If, such being the case, the senses were not to have the specific qualities for their sphere of action, the specific qualities would not at all be known. How then would the mind known them in sequence? Hence the act of sensation consists in the taking in of both the generic and the specific qualities.

This act of taking in is the phenomenon of the senses.

Now he describes the second appearance :—'As to substantive appearance :—'It is the principle of individuality which produces the power of sensation out of its own essence (the Sattva). Hence the instrumentality which is generic nature of the senses and also the action in connection with the appointed sphere of colour, etc., which is the specific quality, both are of the nature of illumination. This is the meaning.

This is their third appearance. The principle of individuality is of course the cause of the senses. Wherever the senses are there must the principle of individuality be. Being thus the common cause of the senses, it is the generic quality of these senses.

The fourth appearance :—The qualities appear as possessing two forms. They are of the nature of things which exist as such; and they are also of the nature of the power which determines the existence of phenomena. Of these the nature of the things in existence as such consists in their being the objects of knowledge; and these are the five Tanmātras, the elements and the things made of the elements. The power again which determines the existence of the phenomena takes up the form of the instruments of knowledge, and consists of the senses together with the principle of individuality. This is the meaning. The rest is easy.—46.

Sūtra 47

ततो मनोजवित्वं विकरणभावः प्रधानजयश्च ।। ४७ ।।

ततः Tataḥ, thence, मनो-जवित्वम् Mano-javitvam, Quickness (as of the mind). विकरण-भावः

Vikaraṇa-bhāvaḥ, uninstrumental perception. प्रधान Pradhāna, over the first cause. जय: Jayaḥ, mastery.

47. Thence come quickness as of mind, un-instrumental-perception and mastery over the Pradhāna (First Cause.)—153.

ततो मनोजवित्वं विकरणभाव: प्रधानजयश्च। कायस्यानुत्तमो गतिलाभो मनोजवित्वम्। विदेहानामिन्द्रियाणामभिप्रेतकालदेशविषयापेक्षो वृत्तिलाभो विकरणभाव:। सर्वप्रकृतिविकारवशित्वं प्रधानजय इत्येतास्तिस्र: सिद्धयो मधुप्रतीका उच्यन्ते। एताश्च करणपञ्चकस्वरूपजयादधिगम्यते।। ४७।।

Vyāsa

Quickness as of mind consists in the attainment by the body of very quick motion.

Un-instrumental Perception means the action of the senses at any time or place without the necessity of the presence of the body.

Mastery over the Pradhāna means the power of control over all the modifications of the Prakṛti. These three attainments are called by the name of Madhupratīkā. These are obtained by conquering the substantive appearance (svarūpa) of the five instruments of sensation.—153.

Vācaspati's Gloss

The author mentions the attainments due to the conquest of the five appearances of the senses :—'Thence come quickness as of mind, un-instrumental perception and mastery over the Pradhāna.'

Un-instrumental perception is the action of the senses outside the body. Place means Kashmir, etc. Time means past, etc. Sphere means the subtle, etc.

Mastery over the Pradhāna means control of the modification of the Prakṛti by the conquest of the senses together with the power of conjunction. These are the attainments which are called the Madhupratīkās by the knowers of Yoga.

Well, it may be that by the conquest of the senses they may come under control. But how their causes, the Pradhāna, etc.? For this reason he says : 'And these, etc.' The five appearances of the senses are their act, etc.

'By their conquest, etc.' The meaning is this : It is not by the mere conquest of the senses that these powers are obtained, but by the conquest of all the five appearances; and the Pradhāna, etc., fall within these.—47.

Sūtra 48

सत्वपुरुषान्यताख्यातिमात्रस्य सर्वभावाधिष्ठातृत्वं सर्वज्ञातृत्वं च।। ४८।।

सत्व Sattva, pure objective essence. पुरुष Puruṣa, consciousness. अन्यता Anyatā, the distinction between. ख्याति-मात्रस्य Khyāti-mātrasya, to him only who recognises. सर्व-भाव Sarva-bhāva, over all states. अधिष्ठातृत्वम् Adhisthātṛtvam, supremacy. सर्व-ज्ञातृत्वम् Sarva-jñātṛtvam, omniscience. च Ca, and.

48. To him who recognizes the distinction between consciounsess and pure-objective-existence comes upremacy over all states of being and omniscience.—154.

सत्त्वपुरुषान्यताख्यातिमात्रस्य सर्वभावाधिष्ठातृत्वं सर्वज्ञातृत्वं च। निर्धूतरजस्तमोमलस्य बुद्धिसत्त्वस्य परे वैशारद्ये परस्यां वशीकारसंज्ञायां वर्तमानस्य सत्त्वपुरुषान्यताख्यातिमात्ररूपप्रतिष्ठस्य सर्वभावाधिष्ठातृत्वम्। सर्वात्मानो गुणा व्यवसायव्यवसेयात्मकाः स्वामिनं क्षेत्रज्ञं प्रत्यशेषदृश्यात्मत्वेनोपस्थिता इत्यर्थः। सर्वज्ञातृत्वं सर्वात्मनां गुणानां शान्तोदिताव्यपदेश्यधर्मत्वेन व्यवस्थितानामक्रमोपारूढं विवेकजं ज्ञानमित्यर्थः। इत्येषा विशोका नाम सिद्धियां प्राप्य योगी सर्वज्ञः क्षीणक्लेशबन्धनो वशी विहरति।। ४८।।

Vyāsa

Supremacy over all states of being comes to him who, having the essence of the Will-to-be in the highest state of purity on account of the impurities of the Rajas and the Tamas having been destroyed, and when the consciousness of power is at the highest, takes his stand at the manifestation of the distinction between the Objective Essence and consciousness (Puruṣa). It means that the 'Qualities' which are the substruction of all phenomena, being of the nature of the things that are in existence, as well as of the power which determines this existence, present themselves before the Lord, the knower of the field, as one whole.

Omniscience means the simultaneously discriminate knowledge of the 'qualities' being as they are of the nature of all phenomena, and showing fourth as they do separately the quiescent, he disturbed and the unpredicable characteristics. This attainment is known as the 'Sorrowless' (viśoka).

Reaching this the Yogī moves omniscient and powerful, with all his afflictions ended.—154.

Vācaspati's Gloss

Now the author shows the attainments subsidiary to the attainment of the knowledge of the distinction between the Objective Essence and the Puruṣa, with the object of attaining which are performed the Saṁyamas which bring about power of knowledge and action, and which by direct knowledge, and one after the other, go on strengthening faith in the object promised, by means of the presents of the attainments that are being made constantly :—'To him who realizes the distinction between the Objective Existence and consciousness, comes just then supremacy over all the states of being and omniscience.' Purity comes by the dirt of Rajas and Tamas being removed. Thence comes the consciousness of the highest power. The mental Essence was before the attainment of this state covered by the Rajas and the Tamas. On the removal thereof it becomes subject to the power of the masterful Yogī. When it becomes subject to the Yogī who has just attained to the possession of the knowledge of the distinction between Objective Essence and consciousness then the Yogī becomes supreme over all states of being. The Commentator explains the state :—'The Guṇas which are the substrata, etc.' The objects to be determined and the determination meaning the intelligent and the non-intelligent phenomena. The power of action is explained by this.

He mentions the power of knowledge : 'Omniscience, etc.' and gives a name to this two-fold attainment well-known to the Yogīs, with the object of inclining towards desrielessness : "This is named the 'Sorrowless." Such a Yogī is described to be one whose afflictions and bonds, *i.e.*, Karmas have been destroyed.—48.

Sūtra 49

तद्वैराग्यादपि दोषबीजक्षये कैवल्यम् ।। ४९ ।।

तद्–वैराग्यात् Tadvairāgyāt, by desirelessness for that. अपि Api, even. दोष–बीज Doṣa-bīja, of the seed of bondage. क्षये Kṣaye, on the destruction. कैवल्यम् Kaivalyam, absolute independence.

49. The seed of bondage having been destroyed by desirelessness even for that, comes absolute-independence (Kaivalya).—155.

तद्वैराग्यादपि दोषबीजक्षये कैवल्यम्। यदास्यैवं भवति क्लेशकर्मक्षये सत्त्वस्यायं विवेकप्रत्ययो धर्मः सत्त्वं च हेयपक्षे न्यस्तं पुरुषश्चापरिणामी शुद्धोऽन्यः सत्त्वादित्येवमस्य ततो विरज्यमानस्य यानि क्लेशबीजानि दग्धशालिबीजकल्पान्यप्रसवसमर्थानि तानि सह मनसा प्रत्यस्तं गच्छन्ति। तेषु प्रलीनेषु पुरुषः पुनरिदं तापत्रयं न भुङ्क्ते। तदेतेषां गुणानां मनसि कर्मक्लेशविपाकस्वरूपेणाभिव्यक्तानां चरितार्थानामप्रतिप्रसवे पुरुषस्यात्यन्तिको गुणवियोगः कैवल्यं तदा स्वरूपप्रतिष्ठा चितिशक्तिरेव पुरुष इति ।। ४९ ।।

Vyāsa

When he comes to think that the discrimination of the distinctive natures, is after all a manifestation of the quality of Essentiality (Sattva) and that the quality of essentiality has been classed with avoidable pains; and that the Pusuṣa is unchangeable, pure and other than the quality of essentiality (Sattva) then he begins to lose his desire for that, and then the afflictions having had their seed burnt up, become incapable of sprouting again like the burnt up seeds of rice.

Then all the seeds of afflictions pass, together with the mind, into latency. When they have become latent, the Puruṣa does not then suffer from the triad of pain. This then, the state, that is to say, in which the qualities manifest in the mind as afflictions, actions and fruitions do not, having fulfilled their object, come back to action, is the final separation of consciousness form the qualities. This is the state of absolute independence, when the Puruṣa remains consciousness alone, as in its own nature.—155.

Vācaspati's Gloss

Because the other Saṁyamas are all but the semblances of the object of the Puruṣa the author now shows that the Saṁyama for the attainment of discriminative knowledge is the fulfilment of the purpose of the Puruṣa, inasmuch as its fruit is the attainment of the absolute independence by means of the manifestation of desirelessness : 'On the destruction of the seed of afflictions by desirelessness even for that, comes absolute independence.' When on the destruction of actions and afflictions, the Yogī becomes conscious of what he says is knowledge of discrimination as a characteristic of the Sattva, etc.' The rest has been described here and there and is therefore easy.—49.

Sūtra 50

स्थान्युपनिमन्त्रणे सङ्गस्मयाकरणं पुनरनिष्टप्रसङ्गात्।।५०।।

स्थानि-उपनिमन्त्रणे Sthāni-upanimantraṇe, on the invitation by the presiding deities. (निमन्त्रण) (स्थानिन्) सङ्ग Saṅga, attachment. स्मय Smaya, smile of satisfaction. अकरणम् Akaranam, non-performance of. पुन: Punah, again. अनिष्ट Anista, with the undesirable. प्रसङ्गात् Prasaṅgāt, contact being possible.

50. When the presiding-deities ivnite, there should be no attachment and no smile of satisfaction; contact with the undesirable being again possible.—156.

स्थान्युपनिमंत्रणे सङ्गस्मया करणं पुनरनिष्टप्रसङ्गात्। चत्वार: खल्वमी योगिन: प्रथमकल्पिको मधुभूमिक: प्रज्ञाज्योतिरतिक्रान्तभावनीयश्चेति। तत्राभ्यासी प्रवृत्तमात्रज्योति: प्रथम:। ऋतम्भरप्रज्ञो द्वितीय:। भूतेन्द्रियजयी तृतीय:। सर्वेषु भावितेषु भावनीयेषु कृतरक्षाबन्ध: कृतकर्तव्य: साधनादिमान्। चतुर्थस्त्वतिक्रान्तभावनीयस्तस्य चित्तप्रतिसर्गएकोऽर्थ: सप्तविधा अस्य प्रान्तभूमिप्रज्ञा:। तत्र मधुमतीं भूमिं साक्षात्कुर्वतो ब्राह्मणस्य स्थानिनो देवा: सत्त्वविशुद्धिमनुपश्यन्त: स्थानैरुपनिमन्त्रयन्ते भो इहास्यतामिह रम्यतां कमनीयोऽयं भोग: कमनीयें कन्या रसायनमिदं जरामृत्युं बाधते वैहायसमिदं यानममी कल्पद्रुमा: पुण्या मन्दाकिनी सिद्ध महर्षय उत्तमा अनुकूला अप्सरसो दिव्ये श्रोत्रचक्षुषी वज्रोपम: काय: स्वगुणैस्सर्वमिदमुपार्जितमायुष्मता प्रतिपद्यतामिदमक्षयमजरममरं स्थानं देवानां प्रियमित्येवमभिधीयमान: सङ्गदोषान्भावयेद् घोरेषु संसाराङ्गारेषु पच्यमानेन मया जननमरणान्धकारे विपरिवर्त्तमानेन कथंचिदासादित: क्लेशतिमिरविनाशीयोगप्रदीपस्तस्य चैते तृष्णायोनयो विषयवायव: प्रतिपक्षा:। स खल्वहं लब्धालोक: कथमनया विषयमृगतृष्णया वञ्चितस्तस्यैव पुन: प्रदीप्तस्य संसाराग्नेरात्मानमिन्धनीकुर्यामिति। स्वस्ति व: स्वप्नोपमेभ्य: कृपणजनप्रार्थनीयेभ्यो विषयेभ्य इत्येवं निश्चितमति: समाधिं भावयेत्। सङ्गमकृत्वा स्मयमपि न कुर्यादेवमहं देवानामपि प्रार्थनीय इति। स्मयादयं सुस्थितंमन्यतया मृत्युना केशेषु गृहीतमिवात्मानं न भावयिष्यति। तथाचास्य छिद्रान्तरपेक्षी नित्यं यत्नोपचर्य: प्रमादो लब्ध विवर: क्लेशानुत्तम्भयिष्यति तत: पुनरनिष्टप्रसङ्ग:। एवमस्य सङ्गस्मयावकुर्वतो भावितोऽर्थोदृढीभविष्यति भावनीयश्चार्थोऽभिमुखी भविष्यतीति।।५०।।

Vyāsa

'When the presiding deities invite, there should be no attachment and no smile of satisfaction; contact with the undesirable being again possible.' There are four classes of Yogīs :—(1) The prathama kalpika; (2) The madhubhūmika; (3) The Prajñājyotiḥ; (4) The atikrāntabhāvanīya.

The first is the one who is practising and in whom the light is just appearing. The second is he who has attained the Ṛtambharā cognition. The third is he who has attained power over the elements and the senses, who preserves all that has been known and has to be known, who has been doing what has to be done and who is given to practice. The fourth is the Atikrāntabhāvanīya. His sole object is to make the mind latent in the Pradhāna. Its stages are the seven-fold in finality.

Of these then the Brāhmaṇa to whom opens up the yet unseen plane of Madhumatī, is invited by the gods from their various places. They tell him, 'Come, sit here; enjoy yourselves here; this is a lovely enjoyment, here is a lovely damsel; this is the elixir of life, which counteracts old age and death; here is a vehicle which moves through the skies; these the kalpa trees; this is the pure stream of Mandākinī; these the perfected ones, the great seers, and beautiful and obedient nymphs; here are clairvoyance, and clair-audience; here a body of adamantine strength. You have earned all these by your virtues. Come, take all this. This is an eternal, unfading, undying position which the gods love.'

Thus addressed, let him contemplate upon defects of attachment. 'It is with difficulty that I have procured the light of Yoga, the destroyer of the darkness of afflictions, after having been long backed by the flames of the world and rolled into the darkness of birth and death. These winds of sensuous enjoyment, brought into sensuous existence by desire, are calculated to put that light out. Having seen all this how should I allow myself to be deluded by the mirage of sensuous enjoyments and put myself as fuel again into the burning fire of the same changeful existence. Farewell then, ye sensuous enjoyments; ye are but dreams, fit only to be enjoyed by weaklings.'

Having thus come upon a fixed resolution, let him practise his meditation. Having thus not allowed himself to become attached, let him not indulge himself in a smile of satisfaction that even the gods begged him. If the indulges in such satisfaction, he will never perceive himself as having his hair in the grasp of death, and resting in fancied security. Thus forgetfulness ever on the watch for a hole, and ever full of efforts, would find its way into the mind; and once there it will bring the afflictions back to life; and thence will come in contact with the undersirable. Thus avoiding attachment and mental pride, the high mental state will obtain firm hold upon him and the object that is to be attained, will ever keep in front.—156.

Vācaspati's Gloss

Now seeing that there is possibility of obstacle in the way of the Yogī who is practising the means of perfect freedom (kaivalya), the author teaches the cause of its removal :—'When the presiding deities invite, there should be no attachment and no smile of satisfaction; there being possibility of contact with the undesirable again.'

The presiding deities are Mahendra, etc., who function in the regions of the powers thus obtained by the Yogī. The invitation comes from them. Attachment and a smile of satisfaction should not be indulged therein, because in that case there is again the possibility of the recurrence of the undesirable. Now with the object of determining the class of the Yogī whom the gods invite form their places, the Commentator mentions all the classes possible Yogīs : 'There are four classes, etc.' Now he describes the nature of the Prathama-kalpika :—'Of these he who practises, etc.' In him the light of the knowledge of objects, such as the mind of others, etc., has just appeared; it has not been mastered by him. He mentions the second :—'He who possesses the truth-bearing cognition, etc.' The cognition there is truth-bearing (Ṛtambharā). It is he who desires to conquer the elements and the senses.

He mentions the third :—'He who has conquered the elements and the senses.' By this the elements and the senses have been conquered by Saṁyama over the gross and other appearances and over the act of sensation and other appearances. He described him further :—In all those that have been achieved by the conquest of the elements and the senses, such as knowing the mind of others, etc., he makes up his mind to preserve, so that they may not be destroyed. In those again which have still to be achieved, such as the 'Sorrowless, etc.," up to the higher desirelessness, he resorts to all the means that should be adopted. The effort of many achieves the object of attainment by resorting to the proper means only.

He mentions the fourth :—'The fourth, etc.' This worshipful being absolutely free while yet in life, and possessing only the last body, has the sole object of making the mind latent in the First Cause (Pradhāna).

Out of the these he determines the Yogī who is invited by the gods :—'To whom opens up the yet unseen plane of Madhumatī, etc.'

As to he neophyte (Prathama-kalpika) there is not the least suspicion in the mind of Mahendra, etc., that he will get to the end of Yoga. The third also is not to be invited by them, because he has got what they invite him for, by his conquest of the elements and the senses. In the fourth also the suspicion of attachment is removed the farthest on account of his having reached the state of higher desirelessness. He who remains is the second alone, fit to be the object of invitation. It is he alone whose cognition is truth-bearing, that can be the object of invitation. 'Undying' is that which is not destroyed. 'Unfading' is that which is ever renewed.

He describes the fault of the smile of satisfaction :—'If he indulges in the smile of satisfaction, etc.' He will never understand impermanency, being possessed of a false sense of security on account of satisfaction. The rest is easy.

In different places it has been said that omniscience results from Saṁyama. That, however, does not mean the knowledge of everything without exception. It only describes the nature of the knowledge, as when they say, 'We have tasted all vegetables.' The meaning here is that we have tasted all sorts of sauces, not that there is none left. The word 'all' (sarva) does signify that nothing remains; as in the word 'The eater has eaten all the food that was given to him.' Here the meaning is that nothing remains.—50.

Sūtra 51

क्षणतत्क्रमयोः संयमाद्विवेकजं ज्ञानम् ।। ५१ ।।

क्षण-तत्क्रमयोः: Kṣaṇa-tat-kramayoḥ, (क्षण) over the moments. (तत्) And their. (क्रम)

succession. संयमात् Saṁyamāt, by Saṁyama. विवेकजम् Vivekajam, born-of-discrimination. ज्ञानम् Jñānam, knowledge.

51. By Saṁyama over the moments and their succession, comes knowledge born-of-discrimination.—157.

क्षणतत्क्रमयोः संयमाद्विवेकजं ज्ञानम्। यथा अपकर्षपर्यन्तं द्रव्यं परमाणुरेवं परमापकर्षपर्यन्तः कालः क्षणो यावता वा समयेन चलितः परमाणुः पूर्वदेशं जह्यादुत्तरदेशमुपसम्पद्येत स कालः क्षणः तत्प्रवाहाविच्छेदस्तु क्रमः क्षणतत्क्रमयोर्नास्ति वस्तु समाहार इति। बुद्धिसमाहारो मुहूर्ताहोरात्रादयः। स खल्वयं कालो वस्तु शून्योऽपि बुद्धिनिर्माणः शब्दज्ञानानुपाती लौकिकानां व्युत्थितदर्शनानां वस्तुस्वरूप इवावभासते। क्षणस्तु वस्तुपतितः क्रमावलम्बी। क्रमश्च क्षणानन्तर्यात्मा तं कालविदः काल इत्याचक्षते योगिनः। न च द्वौ क्षणौ सह भवतः। क्रमश्च न द्वयोः सह भुवोरसंभवात्पूर्वस्मादुत्तरस्य भाविनो यदानन्तर्यं क्षणस्य स क्रमस्तस्माद्वर्तमान एवैकः क्षणो न पूर्वोत्तर क्षणाः सन्तीति तस्मान्नास्ति तत्समाहारः। ये तु भूतभाविनः क्षणास्ते परिणामान्विता व्याख्येयास्तेनैकेन क्षणेन कृत्स्नो लोकः परिणाममनुभवति तत्क्षणोपारूढाः खल्वमी सर्वे धर्मास्तयोः क्षणतत्क्रमयोः संयमात्तयोः साक्षात्करणं ततश्च विवेकजं ज्ञानं प्रादुर्भवति।। ५१।।

Vyāsa

As an atom is a substance in which minuteness reaches its limit, so, a moment is a division of time in which minuteness reaches its limits. Or a moment is that much of time which an atom takes in leaving the position in space it occupies and reaching the next point. The succession of moments is the non-cessation of the flow thereof. The moments and their collection do not fall into a collection of actual things. The Muhūrta, the day and night are all aggregates of mental conceptions. This time which is not a substantive reality in itself, but is only a mental concept, and which comes into the mind as a piece of verbal knowledge only, appears to people whose minds are given to out-going activities, as if it were an objective reality. The moment falls under the head of reality, and is maintained by succession. This succession consists in the sequence of moments. The Yogīs who know time call this by the name of time.

Further two moments cannot co-exist. There can be no succession of two co-existent moments. It is impossible. The uninterrupted sequence of the first moment and of the one which follows, is what is called succession. For this there is but one moment existing in the present; the antecedent and postcedent moments do not exist. Therefore, there cannot be any collection of them.

Further, the moments that have passed and those that have yet to come, should be described as existing in consequence of universal change in evolution. For this reason the whole world undergoes change every moment, all these characteristics are relatively established in that one moment of time. By Saṁyama over the moments and their succession, direct knowledge is obtained of them both, and thence is manifested discriminative knowledge.—157.

Vācaspati's Gloss

Here the author describes the saṁyama which is the means of obtaining the knowledge born out of discrimination :—'By Saṁyama over moments and their succession comes knowledge born of discrimination.' The Commentator gives the meaning of the word 'moment' by an illustration :—'As the atom, etc.' Wherever in a piece of stone, which is being divided and divided again and again, smallness reaches a point beyond which it cannot go, it is said to reach the limit of minuteness. That is called an atom. Similarly, the uttermost limit of minuteness of time, is a moment, a division of time which is not related to any other division of time as a part antecedent and postcedent.

He describes the same moment in another way :—'Or, as much as, etc.' The meaning is that a moment is that much of time in which a mere atom may go off its present place.

He describes the meaning of the word succession :—'The non-cessation of the flow, etc.' 'Thereof' means of the moments.

Further this sort of succession is not real. It is, on the other hand, a mental concept. Because it is impossible that a collection of them should be contemplated as real, seeing that they do not exist simultaneously, he says this :—'The moments and their succession, etc.' Because succession has for its characteristic the existence of a moment not in simultaneity, and because the collective existence of moments is devoid of objective reality, the collective existence of moments and their succession is also void of objective reality. Men without the natural excessive intellection of a Vaibāntika, being every moment given to knowledge which consists in out-going activity, and who are, therefore, confused, think that this Time is a reality.

Well then, is the Moment also unreal ? He answers in the negative. 'The moment, however, is classed among realities,' is a real substance. 'It is given support to by succession' :—The succession that gives support to the moments is only a mental concept, the result of imagination (vikalpa).

He gives the reason for the succession giving support to the moment :—'As to succession, etc.'

He gives the reason for the succession being unreal :—'And two moments etc.' The word 'and,' here signifies the reason 'why'.

He says to him who holds that the moments each belonging to a different class may co-exist :—'There can be no succession, etc.'

Why is it impossible? For this reason he says :—'Succession is, etc.' He concludes :—'For this reason.'

Well, then, are the antecedent and postcedent moments of the nature of the horns of a hare only? He says, No. 'The moments that are gone and those that are yet to come, etc.'

Existing in consequence of universal change :—This means followed in sequence similar. Concludes :—'Therefore, etc.' Because the present only has the power over the actions of objects proper to it.—51.

Sūtra 52

जातिलक्षणदेशैरन्यतानवच्छेदात् तुल्ययोस्ततः प्रतिपत्तिः ।। ५२ ।।

जाति Jāti, genus. लक्षण Lakṣaṇa, differentia. देश Deśa, position in space by all these.

अन्यता Anyatā, by separateness. अनवच्छेदात् Anavacchedāt, there being no distinction. तुल्ययोः Tulyayoḥ, of two similars. ततः Tataḥ, thereby. प्रतिपत्तिः Pratipattiḥ, the distinction.

52. Two-similars are thereby distinguished when not separately distinguishable by genus, differentia and position-in-space.—158.

तस्य विषयविशेष उपक्षिप्यते। जातिलक्षणदेशैरन्यतानवच्छेदात्तुल्ययोस्ततः प्रतिपत्तिः। तुल्ययोदेशलक्षणसारूप्ये जातिभेदोऽन्यतायां हेतुः। गौरियं वडवेयमिति। तुल्यदेशजातीयत्वे लक्षणमन्यवत्करं कालाक्षी गौः। स्वस्तिमती गौरिति। द्वयोरामलयोर्जातिलक्षणसारूप्याद् देशभेदोऽन्यत्वकर इदं पूर्वमिदमुत्तरमिति। यदा तु पूर्वमामलकमन्यव्यग्रस्य ज्ञातुरुत्तरे देश उपावर्तते तदा तुल्यदेशत्वे पूर्वमेतदुत्तरमेतदिति प्रविभागानुपपत्तिः। असन्दिग्धेन च तत्त्वज्ञानेन भवितव्यमित्यत इदमुक्तम्। ततः प्रतिपत्तिर्विवेकजज्ञानादिति कथं पूर्वामलकसहक्षणोदेश उत्तरामलकसहक्षणाद् देशाद्भिन्नः। ते चामलके स्वदेशक्षणानुभवभिन्ने। अन्यदेशक्षणानुभवस्तु तयोरन्यत्वे हेतुरिति। एतेन दृष्टान्तेन परमाणोस्तुल्यजातिक्षणदेशस्य पूर्वपरमाणुदेशसहक्षणसाक्षात्करणादुत्तरस्य परमाणोस्तद्देशात्तद्देशानुपपत्तावुत्तरस्य तद्देशानुभवो भिन्नः सहक्षणभेदात्तयोरीश्वरस्य योगिनोऽन्यत्वप्रत्ययो भवतीति। अपरे तु वर्णयन्ति। येऽन्त्या विशेषास्तेऽन्यताप्रत्ययं कुर्वन्तीति। तत्रापि देशलक्षणभेदो मूर्तिव्यवधिजातिभेदश्चान्यत्वे हेतुः। क्षणभेदस्तु योगिबुद्धिगम्य एवेत्यत उक्तं मूर्तिव्यवधिजातिभेदाभावान्नास्ति मूलपृथक्त्वमिति वार्षगण्यः।।५२।।

Vyāsa

Its sphere is defined :—'Two similars are thereby distinguished, when not separately distinguishable by genus, differential and position in space.' When position and secondary qualities are the same, the genus causes distinction between two similars. Thus 'This is a cow,' 'This is a mare.' When position and genus are common the secondary quality causes distinction, as is the case with a black-eyed cow and an auspicious cow. Between two emblic fruits in which the genus and secondary qualities are the same, difference of position causes distinction. This is anterior and this is posterior. When, however, the anterior emblic fruit moves on to the position of the posterior one in space, at a time when the seer may be looking elsewhere, the position becoming the same, it can no longer cause distinction (as to which it was originally), the anterior or the posterior? In the knowledge of truth, however, there should be no doubt. Hence has it been said, 'They are thereby distinguished.' It means, by discriminative knowledge How? The space correlated to the moment of time of the anterior emblic fruit, is different from the space correlated to the moment of time of the posterior emblic fruit. And the emblic fruits are separate in the sequential notions of the movements in time correlated to their distinct positions in space. The sequential notion of space correlated to another moment of time is the means of their distinction.

As in this case, so in the case of atoms which have community of genus, secondary quality and position in space. By discovering the yet unknown correlation of every

atomic position in space to a different moment of time, the sequential notion of such a position in space for the anterior atom becomes distinct from such a position in space for the distinction of atoms, on the analogy of this illustration. The powerful Yogī knows this distinction by the correlated moment.

Others however say :—It is the last peculiarities (the Viśeṣa of the Vaiśeṣikas) that cause the notion of distinction. Even there the distinction is the difference of space and secondary quality and the difference of form, distance and genus. The distinction on account of the moment of time can, however, be grasped by the intellect of a Yogī alone.

As has been said by Vārṣagaṇya :—'On account of the absence of the difference of form, intervening space and genus, there is no separation in the root.'—158.

Vācaspati's Gloss

Although this knowledge born of discrimination has all existences for the sphere of its operation, as will be shown further, still being very subtle, one particular sphere is first defined :—'Two similars are thereby distinguished, when not separately distinguishable by genus, differentia and position.' For ordinary men the difference of genus is the cause of the knowledge of distinction. When genus such as the characteristic of a cow is the same; when also space, such as presence in the east, etc., is the same; then the distinction of the black-eyed and the auspicious is the other means of distinction. In two emblic fruits the genus of emblic fruit is the same, the differentiae of roundness, etc., are the same. The difference of space, however, is another means of distinction. When, however, some one desirous of testing the knowledge of the Yogī, takes the anterior fruit when he has his attention turned towards something, and places it is the spot previously occupied by the other fruit, having removed the other fruit from there or having concealed it, then the space also becomes the same, and it can no longer be decided that this is the former and this is the latter. The ordinary wise man who is clever in the use of the three means of knowledge, will not be able to distinguish the two under such circumstances. The knowledge of realities, however, should be free from doubt. It is not proper that a Yogī who is possessed of discriminative knowledge should remain doubtful. Hence has the author of the aphorism said :—'Are thereby distinguished, etc.'

Explains 'thereby.' It means by discriminative knowledge. The question now is : How can knowledge born by Saṁyama over moments and their succession distinguish an emblic fruit from another which is the same with reference to genus, secondary quality and position in space ? The Commentator gives the answer :—'The space correlated to the moment of time of the anterior emblic fruit, is different from the space correlated to the moment of time of the posterior emblic fruit.' 'The space correlated to the moment of time of the anterior emblic fruit, means the space which coincides with the one moment of time of the anterior emblic fruit; or in other words, the change which has no interval between itself and the one moment of time. It is different from the position in space correlated to the moment of time of the posterior fruit, *i.e.*, from the un-interrupted change of the posterior fruit.

Let there be the difference of positions in space; but how does it affect the distinction of the fruit? For this reason he says :—'And the emblic fruits are separate in the sequential notions of their moments of time correlated to their positions in space. The moment of time that is correlated to the distinct position in space of the emblic fruit, is that portion of time which is indicated by the change of anteriority and posteriority in its own position in space. The notion of this moment of time correlated to its distinct position means the knowledge thereof. It is by this knowledge that the fruits are distinguished. The performer of Saṁyama knows that the two emblic fruits are different, by the knowledge of their becoming characterized by a moment of time correlated to the change of anteriority and posteriority, in a position other than that in which the changes of anteriority and posteriority in a moment of time existed formerly. Now although the former place has been changed, the Saṁyama is performed with reference to the moment of time correlated to the present changed position of the same object, qualified by the change of position in space different from the former one. By the performance of this Saṁyama direct knowledge is obtained of the change in time in the other position. For this reason it has been said :—'The sequential notion of the moment of time correlated to another position in space, becomes the cause of their distinction.'

Now he says that by the analogy of this very illustration, the same sort of distinction should be believed as existing among atoms, on the authority of a Yogī who alone can conceive of the distinction. 'On the analogy of this illustration, etc.'

'Others however say :' (he cites their opinion) 'it is the last, etc.' The Vaiśeṣikas say that there are certain ultimate perculiarities which are manifest in the permanent substances. It is thus argued. The Yogīs who are absolutely free do not distinguish between objects whose genus, position in space and secondary qualities are the same, and in which there is no interval; and cannot specify either by pointing out mutual differences or by defining their realities. There must, therefore, be some ultimate peculiarity (Viśeṣa) : and it is that, that they make out to be the differentiating quality of permanent substances, such as atoms, etc.

He refutes this theory :—'Even there, etc.' Genus, space and secondary quality have been illustrated. Form is a manifestation of arrangement along certain lines. Thus having removed a thing whose parts are beautifully arranged, another object whose parts are ugly in arrangement, is placed in the same position when the seer is otherwise employed. In this case the knowledge of distinction is obtained by the difference of arrangement.

Or, form may mean the body. It is by relation to the body that the selves whether in evolution or free are distinguished by means of the action of the elements, such as it may be. Thus when the notion of distinction is caused anywhere by other means, it is not necessary to posit a differentia in the shape of ultimate peculiarity (Antya Viśeṣa), as the cause of the distinction. This is similar to the case of the Dvīpas of Kuśa and Puṣkara in their aspect of planes of space.

Inasmuch as it has been said that the differences of genus, position and time, etc., are known by the intellect of the ordinary man, it is said that the difference of moment of time (kṣana) is known by the intellect of the Yogī alone. The word 'alone' signifies the difference of the moment of time, not that of the intellect of the Yogī. It is inferred that the distinction between released Puruṣas also is known by the intellect of the Yogī by their relation to the body moving in the elements (bhūtacara).

The teacher thought that in the case of those who do not possess the means of distinction, there are no distinctions in the case of the Pradhāna. Therefore, he said :—'Although' destroyed with reference to those whose objects have been gained, it is not destroyed with reference to others, being common to the others.'

He says this :—'On account of the absence of form, etc.' The meaning is that the universe has difference indicated by the causes mentioned. But there is no distinction in the root, the Pradhāna.—52.

Sūtra 53

तारकं सर्वविषयं सर्वथाविषयमक्रमं चेति विवेकजज्ञानम् ।। ५३ ।।

तारकम् Tārakam, the intuitional. सर्वविषयम् Sarva-viṣayam, having everything (सर्व) for its Sphere of operation (विषय). सर्वथा-विषयम् Sarvathā-viṣayam, (सर्वथा) having all conditions (विषय) For its sphere of operation. अक्रमम् Akramam, having no succession. च Ca, and. इति Iti, this.

53. And it is the intuitional; has everything for its sphere-of-operation; has all-condition for its sphere-of-operation; has no succession. This is the entire discriminative knowledge.—159.

तारकं सर्वविषयं सर्वथाविषयमक्रमं चेति विवेकजज्ञानम् । तारकमिति स्वप्रतिभोत्थमनौपदेशिकमित्यर्थः। सर्वविषयत्वान्नास्य । किंचिदविषयीभूतमित्यर्थः। सर्वथाविषयमतीतानागतप्रत्युत्पन्नं सर्वं पर्यायैः सर्वथा जानातीत्यर्थः। अक्रममित्येकक्षणोपारूढं सर्वं सर्वथा गृह्णातीत्यर्थः। एतद्विवेकजं ज्ञानं परिपूर्णमस्यैवांशो योगप्रदीपो मधुमतीं भूमिमुपादाय यावदस्य परिसमाप्तिरिति ।। ५३ ।।

Vyāsa

It is intuitional :—This means that the knowledge comes by one's own prescience and no by teaching.

Has everything for its sphere of operation :—This means that there is nothing yet known, which might not be made its object.

Has all conditions for its sphere/:—The all, as it was or will be, or is with all minor modes of expression. It means that he knows all the conditions of these objects.

Has no succession :—It means that he takes in the 'all' as correlated to but one moment.

This is the entire discriminative knowledge :—The light of Yoga is part of this only, beginning with the Madhumatī up to the end of this knowledge.—159.

Vācaspati's Gloss

Having thus described one branch of discriminative knowledge, the author now describes discriminative knowledge :—'It is intuitive; has everything as the sphere of its operation; has all conditions as its sphere; has no succession; this is the entire discriminative knowledge.'

'Discriminative knowledge' : This is the statement of the thing defined. The rest is the description. Intuition is called Tāraka, because it becomes the cause of crossing the ocean of the universe. He distinguishes this from the knowledge by prescience already described :—'Has all conditions for the sphere of its operation.'

'Modes of expression' : means minor modes of differentiation. For this reason the knowledge of discrimination is complete. There is nothing anywhere which may not at any time or in any way be its object. This is he meaning. There may be other knowledge obtained by cognitive trance, but that also is a part of this, and where therefore can there be any knowledge beyond this? It is for this reason complete. The Commentator says this :—'The light of Yoga, *i.e.*, the Cognitive Yoga, is a part thereof.'

Now he says what is the beginning and what is the end :—'Beginning with the Madhumatī, etc.' The truth-bearing cognition is the Madhu, honey, because it causes, such sweet bliss. The meaning is, 'having obtained the purity of cognition as described.' The Madhumatī is that state which is possessed of that and gives sweet bliss. The mind having reached that state, manifests up to the end of that state, passing through seven-fold stages of intellectual progress. It is for this reason that discriminative knowledge becomes intuitional, inasmuch as its branch, the light of Yoga, is intuitional.—53.

Sūtra 54

सत्त्वपुरुषयोः शुद्धिसाम्ये कैवल्यम् ।। ५४ ।।

सत्त्व-पुरुषयो: Sattvapuruṣayoḥ, of the objective essence and the consciousness. शुद्धि Śuddhi, of the purity. साम्ये Sāmye, on their becoming equal. कैवल्यम् Kaivalyam, absolute independence.

54. When the purity of the Objective-Essence and that of the Puruṣa become equal, it is absolute independence.—160.

प्राप्तविवेकजज्ञानस्याप्राप्तविवेकजज्ञानस्य वा । सत्त्वपुरुषयोः शुद्धिसाम्ये कैवल्यमिति । यदा निर्धूतरजस्तमोमलं बुद्धिसत्त्वं पुरुषस्यान्यताप्रतीतिमात्राधिकारं दग्धक्लेशबीजं भवति तदा पुरुषस्य शुद्धिसारूप्यमिवापन्नं भवित तदा पुरुषस्योपचरितभोगाभाव: शुद्धिस्तस्यामवस्थायां कैवल्यं भवति । ईश्वरस्यांनीश्वरस्य वा विवेकजज्ञानभागिन इतरस्य वा । नहि दग्धक्लेशबीजस्य ज्ञाने पुनरपेक्षा काचिदस्ति सत्त्वशुद्धिद्वारेणैतत्समाधिजमैश्वर्यं ज्ञानं चोपक्रान्तं परमार्थतस्तु ज्ञानाददर्शनं निवर्तते तस्मिन्निवृत्ते न सन्त्युत्तरे क्लेशा: क्लेशाभावात्कर्मविपाकाभावाच्चरिताधिकाराश्चैतस्यामवस्थायां गुणा न पुरुषस्य दृश्यत्वेन पुनरुपतिष्ठन्ते तत्पुरुषस्य कैवल्यं तदा पुरुष: स्वरूपमात्रज्योतिरमल: केवली भवति ।। ५४ ।।

।। इति श्रीपातञ्जलभाष्ये सांख्यप्रवचने विभूतिपादस्तृतीय: समाप्त: ।। ३ ।।

Vyāsa

In the case of him who has obtained discriminative knowledge as well as in the case of him who has not obtained discriminate knowledge, it is absolute independence (kaivalya), when the purity of the Objective Essence and the Puruṣa become equal. When the essence of the Will-to-be with the dirt of the Rajas and the Tamas removed, has the notion of the distinctness of the Puruṣa as its sole remaining object, and all the seeds of affliction have been burnt up, then does it, as it were, assume a state of purity similar to that of the Puruṣa. In that state the purity of the Puruṣa consists in the absence of that enjoyment which is attributed to him, as it were, figuratively. In that state comes absolute independence (kaivalya), whether it be to the master or to the ordinary man, to him who is possessed of discriminative knowledge or to him who is not.

He in whom the seed of affliction is burnt up, has no longer any need of knowledge anywhere. It is as the means of purifying the substance of the Will-to-be that knowledge and the powers born of trance have been touched upon. In reality ignorance is removed by knowledge. On its cessation there are no longer any afflictions. When there are no afflictions, there is no fruition of actions. The Guṇas in that state have fulfilled their object. They, therefore, no longer present themselves to be seen by the Puruṣa. Then the Puruṣa shining in this own pure light, becomes absolutely independent (kevala).—160.

Vācaspati's Gloss

Having now described the means of absolute independence, the Saṁyamas together with the attainments, the author now introduces this aphorism in order to show that the knowledge of the distinction between the Objective Essence and the Puruṣa is the direct means of absolute independence :—'In the case of him who has obtained, etc.' The meaning is that the knowledge born of discrimination does, all the same, become the means of absolute independence, whether or not there is the knowledge born of discrimination. 'It is absolute independence (kaivalya) when the purity of the Objective Essence and that of the Puruṣa become equal.'

'The master' is he who has by the performance of Saṁyama obtained the power of knowledge and action. The ordinary man is he who has not obtained these powers. To him who is possessed of discriminative knowledge by the performance of Saṁyama described just before, or, to another who has obtained knowledge otherwise, in either case, the attainments are never under requisition for the purpose. 'He in whom the seeds of affliction, etc.'

Well, but if they are unnecessary for absolute freedom their teaching is useless. For this reason the Commentator says :—'As a means of the attainment of the purity of the Objective Essence, etc.'

The attainments are not absolutely unnecessary in attaining absolute independence. They are not its direct means. The knowledge born of discrimination and that which is attained by the successive performance of Saṁyama is only an indriect cause. The principal cause is the knowledge of distinction. This is the meaning. Ignorance is removed by knowledge. Knowledge means the Highest Intellection.—54.

In this chapter the direct means of Yoga have been described. Also the evolutionary changes have been dilated upon. Also the conjunction with the elements by Saṁyama. Also the knowledge born of discrimination. This is the third chapter of Vācaspati's Gloss on Vyāsa's Commentary of the aphorisms of Yoga. The third Chapter, the Chapter on Attainments, in finished.

4
Absolute Independence (Kaivalya)

Sūtra 1

जन्मौषधिमन्त्रतपःसमाधिजाः सिद्धयः ।। १ ।।

जन्म Janma, birth. औषधि Auṣadhi, drugs. मन्त्र Mantra, incantations. तपः Tapaḥ, purificatory rites. समाधि Samādhi, trance. जाः Jāḥ, born. सिद्धयः Siddhayaḥ, attainments.

1. The attainments are by birth, drugs, incantations, purificatory action (tapas) or trance.—161.

जन्मौषधिमन्त्रतपःसमाधिजाः सिद्धयः। देहान्तरिता जन्मसिद्धिः ओषधीभिरसुरभवनेषु रसायनेनेत्येवमादिः। मन्त्रैराकाशगमनमणिमादिसिद्धिः। तपसा सङ्कल्पसिद्धिः। कामरूपी यत्र तत्र कामग इत्येवमादिसमाधिजाः सिद्धयो व्याख्याताः।। १ ।।

Vyāsa

Attainments by birth exist in the body.

By drugs, in the houses of the Asuras, by elixir and such like :

By incantations, motion in space and the powers of attenuation (aṇimā), etc.

By purificatory action (tapas) the achievement of wishes. He takes such forms and goes to such places as he may like, and does other similar things.

The attainments born of trance have been described.—161.

Vācaspati's Gloss

Now trance, its means and its attainments, have been described chiefly in the first, second and third chapters. Other subjects which it became necessary to take up by context, or by way of introduction, have also been discussed. Here is to be discussed Absolute Freedom (Kaivalya), which is the ultimate of all these practices, etc. And this is impossible to explain without explaining the nature of the mind inclining towards the state of absolute independence, as also the other world and the self which being something beside knowledge alone (Vijñāna), is related to the other world, and which enjoys through the instrumentality of the mind, pleasurable sound, etc. All this has to be described in this chapter, besides what might become necessary by context or by way of introduction.

First of all, he describes the five-fold attainment, with the object of ascertaining which of the minds possessed of attainments is passing towards the state of absolute independence.

'The attainments are by birth, incantations, purificatory action or trance.' He explains :— Exists in the body :—Some one has the power of attenuation in the body, just as he is born because actions done by him as man, which are calculated to cause the enjoyments of Heaven, have developed them into fruition in some heavenly region.

He describes the attainments due to drugs :—'In the house of the Asuras.' Man passes to the places of the Asuras for some reason. He is met there by lovely Asura damsels, and given an offering of elixir. Using that he comes to possess the attainments of freedom from decay and death, and other attainments. Or, the same may take place even here by the use of elixir, as in the case of the thinker Māṇḍavya, who resided in the Vindhya Mountains and who used the elixir.

He next describes the attainments due to incantations :—'By mantras.'

He next describes the attainments of purificatory actions :—'By purificatory action.'

He next describes the attainment of wishes :—Assuming such forms as desired. Whatever does he desire, be it the attainment of Aṇimā or any other, that he attains at once. Whatever he desires to hear or to think anywhere, that he hears or thinks there. By the word, etc., seeing etc., have been included.—1.

Sūtra 2

जात्यन्तरपरिणामः प्रकृत्यापूरात् ।। २ ।।

जात्यन्तर Jātyantara, to another life-state. परिणामः Pariṇāmaḥ, change. प्रकृति Prakṛti, of the creative causes. आपूरात् Āpūrāt, by the filling up.

2. Change to another life-state by filling up of the creative causes (Prakṛtyāpura).—162.

तत्र कायेन्द्रियाणामन्यजातिपरिणतानाम् । जात्यन्तरपरिणामः प्रकृत्यापूरात् । पूर्वपरिणामापाये उत्तरपरिणामोपजनस्तेषामपूर्वावयवानुप्रवेशाद्भवति कायेन्द्रियप्रकृतयश्च स्वं स्वं विकारमनुगृह्णान्त्यापूरेण धर्मादिनिमित्तमपेक्षमाणा इति ।। २ ।।

Vyāsa

Here 'change to another life-state by the filling up of the creative causes,' takes place of the life-state into which the body and the powers have already changed and exist. On the former change going out comes the close appearance of their next change by the sequential showing forth of organ and parts which did not exist before; and the creative causes of the body and the powers favour each their own modifications by filling up, which again has the necessity of virtue, etc., as the incidental cause (of removing the impediment).—162.

Vācaspati's Gloss

The attainments due to the trance have been described in the previous chapter. It is now desirable to say that the change into another life-state brought about by the four classes of attainments due to the use of herbs, etc., is also of the same body and the powers thereof. This, however, does not come about by mere material causes. The material itself, so far as it goes, does not prove to be competent to intensify or weaken the state of the divine and the not-divine, in him. It is plain that a cause having no elements of difference in itself cannot operate to produce different effects. In order to guard against the possibility of he change being taken as due to accident alone, he completes and reads the aphorism :—'Change to another life-state by the filling up of the creative causes.'

Here it is only the change of the body and the powers as they are in one state, that takes place into those suitable to another state. The change takes place of the body and the powers as they appear in man, into the life-state of the animals and gods by the filling up of the creative causes.

The creative causes of the body are the elements of Pṛthvī, etc. The creative cause of the 'powers' is the principle of egoism.

'Filling up' means the sequential showing forth, entrance therein, of these causes. By this comes about the change.

Says this :—'By the former change going out, etc.'

Well, but if the change is favoured by the 'filling up' why does it not take place always? For this reason he says :—'Has the necessity of virtue, etc.

By this have been described the changes of the state of the body into childhood, boyhood, youth, old age; the change of the seed of the Nyagrodha into the tree; the change of the small piece of fire thrown into a heap of straw, into a large fire throwing out flames by thousand and embracing the sky itself.—2.

Sūtra 3

निमित्तमप्रयोजकं प्रकृतीनां वरणभेदस्तु ततः क्षेत्रिकवत्।। ३।।

निमित्तम् Nimittam, incidental causes. अप्रयोजकम् Aprayojakam, are those which do not move into action. प्रकृतीनाम् Prakṛtīnām, the creative causes. वरण Varaṇa, of the obstacle. भेदः Bhedaḥ, piercing through. तु Tu, but. ततः Tataḥ, from that. क्षेत्रिकवत् Kṣetrikavat, like a husbandman.

3. The creative-causes are not-moved-into-action by any incidental-cause; but that pierces-the-obstacle from it like the husbandman.—163.

निमित्तमप्रयोजकं प्रकृतीनां वरणभेदस्तु ततः क्षेत्रिकवत्। नहि धर्मादिनिमित्तं तत्प्रयोजकं भवति प्रकृतीनाम्। न कार्येण कारणं प्रवर्त्यत इति। कथं तर्हि। वरणभेदस्तु ततः क्षेत्रिकवत्। यथा क्षेत्रिकः केदारादपां पूर्णात्केदारान्तरं पिप्लावयिषुः समं निम्नं निम्नतरं वा नापः पाणिनापकर्षत्यावरणं त्वासां भिनत्ति तस्मिन्भिन्ने स्वयमेवापः केदारान्तरमाप्लावयन्ति तथा धर्मः प्रकृतिनामावरणमधर्मं भिनत्ति तस्मिन्भिन्ने स्वयमेव प्रकृतयः स्वं स्वं

विकारमाप्लावयन्ति। यथा वा स एव क्षेत्रिकस्तस्मिन्नेव केदारे न प्रभवत्यौदकान्भौमान्वा रसान्धान्यमूलान्यनुप्रवेशयितुम्। किं तर्हि मुद्गगवेधुकश्यामाकादींस्ततोऽपकर्षति। अपकृष्टेषु तेषु स्वयमेव रसा धान्यमूलान्यनुप्रविशन्ति। तथा धर्मो निवृत्तिमात्रे कारणमधर्मस्य शुद्ध्यशुद्ध्योरत्यन्तविरोधात्। नतु प्रकृतिप्रवृत्तौ धर्मो हेतुर्भवतीति। अत्र नन्दीश्वरादय उदाहार्याः। विपर्ययेणाप्यधर्मो धर्मं बाधते। ततश्चाशुद्धिपरिणाम इति। तत्रापि नहुषाजगरादय उदाहार्याः। यदा तु योगी बहून्कायान्निर्मिमीते तदा किमेकमनस्कास्ते भवन्त्यथानेकमनस्का इति।। ३।।

Vyāsa

This incidental causes in the shape of virtue, etc., do not move the creative causes into action; because the cause is not moved into action by the effect. How then? 'That pierces the obstacle like the husbandman.'

As the husbandman desirous of carrying water from an already well-filled bed to another, does not draw the water with his own hands to places which are on the same or a lower level; but simply removes the obstacles, and thereupon the water flows down of itself to the other bed, so it pierces through vice which is the obstacle to virtue, and that being pierced through, the creative causes pass through their respective changes.

Or, similarly, the same husbandman does not possess the power of transferring the earthy and watery juices to the roots of rice in the same bed. What then? He weeds the 'ring', the 'Gavendhuka' and the 'Śyāmaka' out of the common bed, and when they have been weeded out, the juices themselves enter the roots of rice.

Similarly virtue only becomes the cause of the removal of the vice, because purity and impurity are diametrically opposed to each other. It is not that virtue becomes the cause of the creative cause moving into action. On this point Nandīśvara, etc., are illustrations. On the other side, too, vice counteracts virtue and thence comes the change to impurity. Here too Nahuṣa, the Ajagara, etc., should be taken as illustrations.—163

Vācaspati's Gloss

It has been said, 'By the filling up of the creative causes.' Here the doubt arises. Is this filling up of the creative causes natural, or due to some incidental cause such as virtue and vice? What is proved? Well, because the creative causes, notwithstanding existence, fill up only sometimes, and because it is said that virtue and vice are the incidental causes; it is, therefore, proved that virtue, etc., are the incidental causes of the creative causes moving into action. For this reason he says :—'The creative causes are not moved into action by any incidental cause; that pierces the obstacle like the husbandman.'

It is true that virtue, etc., are the incidental causes, but they do not set the creative causes into action; because virtue and vice are themselves the effects of creative causes. And the effect does not move the cause into action, because the birth of the effect depending upon the cause, it is subject the action of the cause. What is self-dependent can only set an action in something which is dependent on it. The jar which is desired to be made or which has already been made,

cannot certainly use the clay, the wheel and water for that purpose without the potter. Nor is it similarly the object of the Puruṣa that sets the creative causes into action. It is only Īśvara who does this with that object in view. The object of the Puruṣa is said to be the power which sets in action, by virtue of its being the aim thereof. Further, if it were, so the tending of the aim of the Puruṣa towards fulfilment would very properly become the cause of the stopping of the operations of the phenomenal world.—3.

But it is not by this much that virtue, etc., cease to be the means of change altogether. Because they become he means of effecting changes even by removing the obstacles only, like the husbandman. As to Īśvara, His action too should be understood to be of the nature of the removal of obstacles, so that virtue may be practised. This is what has been commented upon by the Commentary already explained.

Sūtra 4

निर्माणचित्तान्यस्मितामात्रात् ।। ४ ।।

निर्माण Nirmāṇa, of creation, created. चित्तानि Cittāni, minds. अस्मिता Asmitā, from egoism. मात्रात् Mātrāt, alone.

4. Created minds proceed from egoism alone.—164.

निर्माणचित्तान्यस्मितामात्रात् । अस्मितामात्रं चित्तं कारणमुपादाय निर्माणचित्तानि करोति ततः सचित्तानि भवन्तीति ।। ४ ।।

Vyāsa

When however the Yogī makes many bodies, then, are these bodies possessed of many minds or all one only? 'Created minds proceed from egoism alone?' Taking as cause the mind which is egoism alone, he makes the created minds. Thence do the bodies become possessed of mind.—164.

Vācaspati's Gloss

Now he considers the unity or manifoldness of the minds in the many bodies made by perfected powers, after the attainments have been achieved by the filling in of the creative causes (Prakṛtis) :—'When however.'

Here if the bodies possessed more than one mind, the desire of each such mind would be different from those of the others; and there would not thus be obedience to the desired of one mind and no mutuality in relationship, just as in the case of two individual selves (Puruṣas). It, therefore, comes to this that it is only one mind which pervades more created bodies than one, just as the light of a lamp is diffused on all sides and illuminates more bodies than one. Says he thereupon :—'Created minds proceed from egoism alone.'

All living bodies, as long as they live, are found to be possessed of one ordinary mind each. Take, for example, the bodies of Caitra and Maitra, etc. So are the created bodies (the Nirmāṇakāyas). Thus is it proved that each of these bodies has a mind of its own.

Says with this in mind :—'Taking as cause the mind which is egoism alone.'—4.

Sūtra 5

प्रवृत्तिभेदे प्रयोजकं चित्तमेकमनेकेषाम्।। ५।।

प्रवृत्ति Pravṛtti, of activity. भेदे Bhede, there being difference. प्रयोजकम् Prayojakam, the director. चित्तम् Cittam, the mind. एकम् Ekam, one. अनेकेषाम् Anekeṣām, of the many.

5. There being difference of activity, one mind the director of-the-many. 165.

प्रवृत्तिभेदे प्रयोजकं चित्तमेकमनेकेषाम्। बाहूनां चित्तानां कथमेकचित्ताभिप्रायपुर:सरा प्रवृत्तिरिति सर्वचित्तानां प्रयोजकं चित्तमेकं निर्मिमीते ततः प्रवृत्तिभेदः।। ५।।

Vyāsa

How may it be that many minds may follow in their activities, the desires of one mind? With this object he makes one mind as the director of all the minds; and thence proceeds the difference of activities.—165.

Vācaspati' Gloss

The aphorism is a reply to what has been said, that in the case of there being more minds than one, there would not be obedience to one mind, nor mutuality of relationship :—'There being difference of activity, one mind the director of the others.' This might be a defect if the Yogī did not make one mind to be the director of more minds than one acting in more bodies than one. When that is made, no defect remains.

It should not be said that there is no use in more minds than one that is one for each body, when one such mind is posited; nor should it be said that there is no use in making a directing mind, because one's own mind can serve that purpose. The reason is that that which has been proved to exist by right reasoning, need no more be subjected to the test of being placed in consonant and dissonant positions.

On this says the Purāṇa :—'The one Lord becomes many by his power of Lordship. For this reason and because having become many he again becomes one, these are certainly born by the differences of the mind, one-fold, two-fold, three-fold and manifold. The Yogīśvara makes his bodies in this way and unmakes them. By some he enjoys objects of enjoyment and by other performs hard penances. He again draws in the bodies as the Sun draws in his ray.' It is with this object that he says :—'How is it that all these minds act according, etc.'—5.

Sūtra 6

तत्र ध्यानजमनाशयम्।। ६।।

तत्र Tatra, of these. ध्यानजम् Dhyānajam, the meditation born. अनाशयम् Anāśayam, is free from the vehicles.

6. Of these the meditation-born is free-from-the-vehicles.—166.

तत्र ध्यानजमनाशयम्। पञ्चविधं निर्माणचित्तं जन्मौषधिमन्त्रतपःसमाधिजाः सिद्धय इति। तत्र यदेव ध्यानजं चित्तं तदेवानाशयं तस्यैव नास्त्याशयो रागादिप्रवृत्तिः ततः पुण्यपापाभिसम्बन्धः क्षीणक्लेशत्वाद्योगिन इति।। ६।।

Vyāsa

The created mind is five-fold, as said :—'The attainments are by birth, drugs, incantations, purificatory action or trance.' Of these the one that is born of meditation is alone free from the vehicles. It does not possess the vehicles, which cause the manifestation of desire, etc. Thence is there no coming into relationship with virtue and vice, inasmuch as the afflictions of a Yogī have ceased to exist.—166.

Vācaspati's Gloss

Now he determines the mind, which tends to emancipation, out of the five descriptions of the minds of the perfected ones (siddhas), which have been described :—'The meditation-born is free from the vehicles.' The vehicles are those that take possession of the mind as the impressions of the actions and the impressions of the afflictions. The mind free from the vehicles is that in which these do not exist. The meaning is that it becomes inclined towards emancipation. Inasmuch as there does not exist in this condition the manifestation of desires, etc., there is no coming into relationship with virtue and vice. But then why do not desires, etc., come into manifestation? For this reason he says :—'Because the afflictions of a Yogī have ceased to exist?'—6.

Sūtra 7

कर्माशुक्लाकृष्णं योगिनस्त्रिविधमितरेषाम्।। ७।।

कर्म Karma, Karma, action. अशुक्ल Aśukla, neither white. अकृष्णम् Akṛṣṇam, nor black. योगिनः Yoginaḥ, of a Yogī. त्रिविधम् Trividham, threefold. इतरेषाम् Itareṣām, of the others.

7. A Yogī's karma is neither-white nor-black; of-the-others it is three-fold.—167.

इतरेषां तु विद्यते कर्माशयो यतः। कर्माशुक्लाकृष्णं योगिनस्त्रिविधमितरेषाम्। चतुष्पात्खल्वियं कर्मजातः। कृष्णा शुक्लकृष्णा शुक्लाऽशुक्लाकृष्णा चेति। तत्र कृष्णा दुरात्मनाम्। शुक्लकृष्णा बहिः साधनसाध्या तत्र परपीडानुग्रहद्वारेणैव कर्माशयप्रचयः। शुक्ला तपः स्वाध्यायध्यानवताम्। सा हि केवले मनस्यायत्तत्त्वाद् बहिः साधनानधीना न परान्पीडयित्वा भवति। अशुक्लाकृष्णा संन्यासिनां क्षीणक्लेशानां चरमदेहानामिति। तत्राशुक्लं योगिन एव फलसंन्यासादकृष्णं चानुपादानात्। इतरेषां तु भूतानां पूर्वमेव त्रिविधमिति।। ७।।

Vyāsa

The vehicle of actions exists in the case of others. Hence, 'A Yogī's karma is neither white nor black; of the others it is three-fold.'

This class of actions has four locations : the black, the black-white, the white, nor white nor black. Of these, the black is of the wicked. The black-white is brought about by external means, as in this the vehicle of actions grows by means of causing pain to, or acting kindly towards others.

The white is of those who resort to the means of improvement of study and meditation. This is dependent upon the mind alone. It does not depend upon external means and is not, therefore, brought about by injuring others.

The one which is neither white nor black exists in the case of those who have renounced everything (the Sannyāsīs), whose afflictions have been destroyed, and whose present body is the last one, they will have. It is not white in the case of a Yogī, because he gives up the fruit of action; and it is not black, because he does not perform actions. Of the other creatures, it is of the three former descriptions only.—167.

Vācaspati's Gloss

Says that the others are possessed of the vehicles, with the object of showing the differences of the other minds from the meditation-born, which is not possessed of the vehicles :—'In the case of others, etc.'

In the same connection he introduces the aphorism as describing the cause thereof :—'A Yogī's karma is neither black nor white; of the others it is three-fold.'

'Has four locations'—Location means place (of manifestation). It has four locations because it manifests in four such places.

'Brought about by external means'—In all such cases injury is sure to be caused to others. It is not that even in action done for the preparation of barley, etc., for food, etc., there exists no injury. It is possible that ants, etc., might be killed at the time of pounding them, and finally the arrangement is that trunk, etc., are produced by the destruction of seeds as such.

'Acting kindly' means the favouring of Brāhmaṇas, etc., by giving them presents, etc.

The white is of those who are not Sannyāsīs, but who perform purificatory action, study and meditation. He shows how it is white :—'This is dependent upon the mind alone, etc.'

That which is neither white nor black, is the karma of the Sannyāsīs (those who have renounced everything. He shows who are the Sannyāsīs :—'Whose afflictions have been destroyed, etc.'

Those who have renounced actions (the karma-sannyāsīs) are not anywhere found performing actions which depend upon external means. They have not got the black vehicle of actions, because they do not perform such actions. Nor do they possess the white vehicle of actions, because they dedicate to Īśvara the fruits of the vehicle of action brought about by the practice of Yoga. That whose fruit is not bad, is called white. That which has no fruit itself, how can it have any bad fruit?

Having thus described the four-fold division of karma, now the specifies which refers to which :—'Of these it is not white, etc.'—7.

Sūtra 8

ततस्तद्विपाकानुगुणानामेवाभिव्यक्तिर्वासनानाम् ॥ ८ ॥

ततः Tataḥ, thence. तद् Tad, their (of residual potencies). विपाक Vipāka, fruition. अनुगुण Anuguṇa, following. विपाकानुगुणानाम् Vipākānuguṇānām, of those that are competent to bring about their fruition. एव Eva, only. अभिव्यक्तिः Abhivyaktiḥ, the manifestation, proceeding. वासनानाम् Vāsanānām, of the residual potencies.

8. Thence proceed the residual-potencies competent-to-bring-about their fruition alone.—168.

ततस्तद्विपाकानुगुणानामेवाभिव्यक्तिर्वासनानाम्। तत इति त्रिविधात्कर्मणस्तद्विपाकानुगुणानामेवेति। यज्जातीयस्य कर्मणो यो विपाकस्तस्यानुगुणा या वासनाः कर्मविपाकमनुशेरते तासामेवाभिव्यक्तिः। नहि दैवं कर्म विपच्यमानं नारकतिर्यङ्मनुष्यवासनाभिव्यक्तिनिमित्तं संभवति। किंतु दैवानुगुणा एवास्य वासना व्यज्यन्ते। नारकतिर्यङ् मनुष्येषु चैवं समानश्चर्चः॥ ८॥

Vyāsa

'Thence' means from the three-fold karma.

'Competent to bring about the fruition thereof.' Whatever is the fruition of whichever class of karma, as such residual potencies only as are competent to bring about the fruition of those actions, are manifested. When the karma relating to the state of the gods is fructifying, the residua which are adequate to the state of the hell-born, the animals and men cannot manifest. On the contrary, it is only the impressions which are adequate to the state of the gods that are manifested. The operation of the rule is the same in the case of the hell-born, the human and the animal tendencies.—168.

Vācaspati's Gloss

Having ascertained the vehicle of actions, now he describes the developments of the vehicle of afflictions :—'Thence manifested the residual potencies competent to bring about their fruition.' He describes the impressions which are competent to bring about the life-state, life-experience and life-period, whether hellish or divine, which are the results of the fruition of good and bad karma :—'The residual potencies competent to bring about the fruition thereof.' The residua which are born of divine experience are competent to bring about the fruition of divine karma. It is not possible that in the case of the manifestation of the residua of human experiences, the enjoyment of the fruitage of divine actions should take place. For this reason the impressions whose manifestation is brought about by karma are of the same class as the fruition thereof. This is the meaning of the Commentary.—8.

Sūtra 9

जातिदेशकालव्यवहितानामप्यानन्तर्यं स्मृतिसंस्कारयोरेकरूपत्वात् ॥ ९ ॥

जाति Jāti, of life state. देश Deśa, of locality. काल Kāla, of time. व्यवहितानाम् Vyavahitānām,

these being distinct. अपि Api, even. आनन्तर्यम् Ānantaryam, sequential non-interruption. स्मृति Smṛti, of memory. संस्कारयोः Saṁskārayoḥ, and of potential residue. एकरूपत्वात् Ekarūpatvāt, because of their being the same in appearance.

9. Memory and potential-residua being the same in appearance, there is sequential non-interruption, even when there is distinction of life-state, locality and time.—169.

जातिदेशकालव्यवहितानामप्यानन्तर्यं स्मृतिसंस्कारयोरेकरूपत्वात्। वृषदंशविपाकोदयः स्वव्यञ्जकाञ्जनाभिव्यक्तः। स यदि जातिशतेन वा दूरदेशतया वा कल्पशतेन वा व्यवहितः पुनश्च स्वव्यञ्जकाञ्जन एवोदियाद्रागित्येवं पूर्वानुभूतवृषदंशविपाकाभिसंस्कृता वासना उपादाय व्यजेत। कस्मात्। यतो व्यवहितानामप्यासां सदृशं कर्माभिव्यञ्जकं निमित्तीभूतमित्यानन्तर्यमेव। कुतश्च स्मृतिसंस्कारयोरेकरूपत्वात्। यथानुभवास्तथा संस्काराः। ते च कर्मवासनारूपाः। यथा च वासनास्तथा स्मृतिरिति। जातिदेशकालव्यवहितेभ्यः संस्कारेभ्यः स्मृतिः स्मृतेश्च पुनः संस्कारा इत्येवमेते स्मृतिसंस्काराः कर्माशयवृत्तिलाभवशाद्व्यज्यन्ते। अतश्च व्यवहितानामपि निमित्तनैमित्तिकभावानुच्छेदादानन्तर्यमेव सिद्धमिति। वासनाः संस्कारा आशया इत्यर्थः।। ९ ।।

Vyāsa

The rise of fruition in the shape of a cat takes place by virtue of the powers competent to show them forth. Even if that rise is separated even by a hundred life-states, or by distance in space, or by a hundred kalpas, it will rise whenever it does, by the operation of its own appropriate cause. Thus will it appear by taking up the residua which are present in the mind on account of the experience of the feline state in some former life. Why? Because even if there be an interval between them, the residua are manifested by the similar manifesting karma becoming the operative cause thereof. Thus there is but sequential appearance. And for what other reason? Because memory and residual potency are but one in appearance. As are the experiences, such are the residual potencies; and they are of the nature of the residual of actions. And memory is similar to the residual. Memory comes by the residual potencies separated therefrom the by life-state and by time and space. From memory come again residua potencies. Thus it is that memory and residua potency are manifested by virtue of the vehicle of action coming into manifestation. Thus even though separated in time, etc., there is sequential non-interruption, inasmuch as the relation of cause and effect does not break.

The Vāsanas (aroma) are residual potencies, the vehicles.—169.

Vācaspati's Gloss

Let that be. But, when the state of a cat is put on after the death of a man, it must be due to the manifestation of the residual of the human state of existence, inasmuch as the one immediately follows the other. It is not possible that the experience of the day immediately preceding be not remembered, but that the experiences of another day more distant therefrom be remembered.

For this reason he says :—'There is sequential non-interruption, even when there is separation in time, life-state and space, on account of the memory and residual potency being the same in appearance.' There may be separation in life-state, etc., from the life of a cat. Still there is non-interruption on account of the fruit thereof, because the same memory is generated when the manifestation is according to its own fruit and in consonance with karma which must fructify into the feline state. 'The rise of a state' is the vehicle of action, because it is from this state that the fruition arises. Further it takes rise in accordance with its own manifesting cause.

'Manifestation' means tending towards the beginning of fruition.

'Thus will it rise again by taking up the residua which are, etc.' The meaning is that if it does manifest, it would manifest by taking up the residua which manifest its own fruition.

Having established the absence of interruption through the operation of the cause, now he establishes the same through the operation of the effect :—'And for what other reason?'

'One in appearance' means similarity. He says the same :—'As are the experiences, etc.'

The question is that if the experiences are of the same appearance as the residual potencies, then inasmuch as the experiences are seen disappearing very soon, the potencies also must be taken as disappearing very soon. That being the case, how is it possible that the potencies, being subject to speedy desertions, should be competent to bring about experiences, after a great lapse of time?

For this reason he says :—'And they are of the nature of the residua of actions.' As the new residuum brought about by momentary action is permanent, so also is the potency generated by momentary experience. There must always be some difference in similarity. If it were otherwise and there were no difference, there would be no similarity. The rest is easy.—9.

Sūtra 10

तासामनादित्वं चाशिषो नित्यत्वात्।। १०।।

तासाम् Tāsām, for them. अनादित्वम् Anāditvam, no beginning. च Ca, and. आशिष: Āśiṣaḥ, of the desire to live. नित्यत्वात् Nityatvāt, owing to the eternity.

10. And there is no-beginning for them, the desire-to-live being eternal.—170.

तासामनादित्वं चाशिषो नित्यत्वात्। तासां वासनानामाशिषो नित्यत्वादनादित्वम्। येयमात्माशीर्मानभूवं भूयासमिति सर्वस्य दृश्यते सा न स्वाभाविकी। कस्मात्। जातमात्रस्याननुभूतमरणधर्मकस्य द्वेषो दुःखानुस्मृतिनिमित्तो मरणत्रासः कथं भवेत्। न च स्वाभाविकं वस्तु निमित्तमुपादत्ते। तस्मादनादिवासनानुविद्धमिदं चित्तं निमित्तवशात्काश्चिदेव वासनाः प्रतिलभ्य पुरुषस्य भोगायोपावर्तत इति। घटप्रासादप्रदीपकल्पं संकोचविकासि चित्तं शरीरपरिमाणाकारमात्रमित्यपरे प्रतिपन्नाः। तथा चान्तराभावः संसारश्च युक्त इति। वृत्तिरेवास्य विभुनश्चित्तस्य संकोचविकासिनीत्याचार्यः। तच्च धर्मादिनिमित्तापेक्षम्। निमित्तं च द्विविधम्। बाह्यमाध्यात्मिकं च। शरीरादिसाधनापेक्षं बाह्यं स्तुतिदानाभिवादनादिचित्तमात्राधीनं श्रद्धाद्याध्यात्मकम्। तथा चोक्तम् ये चैते मैत्र्यादयो ध्यायिनां विहारस्ते बाह्यसाधननिरनुग्रहात्मानः प्रकृष्टं धर्ममभिनिर्वर्तयन्ति तयोर्मानसं

बलीयः कथं ज्ञानवैराग्ये केनातिशय्येते दण्डकारण्यं च चित्तबलव्यतिरेकेण शरीरेण कर्मणा शून्यं कः कर्तुमुत्सहेत समुद्रमगस्त्यवद्वा पिबेत्।। १०।।

Vyāsa

There is no beginning for them, the residua, inasmuch as the desire are ever present. The desire, 'Would that I may not cease to be,' 'Would that I may live on,' is found in everybody. This self-benediction is not inherent. Why not? How could there be fear of death and desire to avoid pain, in any being who has only been born, if he has had no experience of liability to death, it being understood that desire to avoid anything is only caused by remembrance suffered in consequence thereof; and that nothing which is inherent in anything stands in need of a cause. The mind therefore, possessed as it is of residua from eternity, brings into activity by the operation of exciting causes, certain residua only, for the purpose of giving experience to the Puruṣa.

Some philosophers say that the mind has only a form which is commensurate with the body with which it may, for the time, be connected; it contracts or expands like light placed in a jar or a house as the case might be. And thus they say that non-interruption and repeated are proper. The author holds that it is the manifestation alone of the self-existing mind that expands or contracts, and that it is this which has the necessity of the operation of the exciting causes of virtue, etc.

These exciting causes are two-fold, external and internal. The external are those that stand in need of body, etc., as instrument, such as praising, giving of charity, and the performance of obeisances. The internal are those that stand in need of the mind alone, such as faith, etc. And so it has been said :—'These acts of friendliness, etc., are the sports of the thinkers; they do not from their very nature depend upon external causes, and cause the expression of the highest virtue.'

Of these two means the mental ones are more powerful. How? What can excel knowledge and desirelessness? Who can without the power of the mind render the Daṇḍaka forest empty, or drink the ocean like Agastya, by the mere action of the mind alone?—170.

Vācaspati's Gloss

It may be so. The residua laid by in a former and yet again in a former life may manifest themselves, if there be authority for the existence of previous and further previous lives. But there is no authority for such a proposition. Merely the pleasure and pain felt by a creature just born cannot be accepted as authority, because that can be explained by taking it to be natural, like the budding and opening of a lotus flower.

For this reason he says :—'And there is no beginning for them, the desire to live being eternal.'

The meaning of 'and' is that the residua are not only un-interrupted in their fruition, but they are eternal as well, because self-benediction, the desire to live is ever-present. Self-benediction does not fall short of eternity, on account of the residua being eternal.

But inasmuch as this is established by taking them to be inherent, the eternity of self-benediction is not established.

For this reason he says :—'The self-benediction, etc.'

The unbeliever asks :—'Why?' The answer is :—'Of the creature who is just born, etc.' For this very reason, how should it be that a child who has not experienced his liability to death in the present life, who does not know, that is to say, from the experience of the present life that death also is a characteristic of his, should, as he may be falling away from the mother's lap, begin to tremble and hold with his hands tightly the necklace hanging on her breast, marked with the suspicious discus, etc.? And how is it that such a child should experience the fear of death, which can only be caused by the memory of the pain consequent upon aversion to death, whose existence is inferred by the trembling of the child.

Well, has it not been said that this is inherent and natural?

For this reason he says :—'Anything that is inherent, does not stand in need of an operating cause for its birth.' This is the meaning. Such a trembling as becomes visible in the child must be due to fear, just like our own trembling of the same description. The fear of the child must be taken to have been caused by the memory of aversion and pain, for the reason that it is fear just like our own, and the fear due to expected losses that might be coming, is not brought about by the mere memory of pain. Further, from whatever one is afraid, he infers to be the cause of some loss, and then expects that loss would even now cause pain. For this reason pain is caused by the aversion brought about by the memory of pain. Remembering that he infers the cause of pain, which is of the same class which is being felt at the time. The child, however, has not in the present life experienced the pain of falling in any other place. Nor has that sort of pain been felt. Thence the experience of a former life only remains as the explanation, by the canon of residues.

And this is thus applied. The memory of the child just born is due to the experience of former lives, because otherwise it would not be memory. It acts just like our own memory. Even the budding and opening of a lotus is not inherent, because what is inherent in anything, does not stand in need of any other cause for its manifestation. Even fire stands in need of other causes for the manifestation of its heat. In the same way, the cause of the opening of a lotus flower is the contact from outside of the rays of the rising sun : and the cause of the shutting up of the petals is the residual potency, which maintains the inactivity. Similarly the happiness of a baby which is inferred from smiles, etc., should also be considered a proof of a previous life.

An 'exciting cause' is action just in point at the time of fruition. 'Bringing into operation,' means manifestation.

As the context demands, he mentions the opposite theory of the mind having a measure, with the object of refuting it :—'The mind contracts and expands like light in a jar or a place, etc.'

Seeing that action takes place only where the body is found to be, there is no authority for the existence of the mind at any place outside the body. The mind further is not atomic in size, because in that case it would mean the simultaneous non-production of the five sorts of sensation when the large cake is devoured. Further there is no justification for adopting the theory that there is a succession in the case of these sensations, and that they are not being felt simultaneously. No such thing is seen. One atomic mind cannot be competent to come into relationship with the sensations located in more places than one. Hence the only theory that remains is that, the mind is of the dimensions of the body it inhabits, like the light of lamp which is confined either to a jar or a palace. Contraction and expansion of the mind in the bodies of an ant and an elephant manifest themselves therein. The opposite theorists thus say that the form, *i.e.*, the dimensions of the mind are the same as those of the body.

The question arises that if it be so, how can it come into contact with the seed and the field? It does not certainly go out of the dead body without any support, to come into contact with the germ and sperm cells in the bodies of the parents, being dependent as it is for its actions upon others. The shadow of a pillar and such other things does not move if the things themselves do not move. Nor do the pictures disappear, when the picture cloth comes in. This being so, there would not be evolution of souls through births and deaths (Saṁsāra).

For this reason he says :—'For this reason the absence of interruption and for that reason Saṁsāra is proper.'

And further, if there were a measure for it like that of the body, then the leaving of the former body and the taking up of the other body would be secured for it, by taking in the interval another body which would serve for it as a vehicle for the intermediate space. It is of course along with this vehicle that it moves in the other body. So also says the Purāṇa :—'The Yama drew out of the body with force the Puruṣa of the size of the thumb.' This then is the meaning of the absence of interval (Antara). And for this reason evolution by repeated birth is proper.

Not agreeing with this view, the author states his own theory :—'It is the manifestation alone of the self-existing mind that contracts and expands.' The Ācarya (author) here is the Svayambhu.

The doubt here is that if the mind cannot move into another body without some vehicle to support it on its way, how is it that it enters the intermediate vehicle itself? If another body is posited for taht purpose also, then there would be no stopping anywhere. Nor is it possible that the mind should go out of the body along with the intermediary vehicle, because it is understood to take up the intermediary vehicle after it has left the previous body.

It that case let us posit a subtle body, existing permanently from the beginning of creation up to the Great Latency. It would then be that this subtle body would remain in the physical body, and it is along with this that the mind would enter the bodies appropriate to the different regions from the Satyaloka down to the Avici. It would further be proper to speak of this body as being drawn out, because that being permanent, the difficulty of providing for an interval would also disappear.

But then there is no authority for such a proposition, that a subtle body of this description exists. It is certainly no visible to the senses. Nor can it be inferred as a necessity of evolution by passing from one body to another, because that can be explained even on the theory of the author. As to the verbal authority cited, the texts speak of the being drawn out of the Puruṣa, not of the mind, nor of a subtle body, but of the self. The self, however, the power of consciousness is non-transferable from one place to another. This drawing out, therefore, is to be described as being spoken of in a metaphorical sense. And thus the drawing out of the mind or of consciousness means wherever it may be, the absence of manifestation. It does not mean anything else.

We allow that has been said in the Purāṇas, the Itihāsas and the Smṛtis about the mind coming after death possess the body of a Preta (departed spirit) and also the release from that Preta body by the performance of the ceremonies of Sapiṇḍīkaraṇa, etc. But we do not submit to that body being the intermediary vehicle. There is no authority in the Vedas for the existence of such an intermediary vehicle. What happens is that the mind takes up the body of a Preta, and is therein taken away by the men of Yama; not that this body serves as the intermediary vehicle. For this reason, the mind being of the nature of the principle of individuality, and that principle like Ākāśa in all the three worlds, the mental principle is all-pervading.

If this be so, then its functioning also must be all-pervading, and this would mean that the mind is omniscient. For this reason, has it been said, that the manifestation alone of this all-pervading principle is liable is liable to contract or expand.

Let us grant that, but then how is it that the contraction and expansion of the manifestation of the mind take place only now and then. For the reason be says :—'And the mind has need of virtue and vice.'

Divides the cause of the manifestation :—'And the cause is two-fold.'

By the, 'etc.,' in body, etc., the senses and wealth, etc., are meant.

'Faith, etc.' :—Here too energy, memory, etc., are to be understood.

Mentions the consensus of opinion of the Ācāryas, on the question of intermediation :—'As has been said.'

Vihāra means activity (Vyāpāra).

The 'highest virtue' means the white Karma.

'Of the two' :—Out of the internal and external.

Knowledge and desirelessness :—The Dharma born of these is understood here.

By what ? This means by what Dharma brought about by external means. It is knowledge and desirelessness alone that overpower these, *i.e.*, destroy their seed-power. This is the meaning.

He mentions in this case the well-known illustration.—'The Daṇḍaka forest empty.'—10.

Sūtra 11

हेतुफलाश्रयालम्बनैः संगृहीतत्वादेषामभावे तदभावः ।। ११ ।।

हेतु Hetu, cause. फल Phala, motive. आश्रय Āśraya, substratum. आलम्बन Ālambana, object by all these four. संगृहीतत्वात् Saṅgṛhītatvāt, being held together. एषाम् Eṣām, of these. अभावे Abhāve, on the disappearance. तद् Tad, of them. अभावः Abhāvaḥ, disappearance.

11. Being held together by Cause, Motive Substraum and Object they disappear on-the-disappearance of-these.—171.

हेतुफलाश्रयालम्बनेः संगृहीतत्वादेषामभावे तदभावः। हेतुर्धर्मात्सुखमधर्माद्दुःखम्। सुखाद्रागो दुःखाद् द्वेषस्ततश्च प्रयत्नस्तेन मनसा वाचा कायेन वा परिस्पन्दमानः परमनुगृह्णात्युपहन्ति वा ततः पुनर्धर्माधर्मौ सुखदुःखे रागद्वेषाविति। प्रवृत्तमिदं षडक्षरं संसारचक्रमस्य च प्रतिक्षणमावर्तमानस्याविद्या नेत्री मूलं सर्वक्लेशानामित्येष हेतुः। फलं तु यमाश्रित्य यस्य प्रत्युत्पन्नता धर्मादेः। नह्यपूर्वोपजनः। मनस्तु साधिकारमाश्रयो वासनानाम्। नह्यवसिताधिकारे मनसि निराश्रया वासनाः स्थातुमुत्सहन्ते। यदभिमुखीभूतं वस्तु यां वासनां

व्यनक्ति तस्यास्तदालम्बनम्। एवं हेतुफलाश्रयालम्बनैरेतैः संगृहीताः सर्वा वासनाः। एषामभावे तत्संश्रयाणामपि वासनानामभावः।। ११।।

Vyāsa

The cause :—By virtue comes pleasure, by vice pain. From pleasure comes attachment; from pain aversion. Thence comes effort. Thereby, acting by mind, body and speech, one either favours or injures others. Thence come again virtue and vice, pleasure and pain, attachment and aversion. Thus it is that revolves the six-spoked wheel of the world. And the driver of this wheel is Nescience, the root of the afflictions. This is the Cause.

Motive or Fruit is that with a view to which appropriate virtue, etc., is brought about. There is no non-sequential manifestation.

The Substratum is the mind which has yet a duty to perform. It is there that the residua live. They no longer care to live in a mind which has already performed its duty; their substratum is gone.

The Object (ālambana) of the residua is the substance which when placed in contact calls them forth.

Thus are all the residua held together by Cause, Fruit, Substratum and Object.

When these exist not, the residua which depend upon them for existence, disappear too.—171.

Vācaspati's Gloss

Now if these mental modifications and the residua are without beginning, how can they be destroyed? The power of consciousness which is eternal is not destroyed. For this reason he says :—'Being held together by Cause, Fruit, Substratum and Object, they disappear in the absence of these.'

It is observed that those that have no beginning are also destroyed. Take, for example, the case of futurity. The proposition, therefore, fails and is no proof. The power of consciousness is not destroyed, because there is cause which might cause its destruction, not because it has no beginning. And the aphorism too mentions the causes of the destruction of the residua although they are without a beginning. Kindness and injury too point to the causes of virtue and vice, etc. By this the use of spirituous liquors, etc., is also understood.

He mentions the reason thereof :—'The root of the afflictions, etc.'

'Is brought about' means that it is present. It does not mean that the substance virtue is produced.

Mentions reason thereof :—'There is no, etc.'

'With a view to which' means the substance which is in front, contact with the beloved, etc. The meaning of the aphorism is that, in the absence of the pervader the pervaded is absent.—11.

Sūtra 12

अतीतानागतं स्वरूपतोऽस्त्यध्वभेदाद्धर्माणाम्।। १२।।

अतीत Atīta, the past. अनागतं Anāgatam, the future. स्वरूपत: Svarūpataḥ, in reality. अस्ति Asti, exist. अध्व Adhva, of the paths of being. भेदात् Bhedāt, there being difference. धर्माणाम् Dharmāṇām, of the characteristics.

12. The past and the future exist in-reality, there being difference of the paths of being of the characteristics.—172.

नास्त्यसत: सम्भव:। न चास्ति सतो विनाश इति द्रव्यत्वेन सम्भवन्त्य: कथं निवर्तिष्यन्ते वासना इति। अतीतानागतं स्वरूपतोऽस्त्यध्वभेदाद्धर्माणाम्। भविष्यद्व्यक्तिकमनागतमनुभूतव्यक्तिकमतीतं स्वव्यापारोपारूढं वर्तमानं त्रयं चैतद्वस्तु ज्ञानस्य ज्ञेयम्। यदि चैतत्स्वरूपतो नाभविष्यन्नेदं निर्विषयं ज्ञानमुदपत्स्यत तस्मादतीतानागतं स्वरूपतोऽस्तीति। किंच भोगभागीयस्य वा पवर्गभागीयस्य वा कर्मण: फलमुत्पित्सु यदि निरूपाख्यमिति तदुद्देशेन तेन निमित्ते न कुशलानुष्ठानं न युज्येत। सतश्च फलस्य निमित्तं वर्तमानीकरणे समर्थं नापूर्वोपजनने सिद्धं निमित्तं नैमित्तिकस्य विशेषानुग्रहं कुरुते नापूर्वमुत्पादयतीति। धर्मी चानेकधर्मस्वभावतस्य चाध्वभेदेन धर्मा प्रत्यवस्थिता:। न च यथावर्तमानं व्यक्तिविशेषापन्नं द्रव्यतोऽस्त्येवमतीतमनागतं च। कथं तर्हि स्वेनैव व्यङ्ग्येन स्वरूपेणानागतमस्ति स्वेन चानुभूतव्यक्तिकेन स्वरूपेणातीतमिति। वर्तमानस्यैवाध्वन: स्वरूपव्यक्तिरिति। न सा भवत्यतीतानागतयोरध्वनोरेकस्य चाध्वन: समये द्वावध्वानौ धर्मिसमन्वागतौ भवत एवेति नाभूत्वा भावस्त्रयाणामध्वानामिति।। १२।।

Vyāsa

There is no existence for that which exists not, and no destruction for what exists. How then can residua which exist as substances be destroyed? 'The past and the present exist in reality, there being difference of the paths of being of the characteristics.'

The future is the manifestation which is to be. The past is the appearance which has been experienced. The present is that which is in active operation. It is this three-fold substance which is the object of knowledge. If they did not exist in reality, there would not exist the knowledge thereof. How could there be knowledge in the absence of anything that might be known. For this reason the past and the present exist in reality. Further, if the fruit of either the actions which cause experience, or those which cause absolute freedom were impossible of being defined for the aspirer, the actions of the wise with that aim and object would not be proper. And the means has the power of only bringing into the present state the actually existing though as yet un-manifested fruit, not of creating it anew. The means when in full manifestation specifically favours the sequential manifestion of its object; it does not create it anew.

Besides, the substratum exists as characterized by more characteristics than one; and its characteristics have a distinct order of existence in consequence of the distinctions of the paths of being.

It is not that the past and the future states of the object exist in substance in the same sense in which the specific appearance of the present exists. How then? The future exists as an appearance in itself to be manifested. The past exists by an appearance of its own which has been experienced. The present path of being alone is that which shows its own appearance as such. The same does not happen with reference to the past and the future paths of being. Of course at the time of one of these paths of being, the others remain conjoined with the substratum. Hence the existence of the three paths of being does not come out of non-existence.—172.

Vācaspati's Gloss

With the object of introducing the next aphorism the Commentator expresses a doubt :—'There is no existence for the non-existing, etc.'

There is no existence for the non-existent :—This may either be taken as a necessary sequence of the preceding, or, it may be taken as having been introduced anew as an illustration.

'The past and the future really exist, there being difference of the paths of being of the characteristics.'

The non-existent is not born and the existent is not destroyed. The meaning of the aphorism is that the change of the path of being of the existing characteristics alone means the rise and disappearance of the characteristics. The appearance which has been experienced, means the appearance which it has taken up already, or in other words, that of which there is no manifestation in the present. Thus the characteristic is existent in all three times.

He says this :—'If they did not exist in reality, etc.' The non-existent does not become the object of knowledge : it is therefore indefinable.

Knowledge is but the shining out of its object in consciousness. It cannot exist in the absence of the object. Whether it be the knowledge of the Yogī which has all the three times for its sphere of operation, or the knowledge of men like ourselves, it cannot be born in the absence of the object. But the knowledge is born. For this reason, the knowledge of him who feels that the past and the future ordinarily exist along with the present, is said to be a reason for the existence of the object itself.

Now he says that even on account of its being the aim (the object of action) the yet unmanifested exists :—'Further, the fruit of either the action which causes experience, etc.'

The wise are those who can distinguish. And even in the case of what is to be done, whatever may be the cause of whatever, becomes specialized in case of the existence of the object alone. As is the case with the farmer and the student of the Veda, so is the case here. They do not certainly create non-existing things. Similarly, the potter, etc., are the causes of the coming into present existence of the jar which already exists. He says this :—'And the means has only the power of bringing the future into present existence, etc.' If, however, the past and the future do not exist because they do not exist in the present, why then, the present also does not exist, because they do not exist in the present, why then, the present also does not exist, because it does not exist in the past and the future. The existence of all the three, however, is unqualified, on account of there being no specialization of the substratum, and the paths of being. With this object he says :—'Besides a substratum exists, etc.'

Have a distinct order of existence :—This means that each exists established in itself.

In reality : means the real object, the substratum.

If the past and the future did not exist as scuh in the past and the future, they would not exist even in the present, because then, they would be nothing in reality. For this reason he says :—'Of course at the time of these paths of being, etc.'

He summarizes the subject :—'Hence the existence of the three paths of being, etc.'—12.

Sūtra 13

ते व्यक्तसूक्ष्मा गुणात्मानः ।। १३ ।।

ते Te, they. व्यक्त Vyakta, manifested. सूक्ष्माः Sūkṣmāḥ, and subtle. गुणात्मानः Guṇa-Ātmānaḥ, and of the nature of the (आत्मन्) qualities (गुण).

13. They are manifested and subtle, and of the nature of the qualities.—173.

ते व्यक्तसूक्ष्मा गुणात्मानः। ते खल्वमी त्र्यध्वानो धर्मा वर्तमाना व्यक्तात्मानोऽतीतानागताः सूक्ष्मात्मानः षडविशेषरूपाः। सर्वमिदं गुणानां सन्निवेशविशेषमात्रमिति। परमार्थतो गुणात्मानस्तथा च शास्त्रानुशासनम्। गुणानां परमं रूपं न दृष्टिपथमृच्छति। यत्तु दृष्टिपथं प्राप्तं तन्मायेव सुतुच्छकमिति।। १३ ।।

Vyāsa

They, *i.e.*, these characteristics which are possessed of the three paths of being, are of the nature of the manifested, when they exist in the present, and are of the nature of the subtle when they passed into the past or are yet unmanifested. They are the six unspecialized appearance. All this is but the specific arrangement of the 'qualities.' In truth, therefore, they are of the nature of the 'qualities.' So teaches the Śāstra :—'The real appearance of the qualities does not come within the line of vision. That, however, which comes within the line, is but paltry delusion.'—173.

Vācaspati's Gloss

Let that be. This detail, however, of the differences of the world which puts forth the appearance of the changes of the characterized, the characteristic, the secondary quality and condition in many ways, is not capable of appearance from one Mūlaprakṛti. For this reason says :—They are manifested and subtle and of the nature of the 'qualities.' They, the characteristics possessed of the three paths of being, are both manifested and subtle, and they are of the nature of the qualities. There is nothing beyond the three qualities. The variety of manifestation is due to the variety which comes in sequence of the eternal miseries and their residual which they have given birth to.

As has been said in the Vāyu Purāṇa :—This change of the Pradhāna is wonderful on account of showing forth all appearances. It is the six unspecialized manifestations, which in such a way as it may be, constitute the past, the present and the future of the manifested Pṛthvī, etc., and of the eleven instruments of action, sensation and thought.

Now describes the eternal appearance of the universe, with the object of dividing the appearances thereof into the eternal and the non-eternal : All this is but the specific appearance of the 'qualities'. The meaning is that evolutionary changes which are visible consist of different arrangements and forms. On this subject is the teaching of the Śāstra possessed of sixty Tantras.

'Is but paltry delusion' :—This means that it is paltry as if it were delusion, not that it is delusion and nothing else. Paltry means destructible. As delusion changes even in a day, so also the modifications possessing the characteristics of manifestation and disappearance assume other appearances every second. The Prakṛti is possessed of the characteristic of eternity, and in this way is different from the Māyā, it is so far real.—13.

Sūtra 14

परिणामैकत्वाद्वस्तुतत्त्वम् ।। १४।।

परिणाम Pariṇāma, of modification. एकत्वात् Ekatvāt, on account of the unity. वस्तु Vastu, of the object. तत्त्वम् Tattvam, the reality.

14. The reality of the object on account of the unity of modification.—174.

यदा तु सर्वे गुणाः कथमेकः शब्द एकमिन्द्रियमिति । परिणामैकत्वाद्वस्तुतत्त्वम् । प्रख्याक्रियास्थितिशीलानां गुणानां ग्रहणात्मकानां करणभावेनैकः परिणामः । श्रोत्रमिन्द्रियं ग्राह्यात्मकानां शब्दतन्मात्रभावेनैकः परिणामः शब्दो विषय इति । शब्दादीनां मूर्तिसमानजातीयानामेकः परिणामः पृथिवीपरमाणुस्तन्मात्रावयवस्तेषां चैकः परिणामः पृथिवी गौवृक्षः पर्वत इत्येवमादिर्भूतान्तरेष्वपि स्नेहौष्ण्यप्रणामित्वावकाशदानान्युपादाय सामान्यमेकविकारारम्भः समाधेयः । नास्त्यर्थो विज्ञानविसहचरः । अस्ति तु ज्ञानमर्थविसहचरं स्वप्नादौ कल्पितमित्यनया दिशा ये वस्तुस्वरूपमपह्नुवते ज्ञानपरिकल्पनामात्रं वस्तु । स्वप्नविषयोपमं तु न परमार्थतोऽस्तीति ये आहुस्ते तथेति । प्रत्युपस्थितमिदं स्वमाहात्म्येन वस्तु कथमप्रमाणात्मकेन विकल्पज्ञानबलेन वस्तुस्वरूपमुत्सृज्य तदेवापलपन्तः श्रद्धेयवचनाः स्युः ।। १४।।

Vyāsa

When all are 'qualities', how is it that one modification is sound and the other the sense? 'The reality of the object on account of unity of modification.' One modification of the qualities possessed of the nature of illumination, activity and inertia, and being of the nature of an instrument, appears in the shape of organs. This is the sense of hearing. Another modification of the 'qualities' appears in the objective state as the soniferous ultimate atom (Śabda Tanmātra). This is the object sound.

The atom of Pṛthvī is a modification of sound, etc., existing along with the generic quality of form (mūrti). It is a portion of the tanmātra. Single modifications of these atoms are the earth, the cow, the tree, the hill and so forth. In the case of other elements also, taking up the generic qualities of smoothness, temperature, impulsion and space, single modifications are to be understood by meditation.

There is no object not co-existent with ideas. There are, however, ideas, which are not co-existent with objects, such as those that are fancied in dreams.

There are people who try to do away with the reality of objects by this reasoning, saying that objects are but the fabrications of the mind, like the fancies of a dream, and that they are nothing real. The objective world is present by its own power. How is it that they give up the objective world on the strength of imaginative cognition, and even then go on talking nonsense about it? How is it possible to have faith in them?—174.

Vācaspati's Gloss

Well there may be this sort of variety of modification of the three qualities. But how is a single modification brought about in the shape of any one element, say the Pṛthvī or the Apas. This unity is contradicted by its nature. With this doubt the author introduces he aphorism :—'The reality of the object on account of the unity of modification.' A single modification of more than one is also observed. That as follows :—The cow, the horse, the buffalo, the elephant, all of them modify into a single substance, the salt, when they are thrown into a mine of salt. Wick, oil and fire change into a lamp. In this way, although the qualities are more than one, a single modification does take place. For this reason, the Tanmātra, the elements and the objects made of the elements have each a real unity.

In the case of instrumental appearances, being as they are the effects of the principle of individuality, and possessed as they are of the nature of illumination on account of the preponderance of the quality of essentiality (Sattva), the modification is a single one in the shape of an organ, such as the organ of hearing. Of the same qualities, another single modification in the shape of Tanmātra is sound, the object, when they appear as objective phenomena, in the shape of non-intelligent appearances with the quality of Tamas preponderating.

Sound, the object :—Sound here means the soniferous ether (tanmātra). The word 'object' (viṣaya) signifies non-intelligence, because the tanmātra cannot possibly become the object of sensation. The rest is easy.

Now brings in the Vaiśeṣika with his idealistic theory :—'There is no object which is not co-existent with an idea.'

If the elements and physical objects be something different from mere ideation, then it may be that such a Prakṛti be put up as the cause of their production. They are not, however, different from ideas in reality. How is it then that the Pradhāna is put up as a cause? How is it again that the instrumental appearances are fancied to exist as the modifications of the principle of individuality? Thus seeing that a non-intelligent object is not self-illuminative, it does not exist unless it co-exist with the idea. Co-existence means relation. The denial of co-existence means its absence. The meaning is that without coming into relationship with the idea it is of no use in practice. The idea, however, exists without being co-existent with the object, because it is self-illuminative. It can exist as its own field of knowledge. It does not stand in need of a non-intelligent object in practice. These are the two rules that are brought to notice by idealistic philosophers as going along with knowability. They are applied thus :—That which is known by any act of knowledge, does not differ therefrom, in the same way as knowledge does not differ from the self. And the elements and the physical phenomena thereof are known by an act of knowledge. This leads to a knowledge of the pervaded which contradicts it. Knowability as it is seen, is pervaded by similarity, which contradicts the difference to be denied, bringing into consciousness the similarity which pervades itself, it does away with the difference which contradicts it. Thus :—That which is perceived with something else always invariably, does not differ from it. Just as one moon does not differ from another moon. And an object is invariably perceived together with the idea. This knowledge is perceived as being contradictory of the pervader. It contradicts the rule of the pervader consisting of the difference to be denied. This rule does away with arbitrariness, and brings into consciousness the difference which consists in the pervaded.

Let it be. If the object is not different from the idea, how is it that it looks as if it were different. For this reason he says :—'Fancied etc.' As say the Vaināṣikas :—There is no difference on account of the rule of coincident perception. The difference between the yellow and the blue, etc., and their ideas, is brought about by delusive cognitions.

Explains the nature of the fancy :—'An object is merely an ideation,' etc. Refutes :—'How is it possible, etc.' This is connected with the words 'have faith in them.'

'Is present as contradictory knowledge' :—How is it present? 'In the way, etc.' In whatever way it shines as being the meaning of the word 'this,' in the same way it is present by its own power.

Now he shows that the object is the cause of the idea :—'Inasmuch as the object has given birth to the idea thereof by the power of its own perceptibility, it is not for this reason the perceiver of the object. Such a real object cannot be done away with by the unauthoritative force of imaginative cognitions. Inasmuch as imagination is unauthoriatative, its power also is unauthoritative, because the power is of the same nature with it.

'The giving up of the objective world thereby' means ignoring it as if it were removed from sight.

In some places the reading is 'Upagṛhyate' in place of 'Utsṛjyate.' The meaning is the same in either case. They ignore the existence of the outside world, and yet go on talking about it. How can there be faith in them? The meaning here is this. The causes which have been mentioned, *i.e.*, invariable coincident perception and knowability, are not final, because application to the cannon of difference is doubtful. Further the externality and the grossness which are perceived to exist in the elements and the physical phenomenal thereof, which possess the forms of the ideas, are not possible of existence in the case of ideas themselves. Because externality means being related to separate space. Grossness means the pervading of more portions of space than one. It is not possible that one idea may exist in more places than one, and also exist in a place separated from itself. When a certain thing exists in a certain place, there cannot exist in the same place, something else characterized by a quality opposite to the characteristic of being present in the same place. If it were possible the three worlds themselves would become but one.

It may be said, let then there be difference of ideas. It this be so, whence does this consciousness of grossness come in the case of notions, whose sphere of operations is very subtle, and which do not know of the existence and operation of each other, and which are only in relation to their own sphere of operation only. There should be no high talk about its being the sphere of imagination only, because there is in that case no contact and because the reflection is very clear. Further the gross has never been made the object of thought, so that the idea qualified thereby may be clearly perceived, even though at the back of it there may exist imaginative cognition. Further imagination is not confined to the knowledge of the thing itself as it exists in its own sphere, in the same way as knowledge free from the taint of imagination is. Further as imagination is not gross, it is not proper that it should be acting in the sphere of the gross. Therefore it is not possible that in the external cause there should be perceived grossness and externality, and hence it should be considered to be false. And the false is not inseparable from the idea, because if it were, the idea itself would become contemptible like the false, on account of its not comprehending everything. Further knowability being not pervaded by identity, how can it be the opposite of difference (bheda). As to the rule of coincidence of perception of the idea and of grossness, it is capable of explanation like that of the Sat and the Asat (the existent and the non-existent) either by their nature or by obstruction from some cause, even though both of them exist independently. Hence these two arguments are not complete, and are therefore merely false similitudes of arguments, and they merely give rise to an imaginary conception of the non-existence of the external. Further the power of perception cannot be done away with by mere imagination. It is therefore well said, 'How do they give up the objective world on the strength of imaginative cognitions?'

By this also stands refuted the assertion that notions may be generated without there being any actual basis for them, as in the case of dream cognitions.

The imaginative creation of the thing to be known, has been refuted by establishing the existence of the substratum, the whole as being independent of the parts. Details will be found in the Nyāya-Kanika. More details need not be entered into here.—14.

Sūtra 15

वस्तुसाम्ये चित्तभेदात्तयोर्विभक्तः पन्थाः ।। १५ ।।

वस्तु Vastu, in the case of the external object. साम्ये Sāmye, in the being the same. चित्त Citta, of mentality. भेदात् Bhedāt, there being difference. तयो: Tayoḥ, their. विभक्तः Vibhaktaḥ, different. पन्था: Panthāḥ, ways of being.

15. There being difference of mentality in the case of the external-object being the same, their ways-of-being are different.—175.

कुतश्चैतदन्याय्यम्। वस्तुसाम्ये चित्तभेदात्तयोर्विभक्त पन्थाः। बहुचित्तालम्बनीभूतमेकं वस्तु साधारणं तत्खलु नैकचित्तपरिकल्पितं नाप्यनेकचित्तपरिकल्पितं किंतु स्वप्रतिष्ठम्। कथं वस्तुसाम्ये चित्तभेदाद्धर्मापेक्षं चित्तस्य वस्तुसाम्येऽपि सुखज्ञानं भवत्यधर्मापेक्षं तत एव दुःखज्ञानमविद्यापेक्षं तत एव मूढज्ञानं सम्यग्दर्शनापेक्षं तत एव माध्यस्थ्यज्ञानमिति। कस्य तच्चित्तेन परिकल्पितम्। न चान्यकल्पितेन चित्तेनार्थेनान्यस्य चित्तोपरागो युक्तस्तस्माद्वस्तुज्ञानयोर्ग्राह्यग्रहणभेदभिन्नयोर्विभक्तः पन्थाः। नानयोः सङ्करगन्धोऽप्यस्तीति। साङ्ख्यपक्षे वस्तु पुनस्त्रिगुणं चलं च गुणवृत्तमिति। धर्मादिनिमित्तापेक्षं चित्तैरभिसम्बध्यते निमित्तानुरूपस्य च प्रत्ययस्योत्पद्यमानस्य तेन तेनात्मना हेतुर्भवति। केचिदाहुः। ज्ञानसहभूरेवार्थो भोग्यत्वात्सुखादिवदिति। त एतया द्वारा साधारणत्वं बाधमानाः पूर्वोत्तरक्षणेषु वस्तुस्वरूपमेवापह्नवते।। १५ ।।

Vyāsa

And how otherwise is it untrue? 'There being difference of mentality in the case of the external object being the same, their ways of being are different.'

One thing coming within the sphere of many minds is common to them all. It has certainly not been imagined by one mind. Not yet has it been imagined by more minds than one. It is established in itself. How is this? There being difference of mentality when the external object is the same. Even though the external object be the same the mind feels pleasure on account of virtue. The same object excites a feeling of pain on account of vice. The same causes forgetfulness on account of Nescience. The same causes the feeling of indifference on account of right knowledge. Now by whose mind has all that been imagined? Further it is not proper that another mind be coloured by an object which has been imagined by another. For this reason the lines of existence of the external objects and the ideas are different, as they exist as objective and instrumental appearances. There is not even the least suspicion of confusion between them.

Further in the Sāṅkhya philosohy, an object is made of the three qualities, and the functioning of the qualities is ever changeful. The object comes into relationship with the minds on account of the exciting causes of virtue, etc.; and it becomes the cause of the notions as they are produced, each as such, in accordance with the exciting causes.

Some say that the object is co-existent with the idea, inasmuch as it is to be enjoyed thereby like the feelings of pleasure and pain. They do away by means of this conception, the common nature of the object with reference to minds, and this but do away with the being of the object in previous and subsequent moments.—175.

Vācaspati's Gloss

Having now mentioned the reasons for believing that the object is different from and independent of the idea, the Commentator now indtroduces another reason given in the aphorism to establish the same :—And how otherwise is it untrue?

'There being difference of mentality, even though the external object remains the same, their paths of existence are different.' When a certain thing remains the same although the other changes into many states, they both differ from each other altogether. As the one idea of Caitra differs from the different ideas of Devadatta, Viṣṇumitra and Maitra, and although the ideas are different the object remains the same, the object must be different from the idea. And the identity of the object even in the case of the difference of ideas, is ascertained by the knowers by comparison of notes. If one woman is beloved, hated, ignored and approached with indifference by many different people, they can always compare notes that the object of all these varying feelings is the same. For this reason, there being difference of mentality, *i.e.*, of feeling, the paths of being of the two, *i.e.*, of the object and the idea, are different. The path of being means that by which one thing differs from another in nature. The lover feels pleasure in the society of the beloved. The co-wife feels pain. Caitra who has not been able to possess her, feels disappointed and forgets himself.

Let it be so. But wherever an object in the shape of a beautiful woman has been fancied by the mind of one man, the minds of others also admit of being coloured by the same fancied object, and it is for this reason that the object even though fancied, becomes the common object of all the minds.

For this reason says :—'It is not proper that the object fancied by one mind, etc.' If that were so, then in case one of them possessed the knowledge of blue, all would come to possess the knowledge of the blue.

The question arises that inasmuch as there is but one object in the opinion of those, who believe in the independent existence of objects, how is it that one object becomes the cause of different feelings of pleasure and pain, etc. It is not proper that the cause remaining the same same, the effects should be different. For this reason says :—'In the case of the Sāṅkhya philosophy, etc.' Even a single external object changing according to the three qualities, admits of three-fold appearance. But in this way too, all without distinction would have the three-fold knowledge of pleasure, pain and forgetfulness with reference to the same object. For this reason says :—'Depends upon the operative causes of virtue, etc.' The Sattva together with the Rajas gives birth to the feeling of pleasure which depends upon virtue. The same Sattva when free of the Rajas, creates the feeling of indifference which depends upon knowledge. And these virtues, etc., do not exist, all of them, in all the Puruṣas everywhere. It is only any one of them that exist anywhere at any time. Therefore the difference is proper.

Some talkers say on this subject :—'The object certainly co-exists with the idea, because it is enjoyable by the Puruṣa like pleasure and pain. The meaning is this. Let an object be different from the idea. Still it being non-intelligent, does not admit of being known without the idea. The idea it is that illuminates it. Similarly it exists at the time of being known only. It cannot be said to be existing at any other time, because there is no authority for its existence at a time when it is not the object of immediate knowledge.

This the Commentator refutes without the help of the aphorism :—'They by this, etc., An object is certainly common to all minds. It keeps on being cognized for a succession of more moments than one as possessed of the characteristic of change. If that co-exists with the idea, it will be thus, it is such. Now what check is there upon the portion 'It,' that this may not disappear too ?—15.

Sūtra 16

ने चैकचित्ततन्त्रं चेद्वस्तु तत्प्रमाणकं तदा किं स्यात्।। १६।।

न Na, not. च Ca, and. एक-चित्त Eka-citta, on one mind. तन्त्रम् Tantram, depedent. चेद् Ced, if. वस्तु Vastu, an object. तत् Tat, by that. प्रमाणकम् Pramāṇakam, to be cognized by that. तदा Tadā, then. किम् Kim, what (only to denote the question). स्यात् Syāt, would it exist.

16. And if an object dependent upon one mind were not cognized by that, would it then exist?—176.

न चैकचित्ततन्त्रं चेद्वस्तु तत्प्रमाणकं तदा किं स्यात्। एकच्चित्ततन्त्रं चेद्वस्तु स्यात्तदा चित्ते व्यग्रे निरुद्धे वा स्वरूपमेव तेनापरामृष्टमन्यस्याविषयीभूतमप्रमाणकमगृहीतस्य भावकं केनचित्तदानीं किं न स्यात्। सम्बध्यमानं वा पुनश्चित्तेन कुत उत्पद्येत ये चास्यानुपस्थिता भागास्ते चास्य न स्युरेवं नास्ति पृष्ठमित्युदरमपि न गृह्येत तस्मात्स्वतन्त्रोऽर्थः सर्वपुरुषसाधारणः स्वतन्त्राणि च चित्तानि प्रतिपुरुषः प्रवर्तन्ते तयोः सम्बन्धादुपलब्धिः पुरुषस्य भोग इति।। १६।।

Vyāsa

If an object were dependent upon the mind, then in case the mind were restrained, or attending to some other object, the object would not be touched thereby, nor would it come into objective relationship with any other mind. It would not be cognized, *i.e.*, its nature would not be taken in, by any mind. Will it cease to exist at the time? Or, coming into relationship again with the mind, whence would it come back to life?

Further the parts of an object which are not in contact with the mind, would not exist. Thus there would be no back, and how could then there be the front itself? For this reason, the object is self-dependent, and common to all the Puruṣas. Minds also are self-dependent. They come into relationship with the Puruṣas. By their relationship is secured perception, which is enjoyment (bhoga).—176.

Vācaspati's Gloss

Or, there may not be this disappearance of a portion; let the object be co-existent with the idea. On this also says :—'And if an object dependent upon one mind were not cognized by that, would it then exist? If the mind which cognizes a jar, does not at any time turn towards it on account of attention being directed towards a cloth, or if an object having been the object of discrimination the mind thereby becomes restrained, then the idea of the jar and the knowledge of discrimination would not be in existence at the time, and the jar and the knowledge being dependent for their existence upon the co-existence of the idea thereof in the mind, would no doubt cease to exist. Says this :—'One mind, etc.'

'Would it then exist? :'—Means it would not exist.

Further coming into relationship with the mind, how would the jar or the discrimination be born again. Effects have constant causes and lead to them invariably by both the canons of agreement and difference. Effects cannot be born from causes other than their own appropriate causes. In the absence of the cause there would be no occasion for their existence. For, is it proper that an object being the cause of the knowledge thereof, it should also be the cause of itself? If this were so, then the sweets which one might be expecting to get, and the sweets which one might be really using, would be equally placed with reference to taste, strength and digestion. It has therefore been well said :—'If it come into relationship with the mind, etc.'

Further the front portion of any object is always pervaded by the middle and posterior parts, *i.e.*, it cannot exist without the simultaneous existence of the middle and posterior parts. If the existence of an object depended upon being perceived, then the middle and posterior parts would not exist, and thus on account of the cessation of pervasion the front part also would cease to exist. The object itself would not thus be in existence, how then would it in existence along with the idea itself? Says this :—'The portions thereof which are in contact, etc.' Not in contact means not known. Concludes :—'For this reason, etc.' The rest is easy.—16.

Sūtra 17

तदुपरागापेक्षित्वाच्चित्तस्य वस्तु ज्ञाताज्ञातम्।। १७।।

तद् Tad, thereby. उपराग Uparāga, colouring. अपेक्षित्वात् Apekṣitvāt, because of the needing. चित्तस्य Cittasya, for the mind, by the mind. वस्तु Vastu, an object. ज्ञात Jñāta, known. अज्ञातम् Ajñātam, or unknown.

17. The mind needing to be coloured thereby an object may be known or unknown.—177.

तदुपरागापेक्षित्वाच्चित्तस्य वस्तु ज्ञाताज्ञातम्। अयस्कान्तमणिकल्पा विषयाः। अयः सधर्मकं चित्तमभिसम्बन्ध्योपरञ्जयन्ति येन च विषयेणोपरक्तं चित्तं स विषयो ज्ञातस्ततोऽन्यः पुरुषोऽज्ञातः। वस्तुनो ज्ञाताज्ञातस्वरूपत्वात्परिणामि चित्तम्।। १७।।

Vyāsa

'The mind standing in need of being coloured thereby, an object may be known or unknown.' Objects are in nature similar to that of loadstone; the mind is similar in characteristic to iron. Objects coming into contact with the mind colour it. Whatever object colours the mind, that object becomes known. That which becomes known is an object. That which is not thus known is the Puruṣa and is unknown. The mind is changeful, because it assumes the natures of known and unknown objects.—77.

Vācaspati's Gloss

Let that be, If the object were self-dependent and also unintelligent, it would never be illuminated. If now it were to become illuminated, its non-intelligence too would disappear. No existence can remain as such when it gives up its nature. Nor is it proper that the nature of an unintelligent object should receive the illumination of its characteristic by being the receptacle of the action of the senses. Because if it became the characteristic of the object then it would, like the qualities of blueness, etc., be the common attribute of all the Puruṣas. This being so, if one man became learned, all would become learned. No one would remain ignorant. Nor is it proper that the present should be characteristic of the past and the yet unmanifested. Hence to say that an object is self-dependent and that it is the sphere for the act of perception is but a wish of the mind. For this reason says :—'The mind needing to be coloured by contact therewith, an object may be known or unknown. Even though an object is by nature non-intelligent, it colours the mind by coming into contact therewith through the passage of the senses, because such is the mirror of the mind, the power of consciousness being reflected into it, enlivens the mind with the colour of the object therein, and thus knows it. It does not however produce any sort of clearness, etc., in the object. Nor is it that the power of consciousness is unrelated to the mind, because it has been said that its reflection passes into it. Although the mind being all-pervading, and the senses being of the nature of the principle of individuality, cannot come into relationship with the object, still the relationship of the object is with the mind which function in the body. It is for this reason that they have been said to be of the nature of the loadstone, and that the mind possesses a characteristic similar to iron and that they colour it by having come into contact with it through the passage of the senses. Says that it is for this reason that the mind is changeful : 'On account of the object being known, etc.'—17.

Sūtra 18

सदा ज्ञाताश्चित्तवृत्तयस्तत्प्रभोः पुरुषस्यापरिणामात्।। १८।।

सदा Sadā, always. ज्ञाताः Jñātāḥ, are known. चित्तवृत्तयः Citta-vṛttayaḥ, the modifications of the mind. तत्-प्रभोः Tat-prabhoḥ, to its lord. पुरुषस्य Puruṣasya, the Puruṣa, अपरिणामात् Apariṇāmāt, on account of the unchangeability.

18. To its lord, the Puruṣa, the modifications of the mind are always known on-account-of-unchangeability.—178.

यस्य तु तदेव चित्तं विषयस्तस्य सदा ज्ञाताश्चित्तवृत्तिस्तत्प्रभोः पुरुषस्यापरिणामित्वात्। यदि चित्तवत्प्रभुरपि पुरुषः परिणामेत्ततस्तद्विषयाश्चित्तवृत्तयः शब्दादिविषयवज्ज्ञाताज्ञाताः स्युः सदा ज्ञातृत्वं तु मनसस्तत्प्रभोः पुरुषस्यापरिणामित्वमनुमापयति।। १८।।

Vyāsa

To its lord, the Puruṣa, whose sphere of functioning the mind itself is, mental modifications are ever known, because he is unchangeable. If the lord, Puruṣa, too changes like the mind, the mental modifications too in which it functions would be both known and unknown, like the objects of sound, etc. The mind however is always known to its lord the Puruṣa. By this is inferred its unchangeability.—178.

Vācaspati's Gloss

Having thus established the mind and the object to be separate from each other, the author now reads the aphorism, filling up the omissions, with the object of showing that the self is different from these changeful objects and that the characteristic of the Puruṣa is unchangeability, which is the opposite of the characteristic of the objects and the mind. 'To the lord, Puruṣa, whose sphere of functioning the mind itself is, etc.' The modifications of the mind are always known to the Puruṣa, because he is unchangeable. The mind with its modifications is always followed by the Puruṣa in all its modifications of the wandering, the distracted, the one-pointed, up to the state of inhibition. By what reason then is the Puruṣa, unchangeable? 'If the Puruṣa were unchangeable, it would both be known and unknown like the mind (citta). It is however always known. It is therefore unchangeable and for this reason differs from other changeable objects. Says this :—'If the lord Puruṣa changed, etc.' The lord who is the enjoyer of the mind knows it constantly along with its modifications. This fact establishes by inference the unchangeability of the Puruṣa. Thus the meaning is that this unchangeable Puruṣa is different from the changing mind.—18.

Sūtra 19

न तत्स्वाभासं दृश्यत्वात्।। १९।।

न Na, is not. तत् Tat, it. स्वाभासम् Svābhāsam, self-illuminating. दृश्यत्वात् Dṛśyatvāt, because of its knowability; because it is the knowable.

19. It is not self-illuminating, being the knowable.—179.

स्यादाशङ्का चित्तमेव स्वाभासं विषयाभासं च वैनाशिकाणां चित्तात्मवादिनां च भविष्यतीत्यग्निवत्। न तत्स्वाभासं दृश्यत्वात्। यथेतराणीन्द्रियाणि शब्दादयश्च दृश्यत्वान्न स्वाभासानि तथा मनोऽपि प्रत्येतव्यम्। न चाग्निरत्र दृष्टान्तः। न ह्यग्निरात्मस्वरूपमप्रकाशं प्रकाशयति। प्रकाशश्चायं प्रकाश्यप्रकाशकसंयोगे दृष्टो न च स्वरूपमात्रेऽस्ति संयोगः। किंच स्वाभासं चित्तमित्यग्राह्यमेव कस्यचिदितिशब्दार्थः। तद्यथा स्वात्मप्रतिष्ठमाकाशमित्यप्रतिष्ठमेवेत्यर्थः। स्वबुद्धिप्रचारप्रतिसंवेदनात्सत्त्वानां प्रवृत्तिर्दृश्यते। क्रुद्धोहं भीतोऽहममुत्र मे रागोऽमुत्र मे क्रोध इत्येतत्स्वबुद्धेरग्रहणेन युक्तमिति।। १९।।

Vyāsa

A doubt may arise that the mind itself may be-illuminating as well as the illuminator of the objects, as in fact it is believed by the Vaināśikas to be like fire, which illuminates itself as well as other objects. Therefore says :—'It is not self-illuminating being the knowable.' As the other organs and the object of sound, etc., are not self-illuminative on account of their being knowable, so also should the mind be understood to be. Fire is no analogy here. Fire does not illuminate any form of itself which might have been non-luminous before.' The illumination spoken of here is meant to be the illumination which is brought about by the contact of the luminous and the dark, not of the self-luminous. There can be no contact of anything with its own nature. Further, the statement that the mind is self-illuminating means that it is not perceivable by any other entity. This is in the same way as when it is said that the Ākāśa is self-supporting, it is meant that it has no support at all. Living beings are seen acting in accordance with the consciousness of the movements of their Will-to-be. 'I am angry,' 'I am afraid,' 'I am attached here,' 'I am repelled there,' these notions are proper only on account of the knowledge of self-identification not being taken in.—179.

Vācaspati's Gloss

Mentions the Vaināśikas :—'A doubt may arise, etc.' This is the meaning. It may be so if the mind be the sphere for the functioning of the Self. The mind however is self-illuminative and it illuminates other objects also as it illuminates itself. How then can it be the sphere for the constant knowledge of the Puruṣa ? How moreover does it in its unchangeability differ from the changeable mind. Therefore, 'It is not self-illuminating, being knowable.' It might be so if the mind were self-illuminating, (self-knowing), but it is not. Being changeable, the mind is pervaded by perceptibility, like the colours of blue, etc. Whatever is pervaded by perceptibility, is not capable of becoming self-illuminative, because the modification contradicts itself. The act and the object cannot both be the same. The cooking is not cooked : the cutting is not cut. The Puruṣa, however, being unchangeable as he is, is not the object of the act of consciousness. In him therefore self-illumination is not improper. His illuminativeness does not depend upon any other, he is self-illuminative and is not the object of the act of consciousness. Hence the mind is the object of the act of knowing on account of its being the knowable; it is not self-illuminative. The meaning is that because the mind is seized of the reflection of the self the object of its modifications are illuminated.

But the fire is both the knowable and the self-illuminous as a jar, etc., are brought to light by fire not so fire is brought to light by another fire. For this reason says :—Fire is no analogy here. Why not? 'The fire does not illuminate, etc.' The meaning is that fire may not be brought to light by other fire, but it is illuminated by consciousness. It is thus not illuminated by itself, and for this reason there is no over-lapping (Vyabhicāra). 'The illuminated spoken of here, etc.' The words 'spoken of here' differentiate from the illumination which is of the nature of the Puruṣa, the illumination, that is to say, which is of the form of the action. This is intended to be said : Whatever action there may be, it is seen in relation to the subject, the instrument and the object. As cooking is seen in relation to Caitra, fire and rice, so also illumination. Illumination also is action. This also must therefore be like that. Relation lives in different objects; it is not possible in the absence of distinction. Further the assertion that the mind is self-illuminating, means that the mind is not perceivable by any other entity.

Let that be. Let the mind be no perceivable by any other entity. The mind would not cease to be if the act of knowing, which is neither its cause, nor its pervade, ceased to be. For this reason he says : 'By the consciousness of the movements of his own Will-to-be.' The Will-to-be is the mind. Its movements are its functioning. Living beings are creatures. The various mental modifications of anger, greed, etc., are felt by each mind for itself, together with their substratum the mind, and also together with their objects. They in this way establish the objectivity of the mind. Renders the consciousness of the movements of the Will-to-be plainer :—'I am angry, etc.'—19.

Sūtra 20

एकसमये चोभयानवधारणम्।। २०।।

एकसमये Eka-samaye, at the same time. **च** Ca, and. **उभय** Ubhaye, of both. **अनवधारणम्** Anavadhāraṇam, impossibility of being cognised.

20. Nor can both be cognized at the same time.—180.

एकसमये चोभयानवधारणम्। न चैकस्मिन्क्षणे स्वपररूपावधारणं युक्तं क्षणिकवादिनो यद्भवनं सैव क्रिया तदेव च कारकमित्यभ्युपगमः।। २०।।

Vyāsa

And it is not proper that in one moment both one's own nature and the nature of other objects may be ascertained. The conception of the advocates of momentary existence however is that acting is the same as being; and the subject, object, instrument, etc., are the same too.—180.

Vācaspati's Gloss

'And both cannot be cognized at the same time.' To him who says that the mind is both self-illuminating and the illuminator of objects, it cannot of course be possible that the object may be understood at the same time as the self of the mind, and by the same act. An act which is not different from any other is not competent to bring about an effect which is not different. Therefore a difference of function must be recognized. And to the Vaināśikas there is no separation of operation for difference of effects. And it is not possible that there should be a difference of effects brought about by a single birth which is common to all and does not differ from itself. For this reason the knowledge of the object and the act of knowledge cannot be ascertained in one moment of time. This is what the Commentary renders clear :—'And in one moment of time, etc.' And so the Vaināśikas say :—Whatever is the being of a thing the same is their action and the same the subject object. 'Instrument, etc.' Hence the knowability of the mind is for ever; and this removes the idea of its being self-illuminating. This also shows that the seer is unchangeable. Thus all is proved.—20.

Sūtra 21

चित्तान्तरदृश्ये बुद्धिबुद्धेरतिप्रसङ्गः स्मृतिसङ्करश्च।। २१ ।।

चित्तान्तरदृश्ये Cittāntara-dṛśye, in case of being knowable by another mind. बुद्धि-बुद्धेः Buddhi-Buddheḥ, of the wills to know, the wills to know. अतिप्रसङ्गः Atiprasaṅgaḥ, too many, abundance, superfluity. स्मृति-सङ्करः Smṛti-Saṅkaraḥ, confusion of memories. च Ca, and.

21. In case of being knowable by another mind, there will be too many wills-to-know the Wills-to-know; and there will be confusion of memories.—181.

स्यान्मतिः स्वरसनिरुद्धं चित्तं चित्तान्तरेण समनन्तरेण गृह्यत इति। चित्तान्तरे दृश्ये बुद्धिबुद्धेरतिप्रसङ्गः स्मृतिसङ्करश्च। अथ चित्तं चेच्चित्तान्तरेण गृह्येत बुद्धि बुद्धिः केन गृह्यते साप्यन्यया साप्यन्ययेत्यतिप्रसङ्गः स्मृतिसङ्करश्च। यावन्तो बुद्धिबुद्धिनामनुभावास्सावत्यः स्मृतयः प्राप्नुवन्ति तत्सङ्कराच्चैकस्मृत्यनवधारणं च स्यादित्येवं बुद्धिप्रतिसंवेदिनं पुरुषमपलपद्भिर्वैनाशिकैः सर्वमेवाकुलीकृतं ते तु भोक्तृस्वरूपं यत्र क्वचन कल्पयन्तो न न्यायेन सङ्गच्छन्ते। केचितु सत्त्वमात्रमपि परिकल्प्यास्ति ससत्त्वो य एतान्पञ्चस्कन्धान्निक्षिप्यान्यांश्च प्रतिसन्दधातीत्युक्त्वा तत एव पुनस्तप्यति तथा स्कन्धानां महन्निर्वेदाय विरागायानुत्पादाय प्रशान्तये गुरोरन्तिके ब्रह्मचर्यं चरिष्यामीत्युक्त्वा सत्त्वस्य पुनः सत्त्वमेवापह्नुवते। साङ्ख्ययोगादयस्तु प्रवादाः स्वशब्देन पुरुषमेव स्वामिनं चित्तस्य भोक्तारमुपयन्तीति।। २१ ।।

Vyāsa

There may be an opinion that the mind restrained in its own being may be known by another mind just in contact with it. 'In case of being known by another mind there will be too many wills-to-know the Wills-to-know; and there will be confusion of memories.' If the mind be cognized by another mind, by what may the wills-to-know the Wills-to-know be cognized. Even that by another; and that again by another. There will thus be too many of such Wills-to-know. And there will be confusion of memories. As many will be the cognitions of the various Will-to-be, so many will be the memories. One memory will not be capable of determination on account of their confusion. Thus the Vaināśikas have confused everything by denying the existence of the Puruṣa who knows by reflex action the Will-to-know. Further, they are not logical in imagining as they do, the existence of the Puruṣa in some places. Some there are who say that there does exist a pure being, and that that being throw away the existing five Skandhas and takes up others. Having asserted so much they fight shy again of the same.

Further they say that for the purpose of entirely doing away with the Skandhas, and for securing desirelessness, non-production and calmness, they would go to a teacher and with him live the life of a student. And having said this they begin again to conceal the very existence of that being.

As to the Sāṅkhyayoga theories, they declare by the word SVA (on one's own) applied to the mind that there does exist the lord in the shape of the enjoyer of the mind.—181.

Vācaspati's Gloss

Introduces the Vaināśikas again :—There may be a theory that although the mind may not know itself by its own life, on account of its being objective by nature, yet even that fact does not prove the existence of the self-restrained moment of the mind which generates the next may well be taken in by the last mental moment of its own succession. This is the meaning. 'Another mind just in contact therewith. This other mind is equal in knowledge, and between the two there is nothing else intervening.' Therefore, 'In case of being knowable by another mind, etc.' The Will-to-be stands here for the mind. If the last act of mentality is not itself perceived, it cannot have the power of perceiving the previous act of mentality. It is not proper that the previous Will-to-know should be known without coming into contact with the present Will-to-know itself. No one who does not take hold of the connecting rod can reach the holder of the rod himself. Hènce there is *regrussus ad infinitum.*

The Skandhas are five :—Vijjñāna, Vedanā, Saṁjñā Rūpa and Saṁskāra.

'The theories of the Sāṅkhya yoga, etc.' This means the theories of the Sāṅkhyas and the Yogas and of the Vaiśeṣikas, etc., which are preceded by the Sāṅkhyas and the Yogas. The rest is easy.—21.

Sūtra 22

चित्तेरप्रतिसङ्क्रमायास्तदाकारापत्तौ स्वबुद्धिसंवेदनम्।। २२।।

चित्ते: Citteḥ, of the consciousness. अप्रतिसंक्रमाया: Apratisaṁkramāyāḥ, of such as is notable to transform from place to place. तद् Tad, its. आकारापत्तौ Ākārāpattau, by transforming appearance. स्वबुद्धि-संवेदनम् Sva-Buddhi Saṁvedanam, knowing of. संवेदनम् its own. स्व, will to be. बुद्धि.

22. Consciousness knows its own Will-to-be by transforming its appearance, though not-itself moving-from place-to-place.—182.

कथम्। चित्तेरप्रतिसङ्क्रमायास्तदाकारापत्तौ स्वबुद्धिसंवेदनम्। अपरिणामिनी हि भोक्तृशक्तिरप्रतिसङ्क्रमा च परिणामिन्यर्थे प्रतिसङ्क्रान्तेव तद्वृत्तिमनुपतति तस्याश्च प्राप्तचैतन्योपग्रहस्वरूपाया बुद्धिवृत्तेरनुकारमात्रतया बुद्धिवृत्त्यविशिष्टा हि ज्ञानवृत्तिराख्यायते। तथा चोक्तम्। न पातालं न च विवरं गिरीणां नैवान्धकारं कुक्षयो नोदधीनां गुहा यस्यां निहितं ब्रह्म शाश्वतं बुद्धिवृत्तिमविशिष्टां कवयो वेदयन्त इति।। २२।।

Vyāsa

How? 'Consciousness knows its own Will-to-be by transforming its own appearance, though not itself moving from place to place. The power of enjoyment is of course unchanging. It does not also go from place to place. In the changing object it looks as though transferred thereto; and there it follows its manifestations. And it imitates, as it were, the modifications of the Will-to-be whose form is now enlivened by the consciousness which has entered therein. By that imitation it is called a manifestation or modification of consciousness, without being actually qualified by the modifications of the Will-to-be. This means that it does not at all appear to be different from the modifications thereof.

And so it has been said :—

Nor nether worlds, nor mountain caves, nor darkness, nor seas, nor ravines are the hollows in which is placed the Eternal Brahma. The wise points out to the modification of the Will-to-be which does not look different from him.— 182.

Vācaspati's Gloss

Let that be. If however the mind is not self-illuminative nor knowable by another mind, how should it be enjoyed by the Self himself? For although the Self is no doubt self-illuminating, it does not put forth any action anywhere. Without putting forth any action he cannot be the actor. Nor can he be the enjoyer of the mind without coming into relationship with the mind through action. That would be going beyond the ordinary rule.

With this in mind puts the question :—'How?'

Gives the answer by the aphorism :—'Consciousness knows its own Will-to-be by transforming into its own shape, although not itself moving from place to place.'

What was said before, 'Identification with modifications elsewhere' (P.I. 4) has its origin here. The knowing by the Puruṣa of his Will-to-be is achieved when the Will-to-be takes the form of the Puruṣa, *i.e.*, when it takes on he appearance thereof by receiving into itself the reflection of the Puruṣa. Similarly is the case with the moon, when reflected in pure water. Although the moon is not in motion, yet the she appears to be in motion on account of the movements of the water, without any action of her own. In the same way without any sort of action on the part of consciousness, the mind in which the reflection of consciousness has taken its place, shows the power of consciousness to be active by its own movements, and makes it appear to be following itself, although in reality it does not follow it. It is by acting in this way that the mind brings about the experience of the Puruṣa and gives him the nature of the enjoyer. This is the meaning of the aphorism. The commentary does not explain the meaning here, because it has explained the same in many places already here and there. The Commentary here describes the meaning of the modifications of consciousness as not being independent of the modifications of the Will-to-be. As has been said :—'Neither the nether worlds, etc.' They say that the mental modification in which the reflection of consciousness has made its place is on account of that very reflection, the cave of Brahma, who is pure in nature, eternal and auspicious. It is in that cave alone that the hidden Brahma is to be found. When that is removed, he shines by his own light, there being no obstruction and no defect. This is the case with the revered one who has reached his last body.—22.

Sūtra 23

द्रष्टृदृश्योपरक्तं चित्तं सर्वार्थम्।। २३।।

द्रष्टृदृश्योपरक्तम् Draṣṭṛ-Dṛśya-Upraktam, being coloured by. उपरक्तम्, the knower (दृष्ट), and the knowable, दृश्य. चित्तम् Cittam, the mind. सर्वार्थम् Sarvārtham, omni-objective.

23. The mind being coloured by the knower and the knowable is omni-objective (sarvārtha).—183.

अतश्चैतदुपगम्यते। द्रष्टृदृश्योपरक्तं चित्तं सर्वार्थम्। मनो हि मन्तव्येनार्थेनोपरक्तं तत्स्वयं विषयत्वाद्विषयिणा पुरुषेणात्मीयया वृत्त्याभिसम्बद्धं तदेतच्चित्तमेव द्रष्टृदृश्योपरक्तं विषयविषयिनिर्भासं चेतनाचेतनस्वरूपापन्नं विषयात्मकमप्यविषयात्मकमिवाचेतनं चेतनमिव स्फटिकमणिकल्पं सर्वार्थमित्युच्यते। तदनेन चित्तसारूप्येण भ्रान्ताः केचित्तदेव चेतनमित्याहुः। अपरे चित्तमात्रमेवेदं सर्वं नास्ति खल्वयं गवादिर्घटादिश्च सकारणो लोक इति। अनुकम्पनीयास्ते कस्मादस्ति हि तेषां भ्रान्तिबीजं सर्वरूपाकारनिर्भासं चित्तमिति। समाधीप्रज्ञायां प्रज्ञेयोऽर्थः प्रतिबिम्बी भूतस्तस्यालम्बनीभूतत्वादन्यः स चेदर्थश्चित्तमात्रं स्यात्कथं प्रज्ञयैव प्रज्ञारूपमवधार्येत तस्मात्प्रतिबिम्बी भूतोऽर्थः प्रज्ञायां येनावधार्यते स पुरुष इति। एवं ग्रहीतृग्रहणग्राह्यस्वरूपचित्तभेदात्रय- मप्येतज्जातितः प्रविभजन्त ते सम्यग्दर्शिनस्तैरधिगतः पुरुषः।। २३।।

Vyāsa

And it is known in this way :—'The mind being coloured by the knower and the known, is omni-objective.' The mind is of course coloured by the objects of thought. The mind being itself an object comes into relationship with the subjective Puruṣa through its modification as Self. Thus it is that the mind is coloured by both subjectivity and obejctivity, the knower and the knowable; it assumes the nature of both the conscious and unconscious. Although it is of the very nature of the objective, it appears as if it were of the nature of the subjective. Although it is devoid of consciousness by its

nature, it appears as if it were consciousness. Being of the nature of the crystal, it is termed omni-objective.

It is by this similarity of mental appearance that some people are deceived into saying that the mind itself is the conscious agent. There are others again who say that all this is but the mind only and that there is nothing in existence of the objective world, such as the cow or jar, all of which are governed by the law of causation. They are to be pitied. For what reason? Because they are possessed of a mind which is the cause of confusion, shining forth as it does in the shape of all appearances.

In the case of the trance cognition, the cognizable object is reflected into the mind, and it is different from the trance cognition, because it is the object upon which the act of cognition rests. If that object were the mind alone, how could it be that the phenomenon of cognition would be taken in by the cognition itself. For this reason, he who takes in the object reflected in the mind, is the Puruṣa. Thus those who teach that the knower, the knowable and the means of knowledge are the three modifications of the mind, and thus divide the phenomena into three classes are the only true philosophers. It is to them that the Puruṣa is known.—183.

Vācaspati's Gloss

Thus has been established the existence of the Puruṣa, the unchangeable as a separate entity from the mind which is by nature changeable, being as it is by nature the knowable. Now he gives also the authority of the perceptions of the world to prove the same, 'And it is known in this way.' The meaning is that it must be so. 'The mind coloured by both the knower and the knowable is omni-objective.' As the mind coloured by the blue and other objects establishes their existence by perception itself, so also coloured by the reflection of the knower into itself, the mind establishes the existence of the knower too by perception. A notion is evidently made up of two percepts 'I know the blue object.' Therefore the subject also is of a nature similar to that of the objcct. Although proved by perception, it is not shown thereby as existing separately from the mind, like the reflection of the moon which is perceived to be quite distinct from the water into which it is reflected. The mental perception of the Self does not cease to be perception merely by this much.

Further inasmuch as the reflection in the water does not exist in reality as a moon it cannot be said that because the reflection is only a reflection and not the substance itself, that therefore the moon herself does not exist. In the same way, although consciousness becomes the objective in its state of mental reflection, it does not so become in its own nature. This is what is meant by the mind being omni-objective. Says this :—'The mind coloured by the object of thought, etc.' It is not by the external object alone that the mind is coloured by assuming its shape; it is coloured by the Puruṣa too. The reflection of the Puruṣa is his, the Self's manifestation (vṛtti). This reflection of the Puruṣa is to be accepted by the Vaināśikas also. How? If this be not so they must fasten the consciousness upon the mind, saying that there is consciousness in the mind. Says so :—'Misled by this similarity of the mind, etc.' There are some Vaināśiksas who speak of the existence of an eternal object. There are others who speak of the existence of an idea. The question now is that, if the mind shines forth both as a subject and an object, there

must certainly be a difference between the knower and the knowable. As they say :—Although the Self of the Will-to-be is not deferent, yet those who are given to seeing things separated from each other, see it as possessed of the differences of the concepts of the subjective and the objective. This being the case, how are they to be pitied? Says for this reason :—'In the case of the trance cognition, etc.' They must be brought round by first convincing them by the above reasoning that the Puruṣa must be something different from the mind, and hen bringing them into touch with the trance cognition, which has the self as the sphere of its operation by teaching them the eight branches of Yoga. That is to be done in this way. In the trance cognition the object of knowledge is the Self reflected into the mind. It is different from the real Self, because it becomes the support to that Self (Ātmā). If he begin to say notwithstanding that he is given the reasons, that the support may be the mind itself, it is said :—If the object which appears as the Self, be the mind itself and nothing different from it, then how is it possible that the mind may be known by the mind itself (the act of knowing that is to say, by the act of knowing itself). It is self-contradictory to speak of the action of a mental modification upon itself. Concludes :—'Therefore, etc.' They are to be pitied and taught the truth. Says this :—'In this way, etc.' Class means nature.

Sūtra 24

तदसङ्ख्येयवासनाभिश्चित्तमपि परार्थं संहत्यकारित्वात्। २४।।

तद् Tad, that. असंख्येय-वासनाभि: Asaṅkhyeya-Vāsanābhiḥ, (variegated) by innumerable. (असंख्येय) residua (वासनाभि:) चित्तम् Cittam, mind. अपि Api, also. परार्थम् Parārtham, exists for another. संहत्य-कारित्वात् Saṁhatya-Kāritvāt, because it acts by combination.

24. And the mind exists-for-another, also because it is variegated by innumerable residua, inasmuch as it acts by combination.—184.

कुतश्चैतत्। तदसङ्ख्येयवासनाभिश्चित्तमपि परार्थं संहत्यकारित्वात्। तदेतच्चित्तमसङ्ख्येयाभिर्वासनाभिरेव चित्रीकृतमपि परार्थं परस्य भोगापवर्गार्थं न स्वार्थं संहत्यकारित्वाद् गृहवत्संहत्यकारिणा चित्तेन न स्वार्थेन भवितव्यं न सुखं चित्तं सुखार्थं न ज्ञानं ज्ञानार्थमुभयमप्येतत्परार्थं यश्च भोगेनापवर्गेण चार्थोनार्थवाद्पुरुषः स एव परो न परः सामान्यमात्रम्। यत्तु किंचित्परं सामान्यमात्रं स्वरूपेणोदाहरेद्वैनाशिकस्तत्सर्वं संहत्यकारित्वात्परार्थमेव स्यात्। यस्त्वसौ परो विशेषः स न संहत्यकारी पुरुष इति।। २४।।

Vyāsa

And for what other reason is this the case? 'And it exists for another, also because it is variegated by innumerable residua, inasmuch as it acts by combination.' This mind is variegated by innumerable residua. It must therefore exist for another, *i.e.*, for achieving the enjoyment and emancipation of another, not for the achievement of its own object. Because it acts by combination. As a house which has assumed its shape as such, by various materials being brought together, cannot come into existence for itself, so also the mind which assumes a particular shape by more things than one coming together.

The mental phenomenon of pleasure does not exist for its own sake; nor does knowledge exist for itself. On the contrary both these exist for the sake of another. That other is the Puruṣa who has objects to achieve in the shape of enjoyment and emancipation. It cannot be another of the same class. Whatever else the Vaināśika speaks of beyond this as being of the same class, all that must be of the same class, acting as that also would do by combination. The other however is peculiar to itself and differs from the others in not acting by combination. That is the Puruṣa.—184.

Vācaspati's Gloss

Introduces another for believing that the mind is different from the Self :—And for what other reason ? 'And it exists for another, also because it is variegated by innumerable residua, inasmuch as it acts by combination.' The meaning of the aphorism is this. Although innumerable residua of action and affliction live in the mind and not in the Puruṣa, and although further, the fruitions depending upon the residua also live in the mind and this fact seems to establish the contention that the mind itself is both the enjoyer and the object of enjoyment existing for the enjoyer, and that everything therefore exists for the mind, still that mind, notwithstanding its being variegated by innumerable residua exists for another. Why? Because it acts by combination. This is the meaning of the aphorism. Explains :—'The mind, etc.'

Some one may say that although it may be granted that the mind acts by combination, yet notwithstanding this, why should it not be conceived as existing and acting for the sake of itself? Where is the contradiction in this theory? Says to him :—'Because it acts by combination.'

'The mental phenomenon of pleasure.' These words indicate experience side of nature and the painful mind is also understood thereby. The knowledge indicates the emancipation side. This is the meaning. The pleasurable and painful minds consisting as they do of similar and opposite impression are not possible of the Self, because the manifestations in that case would contradict themselves. Nor can anything else acting by combination either directly or indirectly and thus causing pleasure or pain, be either favoured or disfavoured by them. Therefore he alone who does not operate as pleasure and pain directly or indirectly can either be favoured or disfavoured by them. This can only be the Puruṣa who is always indifferent and who can thus be emancipated. His knowledge too being dependent upon the object of knowledge, and being thus contradictory in its own manifestation, it cannot be said that the knowledge is its own object. For this reason emancipation from external objects becomes impossible, in the same way as emancipation is not possible in the case of the Videhas and the Prakṛtilayas. Therefore knowledge also exists for the sake of the Puruṣa, not for the sake of the mind itself.

Nor is the mind in existence for the sake of another of the same kind, because that would mean infinite regression. He therefore for whose sake the mind exists must be the Puruṣa Who does not act by conjunction.—24.

Sūtra 25

विशेषदर्शिन आत्मभावभावनाविनिवृत्तिः ।। २५ ।।

विशेष Viśeṣadarśinaḥ (दर्शिनः), for the seer (दर्शिन्) of the distinction (विशेष). आत्म Ātma, of the self. भाव Bhāva, of the nature and relation of. भावना Bhāvanā, of the curiosity.

विनिवृत्तिः Vinivṛttiḥ, the cessation. आत्म विनिवृत्तिः Ceases the curiosity as to the nature and relations of the Self.

25. For the seer of the distinction, ceases the curiosity as to the nature-and-relations of the Self.—185.

विशेषदर्शिन आत्मभावभावनानिवृत्तिः। यथा प्रावृषि तृणाङ्कुरस्योद्भेदेन तद्बीजसत्तानुमीयते तथा मोक्षमार्गश्रवणेन यस्य रोमहर्षाश्रुपातौ दृश्येते तत्राप्यस्ति विशेषदर्शनबीजमपवर्गभागीयं कर्माभिनिर्वर्तितमित्यनुमीयते तस्यात्मभावना स्वाभाविकी प्रवर्तते यस्याभावादिदमुक्तं स्वभावं मुक्त्वा दोषाद्येषां पूर्वपक्षे रुचिर्भवत्यरुचिश्च निर्णये भवति तत्रात्मभावभावनाकोऽहमासं कथमहमासं किंस्विदिदं कथंस्विदिदं के वा भविष्यामः कथं भविष्याम इति। सा तु विशेषदर्शिनो निवर्तते। कुतः। चित्तस्यैवैष विचित्रपरिणामः पुरुषस्त्वसत्यामविद्यायां शुद्धश्चित्तधर्मैरपरामृष्ट इति। ततोऽप्यस्यात्मभाव भावनाकुशलस्य विनिवर्तत इति।। २५।।

Vyāsa

As the existence of seeds is inferred from blades of grass shooting forth in the rainy season, so it is inferred that he whose tears flow and whose hair stand on end when he hears of the path of liberation, has a store of Karma tending to liberation as the seed of the recognition of the distinction (between the Puruṣa and the Sattva). The curiosity as to the nature for the Self is naturally manifested in him. In the absence thereof, however, he gives up the nature thus described; and by the defect he loves the antithesis and dislikes the thesis.

Here the curiosity as to the nature of the Self appears as—

'Who was I?' 'How was I?' 'What is this?' 'How is this?'

'What shall we become?' 'How shall we become? This however ceases in the case of him who sees the distinction (between the Puruṣa and the mind). Why? This varied change is of the mind alone. The curiosity however in the absence of Nescience is pure, that is, not touched by the characteristics of the mind. For this reason too the curiosity as to the nature and relations of Self ceases for the wise.—185.

Vācaspati's Gloss

Having thus described the reasoned philosophy of the Self, which is the very seed of absolute independence, he now shows that the Puruṣa who has reached that stage of fitness is different from any other Puruṣa, who has not reached that stage of fitness. 'For the seer of the distinction, ceases the curiosity as to the nature and relations of the Self.'

The curiosity as to the nature of the Self ceases in the case of him who possesses that curiosity, when he sees the distinction between the Subjective Puruṣa and the Objective Existence, by the practice and effective achievement of the means of the Yoga. As to the nihilist who does not possess this curiosity, he is not fit to be taught. There can be teaching in the case of him who has not first ascertained the fact of the existence of the Self in the world outside the present body. He cannot, therefore, come to know the distinction between the two and hence in the case of him there cannot be the possibility of any curiosity ceasing to be.

But the question is. How is the curiosity to know the nature of the Self known to be existing in any mind? Says he for this reason :—'As in the rainy season, etc.' It is inferred that there exists some Karma done in the previous birth in the shape of the practice of the eight accessories of Yoga or of some portion thereof. Which is the seed out of which is to grow the knowledge of the reality, and which tends towards emancipation. And in the case of such one, the curiosity to know the nature of the Self must necessarily exist without even the necessity of practice.

Shows who has not the capacity, by the authority of the Āgamis. 'In the absence, etc.' The antithesis is that there is no fruit of action, there being no entity existing in another sphere of existence, or say there being no other world beyond this. The nihilist is he who likes this view, but does not like the thesis, which has the determination of the twenty-five tattvas in view. The curiosity as to the nature of the Self has been described before. Speaks of the thought of him who sees the distinction :—'This varied change, etc.' The meaning is that the curiosity as to the nature of the Self ceases in the case of him who is wise enough to know the distinction.—25.

Sūtra 26

तदा विवेकनिम्नं कैवल्यप्राग्भारं चित्तम्।। २६ ।।

तदा Tadā, then. विवेक-निम्नम् Viveka-nimnam, inclining towards discrimination. (निम्नम् विवेक) कैवल्य Kaivalya, absolute independence. प्राग्भारम् Prāgbhāram, gravitating towards. चित्तम् Cittam, the mind.

26. Then the mind inclines towards discrimination and gravitates towards absolute-independence (kaivalya).—186.

तदा विवेकनिम्नं कैवल्यप्राग्भारं चित्तम्। तदानीं यदस्य चित्तं विषयप्राग्भारमज्ञाननिम्नमासीत्तदस्यान्यथा भवति कैवल्यप्राग्भारं विवेकजज्ञाननिम्नमिति।। २६ ।।

Vyāsa

The mind which ere now was heavy with sensuous enjoyment and tended towards ignorance, takes now the reverse course.

It is now heavy with independence and tends towards discriminative knowledge.—186.

Vācaspati's Gloss

Now describes the nature of the mind of him who sees the distinction :—'The mind' is then inclined towards discrimination and gravitates towards absolute independence. 'This has been explained.'—26.

Sūtra 27

तच्छिद्रेषु प्रत्ययान्तराणि संस्कारेभ्यः।। २७।।

तच्छिद्रेषु Tacchidreṣu, in the breaks in it. प्रत्ययान्तराणि Pratyayāntarāṇi, arise other thoughts (प्रत्यय). संस्कारेभ्यः Saṁskārebhyaḥ, from residua.

27. In the breaks arise other thoughts from residua.—187.

तच्छिद्रेषु प्रत्ययान्तराणि संस्कारेभ्यः। प्रत्ययविवेकनिम्नस्य सत्त्वपुरुषान्यताख्यातिमात्रप्रवाहारोहिणश्चित्तस्य तच्छिद्रेषु प्रत्ययान्तराण्यस्मीति वा ममेति वा जानामीति वा कुतः क्षीयमाणबीजेभ्य पूर्वसंस्कारेभ्य इति।। २७।।

Vyāsa

In the mind inclining towards discriminative knowledge of the notions, and which has just entered the stream of the distinctive knowledge of the Puruṣa and Objective Existence, other thoughts appear in the intervals such as 'I am,' 'This is mine,' 'I know,' etc. Whence? From previous residua, whose seeds are being destroyed.—187.

Vācaspati's Gloss

It may be so if discriminative knowledge is established in discrimination and never inclines towards outward activity. It is, however, seen in the case of one who is begging his food, that is, inclined towards outward activity. For this reason says :—'In the breaks arise other thoughts from residua.'

Thoughts (Pratyaya) are those by which something is known, the essence of the mind. By that arises the discrimination of consciousness. It is of him that are shown the notions, 'I know', when absolute freedom is directly shown as separated from anything else. Or the forgetfulness that I do not know. As also the egoism with reference to that, 'I am,' or 'This is mine.' By previous residua means the residua of outgoing activities.—27.

Sūtra 28

हानमेषां क्लेशवदुक्तम्।। २८।।

हानम् Hānam, removal. एषाम् Eṣām, their. क्लेशवत् Kleśavat, like that of the afflictions. उक्तम् Uktam, has been described.

28. Their removal has been described like that of the afflictions.—188.

हानमेषां क्लेशवदुक्तम्। यथा क्लेशा दग्धबीजभावा न प्ररोहसमर्था भवन्ति तथा ज्ञानाग्निना दग्धबीजभावः पूर्वसंस्कारो न प्रत्ययप्रसूर्भवति। ज्ञानसंस्कारास्तु चित्ताधिकारिसमाप्तिमनुशेरत इति न चिन्त्यते।। २८।।

Vyāsa

As the afflictions are no longer capable of budding forth when their seed-power has been signed, so also does not the conserved energy of previous residua give birth to

notions when its seed-power has been singed by the fire of knowledge. The residua of knowledge, however, live on until the duty of the mind has been fulfilled. They are, therefore, not considered.—188.

Vācaspati's Gloss

Let that be. But if in the face of the existence of discriminative knowledge too, other thoughts arise, what is the cause of their utter removal so that these other thoughts may not rise again at all ? For this reason says :—'Their removal has been described like the afflictions.' The outgoing activities in their potential state are not altogether destroyed as long as the discriminative knowledge is not firmly established. In the case however of discriminative knowledge being firmly established the other thoughts are utterly destroyed and are no longer fit to be born again.

By what cause does it come about that the afflictions born in the intervals of discrimination even cease to give birth to other potentialities? The cause is that the seed-power of the afflictions is burnt up by the fire of discriminative knowledge. In the same way the residua of the outgoing activities are burnt up.

But the residua of outgoing activities are to be restrained by the residua of discriminative knowledge, and the residua of discrimination are to be restrained by the potencies of restraint. And it has been shown that the potencies of restraint have not the external objects for their sphere of operation. The means of restraint are, therefore, to be considered. For this reason says :—'The residua of knowledge, however, etc.' The residua of knowledge are the potencies of higher desirelessness.—28.

Sūtra 29

प्रसङ्ख्यानेऽप्यकुसीदस्य सर्वथा विवेकख्यातेर्धर्ममेघः समाधिः ।। २९ ।।

प्रसङ्ख्याने Prasaṅkhyāne, in the highest intellections. अपि Api, even. अकुसीदस्य Akusīdasya, having no interest left. सर्वथा Sarvathā, constant. विवेक-ख्याते: Viveka-khyāteḥ, from discrimination. धर्म-मेघ: Dharma-meghaḥ, the cloud of virtue. समाधि: Samādhiḥ, the trance.

29. Having no-interest left even in the Highest-intellection there comes from constant discrimination, the trance known as the Cloud-of-Virtue.—189.

प्रसङ्ख्यानेऽप्यकुसीदस्य सर्वथा विवेकख्यातेर्धर्ममेघः समाधिः। यदायं ब्राह्मणः प्रसङ्ख्यानेऽप्यकुसीद-स्ततोऽपि न किंचित्प्रार्थयते तत्रापि विरक्तस्य सर्वथा विवेकख्यातिरेव भवतीति संस्कारबीजक्षयान्नास्य प्रत्ययान्तराण्युत्पद्यन्ते तदास्य धर्ममेघो नाम समाधिर्भवति।। २९ ।।

Vyāsa

When this Brāhmaṇa has no interest left in the Highest Intellection, *i.e.*, desires nothing even from that, then unattached even to that, he has discriminative knowledge ever present, and thus by destruction of the seed-power of potencies, other thoughts are not born. Then does he attain the trance known as the Cloud-of-Virture.—189.

Vācaspati's Gloss

Thus the author of the Aphorism having described the Highest Intellection to be the means of the restraint of outgoing activities, now speaks of the means of restraining even the Highest Intellection :—'Having no interest left even in the Highest Intellection there comes from constant discrimination the trance known as the Cloud of Virtue.' By that Highest Intellection, he does not desire the possession of anything, even of the power of becoming the master of all existence. Nay he begins to feel pain even there. Having become desireless even there by seeing the defect of change, he comes to the possession of constant discriminative knowledge (undisturbed). Explains the same :—'Thus unattached even to that, etc.' As long as the notions of outgoing activities exist, the Brāhmaṇa does not come to possess the constant manifestation of discriminative knowledge. When however he arrives at the stage when all other thoughts cease to exist, then he becomes possessed of constant discriminative knowledge. Then comes to him the trance known as the Cloud of Virtue (dharma-megha). This is the meaning. Dissatisfied with the Highest Intellection and desiring restraint of that even, let him practise the trance known as the Cloud of Virtue. By the practice of that he becomes constantly possessed of discriminative knowledge.—29.

Sūtra 30

ततः क्लेशकर्मनिवृत्तिः ।। ३० ।।

ततः Tataḥ, thence, क्लेश-कर्म Kleśa-karma, of action and afflictions. निवृत्तिः Nivṛttiḥ, the removal.

30. Thence the removal of actions and afflictions—190.

ततः क्लेशकर्मनिवृत्तिः। तल्लाभादविद्यादयः क्लेशाः समूलकाषं कषिता भवन्ति। कुशलाकुशलाश्च कर्माशयाः समूलघातं हता भवन्ति। क्लेशकर्मनिवृत्तौ जीवन्नेव विद्वान्विमुक्तो भवति। कस्मात्। यस्माद्विपर्ययो भवस्य कारणम्। नहि क्षीणक्लेशविपर्ययः कश्चित्केनचित्क्वचिज्जातो दृश्यत इति।। ३०।।

Vyāsa

By the attainment thereof, the affliction of Nescience, etc., are removed, even to the very root. And the good and bad vehicles of action are utterly uprooted. On the afflictions and the actions being removed, the wise man becomes free even while alive (the Jīvanmukta). How? Because Unreal Cognitions are the cause of existence. No one being free from the affliction of Unreal Cognitions is seen being born by anybody anywhere.—190.

Vācaspati's Gloss

Thus does he become capable of restraining that. And now describes the object thereof :—

'Thence the removal of actions and afflictions.' But then how does it come to pass that the wise become free while yet in the bonds of life? Gives the answer :—'Because, etc.' It is the vehicle of action grown strong by the residua of afflictions and actions that surely becomes the cause of life-state, etc.' And when there is no root, the shoots thereof cannot exist. As says on this subject the revered Akṣapāda :—'By not seeing the birth of one who has no desires.'—30.

Sūtra 31

तदा सर्वावरणमलापेतस्य ज्ञानस्यानन्त्याज्ज्ञेयमल्पम् ।। ३१ ।।

तदा Tadā, then. सर्वावरणमलापेतस्य Sarva-āvaraṇa, mala, apetasya, from which is removed (अपेत) all (सर्व) obscuring (आवरण) impurities (मल). ज्ञानस्य Jñānasya, of knowledge. आनंत्यात् Ānantyāt, because of the infinity of. ज्ञेयम् Jñeyam, the knowable. अल्पम् Alpam, but little.

31. The knowable is but little then, because of knowledge having-become-infinite, on account of the removal of all obscuring impurities.—191.

तदा सर्वावरणमलापेतस्य ज्ञानस्यानन्त्याज्ज्ञेयमल्पम्। सर्वैः क्लेशकर्मावरणैर्विमुक्तस्य ज्ञानस्यानन्त्यं भवति। तमसाभिभूतमावृतमनन्तं ज्ञानसत्त्वं क्वचिदेव रजसा प्रवर्तितमुद्घाटितं ग्रहणसमर्थं भवति। तत्र यदा सर्वैरावरणमलैरपगतं भवति तदा भवत्यस्यानन्त्यम्। ज्ञानस्यानन्त्याज्ज्ञेयमल्पं सम्पद्यते। यथाकाशे खद्योतः। यत्रेदमुक्तम्। अन्धो मणिमविध्यत्तमनङ्गुलिरावयत्। अग्रीवस्तं प्रत्यमुञ्चत्तमजिह्वोऽभ्यपूजयदिति।। ३१ ।।

Vyāsa

Knowledge when rid of all the impurities of affliction and action, becomes infinite. The essence of knowledge covered by the veil of Tamas, is but seldom shown forth and becomes capable of recognition by the activity of Rajas. Here, when all the impurities have been removed, then knowledge becomes infinite. When knowledge becomes infinite, but little remains to know, like the shining insect in space. On this it has been said :—'The blind man pierced the pearl; the fingerless put a thread into it; the neckless wore it and the tongueless praised it.'—191.

Vācaspati's Gloss

Now describes the state of the mind at the time when the Cloud of Virtue has been reached :—'The knowable is but little then because of knowledge having become infinite on account of their removal of obscuring impurities. The impurities which cover up the essence of the mind, are spoken of as the obscuring impurities. These are the afflictions and actions. When the mental essence is freed from alloy these obscuring impurities, knowledge, *i.e.*, the power of knowing becomes infinite, *i.e.*, immeasurable, and therefore the knowable remains but little. As in the season after the rains, the sun being freed of the clouds shines brightly all round and his light becomes infinitely strong, and for this reason, the jar and other such things that are to be lighted remain but little, so also the light of the essence of the mind, when freed from the

Rajas and Tamas, becomes inifinite, and but little remains to be lighted up. Says the same :—'When that becomes freed from all the impurities etc. Renders the same plainer by means of the canon of difference :—'When overpowered, etc.' The meaning is that the Tamas is put into motion by the active Rajas and is for this very reason carried away from the place. For this very reason it is called the Cloud of Virtue, inasmuch as it pours forth showers of light upon all the virtues of things to be known.

Well, this trance, the Cloud of Virtue, may be the cause of the calming down of the vehicle of actions along with the afflictions and the residua; but then how is it that when the Cloud of Virtue makes its appearance, the man is not born again? For this reason says :—'As has been said on the subject.'

If an effect can be brought into existence even when the cause no longer exists, then the acts of piercing the pearl, etc., may well be performed by blind people, etc. Or, it may well be that whatever nonsense an ignorant world may talk about improper things, may be considered as very proper.—31.

Sūtra 32

ततः कृतार्थानां परिणामक्रमसमाप्तिर्गुणानाम्।। ३२।।

ततः Tataḥ, by that. कृतार्थानाम् Kṛtārthānām, having fulfilled their object. परिणाम Pariṇāma, of the changes. क्रम Krama, of the succession. समाप्तिः Samāptiḥ, end. गुणानाम् Guṇānām, of the qualities.

32. By that, the qualities having fulfilled their object, the succession of their changes ends.—192.

ततः कृतार्थानां परिणामक्रमसमाप्तिर्गुणानाम्। तस्य धर्ममेघस्योदयात्कृतार्थानां गुणानां परिणामक्रमः परिसमाप्यते। नहि कृतभोगापवर्गाः परिसमाप्तक्रमाः क्षणमप्यवस्थातुमुत्सहन्ते।। ३२।।

Vyāsa

By that, *i.e.*, by the rise of the Cloud of Virtue, the succession of the changes of the qualities is over, inasmuch as they have fulfilled their object, by having achieved experience and emancipation, and their succession having ended, they no longer care to stay even for a moment.—192.

Vācaspati's Gloss

Well, the highest culmination of the Cloud of Virtue being the purity of the light of knowledge, which is the same as the Higher desirelessness, it may well uproot the potencies of the vehicles of outgoing activities and of trance together with the vehicles of afflictions and actions. But the qualities are of the nature of the things which go on performing their actions of their own power. How is it then that they do not go on making the same sort of a body for such Yogīs as they do for all men? For this reason says :—'By that, qualities having fulfilled their object, the succession of their changes ends.' The meaning is that the nature of the qualities, that they do not function with respect to him for whom they have already achieved their object.—32.

Sūtra 33

क्षणप्रतियोगी परिणामापरान्तनिर्ग्राह्यः क्रमः ।। ३३ ।।

क्षण Kṣaṇa, of moments. **प्रतियोगी** Pratiyogī, the uninterrupted sequence. **परिणाम** Pariṇāma, of evolutionary change. **अपरान्त** Aparānta, on the cessation. **निर्ग्राह्यः** Nirgrāhyaḥ, to be cognised as distinct. **क्रमः** Kramaḥ, succession.

33. Succession is the uninterrupted-sequence of moments, cognized as distinct on the cessation of evolutionary change.—193.

अथ कोऽयं क्रमो नामेति। क्षणप्रतियोगी परिणामापरान्तनिर्ग्राह्यः क्रमः। क्षणानन्तर्यात्मा परिणामस्यापरान्तेनावसनेन गृह्यते क्रमः। नह्यननुभूतक्रमक्षणान्नवपुराणता वस्त्रस्यान्ते भवति। नित्येषु च क्रमो दृष्टः। द्वयी चेयं नित्यता कूटस्थनित्यता परिणामिनित्यता च। तत्र कूटस्थनित्यता पुरुषस्य। परिणामिनित्यता गुणानाम्। यस्मिन्परिणाममाने तत्त्वं न विहन्यते तन्नित्यम्। उभयस्य च तत्त्वाभिघातान्नित्यत्वं तत्र गुणधर्मेषु बुध्यादिषु परिणामापरान्तनिर्ग्राह्यः क्रमो लब्धपर्यवसानो नित्येषु धर्मिषु गुणेष्वलब्धपर्यवसानः। कूटस्थनित्येषु स्वरूपमात्रप्रतिष्ठेषु मुक्तपुरुषेषु स्वरूपास्तिता क्रमेणैवानुभूयत इति तत्राप्यलब्धपर्यवसानः शब्दपृष्ठेन अस्तिक्रियामुपादाय कल्पयत इति। अथास्य संसारस्य स्थित्या गत्या च गुणेषु वर्तमानस्यास्ति क्रमसमाप्तिर्न वेति। अवचनीयमेतत्। कथम्। अस्ति प्रश्न एकान्तवचनीयः सर्वो जातो मरिष्यति मृत्वा जनिष्यत इति। ॐ भो इत्यथ सर्वो जातो मरिष्यतीति मृत्वा जनिष्यत इति विभज्य वचनीयमेतत्प्रत्युदितख्यातिः क्षीणतृष्णः कुशलो न जनिष्यत इतरस्तु जनिष्यते। तथा मनुष्यजातिः श्रेयसी न वा श्रेयसीत्येवं परिपृष्टे विभज्य वचनीयः प्रश्नः पशूनधिकृत्य श्रेयसी देवानृषींश्चाधिकृत्य नेति। अयं त्ववचनीयः प्रश्नः संसारोऽयमन्त- वानानन्तवान्वाथानन्त इति। कुशलस्यास्ति संसारक्रमपरिसमाप्तिर्नेतरस्येति। अन्यतरावधारणे दोषस्तस्माद्व्या- करणीयं एवायं प्रश्न इति।। ३३ ।।

Vyāsa

Well, but what is this succession? 'Succession is the uninterrupted flow of moments; it is taken in by last end, the cessation of changes. A cloth which has not undergone the succession of moments, does not give up its newness and become old all at once in the end.

Further, succession is found in the permanent also. This permanence is two-fold, the Eternal in Perfection; and the Eternal in Evolution. Of these, the perfect eternity belongs to the Puruṣa. The evolutionary eternity belongs to the qualities. The Permanent or Eternal is that in which the substance is not destroyed by changing appearances. Both are permanent because their substance is never destroyed.

Now with regard to the appearances of the qualities, the Will-to-be and others, succession has an end which is cognized by the cessation of the changes. In the eternal qualities however, whose appearances these are, it has no end. In the case of the Permanent ones, the existence of the released Puruṣas who are established in their own natures, is also known by succession. In their case too, therefore, it has no end. It is however conceived there, with reference to the necessary conception of the act of being attached to the word.

But then is there or is there not an end to the succession of evolutionary changes of the universe, which is ever present in the qualities, by motion or by cessation of motion? This cannot be answered as such. How?

There is a question to which only a one-sided answer may be given :—'All that is born must die and having been dead be born again.' Well, but if the question is put in this form—

Is it that all that is born must die, and having been dead be born again?

The answer that can be given to this is not a single one but must be divided in two.

He in whom the light of knowledge has appeared, and whose desires have been destroyed, that wise man is not born; the rest are born. Similarly the question is, Is mankind good or not? The answer is again to be divided in two. The humankind is better in comparison with the animals, but is inferior in comparison with gods and seers (Ṛṣis).

As to the question, Has the universe an end or has it not? Why this question cannot be answered as such? For the wise there is cessation of the successions of the universe. Not for the others. There is defect in formulating any other theory. Hence the question must necessarily be divided into two—193.

Vācaspati's Gloss

Puts a question in the context about the succession of changes (krama) :—'Well but what is this succession?' The answer is :—'Succession is the uninterrupted sequence of moments cognized as distinct on the cessation of evolutionary change.'

That to which is mutually related the moment relating backward and forward to the moment of the succession of changes is so called. The meaning is that succession is that which is the support of a group of moments. There can of course be no succession ascertained without the existence of that of which it is the succession. Nor can there be a succession of one moment only. The inference by residue therefore points only to the dependence thereof upon a group of moments. Says this :—'Succession is the uninterrupted flow, etc.' Mentions authority for the existence of the succession of changes :—It is taken in by the last end, the cessation of changes.

Even in new cloth preserved with care, oldness becomes visible after a long time. This is the last end of change, otherwise called its cessation. It is for this very reason that a succession of change exists. And before that too is inferred the smallness, the greater smallness and the greatest smallness as well as the grossness, the greater smallness and the greatest smallness of oldness in regular sequence of one after the other.

Shows the same by the canon of difference :—'A cloth which has not undergone, etc.' That which has not been subjected to the succession of moments, is spoken of as not having undergone that.

Well, but this succession cannot be posited of the Pradhāna, Because that is eternal. For this reason says :—'Succession is seen in those that are permanent. By using the plural number shows that succession pervades all permanent objects.

Now shows the modes of permanence and then establishes how succession pervades the eternal :—'Permanence is two-fold, etc.'

Well, the constantly eternal may be eternal, because it never gives up its nature such as it is. As to the changing substances, they are constantly giving up their appearances; how can they be called permanent? For this reason says :—'The Permanent or Eternal is that, etc.' Characteristic, secondary quality and condition possess the qualities of appearance and disappearance; the characterized however remains the same in substance.

Well, are all successions known by the cessation of changes? Says, No :—'Now with regard to the appearances of the qualities, the Will-to-be, etc.' Because the succession of the characteristics ends on account of their being destructible. Not so however the succession of the Pradhāna ends.

Well, the Pradhāna might be said to be possessed of the succession of changes, because of the change of its characteristics. But the Puruṣa never changes. How then can there be a change of succession in the case of the unchanging Puruṣa? For this reason says :—'In those that are constantly permanent, etc.'

There in the case of those that are bound, they have the notion of non-separation from the mind; there is therefore a fastening of the change on them on account of the changes of the mind. In the case of those however that have been released, the existence of an unreal change has been fancied by ignorance with reference to the action of the word to be. Because the word precedes, fancy comes thereafter and puts on the appearance of the action of the word to be.

It has been said that the succession of changes does not find an end in the qualities. Not suffering that assertion puts the question, 'Is there an end to succession, etc.'?

Cessation of motion means the Great Latency, the Mahāpralaya. Motion signifies creation. This is the meaning.

If there were no end of the change of the universe (Saṁsāra) on account of eternity, how then should it be in the Great Latency, that all the Puruṣas should all at once have an end of the succession of changes in their case, and again should the same succession of changes come into being all at once at the beginning of a manifestation? For this reason it would follow that one Puruṣa alone being released, the universe of evolution would cease to exist for all, and thus all the Puruṣas would become released. In this way would come the end of the succession of the changes of the Pradhāna, and the Pradhāna also would thus come to be impermanent.

Further it is not allowed that the manifestation of existence which did not exist before is possible, and this assertion cannot therefore be taken to prove its infinity. When this becomes the case, it can no longer be said that the Pradhāna is beginningless. All the teachings of the Śāstras thus come to be futile. This is the meaning.

Gives the answer :—It cannot be answered; the question does not deserve to be answered. With the object of showing that this question cannot be answered, shows a question which admits of a one-sided answer. 'There is a question, etc.' The answer to the question, Will all those that are born die? is Yes. This is true. Now speaks of a question which admits of an answer after being divided into two :—Are all those that are born bound to die and dying be born again ? The answer that can be given to this is only possible after a division.

In order to make the matter clear, mentions another question which admits of an answer only after being divided :—'Similarly the question, etc.' This question does not admit of a one-sided answer. It is impossible to say that the evolution of the wise and unwise is in general indefinite or finite. There can be no community between them.

This is similar to the impossibility of ascertaining the goodness or otherwise of every living being all at once. The same is the case with the death of one who is just born. This can, however, be ascertained after a divison. Says this :—The wise man is not born, etc. This is the meaning.

The inference is that there being emancipation of all in the case of the freedom of one only from succession, the world must come to end. And this depends upon the emancipation proved to exist by the authority of the Śāstras. Thus here is the authority of the means of knowledge known as verbal authority, which establishes the emancipation understood. How can it be that the same Śāstras should, by a certain teaching of theirs, stultify another authority of the Śāstras establishing the eternity of the modifications of the Pradhāna? Therefore, the inference which militates against the authority of the Āgama cannot be considered an authority. It is of course in the Veda, the Smṛti and the Purāṇas that the succession of creation after creation is without beginning and without end. Further it is not possible that all the souls should cease to be born and die all at once. Even in the case of learned men who have been practising and working for more lives than one to achieve discriminative knowledge, this knowledge does not become well established. How is it then possible that in the case of all living beings, whether they belong to the class of the moving or the unmoving creatures, it should manifest all at once by some chance.?

Further it is not proper that the effects should manifest at one and the same time although the causes are not in existence at one and the same time. In the case of the manifestation of discriminative knowledge by succession, innumerable souls may be released by succession, but the destruction of the universe will not follow, because creatures are infinite and innumerable. Thus all is plain.—33.

Sūtra 34

पुरुषार्थशून्यानां गुणानां प्रतिप्रसवः कैवल्यं स्वरूपप्रतिष्ठा वा चितिशक्तिरिति।। ३४।।

पुरुषार्थ-शून्यानाम् Puruṣārtha-Śūnyānām, of those that are devoid of the object of the Puruṣa. गुणानाम् Guṇānām, of the qualities. प्रतिप्रसवः Pratiprasavaḥ, becoming latent. कैवल्यम् Kaivalyam, absolute freedom. स्वरूप-प्रतिष्ठा Svarūpa-pratiṣṭhā, established in its own nature. वा Vā, or. चितिशक्तिः Citi-Śaktiḥ, the power of consciousness. इति Iti, so, thus.

34. Absolute freedom comes when the qualities, becoming devoid of the object of the Puruṣa, become latent; or the power of consciousness becomes established in its own nature.—194.

Vyāsa

गुणाधिकारक्रमपरिसमाप्तौ कैवल्यमुक्तं तत्स्वरूपमवधार्यते। पुरुषार्थशून्यानां गुणानां प्रतिप्रसवः कैवल्यं स्वरूपप्रतिष्ठा वा चितिशक्तिरिति। कृतभोगापवर्गाणां पुरुषार्थशून्यानां यः प्रतिप्रसवः कार्यकारणात्मकानां

गुणानां तत्कैवल्यं स्वरूपप्रतिष्ठा पुनर्बुद्धिसत्त्वानभिसम्बन्धात्पुरुषस्य चितिशक्तिरेव केवला तस्याः सदा तथैवावस्थानं कैवल्यमिति ।। ३४ ।।

Vyāsa

It has been said that absolute freedom comes when the succession of the functioning of the qualities in the performance of their duties is over. Its nature is now ascertained. Absolute freedom is the latency of the qualities on becoming devoid of the object of the Puruṣa, or it is the power of consciousness established in its own nature. Absolute freedom is the becoming latent by inverse process, of the qualities, when they are devoid of the object of the Puruṣa, after having achieved the experience and emancipation of the soul.

The power of consciousness is absolute when it is not again limited.—194.

Thus ends the Commentary of Vyāsa, the Sāṅkhya-pravacana, the Fourth Chapter on Absolute Freedom.

The Book is Finished

Vācaspati's Gloss

Describes the connection of the aphorism defining the nature of absolute freedom (kaivalya) with the previous aphorism :—'It has been said, etc.' Absolute freedom is the becoming latent of the qualities when they become devoid of the objects of the Puruṣa.'

The becoming latent of the qualities in their cause, the Pradhāna, when they are devoid of the objects of the Puruṣa, having achieved them :—The out-going and the trance and the inhibitive potencies of the qualities which appear both as the causes and the effects, become latent in the mind. The mind becomes latent in the principle of egoism. The principle of egoism becomes latent in the undifferentiated phenomenal, and the undifferentiative phenomenal into the noumenal.

This backward disappearance of the qualities which appear as both the causes and the effects, is called absolute freedom of the Puruṣa, in relation to the Pradhāna from which he is released. Or, freedom is the establishment of the Puruṣa in his own nature. Says this, 'Or, it is the power, etc.' Inasmuch as in the Mahāpralaya, too, the power of consciousness is established in its own nature, but that is not Mokṣa, he says :—'Does not come into relationship again, etc.' The word 'ITI' in the aphorism means the end of the book.

In this Chapter have been described the mind fit for freedom, and the trance known as the Cloud of Virtue, for establishing the Puruṣa, as he appears in the other world; also two descriptions of Mukti have been described and other things also by context.

The root of the afflictions has been described, as also the affliction; both the Yogas are described together with the eight accessories. The way of Mokṣa in the shape of the knowledge of the distinction between the Puruṣa and the qualities has been rendered plainer. Absolute freedom has been ascertained to be the power of consciousness free from the afflictions.

Thus ends the Fourths Chapter of Absolute Freedom in the Gloss of Vācaspati Miśra on the Commentary of Vyāsa.—34.

Om Tat Sat

For the service of Brahma.

Index of the Sūtras